H. ISAACS

perspectives

Comparative Politics

Academic Editor
Eve Sandberg
Oberlin College

D1404189

Boulder • Bellevue • Dubuque • Madison

Our mission at **coursewise** is to help students make connections—linking theory to practice and the classroom to the out-side world. Learners are motivated to synthesize ideas when course materials are placed in a context they recognize. By pro-viding gateways to contemporary and enduring issues, **coursewise,** publications will expand students' awareness of and context for the course subject.

For more information on **coursewise** visit us at our web site: http://www.coursewise.com

coursewise publishing editorial staff

Thomas Doran, ceo/publisher: Journalism/Marketing/Speech
Edgar Laube, publisher: Geography/Political Science/Psychology/Sociology
Linda Meehan Avenarius, publisher: **courselinks**™
Sue Pulvermacher-Alt, publisher: Education/Health/Gender Studies
Victoria Putman, publisher: Anthropology/Philosophy/Religion
Tom Romaniak, publisher: Business/Criminal Justice/Economics
Kathleen Schmitt, publishing assistant

coursewise production staff

Lori A. Blosch, permissions coordinator
Mary Monner, production coordinator
Victoria Putman, production manager

Cover photo: Copyright © 1997 T. Teshigawara/Panoramic Images, Chicago, IL. All Rights Reserved.

Interior design and cover design by Jeff Storm

Printed in the United States of America by **coursewise publishing,** Inc.
1379 Lodge Lane, Boulder, CO 80303

10 9 8 7 6 5 4 3 2 1

from the
Publisher

coursewise publishing

Edgar Laube

Many years ago the State Department "invited" me to interview for a position as a Foreign Service Officer. I had passed an initial written test, and this two-day interview was the next of several hurdles. On the second day, I spent several hours in a small room with two FSOs. One of the mistakes I made in that interview was to mention that I could speak and read the Chinese language. The first time I mentioned it, the FSOs seemed to ignore the information—which I had thought they would be delighted to learn. So I mentioned it again, at which point one of them said crossly, "We'll teach you want we want you to know."

Whoa. Talk about eye-openers. This was a big one. These two men—trained interviewers and Foreign Service Officers—didn't want to know that I had dirtied my fingernails, culturally and intellectually, learning a difficult language, one spoken by over a billion people who constitute the world's next superpower. At first I was concerned only that I had hurt my chances of being hired. Then for a few days I was perplexed. It took a while for the anger to set in. I never got any further in the hiring process.

In retrospect I think the State Department was looking for people whom they could indoctrinate with a certain world view—that the United States is right, and there's something wrong with just about everybody else. Our government is constantly suggesting that other countries are undemocratic, that they're protectionist, that they perpetrate human rights abuses . . . that they're not on the side of the angels, as we are.

A volume such as this can help you cut through some of this fog. Countries act the way they do for reasons, good or otherwise. Leaders are elected or allowed to lead, cultural and political baggage constrains choices, and poverty and ignorance paralyze entire populations. Knowledge of these contexts within countries will help you make sense of events on the world stage. A presentation of external forces, such as pressure from world financial markets and environmental considerations, provides additional context for understanding.

Eve Sandberg has done a remarkable job of imposing coherence on this complicated international mosaic. Eve has taught in contexts that presented a variety of challenges. She is both a thinker and a doer. She has written extensively, consulted for officials of foreign governments, worked on political campaigns, and gotten her fingernails dirty with various types of advocacy. Above all, Eve is a committed teacher. Working with Eve has been a source of inspiration and delight for me.

Students, I commend this reader to your attention. In it you will find a microcosm of the world as it is, not as the U.S. State Department or anyone else wants it to be. Check out the additional resources at the **courselinks**™ site. If so inclined, please let Eve and me know what you think. (You can contact me via the **coursewise** site.) I sincerely hope that this reader sparks your further interest in people and events beyond our borders. And good luck as you get your own nails dirty. It actually feels pretty good.

from the
Academic Editor

Eve Sandberg
Oberlin College

New strategies and new areas of focus in the study of comparative politics often reflect scholars' responses to their changing world. I agreed to compile this reader because, while the scholarly literature has attempted to keep pace with our changing world, I was frustrated that many of the comparative politics readers remain mired in Eurocentric-dominated approaches. One of the leading comparative politics readers, for example, devotes its initial 187 pages to the largely white male concerns of Europe before turning to another part of the globe. Additionally, its comparative consideration of countries on the African continent includes a total of two articles in the school of thought that some have labeled Afro-pessimism.

In compiling this reader, I did not neglect the important task of studying European politics comparatively, but I expanded the focus of the geographical areas and range of comparative issues covered. We will face global, not just national, challenges in the coming century, and you deserve an introduction to a wide range of comparative issues and to the many forms of political economies that comprise the countries of the world.

Perspectives: Comparative Politics introduces traditional topics such as political parties and party systems in Western style democracies. However, you are also invited to sample a range of current scholarship and reports on such topics as the constraints that global liberalism and economic competition impose on the nation state, the role of structural adjustment programs, regional integration, and comparative strategies for democratization. Moreover, sections on peasants and labor emphasize the special challenges that these groups face in today's domestic political arena and have been included because the majority of people in the world are not European policy makers, but rather belong to one of these two groups.

Comparative women's issues in this reader have not been segregated in one section. Rather, they are discussed where they have relevance within topic areas. This parallels the appearance of women's issues in the real world.

Some readings focus on the obstacles facing democracy activists as we near the year 2000. Journalists are especially visible and vulnerable to anti-democrats in many countries. Thus, issues of electoral corruption and the fight to preserve a free press in fledgling democracies are relevant.

Several readings deal with elected policy makers who find themselves in various dilemmas. In one case, politicians hope to act with environmental responsibility but also must accelerate industrial and other development strategies within their states. Likewise, today's political leaders, especially those in late industrializing states, find themselves imposing harsh economic adjustment programs while facing angry, newly democratized electorates at the polls.

Later readings suggest that political scientists, especially those of a liberal or Marxist orientation, need to broaden their view of comparative politics beyond an exclusively political economy lens and begin to take account of identity issues and how those issues are mobilized for political purposes.

Just as the world is changing, so, too, are the pedagogical techniques employed in teaching. The study questions in this reader require you to find additional background information at selected Internet sites, for comparisons with the readings in this volume. Such exercises promote your ability to find resources related to comparative politics and also raise your awareness and comfort level in using the web as a dynamic learning tool.

The world is changing at a rapid pace. The topics in this reader will give you key insights into the major comparative issues of this decade. While space prevents a detailed examination of all areas of comparative politics, I have tried to include readings that address the most important and, in some cases, the most contentious issues of our time. I am grateful to all those who allowed us copyright permission for reprinting the articles in this reader. I am especially grateful to Mr. George Soros for permission to use his article, "The Capitalist Threat," which appeared in the *Atlantic Monthly*, February 1997. "The Capitalist Threat" will also appear in a forthcoming book of collected essays by Mr. Soros, a book that undoubtedly will be of interest to the students and faculty familiar with this reader.

I would like to thank my editor, Edgar Laube, for his incredible professionalism, good humor, and enthusiasm for this project. I would like to thank James Lindsay for his support and for his encouragement to undertake this project. I am also pleased to acknowledge staff members and students at Oberlin College without whom this project would not have been completed: Tracy Tucker and Janet Paskin for their after-hours/extra hours of hard work and competent contributions; Eve Bratman, Christina Evans, Rebecca Rich, and Elizabeth Sommerfield for their timely and accurate work. My thanks to Jan Cooper for her careful readings on short notice of various writing I sent her way. As always, my thanks to Ann Cohen and Dorothy Sandberg for their continuing enthusiasm for whatever I undertake. Finally, my appreciation to Sandra Zagarell for the day-to-day support and encouragement that helps to make each undertaking enjoyable and productive.

WiseGuide Introduction

Question Authority

Critical Thinking and Bumper Stickers

The bumper sticker said: Question Authority. This is a simple directive that goes straight to the heart of critical thinking. The issue is not whether the authority is right or wrong; it's the questioning process that's important. Questioning helps you develop awareness and a clearer sense of what you think. That's critical thinking.

Critical thinking is a new label for an old approach to learning—that of challenging all ideas, hypotheses, and assumptions. In the physical and life sciences, systematic questioning and testing methods (known as the scientific method) help verify information, and objectivity is the benchmark on which all knowledge is pursued. In the social sciences, however, where the goal is to study people and their behavior, things get fuzzy. It's one thing for the chemistry experiment to work out as predicted, or for the petri dish to yield a certain result. It's quite another matter, however, in the social sciences, where the subject is ourselves. Objectivity is harder to achieve.

Although you'll hear critical thinking defined in many different ways, it really boils down to analyzing the ideas and messages that you receive. What are you being asked to think or believe? Does it make sense, objectively? Using the same facts and considerations, could you reasonably come up with a different conclusion? And, why does this matter in the first place? As the bumper sticker urged, question authority. Authority can be a textbook, a politician, a boss, a big sister, or an ad on television. Whatever the message, learning to question it appropriately is a habit that will serve you well for a lifetime. And in the meantime, thinking critically will certainly help you be course wise.

Getting Connected

This reader is a tool for connected learning. This means that the readings and other learning aids explained here will help you to link classroom theory to real-world issues. They will help you to think critically and to make long-lasting learning connections. Feedback from both instructors and students has helped us to develop some suggestions on how you can wisely use this connected learning tool.

WiseGuide Pedagogy

A wise reader is better able to be a critical reader. Therefore, we want to help you get wise about the articles in this reader. Each section of *Perspectives* has three tools to help you: the WiseGuide Intro, the WiseGuide Wrap-Up, and the Putting It in *Perspectives* review form.

WiseGuide Intro

In the WiseGuide Intro, the Academic Editor introduces the section, gives you an overview of the topics covered, and explains why particular articles were selected and what's important about them.

Also in the WiseGuide Intro, you'll find several key points or learning objectives that highlight the most important things to remember from this section. These will help you to focus your study of section topics.

At the end of the Wiseguide Intro, you'll find questions designed to stimulate critical thinking. Wise students will keep these questions in mind as they read an article (we repeat the questions at the start of the articles as a reminder). When you finish each article, check your understanding. Can you answer the questions? If not, go back and reread the article. The Academic Editor has written sample responses for many of the questions, and you'll find these online at the **courselinks**™ site for this course. More about **courselinks**™ in a minute. . . .

WiseGuide Wrap-Up

Be course wise and develop a thorough understanding of the topics covered in this course. The WiseGuide Wrap-Up at the end of each section will help you do just that with concluding comments or summary points that repeat what's most important to understand from the section you just read.

In addition, we try to get you wired up by providing a list of select Internet resources—what we call R.E.A.L. web sites because they're **R**elevant, **E**xciting, **A**pproved, and **L**inked. The information at these web sites will enhance your understanding of a topic. (Remember to use your Passport and start at http://www.courselinks.com so that if any of these sites have changed, you'll have the latest link.)

Putting It in *Perspectives* Review Form

At the end of the book is the Putting It in *Perspectives* review form. Your instructor may ask you to complete this form as an assignment or for extra credit. If nothing else, consider doing it on your own to help you critically think about the reading.

Prompts at the end of each article encourage you to complete this review form. Feel free to copy the form and use it as needed.

The courselinks™ Site

The **courselinks**™ Passport is your ticket to a wonderful world of integrated web resources designed to help you with your course work. These resources are found at the **courselinks**™ site for your course area. This is where the readings in this book and the key topics of your course are linked to an exciting array of online learning tools. Here you will find carefully selected readings, web links, quizzes, worksheets, and more, tailored to your course and approved as connected learning tools. The ever-changing, always interesting **courselinks**™ site features a number of carefully integrated resources designed to help you be course wise. These include:

- **R.E.A.L. Sites** At the core of a **courselinks**™ site is the list of R.E.A.L. sites. This is a select group of web sites for studying, not surfing. Like the readings in this book, these sites have been selected, reviewed, and approved by the Academic Editor and the Editorial Board. The R.E.A.L. sites are arranged by topic and are annotated with short descriptions and key words to make them easier for you to use for reference or research. With R.E.A.L. sites, you're studying approved resources within seconds—and not wasting precious time surfing unproven sites.

- **Editor's Choice** Here you'll find updates on news related to your course, with links to the actual online sources. This is also where we'll tell you about changes to the site and about online events.

- **Course Overview** This is a general description of the typical course in this area of study. While your instructor will provide specific course

objectives, this overview helps you place the course in a generic context and offers you an additional reference point.

- **www.orksheet** Focus your trip to a R.E.A.L. site with the www.orksheet. Each of the 10 to 15 questions will prompt you to take in the best that site has to offer. Use this tool for self-study, or if required, email it to your instructor.

- **Course Quiz** The questions on this self-scoring quiz are related to articles in the reader, information at R.E.A.L. sites, and other course topics, and will help you pinpoint areas you need to study. Only you will know your score—it's an easy, risk-free way to keep pace!

- **Topic Key** The Topic Key is a listing of the main topics in your course, and it correlates with the Topic Key that appears in this reader. This handy reference tool also links directly to those R.E.A.L. sites that are especially appropriate to each topic, bringing you integrated online resources within seconds!

- **Web Savvy Student Site** If you're new to the Internet or want to brush up, stop by the Web Savvy Student site. This unique supplement is a complete **courselinks**™ site unto itself. Here, you'll find basic information on using the Internet, creating a web page, communicating on the web, and more. Quizzes and Web Savvy Worksheets test your web knowledge, and the R.E.A.L. sites listed here will further enhance your understanding of the web.

- **Student Lounge** Drop by the Student Lounge to chat with other students taking the same course or to learn more about careers in your major. You'll find links to resources for scholarships, financial aid, internships, professional associations, and jobs. Take a look around the Student Lounge and give us your feedback. We're open to remodeling the Lounge per your suggestions.

Building Better Perspectives!

Please tell us what you think of this *Perspectives* volume so we can improve the next one. Here's how you can help:

1. Visit our **coursewise** site at: http://www.coursewise.com

2. Click on *Perspectives*. Then select the Building Better *Perspectives* Form for your book.

3. Forms and instructions for submission are available online.

Tell us what you think—did the readings and online materials help you make some learning connections? Were some materials more helpful than others? Thanks in advance for helping us build better *Perspectives*.

Student Internships

If you enjoy evaluating these articles or would like to help us evaluate the **courselinks**™ site for this course, check out the **coursewise** Student Internship Program. For more information, visit:

http://www.coursewise.com/intern.html

Brief Contents

Comparative Political Systems in Western-Style Democracies   1

section 2 Post-World War II Comparative Political Economies of Late Industrializing/ Third World States   46

Issues of Democratization   99

Changing Business and Labor Systems in Comparative Perspective   129

Peasants in Comparative Perspective   152

The International System Constrains State Choice   171

section
3

section
4

section
5

section
6

Contents

National Front Party was achieving success and attracting followers in voting districts where it had never before achieved a visible presence. Mairowitz traces the efforts of the extremist right wing to achieve a dominant position in local politics and to use that position as a springboard for capturing national power in the near future.   **8**

England

Germany

Russia

section 2

Post-World War II Comparative Political Economies of Late Industrializing/Third World States

South Africa

(GNU) to accelerate social change in South Africa. Hard-liners won the top National Executive Committee (NEC) slots at the ANC after defeating President Nelson Mandela's proposal to design measures that would elect more provincial and minority representatives to the NEC in order to find new blood and democratize the party. Other parties are also convening their representatives to determine their positions in the new South Africa.   **85**

33 **Bill Introduces Compulsory Schooling and Outlaws Exclusion on Grounds of Race,** Patrick Bulger and Adam Cooke. *The Star* (South Africa), August 15, 1996.
Though change in South Africa comes slowly, the new education minister has introduced a law that would force parents to send children ages seven to fifteen to school or face three months in jail or a fine. In addition, the law stipulates that no child may be refused entry to a school on the basis of race. Corporal punishment is also outlawed in schools. This law, however, does not settle a number of contentious issues. These include prohibiting schools from requiring fees from parents, as well as curriculum decisions concerning the teaching of religion and language. In addition, the bill does not resolve the teacher situation in which more teachers are currently employed and teaching in Model C schools than the government allows.   **89**

34 **Killing Machine: Witnesses Tell TRC of Life in the Shadow of Hit Squads.**
Sowetan, August 16, 1996.
The Truth and Reconciliation Committee (TRC) heard testimony about white South Africa's apartheid hit squads, which attempted to assassinate exiled African National Congress officials throughout Europe. By offering truth so that all may understand what took place throughout the apartheid years, those who give testimony hope to be pardoned by the committee in the spirit of national reconciliation.   **90**

South Korea

35 **The Trouble with South Korea.** *The Economist,* January 18, 1997.
In recently passed laws, the South Korean government has sided with corporations and against workers and unions, making it easier for companies to legally fire workers. In response, 15,000 students and union members battled police for days. *The Economist* argues that millions of workers are not taking part, so things are not as bad as they seem. In addition, *The Economist* argues that the new laws themselves are not problematic. Rather, it was the South Korean government's passage of these laws in a secret session of parliament that allowed the opposition to frame the debate around issues of democracy and national security. The real problem was only one of public relations, argues *The Economist.*   **91**

36 **A Korean Deal Emerges,** Damon Darlin. *Forbes,* September 12, 1994.
South Korea's main problem is how to achieve unification with North Korea, which does not seem to want unification. South Korea does not want to promise to bail out North Korea financially, as West Germany attempted to do in East Germany with the resultant political problems. Experts advise giving technical assistance and aid to North Korea to help its economy over the next few years before attempting any unification initiatives.   **93**

37 **Ex-Enemy of the State Sees His Chance to Lead It,** Nicholas D. Kristof.
New York Times, September 24, 1997.
Kim Dae Jung, South Korea's perennial opposition leader, who has lived in exile and campaigned within South Korea in a system that would never permit him to ever achieve leadership, could become South Korea's next president following the December 1997 elections. Kim, leader of the National Congress for New Politics, has escaped many assassination attempts by government leaders. Now, Rhee In Je, who has left the ruling party to found and lead the New Korea Party, may well split the vote of those who do not support Kim, allowing Kim to win a national plurality. Lee Hoi Chang, the current ruling party candidate, trails both Kim and Rhee in the polls. Kim is seeking alliances with the leaders of a number of small parties who also are competing in the election.   **96**

WiseGuide Wrap-Up   **98**

section 3

Issues of Democratization

section 4

Changing Business and Labor Systems in Comparative Perspective

section 5

Peasants in Comparative Perspective

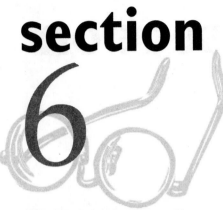

section 6

The International System Constrains State Choice

section 7

Environment and Development

section 8

Structural Adjustment in Comparative Perspective

than fifty developing countries have lost their banking system's capital. Speculators and bankers have been running the international monetary system for years. The IMF seems only proficient at finding new jobs for new employees in its own organization. Hanke argues that we need to stop rewarding the IMF, stop its funding, and have it either meet standards of professional accomplishment or close down. **236**

WiseGuide Wrap-Up   238

WiseGuide Intro   239

section 9

Religion, Ethnicity, and Nationalism: Special Challenges to the State?

Topic Key

This Topic Key is an important tool for learning. It will help you integrate this reader into your course studies. Listed below, in alphabetical order, are important topics covered in this volume. Below each topic you'll find the reading numbers and titles relating to that topic. Note that the Topic Key might not include every topic your instructor chooses to emphasize. If you don't find the topic you're looking for in the Topic Key, check the index or the online topic key at the **courselinks**™ site.

African National Congress
26 Mandela's Group Accepts 5 Years of Power-Sharing
31 South Africa's Indians Changing Loyalties: Domination by the Blacks Now Feared
32 South Africa ANC Conference
34 Killing Machine: Witnesses Tell TRC of Life in the Shadow of Hit Squads

Agriculture
20 Globalization and Resistance: The Remaking of Mexico
48 Land and Democracy: Reconsidering the Agrarian Question
49 Peasant Challenge in Post-Communist China

Anticolonialism
63 Color Lines: Africa and Asia in the Twenty-First Century

Apartheid
26 Mandela's Group Accepts 5 Years of Power-Sharing
33 Bill Introduces Compulsory Schooling and Outlaws Exclusion on Grounds of Race
34 Killing Machine: Witnesses Tell TRC of Life in the Shadow of Hit Squads
50 Transforming a Pariah State: International Dimensions of the South African Transition

Beijing Conference
53 The Fourth World Conference on Women
54 Women Redrawing the Map: The World after the Beijing and Cairo Conferences

Cairo Conference
54 Women Redrawing the Map: The World after the Beijing and Cairo Conferences

Civil Society
41 Book Review: *Making Democracy Work: Civic Traditions in Modern Italy*
43 The Capitalist Threat

Class
46 The "Late Blooming" of the South Korean Labor Movement

Coalitions
3 French Voters Rebuff Deficit-Cutting to Qualify for a New European Currency
26 Mandela's Group Accepts 5 Years of Power-Sharing

Corruption
17 Political Action Man
19 In Mexico's House, Speaker's Stature Signals a New Day
20 Globalization and Resistance: The Remaking of Mexico

Crime
11 German Chancellor Helmut Kohl Launched His Reelection Campaign

Democracy, Democratization
9 Crisis of Unification: How Germany Changes
18 Gains by Opposition Confirmed in Mexico
19 In Mexico's House, Speaker's Stature Signals a New Day
24 Harassment of the Opposition
25 U.S. Envoy to Nigeria Gets a Stormy Farewell
29 Final Election Results
30 The Main Party and Leaders
37 Ex-Enemy of the State Sees His Chance to Lead It
38 Towards Impartial Poll Refereeing
39 Governors Should Be Equal to Ministers
40 Call to Transparency
41 Book Review: *Making Democracy Work, Civic Traditions in Modern Italy*
42 Freedom Favors Development
43 The Capitalist Threat
44 Out of the Closet and into *La Calle*
48 Land and Democracy: Reconsidering the Agrarian Question

Drug Control
51 Mexican Foreign Policy in Focus

Ecology and Environmentalism
49 Peasant Challenge in Post-Communist China
51 Mexican Foreign Policy in Focus
56 Tourism: Think and Think Again
57 Rain Forest Conservation, the Direct or Indirect Approach?

Education
33 Bill Introduces Compulsory Schooling and Outlaws Exclusion on the Grounds of Race
53 The Fourth World Conference on Women

Employment, Jobs, Unemployment
2 Left Wins Strong Mandate as Voters in France Reject Austerity in Favor of Jobs: Conservatives Out
3 French Voters Rebuff Deficit Cutting to Qualify for a New European Currency
5 Populist Pomp: Just Call Me Tony
9 Crisis of Unification: How Germany Changes
10 The Progress of German Unification
15 Japan Market Forces Are Allowed to Advance
20 Globalization and Resistance: The Remaking of Mexico
22 Brazil: Real-Politics
35 The Trouble with South Korea
45 Dismantling Germany's Welfare State

Ethnicity, Ethic Cleansing
62 Nation-States and States of Mind: Nationalism as Psychology
64 The Clash of Civilizations?

European Union, Euro
1 The French Message
12 EMU to Lead Germany from Riches to Rags
55 'I Cannot Accept an a La Carte Europe'

Fundamentalism
64 The Clash of Civilizations?

section 1

Comparative Political Systems in Western-Style Democracies

WiseGuide Intro Today's political party systems in Western democracies take various forms. In the United States, only two viable political parties compete electorally (though many more parties appear on the ballot). In Europe and Japan, many parties are viable contenders for political office, and these parties represent the extreme left and right, as well as various positions in the center.

In some Western political party systems, no single party can capture enough of the vote to win a majority in the Congress or Parliament. Thus, no party can govern alone, assured that it has enough votes to pass its legislative agenda. Party leaders, therefore, must find allies in rival parties with whom to build a majority vote and then govern in coalition. This may require some compromises on policy positions during the election period or afterward. Such compromises are apparent in the readings in this section on the French election, which identify the policy positions that the Communist Party required when it entered into a political alliance with the Socialist-Party–led coalition. The readings on Japan show that building a governing coalition has meant awarding cabinet positions to unpopular party leaders from smaller parties.

Three trends appeared in the political party contests in Western-style democracies in the European national elections of the 1990s. First, following the Bill Clinton model of appealing to younger voters and women, and of using television for communicating to the "average" voter, politicians such as Britain's Tony Blair are adopting a "populist" image.

Second, left-of-center political parties, such as the Labour Party in Britain and the Socialist Party in France, recognize that their main support base consists of workers and unionists who are being hurt by the dismantling of the welfare state and the conservative economic programs being adopted in the name of global competitiveness. Today's European leaders appear to be caught in the horns of a dilemma. They must search for ways to cushion the burden of economic reform on working people and the poor. However, they are also planning to pursue the tough economic reforms that will contribute to their country's global competitiveness.

Finally, the third trend of the 1990s is that women are becoming more important—both as voters and as candidates—to the fortunes of political parties. A new image of women as productive workers, as voters who care deeply about such issues as job security, education, and health care, and as decision makers who are the equals of men has emerged during the national election periods of the 1990s.

The financial and social consequences of the unification of Eastern and Western Germany continue to play a role in today's political arena.

Additionally, to truly understand the role of political leaders today in European Western democracies, we must understand how a politician's stance toward the regional organization of the European Union, which requires domestic budget restraints and many pro business policies that organized labor claims hurt the working poor, helps to determine voters' views of rival political parties.

? Questions ?

1. How does the Mairowitz article (Reading 4) change your view of what happened in the French elections from the view you would have had if you had only read the *New York Times* accounts by Cohen and Whitney (Readings 1 and 2)?

2. How do the prospects for a strong regional European Union affect political issues in France, Germany, Russia, and England?

3. Because the Communist Party made the greatest gains in Russia's parliamentary elections, some might anticipate that the new parliament would reverse the economic reforms of the recent past. In Reading 13, why does the news analyst for the *Economist* believe that the economic reforms will not be reversed?

The French Message

Chirac failed to read mood of a country wary of a world that demands reforms.

Roger Cohen

PARIS, June 1—It was not just France's center-right government that was swept out of office today by a remarkable Socialist resurgence. It was also the previously unassailable dignity of the presidential office as well as assumptions about France's need for market reforms and the coherence of the French right as a political movement.

Lionel Jospin's Socialists are not Tony Blair's Labor Party. They have said that they would create 350,000 jobs in the state sector and have suggested that they would halt the country's privatizations. By voting this party back into office just four years after it suffered a crushing defeat, the French have expressed their deep reservations about the American-led economic reforms they see sweeping the world.

Far from suggesting opportunity, globalization is widely equated here with menace and with the country's 12.8 percent unemployment. "The essential message is that our entire political system is in crisis," said Philippe Séguin, a leader of President Jacques Chirac's defeated Gaullist Party. "The French

continue to look for the means to master the new world that is upon them and that they do not want to equate always with regression and loss of jobs."

That message has been clear enough for a while, intensified by uneasiness over France's planned adoption in 1999 of a single European currency, the euro, and anger over austerity measures taken to prepare for it. But, in a gross miscalculation, Mr. Chirac failed to heed the disoriented national mood.

His decision to call elections 10 months early in an effort to secure a right-wing parliamentary majority for the remaining five years of his presidency, and then to place his deeply unpopular Prime Minister at the head of the campaign, backfired disastrously. Seldom, if ever, has a French President shot himself so conspicuously in the foot.

The institutional consequences already appear far-reaching. This was Mr. Chirac's election, specifically willed by him, and he lost it. By committing such a blunder, the President has punctured the aura that has surrounded the pivotal office of the Fifth Republic since it was founded in 1958.

Gen. Charles de Gaulle, who fashioned the presidency to his ambitions, declared in 1964 that, "The undivided authority of the state is entirely conferred on the President by the people who have elected him." He added: "There is no other authority—ministerial, civil, military or judicial—that is not conferred and maintained by him."

For almost four decades, and certainly under Mr. Chirac's wily predecessor François Mitterrand, this extraordinary concentration of power has been maintained. The President, all powerful, has stood above the fray. But because of an inept campaign in which he took part, and now an ignominious defeat, Mr. Chirac appears to have placed himself in a situation of acute weakness.

It is already clear that in the initial period of "cohabitation" with a Socialist Prime Minister—almost certainly Mr. Jospin himself—the balance of power will lie very much with a newly installed Socialist leader endorsed by the people against the specific will of the President.

Although there have been other such "cohabitations," including Mr. Chirac's own period as Prime Minister under Mr. Mitterrand from 1986 to 1988, none has previously emerged in circumstances so personally demeaning to the head of state.

How Mr. Jospin will exploit this new situation is not yet clear. France's position today is full of contradictions to which the Socialist program appears to offer no ready solutions. The country is formally committed to European integration and to the euro—objectives that in turn seem to require privatizations, deregulation and austerity—yet it has voted for a party that has expressed clear reservations over those economic policies.

Mr. Jospin said today that "the reorientation of European construction" would be central to his program, and that social and economic policy would be "placed at the service of man." These are vague slogans that have convinced many French people that Mr. Jospin wants a Europe that creates jobs rather than rewards capital. But if fiscal austerity goes, Germany's commitment to the euro will go with it, and Mr. Jospin is well aware of this.

So he will quickly find himself navigating in treacherous waters, needing to signal a change in economic and political direction without bringing the franc, the stock market and the entire euro project crashing down around him. Already, since the left's gains in the first round of voting a week ago, the stock market has fallen by 6.48 percent.

It will certainly fall again if, as Mr. Jospin has suggested, he suspends the planned and supposedly imminent privatization of the state telecommunications company, France Télécom. The Socialists' plans to create state jobs without raising taxes and to lower the work week to 35 hours with no loss of pay will also be the object of scrutiny by markets and the German central bank.

Nonetheless, Mr. Jospin is likely to enjoy a honeymoon of several weeks. His modest campaign, his talk of a "new political contract," and his promise to listen to the people have all proved very convincing to the public angry at perceived Government corruption and arrogance. Mr. Jospin's promise of a "profound renovation of public life" appears sincere and deeply felt.

It is precisely because the departing Prime Minister, Alain Juppé, and Mr. Chirac missed this disenchantment—to which Mr. Jospin was attentive—that anger in the French political right was at such a high pitch today. Nicolas Sarkozy, a Gaullist, came closest to pointing the finger at the President and at Mr. Juppé by declaring that, "I am convinced that it is not our ideas that were defeated today but the manner in which they were presented."

That manner did indeed appear often to be entirely lacking in coherence. For two years, with a crushing parliamentary majority behind them, Mr. Chirac and Mr. Juppé veered between promises of reforms intended to cut the state's preponderant role in the economy and equally vehement promises that the unusually state-heavy French economic model would not be touched.

A country full of contradictions and no ready solutions.

France, it is said, is hard to reform, preferring upheaval to gradual change. Certainly there were repeated strikes over the attempts to touch anything, from the state-owned railroads to the social security system.

But the Government's uncertainty about which direction to take has been palpable, finally finding expression in Mr. Chirac's bizarre decision to entrust the last

week of campaigning for his cause to Mr. Séguin and Alain Madelin, a team as unlikely and apparently incoherent as, say, a ticket comprised of Mario Cuomo and Ronald Reagan.

Indeed, the exposure of the paralyzing splits on the right between a Gaullist wing that is attached above all to a strong French state and a reformist wing that believes in sweeping market reforms has been one of the most striking aspects of the election campaign. Edouard Balladur, a former Prime Minister and a member of the centrist Union for French Democracy, declared today "We simply have to start being coherent and stop affirming one thing and then the contrary."

He was one of several center-right politicians to talk today of a need to rebuild France's political right completely. A period of bloodletting is almost certainly imminent.

What is already clear is that the confusion of the Gaullists and of Mr. Balladur's party helped Jean-Marie Le Pen's extremist National Front—for the simple reason that the party's blunt and racist message was instantly comprehensible while that of the center-right was a blur. The National Front has emerged as a third right-wing force with about as much popular backing as each of the other two parties, even though it won only a single seat in Parliament.

"Mr. Chirac should resign because the French people have declined to show confidence in him," Mr. Le Pen declared tonight.

Article Review Form at end of book.

Left Wins Strong Mandate as Voters in France Reject Austerity in Favor of Jobs

Conservatives out

Socialists are expected to form a coalition with communists.

Craig R. Whitney

PARIS, Monday, June 2—In a stunning rejection of President Jacques Chirac's economic austerity policies, French voters on Sunday gave the Socialist Party and its Communist allies a mandate to form a Government that would make jobs its absolute priority for the next five years.

Mr. Chirac called the parliamentary elections a year ahead of schedule, appealing to voters to allow his conservative coalition to keep reducing budget deficits and government spending so France could qualify for membership in a new common European currency by the end of the century.

Instead, the left won on promises by the Socialists and the Communists to try to loosen the budget-deficit limits that Germany has insisted on for undergirding the common currency, and to give priority to strong measures to reduce the country's 12.8 percent employment rate.

The final official count by the Interior Ministry this morning gave the Socialists and smaller leftist parties allied with them 268 seats in the 577-seat Parliament.

They need 289 seats to form a majority, and the Communists, no longer the totalitarian party they were during the cold war, will support them with the 39 seats they won. The environmentalist Greens party, which also said it was ready to serve in a Socialist-led government, won 7.

Mr. Chirac's conservative coalition and its allies, which had 464 seats in the Parliament he dissolved, shrank to 262. The far-right National Front, which had vowed to defeat the Government even if that meant helping the Socialists win power, won one seat, from Toulon, the Mediterranean navy port where it has controlled city hall for the last two years.

"I wish good luck to those who are now going to govern France, and I wish good luck to France," said Mr. Chirac's conservative Prime Minister, Alain Juppé, who had already announced that he would resign today because of the poor conservative showing in the first round of voting a week ago.

As the French Constitution prescribes, Mr. Chirac will appoint the new Prime Minister, possibly today. It will almost certainly be Lionel Jospin, the 59-year-old Socialist Party leader and former Education Minister who ran against him for the presidency two years ago.

Speaking to supporters in his district in southwest France on Sunday night, Mr. Jospin described the leftist victory in terms of tempered triumph.

"It isn't a demand for everything at once, which nobody believes in anymore," he said. "It isn't naïve belief in promises that have several times not been kept in the past. It is a reasoned and pressing demand for real long-term progress for the French people, especially the least privileged among them."

As the election returns rolled in on Sunday night and reverberated across Europe, there was silence from Mr. Chirac.

In Germany, a leading member of Chancellor Helmut Kohl's conservative party said on the German radio, "I would expect the debate that has already begun to take place over the direction of economic and social policies to intensify."

Mr. Kohl's Government is in the throes of its own struggle with high unemployment and budget deficits. Last week it caused a furor and drew criticism from the head of Germany's independent central bank by saying the deficit could be brought down, on paper, by revaluing the bank's gold and currency reserves.

Jacques Santer, president of the European Union's Executive Commission, said on Sunday night that the plan for the common currency by 1999 would remain on schedule.

"I know what President Chirac's program is, and he's still in office," he said. "I look forward to seeing what the new Government's program will be." Mr. Chirac's term does not expire until May 2002.

Raymond Barre, a conservative former Prime Minister, warned the left that it would have to take account of international realities.

"Let it avoid, on the European stage, any step that could lead our partners, especially Germany, to be mistrustful, or lead to a failure of economic and monetary union," Mr. Barre said on French television.

Coming soon after Tony Blair's Labor Party sweep of the British elections a month ago, the outcome in France could help swing the center of gravity at a European Union summit meeting in Amsterdam this month away from the conventional wisdom that continued austerity now is the best way to prosperity with a common European currency later.

The French election result was a clear slap in the face for Mr. Chirac, who appealed to voters on Tuesday not to do this to him.

 Article Review Form at end of book.

French Voters Rebuff Deficit-Cutting to Qualify for a New European Currency

The vote was not a rejection of plans for closer European union, Mr. Jospin said on Sunday night. That, he said, the Socialists would continue to support as they did when their former leader, François Mitterrand, held the French presidency.

But it was, to use Mr. Jospin's words, a call for "reorienting the building of Europe" to put at the center of the project the fight against unemployment rather than arcane financial criteria few people understood.

He also wants Italy and Spain to be in on the common currency from the start, though Germany has insisted that they could not join unless they met the budget-deficit limit of 3 percent of gross domestic product prescribed by the 1992 Treaty on European Union.

The Communists have always opposed the common currency project.

Mr. Jospin could reassure most of France's European partners about his intentions if, as rumored in recent days, he appoints Jacques Delors, Mr. Santer's highly respected predecessor, as Foreign Minister. Mr. Delors is widely regarded as one of the guiding forces behind the treaty.

Mr. Delors's daughter, Martine Aubry, was also elected to Parliament by her district near Lille.

But the central problem for Mr. Jospin, as it was for Mr. Juppé, will be how to reconcile France's European ambitions with its chronic and debilitating unemployment problem.

Unless he does something soon, he could find himself in the same kind of political hot water Mr. Chirac unwittingly got into by calling new elections. Two years ago, Mr. Chirac won the presidency on a pledge to attack unemployment, but his conservative Government could not deliver.

The Socialists and Communists campaigned jointly on promises to create 700,000 jobs, half of them in the public sector without raising taxes, and to reduce the work week from 39 to 35 hours without cutting salaries—promises the conservatives derided as pie in the sky.

But as it became clearer during the last 10 days that the left might win, Mr. Jospin qualified the pledges. Both promises could not be kept simultaneously or right away, he said, an observation he may have been alluding to on Sunday night in saying the voters did not believe they could have "everything at once."

But people did want results right away, Robert Hue, the Communist leader, insisted on Sunday night. After he spoke by telephone with Mr. Jospin, he called for "a radically new policy clearly oriented to the left and significant measures at the very outset of the legislature."

Asked if the Communists would join the Government, as they did during the cold war at the outset of Mr. Mitterrand's first term in 1981, Mr. Hue said, "All that is open; we will discuss it."

The leftist campaign program, which may not turn out to be identical to a concrete Government program, called for a conference of labor unions, employer groups and Government officials this month to discuss jobs, working hours and salaries.

On salaries, the Communists wanted an immediate result—a raise of more than a dollar an hour for the minimum wage, now the equivalent of $6.79 an hour, by July 1.

The left's program would lower the 20.6 percent value-added tax on goods deemed necessities and halt the current Government's plans to lower taxes on unearned income. It would also call off the planned privatization of France Telecom, the Government telecommunications enterprise, that the conservatives intended to go ahead with after the election.

 Article Review Form at end of book.

R E A D I N G 4

Fascism À La Mode

In France, the far right presses for national purity

David Zane Mairowitz

Last May, on the night of the first round of nationwide French elections, I left my Avignon apartment, turned a corner, and headed down the Rue Séverine toward the local headquarters of Jean-Marie Le Pen's far-right National Front Party. Le Pen's group had just won 24 percent of the Avignon vote—over twice what it needed to qualify for the runoff round a week later but nowhere near enough to allow for hopes of victory—and I was curious to see what mood the party faithful were in. Normally the headquarters are easy to miss. There is no

sign on the door, no posters or stickers in the window, not even a bell—only a seemingly empty, anonymous storefront. In part this is attributable to the astonishing paranoia of Le Pen and his cronies, who see themselves as beleaguered and marginalized, fighting a war of resistance against the strains of impurity that would sully France. But there are practical reasons for their concern as well. Although popular throughout the south, and growing ever more so, the Front still has plenty of detractors, and some of them don't mind throwing bricks through windows.

Tonight, however, there were no bricks, and there was certainly no missing the place. As soon as I

rounded the corner I could see people spilling out onto the sidewalk—people I knew. My local mechanic was there, and the *boulangerie* woman, and enough of my neighbors that it took some time to get through all the *bonsoirs* and small talk required of me. Were these people the neofascists I had come to fear as the Front swept town after town in the south? Were they brownshirts? No, just the shopkeepers and skilled workers you'd expect to find in any small European town. They were good people, decent and well-meaning, legitimately concerned about their future, if perhaps not fully aware of the historical implications of a Front victory.

Inside they were celebrating. The Front's candidate, a man by the very un-working-class-sounding name of Thibaut de La Tocnaye (and the victim of countless Hitler mustaches drawn on his campaign posters), had no chance at all in the next week's runoff, but the party was sensing victory nonetheless. For de La Tocnaye was about to do locally what Le Pen had candidates positioned to do across the nation: he was going to spoil the election for the conservatives. By staying in the race, de La Tocnaye and his compatriots would split the right-wing vote and force a Socialist victory. In the short run such a tactic would weaken the right, but in the long run the Front would benefit from the destruction of the centrist obstacle in its path—specifically, President Jacques Chirac and those legislators rallied around him. Le Pen had made no secret of his hatred for Chirac, and in a week's time he would have cause for glee: Chirac would lose his majority, and although the Front would take only 15 percent of the national vote and win but one parliamentary seat, its future would be brighter than ever before.

On June 2, the morning after the election's final round, I opened my *International Herald Tribune* and was greeted by the optimistic headline FRANCE'S LEFT TURN. Fair enough, but over the next few days the media seemed to lose sight of the fact that the turn was made by an extremely right-wing backseat driver. In the post-vote autopsy columns provided by the national daily *Liberation*, for example, the Front was being considered almost as great a loser as Chirac, and some commentators were even predicting that we had seen the last of the neofascists. In fact,

most of the French newspapers stuck to the same easily digestible story—victorious left crushes never-to-be-seen-again right—and did not worry over what the ability to decide a national election implied about the Front's future.

Such is the view of the Paris-based journalist. But I live in Avignon, and in Avignon we know better. The Front isn't finished. In fact, it's getting stronger.

Now and then my son and I go out with a set of scraping tools and attempt to remove the Front stickers that clutter the lampposts and street signs throughout our neighborhood. *"Mains Propres, Tête Haute"* ("Hands Clean, Head High") they read, both proclaiming and appealing to the latest wave of French disgust with government corruption. The tactic has been effective, if somewhat hypocritical. Last February, in the southern industrial city of Vitrolles, the party toppled the Socialist mayor, currently under investigation for fiscal impropriety, and replaced him with Catherine Mégret, the wife of Front bigwig Bruno Mégret, who was himself disqualified from running for having overspent the legal limit on campaign funding. Although largely an unknown quantity, she cannot as yet be accused of corruption herself, and this is what counts most in the local context. For decades the Front has been denied access to the legislature, and its strategy has been instead to build a power base on the municipal level. In the summer of 1995, Front candidates won mayoral races in three fair-size southern towns—Marignane, Orange, and Toulon. If these people can stay out of prison (where a fair number of French mayors, especially here in the south, spend part of their retirement), there is

hope that they may be able to gain a respectability that will allow them to infiltrate the national system from below. It is, after all, perfectly acceptable in France to hold a federal post and a mayorship simultaneously. The last prime minister was also the mayor of Bordeaux, and the Front's single parliamentary seat in this election was won by Jean-Marie Le Chevallier, the mayor of Toulon.

And so the game is played out on the local level. The Front intends to capture as many "model cities" as possible and drum up grass-roots support. Hence the stickers covering everything in sight. Hence the alarmist handbills citing attacks on "French" citizens by local "Arabs" or "blacks." Hence the doorbells rung by proselytizers, the youth clubs organized, the small three- or four-person cells that seek out new recruits. The Front has managed to make frightening progress with the military and police communities; it has even established a union, FN-Police, to encourage their loyalty. In order to influence the national education agenda, the party also is attempting to create its own Parent-Teacher Association.

In other words, Le Pen and the Front do not, for the moment, need seats in Parliament. Towns will do just fine. In Paris, Le Chevallier will be hooted down, but in Toulon he is king. When, last year, a group of booksellers invited the Polish-French author Marek Halter to receive a special award at the Toulon Book Fair, Le Chevallier vetoed the notion, saying, "He comes from Poland, is a naturalized French citizen, is in favor of immigration and of imposing a cosmopolitan culture on France." Subtext: Halter is a Jew.

Le Chevallier instead chose none other than Brigitte Bardot (whose memoirs are a bestseller in France) to receive the Book Fair's prize, though she refused the honor, apparently reasoning that her reputation had been tarnished enough by the very things that so impressed Le Chevallier: the string of racist remarks she has made in public over the last few years and the fact that her latest spouse, Bernard D'Ormale, is a leading member of the Front and one of Le Pen's acolytes. In the end, the Toulon Book Fair resembled nothing so much as a National Front convention, with stalls devoted to the collected speeches of Marshal Pétain, the 1958 right-wing putsch in Algeria, and books about Clovis I, the fifth-century king of the Franks who united "French" territory and has become the party's unofficial patron saint. With a reversal of reality typical of Le Pen and his ilk, all of this was carried out in the name of "pluralism," the idea being that with the media in the hands of "internationalists" (in case the reference is not clear, the party has at times employed the term "T-lévy-sion"), the Front's viewpoint is underrepresented, if not outright censored.

Nor have the other Front mayors hesitated to heavy-hand their way into their constituents' cultural life. In Orange, Mayor Jacques Bompard decided that the public library would henceforth be directly answerable to the *mairie* (or town hall). Suddenly books that did not reflect Front ideology began disappearing from the shelves—including works on the French Revolution (the sentiment "*Liberté, Égalité, Fraternité*" is anathema to the Front), collections of stories from North Africa, and any book with illustrations showing the races

mixing. Also included, of course, were any works by authors known to be hostile to the party. The replacements? Henry Coston's *The Financiers Who Control the World, Mysteries and Secrets of B'Nai Brith*, the works of the Italian fascist Julius Evola, and the usual smattering of French Holocaust-denial tomes being produced by the negationist history department at the University of Lyon III.

Although he lost his presidential bid, and holds no political office, Le Pen is clearly the one giving the cues. Just after the elections he announced that all grants to local nonprofit cultural and educational groups within the Front's jurisdiction would be "reviewed." Since most aid of this sort occurs on the municipal level in France, and since many organizations—theater troupes, community centers, and the like—simply cannot exist without public assistance, this was no small threat. But Le Pen's mayors did him one better. They eliminated virtually all grants to groups outside the Front's cultural and political sphere. Gone, or soon to be, were those groups run by the Front's political adversaries. Gone were the theater troupes and cinemas not sufficiently in line with the far right. And gone as well were those groups performing such apparently distasteful tasks as giving help and comfort to those dying of AIDS.

Le Pen recently appeared at a public meeting with a plate bearing a plaster model of the severed head of Catherine Trautmann, the mayor of Strasbourg (and now minister of culture in the new Socialist government). Supporting his daughter Marie-Caroline's campaign in the town of Mantes-la-Jolie, he waded into a group of

some 200 anti-Front demonstrators and roughed up the Socialist candidate, a woman. He has also been known to lower his trousers in front of reporters, and this has surely hurt him among swing voters. But for his own hard-core supporters, especially in the more macho culture of the south, such behavior simply reinforces the idea that this is a man who has the courage of his convictions, who "talks straight" while most politicians waffle.

Straight talk goes a long way in this part of France, especially with the so-called *pieds-noirs*, the hundreds of thousands of French Algerians who settled in the south after being chased out of North Africa when Algeria gained its independence in 1962. Historically lied to by all the traditional parties, they bear a particular grudge against De Gaulle for "giving up" Algeria, and many of them would never dream of voting for a Gaullist such as Chirac. Le Pen's populist tactics appeal to their sense of persecution: not only did the Arabs kick us out of Algeria but now they're colonizing *France*. Cynically playing on the famous Arab nationalist slogan "*Algérie algérienne,*" Le Pen warns that we will be facing a "*France algérienne*" unless something is done.*

Daniel Simonpiéri, the Front mayor of Marignane, has been doing something. Responsible as mayor for daily banalities such as school meals, he has eliminated

*Front propaganda tends to inflate the number of foreigners in France, putting the figure at 10 percent of the population and suggesting that the majority of foreigners are from North Africa. The last census, in 1994, put the figure at 6.5 percent out of a total population of 58 million. An educated guess would be that approximately half of this number is North African, with the balance being Spanish, Italians, Portuguese, and black Africans from such former French colonies as Gabon and Senegal.

non-pork lunches from public school cafeterias. This means that on days when pork is on the menu, Jewish or Muslim children have no choice but to eat it or, preferably, leave the premises. Education officials in Marignane claim that this measure is strictly "budgetary." In the Toulon marketplace, vendors of African and West Indian foodstuffs have had their stalls closed on the grounds that only locally grown produce can legally be sold there. More important, family allowances and social security payments are in the hands of Front bureaucrats, who claim that foreign families steal these benefits from Frenchmen. Although local governments cannot legally refuse such payments, they can and do create bureaucratic obstacles that make it almost impossible for "immigrants" to claim their money.

Brigitte Bardot, who last year was fined for defamatory remarks she made in an interview with the newspaper *Le Figaro*, has been doing her part, too. Known defender of animals against the cruelties of man, she has spoken out in particular against the Muslim holy rite of Aidel-Kebir, in which lambs "have their throats cut, one after the other, with dull blades." In Bardot's image of a France overrun by Arabs, one can no longer hear the village church bells ringing for the barbaric cries of the muezzin coming from the omnipresent mosques. Although a complete fantasy, I have heard this sentiment echoed by people here in the Midi, who tell me that they no longer hear French spoken in the streets, only Arabic.

Having been taken to court innumerable times for his own overtly racist remarks, Le Pen now adopts a crypto-vocabulary, employing such terms as "the immigration lobby" and "cosmopoli-

tanism." He knows that he must appear modern and reasonable, concerned with the bread-and-butter issues, all the while keeping his blatantly totalitarian long-term agenda only slightly out of focus. On a radio talk show during the election campaign, he was asked by a caller what he would do about Paris's serious pollution problem if elected. "This is a problem of public transport," he said. "If fewer people drove their cars into town, and took public transport instead, we could conquer the pollution problem." So far, so good. No ecologist could put it better. But why don't people use buses and subways? Because of the large number of daily "aggressions" and "insecurity." Everyone knows that in Le Pen's doublespeak "insecurity" must be read as "immigrant." Thus, with a deft sleight of hand, he is able to pass along the implicit message Pollution = Arabs.

The Front has found other uses for "ecology" as well. As Bruno Mégret puts it, "Why fight for the preservation of animal species while at the same time tolerating the disappearance of certain human races due to general crossbreeding?" The "founder" of modern ecology, according to Le Pen, is the Nobel Prize-winning chemist Alexis Carrel, who, working under Pétain, promoted the idea of enforced euthanasia via gas chamber for criminals and the deranged. In Avignon, as in other French towns, a campaign is under way to change the street name Rue Alexis Carrel; that this push has been unsuccessful is largely due to the Front's growing power.

Aside from its traditional hatred of Arabs, the Front has found and demonized another ideological enemy—American culture. Seen as a bastion of "cosmopolitanism,"

the sworn enemy of "national identity," the degenerate United States, with its mixed races and libertine culture; seeks to impose "l' American way of life" on Europe and in particular on France. The inheritance of this "coca-colonization" is, according to Le Pen, urban ghettos and ethnic violence *à la yankee*. "Fast food is mounting as quickly as immigration" is a typical slogan, and the Front's election literature speaks of defending "the French language against the mounting hegemony of American expressions." Explains Bruno Mégret, "[O]ur model of civilization is far superior to that of the United States of America, far superior to those who are trying to colonize us."

Public enemy number one is rap music. The reasons for this are obvious: rap is anti-establishment, anti-police, black, and clearly American in origin. But the Front has found a way to play the issue against Arabs as well. Mégret again: "Rap is one of the cultural consequences of North African immigration in France; it's contrary to our identity as Frenchmen." Never mind that the majority of rappers are second or third generation and that the language they rap in is French.

The group Suprême NTM—which stands for *Nique Ta Mère*, or Fuck Your Mother—has become the scapegoat for this hostility. Sons of the suburban ghetto (*les cités*), and strongly influenced by their American counterparts N.W.A. (Niggaz With Attitude), NTM built its career by way of an obligatory hatred of the French police. At a concert in 1995, organized to protest the election of the Front in Toulon, NTM verbally insulted the officers present, between refrains of their song "Police":

The fascists are not only in Toulon. . . . They're standing right behind you at the entrance. These people are a threat to our freedom. Our enemies are the men in blue. . . . We piss on them.

When the police took NTM to court for outrage against the public forces of order, a heavy fine was expected. But in addition, the group was sentenced to six months in prison and banned from rapping for six months subsequent to their release, a judgment not seen in the French cultural sphere since the middle of the nineteenth century.

I have a hard time reconciling all of this U.S. bashing with what I know of my mechanic, who still watches *Dallas* reruns and takes his kids for a "Beeg Mac" now and then at the local "Macdo." But it would be just as difficult to convince the leftists at the local *Ras l' Front* ("Fed up with the Front") that this man doesn't wear jackboots and may not even understand the neofascist craziness grinding away at his perfectly reasonable fears. He doesn't hate foreigners, but he *is* genuinely worried about unemployment and the violence in his children's schools. He's a man of the Mediterranean, fiercely independent and suspicious of any wind blowing from Paris. And there's the rub: if the National Front continues to sweep city after city, it will happen not because French people everywhere are turning into fascists but because they have no real idea what they are letting themselves in for. Ignorance, not cruelty, is what allows the Front to thrive, and I have little doubt about the party's ability to install the next round of fascist mayors here in the Mediterranean basin on the shoulders of simple people like the man who fixes my car.

My Avignon neighbors tend to rear up when confronted with the Front's "fascism." They see such charges as indicative of a Paris-inspired conspiracy against them, and this only tends to deepen their commitment to the party. They seem unaware that Le Pen's long-term national program bears a chilling resemblance to the Vichy "*Révolution Nationale,*" even though some of them are the sons and daughters of local Resistance fighters who battled the Nazis in the nearby Provençal forests. I run into my Front neighbors at our local vegetable market all the time. Thugs? No. Mrs. Average Frenchwoman, a local schoolmarm, the butcher's wife:

"Will you sign our petition against giving the vote to immigrants?"

"I'm an immigrant myself, Madame."

"Oh, but you, you're the right kind of immigrant."

Meaning I obviously don't hail from North Africa. Immigrant = Arab. "Immigrants" are those who "invade," and Jean-Marie Le Pen has made his choice clear: "I'd rather be invaded by Germans than by Arabs. At least they had Goethe and Schiller. The Arabs have never done anything memorable."

True, tasting the possibility of continuing electoral victory, and not wanting to frighten off still-wavering constituents, Le Pen has banned all swastikas and "Heil Hitler"s from Front rallies. Time and death have eliminated most of the old Führer nostalgics from the party ranks, their places now filled by a new generation with no direct line to the Vichyists and Gestapo agents among the founding fathers of the party in the Seventies. But Front candidates for the recent elections nonetheless included Jean-Jacques Susini, one of the leaders of the

OAS (Organisation de l'Armée Secrète), a terrorist organization responsible for attacks in both Algeria and mainland France during the early Sixties, as well as for an assassination attempt on De Gaulle; several members of the fascist and anti-Semitic group L'Oeuvre Française; and numerous neo-Nazis and Holocaust deniers.

If the Teutonic image doesn't suit what is essentially a Mediterranean movement only a stone's throw from the Italian border, many Front rallies give off the distinct odor of Duce-ism. The National Front emblem, in fact, is a three-color flame, adapted from that of the now-defunct Italian neofascist party MSI (which, depending on whom you ask, stands for either *Movimento Sociale Italiano* or *Mussolini, Sei Immortale*). And the similarities do not end there. A typical party tactic, well-known to most local anti-Front demonstrators, is to have its own security men pretend to be plainclothes policemen, complete with walkie-talkies, leather gloves, and truncheons. At the recent national convention in Strasbourg, these operatives isolated, shoved, and frisked several of the protesters. This practice continues wherever people come to jeer the Front.

Nationwide, the Front's support stands at a "mere" 15 percent. In the south it is nearly double that, and in some constituencies it has approached, and even topped, 50 percent. I often wonder what it would take to push the percentage high enough to sweep the Front to power here in Avignon. Orange, after all, is only half an hour away, and these are the same fiery southern voters, quite a few of them second- or third-generation immigrants from the nearby Spanish and Italian frontiers who are deeply suspicious of newer "foreigners." It could take anything, I suppose—an Islamic republic in Algeria forcing thousands of Arabs to seek refuge in France, another crime wave in the suburban areas, or even (a likely candidate) the relentless drive toward a unified European currency, which most people here consider a grave insult. But the truth is perhaps more frightening: the Front's ascent may require no catalyst at all. In a country that, after fifty years, still has not completely figured out which side it was on in World War II, it could simply happen.

One recent morning at 8:00, I drove my teenage daughter to the local *lycée*, which overlooks the Rhône and the Pont d'Avignon of nursery rhyme. Just outside the gates, amidst the stream of adolescents sleepwalking by, I noticed a small group of interlopers, alert and active, sliding from student to student with rehearsed professional aplomb, talking animatedly to some, carefully avoiding others. They were too well-dressed, too conspicuous to be the drug dealers that haunt all big-town

schools. Besides, they were handing out leaflets. This was the *Front National de la Jeunesse*, the party's youth sector, on early-morning recruitment duty. My daughter explained that they wouldn't dare show up at lunchtime of after school. But at 8:00 A.M., everyone was too zonked to chase them away.

By their own admission, these Front kids had been to youth camps where "Ride of the Valkyries" was piped into their bedrooms at 6:00 A.M. sharp. Maybe that's why they were so wide awake by 8:00, ready to confront the inevitable avalanche of hostility. And with such efficiency: my daughter told me that once, when their leaflets were confiscated by teachers, the group returned the next day with a new one, titled *"Prof ou Flic?"* ("Teacher or Cop?"), that damned the adults for intervening. Not the Hitler Jugend, no, but certainly a well-oiled machine, and one with its own student unions, its own summer camps, its own youth clubs and discos.

Before long, the recruiters had slithered back into the shadows. They'd learned not to outstay their welcome—three to five minutes, max. But that's all they really needed. Of the 2,000 or so youngsters entering those gates that morning, perhaps several hundred would keep the leaflets and read that the only way to ensure security in our high schools is for every student to join the youth organization of the National Front. Of these, perhaps fifty or so would have been victims of "aggression" and would understand the implicit equation Insecurity = Arabs. And for some of them, the temptation to belong would be all too real.

My daughter assured me that the majority of her high school friends were ready to turn *La Jeunesse* away, by force if necessary. Maybe so, and maybe their mothers and fathers and aunts and uncles would be kicked out of their newly "liberated" city offices in the next elections. She doesn't have the historical perspective, my daughter. She can be optimistic, but I know better. Sooner or later, the Front will be back.

 Article Review Form at end of book.

Populist Pomp
'Just call me Tony'

Warren Hoge

London. Except for the coronation of a monarch, there isn't a more richly traditional occasion on the British ceremonial calendar than the State Opening of Parliament.

The centuries-old pageant includes a separate gilded carriage to carry velvet cushions bearing the diamond studded Imperial State Crown, the Sword of State and the miniver-trimmed crimson Cap of Maintenance. Then the Duke of Norfolk, the Lord Chancellor and the Marquis of Cholmondeley, who address the Queen in the House of Lords, retire from her presence humbly—and carefully—by walking backwards down stairs and through corridors.

The titles of participants are gloriously preposterous—Silver Stick in Waiting, Mistress of the Robes, Rouge Dragon Pursuivant, Maltravers Herald Extraordinary and Lady of the Bedchamber.

Such an absurdly outmoded observance seems an odd way to usher in the new Labor government, but that ceremony remains one of the few things in British public life that earnest new arrivals in the capital cannot change. Only a monarch can do that, and none of them has chosen to since Edward VII reviewed the procedure 90 years ago and pronounced it right up to date.

But Tony Blair, the new Prime Minister, who calls himself the product of the "rock and roll generation," is changing what he can. And with a 179-seat majority in the House of Commons, a tightly disciplined party lectured almost daily about the sanctity of loyalty and an enraptured public behind him, he's free to do as he pleases.

Mr. Blair opened his first cabinet meeting with the instruction "Just call me Tony" and with those four words tossed away centuries of British custom under which ministers always addressed one another by their titles.

Roll Up Your Sleeves

That was not all. Mr. Blair moved his wife and three children not to 10 Downing Street but to the more spacious quarters at 11 Downing Street. And he moved himself out of the cabinet room where his predecessor John Major did business and set up a shirt-sleeved work space behind a sofa in a cramped room.

Any sense that Mr. Blair's relaxed personal style bespeaks a loss of control was dispelled by the cabinet's first action. The members renounced the raises they were entitled to and pledged to trim their budgets.

If anything, the new casual atmosphere suggests great confidence and power. On Wednesday, when the members of the royal family in their tiaras, the ambassadors with their sashes and medals and the judges and bishops in their wigs proceeded solemnly to Westminster in limousines and coaches, Mr. Blair grabbed his wife Cherie by the hand and walked the two blocks from the official residence to Parliament, smiling and waving at onlookers.

A Merry Band

When the sergeant-at-arms, dressed neck to stocking in the ceremonial costume of the Gentleman Usher of the Black Rod, rapped his ebony stick topped with a gold lion's head against the door of Commons and announced, "The Queen commands this honorable house to attend her majesty immediately," the group that rose to follow him over to the House of Lords was like no other ever seen in Parliament.

Of the 659 members, 120 are women, nearly twice the number as in the last Parliament, and they bring welcome splashes of spring color. By one newspaper's reckoning, the beard count has gone from 30 to 50. And the vigor of the young legislators, 260 of whom are new to the Parliament, reminded observers of a freshman class just in from holidays.

The second most powerful man in the new government, the Chancellor of the Exchequer

Gordon Brown, announced he would not wear the traditional white tie when he delivers the yearly Mansion House speech in London's financial district next month. And the third member of the ruling triumvirate, Foreign Secretary Robin Cook, found a new way to present the new foreign policy of Britain. He set up a space-age video display with pounding rock music beneath the globed chandeliers at the Foreign and Commonwealth Office. Both Mr. Brown and Mr. Cook were seen lunching in the department cafeterias, firsts for Whitehall.

When George Stephanopoulos, the former Clinton aide, addressed the Institute of Public Relations on Monday night he recalled that the Clinton administration in its honeymoon days had gone in for what he called the "burger bar stuff," discarding the mystique that sustains governments in trouble. He said he had "one note of caution" for his friends in the Blair Administration: "It is not to overdo the populism."

 Article Review Form at end of book.

U.S. Boom Plays Big in Politics Abroad

Roger Cohen

Paris. Tony and Cherie Blair abandoned their official car for a "Westminster walkabout" on their way to the Opening of Parliament last week, and *The London Times* approvingly noted the American inspiration of such politics, especially the way Mrs. Blair's scarf

fell, like Hillary Clinton's, "with a length hanging down from the left shoulder."

Not to be outdone by the new British Prime Minister, President Jacques Chirac last week took a leaf from the Clinton political manual by departing for China with 55 leading French industrialists on a sell-France mission that has danced lightly over human-rights issues. With a par-

liamentary election just a week away, Mr. Chirac was betting that the president-as-global-salesman (as opposed to exalted statesman) is now a winning image even in France.

Whether it is sartorial style or commercial substance, the impact of America's sustained economic vibrancy, and the "whatever works" President identified with it, is now widely felt.

From Canada through Europe to Japan, big government is out of fashion. The political left is lurching toward the center. And growth has assumed the status of a fully fledged political ideology, the foundation of electoral success.

The first thing Mr. Blair did was to grant control of monetary policy to the independent Bank of England, an extraordinary step for the leader of the British left, and one of the first things he made clear was that "high and stable levels of economic growth" would be a priority. The moves echoed Mr. Clinton's message on taking office in 1993 that he would not interfere with the Federal Reserve or be a big spender.

Global Shift

A huge political shift is under way. It may be radical, as in Britain, faltering, as in France and Germany, or tinged, as in Canada, with dread of American economic Darwinism. But the sheer durability and extent of America's economic expansion—a soaring Wall Street, inflation at 3 percent, joblessness under 5 percent, and only a brief blip in upward growth since 1982—has imparted what seems to be the single strongest political message of the post-cold war decade.

That message is: the areas where the state does things better than the market are extremely limited; fiscal discipline can be combined with strong growth and high employment if the right conditions for entrepreneurship are created, and successful politics in the absence of ideological enemies or pressing security threats amounts to the pragmatism of learning these lessons

combined with sharp marketing— exemplified by the Blairs' stroll and that billowing scarf.

Dissension remains. The best balance between state and market is still widely discussed, a debate that reflects the differing cultural traditions in America, Europe and Japan. American domination naturally meets resentment. Mr. Chirac, in China, pointedly embraces a "multi-polar" world, code for one not dominated by the United States. The Chinese applaud him.

But in a post-ideological and Webbed world, the insistent fact that America works seems, for now, hard to resist.

"I am struck when I travel by the way that Bill Gates of Microsoft and Andy Grove of Intel have become international heroes," said Robert Hormats, the vice chairman of Goldman Sachs International. "They are seen as representing an entrepreneurial renaissance that has, at the same time, placed Clinton's America in the vanguard of international technology and created millions of jobs."

The age of Gates-Groveism is reinforced by the fact that their medium is their message: the technology that is linking and changing the world carries its own political and economic impact, reducing politicians' room for maneuver.

In Japan, once a bastion of regulation, it is now almost universally accepted that government interference in the economy is unhelpful. Parliamentary campaigning last fall was dominated by candidates calling for a freer economy, for in Japan the perception is strong that America leads in new technologies because of its flexible capital markets and Clintonian pragmatism.

In Canada, the central policy of the Liberal government of

Prime Minister Jean Chrétien has been deficit reduction; next budget year, for the first time in nearly three decades, the government may not need to borrow any money at all. Now ministers focus on when to cut taxes and by how much, and debate in the campaign for June 2 elections turns on not whether to shrink government but by how much.

Apolitical Revolution

At the depressed heart of the welfare state, in France, change is less clear cut and more contested. Nonetheless, amid coded signals and continuing taboos over endorsing "Anglo-Saxon" economic models, Mr. Chirac's Gaullist party and other members of his right-of-center coalition have been making clear that they believe the age of the government "fonctionnaire" is over. Jean Arthuis, the Finance Minister, went so far last week as to declare that he was delighted that "the welfare state is finished," adding that "too much state kills the state." In a country where the state's role as guarantor of welfare, engine of industry and nexus of society has long been assumed, and where the number of functionaries has risen to 5.5 million from 4.4 million during the past 15 years, such a statement was revolutionary in its audacity. But it is no longer blasphemy.

In response, France's Socialists talk about being a modern party and providing seed capital to small and medium-sized industry. But the party's discourse is still marked by a brand of socialism that promises 350,000 new state-sector jobs to fight unemployment of 12.8 percent. So far this message seems to have left voters unconvinced, and thus Mr. Chirac's government is favored to win the election despite its deep unpopularity during the past two years.

One interesting aspect of the campaign is the desire expressed in many quarters for an apolitical but effective Prime Minister; voters often voice a preference for Christian Blanc, the blunt, hard-driving, telegenic government employee who has wrested state-owned Air France from disaster and prepared it for privatization.

Mr. Blanc was a socialist, but now says, "I don't give a damn about ideology—all I care about is effectiveness." He says he still values socialism's emphasis on human dignity, solidarity, the gen-eral interest and the need to fight injustice. But economic socialism is bunk.

The words could have come from Mr. Blair, who has not questioned Margaret Thatcher's sweeping privatizations but has put improvements in education and health care at the heart of his program. He has also proposed a "welfare-to-work program" financed by a levy on "the excess profits of the privatized utilities." The very notion of "excess profits" seems unthinkable in America.

It is in such matters where the critical test of the American-led global political revolution may lie. Without genuine sensitiv-ity toward those on the wrong end of the changes, the seeds of upheaval could be planted.

The end of the last century brought a similarly sweeping revolution—the cars, trains and industries that made nations whole and brought the masses closer to political life. Few imagined then how those trends would be exploited by fascists and Communists, leading to tens of millions of deaths. The American-led shift in civilization is full of promise; but its ultimate consequences remain unclear.

 Article Review Form at end of book.

R E A D I N G 7

Untested Tory, a Foe of Europe, Is Picked to Lead Party

Warren Hoge

London, June 19—Britain's bedraggled Conservatives today chose as their new leader William Hague, the most untested and inexperienced of the candidates for the post and a declared opponent of Britain's further integration in Europe.

In a ballot of the 164 Tory members of Parliament, Mr. Hague, 36, the former Secretary for Wales, defeated Kenneth Clarke, 56, the former Chancellor of the Exchequer. The vote was 92 to 70, with one abstention and one spoiled ballot.

The Tories thereby entrusted the job of rebuilding a party that has just suffered its worst electoral defeat since 1832 to the youngest man to head the party since 24-year-old William Pitt, known as Pitt the Younger, in 1783.

Labor, which won a majority of 179 seats in the May 1 election, is led by Tony Blair, 44, the youngest Prime Minister this century.

It was the third and final round in an increasingly bitter contest, which began on June 10 with five candidates vying to succeed former Prime Minister John Major as party leader and saw some startling alliances and some deepening ideological fault lines within the party as the field narrowed.

In naming Mr. Hague, who had been in the Cabinet for less than three years, the Tories were turning their backs on Mr. Clarke, the most outspoken advocate of holding open Britain's options in Europe, the party's most accomplished debater and its most experienced politician as a former Secretary for Health, for Education and Science, for law enforcement as Home Secretary and for finance as Chancellor of the Exchequer.

Mr. Clarke congratulated Mr. Hague tonight on his victory and pledged his "unstinting and loyal support" to the new party leader. But he turned down an offer of a senior position in the shadow cabinet, saying he preferred to take a position on the back benches.

Mr. Hague said he would dedicate himself to healing the divided party and said he looked forward to the day soon when "the words people associate with our party are fresh, clear, open and united."

The only issue that Mr. Hague brought forward in his campaign was opposition to any consideration of Britain's joining the European Monetary Union, and he said he would demand that all members of his shadow cabinet honor that stand under a "collective responsibility" pledge.

Europe was an issue that dogged the Tories through the last of their 18 successive years in government and produced the disarray that contributed to the size of their defeat. The subject has seized Conservatives in Parliament far more than it has the rank and file, who rate the issue only as their seventh or eighth concern in political attitude polling.

For a party needing to recapture the center of the electorate that it lost so convincingly to Mr. Blair's "New" Labor Party, Mr. Clarke seemed the more promising candidate. He consistently attracted the most support among Conservatives countrywide in mandatory "advisory" polling that preceded each of the three rounds of balloting of the Tory members of Parliament.

But the Tories in Parliament, many of them sworn to deny Mr. Clarke's attempt at all costs because of his position on Europe, just as consistently showed less enthusiasm for him, prolonging the choice for three full rounds, a first in the party's history, and setting up today's runoff.

Mr. Hague, who surged into the favored position unexpectedly at the end of the first canvass on June 10, solidified his claim on the Euroskeptic right wing of the party in recent days by his litmus test demand on shadow cabinet members on the Europe issue.

Today's vote had been expected to be closer than it was after the latest in a series of developments that occurred after the second round on Tuesday. Mr. Clarke looked to have headed off the right-wing opposition to his election when he drew the backing of the leader of his ideological foes, John Redwood, after eliminating him from the race.

Mr. Redwood, 45, the most vocal enemy of Britain's remaining in talks about monetary union, had felt himself betrayed by his right-wing colleagues in an earlier round of horse-trading and got his revenge by announcing his support for Mr. Clarke.

The earlier alliance, known as the "A.B.C., Anyone but Clarke" project, collapsed in rancor when the two dropouts from the first round, Michael Howard, 56, the former Home Secretary, and Peter Lilley, 53, the former Social Security Secretary, threw their support not to Mr. Redwood but to Mr. Hague, whose views on Europe were not nearly so pronounced.

That act made the relatively inexperienced Mr. Hague the favorite, but he and his backers still had to reckon with the survival tactics of Mr. Clarke, who suddenly secured Mr. Redwood's support by promising him the opposition job of shadow Chancellor of the Exchequer.

Baroness Thatcher, the former Conservative Prime Minister, found herself so provoked by the Clarke-Redwood ticket that she dropped her stated reluctance to take a stand in the race, denounced the accord as "an incredible alliance of opposites which can only lead to further grief" and came out for Mr. Hague.

The prolonging of the vote, the infighting of the last two weeks and whatever cynicism remains in the party over the back stabbing and the apparent sacrifice of principles for electoral advantage put an immediate strain on the first task facing Mr. Hague—unifying the fractious and depleted ranks of the party.

The new leader expressed concern, saying, "Hard words have been said, but I am determined no grudges will be borne by anyone in our party." He added, "Our supporters in the country are sick and tired of the Conservatives' behaving like a school debating society."

Mr. Hague is a relative newcomer to British politics, but he is a more seasoned observer of public life than his age would suggest. At the age of 15 in his South Yorkshire home he busied himself reading parliamentary reports, learned to recite by heart recorded speeches of Churchill and memorized the names and districts of all Tory members of Parliament.

He burst upon the scene soon after when, as a mop-haired 16-year-old student, he took the podium at the Tory Party conference and captivated the audience with a fiery call to arms in defense of Conservative principles.

 Article Review Form at end of book.

Labor Victory in Britain Reflects Era of 'Girl Power'

Susan Taylor Martin

St. Petersburg Times

London—Something remarkable happened May 1, and it wasn't just that the Labor Party kicked out the Conservatives after 18 years. Britons wound up with a record number of women in Parliament and a prime minister's wife who may forever change the way first ladies are perceived.

Among those hailing this formidable display of "girl power" were the Spice Girls, Britain's pop music fivesome who claim former Prime Minister Margaret Thatcher as their hero and inspiration.

"It's great that girls are successful in the music industry or any other industry," said Melanie Chisholm, the "Sporty Spice."

It takes a lot to shove the Spice Girls and Princess Diana out of the spotlight, but Britain's new first spouse appears to have done just that.

Barely a week after her husband Tony Blair, became prime minister, Cherie Booth was back in court in the traditional barrister's white wig and black gown. A Queen's Counsel, or senior courtroom lawyer, Booth has had a brilliant legal career and once harbored political ambitions herself.

Blair and she met almost two decades ago while applying for the same position. He got it but has praised her ever since as the brains of the family.

During the campaign, Booth, 42, endured a fair amount of comment about her dark wardrobe, which one columnist likened to that of Morticia in the Addams Family, but generally has won the admiration of both the media and public.

"Is Cherie truly our first superwoman?" asked the Express, a leading London daily. Not only will she be the first prime minister's wife to work full time, but the first in more than 40 years to raise a family at 10 Downing Street—three children, ages 13, 11 and 9.

Even more significant, though, is the change in composition of Britain's once stodgy and chauvinistic House of Commons. As a result of Labor's landslide victory, the percentage of women in Britain's chief lawmaking body soared from 10 percent to 18 percent.

As a result of Labor's landslide victory, the percentage of women in Britain's chief lawmaking body soared from 10 percent to 18 percent.

Compare that to 11 percent in the U.S. Congress and just 5.5 percent in France.

At Blair's direction, Labor made a strong effort to woo female candidates, to the point of barring male candidates from some races.

This novel affirmative action scheme was subsequently ruled illegal, but women still managed to win 101 of the 419 seats that went to Labor candidates.

Reflecting the shift away from Labor's blue-collar roots, the women of "New Labor" are for the most part middle class, professional and university educated.

Five of the female MPs have been named to the prime minister's Cabinet in such key positions as Northern Ireland secretary. It's the largest number of women ever to sit in a British Cabinet.

At the same time, more and more British women are entering the work force and confronting many of the same issues as their U.S. counterparts—day care, parental leave, job discrimination.

One group, claiming women too long have endured cramped public lavatories, called on the new female MPs to push for national guidelines on cubicle size.

Observers predict the women will help transform Commons, and, in the process, British society.

Who knows? Perhaps a future prime minister waits in their ranks.

None other than Hillary Rodham Clinton has noted that Britain's parliamentary form of government—in which the prime minister is chosen by the party, not the electorate as a whole—makes it easier for women to reach the top.

"They do not have to go out and sell themselves to the entire country and face all of the various questions that women in public life are often objected to," Mrs. Clinton said earlier this year when asked why the United States has never had a woman president.

"It's very difficult for women to overcome many of the preconceptions and stereotypes the public holds about them."

Nobody expects the Page 3 girls to disappear anytime soon from British tabloids. But, thanks to the women of New Labor, there might be a little less fluff and a lot more substance.

 Article Review Form at end of book.

Crisis of Unification

How Germany changes

Jürgen Kocka

Jürgen Kocka is Professor of Modern History at Freie Universität Berlin.

Germany has changed more in the last four years than it has in the last four decades. How are Germans coping with the opportunities and challenges created by the breakdown of communism and national unification? Will the new Germany be mainly a continuation of the old Federal Republic? Or will it be a different country? In which respects? How does the German case compare with other experiences in the postcommunist world? How should it be evaluated in the light of historical experience?

The Exit from Communism: The German Pattern

The East German revolution has been part of a cycle of interrelated revolutions which dramatically changed Eastern and Central Europe in 1989 and 1990. In basic respects, it resembled the revolutions in Poland, Czechoslovakia, Hungary, Bulgaria, and Romania. Like the German Democratic Republic (GDR), these countries had been the objects of Soviet domination since the end of World War II, and liberation from Soviet rule was a central element of all the revolutions in 1989–1990. There were many underlying, contributing, and facilitating factors, but none was as important as the sudden weakening of Soviet control and the unwillingness of the Soviet government to send troops in support of befriended governments which were challenged by their subjects. With the exception of Romania, the revolutions were nonviolent. They were not prepared in advance. They were not led by clearly defined elite groups striving for power. They were not guided by nor did they bring about new sets of ideas. Rather they were inspired by democratic, liberal, and social-democratic ideas which have become central in Western political thought since the eighteenth century: the norms and ideals of modern civil society. Given the nonviolent, "reformist" character of those revolutions, their immediate structural impact was limited. The change in the political system was significant; but social structures, economic rela-

tions, culture, and collective mentalities have only begun to change.[1]

The postcommunist situation is characterized by elements of breakdown, destruction, and vacuum, in which older traditions regain some weight and new structures emerge rather slowly. Three tasks everywhere seem to be on the agenda: the transition to democracy, the building of an open society, and the introduction of a market economy. As the German sociologist Claus Offe has pointed out, an overlapping of these three major initiatives has been rare in history. It explains why "the exit from communism" has been so difficult. Postcommunist societies are heavily dependent on what Western countries offer or deny them. In every case, transition has been slower than expected and only partly successful. The optimism of 1989 is gone. One is increasingly made to realize how difficult it is to transfer the Western model to a part of the world without the economic, social, and cultural conditions which that model seems to presuppose. Doubts about the universal applicability of the Western model grow, both in the East and the West.[2]

Jürgen Kocka, "Crisis of Unification: How Germany Changes," reprinted by permission of DAEDALUS, Journal of the American Academy of Arts and Sciences, from the issue entitled, "Germany in Transition" Winter 1994, Vol. 123, No. 1.

In these respects, the East German gains and challenges—which have become the gains and challenges of unified Germany—are of a more general nature: part of the fate of "the East."[3] Germany is not only a well integrated part of the West; she has also absorbed part of the East and has to deal with some of its problems.

East Germany's geopolitical situation and advanced industrialization helped the ruling Communist Party elite to integrate large parts of the population and to avoid reforms. Compared with Poland and Hungary, change came late in East Germany; when it came, it came fast, like an implosion. It was heavily based on mass mobilization. The (Protestant) Church played a larger role in changing East Germany than it did in changing other countries. But what made the experience of the GDR really unique was the national situation. The GDR was one of two German states: there was no congruity between state and nation. The GDR had to cope with the existence of a strong noncommunist state of the same nationality, the Federal Republic of Germany (FRG), which never fully accepted the nation's division. It is this particular national situation which distinguished the transition in East Germany from similar transitions in other countries in 1989–1990.[4]

Since 1953, the internal opposition against the regime in East Germany had been remarkably weak. The Polish Solidarnosz, Hungarian reform communism, and the Czech Charta 77 had no equivalent in East Germany. Intellectual dissidents were rare. Part of the explanation is to be found in the fact that there was another German state which always accepted actual and potential dissidents from East Germany, thereby weakening the GDR's internal opposition. While in other communist countries dissidents could use national arguments and refer to national traditions when they wanted to criticize dictatorial rule and Soviet domination, arguments of this kind were taboo for East German intellectuals as long as they did not want or dare to question the existence of an independent GDR altogether (which was virtually impossible inside the country). In 1989–1990, the dissident elite turned out to be small in number and of little weight; they could not act as a counterelite, and they disappeared quickly from positions of power.

It should be stressed that the breakthrough phase of the East German revolution—from late September to November 1989—was an endogenous development, neither engineered nor triggered by the West Germans. But in an indirect way, the Federal Republic played an important role in the East German revolution: the mass exodus of East Germans to the West decisively fueled the internal demands for change, the mass demonstrations, and their powerful challenge to the communist establishment. "Exit" produced "voice" in this case, to use the well-known terms of the political economist Albert Hirschman. This mass exodus would not have been possible without the influence of the West German media in the GDR and the citizenship law of the Federal Republic which served as a standing invitation to all ethnic Germans, including those in the GDR. The East German revolution in its second phase—between the opening of the Wall in November 1989 and the first free elections to the East German *Volkskammer* in March 1990—took a national turn. The demand for reform of the GDR, which would become democratic but stay independent, was gradually eclipsed by the quest for national unity. Large majorities of the population supported this national turn which articulated East German dissatisfaction, their distrust in the changeability of the GDR, and, above all, their hope of quickly improving their lot by joining the more wealthy, more liberal, more attractive FRG. This national turn would not have been possible without the existence of another German state, its principal support for unification, and the promises of its governing elite (which later on were not kept). From December 1989 onwards, the influence of the West German government quickly increased, became direct and open. The East German revolution became a movement for national unification that had no parallel in any other country. The East German exit from communism led into a process of self-dissolution; the East German state finally acceded to the Federal Republic and ceased to exist.[5]

The decisive changes related to unification have been generated within the GDR. This holds with respect to the revolutionary mass movements in the autumn and winter, which brought down the Socialist Unity Party (SED) government, forced the opening of the Berlin Wall, and initiated basic reforms; the ensuing drive towards unification; and the self-dissolution of the GDR.[6] But in this process of unification, within the emerging national framework, the tremendous inequality of the two German societies quickly made itself felt. Already in the winter of 1989–1990 the center of gravity started to move from the East to the West, from Leipzig, Berlin, and other East German cities to Bonn, from the grass roots to the centers of government, from a spontaneously organized movement to the established parties and administrations. Certainly, initiatives from below have continued, albeit in different, less spectacular forms. They have found new bases in the communities, regions, and *Länder* of the East in recent years. But those who had improvised mass actions, had founded groups and parties, and had raised from anonymity to unstable leadership positions in the first phase of the revolution, quickly lost out.

In the following months and years, the revolution became something like an orderly "revolution from outside and above," increasingly controlled by the dominant West and engineered by professional politicians and administrators.[7] Basic constitutional change continued throughout 1990. The process of restructuring the economy, social relations, cultural institutions, the educational system, and other spheres of life speeded up and deepened in 1990 and has continued in the following years. The transition from communism became part of a process of incorporating the East into the West by transferring institutions, resources, elites, and ideas from the West to the East.

No other postcommunist countries have had this experience. Change and recovery in East Germany are based on resources that her Eastern neighbors can only dream of. In East Germany, the transition is faster and more thorough than anywhere else. At the same time, it is less autonomous, less self-controlled, and leads to new contradictions.

Incorporating the East into the West: Achievements, Limits, and *Problématiques*

The Basic Decision

In 1990, an extended debate took place about which constitutional form unification should take. Should it be enacted according to Article 146 of the West German Basic Law which provided that in case of unification a new constitution should be framed and voted upon by the people? Or should unification be brought about along the lines offered by Article 23 which made possible the accession of the GDR to the Federal Republic, whose constitution would remain unchanged and apply to Germany as a whole?

Article 146 would have made necessary an extended process of consulting and bargaining which would have offered the opportunity to bring elements from both the West and the East together into a new and better solution. It would not only liberate the Easterners from their socialist constitution, but also, hopefully, overcome some of the weaknesses of the West German political order. This is how advocates of Article 146—mostly on the Left or left of the center—justified their demand. They also thought that such an extended public debate on the constitutional core of unification would present the necessary platform on which the Germans could find out why and how they wanted to get together. It would help the new Germany and its emerging constitutional order to get popular support and legitimation, for the sake of democratic stability.

This strategy would have taken much time which, as those favoring Article 23 felt, was not available given the unstable international situation. A basic change inside the Soviet Union, which was not altogether unlikely, could easily close the "window of opportunity" for German unification. The very unstable situation within the GDR also seemed to require a quick decision. The Basic Law had proven its strength; it enjoyed broad acceptance among West and East Germans. Why dispose of it and increase the uncertainties of an already risky unification? Advocates of Article 23 doubted that much improvement of the Basic Law could be found in the East German constitution. To find international acceptance for German unification was a difficult task that would only become more difficult if the actors on the international scene had to deal with a new Germany whose constitutional order and basic profile would only slowly emerge in a long and painful debate. The international obligations of the Federal Republic were not to be questioned. Advocates of Article 23 thought that it offered a simple and appropriate way to bring about unification without jeopardizing the basic continuity between the old Federal Republic and the newly emerging Germany.[8]

German unification was enacted on the basis of Article 23. Apart from some minor exceptions, temporary arrangements, and limited amendments to be negotiated later, the constitutional order of West Germany was extended to the East. This debate and its outcome had paradigmatic character. Not only with respect to constitutional law, but in nearly all other respects as well, unification was drafted as a process of transferring the internal order of West Germany to East Germany, with only minimal changes. Unified Germany was not meant to be something new. It was meant to be an enlarged Federal Republic of Germany.[9] Has the strategy worked, so far?

Political System

The official name—the Federal Republic of Germany—has not been changed nor has the national hymn, although alternatives were proposed and discussed in 1990. The West German flag became the flag of united Germany. In general, the constitutional and legal system proved to be flexible enough to be extended to the new *Länder*. The reconstruction of the administrative and judicial system according to the West German model is under way.[10] But there are exceptions and countertendencies.

In the constitutional debates, East German participants—frequently supported by West German speakers representing parties from the Left—tend to emphasize the need for more plebiscitary elements (i.e., referendum) and for a broader formulation of some basic rights especially with respect to social conditions (i.e., the right to work), ecological protection, and gender equality. These preferences may result in part from the East German lack of experience with a representative multiparty system, from memory of the successful mass movements during the autumn and winter of 1989–1990, and from the widespread tendency in the East to expect much from "the state" and less from the market. Such preferences have not had much impact on the national level. Although a Constitutional Committee, consisting of members of the *Bundestag* and representatives of the Länder, has been set up as recommended by the Treaty of Unification, its conclusions as to amending the Basic Law have remained extremely cautious. But those preferences have influenced the framing of the new constitutions of the East German *Länder*.[11] They increasingly influence the general debate.

Political Parties

The West German parties have quickly spread to the East by absorbing some of the SED-dependent parties existing throughout the years in the GDR (in the case of the Christian Democratic Union [CDU] and the Free Democratic Party [FDP]), by fusing with parties newly created in the GDR during the revolution (the Social Democratic Party [SPD] and the Greens), and by trying to establish a new local and regional base. Apart from the Party of Democratic Socialism (PDS), the successor party of the SED (11 percent of the vote in the East and 2 percent in the West in the *Bundestag* elections of December 1990), there has been no significant change in the West German party system as it extended to the East.[12] Roughly the same can be said with respect to the unions and other large associations. This bird's eye view does not, however, allow one to discover the limits of the transfer of such institutions. Party membership is desperately low in the new *Länder*. It is difficult to find enough activists (candidates) for local elections. The decades of dictatorship and the abrupt changes of 1989–1990 seem to have produced a vacuum. East German church membership lags far behind West German. People are reluctant to enter new stable commitments beyond the private sphere.

West German institutions have spread to the East but they have barely taken root in the population. Traditional loyalties have broken down, new ones are not yet established. The social composition and the priorities of the East and West branches of one party frequently differ. Parties, unions, and associations are internally torn by the task of bridging differences and contradictions between their Eastern and Western members. Still, thus far they have managed to avoid being split along regional lines. As of yet, regional parties and movements have not emerged, as least not successfully (apart from the PDS). The system is creaking but not breaking.[13]

Economic Change

In July of 1990, the economic order of the West was abruptly introduced to the East. Custom borders and mobility barriers were removed, and, before it existed as one state, Germany was a single market with a common legal framework and a common currency. This was a political decision against which some economists cautioned. But in the later years, the economic structure of the GDR has been quickly molded according to the West German model.

Privatization has proceeded faster there than anywhere else in the postcommunist countries. The Treuhand-Anstalt, a public, government-controlled, but highly autonomous and controversial corporation, founded in 1990, was charged with taking over and privatizing the state-owned and collectivized enterprises of the GDR. Of a total of roughly sixteen thousand units, the Treuhand, by July 1993, had sold about 78 percent and liquidated 17 percent. Seven hundred and forty units remain under Treuhand control to be sold as soon as possible. When transferred to private investors, entrepreneurs, and managers, most of whom come from West Germany and abroad, the units were usually restructured, rationalized, and reduced, frequently with the help of public money.[14]

Measured by the distribution of the economically active population among industrial sectors, the economy of the GDR in 1989 was far behind Western countries. By 1992, the West-East difference had nearly disappeared.

Before celebrating this dramatic change as a clear indicator of economic modernization, one has to take into account that it was accompanied by an equally dramatic decrease in overall employment. In 1989, 920,000 were employed in East German agriculture; by 1992 this figure had gone down to 280,000 (a 70 percent reduction). Manufacturing industries employed 3.17 million persons in 1989, but only 1.29 million in 1992 (roughly a 60 percent reduction). Employment in mining and energy production decreased by 39 percent from 1989 to 1992. By contrast, the reduction in the services (including state) amounted to only 22 percent (from 4.35 million to 3.41 million), and employment in the construction trades even grew by 10 percent (from 563,000 to 620,000).

In short, the number of jobs available in East Germany decreased by 34 percent between 1989 and 1992, from 9.3 to 6.2 million. Had it not been for the public works programs (now scheduled for elimination), the reduction would have amounted to 38 percent. Three million jobs were lost within the first three years following unification. And the process of erosion seems to be continuing in 1993. The official unemployment figures—in July 1993, 1.67 million or 15.3 percent in the East, 2.33 million or 7.5 percent in the West—do not fully show the dramatic nature of the breakdown. It is not at all clear when the trend will be reversed, and part of the erosion will probably be permanent.[15]

East German industries were overstaffed, with a relatively low degree of productivity, and, thus, were not able to compete with the West. Because Western firms frequently disposed of nonutilized capacities, they could quickly increase their production. Despite vigorous attempts at rationalization and effective improvement of the traffic, transport, and communication system with the help of public investment, the competitiveness of many East German firms was countered by rising labor costs—due to an upsurge in costs of living and the dynamic wage policy of the unions. Other factors, including the breakdown of markets in the East, legal obstacles in the period of transition, inefficiencies of the administration, and the worldwide recession, played a role as well.[16]

Research and Universities

In nonmarket sectors, policy decisions had similar, though less brutal effects. Take research and higher learning as an example. The GDR had adopted the Soviet system which provided for a clear institutional separation between universities oriented towards the training of students (although not exclusively) and the institutes of the Academy of Sciences exclusively responsible for research. In West Germany, research and teaching are integrated under the roof of the universities whenever possible, particularly in the social sciences and the humanities. After unification, the huge research institutes of the East German Academy of Sciences, which employed more than twice as many people as the universities, were evaluated by expert commissions in which Western scholars and officials played the major role. The criteria of evaluation were academic quality and efficiency, measured by international standards as well as compatibility with the basic principles of the West German system of research and higher learning. Among those principles, the autonomy, unity, and decentralized structure of research and teaching ranked high. More often than not, the "international standard" was defined by the situation in the old Federal Republic and in other Western countries.

Evaluation was a complicated process which, in the end, was regarded as relatively fair on both sides. It resulted in the dissolution of most academy institutes, in the founding of many new extrauniversity research institutions, and in a vigorous but difficult attempt to reintegrate some members of the academic staff of the dissolved institutes into the university system. Less than 50 percent—some estimate only 30 percent—of the former personnel of the academy institutes are now employed in newly founded institutes and in the universities.[17]

The GDR universities were tremendously "overstaffed" as compared to West German universities (which is a particularly problematic yardstick since the West German system of higher education is in bad shape and suffers, among other things, from a disadvantageous staff-student ratio). The departments of the GDR universities had been structured to meet the needs of the old regime—particularly in the humanities and social sciences—and the imperatives of the Comecon, particularly in the economic and technical disciplines. In the humanities and social sciences, the degree of specialization was very high, the system of rewards little developed, mobility and communication restricted, and access to international literature frequently difficult to obtain. There had been scholars and achievements of high quality, but far fewer than in the West. Political instrumentalization had played a detrimental role, particularly in the humanities and social sciences.

The East German university system has been deeply restructured in the last three years under the control of the *Länder* governments and with effective participation of Western scholars and administrators according to the West German model. Three processes should be distinguished: 1) The system was reduced in size. 2) University law and organization, the structure of the departments, and the patterns of specialization were deeply altered, and positions and tasks were redefined. As a consequence, existing qualifications were depreciated and new ones were demanded. On the professorial level, the old personnel had to apply and compete with other applicants, in many cases from the West. 3) Screening processes took place (in "commissions of honor" inside the universities) which led to the exclusion of persons found guilty of having discredited themselves by moral and political standards.

The necessary shrinking due to financial limits and pressures as well as the widespread redefinition of qualifications due to the change of system have accounted for many more layoffs and personnel exchanges than did political screening. In Saxony, the universities employed thirty-nine thousand persons (among them fifteen thousand scientists) in

1989. In the future, they will employ only 11,200 persons, among them 7,800 scientists. One can estimate that only a small minority—perhaps 10 percent—of those employed in 1989 were dismissed on political and moral grounds.

The influx of Westerners has remained limited, considering the whole system of research and higher learning. About 10 percent of all positions in the universities and research institutions—mostly the leading positions—have been filled by West Germans and, in a small number of cases, by persons from abroad. In fields like history and sociology, the percentage of Westerners is much higher. Of the twenty-nine professors of sociology in East German universities today, only four come from the East. A similar ratio can probably be found among history professors. But there is less change on the level of the nontenured personnel and in such disciplines as mathematics, the natural sciences, medicine, and the technical fields.[18]

Social Inequalities and Mental Distances

Once the basic political decision had been made to execute unification by transferring the West German order to the East as quickly and completely as possible, the rest followed with a certain necessity: market forces on the one hand, and policy decisions on the other restructured the East German system according to the West German model. A tremendous destruction took place. The present situation is difficult, but it can be hoped and expected that the reduced and deeply restructured system of work in the East will eventually be able to compete and grow again.[19]

It is quite evident that the restructuring and incorporation of East Germany is heavily dependent upon West Germany. Without the know-how and personnel from the West, this process of revolutionary change could not have been undertaken. Without money from the West, it would not have been socially bearable.[20]

Because of the massive financial transfer from West to East, the crisis of restructuring has not led to mass poverty in the East. In fact, a majority of the East Germans seem to be and to feel better off today than before the revolution. The unions negotiated huge pay hikes, applying the bargaining rules and tactics of the West. Those who have work can afford more than they used to, and they have access to a whole variety of goods which most of them only dreamed of under the old regime, including the opportunity to travel. Those who lived on pensions were particularly poor and underprivileged in the GDR; most of them now enjoy improved living conditions. Academics who have managed to stay employed have to work more, but do so under better conditions. Life has become freer, the scope of choices has broadened, and new opportunities continue to arise. There also has begun to emerge a new layer of self-employed persons, both in the trades and in the professions.

Not everyone, however, is enjoying an improved standard of living. Many who held power and privilege because of their proximity to the party apparatus and the state have been déclassé, although some have apparently managed to be well placed again, particularly in the world of commerce and services. Women, the large majority of whom had been part of the labor force in the GDR, combining family and job, are now clearly overrepresented among the unemployed. Those who raise children and work outside the home deplore the breakdown of day-nurseries and the disappearance of other public facilities. Careers for women have become less accessible. In addition, new groups have appeared: the homeless, drug addicts, and the long-term unemployed.[21]

Inequality is growing, between income groups, between mena adn women, between those who hav ework and those who do not, between nouveaux riches and déclassés, between those who manage to hold on to their property and those who must move out. The reinstating of a system of private property after so many years leads to new inequalities and injustices. More than half of the population has experienced some change of vocation, and change in mobility—upward, downward, or laterally.

Does all this mean that life in the East has become more similar to life in the West? Yes and no. The East German situation remains clearly distinguished, in at least three respects.

First, this is a period of revolutionary change in the East, requiring rapid adjustment. Routines have broken down, trust has been shattered, new orientations are needed, anxiety is widespread, and self-assuredness is scarce. Crisis and rapid transition define the lives of many in the East, but not so in the West. Though collective protests have so far remained weak and scattered, the East German crisis is deep. The East German birthrate has fallen by 60 percent, the marriage rate by 65 percent, and the divorce rate by 81 percent between 1989 and 1992. Declines of this quantity are extremely rare in history. Only the

Great Wars offer similar examples. Nothing comparable is happening in West Germany. It is not unreasonable to attribute this demographic breakdown to the crisis caused by transition in East Germany. Early in 1990, the fast pace of unification was justified by the Bonn government by pointing to the East-West mass migration which would not be halted except by economic and monetary unity. Yet, even with such unity, East-West migration continues. Between 1973 and 1989 the East German population hovered around 16.5 and 17 million. By 1992, it had fallen below 16 million, and the loss of population continues.[22]

Second, a mixture of repression and paternalism, specific to politics and life in the GDR, left East Germans little accustomed to quick change, uncertainty, competition, and the risky utilization of new opportunities.

Third, the difference between East and West continues to be pronounced and visible with respect to income, life-style, status, power, and quality of life. In contrast to popular expectations and convincing promises in the first years, it is increasingly clear that equalization of living conditions in East and West will take decades. The resulting feelings of inequality, frustration, and inferiority on the part of the East Germans maintain a psychological distance. Tension and mutual reservation, resentment, and outright rejection play an increasing role.[23] There is, of course, some mixing. A thin layer of West Germans live and work in the East, usually in leading positions. East Germans move to the West to work and be trained. Still, different newspapers are read in the East than in the West, and the best-seller lists differ. West German and East German histori-

ans tend to publish in different journals. Even in united Berlin, the circles of intensive communication and collegiality, friendship, and marriage continue to be dived between East and West.

On the level of social and personal relations, of customs and everyday life, integration and incorporation of the East are clearly limited. In these respects, one can still speak of two different societies, and awareness of this split seems to grow. Some East German intellectuals have begun to consider whether the separate development of an East German society—different and relatively independent from the West—could become a desirable possibility in the long run: two societies within one state.[24]

This may sound unrealistic, but it is not coincidental that such ideas are voiced as it becomes increasingly clear that the Westernization of the East will take much longer and require more effort than originally expected. Perhaps the aims should be redefined.[25]

Political Culture

Public opinion surveys have discovered typical differences between East German and West German attitudes. Easterners seem to expect more from "the state," in terms of securing economic growth, stabilizing prices, and guaranteeing employment. They hold old-fashioned virtues such as obedience, orderliness, modesty, cleanliness, and duty in higher esteem. Work represents a more central value to Germans in the East than in the West. East Germans tend less to hedonistic, postmaterialistic, and individualistic values than do West Germans—although the difference is less significant among the younger respondents. East Germans are less likely to identify with political parties and party democracy, and are more sympathetic towards plebiscitary or grass-root democracy. To some observers, Easterners appear more "German" than Westerners, in that they are more deeply rooted in older German traditions.[26]

Until 1990, East Germans and West Germans were exposed to different interpretations of recent German history. They also differ in formative experiences. Survey-based research has discovered that the national-socialist period, World War II, the German persecution of the Jews, and the immediate postwar developments largely contributed to the historical self-understanding of a multigenerational majority of West Germans. A highly critical view of the Nazi period serves as a negative foil and reference point in contrast to which the political culture of the Federal Republic has frequently been defined. East Germans also lean away from a positive view of the Nazi dictatorship, but the period is less central to their historical self-understanding. The type of "antifascism" which was taught and propagated in the GDR has helped to remove the Nazi experience from the historical self-definition of many East Germans. They seem to have a less abashed view of German national history and are more intent on reconciling their own GDR past.[27]

Such data does not indicate a widening gap between East and West, but the existence of deep cultural and political differences. They can be viewed either as consequences of different patterns of socialization throughout the last decades or as reactions to present problems posing themselves differently in the two parts of Germany. Under the institutional roof of a common constitution and a largely unified party system, there still seem to exist the elements of two different political cultures.

The Parts and the Whole: Conclusions and Outlook

In Germany, prior to unification, nation and state were not congruent. The East German exit from communism took the form of self-dissolution and unification with the West German state. In these most fundamental ways, East Germany differed from all the other countries of East and East Central Europe which were moving away from communism in 1989–1990. Transition proceeds faster and reaches deeper in East Germany than anywhere else, and the long-term prospects seem brighter. At the same time, the East Germans have to bear more destruction and uprooting than do their Eastern and Southeastern neighbors. Transition has taken the form of a "revolution from outside and above," again making the East Germans objects of change.

Underlying the transition is the decision to accomplish unification by incorporating the East into the West and by extending the basic order of the Federal Republic to the Eastern part of the country. According to this master plan of 1990, unification meant changing the East but not the West. Unified Germany was not intended to be a new invention nor a compromise between West and East, but an enlarged version of the old Federal Republic.

The transfer of the West German order to the Eastern *Länder* has worked relatively well on the constitutional, legal, and institutional level. However, it has met stiff resistance and has not progressed far on the level of social relations, political culture, and everyday life. On other levels (i.e., the economy), the transfer of the West German order has led to destruction and crisis, as the demographic breakdown shows. Despite efforts to incorporate and integrate the East, a separate GDR identity seems to have been revived, defensively and obstinately documenting the present limits of Westernization.

How will all this affect the system at large? As the role of government in social and economic processes become strengthened, the relationship between *Bund* and *Länder* will be readjusted.

Recovering from unification cannot be solely the responsibility of those in the East. Rather, it demands extraordinary efforts on the part of the whole population. The burden is already beginning to be felt: taxes and fees are raised and the public debt is growing. Unification will put to the test parliamentary institutions and political parties. Will it be possible to reach a consensus on the necessary redistribution? Will it be possible to convince West German voters that it is in their interest to share with the citizens in the East? While unification remains a positive experience for a clear majority of East Germans, in West Germany the skeptics have started to outnumber the supporters.[28]

The crisis in the East brings the weaknesses of the whole to the surface. Take, for example, the right-wing extremist attacks in Hoyerswerda and Rostock. They started in places characterized by high unemployment, disintegration, and dissatisfaction as well as by a weak police force and an evident lack of public authority. But they have triggered waves of extremist attacks on a nationwide scale.

With respect to their basic profiles, the GDR and the old Federal Republic were mutually dependent on each other. For the GDR, the Federal Republic was a permanent challenge and a source of indirect destabilization. For the Federal Republic, the GDR served as a negative foil for comparison and as a source of collective stabilization. Both German states were creations of the Cold War. Their internal structures and external affiliations were deeply influenced by the system of international relations. Now Germany is compelled to find a new place in a changing international environment. This will deeply affect the mood of the country, its self-understanding, and its political substance. Unified Germany will not and cannot be merely an enlarged version of the old Federal Republic. Change, it seems, will extend much farther than the architects of unification intended.

Endnotes

1. Cf. Judy Batt, "The End of Communist Rule in East Central Europe: A four-country comparison," *Government and Opposition* 26 (1991): 368–90. Jürgen Kocka, "Revolution and Nation—1989/90 in Historical Perspective," in Bernd Hüppauf, ed., *United Germany in Europe. Towards 1990 and Beyond: European Studies Journal*, Special Edition (Fall 1993).

2. Cf. Claus Offe, "Capitalism by Democratic Design? Democratic Theory Facing the Triple Transition in East Central Europe," *Social Research* 58 (1991): 865–92; Claus Offe, "Die Integration nachkommunistischer Gesellschaften: die ehemalige DDR im Vergleich zu ihren osteuorpäischen Nachbarn" (forthcoming); Kenneth Jowitt, *The New World Disorder. The Leninist Extinction* (Berkeley, Calif.: University of California Press, 1992).

3. The patterns of change within the Soviet Union and its successor countries were and are different. Because of other differences, Yugoslavia is excluded from the present considerations as well.

4. A good account is Konrad Jarausch, *The Rush to German Unity* (New York: Oxford University Press, 1993).

5. Pending the consent of the international powers, this direction was clear after 18 March 1990, when a large majority of the East Germans voted for parties supporting such a course. Formally, the GDR ceased to exist on 3 October 1990. Albert O. Hirschman, "Abwanderung, Widerspruch und das Schicksal der Deutschen Demokratischen Republik," *Leviathan* 20 (1993): 330–58.

6. The best account and analysis of the mass movements is Hartmut Zwahr, *Ende einer Selbstzerstörung. Leipzig und die Revolution in der DDR* (Göttingen: Vandenhoek & Ruprecht, 1993).

7. I take the term "revolution from outside and above" (*"Revolution von außen und oben"*) from the East German economic historian Jürgen Kuczynski who used it to characterize the basic reforms in Prussia from 1807–1813 which had been triggered by the Napoleonic challenge and which were largely executed by the civil service.

8. Cf. Bernd Guggenberger and Tine Stein, eds., *Die Verfassungsdiskussion im Jahr der deutschen Einheit. Analysen-Hintergründe-Materialien* (München: Hanser, 1991).

9. A central source is Wolfgang Schäuble, *Der Vertrag. Wie ich über die deutsche Einheit verhandelte* (Stuttgart: Deutsche Verlags-Anstalt, 1991).

10. The local self-administration, for example, has been restructured. Qualified personnel is scarce. The problems tend to surmount the capabilities of the agencies. Cf. Martin Osterland and Roderich Wehser, "Kommunale Demokratie als Herausforderung. Verwaltungsreorganisation in der Ex-DDR aus der Innenperspektive," *Kritische Justiz* 24 (1991): 318–32.

11. Cf. Peter Häberle, "Die Verfassungsbewegung in den fünf neuen Bundesländern," *Jahrbuch des Öffentlichen Rechts der Gegenwart* 41 (1993): 70–307.

12. I leave the Deutsche Social Union (DSU) aside, a splinter party on the moderate Right. On the first *Bundestag* elections in united Germany (December 1990), see Ursula Feist, "Zur politischen Akkulturation der Vereinigten Deutschen," *Aus Politik und Zeitgeschichte. Beilage zur Wochenzeitung Das Parlament*, B 11–12, 8 March 1991, 21–32.

13. Articles on the major parties after unification are in Ibid., B 5, 24 January 1992. A good case study is Stephen Silvia, "Left Behind: The Social Democratic Party in Eastern Germany," *West European Politics* 16 (2) (April 1993): 24–48. Heinrich Tiemann et al., "Gewerkschaften und Sozialdemokratie in den neuen Bundesländern," *Deutschland-Archiv* 26 (1993): 40–51. Of the East German population in 1991, 6 percent belong to the Roman Catholic Church, 27 percent to the Protestant Church. The West German figures are 42 percent and 45 percent respectively. "Committees for justice" were launched in the summer of 1992, trying to work on a multipartisan basis and serve as a platform for formulating East German interests. It did not amount to much.

14. *Treuhand Information* (19) (29 July 1993): 7–10. On this peculiar institution, in general, see Jürgen Turck, "Treuhand-Anstalt," in Werner Weidenfeld and Karl-Rudolf Korte, eds., *Handwörterbuch zur deutschen Einheit* (Frankfurt: Campus, 1992), 667–73.

15. The figures are taken and tabulated from an unpublished paper by Jürgen Müller, "Strukturelle Auswirkungen der Privatisierung," Deutsches Institut für Wirtschaftsforschung, preliminary version June 1993, tables II.1 and III.1; and from Rainer Geißler, *Die Sozialstruktur Deutschlands. Ein Studienbuch zur gesellschaftlichen Entwicklung im geteilten und vereinten Deutschland* (Opladen: 1992), 118.

16. Cf. W. R. Smyser, *The Economy of United Germany. Colossus at the Crossroads* (New York: St. Martin's Press, 1992).

17. Cf. several articles in *Aus Politik und Zeitgeschichte. Beilage zur Wochenzeitung Das Parlament*, B 51, 11 December 1992, especially by Wilhelm Krull and Dieter Simon. Figures from "Wissenschaft in Deutschland," *WZB-Mitteilungen* (Wissenschaftszentrum Berlin für Sozialforschung) 58 (December 1992): 38–42.

18. Ibid., 41; Hansgünther Meyer, "Konkordanz und Antinomie der Hochschulerneuerung in Deutschland nach der Wiedervereinigung" (lecture

manuscript, 20 April 1993, unpublished), 8, table 7. M. Rainer Lepsius, "Zum Aufbau der Soziologie in Ostdeutschland," *Kölner Zeitschrift für Soziologie und Sozialpsychologie* 45 (1993): 305–37; Gerhard A. Ritter, "Der Neuaufbau der Geschichtswissenschaft an der Humboldt-Universität zu Berlin—ein Erfahrungsbericht," *Geschichte in Wissenschaft und Unterricht* 44 (1993): 226–38.

19. Signs of recovery are clearly visible. For one example cf. Bernhard A. Sabel, "Science Reunification in Germany: A Crash Program," *Science* 260 (1993): 1753–758, also see the report by Patricia Kahn in Ibid., 1744–746. On the rise of a new stratum of self-employed persons both in industry and the professions, cf. Rudolf Woderich, "Neue Selbständigkeit in Ostdeutschland," *Public. Wissenschaftliche Mitteilungen aus dem Berliner Institut für Sozialwissenschaftliche Studien* 11 (1993): 57–67.

20. About DM 150 billion are annually transferred from the West to the East.

21. Cf. Christine Bialas and Wilfried Ettl, "Wirtschaftliche Lage, soziale Differenzierung und Probleme der Interessenorganisation in den neuen Bundesländern," *Soziale Welt* 44 (1993): 52–74; Geißler, *Die Sozialstruktur Deutschlands,* chaps. 5–7.

22. Cf. Wolfgang Zapf and Steffen Mau, "Eine demographische Revolution in Ostdeutschland?," *ISI. Informationsdienst Soziale Indikatoren* 10 (July 1993): 1–5; Siegfried Grundmann, "Thesen und Hypothesen zur Entwicklung der ostdeutschen Binnen- und Außenwanderung," *Public. Wissenschaftliche Mitteilungen aus dem Berliner Institut für Sozialwissenschaftliche Studien* 9 (1992): 89–100.

23. Cf. the articles by the Greiffenhagens and by Hans-Joachim Maaz and Ursula Meckel in Werner Weidenfeld, ed., *Deutschland. Eine Nation—doppelte Geschichte* (Cologne: Verlag Wissenschaft und Politik, 1993).

24. Cf. the debate in *Public* 9 and 10 (1992–1993), especially the articles by Thomas Koch, Rudolf Woderich, and Rolf Reißig.

25. Cf. the interview with two important East German intellectuals and political speakers: Jens Reich (Neues Forum) and Friedrich Schorlemmer (SPD), "Wer ist das Volk. Die deutschen Integrationsformeln greifen zu kurz," *Blätter für deutsche und internationale Politik,* February 1993, 158–70.

26. From articles by Martin and Sylvia Greiffenhage, Helmut Klages and Thomas Gensicke, Jörg Ueltzhöffer and Bodo Berhold Flaig, Hans-J. Misselwitz and Wilhelm Büprkling in Weidenfeld ed., *Deutschland;* "Ökonomische Kultur in Ostdeutschland," *WZB-Mitteilungen* 58 (December 1992): 27–30; *Allensbacher Jahrbuch der Demoskopie 1984–1992* 9 (1993): 718–19 (on parties and grass-roots democracy); Thomas Gensicke, "Lebenskonzepte im Osten Deutschland," *Public* 9 (1992): 101–122.

27. Cf. the articles by Felix Ph. Lutz, Bernd Faulenbach, and Bodo von Borries in Weidenfeld, ed., *Deutschland,* 157–208.

28. The change came in the middle of 1992. *Allensbacher Jahrbuch,* 452–53.

Article Review Form at end of book.

The Progress of German Unification

When the Iron Curtain fell in 1989, there was no more important consequence than the reunification of Germany. Seven years later the joining of East and West Germany attracts less attention but is no less critical to the future of Europe. Fortunately, for an undertaking this gargantuan, unification is progressing relatively well. It seems to be meeting everyone's expectations—except the Germans'.

Half of western Germans say in opinion polls they are dissatisfied with unification, and 38 percent of eastern Germans agree. One in five easterners would like Communism back. This nostalgia is more understandable in Eastern European countries now stripped of their security blankets. Unification has thrown East Germans into the arms of one of the world's most generous welfare states.

Bonn is pouring well over $100 billion annually into Germany's five new eastern states, more each year than the total cost of the Marshall Plan in today's dollars. Eastern Germans are richer and freer than their former Communist neighbors and richer and freer than ever before. Yet they do not seem very happy about it.

Chancellor Helmut Kohl cast unification's fate in July 1990, when he allowed East Germans to convert Ostmarks to Deutsche marks at an overvalued one-to-one exchange rate. That stopped the stampede of East Germans west, and pleased the East German majority, who wanted to dump everything Socialist and become West Germans as fast as possible. Mr. Kohl also decided to raise eastern wages as close to western wages as possible. The policies enabled eastern consumers to buy western goods. But

they killed East German factories and cut investors' incentives to build new ones in a place whose infrastructure has been largely untouched since Hitler's time.

Today eastern Germans are paid at 81 percent of western levels, but they are only 55 percent as productive. Unemployment in eastern Germany is now over 15 percent, while in the west it is 9 percent. Women have been particularly hard hit.

But the east has grown, in recent years, at the fastest rate in Western Europe. At current investment levels, productivity may equal the west's in 10 years. Meanwhile, the welfare state cushions the blow. The unemployed make more than they did working under Communism.

The Kohl Government is now proposing to cut these and other programs to help an east that westerners see as ungrateful. Particularly unpopular is a 7.5 percent unification tax, especially because Mr. Kohl told West Germans the process would not require a tax increase.

But unification deserves only some of the blame. Scandinavian nations are trimming their social programs. Unemployment is high all over Europe. Some of

Germany's cuts—like free stays at a health spa every four years instead of three—hardly seem onerous. Indeed, parts of the west, notably Bavaria, are booming. The surprise is how well Germany is doing despite its burden.

The easterners' underlying problem may be less financial than psychological. While the Czechs and Poles are proud to be building their new nations, victorious over Communism, each new day reminds eastern Germans that they lost the cold war and must defer to the victors.

The most powerful position any easterner holds in Germany today is provincial governor. To many in eastern Germany, closing a factory is not a necessary economic adjustment but a cruel penalty of capitalism. East Germans thought of themselves as the stars of the Socialist economy. Now they are told their work was second-rate. Even if Dresden became as rich as Düsseldorf overnight, many eastern Germans would resent a process that seems to them less a marriage than an adoption.

 Article Review Form at end of book.

German Chancellor Helmut Kohl Launched His Reelection Campaign

Erik Kirschbaum

Bonn, Sept. 28 (Reuter)—German Chancellor Helmut Kohl launched his reelection campaign on Sunday, vowing to fight crime and pin the blame firmly on opposition Social Democrats (SPD) for thwarting his grand plan to cut taxes.

Exactly 52 weeks before the general election, Kohl said in a series of speeches and interviews that he would try again to push through his failed tax reform proposals next year if he won a record fifth term.

Talks on tax reform between Kohl's coalition and the SPD collapsed last week, prompting economists and industry groups to decry the failure as a blow for Germany's 4.5 million jobless and a handicap for Bonn in the runup to the planned 1999 launch of Europe's single currency.

Kohl, shrugging off opinion polls showing him trailing the SPD's leading challenger Gerhard Schroeder, said he planned to make the emotive issue of crime a centerpiece of his campaign.

"Fighting crime belongs to the top one or two issues that will be focused on in the election," Kohl said in an interview with a local Berlin radio station on Sunday.

Violent crime has risen sharply in the last few years in many of Germany's major cities, a trend that parallels an influx of illegal immigrants from eastern Europe and has frightened many inner city dwellers.

"The public's fears and making our streets safe have to be taken seriously, even if they are sometimes exaggerated," Kohl told "Radio 100.6" in the hour-long interview. "People want more police on the streets and are calling for a stronger state."

The SPD, out of power in Bonn for 15 years, stumbled on the crime issue in a state election in Hamburg last Sunday when the party, long viewed as soft on crime, made a late and feeble effort to take a harder approach in Germany's second largest city.

The SPD unexpectedly slumped in Hamburg by four points to 36 percent, its lowest score in the left-wing bastion since World War Two. Kohl's Christian Democrats (CDU), who have a tougher reputation on crime issues, gained five points to 30 percent.

Kohl told a CDU party congress in the eastern city of Magdeburg that he would make sure voters knew that the SPD, which controls the upper house of parliament, were to blame for blocking his plans to cut taxes by 30 billion marks.

The SPD said Kohl's plans were unbalanced and would tear huge holes in government finances. The talks collapsed on Friday, ending seven months of bitter negotiations.

"We will go door to door and village to village to make sure the people know the SPD is responsible for the collapse of the tax reform," Kohl said.

The SPD governs in 13 of Germany's 16 states and will maintain its hold on the upper

Erik Kirschbaum, "German Chancellor Helmut Kohl Launched His Reelection Campaign," REUTERS, September 28, 1997. Reprinted by permission of Reuters.

house no matter what happens in the federal election. But Kohl said he expects the SPD to drop its opposition to tax reform if it loses in the September 27, 1998, election.

"The SPD would not dare to block the tax reform any more after their defeat," Kohl said. "But that means that two and a half years will be wasted before tax reform is implemented."

SPD chairman Oskar Lafontaine said in a separate interview with German Radio that Kohl's centre-right coalition was so badly split internally and incapable of governing that it should call early elections rather than wait 12 months.

"They cannot cover up the fact any longer that . . . the coalition is as badly split as an unhappily married couple," Lafontaine said. "It is just not working any more . . . Either they should get their act together or call early elections."

Lafontaine said Hamburg was a setback for the SPD but that it may ironically raise the left-leaning party's chances of defeating Kohl in the 1998 poll.

Opinion polls show the SPD and its probable Greens coalition partners five to eight points ahead of Kohl's centre-right coalition. Schroeder, the premier of Lower Saxony considered likely to be Kohl's challenger, leads him in polls by some 30 points.

"Hamburg was a warning signal for us," Lafontaine said. "Because of our strong results in the opinion polls, some of us were already acting as if we had won the election. We haven't."

 Article Review Form at end of book.

R E A D I N G   1 2

EMU to Lead Germany from Riches to Rags

Monetary Union: Well-off nations will become poorer, and the poor ones richer.

Brian Reading

Two weeks ago *The European* commented "Thatcher has crossed the channel, heading for Bonn not Paris". With a vengeance. German finance minister Theo Waigel has embarked upon a quintessential Thatcherite campaign—demanding big cuts to Germany's EU budget contributions. There is some justice in this. Germany's gross contribution to Brussels pays for over 60 per cent of EU expenditure. On a net basis, after deducting its share of Brussels handouts, it pays over Dm20 billion ($10.91bn) or 0.6 per cent of gross domestic product. This is double the contribution per person from the next largest payer, Britain, and five times that of Belgium and France which have higher GDPs per head than Germany. Yet the main reason why German and British net contributions are so high is that both get very little out of the Common Agricultural Policy, which accounts for more than half of EU expenditure. Germany should push, like Britain, for a decent reform of the iniquitous CAP (preferably for its abolition).

Brian Reading, "EMU to Lead Germany from Riches to Rags," The European, pp. 14-20, August 1997. Reprinted by permission of European/Solo Syndication.

But the German government has no stomach to take on special interest groups such as farmers.

Perhaps Waigel may soon gripe about a less obvious increase in Germany's contribution to the EU which is in the pipeline.

Seignorage is "money-for-nothing", the profit a government makes from printing notes and minting coins. Every increase in notes and coins in circulation provides the government with revenues equal to their face value at only fractional production costs. There are some Dm270bn worth of notes and coin in circulation, seven percent of GDP. Other countries print less money. French currency in circulation is three percent of GDP.

A significant part of German money-for-nothing comes from deutschmark notes circulating outside Germany, notably in east Europe. Seignorage is a valuable source of budgetary support. German currency in circulation increased by Dm12bn in 1996.

But if and when monetary union takes place, responsibility for the issue of notes and coin will pass to the European Central Bank. The profit from printing deutschmarks which circulate outside Germany will be lost.

Germany will get a share of ECB seignorage profits, but calculated on the basis of its lower share in EU's total population and GDP. This could cost Dm5bn a year or more. Budgetary problems are making the Germans increasingly tetchy about their payments to Brussels.

They fear that both the widening and deepening of the EU will increase the transfers to poorer and less prosperous countries as the union expands to 20 or more members.

This is the wrong worry. Payments to foreigners which German companies choose to make far exceed public transfers to Brussels. In 1996 German net foreign direct investment was Dm50bn. German industry is relocating abroad, where costs are lower and labour markets more flexible.

German jobs are going to foreigners. Industrial production currently accounts for 36 per cent of German GDP, ten percentage points more than in Britain, France and the US. Industrial jobs accounted for 36 per cent of German employment in 1996, a share last seen in Britain in 1980. British industrial jobs are now at 27 per cent.

Germany is de-industrialising more than a decade after Britain, a process which will accelerate if European monetary union (EMU) goes ahead. Exchange rates will be fixed at levels which over-value the D-mark.

Assuming they are fixed at existing exchange rate mechanism central rates (with Britain in with the pound at Dm2.95) then on a 1996 purchasing power parity basis, Portugal's escudo would be undervalued by 40 per cent against the deutschmark, the Irish punt and Spanish peseta by 25 per cent, the Italian lira by 20 per cent and the pound and the French franc by five per cent.

But purchasing power parities are calculated from relative prices of all goods and services, whether traded or not. The strength of the deutschmark reflects higher German productivity in traded goods, which offsets higher labour costs, bringing their prices closer to competitors' levels. For example, British average manufacturing output per hour worked, calculated using purchasing power parity exchange rates, is 15 per cent below the German level, Spanish productivity is 20 per cent lower.

Unfortunately for Germany, while average productivity which affects existing exchange rate is higher, marginal productivity determines the location of new industry. It is about the same wherever new plant is located.

Bonn could find itself DM5bn a year out of pocket.

Wage costs, taxes and social security contributions differ widely. In the single market, goods can be transported cheaply across frontiers and sold freely anywhere.

In EMU exchange risks will disappear. New investment will be extremely mobile. It will flee Germany with its high costs and its inflexible labour market in favour of Portugal, Ireland and Spain. Germany and its northern European neighbours will become the depressed regions. In the EU, the periphery will be prosperous.

In EMU, the Germans won't be able to do much to restore prosperity. There will be no monetary levers to pull. Fiscal policy will be constrained by high and rising unemployment, widening the cyclical and overall budget deficit. Devaluation, the shortcut to improved competiveness, will be ruled out.

All that will remain will be for jobless German to move to Spain in search of lower paid jobs (which they won't) or for poor Spanish taxpayers to help pay the generous German dole (which they won't). EMU will make rich

Germany depressed and poor Spain prosperous—the reverse of what most people expect. For Germany, EMU is a road from riches to rags.

The depressed countries of northern Europe, however, will be politically powerful. They will complain of unfair competition and social dumping. Waigel has already started. He claims taxes are unfairly low in other countries. Brussels will press for greater harmonisation of tax, social security and labour market systems. Instead of wage costs falling in depressed Germany, they will be forced higher in prosperous Spain, Ireland, Italy and Portugal.

The ECU will then have to be a weak currency to keep an inflationary Europe globally competitive.

Article Review Form at end of book.

The Devil They Don't Know

The consequences of the Communist victory in Russia's parliamentary election look modest in the short term, unpredictable after that.

Moscow. Nobody could sensibly accuse Russians, of all people, of voting for Communists in ignorance of the possible consequences. Yet vote they did by the million, on December 17th, for the Communist Party of the Russian Federation, awarding it around one-third of the seats in the Duma, Russia's lower house of parliament.

Some voters backed the Communist Party because they believed it had changed, others because they believed it was still the same, unlike everything else around them. Gennady Zyuganov, the party leader, was careful to leave both camps none the wiser. On the campaign trail he told different audiences what he thought they wanted to hear. He seems to have guessed pretty well.

Winning (according to preliminary estimates) 21% of the vote, nine percentage points more than their share in 1993, the Communists have been the main beneficiaries of a popular reaction against the government, against the status quo and, by extension, against President Boris Yeltsin. Some way after the Communists came another anti-government party, the far-right Liberal Democrats, led by Vladimir Zhirinovsky. Its 11% was half what it won in 1993, when it dominated the protest vote. Third came Our Home is Russia, a fat-cat party led by the prime minister, Viktor Chernomyrdin, which won 10%. Its near 20% share of the vote in Moscow offset a patchy showing in the provinces. Grigory Yavlinsky's Yabloko, the best-placed reformist group, came fourth with 7%, roughly the same as last time.

The biggest losers were found among the nationalists and the liberals. The Congress of Russian Communities, a nationalist group headed by Yuri Skokov and Alexander Lebed, a populist former general, won only 4% of the national vote. Their failure, and that of other nationalist groups such as the party of the former vice-president Alexander Rutskoi, suggests that aggressive nationalism has a greater hold on the Russian elite than it does on the electorate.

Yegor Gaidar, leader of Russia's Democratic Choice, which formed the radical core of the government that brought in the first wrenching changes after 1991, looked likely to fall out of the Duma altogether. His party ended up with 4.4% of the vote—slightly less even than a entirely unreconstructed hardline Communist block called Working Russia, whose 4.5% was as striking in its way as the 21% won by its more modern sibling.

As for the rest, the election was a brutal exercise in the need for reasonably large parties in a democracy. The existence of a threshold meant that "divan parties" (all members able to sit on a sofa) were massacred: 39 of the 43 parties on the ballot paper seemed likely to win less than the 5% of the vote needed to take a share of the 225 seats allocated by proportional representation. This meant that no less than 50% of the votes were "wasted"—that is, were cast for parties which failed to get into parliament on party lists. The other 225 seats are filled from single-member constituencies across the country, an avenue for independents and an alternative way for those who fail to enter the 450-seat Duma through the party lists.

The result is a triumph for the dogged Mr Zyuganov. His party has won a dominant position in Russian politics, but has not burdened itself with the degree of power in the Duma that might oblige it to start putting its policies, whatever they may be, into practice. Mr Zyuganov has taken on the mantle of Russia's leader of the opposition and has impressed even his rivals with his prudence and professionalism (a charge that could never have been levelled against Mr Zhirinovsky).

In the month or two ahead, as other party leaders chase alliances to give them more leverage in the new Duma, Mr Zyuganov will be able to sit back and field the offers. The first signs are that he will be seeking friendship with as many parties as possible, rather than any tight coalition that might project the sense of a Communist-controlled chamber. On December 18th he said the Communists were prepared to "deal with any party, Zhirinovsky's included"—a catholicity of taste less improbable when set against Mr Zyuganov's role three years ago in assembling the rudiments of a "national salvation front" that was to unite his then-banned Communist Party with the extreme right to make common cause against the democratic centre.

This time, Mr Zyuganov is trying to make democracy work in his favour. Probably, his Communists will want to deal cordially even with Mr Chernomyrdin, against whose government they campaigned so trenchantly. The prime minister's job is the last thing that Mr Zyuganov (or, for the reformers, Mr. Yavlinsky) would want for himself because neither would relish going into the presidential election due next June answering for the shortcomings of a government. If Mr Chernomyrdin finds himself wanting to resign for much the same reason—his ambitions for the presidency are still unclear—the problem will be one of finding a plausible stop-gap.

If Mr Zyuganov, Mr Yavlinsky and Mr Chernomyrdin do indeed plan to spend the next six months avoiding any action that might alienate any significant part of the electorate, that will probably presage a dull parliament with mainly negative achievements. Fiscal discipline may slide, not because of any fundamental policy changes, but because the Duma will be less tolerant of the brutal month-by-month cash-limiting that has kept Russia's public finances on course in 1995. Pensions have gone unpaid for weeks, and power stations left to run short of fuel.

It follows, too, that Mr Zyuganov is unlikely to push any anti-reform agenda extending to renationalisation or expropriation of property—a prospect that was causing businessmen sleepless nights only a few weeks ago. Some within his party might wish him to do so, but Mr Zyuganov is strong enough to keep them in check. Having crept back to the fringe of real power, he has no interest in rallying moderate and democratic forces against him.

If he needs something to say, he will be on safe enough ground merely denouncing further privatisation. Mr Chernomyrdin, too, would probably prefer not to repeat some of the more grotesque struggles for control of government stakes in large public companies that marred the final weeks of 1995. Mr Zyuganov will be on safe ground, too, in condemning the war in Chechnya—another common cause with liberals, and a way of undermining Mr Yeltsin, for whom the war has been a disaster. Mr Zyuganov will probably call for all manner of improvements to Russia's impoverished health and social-security systems, confident that nobody will contradict him. He will evoke nostalgically the old Soviet Union, and call for it to be reassembled "voluntarily". That should be more than enough to carry him through the next six months. Will it be enough to carry him to the Kremlin? It is hard to credit the thought, but less hard than it was before the Duma results starting coming in.

The main obstacle to any challenger for the Kremlin still looks like being Mr Yeltsin, his two recent heart attacks notwithstanding. For the moment the incumbency factor is working against him. But if Mr Yeltsin is well enough to campaign properly in May and June, he may work wonders. He is a seasoned politician, a populist campaigner, and it can only help him that an economic upturn seems imminent.

Of other potential runners, Mr Chernomyrdin is the hardest to read. He has said he will not run against Mr Yeltsin, but he may find the temptation irresistible. He has gravitas but not the common touch. If Russian voters were looking for a safe, stolid, business-as-usual leader, Mr Chernomyrdin would be a gift

from central casting. But they are not, and nor is he.

Mr Lebed now looks like a busted flush: he squandered his appeal as an incorruptible "strongman" by agreeing to be number two in a party led by the uncharismatic Mr Skokov. If Mr Lebed can find a point of principle on which to resign from the Duma in the spring, he could yet campaign for the presidency on a platform of hostility to the entire political establishment (Mr Zhirinovsky has the same aim). But the exgeneral's bamboozling by Mr Skokov must raise a serious question-mark over his political instincts.

Mr Yavlinsky looks good, but not that good. Yabloko's performance was more of a holding action for reform than a personal triumph. At 43, bright, bumptious and curly-haired, he attracts disparate groups of voters, young and old, rich and poor, who seem to view him as a useful ingredient

in the mix of parliamentary politics. But it may be another ten years before he has about him the ring of a plausible president.

Surveying the field, Mr Zyuganov must sense that events are conspiring in his favour. He will probably run, and might win. Only then would he be obliged to stop talking and start doing. Only then would voters discover just whom they had elected—the social democrat who could charm the American Chamber of Commerce, or the Communist throwback who declared on this year's anniversary of the October revolution that Russia was again approaching "a pre-revolutionary situation". For the moment, Mr Zyuganov is not saying. And that, for the moment, is the secret of his success.

 Article Review Form at end of book.

A Shaky Year Over, the Yeltsin of Old Flies to the Summit

Michael Specter

Moscow, June 19—A year ago President Boris N. Yeltsin was practically a dead man. Desperate to win a second term, and to vanquish Communism in Russia for good, Mr. Yeltsin had a heart attack in the middle of the campaign and promptly disappeared from sight.

He won anyway, but by his inauguration last August many Russians were convinced that the feeble, robotic leader who struggled so visibly just to take the oath of office was through. Jokes comparing Mr. Yeltsin to Leonid I. Brezhnev—the ultimate symbol of fossilized Russian rulers—became common. For many critical months no new laws were passed, no initiatives were offered and nobody ran the country.

"It couldn't have been worse," said Andrei A. Piontkowsky, director of the Center for Strategic Studies, a liberal research group here. "The best anybody was hoping for was that he would have the grace to resign quietly. But it's as if he is a different human being now. Look around the summit table this week and ask yourself which President is more vigorous, active or successful than Boris Yeltsin."

That might be a stretch, but Mr. Yeltsin surely gets written off and then rises from the ashes more often than any other world leader. Still, even by his own standards, his most recent resurrection—both physically, after bypass surgery, and as a commanding and active political leader—has been mesmerizing.

Less than a year after he was dismissed as a near-zombie by politicians here and abroad, Mr. Yeltsin, 66, flew in triumph to Denver today for the summit meeting of industrialized countries beginning Friday. And now Russia has become associated with the Group of Seven, and the meeting being called the Summit of the Eight.

It would be hard to argue that Russia—with its astonishing post-Soviet economic decline only now beginning to level off—deserves to be considered one of the world's leading economic powers.

Millions of workers are still waiting for wages promised by a Government that does not have the money to pay them. Nor can one forget that the Russian military is, in the words of its air force chief, "incapable even of buying

Moscow and its leader are once again asserting themselves.

spare parts or dressing its soldiers properly."

But summit meetings are about symbols, and the symbolism of Mr. Yeltsin's new stature is hard to deny. Mr. Yeltsin's has emerged in one piece from difficult negotiations with NATO over the Western alliance's expansion. Though he and most other political leaders were opposed to expansion, once the decision was made the issue disappeared from the agenda here. Not even his Communist opponents talk about it much anymore.

In the last month, Mr. Yeltsin has signed important new agreements with Ukraine and Belarus, cementing his leadership of the Slavic world and helping bring it closer together than it has been since the Soviet Union dissolved in 1991. He has made strong new overtures to Japan, India and China. And he recently greeted the freely elected President of Chechnya in Moscow and referred to that secessionist region of southern Russia by the name its natives prefer, Ichkeria, which he had never before uttered in public.

But Mr. Yeltsin's domestic achievements may be even more significant. Even if it is successful, it will take years—perhaps decades—for Russia to make the transition from command economy serving a totalitarian state to free market. Still, most economic analysts believe that the tremendous depression that fell on Russia in 1991 is either slowing or at an end.

Mr. Yeltsin has asserted himself with unruly political leaders in Russia's many regions, successfully stripping the most outlandish of them—the Governor of the region that includes Vladivostok—of most of his power. And while his young market-oriented team of Government leaders often clash with the Communist-led Parliament, there is today more room for compromise than there has been in years.

"We oppose many of the Government's initiatives," said Gennadi Seleznyov, the Communist Speaker of Parliament and the most eloquent voice of the elected opposition. "We have a strong view that his Government is wrong on many issues. But of course we must work with them and we will. If we don't, it is only the people of Russia who suffer."

It has been less than six months since the Communists in Parliament, led by Mr. Seleznyov, vowed that they would never work with Anatoly B. Chubais, Mr. Yeltsin's Deputy Prime Minister in charge of economics and an object of pure hatred for many who oppose the pace and reasoning of reform. Since then they have worked together often.

"He has many problems to resolve but is facing them," said Masha Lipman, deputy editor of the highly respected weekly magazine Itogi. "He has done the best thing a President can do: hire smart energetic people and let them work."

Mr. Yeltsin rarely used to appear on television, not even in the old days when he was healthy. Now he appears nearly every day with some new edict. This week he has ordered that the gas monopoly, Gazprom, cut its bloated prices to industry by 40 percent. He has annulled a 1995 law that restricted civil liberties. The number of those who would seek Mr. Yeltsin's resignation has fallen sharply in the last six months: from more than 50 percent to less than 30 percent, according to one recent national poll.

"Nobody who has watched him for a long time would say that Mr. Yeltsin has finally turned the corner," Ms. Lipman said. "He is always up and down. But right now he is about as up as he has ever been."

 Article Review Form at end of book.

Japan
Market forces are allowed to advance

Official deregulation is just one symptom of a wider, spontaneous acceptance of market forces. Old business alliances are being reviewed in a harsher, more market-oriented light, writes William Dawkins.

William Dawkins

Change is hard to spot in Japan because it tends to happen incrementally, without great fanfare.

But to many people's surprise, not least that of the Japanese themselves, there have been significant changes this year. Market forces have been allowed to advance into several hitherto protected sectors of the most tightly controlled economy in the developed world.

The archetypal Japanese convention that the broad interests of

William Dawkins, "Japan: Market Forces Are Allowed to Advance," FINANCIAL TIMES, Tuesday, July 15, 1997. Reprinted by permission.

society come before market efficiency and the interests of individuals has been thrown open for reassessment. In several important areas, such as financial services, transport, and energy, it has even begun to break down, with potentially wide-ranging consequences.

All this comes, curiously, with an enthusiastic shove from the Liberal Democratic party government, formerly conservative by instinct and tradition. The administration of Mr Ryutaro Hashimoto was wrongly seen by many as a symbol of return to the old system when it took office last October. It appeared to mark the end of a four-year political struggle between advocates of a "new Japan" and the scions of the old system, based on defending, not challenging, vested interests.

Instead, Mr Hashimoto has adopted the deregulation policies of his political opponents and carried them out with unexpected energy. This is in line with the LDP's tradition of occupying the opposition's territory, but it has also brought the ruling party on to genuinely new ground.

Foreign attention has focused on the government's 2,800-point deregulation programme which includes the so-called "Big Bang" proposals to make financial markets as efficient and competitive as London or New York by 2001.

A gauge of how real is the Big Bang plan is the speed with which parliament agreed in April to abandon exchange controls from next year. Theoretically, this makes more, sweeping deregulation inevitable—as it was in the UK after the abandonment of exchange controls in 1979—because it leaves the authorities with no means to stop financial business leaving Tokyo in search of cheaper markets abroad.

The only option now is to bring Tokyo market costs and efficiency to the same level as its best competitors. In defiance of cynics, the government has adopted a rigorous timetable intended to bring this about.

Finance is not the only sector where Japan is undergoing a culture change. In energy, for example, the end of a cartel on oil imports last year has since caused petrol prices to fall by a fifth, forcing a collapse in domestic oil refiners' profits. In transport, permission was granted last October for the formation of four new domestic airlines, the first in 46 years, to operate on the world's busiest route, from Tokyo to Sapporo.

In telecommunications, Nippon Telegraph and Telephone, the dominant carrier, is to be split, along US lines, between a long-distance and international group and two local operators by 1999. It has been obliged to open domestic lines to foreign companies.

But official deregulation is just a symptom of a wider, spontaneous acceptance of market forces. Equity investors, for example, have, over the past nine months or so, begun to recognise that it is no longer realistic to value companies on the basis of their membership of a group or sector. Share prices no longer move in predictable bands between and within sectors, as they once did, on the assumption that stronger companies would always bail out weaker brethren.

Elsewhere, old business alliances are being reviewed in a harsher, more market-oriented, light. Cracks have opened in the *keiretsu* system of corporate families, loose alliances between suppliers, manufacturers, distributors and banks linked by dozens of cross-shareholdings and an un-

spoken preference to do business with each other. Now, it is no longer heresy for a *keiretsu* member to buy supplies outside the group, or to borrow from an unrelated bank.

Why are all these changes happening only now, more than a decade after the US and much of Europe underwent their own version of economic deregulation?

One answer is that policy debate has always taken a long time to become action in Japan. Many of the reforms now occurring have been under consideration by various government panels for years. Deregulation was the rallying call of the two unstable coalitions which ruled when the LDP was forced into opposition for the first time in its life for nearly a year until mid-1994, as it was for all leading parties in last autumn's general election.

Another factor is the moderate strength of the economy. After the longest slowdown since the 1930s, Japan's gross domestic product grew by 3.6 per cent last calendar year, the best performance in the Group of Seven. Growth in the first quarter of this year was a solid 2.5 per cent over the same period last year.

Unemployment, while high by Japanese standards at 3.3 per cent, is still far from being a social problem. Meanwhile, manufacturers' pre-tax profits rose by a healthy 20 per cent in the year to March, a tribute to the efficiency gains made under pressure of the recession, but also helped by the impact of a weak yen on their foreign competitiveness.

In consequence, policy makers and businessmen feel that the economy is just about robust enough to cope with the short-term pains—a rise in bankruptcies and possibly unemployment— that go with greater competition.

The exception that proves the rule, of course, are the weaker financial institutions, still burdened with bad debts inherited from the rush of irresponsible lending during the late 1980s asset price bubble. They are ill-equipped to face full competition. But, as one stockbroker points out, the alternative to radical deregulation is worse; the long-term decline of the Tokyo markets, with the wider economic damage that implies.

At the same time, however, the changes in Japan over the past year should not be exaggerated. Some features of the traditional inward-looking, system are still strong, for better or worse.

Foreigners are not always welcome in some of the more conservative industries, as Mr Rupert Murdoch, the Australian media magnate, discovered when he had to sell a stake in TV Asahi only nine months after buying it.

But a few months later, he found a new partner, Fuji TV, which bought a stake in Mr Murdoch's Japanese digital television joint venture.

Faction politics, the foundation of the defence of vested interests, are still dominant, in that faction bosses have the power to share out cabinet jobs.

Then again, there are signs of strain in the biggest LDP, factions as followers begin to demonstrate a measure of independence from faction bosses.

The current scandal surrounding questionable payments by Nomura Securities, Japan's largest stockbroker, and Dai-Ichi Kangyo Bank, the leading commercial bank, to gangsters, recalls a similar wave of corruption scandals seven years ago.

The message is that, at some companies, corporate governance, a vital feature of an efficient market, remains undeveloped.

The durability of those remaining bulwarks against market forces invites what must be the biggest question facing Japan over the next few years.

That is, to what extent can it embrace the market forces needed to enable its companies to compete in an increasingly international world, while at the same time retaining valued traditional features such as low unemployment and social stability?

Many Japanese hope that change can come with a minimum of pain. But governments in the west have long become used to surrendering significant economic sovereignty to the markets, with uncontrollable consequences.

It is getting harder for modern Japan to be as different from the west as it used to be.

 Article Review Form at end of book.

R E A D I N G 1 6

Liberal Democrats Regain Control in Japan

Sheryl WuDunn

Tokyo, Sept. 5—Four years after Japanese voters rejected the Liberal Democratic Party from its

longtime lock on power, the party regained control today with an effective majority in Japan's influential lower house of Parliament.

With the Liberal Democratic leader, Ryutaro Hashimoto, as

Prime Minister, the party was already able to set the political agenda in Japan. But the defection of a legislator from the opposition New Frontier Party, giving the

Liberal Democrats a bare majority, makes it easier for them to pass legislation over the heads of the opposition.

The Liberal Democrats won control when Naoto Kitamura, a former member who deserted in 1993, rejoined them today.

The party met and hastily approved Mr. Kitamura's application for membership, giving it 250 seats out of the 500-seat lower house. Another 249 members belong to the New Frontier or other parties or are independents. The final member is the speaker, whose loyalties are with the Liberal Democrats and can vote to break a tie.

The New Frontier Party declined to comment on today's development, but it issued a copy of an earlier statement denouncing members who defected to the Liberal Democrats.

"These individuals elected by the people under the new electoral system have betrayed the will of the voters and joined the force that refuses to execute reform," said the statement. "We must try to explain these facts to the people."

The Liberal Democrats will maintain their alliance with two other smaller parties, in part because they need the smaller parties to have a working majority in the Parliament's upper house. In the upper house, the Liberal Democrats have a much smaller share of the seats, although they hope to rectify that in elections next summer.

At a news conference today, Koichi Kato, the Liberal Democratic Party secretary general, tried to play down his party's dominance. He expressed doubt that many more opposition members in the lower house would join his party.

"We must practice politics humbly by listening to various concerns," he said.

Still, just four years after their humiliating loss in the polls, the Liberal Democrats are growing stronger every day. Mr. Hashimoto is almost certain to be re-elected this month as his party's leader, meaning that he would probably stay on as Prime Minister for at least two years.

He has already lasted more than 20 months as Prime Minister, a post that was turning into a merry-go-round as administrations rose and fell, sometimes every few months. Moreover, in a poll last month, Mr. Hashimoto's support rose to 44 percent, the highest level since he first took office in January 1996.

Mr. Hashimoto may be the leader of the party with the deepest roots in the Japanese bureaucracy, but he has worked hard to fashion an image as a reformer, setting up special advisory councils to evaluate programs to restructure the Government and championing a program to modernize Japan's financial markets.

Still, there is widespread skepticism about how much change he will actually achieve. At a recent conference, a Government panel on restructuring the administration decided, to leave the most criticized ministries, like the Ministry of Finance, largely intact.

In recent months, the Liberal Democrats have been vigorously lobbying members of the New Frontier Party, the main opposition group, and offering them attractive posts and party positions to encourage them to defect and rejoin the Liberal Democrats. They even lured one member, Hajime Funada, who had once reportedly said, "I will put an end to the L.D.P.," as the Liberal Democrats are known. Mr. Funada was a close aide to Ichiro Ozawa, the New Frontier leader.

Mr. Kitamura's move today highlights the disarray at the New Frontier Party and its rapidly declining influence. For months, New Frontier stalwarts have been walking out the door one by one, unhappy with the inner factionalism and dogmatic style of Mr. Ozawa. A brilliant strategist with a startling vision of reform for Japan, Mr. Ozawa is often criticized as secretive, manipulative, stubborn and overbearing.

So far, more than 30 New Frontier legislators have left that party, including former Prime Ministers Morihiro Hosokawa and Tsutomu Hata.

In the poll taken last month, the New Frontier Party gathered support from only 5 percent of those surveyed. Even the Japan Communist Party is attracting more Japanese followers, with 6 percent support.

In contrast, the Liberal Democratic Party far outdistanced both parties, winning support from 33 percent of those polled.

Article Review Form at end of book.

Political Action Man
Ryutaro Hashimoto

Paul Abrahams on the risks taken by Japan's prime minister.

Paul Abrahams

Japanese prime ministers seem to come in two varieties: the common besuited bureaucrat and the dynamic, outward-looking reformer. The latter is a rare and exotic species, best exemplified by Yasuhiro Nakasone, who led the country between 1982–87. Now, the current prime minister, Ryutaro Hashimoto, is displaying some characteristics of that species.

In the past week, he has successfully strutted around on the international stage, concluding a triumphant trip to China, and announcing an autumn summit in Siberia with Boris Yeltsin, the Russian president.

At home, his Liberal Democratic party has regained a majority in the lower house and re-elected him as leader, offering him the possibility of another two years as prime minister. Opinion polls late last month gave him a public approval rating of nearly 50 per cent. That is unprecedented for a Japanese prime minister after two years in power.

But instead of being able to celebrate, Mr Hashimoto has been on the defensive, subject to a barrage of media and popular criticism. The reason is his decision to appoint Koko Sato to his cabinet during Thursday's reshuffle.

The problem with Mr Sato is that he was convicted in 1986 of receiving a Y2m ($16,700) bribe from All Nippon Airways in a scandal involving the US aircraft maker Lockheed. Dubbed the "cabinet convict", he is the first politician with a conviction to serve in a postwar government.

It was not supposed to be this way. Mr Hashimoto was supposed to represent a new breed of Japanese politician, outspoken, dynamic, perhaps even brash, and most of all honest.

Mr Hashimoto's decision to appoint Mr Sato is particularly shocking because the prime minister has nailed his colours to the mast of open, honest government, publicly stating his intention to sever the links "between politics and dirty money".

The press has been quick to portray Mr Hashimoto's cabinet decision as a betrayal, a return by his ruling Liberal Democratic party to its bad old ways. In 1993, after nearly 40 years in power, the LDP was ousted from power mainly because of the public's disgust for its faction-fighting, cronyism and corruption.

The media have also argued that the prime minister's decision could indicate a weakening of his resolve to carry out a comprehensive reform of the country's powerful bureaucracy, and his determination to speed up the economy's stuttering growth through deregulation. Their fears were heightened by the fact that Mr Sato has been made director-general of the government's management and co-ordination agency, the body that will take charge of the bureaucracy reforms.

In reality, the uproar over Mr Sato probably does not endanger the prime minister's agenda of reform. But what the promotion does demonstrate is that for Mr Hashimoto to modernise the country, he must still indulge in old-fashioned political faction-fighting.

So far, Mr Hashimoto has scored top marks for his reformist rhetoric—but lower ones for actual results. To implement his plans, he needs political support from broad sections of his own party in both the lower and upper houses.

Paul Abrahams, "Political Action Man," FINANCIAL TIMES, September 13/14, 1997. Reprinted by permission.

The trouble is that the LDP is split. Mr Hashimoto belongs to the wing that wants to continue the LDP's current coalition with the Socialists and the centrist Harbinger party. The idea is that this would provide continuity and stability. The other wing wants to ally with the centre-right New Frontier party, which comprises former LDP members.

Mr Hashimoto's new cabinet reflects a deal by which the coalition could continue and a number of strategically important LDP jobs stayed in the hands of the prime minister's allies, rather than centre-right candidates. To placate the right, Mr Hashimoto, reluctantly agreed to offer Mr Sato a cabinet job—doing so, paradoxically, at the behest of Mr Nakasone, the prime minister's dynamic predecessor.

"The right did not get what it wanted and had a lot of egg on its face," explains Dan Harada, a political analyst at the Nagatacho Forum, a policy discussion group. "Mr Sato's appointment was a sop. Without it, Mr Hashimoto could have found the right wing of the party even more reluctant to push through his reforms."

Such political expediency has not proved popular, but the effects could prove short-lived. Mr Hashimoto is greatly admired. He is not only a skilled technocrat, having held four cabinet posts, but also a master of selling unpopular policies.

He won widespread respect when, as finance minister, he introduced the hugely unpopular sales tax in 1989. In his efforts to convince a sceptical Japanese population, he invited those opposed to the tax to write to him. He personally responded to 19,000 letters.

As minister of transport he also managed to push through the break-up and privatisation of Japan National Railways, despite the opposition of the company, unions and many in his own party.

Mr. Hashimoto is also personally liked for his youth and energy which is unusual in a country where many politicians are in their late 60s and 70s. Still only 60, he remains a keen practitioner of Kendo, Japanese fencing, fighting three times a week at his former university or on the roof of the ministry of international trade and industry. He is also a mountaineer and has climbed to Mount Everest's base camp in the Himalayas.

By Japanese standards he is a maverick, on one occasion during negotiations with the US turning up in a lime-green leather jacket. His good looks, Elvis-style sideburns and slicked-back hair (he is known as Mr Pomado after the Japanese word for hair-gel) helps his popularity with female voters, while his record of standing up to US pressure on trade issues also appeals to the public.

Some of that popularity will be damaged by Mr Hashimoto's decision to let Mr Sato into his cabinet. But what will count in the end is his ability to deliver on his promises.

In addition to proposing to shake up the bureaucracy, Mr Hashimoto has undertaken to shake up Japan's restrictive distribution industry; cut electricity prices by deregulating the energy industry, reduce telecoms' costs through liberalisation; and reform agriculture. Above all, he plans a Big Bang reform of Japan's financial sector.

If such noble ends are achievable only through some murky means, such as introducing Mr Sato into his cabinet, Mr Hashimoto may feel they are a price worth paying. On the other hand, he might also recall the dangers of murky dealings: Mr Nakasone was brought down because of a corruption scandal involving the Recruit publishing group.

 Article Review Form at end of book.

WiseGuide Wrap-Up

Mairowitz argues that it is not just the French Left that is making gains at the expense of the moderate conservatives. The Far Right wing is also having a resurgence in France. The Far Right appeals to many on economic grounds but also introduces dangerous policies of national exclusion and xenophobia.

A strong regional European Union (EU) is important so that European countries can compete successfully with U.S. and Japanese businesses. It also will allow France to carve out a global leadership role, since France is a major voice in the EU. However, Germany, which stands to gain a great deal economically from a strong EU, does not want to continue to pay the lion's share of the EU's operating costs, since Germans are reeling under the cost of reuniting the Eastern and Western Germanies. The English, once proud of their status as a global power, are wary of the political and economic coordination required to become part of a regional block. Many in Britain fear the loss of Britain's national sovereignty if Britain becomes a full-fledged member of the new EU.

In Reading 13, the *Economist*'s analyst of Russian politics argues that two factors make it unlikely that the Russian Communist Party will reverse the economic reforms of recent years. First, the Communist Party is now led by Gennady Zyuganov, a pragmatist who can adapt to new circumstances and compromise on many of the previous ideological stances of the Communist Party. Second, international forces have introduced such reforms globally, and the Communist Party is likely to realize that it is too late to turn back the clock.

R.E.A.L. Sites

This list provides a print preview of typical **coursewise** R.E.A.L. sites. There are over 100 such sites at the **courselinks™** site. The danger in printing URLs is that web sites can change overnight. As we went to press, these sites were functional using the URLs provided. If you come across one that isn't, please let us know via email to: webmaster@coursewise.com. Use your Passport to access the most current list of R.E.A.L. sites at the **courselinks™** site.

Site name: BBC Politics 97

URL: http://www.bbc.co.uk/politics97/issues/emuprocon.shtml

Why is it R.E.A.L.? Read and analyze the pros and cons of British participation in the Euro, the European Union's single currency to be initiated in 1999, followed by a second round in 2002. Britain's Tony Blair has announced that Britain will consider joining in 2002.

Key topics: Euro

Site name: AsiaWeek Newsgroup Japan

URL: http://www.asiaweek.com/asiaweek/current/issue/newsgroup/japan.html

Why is it R.E.A.L.? This site provides up-to-date information on contemporary Japanese politics for English readers. Report on how Japanese political party rivalry and efforts at coalition building continue to shift and change. Explain how media reports of corruption reflect on various Japanese political parties.

Key topics: governing political party coalition

Post–World War II Comparative Political Economies of Late Industrializing/Third World States

WiseGuide Intro

The 1990s has been a period of democratic transition for many states, including Third World/late industrializing countries (LICs). As Samuel Huntingon has written, we are living in the historic "Third Wave of Democratization." In some countries, however, governing parties still manipulate any new initiatives to hold democratic elections, and democracy continues to be thwarted. Mexico, for example, permitted elections throughout the decades during which its neighbors suffered under military dictatorships. However, the Institutional Revolutionary Party (PRI) coopted or coerced opponents and never allowed opposition parties to win electoral contests and gov ern. In September 1997, for the first time, Mexico's national governance structures began to change. Opposition members were permitted to claim their rightful victories and take their seats in the national parliament, where they comprised the majority of representatives.

Democratization in newly industrializing countries like Mexico, Brazil, South Africa, and South Korea is occurring in a historic period when national leaders in all states must confront the harsh economic realities of global competition and the economic discipline that such globalism imposes. The leaders in these new democracies walk a difficult line between governing within their economic means and providing enough goods and services that they can win reelection from a newly mobilized, democratic electorate. Additionally, today's leaders must secure the economic capital necessary to accelerate the industrialization and diversification of their economies. Brazil provides an excellent case study. Readings 21 and 22 discuss how Fernando Henrique Cardoso, a former leftist academic and a victim of the military junta that ruled Brazil during its authoritarian period, became a democratically elected president and modified his views about how the state might provide for all Brazilians and how it must be wary of its "dependent" relations with Northern states. Cardoso has had to find ways to pursue conservative economic policies while also remaining electorally popular. It remains a difficult balancing act.

Northern states continue to use their economic leverage to influence Southern states to democratize and liberalize trade and financial sectors. Moreover, citizens in Northern states often lobby their governments to pressure Southern states to achieve better human rights records. Southern state leaders, not surprisingly, resent Northern state economic pressure in any form. Some citizens living in Southern states, such as Nigeria, however, believe that Northern states could do more to protect them from their government. Northern democratic state leaders, though, argue that they are trying to promote democratization and the improvement of human rights, but must be respectful of the national sovereignty of other states.

South Africa is a good example of a state in which democratization does not preclude continuing contestation. Now, however, contestation takes a legal form in which political parties debate their positions on issues among their own membership and then debate each other nationally. Democratization also requires that governments, such as the South Korean government discussed in this section, find new ways of allowing interest groups and their organizations, such as unions or peasant organizations, to participate in the new democratic governing process.

Late industrializing countries deal with their recent authoritarian pasts in a variety of ways. The world has been watching the South African experiment in which the new government has established a Commission on Truth and Reconciliation. After testifying truthfully to this commission about politically motivated crimes committed during the years of repression, individuals can petition in the name of desperately needed national reconciliation for clemency from the commission and for protection from prosecution by the victims of their crimes. Those who do not testify can be tried in the courts. So much is not known about the dark years of repression that many people would rather have the commission shed light and understanding on those years than have juries extract revenge from perpetrators of apartheid crimes. Additionally, it might be difficult to obtain the kind of evidence about these crimes that would be admissible in a democratic court.

Today's late industrializing countries of Africa, Latin America, and Asia are undergoing great changes of democratization and economic liberalization; they face many challenges. Hopefully, these challenges will prove to be opportunities that will improve living standards, political security, and citizen participation.

? Questions ?

1. In what ways are challenging economic times making it difficult for the new reforming politicians in Mexico and Brazil? Reading 35 on South Korea argues that workers must endure hard economic times now and that democratic processes of openness must be guaranteed. How might workers respond?

2. From the evidence presented in the readings, how have Mexico, South Africa, South Korea, and Brazil progressed in securing democratic practices? Compare these countries with Nigeria.

3. Kim Dae Jung and Fernando Henrique Cardoso share a similar political path. What similarities do they share?

Gains by Opposition Confirmed in Mexico

Julia Preston

Mexico City, July 14—Official results have confirmed that opposition parties won a major share of power in national elections this month, bringing new pluralism to a country that had been a one-party state.

The official tallies, issued late Sunday, concluded a vote widely regarded as the cleanest in Mexico's modern history. The final count was very close to preliminary results released by the federal elections council in the hours after the polls closed on July 6.

The outcome was a vindication for the head of the elections council, José Woldenberg, who had pledged to run an election that would give Mexicans new confidence.

The official results showed that the Institutional Revolutionary Party, or PRI, which governed Mexico virtually unchallenged for nearly seven decades, lost its majority in the lower house of Congress. But the party will still have the largest delegations in both houses of the legislature.

According to estimates based on the official figures, the PRI will have 239 seats in the 500-seat lower house.

In a surprise result, the left-of-center Party of the Democratic Revolution will have the second-largest delegation, with 125 seats. The conservative National Action Party, which has been Mexico's second political force, is expected to have 122 seats, and smaller parties will divide the rest.

The PRI will continue to dominate the Senate, but it no longer has the power to approve any significant legislation without forging alliances with opposition lawmakers.

The Party of the Democratic Revolution, known by its Spanish initials as the P.R.D., was buoyed by the decisive victory in the Mexico City mayoral race of its founding leader, Cuauhtémoc Cárdenas, who took 47 percent of the vote in the first election for the post in decades. His party also won 38 of 66 seats in the capital's city council, giving him a free hand to carry out his policies.

Mr. Cárdenas is facing a long transition, since he does not take office until Dec. 5. After an amicable meeting with Mr. Cárdenas late today, President Ernesto Zedillo announced that he would cede some of his powers by allowing the Mayor-elect to name a new police chief and District Attorney for the capital, which is in the grip of a crime epidemic. By law Mr. Zedillo is still entitled to make those appointments.

The elections council will not give its final word on the distribution of seats in Congress until an elections court has ruled on contested returns in some districts, which it must do by Aug. 23. But officials said today that the tally was unlikely to change substantially. The new legislators take office in late August.

The only contest that produced widespread fraud allegations was in the Gulf state of Campeche. In the race for Governor there, Layda Sansores, who broke with the PRI last year to join the P.R.D., was defeated by the PRI candidate, Antonio González Kuri, who won 48 percent of the vote to her 41 percent, according to official tallies.

Mrs. Sansores led a march of an estimated 20,000 sympathizers in the state capital on Sunday and has pledged to wage a campaign of civil resistance.

The opposition parties also organized some protests charging fraud in the central state of Colima, where final results showed a narrow victory for the PRI candidate for Governor. The protests are not expected to affect the outcome of that contest.

In the southern state of Chiapas, more than one-fifth of the precincts never opened after sympathizers of the Zapatista rebels burned polling stations and attacked voters across much of the state. The elections council has not decided whether to call a new election in the state.

Article Review Form at end of book.

R E A D I N G   1 9

In Mexico's House, Speaker's Stature Signals a New Day

Sam Dillon

Porfirio Munoz Ledo, Mexico's powerful new Speaker of the House, recalled recently that when he was first elected as an opposition senator in 1988, he pleaded with leaders of the governing Institutional Revolutionary Party, or PRI, to allow him to serve on a committee. Any committee.

But they just laughed, Mr. Munoz Ledo recalled.

As recently as 1988, the idea that a member of Mexico's opposition would aspire to share in the power wielded by a Senate committee was, to the PRI, well, laughable.

The party's disdainful treatment of Mr. Munoz Ledo is remarkable, since by 1988 he had already held two Cabinet posts and had been president of the PRI as well as Mexico's representative at the United Nations and President of the United Nation Security Council. Finally, one compassionate PRI senator offered to allow Mr. Munoz Ledo to join her Committee on Libraries, he recalled. He accepted immediately.

It is a sign of the speed with which Mexico is changing in the wake of the opposition's landslide victory in July 6 elections that on Monday night, after President Ernesto Zedillo delivered his annual state-of-the-nation address to a joint session of Congress, Mr.

Munoz Ledo's response was the first ever delivered to a sitting Mexican President by a member of the opposition.

Mr. Munoz Ledo spoke with tact and elegance, but he did not shrink from giving a tough message to Mr. Zedillo, who was sitting next to him at the podium of the Congress with millions of Mexicans watching on a nationwide broadcast. The message was that the era of Mexico's godlike presidencies has come to a close.

"Every one of us is equal to you," Mr. Munoz Ledo said, quoting a ritual phrase spoken in the 13th century by representatives of the earliest Spanish Parliaments to Spanish kings who visited their chambers. "And all of us together amount to more than you."

Mr. Zedillo responded with considerable poise, pledging in his own speech to respect the autonomy of the Mexican legislature.

"Both men carried themselves with dignity," said Alberto Aziz Nassif, an author of several studies of Mexico's democratic evolution. "They both lived up to the demands of history."

In their interchange, which several analysts described today as historic, Mr. Zedillo and Mr. Munoz Ledo not only signaled the emerging relationship between the legislative and executive branches but also laid out their respective views of what should be Mexico's broad political agenda during the three-year congressional session inaugurated on Monday.

Mr. Munoz Ledo sketched a list of reforms that is vast by any standards. He said the Congress will seek to reform the judiciary, overhaul the tax laws, strengthen state and municipal governments, establish public rights to referendum and plebiscite, investigate corruption, and if necessary put Government officials suspected of crimes on political trial.

He said the Congress would also review Government economic policy, with an eye to increasing salaries, improving delivery of education and other services, restructuring the unpayable mortgage debts held by millions of poor Mexicans, and promoting small businesses.

Anticipating opposition hopes to steer Mexico along new economic paths, Mr. Zedillo devoted much of his address to defending his free-market, tight-money policies. He reminded Mexicans that the economy grew 7 percent during the first half of 1997.

"It's possible to examine and perfect details and specific programs," Mr. Zedillo said. "But I'm convinced that the essential bases are correct, and if respected will lead to the growth with jobs Mexico needs."

Mr. Munoz Ledo responded sharply.

"Obstinacy is the opposite of wisdom and is a harmful trait in public affairs, which require firmness but also flexibility, imagination and compliance with the will of the electorate," Mr. Munoz

Ledo said. "To know how to govern is to know how to listen and how to correct course."

Analysts characterized that as good counsel that Mr. Munoz Ledo could heed himself.

"Munoz Ledo is one of Mexico's most brilliant men," said Alfonso Zarate, editor of Carta Politica, a bimonthly political newsletter here. "The only thing that exceeds his intelligence is his egotism."

Mr. Munoz Ledo, who is 64, began his career within the PRI, heading the Ministries of Labor and Education during the 1970's, and later representing Mexico at the United Nations, from 1979 to 1985.

He broke with the PRI in 1987 to form an opposition alliance that backed the 1988 presidential candidacy of Cuauhtemoc Cardenas. Many believe Mr. Cardenas lost that election through fraud. (Mr. Cardenas was elected mayor of Mexico City in July.)

 Article Review Form at end of book.

Globalization and Resistance

The remaking of Mexico

Mexico is transforming itself through the interaction of two very powerful forces—the neoliberal project, which is imposing a new set of social and economic relations from above, and the resistance to that project, reorganizing society from below.

David Barkin, Irene Ortiz and Fred Rosen

I

"Deep down, we don't want to bankrupt the system," says José María Imaz to a small press conference in New York City, "but if it comes down to it, we will have to keep our word." [1] Imaz, the dapper-looking director of a Mexican small-business group called the National Entrepreneurial Alliance, spent this past November in New York and Washington, meeting with officials of the leading brokerages doing business in Mexico, representatives of the International Monetary Fund (IMF), key anti-NAFTA congress-people and members of a wide range of think tanks. He came to the seats of power to negotiate on behalf of Mexico's powerful debtor's movement, El Barzón, which has made itself so independent of the country's ruling Institutional Revolutionary Party

(PRI), that it has become the first major opposition group since the days of the Mexican revolution to negotiate with foreign powers about Mexico's future.

A reporter asks Imaz why a middle-class, self-described middle-of-the-road businessman like himself would threaten to shut down his country's financial system? And why would his organization of debt-ridden property owners send him to another country to carry on negotiations? For the *barzonista*, these are not difficult questions to answer. He is angry because small and medium property owners like himself, despite their "natural" conservatism, have been decimated by the economic restructuring of the past 15 years. And his organization sent him abroad because real economic—and therefore political—power in the country has accrued to transnational corporations, U.S. portfolio investors, international financial institutions and the U.S. government—all of whose representatives can most easily be found in New York and Washington.

His trip was motivated by a ruling handed down by the fifth circuit federal tribunal of Mexicali, Baja California. On October 30, the court ruled that Mexico's ten largest banks had been illegally constituted when privatized in 1990 by then-president Carlos Salinas and thus had no "legal existence." Salinas, in effect, had decreed the bank privatizations after the expiration of a 360-day limit established by the Mexican Congress, leading the court to declare that the privatization decrees were "extemporaneous." [2] If the banks have no legal existence, then neither, of course, do the debts owed to them, and on the basis of the ruling, El Barzón is filing for the dismissal of all court proceedings initiated by the banks to enforce the collection of past-due debts. Imaz was in town with one big bargaining chip: Help us restructure the internal debt so that it is payable, and we won't close down the system by legally refusing to make payments on *all* bank debt.

The court's ruling may be based on a technicality, but it

David Barkin, Irene Oritz, Fred Rosen, "Globalization and Resistance, The Remaking of Mexico," NACLA REPORT ON THE AMERICAS; Vol. 30:4, pp. 14–27. Copyright 1997 by the North American Congress on Latin America, 475 Riverside Dr., #454, New York, NY 10115-0122.

highlights the overlay of neoliberal economic restructuring on the traditional corruption of the PRI. The airing of the issue will be somewhat uncomfortable for the Mexican government since the privatization process involved the substantial enrichment of still-powerful *priistas*. Barzón advisor Carlos Marichal, an economic historian at the Colegio de México, says that technicality or no technicality, the banks and the government are taking the situation very seriously. "They are terrified," says Marichal. "The banks have hired some big legal guns, and knowing the Mexican legal system, they will probably get some favorable ruling, but only after hard political negotiations."[3] El Barzón's international-level negotiations seek to convince the brokerages and lending agencies to opt for social and financial stability—and to pressure the Mexican banks to do the same.

Nearly half the bank debt in Mexico is overdue, and much of it is unpayable. The government has kept the banks afloat with a series of "debtor-aid" plans, but the deeply indebted small farmers and entrepreneurs who make up El Barzón claim that these plans have used public money to bail out the banks—and their well-connected owners—while doing nothing to alleviate the burden on the debtors. "Now we want the banks to get us back on our feet," Imaz told Salomon Brothers. "We want them to let us pay what we can afford." El Barzón wants the government to nationalize some 300,000 mortgages which, explains advisor Marichal, would be held by a state housing agency. "That way the government would get points for the 1997 local elections and also resolve part of the problem of the money advanced to the banks to save them. The banks

would simply keep the money and the government would keep the mortgages and charge at a lower rate. But the banks are stupid and avaricious, and the fight will be tremendous."[4]

The brokerages and lenders were dubious when Imaz called, but none refused the soft-spoken businessman a meeting. Such is the power of Mexico's massive co-operative movement. It is also a sign of the delicacy of the issue. The privatized banks—and the semi-autonomous central bank—are meant to efficiently manage the flows of private international capital that are the driving forces of the new Mexican economy. Yet the faltering national banking system has never been up to the task. Indeed, the Latin American banking systems have been called the "Achilles' heel of the global economy today" by IMF Managing Director Michel Camdessus, whose institution is clearly worried about the disruptive power of the Mexican debtors.[5] The savvy *barzonistas*, fighting for their own survival, had found their opponents' weak point.

A hundred miles and cultural light years removed from José Imaz's offices in the comfortable Tlalpan district of Mexico City, at an agricultural training center in Mexico's rugged Eastern Sierra Madre, another sign of political transformation—and another fight for survival—can be found. Professor Benjamín Berlanga, a middle-aged veteran of three decades of radical struggles, teaches his young campesino students why communities like the one in which they live—communities in which perhaps 20 million Mexicans earn their living

and make their homes—have become unlivable. In 1982, Berlanga, along with several colleagues—many from a feminist umbrella group that works with poor women in the countryside—founded a school called the Center for Rural Training and Development (Cesder). Cesder, with the expressed aim of allowing campesinos to remain on the land, teaches techniques of land management and small-scale craft production and marketing. This goal—rebuilding an independent campesino economy and community—runs directly counter to the IMF, World Bank and Mexican government policies which call for the development of larger, more profitable enterprises on the land. Successive local governments, who see the modest endeavors of Cesder graduates as threatening, have tried to shut the center down.[6]

"The relations that campesinos in a community like this have with nature is precarious," the professor tells his students, "because of the fragile conditions of the ecosystems—poor hillside lands, little rain, accelerated processes of erosion and deforestation. The 'modern' propositions and technologies are useless for this kind of land, and the campesinos have lost the technologies that had served them for centuries. This leads to precarious productivity—a little corn, a little beans, and it all stays in the community. And it's like the lottery. One year there's plenty, the next year nothing. There's not enough land or capital to produce even for self sufficiency. The relationship with nature is *jodido* [screwed]."

> **The IMF is clearly worried about the disruptive power of the Mexican debtors' movement. And the savvy *barzonistas*, fighting for their own survival, have found their opponents' weak point.**

Cracks In PRI Unionism

Héctor De la Cueva

For over half a century, Mexico's labor movement has been a model of open subordination to the government and the ruling Institutional Revolutionary Party (PRI). Every member of the country's dominant labor federation, the Mexican Workers Confederation (CTM) has been an automatic dues-paying member of the PRI. The CTM, together with 31 other unions and labor federations, belongs to a larger umbrella organization called the Congress of Labor (CT). Within the CT, the CTM is the undisputed "first among equals," and the CTM president, nonagenarian Fidel Velázquez has, until recently, ruled both groups with an iron hand. In negotiations with the state and with employers, as well as within the official party, it is the CTM which always "represents" the entire "organized workers' movement."

Despite corrupt, nepotistic leaders who run the unions like fiefdoms, the official labor movement thrived during the years of economic growth when it won real social victories. Its support base, however, has now been eroded by the economic crisis and by the imposition of labor discipline by its own party, the PRI. The CTM has bowed to the neoliberal project by signing a series of "pacts" with business and the government over the past ten years which have cut wages and made labor contracts more "flexible." The federation has been so deeply incorporated into the structure of the ruling party that its first instinct has been to defend the PRI rather than its own members. This has cost it rank-and-file support.

Though the unionization rate of Mexican workers continues to hold at around 25%, the official union apparatus is coming apart at the seams. Small but significant groups of Mexican workers in manufacturing, services and education are organizing in trade unions independent of the CT and the PRI. Perhaps even more significant are the struggles for democratization of the unions within the CT. Ten CT-affiliated unions and federations have formed a dissident group called the Forum of Unionism Facing the Nation. Among the most prominent leaders of the group, known as the *foristas*, are Francisco Hernández Juárez, the charismatic leader of the telephone workers, Pedro Castillo of the combative electrical workers, and Elba Esther Gordillo, expresident of the powerful teachers union. A number of independent unions have joined forces with the ten founding Forum members, bringing *forista* membership to 25 unions and federations.

The Forum, initiated essentially as a forum for airing heterodox views, has since become a permanent organization. Some of the group's members have suggested abandoning the CT and forming a new umbrella group, while others have argued for the less drastic step of calling a national workers assembly open to all, including independents. The CTM has responded aggressively, threatening to expel the heretics from the CT. The government, meanwhile, which now sees trade unionism as an impediment to neoliberal reform, has momentarily frozen its union-busting plans and arrived at an understanding with the CTM. This has somewhat strengthened the official federation within the PRI. For now, the CTM has not expelled the *foristas*, but a *de facto* split already exists.

The events surrounding the past two May Day celebrations reflect this split. While the government and the CT decided to cancel labor's official May Day parade in 1995 because they feared being overwhelmed by the discontent from below, hundreds of thousands of people in Mexico City and other large cities filled the streets—and the political vacuum. In the heat of these mobilizations, opposition groups formed the May 1 Interunion Coordinating Council.

May Day, 1996 was even more significant. Over 100,000 *foristas*—disobeying official orders not to march—marched the traditional May Day route from Mexico City's Monument to the Revolution, through the city's Historic Center, ending at the central plaza, the *Zócalo*. Another 100,000 protesters, organized under the banner of the May 1 Interunion Coordinating Council, followed the first group to the *Zócalo* where they held a two-hour rally after most of the *foristas* had left. Opposition leader Cuauhtémoc Cárdenas addressed the demonstrators, and *Subcomandante* Marcos sent a "message of solidarity."

Because of prior May Day clashes between "official" and "independent" unionists, the leaders of the two groups prudently signed a "nonaggression pact" before the march, in which they agreed not to be in the same place at the same time. In another sign of caution, *foristas* agreed among themselves to have no official speeches in order to avoid any public disagreements. Members of *forista* unions, carrying placards denouncing neoliberalism and the Zedillo government, simply marched past the reviewing platform on which the dissident union leadership was standing.

This May Day split may signal a realignment of the labor movement beyond a simple changing of the guard. Following the *forista* march, Hernández Juárez of the telephone workers told reporters that labor's old leadership was not the issue. "We want a change in attitudes, not personalities, and this mobilization is a clear sign that things are changing."

Gordillo, of the teachers' union—a *forista* despite her long years of PRI militancy—held out a hand of friendship to the "independents" of the second march. "Let's hope," she said, "that next year we can march together in one big demonstration that can show the face of the unionism of the future." Such a realignment would spell an end to the current model of labor-government cooperation.

Berlanga, lecturing to a class of entering students in a sprawling adobe building built by a previous generation of students, explains that this precariousness means that very little of the campesinos' output can be sold outside the community. The only thing campesinos can now sell, he says, is "their ability to work—their labor power." Campesinos face the market as sellers of labor power and buyers of just about everything else. "They face double exploitation: *jodido* on the labor market and *jodido* in the markets for the goods imported into the village. This all leads to a loss of dignity and identity, and to increased rates of alcoholism, family dissolution, feelings of impotence and fights among communities. There is a loss of social organization, a degradation of the conditions of life."

Of course, the lack of access to land and capital has long been a problem in Mexico. For decades, rural workers have been streaming into the cities to sell their ability to work, both as permanent migrants and as weekday workers who return to their villages on weekends and holidays. Men have typically sought work in the construction industry, while women have found work as live-in domestics. But with the 1995 collapse of Mexico's domestic market and the consequent shrinking of the demand for labor, there has been a downward displacement of workers, and both sources of work are drying up for migrant campesinos. This is happening just as Mexico's small-scale farmers face a sharp deterioration of their living standards and the unraveling of their communities.

"Every year we realize that these campesino regions fall outside the scope of government plans," says Cesder's Berlanga. "What is necessary is a different type of policy that takes these regions into account. Our vision is a country in which campesinos continue to exist, but in a different kind of society from the one that's developing now. The campesinos don't fit into the government's project—not as producers and not as citizens. They are told to stop being campesinos and to adapt to another mode of life, but there is no room for them in the cities, and there is no policy to incorporate them elsewhere."

Berlanga and his colleagues arrived in the Sierra in the early 1980s, veterans of the radical struggles of the 1960s, whose defining moment was the 1968 massacre of hundreds of protesting students in Mexico City's Tlatelolco Plaza. By the late 1970s, the old radicals had dispersed but by no means disappeared. In addition to being a teacher of alternative agricultural techniques, Berlanga is one of a few hundred "advisors" to the Zapatista Army of National Liberation (EZLN).

"Marcos and I are of the same generation," he says. "At the same time that he went with his people to the guerrilla movement in Chiapas, we came here with a very different perspective having nothing to do with armed struggle. When the Zapatistas emerged in Chiapas, for a moment we wondered whether we should have been armed revolutionaries and fought here, for example, in the Sierra. Marcos did it, why didn't we? Maybe we've been mistaken for the last ten years. But the possibility of this armed group—this new discourse—only appeared after years of working from below with local organizations who gave no thought to armed struggle. Marcos couldn't have existed if we hadn't existed.

And all of our forces were strengthened when the armed struggle broke out in Chiapas. If the Zapatista uprising had never taken place, the emergence of civil society would have been a much slower process." Berlanga becomes momentarily pensive, his thoughts drifting to a group of students assisting in the difficult birthing of a goat. "The work is very slow," he muses, "but we have all been preparing the ground for each other."

Similar stories are told in places as dissimilar as working class *colonias* in the center of Mexico City and impoverished indigenous communities in rural Chiapas. The movements bubbling up from below are sometimes the result of spontaneous reactions to unbearable situations—as in the case of El Barzón. More often they represent a resistance that has been gestating for years, the result of the carefully laid groundwork of social activists. The socially corrosive forces of globalizing neoliberalism have helped give these movements a more unified shape.

Mexico City's working-class Colonia Guerrero, for example, has given life to one of the city's most militant—and still independent—neighborhood organizations, the Assembly of Barrios. It is also home to one of the city's oldest and most socially active Catholic parishes, the Parish of Los Angeles. The parish is the key to the *colonia's* long and continuing role in the social struggle, says Francisco Saucedo, a *colonia* resident and official of the center-left Party of the Democratic Revolution (PRD). Just a few years ago, he says, "on the one hundredth anniversary of the parish, the Padre invited all the *colonia's* social and civic organizations to participate in the celebration.

Suddenly we were all in the same space; the idea of sharing who we were and where we came from led to a process of rediscovery." Saucedo's "rediscovery" is much like Berlanga's realization that despite the slow and painstaking nature of organizing within small communities, many Mexican activists were laying the groundwork for one another. [7]

The Jesuits of the Los Angeles Parish, for example, have long taken a leading role in Colonia Guerrero's social organization. "In the 1960s, the Jesuits led the social movement," says Saucedo. "This was a period of reflection, a great feeling that there was a need to do something, especially after the massacre a Tlatelolco. We began to organize around the need for housing and the rights of tenants." Residents formed the Union of Neighbors of Colonia Guerrero which, by the 1980s, had linked up with similar groups in other *colonias* to become the city-wide Tenants Coordinating Group. And in 1981, a group called the Coordinating Committee of Urban Popular Movements (Conamup) was formed in Guerrero to coordinate the struggles of popular movements throughout Mexico City. "This was the birth of the social left," says Saucedo, "a left closely connected to the daily struggles of the workers. We organized in factories as well as neighborhoods. All these spaces were terrains of struggle. All this came together in the late 1980s as a current of the PRD, which distinguished itself from an older, more party-oriented left." This "social left" is a nonelectoral left, even though it is linked to—and now dominant within—the country's leading leftist electoral force.

The social left grew in the aftermath of the massive 1985 earthquake that killed at least 10,000 people in Mexico City. Neither the government nor the community organizations of the ruling PRI proved capable of organizing rescue actions, post-earthquake relief or housing reconstruction. All these tasks were left to non-governmental organizations (NGOs), informal neighborhood groups and the parish. In the process, community organizations—both church groups and the spontaneously created groups of victims—forged new links with international relief donors. The urban popular movement grew along with victims' groups, and in April, 1987, the Assembly of Barrios was formed as a city-wide organization to fight against evictions and for better housing and reconstruction. "There were none of those interminable discussions of the left," says Saucedo. "It was just like this (he snaps his fingers) and we got it done. The victims' movement became the vanguard of the social left. We did what we said. We were not strictly known as the left, but that's who we were."

"We came here and we learned from the people," say both Berlanga and Saucedo. In both cases leftist organizers brought certain agendas to communities which had agendas of their own, and in the interaction, new forms of political action emerged. In both cases, the linking with popular struggles—for land, work, housing—has narrowed the organizers' agenda. Berlanga says the same of his *compañero* Marcos: "There is a great difference between the project Marcos and his people initiated in Chiapas 15 years ago and the project they have now. They went with a project of guerrilla warfare to seize power. The result was not what Marcos envisioned. But he captured the moment and the circumstances and reworked his discourse into what it is now. And it still needs time to mature in practice."

In a similar way, there is a great difference between the project that former student activists took into Mexico City's Colonia Guerrero and the one they ended up with. They also "captured the moment" and developed a new discourse, one that was a good deal narrower and more concrete, and with more opportunities for small successes.

The El Barzón movement also underwent a profound transformation as its struggle unfolded. Driven first by desperation, these debt-laden entrepreneurs are now holding regular strategy sessions with previously marginalized groups from virtually all sectors of Mexican society. Today, their closest collaborators seem to be the Zapatista guerrillas.

These political transformations will continue, linked to the continuing social crisis of the country—a social crisis linked to its economic policy. The move from social protection to a market-driven globalization has torn the fabric of Mexican society, leaving it to the radicals—of one sort or another—to remake the country from below.

II

Until the early 1980s, four components guided Mexican economic policy: a high degree of state participation in the economy; a strategy of "stable development" which attempted to keep prices, interest rates and the exchange rate under control; the protection of domestic industry with high tariff and non-tariff barriers to international trade and investment; and an attempt to provide a relatively high degree of social security to Mexican citizens.

Beginning with the reforms of President Miguel De la Madrid in 1983—reforms dictated in large part by the international lending agencies which were "helping" the country emerge from its moratorium on international debt payments—economic policy took a 180-degree turn. Embarking on the "free-market" path pioneered by the "Chicago boys" employed by the Chilean dictatorship, Mexico reversed all four directions and entered into a period of reform that privatized and deregulated the economy, opened it to international investment and trade, and cut loose the workforce—especially the peasantry—from its traditional protections and supports.

The goal was the development of an export-based economy, driven by private capital, with a major role for transnational companies and international portfolio investors, all with little regard for domestic productive chains. Many U.S. investors shared this goal, and negotiations to create NAFTA soon became a priority for leaders in all three North American countries. Doubts within the official delegations notwithstanding, the treaty was designed to make economic integration irreversible, forging a hoped-for unbreakable alliance of transnational capital.

Policy makers saw the project as part of a global movement which, in Latin America, had come to be known as "neoliberalism," a word which came into vogue in the early 1980s when its advocates, led by the eloquent Mario Vargas Llosa, spearheaded a stinging attack on the region's "statist" economies. The new movement deliberately evoked the classic liberal commitments—individual rights, civil liberties, private property—and placed these commitments in the context of the late twentieth-century global economy. This celebration of the individual was embedded in the institutional setting of the North-South divide; the global dominance of (mostly) northern-based transnational corporations, which quickly incorporated the wealthiest of the Third-World corporate elites; the government-like role played by the major international financial institutions; and the continually changing global division of labor, in which low wages had become many countries' sole comparative advantage in the international economy.[8]

The basic ideas of what has become the on-the-ground neoliberal economic model are embodied in the development strategies of the International Monetary Fund (IMF), the World Bank and, in Latin America, the Inter-American Development Bank (IDB). Indeed, implementation of the elements of the model is so frequently a condition of receiving IMF support that the term "IMF conditionality"—along with the synonomous "Washington consensus"—has entered the vocabulary of planners and politicians across the region.[9]

The course of neoliberal reform has been embodied by Mexico's determined insertion into the global economy—most dramatically by way of NAFTA—and by the growing importance of foreign private investment as a driving force of economic growth and development. Low costs of production (i.e. low wages) have become the magnet which attracts transnational direct investors, high rates of return (i.e. high interest rates) have brought in the "hot-money" portfolio investors, and disappearing tariff barriers have allowed international retailers to set up shop throughout the country. Declining real wages, meanwhile, are impoverishing Mexican workers and stripping the country's government-controlled union movement of its legitimacy. High real interest rates are crowding out domestic business-people, and radicalizing—at least temporarily—the small business owners of El Barzón. Cheap products from U.S. agribusiness are depriving campesino producers of a market, providing fertile organizing ground for groups like Cesder. To borrow Berlanga's turn of phrase, the whole country is *jodido*.

The "technocratic" economic team that rose to power under Miguel De la Madrid during the latter half of the 1980s consolidated the neoliberal reforms. The new team, one of whose key players was president-to-be Carlos Salinas de Gortari, declared that government had no business in production, but rather should limit itself to creating the conditions within which private groups could operate profitably. It also declared that the country's principal problem was a lack of internal savings, and therefore set itself the task of developing markets capable of receiving foreign capital, and a business environment capable of attracting global producers and financiers.

The new team of Mexican technocrats oversaw the dismantling of the state apparatus that had promoted industrial and agricultural development over the previous four decades. In its place they used policies of slow money growth and fiscal austerity to generate high rates of return for foreign investors. Declining inflation, a stable currency and high interest rates were the anchors of a financial policy that converted Mexico into the *wunderkind* of international finance. Many Mexicans, of course, feared that the "reformers"

The Workforce of the 1990s

Teresa Rendón and Carlos Salas

Over the past decade and a half, the structure of Mexican employment has undergone deep changes. The production-based workforce—the source of stable jobs that pay wages above the poverty line—has ceased to grow. In the meantime, there has been an increase in low-paying, unstable jobs that carry no benefits.

The opening of the economy in 1982 brought with it a slowing down of the growth of domestic demand, and the substitution of imported for domestically produced goods. As a result, the *non-maquila* manufacturing sector is no longer able to generate new jobs.

The contraction of domestic demand has led Mexican investors to look increasingly to commerce and services as vehicles of investment. This has led to the growth of these two sectors as sources of new jobs. [See Table 1.]

While this has brought about the creation of larger firms in these two sectors, the proliferation of tiny, two or three-person businesses, typically employing non-waged family and individual labor, continues unabated. There has thus been a growth of employment in very small-scale enterprises as well as a weakening of the trend toward the creation of a wage-labor force.

These trends, together with the consistent decline in real wages, have led families to send an increasing number of family members into the workforce to bolster household income. Integral to this development is the growing labor-force participation of women and teenagers.

Finally, the *maquiladora* industry has expanded continuously since 1980, and especially in the past few years. Between 1988 and 1993, 41% of all new waged jobs in manufacturing were created in the *maquila* sector. Since most *maquiladoras* are still located near the U.S. border, their growth has led to a movement northward of employment. While not all of this job creation has taken place in the border states, there has clearly been a deepening of regional differences, as jobs move northward. [See Table 2.]

Table 1 Labor Force According to Sector

	1979	1995
Working Population (in thousands)	19,177	33,721
Total	100%	100%
Agriculture	29%	25%
Manufacturing	19%	15%
Other industries	8%	6%
Commerce	14%	19%
Services	30%	35%

Source: Encuesta Continua sobre Ocupación, 1979; Encuesta Nacional de Empleo, 1995.

Table 2 Regional Distribution of the Employed Population (All figures are percentages.)

Region	Manufacturing 1980	Manufacturing 1993	Commerce 1980	Commerce 1993	Services 1980	Services 1993
Central states	59.6	47.4	52.7	48.7	54.2	52.5
Southern states	10.3	9.0	15.5	17.4	16.0	16.2
Northern states	29.9	43.6	31.6	34.0	29.7	31.3

Source: Authors' calculations based on the 1981 and 1994 Economic Census. Northern states include Sinaloa, Durango, Zacatecas, Aguascalientes, San Luis Potosí and all states further north. Southern states include Guerrero, Oaxaca, Veracruz and all states further south.

also had some venal interests in mind when they accelerated the privatization process and tried to make it irreversible. Subsequent events have done nothing to extinguish those fears.

The privatization of state firms has been financed by a combination of on-the-ground and financial foreign investment, and the return of the "flight capital" that had been sent abroad by wealthy nationals. The process has meshed with the old personal connections of the Mexican regime. In an especially egregious example, Telmex, the state-run phone system, was privatized in 1990 in an insider deal in which one man—the well-connected billionaire Carlos Slim—was allowed to create a huge financial base with foreign partners, tender a large international public stock offering, and still retain a very profitable controlling interest.

Neoliberal reform moved into high gear in the early 1990s under the presidency of Carlos Salinas. The banks, which had been nationalized in 1982, were reprivatized in 1990 as part of the market-oriented restructuring of the economy. The banks' rapid integration into the oligopolistic structure of the economy made them—at least until the current playing out of El Barzón's lawsuit—independent of political pressure. When their speculative investments and policies turned out to have been based on poor judgement, or worse, used to finance frankly corrupt activities and practices, they were still able to demand—and receive—government support.

Along with privatization, the economic restructuring promoted by the last three Mexican administrations has called for the creation of an autonomous monetary authority, like the private banks, free from popular pressures. The central bank, the Banco de México—long proud of its reputation for "technocratic"and de-ideologized monetary management—has been given political and functional autonomy as part of a broader effort to remove economic policy from accountability to popular representation. That way, the "bitter medicine" of austerity can be more efficiently imposed through a policy of tight money.

On a global scale, the neoliberal era has seen the rising power of financial capital. The principal financial centers—New York, London, Tokyo and, perhaps, Frankfurt—have become centers for attracting and redistributing financial assets throughout the world. With the demise of the socialist bloc and the emergence of eastern European markets, the leading companies in these centers have gained even more freedom to concentrate and then redistribute money from one country to another with a simple order transmitted by voice or computer. The global trend of fi-

---

Why the Recovery Is Not a Recovery

Over the last two years, Mexicans have been caught in an economic crisis of appalling proportions. The peso devaluation of December, 1994, and the ensuing capital flight and stock market crash, plunged the Mexican economy into its deepest depression since the 1930s. Within two months of the devaluation, the value of the currency had declined by more than half; within four months the level of unemployment had doubled; inflation jumped from 7% in 1994 to 52% in 1995; and the gross domestic product (GDP) had declined by 6.9% at year's end.[1] The economic crisis saw the collapse of the country's internal market, the virtual disappearance of credit for small and medium-size businesses, a dramatic contraction of formal employment and an alarming growth of poverty. Twelve months after the peso debacle, an estimated 75% of Mexican families could not afford the "basic basket" of goods and services considered necessary to bring a family above the official poverty line. 1995 was not a happy year.

1996 saw a halt to the decline, and the beginning of what is now being touted—especially to foreign investors—as a "recovery." Third-quarter GDP growth has been reported at 7.4%, leading Finance Minister Guillermo Ortiz to tell a November press conference that the country's basic institutions were now sound. Mexico, he said, could expect 4% economic growth, 800,000 new jobs, $8 billion of new foreign direct investment and $3 billion in privatization earnings in 1997.[2]

But what Ortiz says is an economic "recovery" is doing nothing to improve living conditions in Mexico. Real wages continue to fall, formal employment continues to be hard to find and the rate of poverty hasn't budged. The decline of GDP was halted only by the robust performance of transnational firms in the automobile industry and in the *maquiladora* sector—firms which import and produce strictly for export and are barely integrated into the national economy. In fact, since the export-oriented firms employ Mexican labor but don't rely on Mexican purchasing power, they have been well placed to take advantage of the country's economic collapse.

This export-driven "recovery" is not without precedent. A sharp devaluation back in 1982 created similar opportunities for the automobile industry to initiate a period of accelerated expansion. A highly automated assembly plant was built by the Ford Motor Company in Hermosillo, Sonora to produce automobiles for the U.S. market. Dozens of additional plants were created by other transnational firms to provide basic parts for autos being assembled in Mexico or for use on the assembly lines in the United States.

This activity was so important, that by the end of the decade, more than one-third of the engine blocks used in cars in the United States were imported

---

nancial deregulation has placed unprecedented amounts of capital at the disposition of these agents, who turn out to be accountable to virtually nobody, as we continually learn when their errors of judgement or corrupt practices provoke failures of a magnitude that require taxpayers in their home countries to bail out the financiers and their agents.

With tremendous accumulations of wealth to be distributed and invested every day, the global

financiers—corporate bankers, underwriting firms, mutual funds, insurance companies and even stockbrokers—have become key decision makers in the so-called "emerging markets." They are under constant pressure since they know that they not only have to search out new profitable opportunities and anticipate future trends, but that each decision will influence the attractiveness of the rest of their portfolio, and those of their competitors. The size of their from Mexico. Almost three-quarters of the wiring harnesses and substantial parts of the brake assemblies, windows and other components were supplied from plants in northern Mexico. In spite of the rapid growth of exports, however, at its height, the industry only employed about 175,000 people.[3]

In a like manner, agro-export groups seized the moment in the early 1980s. In many cases, local producers joined with foreign counterparts or international brokers to obtain the technology and finance the high costs of fruit and vegetable production. The range and value of primary products exported during this period increased dramatically, as producers aggressively sought out new clients in traditional markets, and managed to enter new markets.

The opening of the economy in the 1980s and the declining real incomes of the population rapidly eroded the market for domestic producers of many basic consumer items, especially in the clothing and footwear sectors. Without any adjustment or modernization program, and with soaring interest rates and a lack of credit, Mexican firms simply could not compete with the less expensive products—despite their lower quality—being imported from Asia.

The assault against domestic producers extended to other manufacturing areas, and dramatically to the rural economy. By the late 1980s, small farmers, who had been able to adapt to changing conditions earlier in the decade, found that they could no longer compete with the growing volumes of imported grains, frequently subsidized by foreign governments. To seal their fate, the Salinas administration introduced constitutional changes—the reform of Article 27, which privatized communally owned *ejido* lands—to facilitate the sale of desirable plots to agroindustrial interests.

What we are seeing now—in keeping with the same neoliberal strategy—is a *maquilization* of the Mexican economy. With the loosening of trade barriers and the relentless cheapening of labor power, *maquila* employment has grown from about 550,000 in 1994 to about 800,000 by late 1996. By contrast, employment in non-*maquila* manufacturing has been falling for a decade. Twenty-seven percent of all manufacturing workers are now working in *maquiladoras*—compared to only 7% in 1985.[4] *Maquila* output rose dramatically in 1995 and continued to rise in 1996—from January through August, output was 17% higher than over the same period in 1995. But the *maquila* sector's percentage of local integration—inputs bought from Mexican suppliers—has declined from 2.3% to 1.4% since 1994.[5]

The sector's lack of integration into the Mexican economy can be grasped by comparing the value of its exports with the value of its imports. Over the first eight months of 1996, the value of *maquila* exports stood at $23.3 billion, while the value of *maquila* imports was $19.9 billion.[6] *Maquila* imports consist entirely of intermediate goods—like cloth for shirts or circuits for electrical parts—which must be worked into final goods and re-exported within six months. So while $23.3 billion of maquila output was added to Mexico's GDP over the first eight months of 1996, only $3.4 billion of that total was actually produced in Mexico.

Crucial industries in the non-*maquila* sector are also increasing exports. Transnational automakers, for example salvaged 1995 with a 22.5% increase in the production of passenger cars for export and a 131.6% increase in the production of trucks for export. This trend has continued into 1996. The combined non-*maquila* export value of cars, trucks, vehicle motors and auto parts rose from $7.8 billion for the first eight months of 1995 to $10.9 billion for the same period of 1996, a 40% increase.[7]

All told, as the non-*maquila* sector turned to export-oriented production, its share of total exports (compared to the *maquiladoras*) rose from 56.9 in 1994 to 62.1% over the first eight months of 1996.[8] The longer the current crisis continues, the higher this number is likely to get, as more and more non-*maquila* producers begin looking abroad for their customers, and the domestic market increasingly does without.

—D.B. and F.R.

investments is such that a recommendation about a particular company or country can often determine the success or failure of corporate strategies or national economic policies.

Unlike the multilateral financial institutions emerging from the Bretton Woods accords of 1946, which built up large staffs of professionals who counselled recipients on the management of their economies to promote capital accumulation and development, these new financiers have very short-term horizons. They have to report competitively attractive results to their shareholders, to new investors and to regulatory bodies on a quarterly, semi-annual or annual basis. Their personal fortunes depend upon these performance reports, which are insensitive to long-term considerations of stability—or to the impact of their investment decisions on the social and economic structures or the environmental health of the regions they are entering.

Under the Salinas administration, tens of billions of dollars poured into Mexico, oblivious to the profound disequilibria that were gestating in the productive structure, and oblivious to the growing hardships of daily life for the majority of Mexicans [see "Why the Recovery Is Not a Recovery," p. 58]. Very little of the foreign savings was used for productive purposes. There was some new investment in export-oriented automobile production, in the *maquiladoras* and in a few other manufacturing sectors, but most of the resources were channeled into the stock market, where profits are not taxed and transactions need not be reported to fiscal authorities. In the early 1990s, reports the Bank of Mexico, foreign portfolio investment was the country's main source of foreign-capital inflows.[10]

Money—even "cautious" money—was drawn to Mexico by a government securities market that offered rates of return four or five times higher than prevailing interest rates in the United States or Europe. Of course, overnight devaluation could wipe out the dollar earnings of peso-denominated investments, but the magic of Salinas' relationship with the world press and financial community conquered any reservations. The stock market was awash in money, but little new productive investment was occurring, real incomes were falling, underemployment rising and social malaise deepening.

The massive injections of new money—especially in the early 1990s—created a speculative boom that fed upon itself. Because there were so few players, the financial boom could be cleverly manipulated by knowledgeable brokers to produce sudden cyclical swings that allowed for great fortunes to be made. And since portfolio investment is sensitive to perceptions of very short-term gains and losses, in a lightning-quick loss of confidence, investors reacted to the government's awkward peso devaluation of December, 1994 by removing at least $5 billion of foreign (and a good deal of domestic) capital in a matter of days.

The globalizing strategy has been accompanied all along by a loosening of price controls, exchange-rate controls and interest-rate controls, though not surprisingly, the model has never called for the absence of wage controls. In Mexico such controls have been "semi-voluntary," achieved through the cooperation of the trade-union hierarchy within the PRI corporate structure. Deals with labor unions officially incorporated into the long-ruling PRI have allowed the export sector to take advantage of labor discipline and a cheaper labor force. [See "Cracks in PRI Unionism," p. 53.]

The strategy has also called for a shrinking of the welfare state: cuts in social spending, and the encouragement of market—rather than state—solutions to social problems. Social-security pensions, for example, are now being turned over to privately managed, individually chosen pension funds. The problem of insufficient domestic savings is thereby being addressed with a program that places the private savings of workers at the disposal of private investors, at the same time that it encourages workers to think of themselves as financial entrepreneurs.[11]

The lending agencies have also placed great emphasis on what they call "human resource development"—agency terminology for the neoliberal model's labor policy. In Mexico, this has meant the growth of privately controlled technical training and education, a "residual" social-welfare policy to replace the "institutional" social welfare of the previous model, labor flexibility and the renegotiation of union contracts. It has also meant the encouragement of microenterprise, not so much as a model of private-sector development, but as a substitute for state-sponsored social security—i.e. a way of mopping up the unemployed.

Under the neoliberal model of social welfare, the state will step in only residually—in emergencies of one kind or another that might call the system's legitimacy into question. While there is a great deal of philosophical talk among neoliberals about how individuals (or perhaps families) are responsible for their own welfare, the economic justification is labor discipline, Mexico's comparative advantage in the new global division of labor. Microenterprise—the informal family firm—has become the model's safety net, and has created an enormous reserve labor pool. One of the reasons Mexico's unemployment rate has been so low throughout the economic crisis—hovering around 6%—is precisely the safety valve of the easy-to-enter informal economy, at home and north of the border.

This has created a powerful downward pressure on wages. Internal documents of the National Minimum Wage Commission show that the real minimum wage peaked in 1978 and has since declined to levels lower than those of the populist 1930s. [See Graph, p. 23.]* It now takes 4.8 minimum wages for an urban family of four to rise above the poverty line, but the average wage is between two and three minimum wages. The result is an increasingly desperate, "available" workforce.

Declining real wages has made it necessary for families to send more than one member out to work. Many of those second and third family workers are losing their jobs, however, and find themselves looking for something not quite as good. At the lowest

---

*Does not appear in this publication.

levels, there is no place left to look. This downward displacement of labor has reached the point where there are large numbers of working-age people who are doing absolutely nothing. This has obvious public-safety implications. Crime is rising in all sectors of neoliberal Mexico.

III

A social left has emerged over the past ten years as a response to this disassembling of the country's social and economic networks from above. As the experience of groups like Cesder and the Assembly of Barrios shows, this left has formed around very concrete demands and proposals. While it has achieved success by setting itself narrow, achievable goals, there is a down side. "We were successful with the early stages," says Francisco Saucedo of Colonia Guerrero. "We demanded land and housing. We succeeded and we constructed the Assembly of Barrios. We had tens of thousands of people, almost in permanent mobilization. Now the government has penetrated us and divided us. The organizations are local and small and fighting for the same small things. These small organizations, if not linked to some larger project, lack political impact. They become competitive and parochial."

This recognition, combined with the severity of the current economic crisis has given form to some political alliances that in an earlier day would have been impossible. This past July, for example, 300 once-middle-class *barzonistas* held a two-day conference in the town of La Realidad, Chiapas, under the "protection" of the dirt-poor indigenous Zapatista guerrillas.

It has also given form to a new try at an alliance between the EZLN and the center-left PRD. Marcos and the new PRD general secretary Andrés Manuel López Obrador have announced that the two groups would work together—something they have not been able to do before—to ensure success in the 1997 congressional election. From Marcos' point of view, such a partnership must be embedded in a broader alliance of social forces. "If we had to choose a political force to which to give our support," said Marcos in a talk to members of El Barzón, "that force would be civil society, a force independent of the political parties, or which, including them, was greater than the sum of its parts, more generous than the egoism of their leaderships, more inclusive than particular sectarianisms. A force of forces. That would be the political force the EZLN would support."[12]

The EZLN clearly cannot organize such a national force by itself. Its supporters outside of Chiapas have organized the Zapatista National Liberation Front (FZLN), but realize they have to join forces with other groups in order to have any real effect. "A force of forces must be based on the principle of nonexclusion," says Javier Elorriaga, a leader of the FZLN who spent over a year in jail for being an "alleged Zapatista"—he acted as a go-between for the EZLN and the government in the early days of the uprising. "Zapatismo cannot represent everything. Modestly, we want to be one more force, to build a space that is genuinely democratic. We want to build a popular force which one day can become the government, not through an armed revolution, but

a social revolution in which the people take the destiny of the country in their own hands."[13]

This seems to be the direction that the recently elected leadership of the PRD wants to take. The idea, says party leader López Obrador, is to "build the party both to win elections and defend popular causes."[14] The idea has been taken up by some of the older currents within the party. One of the defeated, "old-left" candidates for party leadership, Amalia García, is now a member of the PRD executive committee with the specific responsibility of reaching out to this social left. The significance of the "flowering of civil society," she says, is that it is "breaking the state's monopoly of political mediation." And beyond that, "Mexico is entering into another electoral dynamic in which other parties are appearing, occasionally winning, and demonstrating that the PRI no longer has an absolute monopoly on the direction of the country. It is no longer the only political actor."[15]

Just how this social left is developing could be glimpsed at a meeting in Mexico City this past summer called the "Convergence," organized by the EZLN-El Barzón alliance. The organizers issued the call around two very broad and fundamental demands: for a new political economy (against neoliberalism) and against corruption and impunity (against the corporatism of the PRI). "People are thirsting for new initiatives," said García, representing the PRD at the Convergence. "But there are more initiatives now than it's possible to coordinate."

In attendance—and therefore "members" of this incipient

organization—were groups and organizations of all stripes. Small and mid-scale entrepreneurs, increasingly squeezed by the ongoing economic crisis, and bank debtors like El Barzón participated alongside housing-advocacy groups and street-vendor representatives. NGOs, typically organized around specific issues, and human rights groups were present, as were feminist groups, Christian base communities, groups formed around the movements for dialogue and peace in Chiapas and other conflictive zones, and a variety of social, cultural, religious and philanthropic "civil associations." Campesino and farmworker organizations, dissident trade unionists and members of opposition political parties—the PRD as well as the smaller Workers Party (PT)—also attended the late-August meeting.

The groups represented in the still-gestating Convergence reflect different aspects of the Mexican crisis and, above all, civil society's response to that crisis. While the Convergence itself may fade away like many other attempts to organize the Mexican opposition, its size, scope and diverse composition highlight the country's current state of affairs: Mexico is transforming itself through the conflictive interaction of two very powerful forces—the globalizing project imposed from above, and the resistance to that project, welling up from below.

Notes: Globalization and Resistance

1. José María Imaz, press conference, November 20, 1996, Bronx, New York.
2. "Inexistentes, los 10 principales bancos," *La Jornada* (Mexico City, October 31, 1996.
3. Carlos Marichal, personal communication to Rosen, December 1, 1996.
4. Carlos Marichal, personal communication, December 1, 1996.
5. Michel Camdessus, press conference, October 4, 1996, Washington D.C.
6. Benjamin Berlanga, interviews with Ortiz and Rosen, July 20–23, 1996, Zautla, Puebla.
7. Francisco Saucedo, interviews with Rosen, November 25, 1995 and July 21, 1996, Mexico City.
8. For a collection of early neoliberal arguments, including Vargas Llosa's widely reprinted "América Latina y la opción liberal," see Barry B. Levine, ed., *El Desafio Neoliberal* (Bogotá: Grupo Editorial Norma), 1992.
9. See John Williamson, ed., *Latin American Adjustment* (Washington, D.C.: Institute for International Economics), 1990.
10. Banco de México, *The Mexican Economy* (Mexico City), 1995, pp. 95–100.
11. For the official perspective, see Banco de México, *The Mexican Economy* (Mexico City), 1996, pp. 178–192.
12. "El aguascalientes de El Barzón, muy distinto al de los zapatistas," *La Jornada* (Mexico City), July 21, 1996.
13. Javier Elorriaga, interview with Ortiz, August 30, 1996, Mexico City.
14. "Promete López Obrador convertir al PRD en primera fuerza política," *La Jornada* (Mexico City), July 22, 1996.
15. Amalia García, interview with Ortiz, September 2, 1996, Mexico City.

Why the Recovery Is Not a Recovery

1. Banco de México, *The Mexican Economy* (Mexico City), 1996, and *Indicadores Económicos*, various months, 1995.
2. "Budget Aims at Economic Recovery," *El Financiero International* (Mexico City), November 11–17, 1996.
3. Institute for Economic and Geographical Statistics (INEGI), *Monthly Industrial Survey*, (Mexico City), various dates.
4. INEGI, *Monthly Industrial Survey*, various dates.
5. INEGI, *Monthly Industrial Survey*, various dates.
6. Banco de México, *Indicadores del sector externo* (Mexico City), August, 1996, pp. 23, 46.
7. Banco de Mexico, *Indicadores del sector externo* (Mexico City), August, 1996, pp. 18, 19.
8. Banco de México *Indicadores del sector externo.* (Mexico City), December, 1995 and August, 1996.

 Article Review Form at end of book.

Brazil's Big Winner

Fernando Henrique Cardoso

James Brooke

Special to The New York Times

Brasilia, Oct. 4—Hooded, hand-cuffed and listening to friends' cries under torture, a leftist sociology professor facing interrogation one night 25 years ago thought that his life might end at the hands of army intelligence agents. Indeed from 1964 to 1985, the years of Brazil's military dictatorship, he suffered exile, imprisonment, blacklisting and the bombing of his social research group.

But today, voting returns and exit polls indicated that Brazilians had elected the professor, Fernando Henrique Cardoso, president by the widest popular margin since a retired army general was chosen to lead the nation in 1945.

The election of Mr. Cardoso as Brazil's first president in decades with a strong political power base was seen to have bolstered the strength of civilian democracy in a country that has had its share of political instability. It also signaled to many that Brazil would stay on a firm course of fighting inflation and spurring economic growth through free market policies, after many false starts and promises.

Indeed, there were many predictions that Mr. Cardoso, a former Foreign Minister and Finance Minister, would also push Latin America's largest economy into a new period of rapid economic growth that would draw in huge new amounts of foreign investments and imports.

With only 5 percent of votes counted by nightfall, Brazilians relied on three exit polls, which gave Mr. Cardoso victory with about 53 percent of the vote, enough to avoid a runoff against his closest challenger, Luis Inácio Lula da Silva, a trade union leader who until a few weeks ago was the front-runner. This evening Mr. da Silva declined to comment on the results, but he in effect acknowledged his defeat by saying his party would not ask for any positions in the new government.

With a reputation in this capital for cordiality and congeniality, the 63-year-old intellectual and senator chosen to lead Brazil is a complex person who defies easy labeling. He described himself today as a leader of "the viable left," and many in Brazil hailed his victory as a vindication for his decades of dissent.

"The generation of the exiles finally reach power," a daily in Rio de Janeiro, Jornal do Brasil, said today, joining virtually all of Brazil's press in informally annointing Mr. Cardoso as the nation's next president.

In some respects, the optimism over Mr. Cardoso's election recalled the hopeful spirit that existed when Brazil's last elected president, Fernando Collor de Mello, took office in 1990. But Mr. Collor later tried to rule by dictating to Congress, and after being disgraced by a congressional corruption inquiry he was forced to resign in 1992.

In contrast, Mr. Cardoso has a reputation as a patient conciliator. "He's a coalition builder, naturally more a prime minister than a president," said Alfred Stepan, a lifelong American friend who is now president of Central European University in Budapest.

In a country where two-thirds of the electorate never finished primary school, Mr. Cardoso vowed in the campaign to spend billions of dollars to guarantee schools and health care for all. "We are an unjust country," he said. "The great Achilles heel of Brazil is injustice."

On the other hand, a survey of executives of Brazil's top 500 companies found that, of the eight presidential candidates, Mr. Cardoso won the support of 97 percent.

"What this guy brings to the table is the power of São Paulo," an admiring American banker said, alluding to Mr. Cardoso's legislative constituency in Brazil's financial capital. "For the first time in memory, Brazil has a political leader not only with moral and technical authority, but also with political authority."

Although he flashes the easy grin of a man born in Rio, Mr. Cardoso will be Brazil's first major president in 65 years from São Paulo. Propelled by opinion polls indicating that Mr. Cardoso would win, São Paulo's stock exchange has risen about 80 percent since July.

Convinced that Brazil is entering a high growth phase similar to the "miracle" years of the 1970's, businessmen cite the free market track record forged by Mr. Cardoso during his one-year tenure as Finance Minister, which ended last April. As a candidate, he promised to maintain a tough anti-inflation fight that has reduced Brazil's monthly inflation from 45 percent in June to 1.5 in September.

Although recent economic growth projections have been encouraging, some skeptics have wondered about the veracity of the numbers. These skeptics pointed out that three days before the vote on Monday, Brazil registered its lowest monthly inflation rate in five years.

Mr. da Silva charged that Mr. Cardoso's business backers were artificially holding back price rises and that the anti-inflation plan would fall apart after the election. In interviews during the campaign, Mr. Cardoso vowed to open oil, telephone, mining and public works construction to foreign companies, to gradually privatize state companies, to maintain Brazil's six-month-old foreign debt accord, and to maintain policies that have rapidly opened to free trade an economy larger than Russia's.

For the first time in almost a decade of civilian rule, Brazilians believe that their president will have the political power to carry out many of his promises. On Monday Mr. Cardoso's three-party coalition apparently won a loose majority in Congress. Centrist candidates also fared well in races for powerful state governorship posts.

On the world stage, Mr. Cardoso is expected to dramatically raise Brazil's low-key profile. Itamar Franco, Brazil's current president, speaks only Portuguese, is visibly uncomfortable around foreigners and often cancels overseas trips on short notice.

With English honed during stints in the 1970's as a visiting lecturer at Berkeley, Oxford, Princeton, Stanford and Yale, Mr. Cardoso also speaks fluent French, the traditional foreign language of Brazil's elite. He is also fluent in Spanish and taught in Chile during one of his periods of exile. Unlike most Brazilians who travel in Latin America, Mr. Cardoso speaks proper Spanish, not a hybrid, improvised "Portunhol."

Arrested and then banned from teaching in Brazilian universities by the military in 1969, Mr. Cardoso founded Cebrap, the Brazilian Analysis and Planning Center. A haven for other blacklisted professors, this São Paulo research center was bombed by a right-wing terror group in 1974.

The author of 21 books, Mr. Cardoso is best known abroad for coauthoring, with Enzo Faletto, "Dependency and Development in Latin America."

Fernando Henrique Cardoso was born on June 18, 1931, in Rio de Janeiro. Drawn into politics 20 years ago, Mr. Cardoso served as a São Paulo senator from 1983 to 1992. In 1988 he helped to found the Brazilian Social Democratic Party, a center-left group that opposed corruption.

Mr. Cardoso's wife, Ruth Corrêa Leite Cardoso, stayed in São Paulo while her husband moved to Brasilia. An anthropologist at Cebrap, she specializes in studying community movements by women and blacks in São Paulo shantytowns. With their three children grown and married, Mrs. Cardoso said last month that she would move to Brasilia if her husband won the race.

Although Mr. Cardoso's inauguration on Jan. 1 will mark the 10th anniversary of civilian rule, the threat of military intervention is never distant. According to a book issued today, "A História Real," Mr. Cardoso helped to defuse an incipient military rebellion against President Franco last February.

 Article Review Form at end of book.

Brazil
Real-politics

Brasilia—The *real* plan, named after the new currency that was part of it, was dreamed up by Fernando Henrique Cardoso, then finance minister, and introduced in mid-1994. It brought him the presidency, and Brazilians low inflation and a degree of economic stability that few could recall. Since he took office in January 1995, his government has enjoyed solid support—until now. Its opinion-poll rating (in São Paulo) fell to 38% in March, 25% last month.

Why? One reason lies in Congress. The government has had some useful constitutional amendments passed, but not the ones it needs to balance the public books. So it has had to rely on tight money and an expensive currency to keep inflation down. This has led to temporary economic stagnation, hurting everyone. On top, the middle classes have been hit by price rises for services such as education, health insurance and housing, which are not subject to competition from imports. Workers and the poor have gained much since inflation stopped eating the cash in their pockets. But they were disappointed by the government's decision a month ago to lift the minimum wage by only 12%—less than annual inflation. In 12 months, unemployment has risen from 4.4% to 6% nationally, and in greater São Paulo, the industrial heartland, to 16%, the highest since 1985.

The trade unions have called a one-day general strike, for jobs and wages, on June 21st. On May 22nd, it was the turn of the bosses: in a rare demonstration, 2,800 businessmen descended on the capital, Brasilia, to protest at high interest rates and Congress's slowness in approving reforms.

Hours later, Congress thumbed its nose at them, and at the president, voting to gut the government's already much weakened proposals to reform the national pension system, one of the big drains on the public purse. And that was despite some crude bargaining in which Mr. Cardoso bowed to the powerful farm lobby, agreeing to withdraw a measure that would help banks to collect overdue debts (which in turn would help them reduce their loan rates).

The government has added to its own troubles. True, the rules require it to assemble a 60% majority from its undisciplined nominal supporters for almost every line of its proposed constitutional changes. But one reason for public suspicion of the pensions shake-up, says Walder de Goes, a political consultant in Brasilia, is that the need for it has not been properly explained.

The uneasy coalition that links Mr. Cardoso's Social Democrats and the (conservative) Liberal Front finds it easier to speak with half-a-dozen voices than one. And they dither. When Jose Serra, the ambitious planning minister, at last announced on May 28th that he would resign to stand for the majoralty of São Paulo, it came only after days of public shilly-shallying.

So is the *real* plan doomed to a slow death from withering political support? Almost certainly, no. Officials admit that the government is going through a bad patch. But Sergio Amaral, Mr. Cardoso's spokesman, says he is confident that the fall in the president's popularity is overstated and will be reversed. He foresees a "new wave of optimism" by the end of 1996, offering two reasons for it: the start of an economic pickup, with retail sales rising in

May; and his conviction that, despite last month's defeat, the government will get reform both of pensions and of the administrative system through Congress by December.

It still has plenty of room for manoeuvre. Brazilian presidents have wide powers of the pen. Mr. Cardoso could rein in public spending (by sacking contract workers, for example) even without constitutional change. The government now plans to reintroduce its original, tougher pension-reform plan in the Senate, where its majority is firmer, returning the measure to the unruly lower house only after October's municipal elections are over.

Yet, say his critics, Mr. Cardoso, more of an academic than a political street-fighter, needs to show more daring leadership. He should appeal to the public to help him prod Congress into approving his reforms. If he did, he might find that his difficulties would actually help him: if the *real* plan, and Brazil's precious economic stability, were perceived to be in serious danger, it should not be too hard to rally both public opinion and Congress round the government's programme of reform.

 Article Review Form at end of book.

Nigeria
Current policy issues

Africa Policy Information

Section 1: Current Policy Issues

The most urgent issue is democracy, understood not only as an end to military rule but also as the establishment of responsive political institutions which promote accountable government, prevent corruption, respect human and civil rights, and ensure popular sovereignty.

For most Nigerians, the pressing problems of everyday survival are the highest immediate priority. Since the oil boom of the 1970s, Nigeria's economy has been in crisis despite continued expansion in oil production. The real income index for urban households dropped from 166 in 1980 to 71 in 1986. The exchange rate for the naira has dropped from one to a dollar in 1985 to 79 to a dollar in 1996. And the list of dismal statistics could go on. Without the establishment of accountable government, however, the chances of addressing other pressing problems—such as the deterioration of living conditions and the collapse of once outstanding educational institutions are very low.

Nigeria has abundant human as well as natural resources to address its problems. Many of its outstanding leaders, however, are instead in prison or in exile. The prerequisite for addressing other problems is having a government that works and is accountable to the Nigerian people.

Nigerian hopes for a return to civilian rule were dashed when the military regime annulled national elections after votes were counted in June 1993. Since then repression has escalated to unprecedented levels, culminating in the execution of environmental activist Ken Saro-Wiwa and his colleagues in November 1995. Millitary ruler General Sani Abacha peddles another complex program, while internal protest is repeatedly quashed and the international community pays only sporadic attention.

Like the anti-apartheid movement in the early 1970s, the Nigerian pro-democracy movement is faced with the challenge of building a coalition that can isolate a systematically abusive regime and promote a democratically accountable alternative. The situations differ in many respects, most notably in the lack of a racially-defined barrier between oppressor and oppressed. Nevertheless, the movement for democracy in Nigeria has similar strengths and faces comparably formidable obstacles as did its South African counterpart twenty years ago.

Despite repression, human rights and environmental coups, trade unionists, educators, and others inside Nigeria continue to resist authoritarian rule. Internal opposition has been supported by a large and well-educated group of Nigerians living abroad, just as the South African exile community played a key role in the anti-apartheid struggle. International human rights groups and environmental groups have joined with Africa advocacy groups in focusing world attention on Nigeria.

In 1993, and again in 1995, the international community and African leaders, including South African President Nelson Mandela, also responded with intensified political, diplomatic, and economic pressure on the Abacha regime to secure the release of imprisoned leaders, to permit the return of exiled activists, and to facilitate the identification of a durable solution to Nigeria's political crisis. The United States, the European Union, and the Commonwealth imposed limited sanctions on Nigeria, including a ban on arms sales and visa restrictions on Nigerian officials. There has also been increased international support for Nigerian organizations working for democracy and human rights.

These pressures have had more symbolic effects than substantive impact. They have fallen far short of more comprehensive sanctions demanded by Nigerian pro-democracy forces. Legislation introduced in the US Congress, but not yet voted on, would authorize additional economic sanctions, while still not including a comprehensive embargo on Nigerian oil.

Sanction proposals have been vigorously opposed by oil companies. Since the discovery of oil in the Niger River delta in 1958, Shell Oil and other international oil companies have caused extensive environmental damage to this area, the homeland of the Ogoni people and other minority groups. Environmental and human rights groups accuse the companies of collaborating with the Nigerian military regime to stifle opposition to the industry's activities.

When public attention and the media spotlight shifts off of Nigeria, diplomats tend to revert to business as usual, relying on the false hope that quiet diplomacy with the Nigerian government will eventually bring about the promised transition to civilian rule and avert further crises. The military regime is running a well-financed public relations campaign to convince African-Americans and others that it is sincere about change. Real progress toward democracy is unlikely, however, unless more significant steps are taken to weaken the military regime and to strengthen popular democratic forces.

Representatives of pro-democracy groups within Nigeria, hampered by difficulties of communication and recurrent repression, are best contacted when travelling or through overseas representatives. The following is a short list of U.S.-based contacts for those willing to get involved in supporting the struggle for democracy in Nigeria. Many more sources can be found on or through the Web sites listed in the section of this paper.

The United Democratic Front of Nigeria (UDFN) was formed in March 1996 at simultaneous summit meetings in South Africa and Norway, as a common platform of pro-democracy organizations. Contact points in the U.S. include (1) the Nigerian Democratic Movement, P.O. Box 91291, Washington, DC 20090; tel: 202-806-4793; fax: 202-806-4632; e-mail: ailto:ndmorg@cldc. howard.edu http://www.cldc. howard.edu/~ndmorg/ndmpa ge.html contact: Bolaji Aluko; and (2) the Organization of Nigerians in the Americas, P.O. Box 200985, Austin, TX 78720-0985; tel: 512-335-0287; fax: 512-471-1061; e-mail: mailto:julius@jeeves.la. utexas.edu contact: Julius Ihonvbere. Other Nigerian pro-democracy groups can be located through the Web addresses in the niger 5.html

The International Roundtable on Nigeria (IRTON) is an informal association of human rights, environmental, labor, and US-based Nigerian pro-democracy groups working to help Nigerians restore a rights-respecting, accountable government. Its meetings are coordinated through the Government Affairs Office of Amnesty International USA, 304 Pennsylvania Ave SE, Washington DC 20003, tel: 202-544-0200, Ext. 234; fax: 202-546-7142. Contact: Adotei Akwei

The Africa Fund which took a leading role in the campaign for local and state government action against the apartheid regime, is now involved with other groups in similar actions

to support the Nigerian pro-democracy movement. Africa Fund, 17 John St., New York, NY 10038; tel:212-962-1210; e-mail: mailto:africafund@igc.apc.org contact: Michael Fleshman.

Of the U.S.-based environmental organizations, the Sierra Club is currently most actively engaged in the Shell Boycott, working with representatives of the Movement for the Survival of the Ogoni People (MOSOP) and other groups. Sierra Club, 408 C St., NE, Washington, D.C. 20002; Tel: 202-675-6691;

e-mail: ailto:stephen.mills@sierraclub.orgweb: http://www.sierraclub.org/human-rights/nigeria.html contact: Stephen Mills, Human Rights and Environment Campaign Director.

Africa Policy Information Center 110 Maryland Ave. NE #509 Washington, DC 20002, USA Tel: (202) 546-7961 Fax: (202) 546-1545

e-mail: mailto:apic@igc.apc.org

 Article Review Form at end of book.

Harassment of the Opposition

Human Rights Watch/Africa

"In case the western world has forgotten the rule of law, we in Nigeria are prepared to teach them."
—Nigerian Minister of Information and Culture Walter Ofonagoro, interviewed in *Tell* magazine, August 19, 1995.

The transition program announced by Gen. Abacha on October 1, 1995 cannot be deemed credible until there is free political activity in Nigeria. Nor can the Nigerian military government expect the internal opposition movement or the international community to take seriously its pledges to restore democracy while the presumed winner of the

June 12, 1993 elections—probably the fairest in Nigeria's history—remains in prison facing charges of "treasonable felony" (a lesser charge than the capital offense of treason). Indeed, the primary credibility problem of the current transition program is that Nigeria has already successfully conducted a similar program, which was prevented from reaching its

Human Rights Watch/Africa, "Harassment of the Opposition" excerpt from NIGERIA "Permanent Transition," Vol. 8, No. 3 (A), pp. 15-20. Reprinted courtesy of Human Rights Watch. Not to be reprinted without permission.

conclusion only by military intervention. Meanwhile, many of the most prominent human rights and pro-democracy activists are in detention, and others are subjected to daily intimidation and harassment or have fled abroad; the independent press is severely restricted, and journalists are also in prison or under the threat of imprisonment; the internal broadcast media are government-controlled propaganda machines; the rights to freedom of assembly and association are regularly violated and hard-won elements of academic freedom are denied; and a military crackdown in Ogoniland remains in progress months after the "judicial murder" of Ken Saro-Wiwa, the leader of Nigeria's first effective grassroots protest movement. Those efforts that have been made to promote reconciliation and dialogue over Nigeria's problems and future appear to be solely cosmetic. No efforts have been made to prevent corruption, brutality and murder by the armed forces, endemic across the Nigerian federation.

The Imprisonment of Chief Abiola

On June 23, 1994, several days after declaring himself president, Chief M.K.O. Abiola was detained at his residence in Lagos. The government ignored two orders by the Federal High Court in Lagos to produce him before the court and justify his detention, and on July 4 the court ordered the federal minister of justice to appear before it on July 7 to answer charges of contempt of court. On July 6, Abiola was brought before a Federal High Court in Abuja, specifically established for his trial, and charged with treasonable felony. On July 14 an application for bail was refused. On

October 21, Justice Gbolahan Jinadu of the High Court in Lagos ruled, bravely, that Abiola's arrest and detention was unconstitutional and "most reckless, irresponsible and an excessive show of executive power"; declaring oneself president did not constitute an offense under the Nigerian criminal code. The government appealed the ruling. On November 4, the Court of Appeal in Kaduna set aside the decision of the Abuja High Court denying him bail; again the government appealed the ruling to the Supreme Court, and the Court of Appeal later allowed a postponement of the release order until the appeal was heard.[23] The bail hearing before the Supreme Court, the highest court of appeal in Nigeria, has been repeatedly adjourned, and appears to be indefinitely on hold, for lack of judges to hear the case. Seven of the eleven Supreme Court judges agreed to recuse themselves from hearing the case in May 1995, as a result of an application that they should do so on the grounds that they are also the plaintiffs in a libel case against *The National Concord*, a newspaper owned by Chief Abiola, in connection with a December 1993 article headed "Chief Justice Mohammed Bello: Kick Him Out Now Lawyers Demand," which alleged that Supreme Court judges had accepted "gifts" of Mercedes Benz cars from former head of state Gen. Babangida. A minimum of five judges is required to hear a case, and the government has failed to appoint further judges to replace those who are disqualified, despite representations from the lawyers representing Chief Abiola.

[23]Amnesty International, Urgent Action, UA 282/94, July 21, 1994; "Abiola's Travails," *Constitutional Rights Journal* (Lagos), October–December 1994.

Chief Abiola has been held in solitary confinement and in poor conditions, has a history of hypertension and other problems, and has frequently been denied access to his personal physician. Dr. Ore Falomo, his doctor, was detained for some time in 1995, after arriving in Abuja on April 20 believing he would be able to see Chief Abiola. Although in general it is difficult for visitors to gain access to him, Chief Abiola has been seen on a number of occasions by visitors from overseas, including the representatives of the U.N. secretary-general who visited Nigeria on a fact-finding mission in April 1996. Chief Abiola is currently believed to be rotated between various different places of detention in Abuja.

The legal situation concerning Abiola's detention was further complicated in early 1996 by disagreements between Kola Abiola, M.K.O. Abiola's eldest son, and Kudirat Abiola, his senior wife since the death of Kola's mother in 1992 and an outspoken campaigner on his behalf, as to the lawyers who should represent the chief.[24] Godwin O.K. Ajayi led the defense team until February 1996, when Kola Abiola wrote to him withdrawing the brief and replacing him with another well-known Lagos lawyer, Rotimi Williams. On Monday May 6, at a hearing in which Ajayi was asking for accelerated hearing of the case, Kudirat Abiola filed an affidavit in the Lagos Federal High Court insisting that Ajayi should continue with the case and accusing Kola Abiola of spearheading a group that wanted Abiola to renounce his claim to the presidency. On May 8, at a hearing in which Rotimi Williams had filed a mo-

[24]Pini Jason, "Abiola in Hock," *New African* (London), May 1996; Reuter, May 6, 1996.

tion urging the court to strike off Ajayi's name, a Federal High Court in Abuja ordered the inspector-general of police to produce Moshood Abiola in court on May 10 to settle the controversy. In issuing his decision, Justice Chris Senligon- criticized persistent police disobedience of court orders: "Such executive rascality is capable of lowering the image and status of the judiciary thereby impeding our march towards democracy."[25] The federal government appealed the ruling, and the controversy remains unsettled.

The Assassination of Kudirat Abiola

While these court cases were proceeding, Kudirat Abiola, the principal campaigner on her husband's behalf, faced harassment from the Nigerian authorities. On May 8, she was charged, with two other people, with "conspiracy to cause misdemeanor and making false publications with intent to cause fear to members of the public." She was released on bail, having been arrested the previous day and held overnight. Police said the charges related to the printing of exercise books with pictures of Chief Abiola describing him as president elect.[26] Mrs. Abiola reported to the press, including in an interview with the outspoken *Tell* magazine on May 27, 1996, that she had on several occasions been trailed by security operatives.

On June 4, 1996, Kudirat Abiola was shot and killed by unknown attackers while driving along the Lagos/Ibadan expressway on her way to visit the Canadian High Commissioner in

Victoria Island, Lagos.[27] Most Nigerians assumed the killing was political, aimed at silencing one of the government's most vocal critics. Nevertheless, the police immediately announced a high-level investigation into the assassination, offering one million naira (about U.S. $12,500) for information leading to the arrest of the killers. On June 5, a student demonstration protesting in Ibadan at the assassination of Kudirat Abiola was broken up by police: the president of the student union was detained overnight.

On June 12, Kola Abiola was arrested in connection with the assassination; over the next few days more than twenty more members of the Abiola family were arrested. Kola was held until June 29, and other members of the family released soon after. On June 17, four senior members of NADECO were also arrested in connection with the killing. The oldest, Chief Solanke Onasanya (80) was released on bail on July 1, but three others—Chief Abraham Adesanya (74), Chief Ayo Adebanjo (69) and Alhaji Ganiyu Dawodu (63)— were kept in detention. Later in July, a Federal High Court in Lagos ordered the release of the remaining three, and awarded them–500,000 damages each. The Nigerian government appealed the order, saying it intended to charge the detainees in connection with the Kudirat Abiola assassination, and kept them in custody, where they remain to date, still uncharged.

[27]There have been a number of other assassinations or assassination attempts on political figures in Nigeria in the last year: on October 6, 1995, Alfred Rewane, veteran politician from the south west of the country and major financial backer of NADECO, was shot dead in his Lagos home; on February 2, 1996, Alex Ibru, publisher of the independent *The Guardian* newspaper and former minister of the interior, was shot and wounded in his car in Lagos.

Opposition activists concluded that the detentions were an attempt to sow discord in the family of the most prominent symbol of the June 12, 1993 elections.

Detentions without Charge under Decree No. 2

The State Security (Detention of Persons) Decree No. 2 of 1984 has been repeatedly condemned by international observers, including the U.N.'s Working Group on Arbitrary Detention. The Working Group has found in cases considered over several years that detentions under Decree No. 2 violate articles 9 (right to liberty and security of the person), 19 (right to freedom of opinion and expression) and 22 (right to freedom of association) of the International Covenant on Civil and Political Rights, to which Nigeria is a party. In 1996, the Working Group has declared a number of detentions carried out under the decree to be arbitrary, and has requested the government of Nigeria to "take the necessary steps to remedy the situation in order to bring it into conformity with the provisions and principles incorporated in the Universal Declaration of Human Rights and in the International Covenant on Civil and Political Rights."[28]

[28]Working Group on Arbitrary Detention, Decision No. 2/1996 (concerning Meshack Karanwi, Batom Mitee and Lekue Loolo), and Decision No. 6/1996 (concerning Gen. Olusegun Obasanjo and nineteen others, Dr. Beko Ransome-Kuti, Dr. Tunji Abayomi and Chima Ubani), adopted on May 22 and May 23, 1996, respectively. In neither case had any response been received from the Nigerian government refuting the allegations in the communications during the ninety days allowed for responses before decisions are published. A communication on a further case was sent following a meeting of the Working Group in July, and is currently awaiting a response from the Nigerian government.

[25]Pan African News Agency (PANA), May 8, 1996.
[26]PANA, May 8, 1996.

Particularly objectionable amongst the provisions of Decree No. 2 are the following:

- a detainee has no right to be informed of the reasons for his or her detention;

- he or she has no right of access to family, lawyers or private medical treatment;

- detention orders are renewable, thus permitting indefinite detention on grounds of "state security" without charge or trial;

- the courts' jurisdiction to review detention orders has been ousted, so that no civil proceedings may be brought in respect of anything done in terms of the decree, nor may the constitutionality of any action be inquired into by any court.

When the regular court system has attempted to ensure that the government complies with its obligations under international law, this has had no effect: court orders that detainees and prisoners be given access to independent medical attention or legal assistance, allowed to see members of their families, or brought to court are routinely ignored by the military authorities.

In June 1996, a number of amendments to Decree No. 2 were announced by the military government. Decree No. 14 of 1994, which had amended Decree No. 2 to exclude courts from granting writs of habeas corpus in respect of persons held under Decree No. 2 was repealed by the State Security (Detention of Persons) (Amendment)(No. 2)(Repeal) Decree, adopted on June 7. A panel was also established to review cases of detention and the review of all existing cases promised. However, the main ouster clause in Decree No. 2, preventing the courts from inquiring into the legality of a detention order, remains in place.

Amongst those currently detained without charge are the following:

Frank Ovie Kokori, secretary-general of NUPENG. He was arrested on August 20, 1994 by plainclothes security operatives who trailed him to the place in Lagos where he was living in hiding. Chief Kokori was one of the leaders of the two-month oil-workers strike of July and August 1994 to protest the military take over of one year earlier and to demand a return to civilian rule. Like many of the other detainees, Chief Kokori has been moved around between a number of different prisons, mostly in the north of Nigeria. He has intermittently been allowed to receive visitors, but is reported to be in poor health as a result of diabetes. Court orders that he be produced in court or released from illegal detention have been ignored by the government.

Ayo Opadokun, national secretary of NADECO. He was detained on October 13, 1994 under Decree No. 2, apparently in connection with his activities opposing continued military rule. Although his release was announced by the government in June 1996, he has not been seen by any colleagues or family members and is presumed still to be in detention.

Kebir Ahmed, chair of the Sokoto state branch of the Campaign for Democracy. He was arrested in his home in Sokoto by a team of plainclothes and uniformed policemen on March 10, 1995. He was questioned in Kaduna in connection with his pro-democracy activities, in particular the distribution of leaflets. It is not known where Mallam Ahmed is being held.

Chima Ubani, secretary-general of Democratic Alternative, a pro-democracy party, and Head of Campaigns at the Civil Liberties Organisation, one of Nigeria's best known human rights groups. He was arrested on July 18, 1995 by seven plainclothes policemen from the State Security Service (SSS), at his home in Lagos. The SSS searched his apartment for "subversive documents," and he is apparently held in connection with his human rights and pro-democracy activities. After being kept in the SSS facility at the Inter-centre, Lagos with Abdul Oroh and Tunji Abayomi, Ubani was transferred after their release to Ikoyi prison, in Lagos. The authorities have ignored a series of court orders demanding that he be produced in court or released from custody.

Milton Dabibi, general secretary of PENGASSAN, until the dismissal of the union's national executive council by military decree in August 1994 and replacement by a sole administrator, was arrested in Lagos on January 25, 1996. He was initially held at the SSS office in Ikoyi, Lagos. News of his detention first appeared in a Nigerian newspaper on February 14. He is believed to be held at a prison in the north of Nigeria, far from his family in Lagos.

Gani Fawehinmi, human rights lawyer and leader of the National Conscience Party (NCP), which has been protesting the government's three year program of transition to civilian rule. Amongst other important cases, he led the defense team for Ken Saro-Wiwa and eight other MOSOP members in the trial before a special tribunal that led to their execution, and launched an action to challenge the constitutionality of that tribunal and of a further tribunal constituted to try nineteen other Ogoni activists. He was detained on January 30 of this year, shortly before he was due to address a rally at the University of Lagos. He has been detained by the military authorities on many previous occasions for his work.

After being held at the headquarters of the State Security Service (SSS) in Shangisha, near Lagos, Chief Fawehinmi was transferred to a prison in Bauchi State, in the north of Nigeria. Although Fawehinmi suffers from hypertension and became seriously ill while in detention on a previous occasion, the military authorities have ignored court orders for him to be allowed to receive medication from his family. Although he was visited once by his wife, he has since been held incommunicado: on June 4, the Court of Appeal sitting in Lagos ordered that Chief Fawehinmi's wife, Ganiat Fawehinmi, and his personal physician should be allowed access to him. On arriving at Bauchi prison, access was denied. Fawehinmi is reported by the Nigerian Medical Association to be in very poor health.

Femi Aborisade, deputy head of the National Conscience Party. Following the detention of Gani Fawehinmi, the NCP campaigned for his release, and also protested the local government elections to be held on a non-party basis at the end of March. On February 13, the government announced that it had promulgated the Transition to Civil Rule Decree which, among other things, made it a criminal offense to "do anything to forestall or prejudice the realization of the political programme." On

February 14, Femi Aborisade was arrested. It is not known where he is being held.

Femi Falana, president of the National Association of Democratic Lawyers (NADEL), and a human rights lawyer who worked with Chief Fawehinmi in the defense of Ken Saro-Wiwa. He was arrested on February 14, 1996, after security police seized files from his chambers, including files relating to a case being brought on behalf of Fela Anikulapo Kuti, musician and brother of well-known democracy activist Beko Ransome-Kuti, against the National Drug Law Enforcement Agency as a result of his detention by that body for five days. He is held in Hadejia prison in Jigawa state, in the north of Nigeria.

George Onah, defense correspondent for *The Vanguard* daily newspaper, arrested by the Directorate of Military Intelligence on May 17, the day after a story appeared under his by-line titled "Army kicks out 220 officers," and held in DMI headquarters, Apapa, Lagos. Released later that day, he was told to report back with his editor the following Monday. The newspaper published an apology to the army. Onah, a former soldier himself, was then rearrested on May 22, and has been held since then. Director of Defense Information Brig. Gen. Fred Chijuka said that Onah was being held in order to find out whether he was properly discharged from the army, and not for any reason to do with the article on the dismissals.

Abraham Adesanya, Ayo Adebanjo and Ganiyu Dawodu, NADECO leaders, arrested on June 17, 1996. While the police have indicated that they intend to charge them in connection with

the assassination of Kudirat Abiola, they have not yet done so (see above).

Recently released after long detentions were Tunji Abayomi, chair of Human Rights Africa, a human rights organization, held from July 1995 to June 1996; Abdul Oroh, executive director of the CLO, held from July 1995 to June 1996; Fred Eno, assistant to Chief Abiola, held from August 1994 to June 1996; Mohammed Sule, writer and filmmaker, held from February 1995 to June 1996; and Nosa Igiebor, editor of the crusading *Tell* weekly magazine, held from December 1995 to June 1996. Others, who were released in January 1996 after a year or more of detention, include Sylvester Odion-Akhaine, secretary-general of CD, held since January 1995; Fidelis Aidelomo and Wariebi Agamene, both of NUPENG, held since August 1994; Olawale Oshun of NADECO, held since August 1994; and Ademola Adeniji-Adele, assistant to Abiola, held since August 1994.

The Nigerian government has also been known to announce releases which have not in fact taken place, apparently in an attempt to influence international opinion to reduce the pressure on Nigeria to improve its human rights record. The release of Chief Ayo Opadokun, national secretary of NADECO, held since October 1994, was announced in June 1996, at the same time as the releases of Abdul Oroh, Tunji Abayomi, Fred Eno and Nosa Igiebor, timed to coincide with the meeting of the Commonwealth Ministerial Action Group in London. However, he has not yet contacted his wife or any NADECO member, and is presumed by his family and colleagues still to be in detention. The release of three students was also announced in June 1996: two of them, Charles Titiloye and Hilary Ojukwu, had been released in January 1996 after spending two months in detention; the third, Matthew Popoola, was among those convicted in the alleged 1995 coup plot, and is presumed to be still in prison.

Numerous activists are detained without charge for shorter periods, in many cases repeatedly, as a result of their human rights or pro-democracy activities. Those who have been held this year include:

Nnimmo Bassey, director of Environmental Rights Action (ERA), a project of the CLO, detained from June 5 to July 19, 1996, at the Alagbon Close police station in Lagos, after being picked up at the international airport while on his way to an environmental rights conference in Ghana. He was told his detention was in relation to student demonstrations in Benin City in 1994, in which he had been involved.

Godwin Uyi Ojo, project officer with ERA, arrested on January 25, 1996, in Lagos, and detained without charge until February 10 in the police station in Surulere, and then at the SSS offices in Shangisha. He was questioned in connection with a report on the January 4 disturbances in Ogoniland, of which he had a draft with him, and asked about his connections with the international community.

Biodun Olamosu, member of Gani Fawehinmi's National Conscience Party, arrested in Kano in May 1996 and held without charge until July 2, when he was released but charged with sedition for distributing NCP posters in the city.

Steve Aluko, Kaduna regional director of the CLO, arrested on February 1, released on February 2, then rearrested on February 5 and held until March 8 by the SSS in Zaria and then Kaduna. He was questioned in connection with recent bomb blasts in Kano, Kaduna and Zaria.

Bunmi Aborisade, editor of *June 12*, a monthly magazine, arrested and detained at the Directorate of Military Intelligence head office in Apapa, Lagos on April 11. He was released on May 6.

John Odion, secretary-general of the National Union of Bank, Insurance and Financial Institution Employees, detained without charge between November 10, 1995 and February 22, 1996.

Other detainees are held for a few hours or a day or two at a time. On June 13, Mahmoud Abdul Aminu, staff attorney with the Civil Liberties Organisation (CLO) in Ijebu-Ode, was arrested and held till the following day. He was ordered to report back to the SSS station, but has gone into hiding. On May 8, Tunde Oladunjoye, publicity secretary of the Committee for the Defense of Human Rights (CDHR), Tunde Olugboji, projects officer at the Constitutional Rights Project (CLO), and three members of the CLO were arrested in Jos, at a workshop on the churches and human rights in Nigeria. They were detained at the SSS headquarters in Jos and released on May 11. On March 20, SSS members arrested Yemisi Odukoya, secretary at the offices of Femi Falana in Lagos, and questioned her about the whereabouts of Jiti Ogunye, secretary-general of the CDHR. She was released later that day. Further detentions are described in the sections on attacks on the independent press and on events in Ogoniland, below. It is impossible to give an accurate figure for the number of detentions without charge on political grounds at any one time; partly because monitoring every state is impossible for local human rights organizations, most of which are based in Lagos; partly because detentions are often for a brief time, and are very difficult to track accurately.

 Article Review Form at end of book.

U.S. Envoy to Nigeria Gets a Stormy Farewell

Howard W. French

Abidjan, Ivory Coast Sept. 25 — When Walter Carrington, a lifelong African specialist, became the American Ambassador to Nigeria four years ago, soon after the military leadership annulled the most democratic elections that country had ever held, he knew that his assignment would not be easy.

From the time of his arrival to his final weeks in the job, before heading to a Harvard University fellowship early next month, Mr. Carrington has found himself butting heads with the leaders of Africa's most populous country on a range of issues that run from democracy and human rights to international drug trafficking.

But nothing could have prepared Mr. Carrington for the seeming final act in his ambassadorship, when state security officials undertook a campaign of intimidation against people who have organized farewell parties for him.

In what Mr. Carrington, a 67-year-old lawyer with a 38-year-long familiarity with Nigeria called "the most surrealistic experience I have had here yet," heavily armed policemen burst into a well-attended reception in Mr. Carrington's honor in Lagos last week, threatened to shoot one speaker and ordered the foreign guests, including the American Ambassador, to leave at once.

After grabbing the microphone away from an elderly man who had begun to make introductory remarks in honor of Mr. Carrington, witnesses said, one policeman threatened to shoot another human rights activist who defiantly grabbed another microphone and sought to address the stunned crowd.

Earlier that evening, Mr. Carrington said, a police unit cordoned off the area where the farewell was originally supposed to take place, and forbade the Ambassador and others entry, forcing the Nigerian human rights and pro-democracy groups that had organized the reception to shift it elsewhere.

Advocacy of human rights angers Nigerians.

"The leader of the police unit could be heard saying loudly on his hand held radio, 'Sir, we have located the place, the U.S. Ambassador is here, and we are going to break up the meeting,'" Mr. Carrington said. "And when we were leaving we could hear the same man saying that they had succeeded, and that the Ambassador was leaving."

Washington has since filed what diplomats call a "strong protest" with the Nigerian Foreign Ministry and the Nigerian Embassy in Washington, calling the breakup of the reception "scandalous."

But the protest did not prompt an official apology from Gen. Sani Abacha's Government. Instead, this week the Nigerian Minister for Special Presidential Affairs, Alhaji Wada Nas, launched into a scathing attack on Mr. Carrington.

Mr. Nas was quoted by Agence France-Presse as saying "his stay in Nigeria must be described as four years of waste during which nothing was accomplished between the two countries in economic, cultural or political terms."

Throughout Mr. Carrington's tenure in Nigeria, senior officials of that country have interpreted the deep chill that permeates ties between Washington and the Nigerian capital, Abuja, as the reflection of Mr. Carrington's efforts to poison relations.

In interviews with local news organizations, Nigerian officials have repeatedly said that Mr. Carrington's outspokenness in favor of human rights and democracy in a country long ruled by the military, did not reflect Washington's official views of their country.

Instead, in a string of attacks that often have a poisonous personal quality, Nigerian officials have depicted Mr. Carrington, who is black, as part of a corrupt African-American elite that publicly criticizes Nigeria in the secret hope that Abuja will offer to buy their silence with generous financial donations.

During a wave of bombing incidents in Nigeria last year, Mr. Carrington was summoned by the Foreign Minister on Christmas Eve for an official dressing down.

Senior Government officials publicly complained about a safety warning by the American Embassy to American travelers to Nigeria, and hinted that Mr. Carrington, who has openly maintained close contacts with opposition groups, had knowledge of the attacks.

In August, the Nigerian police commissioner said Mr.

Carrington's diplomatic immunity should be withdrawn so that he could be brought in for questioning.

For Mr. Carrington, there is no mystery why relations between the United States and Nigeria have been so rocky during his tenure.

"I came here in November 1993, a few months after the annulment of the elections of June '93, and I was here 12 days before the military under Abacha staged its palace coup and took over the Government," Mr. Carrington said. "Our Government put on sanctions in response to the annulment. Before that our Government had already banned flights between the United States and Nigeria because of security concerns.

"And a few months after I arrived, a third set of sanctions were slapped on because of a finding that Nigeria was not cooperating in narcotics matters." In none of these areas, Mr. Carrington said, had there been enough progress in Washington's view to lift sanctions.

Relations between the two countries worsened after the November 1995 execution of the playwright and minority rights advocate Ken Saro-Wiwa. Mr. Carrington and two dozen other ambassadors were temporarily recalled in protest.

As he prepares to leave Nigeria for Cambridge, Mass., where he will work on African issues at the DuBois Institute at Harvard, his alma mater, Mr. Carrington responded to the personal attacks against him by voicing his own of regret over the state of Africa's most populous and potentially most powerful nation.

"'This is a country that I have been coming to since 1959, so I have been able to see the years of boom and bust here," he said. "This is a country richer in human resources than almost anyplace I can think of, and it is rich in natural resources too. And yet Nigeria is a country ranked by the United Nations as one of the poorest places in the world, and ranked by some as one of the most corrupt countries in the world.

"As a black American, this deeply saddens me. This is a place that should be one of the leading countries in the world. But until they are able to resolve the problem of allowing the people to choose their leaders democratically, I am afraid they are not going to be able to realize this potential."

 Article Review Form at end of book.

Mandela's Group Accepts 5 Years of Power-Sharing

Defeating militants, it backs deal with de Klerk.

Bill Keller

Special to The New York Times

Soweto, South Africa, Feb.18.—The African National Congress subdued its angry militant wing today and approved a plan to let minority parties share in governing the country for five years after the end of white monopoly rule.

The agreement, which takes South Africa a major step closer to its first post-apartheid government, creates the prospect that President F.W. de Klerk's National Party would stay on as a junior partner in running the country until near the end of the century.

Until three years ago, the congress and the National Party were bitter antagonists, with the congress outlawed and waging guerrilla warfare against the Government. Sharing executive power with the National Party, which devised apartheid, remains anathema to many blacks.

Cyril Ramaphosa, the secretary general of the congress and its chief negotiator, told reporters that the agreement could not be described as "power sharing"

since the majority party would get its way on most matters.

If the agreement is finally enacted, white rule would end with the election by April 1994 of a 400-seat assembly, the first in which South Africa's 30 million blacks would have the vote. The assembly would write a new constitution and serve as the interim parliament for a term of five years.

The president would be chosen from the most successful party, and any party that won at least 5 percent of the seats in the new parliament would also be entitled to places in the cabinet. It is widely assumed that Nelson Mandela, the congress leader, would become the new president.

Approval of Cabinet

The president would be obliged to get cabinet approval on major decisions—two-thirds approval on certain issues of fundamental importance, which have not yet been specified.

This arrangement already had the endorsement of Mr. de Klerk and must now be sold to other participants in multiparty talks, expected to resume next month.

The proposal has evoked furious denunciations from Mangosuthu G. Buthelezi of the conservative, Zulu-based Inkatha Freedom Party, and from black militant groups like the Pan Africanist Congress, which fear they may be relegated to the margins by a future black-white coalition.

Agreement Called Binding

But the congress and the Government have sworn to treat their new agreement as binding, which means these longtime antagonists in effect reenter the multiparty talks as a formidable team.

The formula for coalition government was worked out by negotiators for the Government and the congress in January, but it caused an uproar among militants within the congress who regard it as a sellout. There was some doubt whether the congress's 100 - member governing committee would endorse it today.

The congress negotiators' task of selling their deal to their broad and fractious leadership was complicated when President de Klerk and his aides described the deal as '"power sharing," an emotionally charged expression that to many black leaders means a permanent white veto.

Anti-apartheid hard-liners like Harry Gwala, the firebrand who heads the congress's war-torn Natal Midlands region, denounced anything short of full-fledged majority rule, and during a three-day debate here, they called unsuccessfully for a nation-wide membership conference to debate the issue.

Dissension in Congress

Even as the congress committee was finishing its work today, Chris Hani, secretary general of the Communist Party and a congress leader, was predicting to a student audience in Cape Town that the congress would reject "this business of five years." Mr Hani said the unity government would endure for perhaps nine months, and then step aside for new elections.

As is customary, when the congress governing body finally voted this afternoon the outcome was unanimous, although some of the more outspoken critics had departed for other engagements.

But President de Klerk, in an interview televised here last Sunday, noted approvingly that the new president would not have as much power "as I have in terms of our present system." Mr. de Klerk appoints and controls the Cabinet and has no obligation to weigh the views of minority parties.

The agreement, by whatever name, is a compromise, and if enacted it would institutionalize an element of compromise in the Future government.

Five Years of Consensus Rule

Mr. de Klerk, who has long insisted that a permanent consensus-style arrangement be enshrined in the constitution, has now agreed to only five years. After that, whites worried about their future must count on the legal checks and balances incorporated in a new constitution.

The congress, which had earlier insisted on full majority rule, has now agreed to wait a bit, assuming that it will win big enough in the first elections to enact most of its policies anyway as the dominant force in the unity government.

The general strategy of inviting the minority into a coalition was embraced by the congress last year at the urging of Joe Slovo, the Communist Party chairman and a leading congress negotiator.

Mr. Slovo contended that abruptly cutting out the white minority would leave civil servants, security forces and businessmen embittered and sow the seeds of a destructive backlash.

"The objective will be to unite our country, to bring about stability, to insure we embark on a reconstruction program with other parties." Mr. Ramaphosa said today.

Mr. Slovo added that holding a second round of "full democracy" elections as soon as a new constitution was drafted would waste time and money, and probably produce an outcome little different from the first election.

In their recent talks, the Government and the congress have also reached a compromise on the divisive question of how to protect the interests of regions.

The Government has dropped its demand that regional powers and borders be permanently entrenched before elections, agreeing instead to leave the final distribution of powers to the new assembly. The congress, in turn, agreed that half of the assembly seats would be apportioned by regions, and that questions of regional power would require a two-thirds vote of those members.

This agreement drew a passionate protest from Mr. Buthelezi, whose support is concentrated primarily in the far eastern Natal province. Along with a few other regional leaders, he has made strong regional powers his highest priority.

Some Issues Unsettled

Congress and Government officials said many details remain to be negotiated, and a few major differences have yet to be bridged, including the future of the army and the police.

The progress could also bog down because of the evident burnout of negotiators.

Mr. de Klerk is rumored to plan a major shake up of his Cabinet, which has been visibly exhausted by trying to govern and negotiate simultaneously.

 Article Review form at end of book.

Voting

From partitions . . .

Organized into four white-run provinces and 10 black "home-lands," ostensibly self-governing, but heavily dependent on South African subsidies.

. . . To provinces

Homelands are abolished. The nine provincial legislatures will each select 10 members of a national Senate. The provinces administer the police, schools, health and other services, but will be subject to the laws of Parliament.

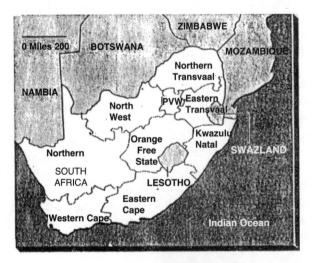

Article Review Form at end of book.

The Voters

Each voter has two votes. Parliament will have two houses: a 400-seat National Assembly, elected by the people, and a 90-seat Senate, with 10 members elected indirectly by each of the nine provincial legislatures. The voter votes twice, once for a single party or organisation on the national lists and once for a single party or organisation on the provincial lists. National Assembly seats are then allocated by proportional representation, 200 from national lists and 200 from provincial lists, except in the case of the National party, which has no national list and will choose all its representatives from provincial lists. Provincial legislatures will range from 30 to 86 members, seats allocated by proportional representation. National Cabinet posts will be allocated proportionately from parties holding a minimum of 20 seats. The President will be elected by a joint session of both houses.

Article Review Form at end of book.

Orange Free State

African	81.4%
White	15.9%
Indian	0.1%
Coloured	2.6%

Pop 2.5m (1.6m voters)
Legislature 30 seats
8 parties

Northern Cape

African	30.6%
White	19.1%
Indian	0.2%
Coloured	50.0%

Pop 0.7m
(0.44m voters)
Legislature 30 seats
7 parties

Western Cape

African	18.4%
White	27.6%
Indian	0.9%
Coloured	53.0%

Pop 3.4m (2.4m voters)
Legislature 42 seats
13 parties

Eastern Cape

African	83.2%
White	8.6%
Indian	0.3%
Coloured	7.8%

Pop 5.9m (3.2m voters)
Legislature 56 seats
8 parties

Natal

African	78.0%
White	9.7%
Indian	10.9%

Coloured	1.4%

Pop 8m (4.6m voters)
Legislature 81 seats
10 parties

North-West

African	88.0%
White	10.5%
Indian	0.3%
Coloured	1.2%

Pop 3.3m (1.7m voters)
Legislature 30 seats
7 parties

Eastern Transvaal

African	86.7%
White	12.2%
Indian	0.5%
Coloured	0.6%

Pop 2.6m (1.6m voters)
Legislature 30 seats
8 parties

Pretoria/Witwatersrand/ Vereeniging (PWV)

African	62.3%
White	32.1%
Indian	2.1%
Coloured	3.4%

Pop 6.5m (4.9m voters)
Legislature 86 seats
14 parties

Northern Transvaal

African	95.5%
White	4.2%
Indian	0.1%
Coloured	0.2%

Pop 4.7m (2.3m voters)
Legislature 40 seats
9 parties

Final Election Results

Total Votes		%
African National Congress	12,237,655	62.6
National Party	3,983,690	20.4
Inkatha Freedom Party	2,058,294	10.5
Freedom Front	424,555	2.2
Democratic Party	338,426	1.7
Pan Africanist Congress	243,478	1.2

African Christian Democratic Party	88,104	0.5
Other Parties, Total Vote		
African Muslim Party	34,466	
African Moderates Congress Party	27,690	
Dikwankwetla Party	19,451	
Federal Party	17,633	
Minority Party	13,433	
SOCCER Party	10,375	

African Democratic Movement	9,886
Women's Rights Peace Party	6,434
Ximoko Progressive Party	6,320
Keep it Straight and Simple	5,916
Workers List Party	4,169
Luso South African Party	3,293

National Assembly Seats: ANC 252, NP 82, IFP 43, FF 9, PAC 5, ACDP 2

Provincial Legislature Seats

Pretoria-Witwatersrand-Vereeniging (PWV)
ANC 50, NP 21, FF 5, DP 5, IFP 3, Others 2

Western Cape
NP 23, ANC 14, Others 5

Northern Cape
ANC 15, NP 12, Others 3

North West
ANC 26, NP 3, Others 1

Northern Transvaal
ANC 38, Others 2

Eastern Transvaal
ANC 25, NP 3, FF 2

Orange Free State
ANC 24, NP 4, Others 2

Eastern Cape
ANC 48, NP 6, Others 2

KwaZulu/Natal
IFP 41, ANC 26, NP 9, Others 5

The ANC has a marginally higher percentage membership in the Constitutional Assembly than in the National Assembly, although still short of the two-thirds majority which would have enabled it to unilaterally rewrite South Africa's constitution.

The Constitutional Assembly (CA), to be constituted on May 24th, comprises the 400 National Assembly (NA) members who were sworn in on May 16th, sitting together with the 90 senators sworn in on May 20th.

The CA is to be tasked with writing South Africa's final constitution over the next two years, applying 34 principles set out in the interim constitution. The ANC will have 252 NA members and 60 senators, giving it 63.67% of the seats in the Constitutional Assembly compared with 63% in the NA.

The NP, with 82 members in the NA and 17 in the Senate, will have 20.25% of the seats in the CA compared with 20.5 in the NA. The IFP has 9.79% of the seats in the CA, the FF 2.85, the DP 2.04, the PAC 1.02 and the ACDP 0.4. Neither the PAC nor the ACDP has any senators.

(GD 7/5, SAPA 19/5: *BBC Mon.*)

Article Review Form at end of book.

The Main Parties and Leaders

African National Congress

The leading anti-apartheid organisation says it will redistribute wealth to redress the great disparity between blacks and whites. But it also stresses support for a mixed economy in which both private enterprise and government can play a role in ending the inequalities created by apartheid. It has backed away from plans to nationalise key industries.

Specific election promises include the provision of better health and education, millions of new homes, and more than two million jobs over the next 10 years.

Its greatest asset is Mr. Mandela, once the most famous prisoner in the world, extremely active and energetic at 75. It is expected to win about 60% of the vote for national parliament.

Nelson Mandela, 75, President of the African National Congress, spent 27 years in prison for his fight against apartheid. The left-wing ANC, which is expected to win a clear majority in the 400-seat National Assembly, has moderated its policies with the approach of the elections and has moved away from its initial entrenched policy of nationalisation. It now officially advocates a mixed economy, and during the campaign Mr. Mandela made a point of appealing to the business vote. The ANC promises lower taxes for those earning less than 4,000 rand (£240) a month. It pledges to provide work and training for 2.5m more people over the next decade.

National Party

In power since 1948, originally on the platform of racial separation, it now claims to be the party which killed apartheid. Open to all races since 1990, it is opposed to a concentration of power in a new central government, and stands for a strong devolution of authority.

It will oppose any socialist experiments to redistribute wealth and will fight moves to raise taxes. Promotion of private enterprise as the driving force in the economy will be the only way to reduce unemployment and poverty, it says.

Coloured, Indians and a majority of whites, but only a minority of blacks are expected to give the party something above 20% of the vote, enough to make Mr. de Klerk, joint Nobel Peace Prize winner with Mr. Mandela, second Vice-President.

Frederik Willem de Klerk, 58, leads the National Party, which institutionalized apartheid and has ruled South Africa since 1948. As state President Mr. de Klerk turned the party on its head in 1990 by announcing that he was abolishing apartheid, freeing Nelson Mandela and "unbanning" black liberation movements. The National Party presents itself as a centre-right, non-racial party with the experience to lead South Africa into the post-apartheid future. Mr. de Klerk, who replaced President Botha in a Cabinet coup in 1989, told *The Times* that he decided to end white rule to avert a "devastating revolution" in the country.

Inkatha Freedom Party

It argues that there will be no peace in South Africa unless the regions are allowed powers and independence which cannot be interfered with by a central government. It also places emphasis on private enterprise to reduce poverty and unemployment.

Essentially Zulu-based, it came into the election late after Chief Buthelezi failed to win more powers for the regions. It is expected to win a third or more of the votes in the KwaZulu-Natal regional assembly, but only about seven per cent or less nationally.

Mangosuthu Buthelezi, 65, took his Inkatha Freedom Party into the election process at the last minute after an agreement to reinforce the status of King Goodwill Zwelithini of the Zulus and its KwaZulu-Natal heartland. Chief Buthelezi split with the ANC in the late 1970s and there has been savage Inkatha-ANC conflict among the Zulus, the largest ethnic group in South Africa. Inkatha advocates conservative, free-market policies and harnessing resources to fight poverty, unemployment, homelessness and hunger. It demands entrenched powers for provincial governments, such as the right to levy taxes and form their own armies.

Freedom Front

Votes for the Freedom Front will be used to assess support, and the possible location of a volkstaat or white homeland. Although this is unlikely to ever be accepted, the constitution guarantees that the issue must at least be considered after the elections.

The party is expected to win about five per cent of the national vote entitling General Viljoen, a retired Chief of the South African Defence Force, to a post in a government of national unity.

Constand Viljoen, 60, the former Chief of the South African Defence Force, broke ranks with white hardliners who were boycotting the elections and demanding an Afrikaner homeland. In March he formed the Freedom Front. This includes former members of the pro-apartheid Conservative Party, which was represented in the last white parliament but opposes the elections. The Freedom Front wants a white homeland or volkstaat, but believes this cannot be achieved by abstaining from the polls. It hopes to pick up votes from the right wing of the National Party. It says that protecting minorities' rights and self-determination will bring peace.

Pan Africanist Congress

Regards itself as the true liberator of South Africa, and only recently suspended the armed struggle, three years after the ANC. It emphasizes the return of the land to Africans as the key to curing all other ills.

Mr. Makwetu was jailed many times for his anti-apartheid activities. The PAC is expected to win about four per cent of the vote nationally.

Clarence Makwetu, 63, leads the radical Pan Africanist Congress, founded in 1959 by a breakaway faction of the ANC. Before suspending its "armed struggle" in January, the PAC used the slogan "one settler, one bullet" and the Azanian People's Liberation Army, its guerrilla

wing, attacked whites. The PAC wants land returned to dispossessed blacks and greater state control of the economy. It seems strongest in the Cape town and Port Elizabeth areas. Militant black youths around Cape Town have identified themselves with the killers of Amy Biehl, the American exchange student who was killed in 1993 by a mob chanting the PAC slogan.

Democratic Party

Like the National Party, it claims to have "killed apartheid." Expected to win about three per cent of the vote nationally it is seen as a voice in parliament to help keep the other parties honest.

Zach de Beer, 65, is a doctor and businessman, as well as a politician. He heads the Democratic Party, which was formed in 1989 when the Progressive Federal Party (PFP), the Independent Party and the National Democratic Movement merged. The PFP had a history of opposition to apartheid. Helen Suzman was its most celebrated member when she sat in parliament. The Democratic Party portrays itself as the only national party with "clean hands." It supports individual rights and a free-market economy. The reform of the National Party has diminished to prospects for the Democratic Party as a liberal anti-apartheid movement.

 Article Review Form at end of book.

South Africa's Indians Changing Loyalties

Domination by the blacks now feared

Kenneth B. Noble
Special to The New York Times

Phoenix, South Africa, April 18— There was nothing obviously threatening about the three black women who knocked on Neele Rajoo's door last month and said they were looking for work. Although she had no use for another housekeeper, Mrs. Rajoo, a 46-year-old shop clerk of Indian descent, offered them a seat and some water.

"They were very well dressed and very educated and spoke perfect English," Mrs. Rajoo said.

Then, matter-of-factly, as though she were buying a packet of gum, one of the women placed a two-rand coin—about 60 cents—into her empty cup. This, she said, was a deposit on Mrs. Rajoo's house. They would return after election day, she added, to take possession of what was rightfully theirs.

Odd encounters like this one have been reported with increasing frequency in the last few months here, part of a campaign that appears to be organized but remains mysterious in its origins.

The Message Seems Clear

For Mrs. Rajoo, however, there was no mystery in the message: blacks are poised to seize not only power but just about anything else they want, confident that the future black Government will do little to stop them. And that explains why she and her sister Kogie, 47, who live together in a comfortable two-story house in one of South Africa's few racially mixed residential areas, say they expect to cast their vote later this month for the National Party, the inventors and enforcers of apartheid.

"I've lived and worked with blacks all my life, and I've always supported their struggle and supported the African National Congress," Mrs. Rajoo said, "But now we're scared. When we look at the blacks, whether it is the A.N.C. or Inkatha, all we see is violence and fighting."

The Rajoos' shift in allegiances illustrate the extraordinary changes under way here on the outskirts of Durban, a port city and commercial center of Natal Province and home to the largest concentration of Indians outside of India. Indians account for not quite 3 percent of South Africa's population of 35 million.

In yet another reverberation from the collapse of South Africa's apartheid system, the bulk of the Indian community, once considered a natural ally of the black opposition, is now inclined to support the National Party, according to recent polls and regional analyses.

For years, South Africa's one million Indians have faced a quandary. They are resented by many blacks, who see them as exploitative outsiders who treat Africans with condescension, if not outright disdain, yet they have never been accepted by whites.

At the same time, people of Indian descent have been to the forefront of those opposed to the apartheid system. India, for instance, was the first country to impose sanctions against South Africa 47 years ago and for decades the Indian Government recognized the African National Congress as the sole representative of the South African people.

The congress has long had numerous Indians at every level.

Perhaps most telling, Mohandas K. Gandhi, who spent two decades here around the start of the century, established the Natal Indian Congress, now the oldest political organization in the country and among the first to mount organized resistance to the policies of successive white governments that disenfranchised blacks.

By most accounts, Gandhi took little interest in blacks, but his theories powerfully influenced the African National Congress, which was founded in 1912 and retained a creed of nonviolence for nearly half a century. Nelson Mandela has regularly invoked Gandhi as his spiritual mentor.

Given the Indian community's long history in the black resistance struggle, analysts initially assumed that Indians would line up squarely behind the black-dominated political parties, mostly the African National Congress but also the Zulu-based Inkatha Freedom Party in Natal. But lately there appears to be a clear shift of support among them toward the National Party.

A Fear of Black Domination

African National Congress officials deny any signs of disaffection by potential Indian voters. "We have people out in the community, and we know that the Indians are strongly behind us," said Jacob Zuma, the congress's senior official in Natal.

But others reject this argument. Among those who believe that the National Party is likely to win big among Indians is Mahmoud Rajab, a former member of the disbanded three-chamber Parliament, which included Indians and people of mixed race, but excluded the country's black majority of 26 million people. He is now a parliamentary candidate of the Democratic Party, traditionally the liberal opposition to the National Party. "People are supporting the National Party because they fear black domination," Mr. Rajab said.

He estimates that in Natal the National Party will win 55 to 60 percent of the Indian vote, while the Democratic Party and the African National Congress will obtain about 15 percent each. By comparison, he estimates that perhaps five years ago, the National Party would have been fortunate to get more than 15 percent of the Indian vote. Other independent polls have shown similar support for the National Party.

Sathie Naidoo, 37, a former public relations man who is now a National Party candidate, said all issues boiled down to one central question: which party can best protect the interests of the majority of Indians who, despite apartheid, have prospered, especially in comparison with blacks.

"The Indian community in South Africa lives better than Indians anywhere else in the world," Mr. Naidoo said. "There is nobody here who goes to bed without a meal in their stomach, and there is nobody here who sleeps on the street.

"The way the Indian looks at it," Mr. Naidoo added, "who does the A.N.C. represent? Do they represent the masses of blacks walking the street, unemployed and uneducated, or are they representing me, who owns a house, whose children are going to school. That's where the fear is coming from."

The former allies of the blacks have turned wary.

Indians Wary of 'the List'

Similar fears have been addressed in similar fashion in the western Cape Province, where surveys show that millions of mixed-race people, whose status has traditionally been only marginally better than that of blacks, are clearly disposed toward voting for the National Party.

Mr. Naidoo said that many Indians were especially concerned that a leftist A.N.C. government would stifle their entrepreneurial skills and money-making potential. Many Indians are also said to look nervously toward the new and often vaguely outlined affirmative action policies that many companies have begun to adopt, and a concept that the African National Congress strongly supports.

Nirode Brawdaw, manager of The Leader, a weekly newspaper in Durban aimed at the Indian community, said:

"The list works like this. If you're a black woman, you're great and you can walk into any door right now. If you're a black man, you're second. Then come colored and Indian women, Indian and colored men, and then whites."

He added, "People are saying, there's my son, he has a B.A. degree, but can't find a job right now because no corporation is hiring an Indian or colored."

Blacks Invade Housing Tract

For Mrs. Rajoo and many other Indians, the fear of black domination is not an abstract notion. In interviews, several dozen Indians almost invariably cited the example of a housing tract of 800 cottages near here called Cato Manor, which was built for Indian families.

In November, just as the finishing touches were being put on the subdivision, several hundred blacks from an overcrowded township nearby scratched their names on the doors and moved in. Perhaps just as astonishing, Mrs. Rajoo said, neither the lame-duck white authorities nor the future black Government leaders made any effort to evict the invaders.

The blacks felt they should be entitled to the houses, and they were adamant about it, Mrs. Rajoo said. "They wrote down on the doors, remember the 1949 riots," she said, a pointed allusion to the massacre in which 142 Indians died when black resentment over their treatment by Indian landlords exploded in an orgy of killing centered on Cato Manor.

"Cato Manor taught Indians a lesson that we'll never forget," Mrs. Rajoo said. "We have to look after our own interests first."

 Article Review form at end of book.

South Africa
ANC Conference

The African National Congress (ANC) gathered in Bloemfontein for its first conference in South Africa since it was unbanned in 1991. It was an opportunity for frank assessment.

President Nelson Mandela, in a frank and measured opening address to the African National Congress's 49th national conference on December 17th, signalled the overthrow of some of the ANC's long-held beliefs about itself and the country.

In a lengthy speech interrupted for a five-minute interval, Mr. Mandela in effect urged the 3,000 delegates to grasp the realities of the new situation and to translate the ANC's April election victory into a campaign "to set the country on a new moral footing".

His speech, which drew frequent applause, took issue with a litany of militantly-held ANC beliefs. He said: The ANC would have lost the election in Kwazulu/Natal even if there had been better security and supervision; that reconstruction and reconciliation were not "separate programmes directed variously at specific racial groups" and that the government was not "pandering to white fears"; that privatisation "depends not on ideological imperatives, but on the balance of economic necessity"; that nonpayment of rent and services, like corruption in the public and private sector, was related to "the nation's morality"; and that fiscal discipline, macroeconomic stability and economic growth which "tend to irritate those justifiably impatient for change" were "neither luxuries nor requirements foreign to the ANC's own policies".

Frank Assessment: Mandela

Mr. Mandela appeared determined to steer the conference away from a "lament over apartheid" and to a balanced assessment of the ANC's strengths and weaknesses. He warned the ANC against concluding that "we are merely in political office—weak, tied hand and foot by some terrible agreements that we reached in negotiations."

"The other extreme is to create the impression that we are all-powerful, ready to realize each and every one of the programmes we would like to implement".

Mr. Mandela dwelt at length on the economy the government of national unity had inherited. South Africa was an "over-taxed society" which could not rely on "handouts from donors or from increasing government debt", he said. "Rather we must operate within our means as we rearrange government spending and create optimum conditions for economic growth". However, "the funds to accelerate reconstruction and ensure economic growth are concentrated in a few white hands".

Local cartels blocking foreign investors were a problem as was tax evasion, industrial competitiveness and productivity. "Visible changes" would need to be the prime feature of government operations in 1995. Jobs had to be created, the state machinery had to be restructured (if necessary using legislation that did not conflict with constitutional guarantees), the budget deficit had to be reduced and wasteful expenditure eliminated. The ANC will continue to urge that the belt-tightening measures and steps to narrow the wage gap which government has undertaken, is an example that

should be followed by the private sector," said Mr. Mandela. (SAPA 17/12: *BBC Mon.*)

New Strategies: Mbeki

The ANC needed new strategies and tactics to deal with the reality of having come to power, ANC National Chairman Thabo Mbeki said on December 18th. He was speaking during the tabling of his strategy and tactics document "From Resistance to Reconstruction and Development" at the national conference. The document will guide the ANC in the three-year period ahead.

Mr. Mbeki told the 3,000 delegates at the University of the Orange Free State that the ANC had achieved political power but that South Africa remained a racially divided society. He called for thorough transformation of the civil service, saying the sooner this was done the better. The army and the police as well as the judiciary had to be transformed to reflect the composition of South African society. He said the top echelons of the civil service were filled by whites.

Mr. Mbeki said the ANC had made compromises to bring about a transfer of political power but that it had not sold out. Political power now had to be translated into effective economic and social changes. The economy needed to be deracialized and "monopoly domination" ended to bring about economic emancipation.

The document noted that the upliftment of the black majority remains the ANC's central objective, but that this did not mean the ANC's programmes were anti-white in character. Mr. Mbeki said the ANC needed new strategies to insure against the "danger of the ANC and the democratic movement being outflanked by people

and groups that pop up and take advantage of the fact that there are urgent and pressing needs". (SAPA 18/12: *BBC Mon.*)

Financial Problems: Ramaphosa

The ANC has been beset by huge organisational, financial and managerial problems since taking power and must sharpen up its act, delegates at the party's conference were told.

The party's secretary-general, Mr. Cyril Ramaphosa, told the congress in Bloemfontein finances were a shambles, the grassroots felt alienated and were in disarray. MPs needed a code of conduct and ministers had to be more accountable.

Conceding that the ANC was "riddled with problems", he said profligacy at all levels of the party had placed a huge strain on its finances.

"We do have financial difficulties", he said. "We are still addressing the problems of the massive debt we have incurred after the elections. We do have a number of debts still."

His assessment of the past seven months came on the second day of the ANC's first congress since 1991, billed as a time for the party to return "to its roots" and reassess its priorities.

Mr. Ramaphosa's speech to the delegates mirrored the sober mood of grassroots members, who feel the ANC is proving slow to adjust from protest politics to holding office.

He singled out for attack a tendency for indecisiveness, accusing the party leaders and MPS of vacillating when criticised, and of being "reactive", rather than "proactive".

He also gave warning that MPs should beware being beguiled by the torrents of praise for the party and its leader, President Nelson Mandela, lest its lost sight of its primary objectives—redressing the inequalities of apartheid. (D Tel 19/12)

NEC

ANC militants swept the boards at elections for the ANC's National Executive Committee (NEC) on December 21st. Known hardliners won the top NEC positions when results were announced on the final day of the ANC's 49th national conference at the University of the Orange Free State.

Former Transkei military ruler and now Environmental Affairs and Tourism Deputy Minister Bantu Holomisa came in at number one of the 60 NEC positions, voted for with 1,915 votes. The next four positions were taken by leaders who have maintained a consistently hard line in their approach to national and party issues. They are: Posts, Telecommunications and Broadcasting Minster Pallo Jordan, who won 1,879 votes; former ANC Youth League firebrand Peter Mokaba with 1,824 votes; Transport Minister Mac Maharaj with 1,818 votes; and ANC Women's League President Winnie Mandela with 1,802 votes. Their election signalled a possible hardening of attitudes in the NEC in the future.

President Nelson Mandela, whose initiatives to have more leaders from the provinces and minorities elected to the NEC was earlier defeated, called in his closing address for "fresh blood" in the leadership. He said the ANC needed to develop a younger leadership corps if it was to thrive as an organisation. However, the conference had disproved the "prophets of doom" who had predicted leadership battles and

grassroots disenchantment with serving ANC leaders.

The six senior NEC officials are: President—Nelson Mandela; Vice-President—Thabo Mbeki; National President—Jacob Zoma; Secretary General—Cyril Ramaphosa; deputy secretary-general—Cheryl Carolus. Mr. Walter Sisula (82) announced his retirement from the post of Vice-president before the conference.

Resolutions

The ANC would use its majority position in the Government of National Unity (GNU) to accelerate changes to the state and society, the ANC's 49th national conference resolved on December 21st.

Backed by its April election victory, the ANC would transform the civil service and security forces. The ANC's National Executive Committee was instructed to "examine the necessity or otherwise of amending the interim constitution with a view of enabling the government to implement its policies on the civil service." The resolutions noted that while the GNU "imposes some constraints, it is imperative the ANC assumes full responsibility for its overwhelming mandate, and that as a movement we drive forward the process of transformation from our new positions in government".

The liberation of black people remained incomplete and the ANC would remain a broad-based liberation movement whose character would assist the implementation of government programmes to transform society. The resolutions said the ANC would retain its historic bias to the "black working class" and the rural poor. "We reaffirm the liberation of black people in general and the Africans in particular as the main content of our national democratic revolution."

The "total liberation" of the black majority, including "Coloured" and Indian communities, was the "only viable path towards lasting stability and prosperity". Whites were beginning to experience "real freedom and security".

The ANC also said it would review the mandate of the Public Service Commission.

A resolution also called for an independent and representative prosecuting authority, including the possibility of a central Attorney-General's Office. "The restructuring of courts should also examine the possibility of establishing community courts, traditional courts and mechanisms to facilitate accessibility to courts."

The conference said the structure of media ownership and management did not allow for the free flow of information.

ANC Deputy President Thabo Mbeki said the ANC had not adopted any changes to its economic policies, including privatisation. However, the conference called for "reviewing and restructuring of state assets" and endorsed the government's six-point plan to restructure state involvement in the economy.

The ANC would also support a gun-free society.

Transitional local government councils were a bridge between apartheid and democracy and the ANC called on all provincial executive committees to evaluate these councils in terms of the negotiation process and the selection of nominated councillors. A resolution was passed for an ANC strategy workshop for local government elections.

The ANC would launch a campaign, "mobilisation for a learning nation", to mobilise people for the transformation of education. The campaign is expected to take off within two months of the conference.

Conference also mandated the ANC to push for democratic majority rule in the writing of a new constitution. Enforced power-sharing was rejected. The ANC said it had emerged from the conference "stronger and more united than ever before". (SAPA 21/12; *BBC Mon.*)

IFP to Pull Out?

A special Inkatha Freedom Party (**IFP**) conference early in 1995 will consider a plan by party hardliners to quit the government of National Unity and play the role of a Westminster-styled opposition party, IFP insiders revealed in mid-December.

This could be followed with a push to dissolve the IFP-dominated KwaZulu/Natal government as a prelude to a fresh election in the province in a bid to strengthen the IFP's 51% majority, the sources added.

The sources said the IFP plans to throw down the gauntlet to the ANC in KwaZulu/Natal early in 1995. Its strategy will revolve around using the provincial legislature to claim "real federal powers" on issues like policing and housing, thus sparking a major constitutional confrontation with the ANC and central government.

The IFP may also push for a dissolution of the provincial government on the grounds that its attempts to govern are being frustrated and call a snap poll, the sources said. (WM+G 15/12)

Gauteng

The PWV province has been renamed Gauteng by a majority vote in the PWV Legislature. Now Parliament will be asked to act "without delay" to give effect to the change.

Many cries of "Viva Gauteng" and "Mayibuye Gauteng" emanated from the African National Congress side of the House during the "emotionally charged debate". (St 8/12)

 Article Review form at end of book.

Bill Introduces Compulsory Schooling and Outlaws Exclusion on Grounds of Race

**Patrick Bulger
and Adam Cooke**

Education Minister Sibusiso Bengu yesterday introduced a new law to force parents to send their children between the ages of 7 and 15 to school or face a fine or up to three months in jail.

The South African Schools Bill signals the death knell for apartheid education by introducing compulsory schooling and by taking away from school governing bodies the right to exclude children because of race.

But the draft law, which will be scrutinised in the National Assembly and the Senate before being passed into law, leaves the disputed Model C system largely intact. The immovable properties of Model C schools, widely regarded as "privatised apartheid" will now become the property of the state once more.

The bill gives governing bodies a large degree of discretion over matters such as school facilities, fees, religious instruction and language.

Although no child can be turned away from a school on the grounds of inability to pay fees, governing bodies are free to levy school fees and may take legal action against parents who refuse to pay the fees. The governing bodies will comprise parents not employed at schools, educators (teachers), members of staff other than teachers, and learners (pupils) in the eight grade or higher.

The bill also provides for independent schools and for state subsidies for independent schools.

It stops short of creating a situation, once feared by opponents of nonracial education, that the new government would reintroduce highly centralised control of schools. The bill makes provision for public schools on private property, such as farm schools.

The bill outlaws corporal punishment, and teachers who insist on beating their pupils will open themselves to a charge of assault.

Bengu, at a media briefing at Parliament yesterday, hailed the bill as "a charter of democratic empowerment for all schools and school communities".

Kevin Nkoane, a specialist at Wits University's Centre for Education Policy Development, said the approach was also politically more saleable, "especially to poorer communities as it is more democratic and allows parents themselves to decide on whether to pay fees or not".

Johan de Jager, chairman of Gauteng's Association of Governing Bodies, said he was relieved to see educational principles had, in the end, driven the new policy.

He said areas that had been identified as impractical in earlier drafts had now been given serious attention: "The system is now more workable."

Bengu, referring to an intense round of negotiations conducted by the Department of Education and the Model C schools, said the negotiation process was a "magnificent democratic conversation about educational transformation".

One aspect that has not yet been resolved, however, is the position of the about 5,000 teachers employed in Model C schools over and above the quota allowed by the Government. The extra teachers have been given a re-prieve until December 1997 and negotiations until then will be conducted to establish exactly what status extra teachers will enjoy, if any.

Article Review Form at end of book.

Killing Machine

Witnesses tell TRC of life in the shadow of hit squads

Sapa. South African hit squads operating in Europe in the 1980s made several attempts on former African National Congress envoy Mr. Godfrey Motsepe's life, the Truth and Reconciliation Commission heard yesterday.

"At times, I felt like I was walking next to my grave," he told the TRC sitting in Pretoria.

Motsepe, now a director in the Department of Foreign Affairs, said he was instructed to set up an ANC mission in Western Europe in the mid-1980s. He was based in Brussels, Belgium.

The first attempt to assassinate him was on February 4, 1988. He was working late in the ANC office when the doorbell rang. A man posing as a journalist asked for an interview.

Motsepe said he realised the visitor was not telling the truth and turned down the request.

"About 10 minutes later, I went on the balcony. I saw a man with a skull cap and his collar turned up. As I was standing there, he fired two shots at me." Only a splinter hit him.

The next attempt was about six weeks later.

"It was on the night of March 27 when I was awoken by a telephone call from the Belgian authorities," Motsepe said, "They informed me that a 17kg bomb had been found at the entrance to the office."

Callousness of the Attempt

It had been set to go off the next morning at 9am when he usually arrived at the office. Motsepe said even the Belgian authorities had been surprised at the callousness of the attempt as the bomb would have caused extensive destruction.

Two days later SA's killing machine swung into action and the ANC representative in Paris, Ms Dulcie September, was shot dead.

"It seems as if that was the work of the same hit squad, which was travelling around Western Europe at the time, trying

"Killing Machine Witnesses Tell Truth and Reconciliation Committee of Life in the Shadow of Hit Squads," SOWETAN, August 16, 1996. Reprinted by permission.

to eliminate all ANC people or activists," Motsepe said.

The hit squad had been in Britain before travelling to Belgium. "Scotland Yard tipped off the Belgian authorities that there was a group of dubious characters from South Africa coming across. They even sent photographs of these people."

Motsepe said one of them had been with the South African Embassy in London before the British government declared him *persona non grata.* "They showed me a photograph of this man, and this was the same one who had shot at me. Our eyes had met for a split second."

He said the man was a police sergeant at the time, and had later been promoted to captain. "I know who this man is. He lives in Cape Town."

His name was not revealed during the testimony, but it is known to the commission. Commissioner Mr. Wynand Malan said the man had been contacted and asked for his comments.

Parents from townships around Pretoria yesterday also recounted to the TRC the murders and disappearances of their children in the 1980s. Some said they had suffered harassment by police hunting their children for political activities.

Mr. Piet Mothupi of Atteridgeville said his son Daniel (13) was shot dead by a policeman on February 10, 1986. "When I left for work in the morning, Daniel was preparing to go to school. At about noon I received a telephone call informing me that he was dead."

Mothupi said he later heard that his son had been forced by activists to boycott school that day. Daniel was shot by an elderly policeman who had been driving past a roadblock set up by protesters.

Ms Ellen Morudu said police had often visited her home asking about her son Moss, who disappeared in 1987. "They pestered me."

Her home was once ransacked and her furniture damaged while she was at work. Her son was a member of the Council of SA Students.

Ms Selína Makao said her Saulsville house was bombed by police in April 1986.

This was after countless visits by police looking for her son Stanley, who was a member of the ANC. "I woke up at 1am and saw my house was on fire," Makao said. She suffered serious burns.

Article Review Form at end of book.

The Trouble with South Korea

In politics, if not in economics, ordinary South Koreans appear much more sophisticated than their rulers.

Students and unionists, 15,000 of them, fought running battles with the riot police in Seoul on Wednesday—iron bars and stones against tear-gas cluster bombs. Pickets outside the Hyundai shipyard in Ulsan punched and poured yellow paint over strikebreakers, who smashed their way into work on bulldozers. Things are getting so out of hand, says the government, that communist North Korea may take advantage of the situation to start a revolution in the South.

To anyone standing outside Myongdong cathedral in Seoul, where the leaders of the outlawed

Korean Confederation of Trade Unions have been seeking sanctuary from arrest, listening to the yells of protest, smelling the teargas and watching the riot police in action, South Korea might seem to be on the brink of chaos. It is not.

True, hundreds of thousands of workers have downed spanners and taken to the streets to complain about the new labour laws passed on December 26th, which make it easier for companies to sack workers. True, there has been violence and the authorities have begun to arrest union leaders. But no one has been killed (touch wood). And the millions who were supposed to take part in this week's scheduled general strike have, for the most part, clocked in as usual. The army, on standby to man the buses and power stations, has not been needed. The strike-busters at Hyundai are numerous enough to keep the shipyard running at almost full capacity.

Much of the comment abroad about how extraordinary it is to see an "Asian tiger" suffering from labour disputes is amnesic. The strikes at Hyundai in 1989 were much worse, when workers barricaded themselves in for 109 days and could be dislodged only by thousands of riot policemen in speedboats and helicopters. This year's strikes will be expensive; the cost in lost output is at least $2 billion so far. But South Korea's system of government is not under threat.

The government of President Kim Young Sam has handled the dispute extraordinarily badly. By forcing the laws through in a secret parliamentary session, and then trying to turn the protests into an issue of "national security", it has made a freely elected government look like an authoritarian rabble. That has obscured the real case for a more flexible labour market in South Korea, which is that the ban on laying off labour obliges big companies to hang on to redundant workers, while small firms fail because they cannot find enough good people to work for them.

South Korea's economy is dominated by a few vast diversified conglomerates, the *chaebol*. Four groups—Hyundai, Samsung, Daewoo and LG (formerly Lucky Goldstar)—account for a third of the total sales of South Korea's companies and over half the country's exports. These firms are so important to the economy that the government could not let them go bust. So banks consider them super-safe borrowers, and lend them a disproportionate amount of the country's available capital. Small firms then find it hard to raise money.

As the *chaebol* put smarter robots on their production lines and dream up better ways of organizing their sales teams, they often find that they can produce and sell the same number of widgets with fewer staff. Since they are not allowed to sack people, they are always having to make work for idle hands. This drives them constantly to diversify into areas where they have no expertise. Hyundai, for example, makes ships, cars and building equipment—and also runs department stores and sells insurance. With unemployment a negligible 2%, and the *chaebol* hanging on to most of the best workers, start-ups wither and small firms stay small.

Deregulating the labour market is an essential first step to curing these ills. But convincing organised labour of this will not be easy. The government is planning to soften the blow by announcing increases in South Korea's (currently almost nonexistent) unemployment benefits and allowing unions greater freedom to organize. Mr. Kim has also promised that there will be no mass layoffs. He is probably telling the truth. Korea's growth rate slowed from 9% in 1995 to an estimated 6.8% in 1996, but unemployment of the sort that plagues Europe is not on the cards in the foreseeable future.

The government's case would be believed more readily if it were not so transparently lying about other things. The ruling party claims that the recent strikes are a protest not only against the new labour laws, but also against the new security legislation passed at the same time. Doubtless, some unionists do object to the fact that Mr. Kim has increased the power of the security police to arrest people for the vaguely defined offence of "praising" or "benefiting" North Korea. But this is clearly not what they are striking about.

Although Mr Kim is constitutionally barred from seeking a second term at the next presidential election, scheduled for December 18th, he would like to ensure that a protégé of his gets the job. By commie-bashing, he hopes to endear himself to his party's conservative wing, which distrusts him for being an ex-dissident.

But the official reason for giving the security services these new powers is absurd. Few people seriously believe that democracy in South Korea is under threat from a fifth column that takes orders from the North. Nonetheless, last October, the public prosecutors' office claimed that South Korea had 10,000 "core leftists" and 30,000 more lukewarm pinkos. The new security law is designed to prevent this group from taking over the country.

This leads to cases such as that of Jin Kwan, a prominent Buddhist leader, who was arrested in October for alleged pro-Northern activities. These included trying to talk to Buddhists on the other side of the barbed-wire border and lobbing on behalf of three aged former political prisoners who wanted to rejoin their families in North Korea. In another episode in October, the editor of the *Dongkuk University Times* and a student journalist were arrested for publicising the views of students who thought that demonstrators should not be arrested so often.

Among the sins proscribed by the national security law are owning North Korean books or magazines (without permission), sending letters to North Korea (ditto) and visiting North Korea's home page on the Internet. The national security agency is worried that this laughable piece of propaganda might fool gullible southerners into believing that life is better in the North. The website shows enticing pictures of North Korean "beauties" (wearing green military uniforms) and describes a "nice meal" obtainable in the people's paradise—clams baked in petrol.

The South Korean government is, of course, right to have some worries about North Korea. Northern commandos have sneaked across the border before to create mischief, and may well do so again. If the North were to collapse suddenly into the arms of the South, which is far from impossible, the burden on the South would be huge. But the one area where the North poses no threat is in the battle for the loyalty of ordinary South Koreans—hard as it may be at present for workers in the South to feel that they live in a model democracy.

Article Review Form at the end of book.

A Korean Deal Emerges

The Korean people cannot live divided forever.
—*South Korean President Kim Young-sam in a speech on Aug. 15, National Liberation Day*

"We want [North Korean President] Kim Jong-il to stay in power, even if we don't like him.
—*Park Jin, an economist at Seoul's influential Korea Development Institute*

Damon Darlin

In the two seemingly contradictory statements above, you have the main problem faced by South Korea today, and its likely solution. The problem is how South Korea can bail out the North without running up the kind of reunification costs West Germany took on when it rescued East Germany in 1990. The solution? Delaying reunification for a few years by supporting Kim Jon-il with economic and technological aid.

North Korea has a population of 22 million, only slightly more than East Germany had; like East Germany, the North's economy is a shambles. Residents in

Damon Darlin, "A Korean Deal Emerges," FORBES, September 12, 1994. Reprinted By Permission of FORBES Magazine © Forbes Inc., 1994.

the countryside, for example, are now told to eat only two meals a day. Per capita, North Koreans earn an eighth of what South Koreans do, and the gap is growing rapidly. (*See chart*).

Where their success makes South Koreans proud, the gap between North and South also makes them worry. If the North's economy were to collapse in a sudden heap, millions of northerners would flee south, destabilizing South Korea just as it is emerging as a full-fledged member—politically as well as economically—of the industrialized world. Putting the two Koreas back together overnight the way West Germany took over East Germany would cost Seoul over $500 billion. At this point in its development, it's doubtful whether South Korea could foot such a bill.

Seoul's talented economic technocrats, many of whom helped lay the foundation for South Korea's spectacular growth during the 1970s and the 1980s, are already hard to work on the reunification problem. "We'll use the same strategy that we used in the 1960s to build our economy," says the Korea Development Institute's Park Jin.

In effect, Seoul (in concert with Washington) is working out a deal with Pyongyang that goes like this: South Korea will extend financial aid to North Korea and encourage its businessmen to start investing there, thus slowly improving the northerners' standard of living and helping Kim Jong-il to secure his hold on office. Right now Seoul is preparing to finance most of a $4 billion nuclear power reactor in the North, if Washington approves the project and if—the big if—North Korea freezes its nuclear weapons program and allows inspections of sites where fuel may be stored. Reliable supplies of

South Korea: Strong and Getting Stronger

	North Korea	South Korea
Population	22.6 million	44.1 million
GNP	$20.5 billion	$328.7 billion
Per capita GNP	$904	$7,466
Economic growth	–4.3%	5.6%
External debt	$10.3 billion	$44.1 billion
As % of GNP	50.3%	13.4%
Military spending	$5.6 billion	$11.9 billion
As % of GNP	27.4%	3.6%
As % of govt budget	30%	25.1%
Iron ore production	476.3 million tons	21.9 million tons
Steel production	186 million tons	3.3 billion tons
Cement production	398 million tons	4.7 billion tons
Textile production	1.9 million tons	60.4 million tons

Source: Korea Development Institute, 1993 figures.

electricity are necessary before significant investment can take place in the North.

The gap between the Koreas is widening because the North spends heavily on its military and has fewer factories.

In return for Seoul's aid, Kim Jong-il will use his army to keep the North Koreans on their side of the border, which will remain closed for the next several years. This is the only way Seoul can delay the enormous cost of bringing the North Koreans up to the South's standard of living overnight.

By keeping the Korean peninsula partitioned for a few more years, Seoul hopes to grow its way out of the reunification problem. South Korea's gross national product of $329 billion is currently 16 times bigger than North Korea's (*see chart*). Next year it will be 20 times bigger, because the South's economy is expanding at a healthy 8% rate while the North's is shrinking at a 4%-plus clip.

By the end of the decade South Korea's economy will have grown 60%. Assuming no sudden

implosion of the North Korean economy, South Korea's planners believe their country can bring North Korea's standard of living up to 40% of the South's in ten years. Cost: about $260 billion over the decade, mainly to feed and clothe northerners, mostly unemployed soldiers and factory workers.

To finance its northern aid package, Seoul will sell some government bonds to its citizens and increase taxes somewhat. Mostly, however, Seoul will finance reunification with overseas borrowings. The country can easily afford to borrow. South Korea is one of the world's most creditworthy countries.

On strictly economic grounds, many South Korean businessmen would probably rather invest in China (where labor costs around $100 a month) or Vietnam ($50 a month) than in North Korea (about $150 a month). On the other hand, wages in South Korea now run at nearly $1,200 a month on the average. so the North doesn't look too bad, especially when noneconomic considerations—common language and culture, South Korean pride, government prodding, fear of the consequences if they don't invest up North—are factored in. Indeed, several of South Korea's *chaebol* conglomerates were eager to start investing in the North in the early 1990s. But the South Korean government reined them in as part of the effort, unsuccessful so far, to pressure Pyongyang into dropping its nuclear bomb building program.

The wild card, of course, is Pyongyang. Assuming his generals don't send him to an early grave, will new leader Kim Jong-il allow the gradual liberalization necessary to keep North Korea's economy from collapsing?

Seoul's officials think Kim has little choice in the matter. Military adventurism would be foolhardy. South Korea now spends only about 3.6% of its GNP on its military, versus 27% of GNP in the North. Yet so much larger is the South's economy that Seoul is outspending Pyongyang 2-to-1. North Korea's old comrades-in-arms in Beijing have their hands full riding China's economic boom. Their interest is the same as Seoul's: stability on the Korean peninsula.

Nuclear war? Always a possibility. But here Seoul is betting that Kim would rather live to indulge his legendary passions for movie actresses and fine French cognac than die in a radioactive whirlwind.

Daryl Plunk, a visiting fellow at the Heritage Foundation in Washington, sums up the view most Korea experts now hold when he says: "If the North Koreans are smart—and we know they are smart—they will move in the direction of reform." Agrees former U.S. Ambassador to South Korea Donald Gregg: "North Korea doesn't want to become another East Germany."

There are signs that Kim is already mincing toward reform. His cousin, Kim Dal-hyon, favors some opening up of the North's economy. As North Korea's deputy prime minister for economic affairs, Kim Dal-hyon welcomed delegations of Seoul's leading industrialists to North Korea in 1991. Several months later he visited the South, where he had surprisingly frank talks with then President Roh Tae-woo and more industrialists, and returned home to push for the development of two free-trade zones along the Russian and Chinese borders—far from Pyongyang's control.

Last year Kim Dal-hyon was demoted, suggesting that hardline isolationists again had the upper hand. But in July the list of participants at the Great Leader's funeral showed that Kim Dal-hyon had been rehabilitated, and with him some other reformers who are playing active roles again.

Another straw in the wind: As he laid his father to rest in a see-through coffin, Kim Jong-il quietly announced that South Korea products imported into North Korea may now carry a label stating their country of origin. This impressed Pyongyang-watchers in Seoul. Under Kim Il-sung's rule, such imports could carry no label. The Great Leader did everything he could to hide from the North Koreans how prosperous capitalism had made the South.

Korea's stock market certainly seems to be signaling the belief that cautious economic reform is on Pyongyang's agenda. The market has doubled from its low in late 1992 and is approaching its historic highs. Referring to the government's recent anti-speculation campaign, Philip Smiley, head of Jardine Fleming Securities in Seoul, says: "The South Korean Finance Ministry's market-cooling policies have done more to hurt the [stock] market here than anything Kim Jong-il has done.

 Article Review Form at end of book.

Ex-Enemy of the State Sees His Chance to Lead It

Nicholas D. Kristof

Seoul, South Korea—It was on the grounds of the sprawling presidential mansion here that Government officials hatched successive plans for eliminating their enemy, first by killing him in a car accident, then by drowning him in the ocean, and finally by having him executed by hanging.

But the presidential staff in those days was more persistent than efficient, and none of these plans worked. And so the next occupant of the presidential mansion may be that onetime enemy; Kim Dae Jung.

Mr. Kim, who would presumably bring a new staff of aides to the mansion, has been an opposition leader in South Korea so long that it is difficult to conceive of him as President. He is still lame from the first attempt to assassinate him, when a truck crashed into his car and killed his driver, but if the polls are right then Mr. Kim may soon be able to limp up the great central stairs of the presidential mansion and claim it as his own.

A somber man with a thickening middle but a full head of jet black hair, a fiery orator one moment and a patient statesman the next, Mr. Kim is consistently leading in all the opinion polls for the presidential election in December. To everyone's surprise—except his own—he is widely regarded as enjoying by far his best chance ever of leading the country.

A victory by Mr. Kim would be a landmark for Korea and East Asia as a whole, marking the first time in Korean history that an opposition leader had been elected President. South Korea has had reasonably free elections in recent years, but the same pattern has emerged here as in Japan and Taiwan: one party dominates the Government and is nagged by an opposition that is free to speak but usually unable to win the top post.

"In the 50 years since we became an independent country, we've never had a peaceful transition of the Government, in which an opposition party became a ruling party," Mr. Kim reflected in a long conversation in his office in the National Assembly. "For that

reason, the Government became corrupted and static, and reform cannot be implemented."

It is a sign of South Korea's increasing maturity as a democracy that Mr. Kim could almost certainly take office if elected. In the 1987 campaign, army officers warned that they might be forced to stage a coup or even kill him if he were chosen President. But now, by all accounts, the army would—if a bit grudgingly—accept him as the country's leader.

Similarly, the secretive Agency for National Security Planning would have to make adjustments if Mr. Kim is elected, such as spying for him instead of on him. Mr. Kim who believes his phones are still wiretapped along with those of many other Koreans—a charge that almost everybody finds credible—says he would like to restructure the intelligence agency to curb its domestic spying. But even the agency could probably accept Mr. Kim as President.

"I don't think that the people at the agency are too afraid of him," a prominent Korean official said with a grin. "They think they can handle anybody."

While Mr. Kim is now the front-runner, some experts still regard his election as unlikely. At the last minute, voters may rally around the ruling party candidate if they think that Mr. Kim would otherwise be elected. A large number of Koreans worry that Mr. Kim is soft on Communism, or else is a demagogue, or else is simply an old man whose time has passed.

"In American age, I'm 71," Mr. Kim mused with a twinkle in his eye (Korean ages often include a year awarded at birth and another at the beginning of each year, instead of waiting for a birthday). "But for 6 years I was in prison and for 10 years I was held under house arrest and exile, so those 16 years should be deducted. Then I'm only 55."

One indication of the suspicions in Korean politics is that the governing party suggests that Mr. Kim is lying about birth date and that he is actually a couple of years older. Indeed, at times Mr. Kim has used a birth date that would suggest that he is now 73.

Another of Mr. Kim's fundamental challenges is that, as his critics see it, he has been reduced to being a regional candidate from his native Cholla area, which is in the south-western part of the country and is stigmatized as poor, uncouth and unruly. Many respectable Korean families today would be appalled if their daughter were to try to marry a man from Cholla, and they sometimes feel the same way about voting for a candidate from Cholla.

In the last presidential race, in 1992, Mr. Kim received 90 percent of the vote from the Choila provinces and just 27 percent in the rest of the country—many of those coming from people who had migrated from Cholla. The bedrock of support from Cholla and from devoted loyalists around the country means that Mr. Kim is likely to receive about a third of the overall vote nationwide, and that could be a plurality if the rest of the vote is split among the three or four other major candidates.

"A lot of people think that this time there is a strong possibility that Kim Dae Jung will win the presidential race," said Kang Tae Hoon, a professor of political science at Dankook University in Seoul.

[The ruling party's crisis worsened—and Mr. Kim's chances of winning the presidency improved—when a popular politician, Rhee In Je, announced he would leave the ruling party and run for President on his own. Polls show that if the election were held now Mr. Rhee would come in second, after Mr. Kim, and that the ruling party candidate Lee Hoi Chang, would come in third.]

Partly because of his search for middle-class votes, Mr. Kim has moderated his political and economic views in recent years. As head of the main opposition party, the National Congress for New Politics, he is still a bit more sympathetic to labor and to a Government role in rescuing failed enterprises than the leaders of the New Korea Party are, but the differences in policy between him and the other candidates are much less than they were in past years.

Ra Jony Il, a political scientist at Kyung Hee University, noted that even as it has moved to democracy in recent years, South Korea has found it difficult to differentiate state power from politics. The tendency is still for the incumbent to use the police, courts, tax authorities and other powers of the state to tilt the playing field against his opponents.

But Mr. Ra argues that Mr. Kim's election would end that tendency.

 Article Review Form at end of book.

WiseGuide Wrap-Up

To be internationally competitive, today's political leaders are restraining the rights of workers to organize and are cutting government budgets so that services such as education and health care are beyond the reach of many citizens. This undermining of labor's possibilities for making gains, combined with economic austerity, threatens the popularity of many reforming governments, who also happen to be the first democratically elected governments in the recent history of their countries. Hence, many citizens are linking economic hardship with democracy and becoming nostalgic for earlier, authoritarian systems.

Despite the enthusiasm of many that we are now in a historic "Third Wave" of democratic reforms, some authoritarian regimes, such as Nigeria, continue to resist democratization and to violate the human rights of their citizens. In some countries that have democratized, new leaders, such as Kim Dae Jung and Fernando Henrique Cardoso, now serve as presidents. Both of these leaders were harassed and at times imprisoned by the officials of previous authoritarian regimes in their countries.

R.E.A.L. Sites

This list provides a print preview of typical **coursewise** R.E.A.L. sites. There are over 100 such sites at the **courselinks**™ site. The danger in printing URLs is that web sites can change overnight. As we went to press, these sites were functional using the URLs provided. If you come across one that isn't, please let us know via email to: webmaster@coursewise.com. Use your Passport to access the most current list of R.E.A.L. sites at the **courselinks**™ site.

Site names: Electronic Mail and Guardian

URLs: http://www.za

Why are they R.E.A.L.? This site shows testimonies offered to the South Africa Truth and Reconciliation Commission. Identify what kinds of testimony South Africans are giving to the commission. Then identify which testimonies the *Mail & Guardian* has chosen to publicize.

Key topics: national reconciliation, apartheid

Site name: Sierra Club Human Rights and the Environment

URL: http://www.sierraclub.org/human-rights/nigeria.html

Why is it R.E.A.L.? This site contains background information on Nigerian human rights and environmental issues, especially in relation to the murder of Nigerian community activist Ken Saro-Wiwa and the Shell Oil Company. Identify at least four responses of the international human rights organizations to the death of Ken Saro-Wiwa.

Key topics: Ken Saro-Wiwa, human rights

section

3

Key Points

- Despite the increasing numbers of countries undergoing transitions to democracy, obstacles to democratic practices remain even in countries that hold national multiparty elections.

- Some theorists argue that while elections facilitate democracy, other facets of democratic society, such as "social capital" and fair economic policies, must be present before a democratic system can be consolidated.

Issues of Democratization

WiseGuide Intro

While the 1990s is clearly a decade in which democratization is making great advances, many aspects of the democratic reforms of this era are being debated. For example, although free, internationally monitored elections brought some of Africa's new leaders to power, these new leaders are finding ways to limit the ability of opposition politicians to campaign, to contest, and to change governments peacefully. In Zambia and Zimbabwe, for example, as readings in this section demonstrate, democratically elected presidents undermine free elections and stack the selection of representatives to parliament to prevent governmental change.

Democracy analysts are also concerned that, just as authoritarian government civil servants looked to the state to provide them with economic largesse, so too, democratic politicians are demanding greater compensation and benefits at the expense of getting on with their tasks of governance and the development of the national economy. Further, despite paying lip service to the principles of democracy, many leaders in newly democratizing countries are attacking the independent press in an effort to eliminate criticism of their administration.

Some scholars argue that democracy cannot be institutionalized until civil society has experienced activities that promote the creation of, in Robert Putnam's phrase (see Reading 41), "social capital," which includes the development of norms, trust, and networks of community organizations. Without this democratic "glue" at the grassroots levels of society, democracies cannot function. Others argue that the severe economic policies that most countries must enact today to become globally competitive require that democratically sanctioned criticisms and political rights be limited until these difficult economic times pass. In response, others, like Amartya Sen (see Reading 42), argue that the quest for economic performance cannot negate political rights.

In the global debate of democratization issues, billionaire capitalist George Soros has gained international attention for his assertion that now that communism has been defeated the next great threat to democracy is capitalism (see Reading 43). Soros argues that those who must live under the laws of the market, rather than according to laws passed by democratic representatives, suffer harsh consequences. Soros asserts that the market is not democratic and that those who suffer under its rule may long for strong authoritarian governments to protect them from the vagaries of unregulated capitalist markets.

Some policy makers argue that democratization can be limited and restricted for some categories of citizens. In Latin America, gays and lesbians are fighting to preserve their new democratic freedoms by contesting so-called "public morality laws" that those who would restrict the democratic rights of sexual minorities are introducing (see Reading 44).

Democratization is a goal for which people in states around the globe undertake great risks. However, the introduction of democratic institutions and practices remains problematic. This section addresses some of the problems inherent in the institutionalization of democratic political systems.

Questions

1. What obstacles do democratic practitioners face in their effort to replace authoritarian rule with democratic political systems?

2. What is "social capital," and why does Robert Putnam argue in Reading 41 that it is crucial to the process of institutionalizing democratic practices in societies?

3. Supporters of authoritarian leaders argue that only authoritarian leaders can make the tough but necessary economic decisions that benefit the country as whole but that the average voter will not support. How does Amartya Sen counter this perspective in Reading 42 and argue that authoritarian leaders do not make better political leaders than democratically chosen heads of state?

4. Why does George Soros, an internationally respected capitalist, argue in Reading 43 that now that communism has been defeated, capitalism is the major threat to democracy?

Towards Impartial Poll Refereeing

A new SADC task force aims to bring free and fair elections to the sub-continent, reports Lewis Machipisa in Harare.

Lewis Machipisa

As controversy continues over whether the Zambian elections were free and fair, electoral commissioners from members of the SADC met last week to propose new methods to deliver honest elections.

Zambia is only the latest case of controversy over polling results—most other countries in the region, including Zimbabwe and South Africa, have faced criticism over manipulated voting figures.

At a meeting in Harare on December 4 and 5, electoral commissioners from SADC members resolved to set up a task force to work out ways of delivering free, fair, transparent and legitimate elections.

That effort must include examining the constitution of the commissions themselves, according to Drene Nupen, director of the Electoral Institute of South Africa (EISA), which convened the meeting.

Whatever the legal basis for the establishment of an electoral body, she says, its members should be appointed in a manner which ensures that they enjoy the

confidence of both the public and political parties.

"Regional cooperation to strengthen democracy and promote greater self-reliance in running elections is a logical and desirable step emerging from the extension of democracy throughout the Southern African region," she adds.

But it could prove difficult for the commissions in some SADC countries to bring about meaningful change if the laws they have to work with remain the same, according to Makumbe.

"The problem with electoral commissions in Africa is that they only review laws that have already been made by the governments. Instead of being reactive they should be playing a more proactive role if they are to be meaningful," she argues.

In Zimbabwe, for example, successive elections have been declared free and fair by the country's electoral commission, but critics maintain that the constitution itself is flawed since it is heavily weighted in favour of the incumbent president.

Section 58 of the constitution empowers President Robert Mugabe to appoint 20 unelected parliamentarians. His Zimbabwe

African National Union-Patriotic Front (ZANU-PF) party also benefits indirectly from the support of 10 chiefs sent into parliament by a college of traditional leaders.

As a result, the opposition notes, ZANU-PF only needs 46 of the 120 contested seats to retain control of the 150-member house.

Moreover, according to the Zimbabwean human rights organisation Zimrights, the constitution's electoral act gives "excessive powers to the president as he can suspend or amend any provisions of the act or any other law insofar as it applies to any election."

He can also overrule the act without having to explain his reasons and no person or court is permitted to query his action. These powers, Zimrights claims, place the whole electoral process in the hands of the incumbent president.

Another case in point is Zambia, where the ruling Movement for Multiparty Democracy (MMD) this year enhanced its electoral chances by changing the constitution.

A nationality clause limiting the presidency to people born to Zambian parents prevented the main challenger to President

Lewis Machipisa, "Towards Impartial Poll Refereeing." IPS/Misa, December 8, 1996.

Frederick Chiluba, former head of state Kenneth Kaunda, from taking part in presidential polls held on Nov. 18. Kaunda is of Malawian origin.

South Africa, on the other hand, is hoping to create its election commissions in a much more transparent way. "I am not saying the way other countries have elected their commissions is not democratic," says Nupen. "But what has happened in these countries is a golden opportunity for us to put in place a process where we can truly nominate and elect and have independent, impartial nonpolitical electoral commissioners."

"The process of nomination and election is incredibly transparent because a body has been put up which includes, among others, the president of the constitutional court, a member from the gender commission, and the public protector and these people take the nominations, interviews and will make recommendations," she explains.

"We have learnt some very valuable lessons from our sister countries," adds Nupen. "We have to look at the laws that we have inherited to see if they fit the conditions of today."

Some analysts argue that, to improve the credibility of electoral commissions, these should be made up of representatives of all registered political parties.

That suggestion was rejected by Judge Bobby Bwalya, chair of the Zambian Electoral Commission, the body that organised the November 18 polls—deemed severely flawed by independent monitors.

"If you pick members from all the political parties, you will have problems. They will never reach consensus because politicians take very rigid political stances and I think it's better to have people who are completely independent," said Bwalya.

Recognising the flaws in the laws they apply and the electoral processes they manage will also be key to the success of the commissioners' bid to improve the quality of elections in Southern Africa.

However, as far as Bwalya is concerned, the recent election in Zambia was flawless. Dismissing the widespread charges that they were not free and fair, he told IPS: "There cannot be rigging of any election in Zambia. There is no chance of double voting or ghost voters in Zambia."

 Article Review Form at end of book.

'Governors Should Be Equal to Ministers'

The Association of Regional Councils (ARC) wants the position of Regional Governor elevated to the status of that of a Minister or Deputy Minister.

Tabby Moyo

At Mariental

At its first Congress held at Mariental over the weekend, the ARC also proposed that in future Regional Governors should be elected by the people in the regions in which they serve.

However, Regional, Local Government and Housing Minister Dr Nicky Iyambo told close-on 100 delegates from all the country's 13 regional councils that, as it stood, the Namibian Constitution made it impossible for Government to make such moves.

Tabby Moyo, "Governers Should Be Equal to Ministers," THE NAMIBIAN, October 13, 1997. Reprinted by permission.

ARC also noted with serious concern the apparent lack of official recognition for the position of Regional Councillor.

The meeting decided that, realising the determination of Government—in particular the Local Government Ministry—to discriminate against Regional Councillors with regard to benefits such as pensions and other perks, the position of Regional Councillor be elevated to that of a full-time politician to supervise and co-ordinate Government activities at constituency offices.

The ARC also proposed that Regional Councillors be remunerated just as other politicians were.

"It is essential that their duties be enacted in an act of parliament," the Regional Councillors meeting resolved.

In this regard, it was also decided that the Regional Councils Amendment Bill, 1997, be amended to cover benefits, including pensions, for Regional Councillors.

Having noted the unclear position with regards the policy of decentralisation in relation to the Constitution, the ARC resolved that policy should acknowledge

that Regional Councils were in charge of the regions and that shared responsibility with Government be emphasised.

Congress also resolved that the regional executive officers of all the 13 regions be made members of the Focal Persons for Decentralisation (FPDs) in order to strengthen the implementation of the decentralisation policy.

ARC also felt that it should also serve on the Ministry's Task Force on decentralisation.

 Article Review Form at end of book.

Call to Transparency

Journalists must lead by example.

Geoff Nyarota

Excerpts from an address on WPFD

The Media Institute of Southern Africa (MISA) says that while the Southern African Development Community information ministers have adopted the 1991 Windhoek Declaration on promoting an independent and pluralistic media in Africa in principle, as far as the Institute is aware, none of the SADC-member governments has used the declaration as the basis of national media policy.

Realistically, this means few of the governments in the region fully subscribe to the notion that the establishment, maintenance and fostering of an independent and pluralistic press is essential to the development and maintenance of democracy in a nation, and for economic development, as stated in the declaration.

While all the governments in the region are democratically elected and espouse democratic principles, in reality they have become increasingly intolerant of press freedom and reliant on the oppressive tools inherited from their dictatorial predecessors to stifle freedom of expression and freedom of the media. The government of Frederick Chiluba of Zambia is a typical example.

Geoff Nyarota, "Call to Transparency," FREE PRESS, the Media Magazine of Southern Africa, Edition 3, 1996.

Reluctant

Corruption, abuse of human rights and other undemocratic practices thrive in an atmosphere where the media are reluctant to expose them. In most cases the people of southern Africa get to know about some of the excesses of their governments by tuning in to the British Broadcasting Corporation (BBC). Demonstrations by teachers in Harare in 1991, riots in the Copperbelt of Zambia in 1982, prisoners dying in prison in Malawi-were BBC reports while the journalists of southern Africa stood aside and watched as spectators. Why do foreign correspondents enjoy more freedom in our countries?

It is absolutely essential, once in a while, for journalists in the region to pause and take stock of themselves; to engage in introspection and assess whether they are doing everything possible to exploit fully even that little freedom which they have at their disposal.

Just as blameworthy as corrupt and undemocratic politicians are the journalists, editors especially who are either passive in combating corruption and injustice or who, for one reason or another, take a definite decision to cover up for it.

There are some among the ranks of journalists who have assumed the role of official censors without being instructed to do so. Usually the objective of their self-censorship is self-seeking. Paradoxically, when it suits them, such journalists also turn around and accuse governments of denying them freedom.

Corruption

Some of the most determined protagonists of press freedom will be found lurking within the ranks of the journalists.

In my discussions with fellow journalists I often get the impression that they entertain a certain expectation that governments will once in a while, in moments of good-naturedness and repentance, grant journalists sanction to reveal their weaknesses, highlight their short-comings, expose their corrupt tendencies and, generally, make known all what is bad about them.

Politicians are human beings and most normal human beings are averse to negative publicity.

Responsibility

Unlike other human beings, however, politicians are publicly accountable. It is a matter of public concern when their actions and decisions run contrary to public expectation. It becomes the onerous responsibility of the journalists to find out the short-comings and bring them to public attention and to call for good governance, accountability and transparency.

But unfortunately for the journalists, most normal politicians are also very powerful people with a vested interest in their continued tenure of office at all costs. Likewise, the leaders of the corporate world are equally, if not more, powerful. They are devoted to maximising profits for their companies. Exposing the wrong-doing of either group through investigative journalism, therefore, carries an element of risk. Yet journalists always expect journalism to be risk-free.

Solidarity

Journalists, however, can also be powerful people. The pen is mightier than the sword, it has been said. Their strength, however, lies in numbers. If there is solidarity among journalists they can become a formidable force. At the individual level, what they need is courage. If journalists lack courage their cry for media freedom becomes a cry in vain.

Fred M'membe, Editor-In-Chief of The Post in Zambia, has become a house-hold name in media circles in southern Africa. He was the winner in 1995 of MISA Press Freedom Award. The government of Zambia continuously harasses him because M'membe dares to challenge Zambia's antiquated and repressive media laws. In March, they locked him up for 24 days. But M'membe is a brave man. He is a courageous journalist.

An obsession with material possessions and wanton-acquisition has reduced many journalists to a level of official praise singers and shameless hero-worshippers. Their determination to expose corruption and undemocratic practices, where they exist, has diminished by inverse proportions to the increase in the level of comfort and luxury in their lives.

In any case, what moral justification do we, as journalists, have to demand that other people behave correctly when we are ourselves not exemplary? Are we as individuals always dedicated to our professional calling; are we always ethical and accountable in carrying out our duties? Is there democracy at our places of work? Is there transparency in the activities of our journalists' organisations?

If the answer to any of these questions is negative then our campaign for media freedom will remain futile, even if every day of the year is declared World Press Freedom Day.

 Article Review Form at end of book.

Book Review

Making Democracy Work: Civic Traditions in Modern Italy

Julie Fisher

Program on Nonprofit Organizations, Yale University

Charles H. Hamilton

J. M. Kaplan Fund, New York

Terms like *civil society, community, civic culture,* and *social capital* now clutter the academic landscape. As Emmet Carson said of the idea of civil society at the 1993 Association for Research on Nonprofit Organizations and Voluntary Action (ARNOVA) meeting, "If my mother doesn't know what it is, it won't work." Fair enough. And yet, these terms attempt to capture a dawning paradigmatic change of academic and practical import. This is due to a combination of factors, including the fall of Communism, the failures of public policy on the Left and Right, yearnings for some kind of togetherness, an abhorrence of powerlessness, and the worldwide explosion of nongovernmental organizations (NGOs) and other alternative institutions. Everywhere, it seems, people are rediscovering the social ties that bind people together.

For several decades we have invested the political process with our hopes and energies only to discover that politics may be more the effect of other social forces than the cause of basic social change. Something has been missing. Put another way, after several decades of "bringing the state back in" to what had become pretty sterile social science, we are now seeing an effort to "reinvent society" from the dual sources of theory and practice.

During the 1970s, Latin American intellectuals, reacting against tired Marxism as well as dictatorial states, began to write about *sociedad civil.* Harkening back to Adam Smith and Hegel, the term *civil society* also reappeared in the literature of Central and Eastern European dissidents as they tried to carve out an understanding of social process that could stand in opposition to the state while being broader and more humane than simply "the market." The proliferation of NGOs throughout the world has also advanced understanding of what Michael Walzer has called "the space of uncoerced human association" (1991, p. 293). Increasingly, the idea of civil society has figured prominently in more and more works; of particular note are those by Victor Perez Diaz (1993) and Ernest Gellner (1994).

The best book of the lot is Robert Putnam's *Making Democracy Work* (coauthored with Robert Leonardi and Raffaella Y. Nanetti). It is beautifully written, based on 20 years of research, and held together by the creative use of many different theoretical threads (collective action, game theory, the new institutionalism, etc.). It is a scholarly bestseller, having already sold nearly 20,000 copies. In the nearly 3 years since its publication, it has had a remarkable impact on several disciplines, its themes have garnered great journalistic attention, and we know of at least two foundations that have made major shifts in their funding priorities as a result of the book. The Kettering Foundation has begun a series of Civil Investing Seminars for foundation executives to explore giving strategies focusing on strengthening civil society.

*Making Democracy Work: Civic Traditions in Modern Italy, by Robert Putnam, Robert Leonardi, and Raffaella Y. Nanetti. (1993). Princeton, NJ: Princeton University Press. 258 pp., $35.00 (cloth), $14.95 (paper).

Julie Fisher and Charles Hamilton, Book Reviews: "Making Democracy Work: Civic Traditions in Modern Italy" by Robert D. Putnam, Robert Leonardi, and Raffaella Y. Nanetti. NONPROFIT AND VOLUNTARY SECTOR QUARTERLY, Vol. 25, No. 1, March 1996. pp. 124-135. Copyright © 1996 Sage Publications, Inc. Reprinted by permission of Sage Publications, Inc.

Making Democracy Work is an important book for researchers and practitioners in the voluntary sector. The book is ostensibly a specific study of democracy in modern Italy. More important, this is a remarkable exploration of the crucial importance of social capital, that is, the "features of social organization, such as trust, norms, and networks, that can improve the efficiency of society by facilitating coordinated actions" (p. 167). That complex discussion enriches the whole concept of a voluntary sector and is tantalizing in its suggestions about what makes society work or not work so well. Yet these same researchers and practitioners in the voluntary sector have important contributions and corrections to make on precisely the topics Putnam has raised.

The book had its origins in 1970 when the Italian government began to implement a constitutional provision to set up regional governments. Although Putnam draws on evidence from all 20 regions, 6 regions that represent the vast diversities of Italy are singled out. Human action offers few such opportunities to systematically study institutional development and the impact of social context over many years. Putnam and his colleagues were there at the beginning; the results of their inquiries make for fascinating reading.

The early chapters focus on 20 years of development, policy formulations, and implementation, attempting to chronicle and measure the contrasts long remarked on between northern and southern regions in terms of their institutional performance. All of this leads the author to ever wider circles of inquiry. Although Putnam's original inquiry grew out of the stark differences in regional governmental performance that began to develop during the 1970s, he found the usual explanations for those differences wanting. He began to suspect alternative explanations outside of the usual political science lexicon. Of particular importance is the link between performance and the character of civic life—what he terms "the civic community" (p. 15). The differences in the level and vitality of civic life turn out to have a determining role in explaining differences in institutional success. Although business and government have a role to play, social capital, according to Putnam, "is the key to making democracy work" (p. 185).

Perhaps even more fascinating are the historical roots of the ability of the North to respond to the opportunities of governmental decentralization and the failure of the South to do likewise. The story he tells really begins in the twelfth century when northerners responded to political anarchy by creating workingmen's guilds, and southerners welcomed the autocratic order provided by Norman invaders for the very same reason. In the city-states of the North, communes sprang from voluntary associations based on groups of neighbors swearing mutual assistance to each other. Eventually, this led to the professionalization of city administration. Economic guilds were organized and credit was invented, "one of the great economic revolutions in world history" (p. 128). Although northern Italy continued to be plagued by poverty and factionalism, horizontal networks moderated conflict and social mobility was high.

In southern Italy, in contrast, the Norman kings reinforced the feudal rights of barons who provided them with military backing. Although the Normans also promoted religious tolerance and commerce, southern towns and cities that showed any desire for autonomy were subjugated by a network of officials responsible to the king.

Making Democracy Work starts out to "explore the origins of effective government" (p. 15), but ends up somewhere else: exploring the foundations for an effective society. Putnam's exploration of why political, economic, and social development seem to flourish differently in areas of similar political decentralization inexorably moves toward the key importance of the local, voluntary associations that make for civil society. Although Putnam does not specifically say it, civic community is also linked to civility. Not only is "collective life in the civic regions . . . eased by the expectation that others will probably follow the rules" (p. 111), but people in northern Italy are less concerned about the need for strong top-down authority.

Note that the real core of democracy may not be "political" in the usual sense of the term, but profoundly social. It is the tension in that subtle shift in emphasis from the political to the social as it unfolds in Putnam's research that makes his intellectual odyssey so interesting and his book so important. For those of us researching and working in aspects of the voluntary sector, the point is especially salient. We, as reviewers, think it valuable to look anew at what makes a society work or not work by dissecting this major issue into four questions arising from the work:

1. What is civil society?
2. What is the relationship of civil society to government performance?
3. What is the relationship of civil society to democracy?
4. What is the relationship of civil society/social capital to socioeconomic development?

What Is Civil Society?

Although there is some debate about what civil society or (in Putnam's words) "civic community" means, and Putnam does not specifically define it, Michael Walzer's definition above is a good beginning. Other more explicit observers include the for-profit as well as the nonprofit sector in their definitions. Perez Diaz (1993, p. 56), for example, defines civil society as "markets, associations and a sphere of public debate." Businesses, as well as nonprofit organizations, help mediate between the citizen and the state. Moreover, businesses and nonprofits are often more than just unrelated members of the same civil society. Just as the craftsmen's guilds formed in northern Italy a thousand years ago were economic in character, so also development NGOs as diverse as the Grameen Bank in Bangladesh or the Foundation for Economic and Social Initiative in Poland are promoting for-profit enterprises. They also work with grassroots organizations such as rotating credit associations, which, as Putnam points out, are found throughout the world.

The importance of a "sphere of public debate" to civil society is clearly understood by grassroots organizations in the Philippines that use large community blackboards as local newspapers. In contrasting the strength of civil society in northern Italy with its weakness in the South, Putnam uses newspaper readership as one of four civic community indicators. Even a partially independent media can help a country move from deferential to autonomous active civility.

Most discussions of civil society, including some of Putnam's,

focus on vertical relationships, down to the citizen and up to the government. Putnam's "tale of detection" (p. xiv), however, also led to "astonishingly deep historical roots" characterized by stronger or weaker horizontal bonds. So much of our lives and theory are implicitly vertical. But as Putnam points out, "the relevant distinction is not between the presence and absence of social bonds, but rather between horizontal bonds of mutual solidarity and vertical bonds of dependency and exploitation" (p. 144). His study measures the dramatic differences between the strength of civic community in northern Italy (where civic bonds are largely horizontal) and southern Italy (where they remain vertical).

Instead of focusing on definitions of civil society or civic community, Putnam and his colleagues put their energies, over 20 years, into a largely successful attempt to measure it. In addition to the incidence of newspaper readership, they measured the vibrancy of associational life, turnout for referenda, and the incidence of preference voting for a particular candidate from the party list (as a negative indicator). They found that the four indicators were "highly correlated" (p. 96) with each other, as well as with support for political equality. Moreover, this "civic community index" was highly correlated with another index of civic community involvement developed for the period 1860–1920. This historical index included the strength of mass parties, the incidence of cooperatives, membership in mutual aid societies, electoral turnout, and local associations founded before 1860. No doubt variations on Putnam's method should be tried on other areas.

The Relationship of Civil Society to Government Performance

What makes government responsive and accountable? What makes for good government some places and bad government elsewhere? Putnam and his collaborators ran detailed assessments of regional government success using 12 diverse measures to create a composite measure of performance, including cabinet stability, budget promptness, and statistical and information services as measures of policy processes; reform legislation and legislative innovations as measures of the content of policy decisions; and 7 measures of policy implementation, including day care centers, family clinics, industrial policy instruments, agricultural spending capacity, local health unit expenditures, housing and urban development, and bureaucratic responsiveness. Not only was there high consistency among these 12 indicators, but his team did two separate indicator analyses in 1978 and 1985 that were highly consistent with each other.

Not surprisingly, he found that there was a strong correlation between regional governmental performance and the strength of the civic community. More remarkably, the success or failure of regional governments in the 1980s was strongly correlated with the team's historical civic society index. Putnam and his team have, in other words, been able to move beyond correlation toward causality. Equally important were some of their negative findings. For example, the success or failure of regional governments was "wholly uncorrelated with virtually all measures of political fragmentation, ideological polarization and social conflict" (p. 117). The highly civic community, in other words, is not necessarily free of strife.

In answering the question of why the relationship between civic community and government performance is so strong, Putnam focuses mainly on political culture. He found, for example, that contacts between citizens and governments in the South are more likely to be personalistic than those in the North, and that northerners, whether they be political leaders or ordinary citizens, are more committed to equality and compromise than their counterparts in the South. Implicit in his argument is the assumption that political culture can only develop slowly, over many years.

Yet evidence from other parts of the world throws doubt on the generalizability of Putnam's powerful Italian findings. In the Third World, for example, the why question is being addressed more directly than in Italy. NGOs operate within a historical context close to that of southern Italy, yet in dealing with issues such as development or human rights, they often have a more direct impact on governments than the choral societies or sports clubs of northern Italy. Third World NGOs are sometimes able to subvert ineffective bureaucratic behavior because some government employees are smart and opportunistic, if not as well educated as NGO leaders. In India, for example, many development ministries and bureaus are collaborating with NGOs, even though the security ministry harasses them. Ties between NGOs and poorly funded subnational governments in many countries are increasingly common because

NGOs can provide human and even financial resources. Many Brazilian cities, for example, work with both grassroots organizations and intermediary grassroots support organizations. In Sao Paulo alone there are over 1,000 neighborhood associations collaborating with the city government on community gardens and sanitation (see Fisher, 1992).

In the Third World, let us go a little deeper and focus on the major factors associated with direct, positive NGO influence on government policy. Even though the dramatic growth of NGOs is already having some impact on political culture, and thus a long-term cumulative impact on governments, it is those NGOs with a high degree of organizational autonomy that are having the strongest impact on government policy. To quote a Philippine NGO leader,

> In dealing with government it is important to make sure that you participate on your own terms. This means you do not access money from governments, nor do you sit down just to be coopted. You must be able . . . to enter into relationships where you can participate in the conceptualization and onward to the implementation of every project. (see Fisher, 1995)

This may, of course, be more difficult in Central and Eastern Europe, where even nonpartisan organizations may be viewed as political opponents.

Measuring local performance and decentralization may be misleading without reference to a larger political context. What, for instance, is the true extent of the decentralization promoted by the Italian government? By the early 1990s, the regional governments were spending 10% of gross domestic product. Yet, with

total government spending in Italy as high as it is, one wonders how important and robust even the northern regional governments really are. Indeed, a huge central governmental sector has to have a dampening effect on both economic development and social capital. Thus Putnam's "central question: . . . What are the conditions for creating strong, responsive, effective representative [political] institutions?" (p. 6) may be answered quite differently at the national level. Without reference to the larger political and economic framework, including the nationally oriented nonprofit sector, regional governments can take on an unsubstantiated importance.

What Is the Relationship of Civil Society to Democracy?

It is curious that, despite the book's title, and Putnam's substantially unassailable assumption that effective government must be responsive, accountable, and, therefore, democratic, the word *democracy* does not appear in the index. To be sure, civil society and democracy are closely intertwined. Indeed, except for a few very small islands in the Pacific and the Caribbean, it is hard to conceive of a democracy not based on a strong civil society. Yet civil society and democracy are not coterminous. Some observers, most notably Perez Diaz (1993) in his discussion of recent Spanish history, have concluded that the development of a strong civil society typically precedes the emergence of a democratic political system. Civil society may grow stronger under a dictatorship, although conflict is probable. Fragile democratic governments can be overthrown even though civil society has grown stronger, although civil society will often become a target as well. Yet, in support of Putnam's findings, a growing civil society can also strengthen democratic institutions or circumscribe the options of dictatorships.

How should we be thinking about this process that advances civil society, responsive democratic government, and, ultimately (Putnam's question), effective policy implementation? A look back at the topic of "political development" is appropriate. In the 1960s, political development was as hot a topic in political science as "civil society" is today. By the 1970s, however, it had been eclipsed by "realistic" writings on topics such as the inevitable rise of bureaucratic authoritarianism and the apparent decline of democracy, particularly in Latin America. Ironically, this shift in political science occurred just as those writing about development were emphasizing local participation for the first time. With the explosion of NGOs in the developing and transitional countries and with the return to democracy in many countries, students of civil society need to look back at the political development literature. Political development can be defined as an interactive public decision-making and learning process based on power creation and power dispersion within and between government and civil society. It leads to increased autonomy from below and responsiveness from above (Fisher, 1993, p. 17).[1]

The toughest issue is, of course, the content of interaction between society and state. But previously excluded groups, newly organized into associations, can enhance the dimensions available for problem posing and problem solving.[2] Attempts to define political development need to focus on process recognition, but need not, indeed should not, imply that change is inevitable. It is a process that may start and be derailed, especially if civil society is only incipient or fragile. Nor is it occurring everywhere. Putnam's findings, however, buttress the view that it is propelled by the long-term growth of civil society. In the developing and transitional countries, there is considerable evidence that short-term deliberate cultivation of civil society can also contribute to political development. In Cambodia, for example, where there were almost no NGOs even 10 years ago, a small women's rights organization called Ponleu Khmer has, with international NGO support, become a major player in the national human rights dialogue, as well as an important organizer of an NGO network.

Regarding civil society's relationship with government performance and democracy, then, Putnam's analysis leads us in interesting directions. He assumes that institutions shape policy and that institutions are shaped by history. Between these two assumptions, however, Putnam argues that the "practical performance of institutions . . . is shaped by the social context within which they operate" (p. 8). Putnam does not undermine the common assumption that institutional change can influence civic culture. That is what he expected to find with the decentralization of Italian government. Yet, to Putnam's initial surprise, the strength of the opposite direction became the real crux of his argument. "Civic context matters for the way institutions work. By far the most important factor in explaining good government is the degree to which social and political life in a region approximates the ideal of the civic community" (p. 120).

The Relationship of Civil Society to Social and Economic Development

In addition to being predictive of effective regional government, Putnam's historic civic community index was much more predictive of current levels of socioeconomic development than were earlier levels of socioeconomic development. "When we use both civic traditions and past socioeconomic development to predict present socioeconomic development, we discover that civics is actually a much better predictor of socioeconomic development than is development itself" (p. 156). "Over the two decades since the birth of the regional governments, civic regions have grown faster than regions with fewer associations and more hierarchy, controlling for their level of development in 1970" (p. 176).[3]

Again, Putnam has surpassed correlation with significant evidence of historical causality. Yet, as Putnam himself points out, civic community in northern Italy embodies a dense mixture of economic as well as political associations that foster competition as well as cooperation. More specifically, he argues that such "social capital" can overcome the proverbial free rider. Rotating credit associations, for example, also ubiquitous throughout the Third World, are based on strong norms of "generalized reciprocity," unsustainable by vertical networks. Moreover, economic institutions such as guilds were part and parcel of the growth of preindustrial civil society in northern Italy.

What Do We Make of This? Where Do We Go from Here?

The unsettling news about social capital in this book relates to Putnam's historical determinism. Indeed, as he notes somewhat pessimistically in the concluding chapter, with respect to social capital, "them that has gets" (p. 169). He also finds that

> the southern territories once ruled by the Norman kings constitute exactly the seven least civic regions in the 1970s. . . . At the other end of the scale, the heartland of republicanism in 1300 corresponds uncannily to the most civic regions of today, followed closely by the areas still further north in which medieval republican traditions, though real, had proved somewhat weaker. (p. 133)

Although these stable and prosperous medieval societies were replaced by autocracies in response to the Black Death and the Hundred Years War, northern rulers still accepted civic responsibilities. Putnam points out that the concept of a "patron of the arts" originated in northern Italy. The nineteenth century saw the use of the "principle of association" (p. 138) as a central element in the ideology of the *risorgimento,* and the emergence of cooperatives throughout the North. "By 1904 Piedmont had more than seven times as many mutual aid societies as Puglia, in proportion to population" (p. 148).

Why were the northern Italians already more prone to organize themselves in the year 1100? The answer, says Putnam, may be "lost in the mist of the Dark Ages" (p. 180). Despite Putnam's persuasive historical determinism, one is tempted to answer his query with the observation that guilds were originally organized because a few people voluntarily decided they were a logical response to a chaotic and threatening environment. By the same token, the dramatic organizational explosion that began in the Third World only 25 years ago—there are now between 35,000 and 50,000 intermediary NGOs in Asia, Africa, and Latin America—was a self-conscious response to worsening poverty, high-level unemployment, and the increased availability of voluntary foreign assistance. To be sure, the new intermediary NGOs or grassroots support organizations were also able to link up to preexisting member serving organizations at the local community level.

Even historical determinism, in other words, must have a starting point. It seems to be in the individual choices and values, the small-scale organizing, and the trust that people can develop in their daily lives. This had to be true during "the mist of the Dark Ages." It was also described by Tocqueville in *Democracy in America* and is now visible in the rise of NGOs in the developing countries (see Fisher, 1993). So, although we agree with Putnam that history can be tenacious, "history" does not fully determine. What Putnam's research does suggest is that context and culture are more negatively tenacious in some places than in others. In places such as southern Italy, historical context may be "harder for would-be reformers to manipulate, at least in the short run, so our research is not likely to suggest shortcuts to institutional success" (p. 10).

NGO organizers in the developing and transitional world, however, have some inherent advantages over the original Italian organizers of guilds and mutual aid societies. In 1100 it was hard to communicate, even between northern and southern Italy. Today international travel and the communications revolution tend to preclude the possibility of the isolated historical accidents that influenced an Emilia Romagna or a Calabria for a thousand years. Today international and Third World NGOs are not just letting civil society sprout by chance. They are, in effect, cultivating it rather deliberately. One value of Putnam's book is that his analysis reinforces the dicey and delicate difference between cultivating civil society and proclaiming or coopting it from above.

On the plus side, one suspects Putnam is right: Civic traditions "have remarkable staying power" (p. 157). To be sure, civil society can be destroyed pretty thoroughly in dictatorial regimes of both the Left and the Right. And American society in recent decades has seen a decline in civility by most accounts. Yet traditions and something bordering on an associational "collective self-consciousness" persist and can be drawn upon. In addition, people seem to be quite deliberately creating civil societies in many parts of the world. If civil society in most of the developing and transitional countries is not yet as strong as it is in northern Italy, it is arguably stronger than in Sicily or Calabria. Moreover, unlike Italy, where choral societies and sports clubs are the most common forms of association, NGOs are tied more closely to socioeconomic results because they are specifically focused on local development and national development policies.

This conclusion provides us with hope that three major trends occurring throughout the developing countries—the growth of development NGOs, the continuing vitality of the informal for-profit sector; and the movement for human rights and democracy—are not just fads. They may even have the long-range potential to reinforce each other. This process of reinforcement and convergence can be accelerated by NGOs focusing on microenterprise development, governments willing to facilitate the widespread creation of new wealth rather than protecting economic exploitation, and political entrepreneurs aware of the need to challenge authoritarian governments.

Civil societies, an informal economy, and concern about democracy are also emerging in the transitional countries of Central and Eastern Europe and the former Soviet Union. Although educational levels are higher in the transitional countries than in much of the Third World, only the continuing growth of civil society can help people challenge habits of economic and political dependency.

What Kind of Research Makes Sense? Twenty Years on Local Organizations?

It is certainly true that nonprofit research can add much to the discussion about civil society. Putnam's book, we think, lacked something because he did not focus more directly on the voluntary sector. And yet, in a recent article called "Bowling Alone," Putnam (1995) reminds us that there are dilemmas in focusing too much on the voluntary sector: "To identify trends in the size of the nonprofit sector with trends in social connectedness would be another fundamental conceptual mistake" (p. 71). Much voluntary sector research has emerged from advocacy, and may not always focus on bureaucratization or self-serving behavior. Nonprofits, just like government, business, and other forms of human interaction, can destroy social capital.

On the other hand, as researchers, we are, paradoxically, often timid about our place: That the third sector comes in "third" underscores the point. Putnam's book, it seems to us, suggests a more upbeat and ambitious research agenda. His exploration of political institutions uncovers the central role that social capital plays in economic and political development for society as a whole. Italy became a case study for a perspective that has relevance domestically and internationally.

We need more works with the larger context provided by Putnam: The big studies more directly and immediately focused on the role of associational life, trust, and the voluntary sector in building democracy and civil society. Microstudies with a sectoral emphasis based on data collection must continue, of course. Yet we need more daring scholars in the tradition of, say, Tocqueville and Max Weber. In the coming years, we would hope to see research begun and other research finally concluded that will give us the longitudinal studies of NGOs and domestic institutional development we need.

"Bowling Alone" allowed Putnam to use some of his insights about America's declining social capital through a discussion of the decline in organized bowling leagues. There is room for serious disagreement about the extent to which this is true. Some people are more inclined to see that we are just going through a process of shifting forms of community (for instance, the rise of a kind of "Internet community"). There is bound to be much disagreement over the causes of any decline in civil society. These are precisely the questions we need to look at. Can we, for instance, develop surveys of civic involvement over time? We need tools that can measure dependency attitudes and participatory attitudes: perhaps using the work of Ellen Langer on learned helplessness. In that way, we could begin to see whether government policies, foundation grants, and voluntary associations actually lead to the destruction of social capital or encourage empowerment.

Putnam is eloquent in his description of this emerging American dilemma. As he writes in "Bowling Alone," more Americans than ever before are in social circumstances that foster associational involvement (higher education, middle age, and so on), but nevertheless aggregate associational membership appears to be stagnant or declining" (p. 73). We suspect that this dilemma afflicts many developed countries today, even as civil society becomes stronger in the developing and transitional countries. Whether we are interested in voluntary sector research, or what makes for a good society, or the state of associational life, a close look at Putnam and others who write about civil society can and should inform our discourse. As Putnam concludes his book, "building social capital will not be easy, but it is the key to making democracy work" (p. 185).

Notes

1. The definition grew out of a reexamination of the political development literature.
2. See Goulet (1986) and Brown (1984).
3. For a recent, wide-ranging look at how and why social capital creates prosperity, see Francis Fukuyama's new book *Trust* (1995).

References

Brown, S. (1984). The logic of problem generation: Form morality and solving to de-posing and rebellion. *For the Learning of Mathematics*, 4(1), 9–20.

Fisher, J. (1992). Local government and the independent sector in the Third World. In K. McCarthy, V. Hodgkinson, R. Sumariwalla, and Associates (Eds.), *The nonprofit sector in the global community: Voices from many nations.* San Francisco: Jossey-Bass.

Fisher, J. (1993). *The road from Rio: Sustainable development and the nongovernmental movement in the Third World.* Westport, CT: Praeger.

Fisher, J. (1995). *Cultivating civil society: NGOs, donors and governments in the Third World* (Unpublished manuscript).

Fukuyama, F. (1995). *Trust: The social virtues and the creation of prosperity.* New York: Free Press.

Gellner, E. (1994). *Conditions of liberty: Civil society and its rivals.* New York: Viking Penguin.

Goulet, D. (1986). Three rationalities in development decision-making. *World Development* 14(2), 301–317.

Perez Diaz, V. M. (1993). *The return of civil society: The emergence of democratic Spain.* Cambridge, MA: Harvard University Press.

Putnam, R. D. (1995, January). Bowling alone. *Journal of Democracy, 6*(1), 65–78.

The Solitary Bowler. (1995, February 18). *The Economist,* pp. 21–22.

Walzer, M. (1991, Spring). The idea of civil society. *Dissent,* pp. 293–304.

Article Review Form at end of book.

R E A D I N G   4 2

Freedom Favors Development

Amartya Sen

Harvard—Something of a "general theory" of the relationship between political liberty and economic prosperity has been articulated in recent years by that unlikely theorist Lee Kuan Yew, the former prime minister of Singapore. He is not alone in praising the supposed advantages of "the hard state" in promoting economic development that goes back a long way in the development literature. Even the sagacious Gunnar Myrdal's extensive skepticism, in *Asian Drama*, of what he called "the soft state" has sometimes been interpreted (rather unfairly to Myrdal) as a celebration of political toughness in the cause of good economics.

It is true that some relatively authoritarian states (such as Lee's Singapore, South Korea under military rule and, more recently, China) have had faster rates of economic growth than some less authoritarian states (such as India, Costa Rica and Jamaica). But the overall picture is much more complex than such isolated observations might suggest.

This article is an updated and revised version of a paper, "Freedoms and Needs" that originally appeared in *The New Republic.*

Amartya Sen, "Freedom Favors Development," NEW PERSPECTIVE QUARTERLY, Vol. 13 & 14, Fall 1996, pp. 23-27. Reprinted by permission of Blackwell Publishers.

Systematic statistical studies give little support to the view of a general conflict between civil rights and economic performance. In fact, scholars such as Partha Dasgupta, Abbas Pourgerami and Surjit Bhalla have offered substantial evidence to suggest that political and civil rights have a positive impact on economic progress. Other scholars find divergent patterns, while still others argue, in the words of John Helliwell, that on the basis of the information so far obtained "an optimistic interpretation of the overall results would thus be that democracy, which apparently has a value independent of its economic effects, is estimated to be available at little cost in terms of subsequent lower growth."

There is not much comfort in all these findings for the "Lee Kuan Yew hypothesis" that there exists an essential conflict between political rights and economic performance. The general thesis in praise of the tough state suffers not only from casual empiricism based on a few selected examples, but also from a lack of conceptual discrimination. Political and civil rights come in various types, and authoritarian intrusions take many forms. It would be a mistake, for example, to equate North Korea with South Korea in the infringement of political rights, even though both have violated many such rights.

The complete suppression of opposition parties in the North can hardly be taken to be no more repressive than the roughness with which opposition parties have been treated in the South. Some authoritarian regimes, both of the "left" and of the "right," such as Zaire or Sudan or Ethiopia or the Khmer Rouge's Cambodia, have been enormously more hostile to political rights than many other regimes that are also identified, rightly, as authoritarian.

It is also necessary to examine more rigorously the causal process that is supposed to underlie these generalizations about the impact of authoritarianism on prosperity. The processes that led to the economic success of, say, South Korea are now reasonably well understood. A variety of factors played a part, including the use of international markets, an openness to competition, a high level of literacy, successful land reforms and the provision of selective incentives to encourage growth and exports. There is nothing to indicate that these economic and social policies were inconsistent with greater democracy, that they had to be sustained by the elements of authoritarianism actually present in South Korea.

The fundamental importance of political rights is not refuted by some allegedly negative effect of these rights on economic performance. In fact, the instrumental connections may even give a very positive role to political rights in the context of deprivations of a drastic and elementary kind: whether, and how, a government responds to intense needs and sufferings may well depend on how much pressure is put on it, and whether or not pressure is put on it will depend on the exercise of political rights such as voting, criticizing and protesting.

Consider the matter of famine. I have tried to argue elsewhere that the avoidance of such economic disasters as famines is made much easier by the existence, and the exercise, of various liberties and political rights, including the liberty of free expression. Indeed, one of the remarkable facts in the terrible history of famine is that no substantial famine has ever occurred in a country with a democratic form of government and a relatively free press. They have occurred in ancient kingdoms and in contemporary authoritarian societies, in primitive tribal communities and in modern technocratic dictatorships, in colonial economies governed by imperialists from the north and in newly independent countries of the south run by despotic national leaders or by intolerant single parties. But famines have never afflicted any country that is independent, that goes to elections regularly, that has opposition parties to voice criticisms, that permits newspapers to report freely and to question the wisdom of government policies without extensive censorship.

Voting and Famine

Is this historical association between the absence of famine and the presence of political freedom a causal one, or is it simply an accidental connection? The possibility that the connection between democratic political rights and the absence of famine is a "bogus correlation" may seem plausible when one considers the fact that democratic countries are typically rather rich, and thus immune to famine for other reasons. But the absence of famine holds even for those democratic countries that happen to be poor, such as India, Botswana and Zimbabwe.

There is also what we might call "intertemporal evidence," which we observe when a country undergoes a transition to democracy. Thus India continued to have famines right up to the time of independence in 1947; the last famine, and one of the largest, was the Bengal famine of 1943, in which it is estimated that between

2 million and 3 million people died. Since independence, however, and the installation of a multiparty democratic system, there has been no substantial famine, even though severe crop failures and food scarcities have occurred often enough (in 1968, 1973, 1979 and 1987).

Why might we expect a general connection between democracy and the nonoccurrence of famines? The answer is not hard to find. Famines kill millions of people in different countries in the world, but they do not kill the rulers. The kings and the presidents, the bureaucrats and the bosses, the military leaders and the commanders never starve. And if there are no elections, no opposition parties, no forums for uncensored public criticism, then those in authority do not have to suffer the political consequences of their failure to prevent famine. Democracy, by contrast, would spread the penalty of famine to the ruling groups and the political leadership.

There is, moreover, the issue of information. A free press, and more generally the practice of democracy, contributes greatly to bringing out the information that can have an enormous impact on policies for famine prevention, such as facts about the early effects of droughts and floods, and about the nature and the results of unemployment. The most elementary source of basic information about a threatening famine is the news media, especially when there are incentives, which a democratic system provides, for revealing facts that may be embarrassing to the government, facts that an undemocratic regime would tend to censor. Indeed, I would argue that a free press and an active political opposition constitute the best "early warning system" that a country threatened by famine can possess.

Mao's Missing Links

The connection between political rights and economic needs can be illustrated in the specific context of famine prevention by considering the massive Chinese famines of 1958–61. Even before the recent economic reforms, China had been much more successful than India in economic development. The average life expectancy, for example, rose in China much more than it did in India, and well before the reforms of 1979 it had already reached something like the high figure—nearly 70 years at birth—that is quoted now. And yet China was not able to prevent famine. It is now estimated that the Chinese famines of 1958–61 killed close to 30 million people— 10 times more than even the gigantic 1943 famine in British India.

The so-called "Great Leap Forward," initiated in the late 1950s, was a massive failure, but the Chinese government refused to admit it and continued dogmatically to pursue much the same disastrous policies for three more years. It is hard to imagine that this could have happened in a country that goes to the polls regularly and has an independent press. During that terrible calamity, the government faced no pressure from newspapers, which were controlled, or from opposition parties, which were not allowed to exist.

The lack of a free system of news distribution even misled the government itself. It believed its own propaganda and the rosy reports of local party officials competing for credit in Beijing.

Indeed, there is evidence that just as the famine was moving toward its peak, the Chinese authorities mistakenly believed that they had 100 million more metric tons of grain than they actually did. Interestingly enough, Mao himself, whose radical beliefs had much to do with the initiation of, and the perseverance with, the Great Leap Forward, identified the informational role of democracy, once the failure was belatedly acknowledged. In 1962, just after the famine had killed so many millions, he made the following observation to a gathering of 7,000 cadres:

> Without democracy, you have no understanding of what is happening down below; the situation will be unclear; you will be unable to collect sufficient opinions from all sides; there can be no communication between top and bottom; top-level organs of leadership will depend on one-sided and incorrect material to decide issues, thus you will find it difficult to avoid being subjectivist; it will be impossible to achieve unity of understanding and unity of action, and impossible to achieve true centralism.

Mao's defense of democracy here is quite limited. The focus is exclusively on the informational side, ignoring the incentive role of democracy, not to mention any intrinsic importance that it may have. Still, it is significant that Mao himself acknowledged the extent to which disastrous official policies were caused by the lack of the informational links that a more democratic system could have provided.

These issues remain relevant in China today. Since the economic reforms of 1979, official Chinese policies have been based on the acknowledgment of the importance of economic incentives without a similar acknowledgment of the importance of political incentives. When things go reasonably well, the disciplinary role of democracy might not be greatly missed; but when big policy mistakes are made, this lacuna can be quite disastrous. The significance of the democracy movements in contemporary China has to be judged in this light.

African Disasters

Another set of examples comes from sub-Saharan Africa, which has been plagued by persistent famine since the early 1970s. There are many factors underlying the susceptibility of this region to famine, from the ecological impact of climatic deterioration—making crops more uncertain—to the negative effects of persistent wars and skirmishes. But the typically authoritarian nature of many of the sub-Saharan African polities also has something to do with the frequency of famine.

The nationalist movements were all anticolonialist, but they were not all pro-democratic, and it is only recently that the assertion of the value of democracy has achieved some political respectability in many of the countries of sub-Saharan Africa. And in this political milieu the Cold War did not help at all. The United States and its allies were ready to support undemocratic governments if they were sufficiently anti-Communist, no matter how anti-egalitarian they might have been in their domestic policies. The Soviet Union and China, of course, also did not recoil from authoritarian regimes. When opposition parties were

banned and newspapers were suppressed, there were very few international protests.

One must not deny that there were African governments, even in one-party states, that were deeply concerned about averting disasters and famine. Examples of this range from the tiny country of Cape Verde to the politically experimental nation of Tanzania. But quite often the absence of opposition and the suppression of free newspapers gave the respective governments an immunity from social criticism and political pressure that translated into thoroughly insensitive and callous policies.

Often famines were taken for granted, and it was common to put the blame for the disasters on natural causes and the perfidy of other countries. In various ways, Sudan, Ethiopia, Uganda, Chad, several of the Sahel countries and others provide glaring examples of how badly things can go wrong without the discipline of opposition parties and the news media. The way toward the Somali crisis was prepared by decades of intolerance, authoritarianism and a general undermining of orderly political processes.

This is not to deny that famines in these countries were often associated with crop failures: When a crop fails, it not only affects the food supply, it also destroys employment and the means of livelihood. But the occurrence of crop failures is not independent of public policies (such as governmental fixing of relative prices, policy regarding irrigation and agricultural research and so on). Moreover, even when crops fail, a famine can be averted by a careful redistribution policy. Botswana, for example, experienced a fall in food production of 17 percent,

and Zimbabwe a fall of 38 percent, between 1979–81 and 1983–84, in the same period in which the decline in food production amounted to a relatively modest 11 percent or 12 percent in Sudan and Ethiopia. Sudan and Ethiopia, with comparatively smaller declines in food output, had major famines. Botswana and Zimbabwe had none. The happy outcome in the latter countries was largely the result of timely and extensive famine-prevention policies by these latter countries. And democracy, which included a relatively uncensored press, made such policies imperative. For had the governments in Botswana and Zimbabwe failed to do this, they would have come under severe criticism from the political opposition. The Ethiopian and Sudanese governments, by contrast, did not have to reckon with such democratic inconveniences.

Some Qualifications

In making such arguments, of course, there is the danger of exaggerating the effectiveness of democracy. Political rights and liberties are permissive advantages, and their effectiveness depends on how they are exercised. Democracies have been particularly successful in preventing disasters that are easy to understand, in which sympathy can take an especially immediate form. Many other problems are not quite so accessible. Thus India's success in eradicating famine is not matched by a similar success in eliminating non-extreme hunger, or in curing persistent illiteracy, or in relieving inequalities in gender relations. While the plight of famine victims is easy to politicize, these other deprivations call for deeper analysis, and for greater and more effective use of mass communication and political participation—in sum, for a further practice of democracy.

A similar observation may be made about various failings in more mature democracies as well. For example, the extraordinary deprivations in health care, education and social environment of African Americans in the US make their mortality rates exceptionally high. American blacks have low survival chances to old age not only compared with American whites, but also compared with the citizens of China, Sri Lanka or the Indian state of Kerala, who are better provided with these public goods (despite being immensely poorer in per capita income). And some American blacks are even more deprived than others; the male residents of Harlem not only have lower survival chances than the corresponding groups in Kerala or Sri Lanka or China, they even fall behind Bangladeshi men by their late 30s.

But, again, the remedy of these failures in the practice of democracy turns, to a great extent, on the fuller use of political and civil rights, including more public discussion, more accessible information and more concrete proposals. To be sure, the difficulties in deciding on the means of eradicating these hardened deprivations remain. Still, the fact that the lack of medical care for many has become more prominent in the politics of the United States is what lends the matter some urgency, what directs new energy toward the solution of the problem. And the same grounds for hope would be true in the case of the poorer countries as well.

Minority Rights

It is important to acknowledge, however, the special difficulty of making a democracy take adequate notice of some types of deprivation, particularly the needs of minorities. One factor of some importance is the extent to which a minority group in a particular society can build on sympathy rather than alienation. When a minority forms a highly distinct and particularist group, it can be harder for it to receive the sympathy of the majority, and then the protective role of democracy may be particularly constrained.

Consider the ineffectiveness of electoral politics in ensuring sensitivity to the rights and the welfare of separatist groups, particularly those groups that are tainted with some use of terrorist methods and with receiving assistance from beyond the border. Illustrations are not hard to find in India, particularly in the case of Kashmir, where there is increasing evidence of the violation of civil rights and personal liberties by the Indian police and military. The frustration of the Kashmiris does not seem to influence the political behavior of the majority of Indians. Even India's large Muslim population, which numbers well over 100 million, does not appear to have much interest in working for the rights of the relatively tiny Muslim population of Kashmir. There is also a basic tension between the separatism of Kashmiri Muslim activists and the deep-seated integrationist beliefs of the immensely larger Muslim population in the rest of the country.

In the rather straitjacketed models of so-called "rational choice theory," which tend to characterize human beings as narrowly self-interested, it is hard to incorporate the satisfaction of minority needs through majority votes. To some extent this skepticism is justified. Even the plight of African Americans has something to do with the fact that blacks constitute a relatively small minority of the American population. And yet politics does not always operate in this way. Much depends on which issues are identified and politicized and made into a concern of those who are not directly involved.

Potential famine victims form a small minority in any country (a famine rarely affects more than 5 percent, and at most 10 percent, of a population), and the effectiveness of democracy in the prevention of famine has tended to depend on the politicization of the plight of famine victims, through the process of public discussion, which generates political solidarity. Outrage at famine deaths moves vast numbers of people who are in no way threatened by starvation themselves.

Population and Freedom

Among the developing countries, China has distinguished itself in its use of coercion to cut down the growth rate of its population, in some regions by means of such measures as a "one-child policy," and more generally by the conditioning of social security and economic rights (such as housing) on adherence to the government's rules about the number of births, the terrible predicament of children in larger families notwithstanding. There are many admirers of such harsh policies and China's success in fertility reduction is often cited as an argument for coercion. The birth rate in China has certainly come down; it is now around 19 per 1,000, which is considerably lower than India's 29 per 1,000 and the average figure of 37 per 1,000 for poor countries other than India and China.

Within India, however, there are wide variations in the birth rate, and these variations relate both to rates of mortality and to education, especially to female education. Consider the state of Kerala, which, with a population close to 30 million people, is larger than Canada. Kerala has the highest life expectancy in India (more than 70 years, in fact 74 years for women, considerably higher than China's), the highest rate of literacy in general, and the highest rate of female literacy (higher than that of China as a whole and higher than that of every province in China). The birth rate in Kerala has fallen sharply over the last few decades, from 44 per 1,000 in the 1950s to 18 per 1,000 by 1991. This birth rate, lower than China's, has not been achieved by compulsory birth control or by the violation of the individual's freedom to decide on these matters, but by the voluntary exercise of the family's right to family planning.

Indeed, when China introduced the policy of "one-child family" and other measures of compulsion in 1979, Kerala had a total fertility rate (roughly the number of children per couple) of 3.0, while China's fertility rate was 2.8. Between then and the early 1990s, the fertility rate in China fell from 2.8 to 2.0, while that in Kerala declined from 3.0 to 1.8, ending up as much below China's fertility rate as it had been above it in 1979. Compulsion did not help China to have a faster fall in fertility rate than cooperation did in Kerala—quite the contrary.

The change in Kerala is owed in part to the operation of economic and social incentives toward smaller families, as the death rate has fallen and family-planning opportunities have been combined with health care. But it is also influenced by a general perception that the lowering of the birth rate is a real need of a modern family; and this perception would not have been possible without public education (especially of women) and enlightened discussion. The emergence of a resolute desire by Keralan women to be less shackled by continuous child-rearing is part of the process of the free formation of values and priorities.

The temptation to impose compulsory birth control arises when the government's view of needs differs from the views of the families themselves. Such a disjunction can lead to deeply disturbing results. Thus, while China has ended up with a birth rate only a little higher than the birth rate of Kerala, one result of official coercion in China has been a much higher level of mortality among female children, quite unlike the situation in Kerala. The traditional "son preference" seems often to have led to extreme responses in China to compulsory birth control measures, including an increase in female infanticide and in the differential neglect of female children. These horrors must be counted among the consequences of a closed society in which the reduction in the birth rate is achieved without an open and educated discussion of personal and economic needs.

While China and Kerala had similar figures of infant mortality in 1979, by the early 1990s Kerala's infant mortality rates (per 1,000) had fallen to 17 for boys and 16 for girls, but those rates for China became 28 for boys and 33 for girls. The generally higher rate of infant mortality in China (not just for girls but especially for them) were partly the result of coercive family-planning policies.

Political rights are important not only for the fulfillment of needs, they are crucial also for the formulation of needs. And this idea relates, in the end, to the respect that we owe each other as fellow human beings. In *Taking Leave*, William Cobbett observed that "we now frequently hear the working classes called 'the population,' just as we call animals upon a farm 'the stock.'" The importance of political rights for the understanding of economic needs turns ultimately on seeing human beings as people with rights to exercise, not as parts of a "stock" or a "population" that passively exists and must be looked after. What matters, finally, is how we see each other.

 Article Review Form at end of book.

The Capitalist Threat

What kind of society do we want? "Let the free market decide!" is the often-heard response. That response, a prominent capitalist argues, undermines the very values on which open and democratic societies depend.

George Soros

In *The Philosophy of History*, Hegel discerned a disturbing historical pattern—the crack and fall of civilizations owing to a morbid intensification of their own first principles. Although I have made a fortune in the financial markets, I now fear that the untrammeled intensification of laissez-faire capitalism and the spread of market values into all areas of life is endangering our open and democratic society. The main enemy of the open society, I believe, is no longer the communist but the capitalist threat.

The term "open society" was coined by Henri Bergson, in his book *The Two Sources of Morality and Religion* (1932), and given greater currency by the Austrian philosopher Karl Popper, in his book *The Open Society and Its Enemies* (1945). Popper showed that totalitarian ideologies like communism and Nazism have a common element: they claim to be in possession of the ultimate truth. Since the ultimate truth is beyond the reach of humankind, these ideologies have to resort to oppression in order to impose their vision on society. Popper juxtaposed with

these totalitarian ideologies another view of society, which recognizes that nobody has a monopoly on the truth; different people have different views and different interests, and there is a need for institutions that allow them to live together in peace. These institutions protect the rights of citizens and ensure freedom of choice and freedom of speech. Popper called this form of social organization the "open society." Totalitarian ideologies were its enemies.

Written during the Second World War, *The Open Society and Its Enemies* explained what the Western democracies stood for and fought for. The explanation was highly abstract and philosophical, and the term "open society" never gained wide recognition. Nevertheless, Popper's analysis was penetrating, and when I read it as a student in the later 1940s, having experienced at first hand both Nazi and Communist rule in Hungary, it struck me with the force of revelation.

I was driven to delve deeper into Karl Popper's philosophy, and to ask, Why does nobody have access to the ultimate truth? The answer became clear: We live in the same universe that we are trying to understand, and our perceptions can influence the events

in which we participate. If our thoughts belonged to one universe and their subject matter to another, the truth might be within our grasp: we could formulate statements corresponding to the facts, and the facts would serve as reliable criteria for deciding whether the statements were true.

There is a realm where these conditions prevail: natural science. But in other areas of human endeavor the relationship between statements and facts is less clear-cut. In social and political affairs the participants' perceptions help to determine reality. In these situations facts do not necessarily constitute reliable criteria for judging the truth of statements. There is a two-way connection—a feedback mechanism—between thinking and events, which I have called "reflexivity." I have used it to develop a theory of history.

Whether the theory is valid or not, it has turned out to be very helpful to me in the financial markets. When I had made more money than I needed, I decided to set up a foundation. I reflected on what it was I really cared about. Having lived through Nazi persecution and Communist oppression, I came to the conclusion that what was paramount for me was

George Soros, " The Capitalist Threat." Work originally appeared in THE ATLANTIC MONTHLY (February 1997) and is reprinted here with the permission of the author.

an open society. So I called the foundation the Open Society Fund, and I defined its objectives as opening up closed societies, making open societies more viable, and promoting a critical mode of thinking. That was in 1979.

My first major undertaking was in South Africa, but it was not successful. The apartheid system was so pervasive that whatever I tried to do made me part of the system rather than helping to change it. Then I turned my attention to Central Europe. Here I was much more successful. I started supporting the Charter 77 movement in Czechoslovakia in 1980 and Solidarity in Poland in 1981. I established separate foundations in my native country, Hungary, in 1984, in China in 1986, in the Soviet Union in 1987, and in Poland in 1988. My engagement accelerated with the collapse of the Soviet system. By now I have established a network of foundations that extends across more than twenty-five countries (not including China, where we shut down in 1989).

Operating under Communist regimes, I never felt the need to explain what "open society" meant; those who supported the objectives of the foundations understood it better than I did, even if they were not familiar with the expression. The goal of my foundation in Hungary, for example, was to support alternative activities. I knew that the prevailing Communist dogma was false exactly because it was a dogma, and that it would become unsustainable if it was exposed to alternatives. The approach proved effective. The foundation became the main source of support for civil society in Hungary, and as civil society flourished, so the Communist regime waned.

After the collapse of communism, the mission of the foundation network changed. Recognizing that an open society is a more advanced, more sophisticated form of social organization than a closed society (because in a closed society there is only one blueprint, which is imposed on society, whereas in an open society each citizen is not only allowed but required to think for himself), the foundations shifted from a subversive task to a constructive one—not an easy thing to do when the believers in an open society are accustomed to subversive activity. Most of my foundations did a good job, but unfortunately, they did not have much company. The open societies of the West did not feel a strong urge to promote open societies in the former Soviet empire. On the contrary, the prevailing view was that people ought to be left to look after their own affairs. The end of the Cold War brought a response very different from that at the end of the Second World War. The idea of a new Marshall Plan could not even be mooted. When I proposed such an idea at a conference in Potsdam (in what was then still East Germany), in the spring of 1989, I was literally laughed at.

The collapse of communism laid the groundwork for a universal open society, but the Western democracies failed to rise to the occasion. The new regimes that are emerging in the former Soviet Union and the former Yugoslavia bear little resemblance to open societies. The Western alliance seems to have lost its sense of purpose, because it cannot define itself in terms of a Communist menace. It has shown little inclination to come to the aid of those who have defended the idea of an open society in Bosnia or any-

where else. As for the people living in formerly Communist countries, they might have aspired to an open society when they suffered from repression, but now that the Communist system has collapsed, they are preoccupied with the problems of survival. After the failure of communism there came a general disillusionment with universal concepts, and the open society is a universal concept.

These considerations have forced me to re-examine my belief in the open society. For five or six years following the fall of the Berlin Wall, I devoted practically all of my energies to the transformation of the formerly Communist world. More recently I have redirected my attention to our own society. The network of foundations I created continues to do good work; nevertheless, I felt an urgent need to reconsider the conceptual framework that had guided me in establishing them. This reassessment has led me to the conclusion that the concept of the open society has not lost its relevance. On the contrary, it may be even more useful in understanding the present moment in history and in providing a practical guide to political action than it was at the time Karl Popper wrote his book—but it needs to be thoroughly rethought and reformulated. If the open society is to serve as an ideal worth striving for, it can no longer be defined in terms of the Communist menace. It must be given a more positive content.

The New Enemy

Popper showed that fascism and communism had much in common, even though one constituted the extreme right and the other the extreme left, because both relied on the power of the state to repress the freedom of the individual. I want to extend his argument. I contend that an open society may also be threatened from the opposite direction—from excessive individualism. Too much competition and too little cooperation can cause intolerable inequities and instability.

Insofar as there is a dominant belief in our society today, it is a belief in the magic of the marketplace. The doctrine of laissez-faire capitalism holds that the common good is best served by the uninhibited pursuit of self-interest. Unless it is tempered by the recognition of a common interest that ought to take precedence over particular interests, our present system—which, however imperfect, qualifies as an open society—is liable to break down.

I want to emphasize, however, that I am not putting laissez-faire capitalism in the same category as Nazism or communism. Totalitarian ideologies deliberately seek to destroy the open society; laissez-faire policies may endanger it, but only inadvertently. Friedrich Hayek, one of the apostles of laissez-faire, was also a passionate proponent of the open society. Nevertheless, because communism and even socialism have been thoroughly discredited, I consider the threat from the laissez-faire side more potent today than the threat from totalitarian ideologies. We are enjoying a truly global market economy in which goods, services, capital, and even people move around quite freely, but we fail to recognize the need to sustain the values and institutions of an open society.

The present situation is comparable to that at the turn of the past century. It was a golden age of capitalism, characterized by the principle of laissez-faire; so is the present. The earlier period was in some ways more stable. There was an imperial power, England, that was prepared to dispatch gunboats to faraway places because as the main beneficiary of the system it had a vested interest in maintaining that system. Today the United States does not want to be the policeman of the world. The earlier period had the gold standard; today the main currencies float and crush against each other like continental plates. Yet the free-market regime that prevailed a hundred years ago was destroyed by the First World War. Totalitarian ideologies came to the fore, and by the end of the Second World War there was practically no movement of capital between countries. How much more likely the present regime is to break down unless we learn from experience!

Although laissez-faire doctrines do not contradict the principles of the open society the way Marxism-Leninism or Nazi ideas of racial purity did, all these doctrines have an important feature in common: they all try to justify their claim to ultimate truth with an appeal to science. In the case of totalitarian doctrines, that appeal could easily be dismissed. One of Popper's accomplishments was to show that a theory like Marxism does not qualify as science. In the case of laissez-faire the claim is more difficult to dispute, because it is based on economic theory, and economics is the most reputable of the social sciences. One cannot simply equate market economics with Marxist economics. Yet laissez-faire ideology, I contend, is just as much a perversion of supposedly scientific verities as Marxism-Leninism is.

The main scientific underpinning of the laissez-faire ideology is the theory that free and competitive markets bring supply and demand into equilibrium and thereby ensure the best allocation of resources. This is widely accepted as an eternal verity, and in a sense it is one. Economic theory is an axiomatic system: as long as the basic assumptions hold, the conclusions follow. But when we examine the assumptions closely, we find that they do not apply to the real world. As originally formulated, the theory of perfect competition—of the natural equilibrium of supply and demand—assumed perfect knowledge, homogeneous and easily divisible products, and a large enough number of market participants that no single participant could influence the market price. The assumption of perfect knowledge proved unsustainable, so it was replaced by an ingenious device. Supply and demand were taken as independently given. This condition was presented as a methodological requirement rather than an assumption. It was argued that economic theory studies the relationship between supply and demand; therefore it must take both of them as given.

As I have shown elsewhere, the condition that supply and demand are independently given cannot be reconciled with reality, at least as far as the financial markets are concerned—and financial markets play a crucial role in the allocation of resources. Buyers and sellers in financial markets seek to discount a future that depends on their own decisions. The shape of the supply and demand curves cannot be taken as given because both of them incorporate expectations about events that are shaped by those expectations. There is a two-way feedback mechanism between the market participants' thinking and the situation they think about—"reflexivity." It accounts for both the imperfect understanding of the participants (recognition of which is the basis of the concept of the open society) and the indeterminacy of the process in which they participate.

If the supply and demand curves are not independently given, how are market prices determined? If we look at the behavior of financial markets, we find that instead of tending toward equilibrium, prices continue to fluctuate relative to the expectations of buyers and sellers. There are prolonged periods when prices are moving away from any theoretical equilibrium. Even if they eventually show a tendency to return, the equilibrium is not the same as it would have been without the intervening period. Yet the concept of equilibrium endures. It is easy to see why: without it, economics could not say how prices are determined.

In the absence of equilibrium, the contention that free markets lead to the optimum allocation of resources loses its justification. The supposedly scientific theory that has been used to validate it turns out to be an axiomatic structure whose conclusions are contained in its assumptions and are not necessarily supported by the empirical evidence. The resemblance to Marxism, which also claimed scientific status for its tenets, is too close for comfort.

I do not mean to imply that economic theory has deliberately distorted reality for political purposes. But in trying to imitate the accomplishments (and win for itself the prestige) of natural science, economic theory attempted the impossible. The theories of social science relate to their subject matter in a reflexive manner. That is to say, they can influence events in a way that the theories of nat-

ural science cannot. Heisenberg's famous uncertainty principle implies that the act of observation may interfere with the behavior of quantum particles; but it is the observation that creates the effect, not the uncertainty principle itself. In the social sphere, theories have the capacity to alter the subject matter to which they relate. Economic theory has deliberately excluded reflexivity from consideration. In doing so, it has distorted its subject matter and laid itself open to exploitation by laissez-faire ideology.

What allows economic theory to be converted into an ideology hostile to the open society is the assumption of perfect knowledge—at first openly stated and then disguised in the form of a methodological device. There is a powerful case for the market mechanism, but it is not that markets are perfect; it is that in a world dominated by imperfect understanding, markets provide an efficient feedback mechanism for evaluating the results of one's decisions and correcting mistakes.

Whatever its form, the assertion of perfect knowledge stands in contradiction to the concept of the open society (which recognizes that our understanding of our situation is inherently imperfect). Since this point is abstract, I need to describe specific ways in which laissez-faire ideas can pose a threat to the open society. I shall focus on three issues: economic stability, social justice, and international relations.

Economic Stability

Economic theory has managed to create an artificial world in which the participants' preferences and the opportunities confronting participants are independent of each other, and prices tend toward an

equilibrium that brings the two forces into balance. But in financial markets prices are not merely the passive reflection of independently given demand and supply; they also play an active role in shaping those preferences and opportunities. This reflexive interaction renders financial markets inherently unstable. Laissez-faire ideology denies the instability and opposes any form of government intervention aimed at preserving stability. History has shown that financial markets do break down, causing economic depression and social unrest. The breakdowns have led to the evolution of central banking and other forms of regulation. Laissez-faire ideologues like to argue that the breakdowns were caused by faulty regulations, not by unstable markets. There is some validity in their argument, because if our understanding is inherently imperfect, regulations are bound to be defective. But their argument rings hollow, because it fails to explain why the regulations were imposed in the first place. It sidesteps the issue by using a different argument, which goes like this: since regulations are faulty, unregulated markets are perfect.

The argument rests on the assumption of perfect knowledge: if a solution is wrong, its opposite must be right. In the absence of perfect knowledge, however, both free markets and regulations are flawed. Stability can be preserved only if a deliberate effort is made to preserve it. Even then breakdowns will occur, because public policy is often faulty. If they are severe enough, breakdowns may give rise to totalitarian regimes.

Instability extends well beyond financial markets: it affects the values that guide people in their actions. Economic theory takes values as given. At the time economic theory was born, in the age of Adam Smith, David Ricardo, and Alfred Marshall, this was a reasonable assumption, because people did, in fact, have firmly established values. Adam Smith himself combined a moral philosophy with his economic theory. Beneath the individual preferences that found expression in market behavior, people were guided by a set of moral principles that found expression in behavior outside the scope of the market mechanism. Deeply rooted in tradition, religion, and culture, these principles were not necessarily rational in the sense of representing conscious choices among available alternatives. Indeed, they often could not hold their own when alternatives became available. Market values served to undermine traditional values.

There has been an ongoing conflict between market values and other, more traditional value systems, which has aroused strong passions and antagonisms. As the market mechanism has extended its sway, the fiction that people act on the basis of a given set of nonmarket values has become progressively more difficult to maintain. Advertising, marketing, even packaging, aim at shaping people's preferences rather than, as laissez-faire theory holds, merely responding to them. Unsure of what they stand for, people increasingly rely on money as the criterion of value. What is more expensive is considered better. The value of a work of art can be judged by the price it fetches. People deserve respect and admiration because they are rich. What used to be a medium of exchange has usurped the place of fundamental values, reversing the relationship postulated by economic theory. What used to be

professions have turned into businesses. The cult of success has replaced a belief in principles. Society has lost its anchor.

Social Darwinism

By taking the conditions of supply and demand as given and declaring government intervention the ultimate evil, laissez-faire ideology has effectively banished income or wealth redistribution. I can agree that all attempts at redistribution interfere with the efficiency of the market, but it does not follow that no attempt should be made. The laissez-faire argument relies on the same tacit appeal to perfection as does communism. It claims that if redistribution causes inefficiencies and distortions, the problems can be solved by eliminating redistribution—just as the Communists claimed that the duplication involved in competition is wasteful, and therefore we should have a centrally planned economy. But perfection is unattainable. Wealth does accumulate in the hands of its owners, and if there is no mechanism for redistribution, the inequities can become intolerable. "Money is like muck, not good except it be spread." Francis Bacon was a profound economist.

The laissez-faire argument against income redistribution invokes the doctrine of the survival of the fittest. The argument is undercut by the fact that wealth is passed on by inheritance, and the second generation is rarely as fit as the first.

In any case, there is something wrong with making the survival of the fittest a guiding principle of civilized society. This social Darwinism is based on an outmoded theory of evolution, just as the equilibrium theory in economics is taking its cue from

Newtonian physics. The principle that guides the evolution of species is mutation, and mutation works in a much more sophisticated way. Species and their environment are interactive, and one species serves as part of the environment for the others. There is a feedback mechanism similar to reflexivity in history, with the difference being that in history the mechanism is driven not by mutation but by misconceptions. I mention this because social Darwinism is one of the misconceptions driving human affairs today. The main point I want to make is that cooperation is as much a part of the system as competition, and the slogan "survival of the fittest" distorts this fact.

International Relations

Laissez-faire ideology shares some of the deficiencies of another spurious science, geopolitics. States have no principles, only interests, geopoliticians argue, and those interests are determined by geographic location and other fundamentals. This deterministic approach is rooted in an outdated nineteenth-century view of scientific method, and it suffers from at least two glaring defects that do not apply with the same force to the economic doctrines of laissez-faire. One is that it treats the state as the indivisible unit of analysis, just as economics treats the individual. There is something contradictory in banishing the state from the economy while at the same time enshrining it as the ultimate source of authority in international relations. But let that pass. There is a more pressing practical aspect of the problem. What happens when a state disintegrates? Geopolitical realists find themselves totally unprepared. That is what happened when the Soviet

Union and Yugoslavia disintegrated. The other defect of geopolitics is that is does not recognize a common interest beyond the national interest.

With the demise of communism, the present state of affairs, however imperfect, can be described as a global open society. It is not threatened from the outside, from some totalitarian ideology seeking world supremacy. The threat comes from the inside, from local tyrants seeking to establish internal dominance through external conflicts. It may also come from democratic but sovereign states pursuing their self-interest to the detriment of the common interest. The international open society may be its own worst enemy.

The Cold War was an extremely stable arrangement. Two power blocs, representing opposing concepts of social organization, were struggling for supremacy, but they had to respect each other's vital interests, because each side was capable of destroying the other in an all-out war. This put a firm limit on the extent of the conflict; all local conflicts were, in turn, contained by the larger conflict. This extremely stable world order has come to an end as the result of the internal disintegration of one superpower. No new world order has taken its place. We have entered a period of disorder.

Laissez-faire ideology does not prepare us to cope with this challenge. It does not recognize the need for a world order. An order is supposed to emerge from states' pursuit of their self-interest. But, guided by the principle of the survival of the fittest, states are increasingly preoccupied with their competitiveness and unwilling to make any sacrifices for the common good.

There is no need to make any dire predictions about the eventual breakdown of our global trading system in order to show that a laissez-faire ideology is incompatible with the concept of the open society. It is enough to consider the free world's failure to extend a helping hand after the collapse of communism. The system of robber capitalism that has taken hold in Russia is so iniquitous that people may well turn to a charismatic leader promising national revival at the cost of civil liberties.

If there is any lesson to be learned, it is that the collapse of a repressive regime does not automatically lead to the establishment of an open society. An open society is not merely the absence of government intervention and oppression. It is a complicated, sophisticated structure, and deliberate effort is required to bring it into existence. Since it is more sophisticated than the system it replaces, a speedy transition requires outside assistance. But the combination of laissez-faire ideas, social Darwinism, and geopolitical realism that prevailed in the United States and the United Kingdom stood in the way of any hope for an open society in Russia. If the leaders of these countries had had a different view of the world, they could have established firm foundations for a global open society.

At the time of the Soviet collapse there was an opportunity to make the UN function as it was originally designed to. Mikhail Gorbachev visited the United Nations in 1988 and outlined his vision of the two superpowers cooperating to bring peace and security to the world. Since then the opportunity has faded. The UN has been thoroughly discredited as a peacekeeping institution. Bosnia is doing to the UN what Abyssinia did to the League of Nations in 1936.

Our global open society lacks the institutions and mechanisms necessary for its preservation, but there is no political will to bring them into existence. I blame the prevailing attitude, which holds that the unhampered pursuit of self-interest will bring about an eventual international equilibrium. I believe this confidence is misplaced. I believe that the concept of the open society, which needs institutions to protect it, may provide a better guide to action. As things stand, it does not take very much imagination to realize that the global open society that prevails at present is likely to prove a temporary phenomenon.

The Promise of Fallibility

It is easier to identify the enemies of the open society than to give the concept a positive meaning. Yet without such a positive meaning the open society is bound to fall prey to its enemies. There has to be a common interest to hold a community together, but the open society is not a community in the traditional sense of the word. It is an abstract idea, a universal concept. Admittedly, there is such a thing as a global community; there are common interests on a global level, such as the preservation of the environment and the prevention of war. But these interests are relatively weak in comparison with special interests. They do not have much of a constituency in a world composed of sovereign states. Moreover, the open society as a universal concept transcends all boundaries. Societies derive their cohesion from shared values. These values are rooted in culture, religion, history, and tradition. When a society does not have boundaries, where are the shared values to be found? I believe there is only one possible source: the concept of the open society itself.

To fulfill this role, the concept of the open society needs to be redefined. Instead of there being a dichotomy between open and closed, I see the open society as occupying a middle ground, where the rights of the individual are safeguarded but where there are some shared values that hold society together. This middle ground is threatened from all sides. At one extreme, communist and nationalist doctrines would lead to state domination. At the other extreme, laissez-faire capitalism would lead to great instability and eventual breakdown. There are other variants. Lee Kuan Yew, of Singapore, proposes a so-called Asian model that combines a market economy with a repressive state. In many parts of the world control of the state is so closely associated with the creation of private wealth that one might speak of robber capitalism, or the "gangster state," as a new threat to the open society.

I envisage the open society as a society open to improvement. We start with the recognition of our own fallibility, which extends not only to our mental constructs but also to our institutions. What is imperfect can be improved, by a process of trial and error. The open society not only allows this process but actually encourages it, by insisting on freedom of expression and protecting dissent. The open society offers a vista of limitless progress. In this respect it has an affinity with the scientific method. But science has at its disposal objective criteria—namely the facts by which the process may be judged. Unfortunately, in human affairs the facts do not provide reliable criteria of truth, yet we need some generally agreed-upon standards by which the process of trial and error can be judged. All cultures and religions offer such standards; the open society cannot do without them. The innovation in an open society is that whereas most cultures and religions regard their own values as absolute, an open society, which is aware of many cultures and religions, must regard its own shared values as a matter of debate and choice. To make the debate possible, there must be general agreement on at least one point: that the open society is a desirable form of social organization. People must be free to think and act, subject only to limits imposed by the common interests. Where the limits are must also be determined by trial and error.

The Declaration of Independence may be taken as a pretty good approximation of the principles of an open society, but instead of claiming that those principles are self-evident, we ought to say that they are consistent with our fallibility. Could the recognition of our imperfect understanding serve to establish the open society as a desirable form of social organization? I believe it could, although there are formidable difficulties in the way. We must promote a belief in our own fallibility to the status that we normally confer on a belief in ultimate truth. But if ultimate truth is not attainable, how can we accept our fallibility as ultimate truth?

This is an apparent paradox, but it can be resolved. The first proposition, that our understanding is imperfect, is consistent with a second proposition: that we must accept the first proposition as an article of faith. The need for articles of faith arises exactly because our understanding is im-perfect. If we enjoyed perfect knowledge, there would be no need for beliefs. But to accept this line of reasoning requires a profound change in the role that we accord our beliefs.

Historically, beliefs have served to justify specific rules of conduct. Fallibility ought to foster a different attitude. Beliefs ought to serve to shape our lives, not to make us abide by a given set of rules. If we recognize that our beliefs are expressions of our choices, not of ultimate truth, we are more likely to tolerate other beliefs and to revise our own in the light of our experiences. But that is not how most people treat their beliefs. They tend to identify their beliefs with ultimate truth. Indeed, that identification often serves to define their own identity. If their experience of living in an open society obliges them to give up their claim to the ultimate truth, they feel a sense of loss.

The idea that we somehow embody the ultimate truth is deeply ingrained in our thinking. We may be endowed with critical faculties, but we are inseparably tied to ourselves. We may have discovered truth and morality, but, above all, we must represent our interests and our selves. Therefore, if there are such things as truth and justice—and we have come to believe that there are—then we want to be in possession of them. We demand truth from religion and, recently, from science. A belief in our fallibility is a poor substitute. It is a highly sophisticated concept, much more difficult to work with than more primitive beliefs, such as my country (or my company or my family), right or wrong.

If the idea of our fallibility is so hard to take, what makes it appealing? The most powerful argument in its favor is to be found in the results it produces. Open societies tend to be more prosperous, more innovative, more stimulating, than closed ones. But there is a danger in proposing success as the sole basis for holding a belief, because if my theory of reflexivity is valid, being successful is not identical with being right. In natural science, theories have to be right (in the sense that the predictions and explanations they produce correspond to the facts) for them to work (in the sense of producing useful predictions and explanations). But in the social sphere what is effective is not necessarily identical with what is right, because of the reflexive connection between thinking and reality. As I hinted earlier, the cult of success can become a source of instability in an open society, because it can undermine our sense of right and wrong. That is what is happening in our society today. Our sense of right and wrong is endangered by our preoccupation with success, as measured by money. Anything goes, as long as you can get away with it.

If success were the only criterion, the open society would lose out against totalitarian ideologies—as indeed it did on many occasions. It is much easier to argue for my own interest than to go through the whole rigmarole of abstract reasoning from fallibility to the concept of the open society.

The concept of the open society needs to be more firmly grounded. There has to be a commitment to the open society because it is the right form of social organization. Such a commitment is hard to come by.

I believe in the open society because it allows us to develop our potential better than a social system that claims to be in possession of ultimate truth. Accepting the unattainable character of truth offers a better prospect for freedom and prosperity than denying it. But I recognize a problem here: I am sufficiently committed to the pursuit of truth to find the case for the open society convincing, but I am not sure that other people will share my point of view. Given the reflexive connection between thinking and reality, truth is not indispensable for success. It may be possible to attain specific objectives by twisting or denying the truth, and people may be more interested in attaining their specific objectives than in attaining the truth. Only at the highest level of abstraction, when we consider the meaning of life, does truth take on paramount importance. Even then, deception may be preferable to the truth, because life entails death and death is difficult to accept. Indeed, one could argue that the open society is the best form of social organization for making the most of life, whereas the closed society is the form best suited to the acceptance of death. In the ultimate analysis a belief in the open society is a matter of choice, not of logical necessity.

That is not all. Even if the concept of the open society were universally accepted, that would not be sufficient to ensure that freedom and prosperity would prevail. The open society merely provides a framework within which different views about social and political issues can be reconciled; it does not offer a firm view on social goals. If it did, it would not be an open society. This means that people must hold other beliefs in addition to their belief in the open society. Only in a closed society does the concept of the open society provide a sufficient basis for political action; in an open society it is not enough to be a democrat; one must be a liberal democrat or a social democrat or a Christian democrat or some other kind of democrat. A shared belief in the open society is a necessary but not a sufficient condition for freedom and prosperity and all the good things that the open society is supposed to bring.

It can be seen that the concept of the open society is a seemingly inexhaustible source of difficulties. That is to be expected. After all, the open society is based on the recognition of our fallibility. Indeed, it stands to reason that our ideal of the open society is unattainable. To have a blueprint for it would be self-contradictory. That does not mean that we should not strive toward it. In science also, ultimate truth is unattainable. Yet look at the progress we have made in pursuing it. Similarly, the open society can be approximated to a greater or lesser extent.

To derive a political and social agenda from a philosophical, epistemological argument seems like a hopeless undertaking. Yet it can be done. There is historical precedent. The Enlightenment was a celebration of the power of reason, and it provided the inspiration for the Declaration of Independence and the Bill of Rights. The belief in reason was carried to excess in the French Revolution, with unpleasant side effects; nevertheless, it was the beginning of modernity. We have now had 200 years of experience with the Age of Reason, and as reasonable people we ought to recognize that reason has its limitations. The time is ripe for developing a conceptual framework based on our fallibility. Where reason has failed, fallibility may yet succeed.

 Article Review Form at end of book.

Out of the Closet and into *La Calle*

Violence against sexual minorities is on the rise in Latin America. While gay and lesbian activists who openly protest this violence face serious risks, they are increasingly willing to take those risks.

Amy Lind

Amy Lind teaches sociology and Latin American Studies at Brown University.

Like many gay-pride marches throughout the world, last year's Gay/Lesbian/Transvestite/Trans-sexual Pride March in Buenos Aires was held on June 28 to commemorate the 1969 Stonewall riots in New York City. Some 1,500 people, representing over 22 organizations from diverse regions of the country, were present—almost double the number of participants in the previous year's march. In many respects, this turnout was an expression of the growing political visibility of sexual minorities in Argentina. While only a small number of gay-rights organizations existed in Argentina—as in other Latin American countries—just two decades ago, today a broad range of organizations have emerged, reflecting the diverse experiences, types of oppression and political activism of sexual minorities.

Many of the marchers in Buenos Aires, fearful of the consequences of "coming out," wore masks or partially covered their faces as they marched through the downtown streets of the capital city. The need felt by many demonstrators to conceal their identities highlights the contradictions of becoming politically visible for sexual minorities in Latin America. On one hand, the demonstrators publicly manifested their pride—and anger—as they walked to the Congress from the Plaza de Mayo, an important public place for political expression in Argentina. The marchers also showed their growing discontent with Argentine laws and institutional practices which legitimize police brutality against gay men, lesbians, transvestites, transsexuals and other sexual minorities. It is precisely because of this violence, however, that many of those who protested in the streets were cautious about publicly revealing their identities.

Yet, while risks remain for gay and lesbian activists who engage in open protest, people are increasingly willing to take them. Pride marches have been organized in other countries, most notably in Mexico and Brazil. And throughout Latin America, gay and lesbian non-governmental organizations (NGOs) have played important roles in launching educational campaigns and in monitoring human rights abuses against sexual minorities.

While many progressive groups have supported this growing activism of Latin America's gay and lesbian community, the increased visibility has also triggered a backlash against gay-rights organizations. Police brutality has increased over the past few years, as have measures harassing sexual minorities, such as raids of gay and lesbian bars. Paramilitary groups have become more visible in their self-styled morality campaigns to "clean the streets" of "disposable" sectors of the population, including gays and lesbians as well as transvestites, transsexuals, male prostitutes, street children and other social "undesirables." Systematic, accurate documentation in recent years by gay-rights groups has highlighted the scope of the problem—and has provided a basis for local organizations to develop alliances with like-minded organizations in their cities and in other regions and countries.

Only a few countries, including Nicaragua, Ecuador and Chile, have laws which criminalize homosexual practices. In some cases, these laws have existed for decades, but in others, new anti-gay laws or legal campaigns have emerged. In Nicaragua, for example, the conservative government of Violeta Chamorro passed an anti-sodomy law in 1992 which mandates prison sentences of up to three years for "anyone who induces, promotes, propagandizes or practices in scandalous form sexual intercourse between persons of the same sex." Such legislation serves as "a constant threat," according to a recent report by the Inter-Church Committee on Human Rights in Latin America, "allowing the police to intimidate, abuse and extort lesbians, gays and transvestites." And in Guadalajara, Mexico, although no national law criminalizes homosexuality, the governing right-wing National Action Party (PAN) passed a local ordinance last December which outlaws "abnormal sexual behavior." The origins of the ordinance date back several decades, but this new version has received public attention because it renews the legal power of the local police to arrest homosexuals, and it makes extra-legal police practices like extortion more likely to occur.

Elsewhere in Latin America, existing laws designed to uphold "public morality" are being applied with renewed vigor against sexual minorities. For example, police in Peru have used laws against prostitution to arrest transvestites and male sex workers. Last January, under the guise of a campaign to crack down on prostitution known as "Operation Thunder," Peruvian police detained over 300 people in a series of raids on gay nightclubs.

A similar wave of police raids of gay and lesbian bars and nightclubs threatened Argentine sexual minorities in 1995 and 1996. While no law in Argentina specifically criminalizes homosexuality, the police have resorted to a number of other legal instruments to harass individuals they consider "dangerous." For example, police edicts, which are not laws as such, but regulations set in place nearly 50 years ago and applied at the discretion of the Argentine police, have been used extensively to harass sexual minorities. The "Edict Against Public Scandals," which punishes those "who disturb with flirtatious remarks" and prohibits "public exhibition of persons wearing or disguised with clothes of the opposite gender," has been used to arrest gay men, lesbians and transvestites. The "Edict Against Public Dancing" punishes any proprietor who "allows men to dance together." Individuals arrested under these edicts have been held by police for up to 30 days and fined. The Buenos Aires group, Gays for Civil Rights (Gays D. C.), says that it documented 331 complaints of arrest under the edicts in 1995—twice the number of complaints documented over the two-year period between September, 1992 and September, 1994. More than 50 transvestites and transsexuals were arrested every night in Buenos Aires in 1995 and the first half of 1996, according to the International Gay and Lesbian Human Rights Commission (IGLHRC), a non-profit organization based in San Francisco. In a single sweep last February, 160 people were arrested under the charges of cross-dressing and prostitution.

More brutal forms of repression against sexual minorities have also risen alarmingly over the past few years, especially in Brazil, Colombia, Ecuador and Peru. Paramilitary groups and "social cleansing" death squads claim to be taking justice into their own hands by "disposing" of those viewed as "dirtying" the social fabric of society. In Brazil, the Gay Group of Bahia (GGB) has documented more than 1,200 cases of assassinations of lesbians, gay men and transvestites since 1982. The group says that at least 12 anti-gay death squads operate in various parts of the country, including the "Group for Hunting Homosexuals" in Belém do Pará and a neo-nazi skinhead group in São Paulo whose members wear t-shirts saying "Death to Homosexuals." And in Colombia, 39 groups have engaged in "social cleansing" activities, according to activist Juan Pablo Ordoñez, including the groups, "Death to Dangerous Homosexuals" and "Death to Homosexuals."

 Article Review Form at end of book.

WiseGuide Wrap-Up

While many are hopeful that democratization is making gains around the world, obstacles remain. Authoritarian leaders who have agreed to hold elections still use intimidation, violence, control of the media, and campaign resources to prevent fair elections. Additionally, they sometimes "stack" the parliament by appointing enough representatives to give their political party control of the parliament, even as they allow elections for other parliamentary seats. Authoritarian leaders harass, jail, and sometimes torture media professionals who offer any criticism of governmental policies. Sometimes, after fair elections have been held, foreign governments pressure democratically elected officials to share power with the allies of the Northern governments.

"Social capital" includes the development of norms, trust, and networks of community organizations. Without citizen socialization into norms of civil behavior and without participation in organizations, where trust in the good will of others develops and the practices of compromise are learned, citizens are unlikely to sustain a democratic society.

Supporters of authoritarian governments argue that authoritarian leaders can make tough decisions for the good of the nation, such as imposing higher taxes to pay for national development projects. These are decisions that average voters concerned with personal special interests would not support. In Reading 42, Amartya Sen argues that political rights must not be taken away in the name of economic effectiveness. Additionally, Sen states that the economic record of authoritarian governments is terrible. Many have allowed famine to kill hundreds of thousands of their citizens without acting effectively.

Capitalism is often thought to go hand in hand with democracy, but in Reading 43, the internationally respected capitalist George Soros criticizes capitalism as being anti-democratic. Individuals who make marketplace decisions that affect all of us are not elected officials. Further, the resources to make decisions in the marketplace are hierarchically distributed, not democratically distributed.

R.E.A.L. Sites

This list provides a print preview of typical **coursewise** R.E.A.L. sites. There are over 100 such sites at the **courselinks**™ site. The danger in printing URLs is that web sites can change overnight. As we went to press, these sites were functional using the URLs provided. If you come across one that isn't, please let us know via email to: webmaster@coursewise.com. Use your Passport to access the most current list of R.E.A.L. sites at the **courselinks**™ site.

Site names: The Post
Zimbabwe Independent

URLs: http://www.zamnet.zm/zamnet/post/post.html
http://www.samara.co.zw/zimin/Index.html

Why are they R.E.A.L.? By looking at the articles posted by *The Post* and the *Zimbabwe Independent*, you can identify which governments are attempting to intimidate their press professionals and prevent them from communicating full and open coverage of events and activities. You can determine what strategies the governments and the press are using to achieve their goals. You can also track the news regarding Southern African leaders and the efforts of the Southern African press to maintain a free press throughout the region.

Key topics: freedom of the press, democratization and a free press

Site name: Center for Voting and Democracy

URL: http://www.igc.apc.org/cvd/

Why is it R.E.A.L.? Newly democratizing states have to choose how to elect their representatives. When you visit this site, list the ways in which the authors argue that proportional elections are superior to the winner-take-all elections used in U.S. congressional districts. Note that the authors of this site would like to see the United States change its vote-counting methods. Election planners and constitution writers in new democracies that favor proportional elections can use these arguments.

Key topics: proportional voting

section 4

Changing Business and Labor Systems in Comparative Perspective

WiseGuide Intro

Many believe that the financial turmoil and hardship that Europeans experienced prior to World War II helped to create the conditions for authoritarian leaders to come to power. Economic hardship promoted the attractiveness of authoritarian leaders on both the left and the extreme right of the political spectrum. Thus, following World War II, Europe's new democratic leaders created welfare states that cushioned citizens from having to endure economic difficulties. They also sought ways to harmonize the interests of labor, capital, and the state; when harmonization was not possible, the state imposed compromises that the contending parties could tolerate. Free health care, full employment, and comfortable retirement benefits were some of the goals of the new European welfare states. Citizens living within a moderately capitalistic economic state had financial stability and security.

In the 1980s, Britain's Prime Minister Thatcher began to dismantle Britain's welfare state. In the 1990s, other countries, which can no longer afford the costly economic programs earlier promised to citizens, are also dismantling the welfare state. As you can see from the readings on Germany in this section, the costs of unifying the former Communist East Germany with West Germany are contributing to the dismantling of the German welfare state. Choices must be made regarding the allocation of resources, and the newly unified German government is giving the needs of East Germany priority. Further, as the readings in this section show, in other parts of the world, such as in Korea and Japan, where the post–World War II state has played a major role in governing, the economy, labor and business relations are similarly changing.

The increasingly global market economy, in which capital and investments can relocate rapidly, has caused corporations around the world to demand "give-backs" from labor unions in the name of competitiveness. In South Korea these came in the form of reduced pay and the right to increase layoffs of workers. Despite a post-war system of corporatism that saw the state manage owner-labor relations, South Korean unions began to reject the state's role as one biased in favor of owners of corporations. Militant unionism grew in South Korea when it joined the Organization for Economic Co-Operation and Development and had to permit some forms of labor organization at the same time that corporations were attacking workers' living standards in the name of competitiveness. The unions began to win nationwide backing for their struggles when they tied their claims for labor democracy to demands for political democracy.

Key Points

- When citizens experience hard economic times, they often turn to authoritarian leaders to solve their problems.

- After World War II, leaders who favored democratic forms of government introduced welfare policies to make certain their populations would not swap authoritarian political reforms for democratic ones. These leaders created the welfare state.

- In the 1980s, many leaders argued that the state could no longer support welfare policies and began to dismantle the welfare state.

- Today's workers must adjust to living with the economic hard times that come when the state does not mediate between labor and business.

- Today, all businesses face global competition. To sell their products cheaply, they try to keep workers' wages and benefits low.

- Many labor unions are becoming more desperate and more militant in their efforts to maintain a decent standard of living for workers.

One of the few places in the world where the globalization of liberal market policies is having an exceptional effect is in the Middle East. As Iqbal argues in Reading 47 in this section, because Islamic citizens must practice Islamic finance, which includes such principles as interest-free transactions, an alternative response from that of the Western states is evolving for Middle Eastern workers and owners who also must cope with global pressures.

Questions

1. Following World War II, how did government leaders justify establishing welfare states and collecting taxes to ensure the well-being of all citizens?

2. How is the idea of "global competitiveness" affecting workers' ability to unionize and to improve their living standards?

3. What are the principles on which "Islamic finance" is based?

Dismantling Germany's Welfare State

Hanna Behrend

"The Federal Republic of Germany is a Democratic and Social Federal State," according to Article 20 of the German Constitution. After the defeat of Nazi Germany, all the newly established political parties in West Germany, including the conservative Christian Democratic Union (CDU) and Christian Social Union (CSU), adopted policies in the immediate post-war period designed to curb the unbridled power of capitalist enterprise. Legislation was passed which authorized organized labor to negotiate agreements on wages and working conditions binding on entire branches of industry and trade. Government policy was designed to balance industrial expansion and public welfare. Free enterprise in the German Federal Republic was thus subject to collective bargaining, staff representation, and other labor and social legislation. A system of general state-operated social insurance, financed since the days of Bismarck by equal contributions from both the gainfully employed and their employers, safeguarded the former from risks arising from their employment and ensured them an old-age pension, as a rule sufficient to live on even unsupported by any private provisions of their own. Social security, the modern and more enlightened successor to the old poor law provisions, then supplied the basic means of support only to those relatively few who had no claim to unemployment benefits or unemployment assistance (to which laid-off employees are eligible after their claim to unemployment benefits lapses).

For almost 40 years, the German welfare state was solidly based "on full employment in a free society." A rubble heap in 1945, West Germany recovered the rank of a leading industrial power within a decade. Benefitting from Marshall Plan aid and paying only token reparations, West Germany blossomed into an economic miracle, which turned the country into a consumers' paradise and ushered in a period of full employment and desirable working conditions. The Cold War ensured that the former enemy would be welcomed into the Western alliance. The social-democratic concept of equal opportunities for all and a network of welfare provisions for those in need was basically approved by even conservatives and liberals. The Federal Republic became, particularly in the eyes of the majority in the other German state, a much envied place. Under conditions of a still bridled global expansion and relatively mild international competition, funds were available not only for West Germany's then up-to-date social, educational and health services, and for the necessary infrastructural ventures, but also for the promotion of science, research and development; even the arts were subsidized on a grand scale. Indeed, not only did industry, big business and finance thrive, but considerable sections of the West German population, including skilled (male) workers, benefitted from the long post-war boom. Their living standards were high and their incomes enabled them to save and invest savings not only in national but also in global financial undertakings, thereby also partaking in the exploitation of the Third World.

Hanna Behrend, "Dismantling Germany's Welfare State," NEW POLITICS, Summer 1996, Vol. VI, No. 1, whole #21. Reprinted by permission.

East Germany: A Unique Testing Ground for Neoliberalism

The social welfare system of the German Democratic Republic (GDR) was superior to West Germany's. While never openly admitted, it did provide a political obstacle to efforts to dismantle the West German welfare state during the 1980s, prior to unification. Standards of living in the GDR were relatively low (though the highest in all the Comecon countries), but there were neither really wealthy nor really poor people. Full employment included 91% of women; adequate childcare provisions and paid leave in case of children's illness permitted mothers to continue working. Education was open to everyone, the health service including prophylactic treatment, and medication was completely free, as were abortion on demand and contraceptives. These "assets" were, understandably, not appreciated by the East German people. They resented the deficient supply of consumer goods, the police state methods, and the state's interference with free travel, as well as the absence of other civil rights.

After unification in 1990, all the welfare and social insurance systems of the GDR were scrapped and replaced by the far more costly and bureaucratic West German versions. The inferior West German welfare state was itself increasingly in jeopardy. The *Anschluss* of East Germany to the Federal Republic, however, provided the conservative government and the industrialists' lobby with an unexpected breathing space, warding off the impending economic recession for two years. The steamrolling of the GDR economy, irrespective of whether enterprises were competitive or not, also rid West German industry of unwanted competitors and presented it with new markets which included the GDR's East European customers.

Unification and complete economic and political hegemony over East Germany also supplied those in power in the Federal Republic with a unique testing ground for their new policy of unbridled neoliberalism. This meant industrial reconstruction totally geared to the vested interests of the major capital owners and riding roughshod over the concerns of the majority, for whom the policy brought mass unemployment, the dismantling of the welfare state, the undermining of national wage/salary agreements, a general deterioration of working conditions, higher prices for commodities and services, higher taxes and rates, growing criminal delinquency and violence, and a general lowering of safety standards and quality controls in all spheres.

This new policy was first practiced in post-unification East Germany on a stunned, confused, and divided population who had been promised changes that would turn the country into a "thriving land." It included ruthless de-industrialization, decimation of the GDR's former research potential, and the takeover of its wholesale and retail trade by West German chains which, for a long time, had boycotted East German products. The attempt to push the efficient agricultural cooperatives into dissolving themselves and to privilege non-viable family farming was only partly successful. In short, the destruction of the GDR's economy and half of its jobs was the outcome of the irresponsible privatization policy practiced, on behalf of the Kohl government, by the Treuhand holding company[1]. By squandering assets and preventing necessary modernization and replacement of obsolete equipment, much valuable property ended up mostly in the hands of West German trusts, which got the choicest bits for a song and, in addition, were given billions of DM subsidies. Meanwhile, quite a few West German companies have closed the East German plants they acquired from Treuhand under such favorable conditions to save their West German plants[2]. When the Treuhand agency closed its books in 1994, German taxpayers were presented with liabilities of about 200 billion DM, while the people of the ex-GDR emerged from this "privatization drive" with nothing to show for two generations' labor.

In addition to this collective expropriation, tens of thousands of East Germans lost their homes through the "restitution of property to former owners before compensation" ruling. This also robbed cooperatives, urban and rural communities, and even whole regions, of property they had used and improved generally for decades. The appropriation of the GDR State Bank by the Federal German Bank, moreover, turned loans granted by the GDR planning authorities to individual and corporate house builders, industrial and agricultural enterprises, and local communities into genuine liabilities. Under centralized administration these "loans" were considered mere bookkeeping operations in keeping with the planned allotment of funds for investment and development ventures; under market conditions, they became crippling burdens on individual home owners, building societies and other enterprises, and local, regional and state administrations.

The mere interest on the capital has meanwhile risen to 1.2 million DM. So far, the government has refused to write off these sham debts, which contribute to enormous rent increases, capital shortages for indigenous East German (small and middle) industrial and agricultural enterprises and, above all, the threat of bankruptcy that hovers over most local, regional and state administrations in the East, already impoverished by shrinking revenue from taxes and rates. They are hard put to provide those unable to earn their own living with the social security to which they are entitled, let alone finance road works or sewer repairs, or keep up social and educational projects. Most urban communities are heavily overdrawn, and they are scrapping or quietly folding up youth, women's, senior citizens' and many other self-help projects, with the subsequent loss of jobs adding, particularly, to the rate of female unemployment in the East.

The ratio of East to West German wages rose from 20–40% in 1994 to the present average of 60%, with East Germans working an annual average of 1,700 hours as against 1,580 hours in the West, but in defiance of 1994 election promises there has been a slowing-down of the adjustment process. A report issued by the Social Democratic Party (SPD) parliamentary group in April 1996 states that

> even five years after unification a market economy is still not working properly in East Germany . . . [It] is, . . . by and large, run by public funds . . . The Federal

Government is playing down the deficit of millions of jobs in East Germany . . . The real problem . . . is the net loss of 3.477 million jobs from 1989 to 1994 and only a feeble rise in the number of gainfully employed since.

The report pleads for a continuation and restructuring of state subsidies to prevent East Germany from "remaining a destitute area with a high rate of unemployment." The coalition government, however, insists that East Germany is prosperous enough to support itself.

According to a 1995 survey, the average four-person household income of employed East German workers and employees was 4,263 DM compared to 5,214 DM in West Germany. While 99.4% of West German household income is earned by one person, the chief wage-earner in East German households provides only 72%.

Low pay and insecure employment have meant poverty even for many of those with jobs: 15.9% of couples with two children and 40.2% of couples with three and more offsprings. Many women are forced by job creation and retraining programs to accept lesser skilled, part-time and temporary low-paying employment. This suits the conservative government, which has tried in vain to push East German women into the "silent labor reserve." According to a 1993 official statement, 43% of those women in full-time employment and 26.5% of the self-employed are unable to support themselves without assistance.

Insecure, part-time employment affects not only women, of course. Single fathers, school dropouts, the elderly, foreigners and the handicapped all belong to "risk groups" in danger of falling

below the poverty line, either as a result of being laid off or being unable to find jobs that would provide them with a living wage. Thus, since the 1.2 million jobs reserved for the handicapped in GDR times were slashed, handicapped people are finding it extremely hard to find qualified jobs or places as trainees. Many are falling below the poverty line because of cuts in social security, or because of low pensions.

Of those claiming social security, however, 88% need it because of unemployment. Unemployment hits East German women, with a rate of 21.5%, twice as hard as men. On average, women who are laid off remain unemployed twice as long as men. More than a quarter of East German children live in households supported by unemployment benefits. While in 1990, 25,000 East German children lived in households whose only source of income was social security, this figure had risen to 63,000 by 1993. Homelessness, which was totally unknown in the GDR, now affects 30,000 people in East Germany; 6,000 of whom actually live permanently on the road. Urban and rural communities are unable to provide them with homes or pay the rent they owe to prevent their eviction.

An investigation undertaken in 1994 into the financial situation of East Germans over age 50 found that only 20% owned any property at all, and no more than 18% owned their own homes. Only 59% of this age bracket, considered by the labor offices as practically unemployable, can fall back on savings. Altogether, the poor sections of the East German population increased from 3.5% in 1990 to 8.9% in 1993.

The policies that brought these results have not been challenged by either the West-dominated German trade unions or the West-dominated German opposition parties. This is consistent with a general move toward the right across the entire political spectrum and has encouraged industry, big business, and finance to clamor more and more vociferously for a "reform" of the welfare state, i.e. its dismantling. Testing neoliberalism in East Germany proved successful since resistance remained local, regional or, at best, involved only the five East German states; the neoliberal program, therefore, could safely be expanded to cover all of united Germany.

The Decline of the West German Welfare State

The West German welfare state had begun to crack long before unification. Even in periods of increasing economic activity the labor market no longer provided the number of jobs to ensure temporary unemployment. This development profoundly affected the foundations of the German welfare state.

Mass unemployment is the result of structural changes. Automated workshops and computerized administration have increased the per capita performance of labor to between three and four times the output of the early 1980s. Even in the boom period from 1983 to 1990 the unemployment rate remained stable in all West European countries. In the mid-1980s, the German Trade Unions Association forecast that by the year 2000, failing regulatory interventions in the labor market, only a quarter of the labor force would still hold secure jobs

at negotiated rates of pay, while another quarter would make do with insecure, low skilled and badly paid jobs. The remaining 50% would be permanently out of work or have temporary, part-time, casual, seasonal, or menial jobs. This prognosis is well on its way to being realized.

To cope with the need to transform industrial enterprises to keep up with the leap in technology and with the increasing pressure of global competition, German employers, as early as the 1980s, began to press for a policy of deregulating labor and scaling back social legislation. Wage agreements were undermined by local exceptions to the national rates. Provisions for part-time work, shorter hours without higher pay, farming work out to subcontractors or homeworkers, etc., led to a gradual erosion of "normal gainful employment." In 1982, wages still made up 72% of the gross national product; by 1994 this figure had dropped to 66%.

As mass unemployment became a permanent reality, more and more people failed to find work when they gave up or lost their jobs and thus became long-term unemployed. After their claims to unemployment benefits or assistance lapsed, they had to resort to social security, thus becoming a burden on local, regional, and state authorities rather than a tax-paying asset to them. The December 1995 unemployment figures of 3.79 million were the highest since 1945. The rate of unemployment (excluding those not registered, in job creating schemes, in early retirement, and in retraining) stands officially at 8.7% in the West and 14.9% in the East. *Every tenth employable German is out of work.* Forecasts

emphasize that this trend will continue.

Poverty, defined by the European Community (EC) as affecting people with incomes of 50% below average, is growing fast in all of Germany. Among those claiming social security, 56% in the West and 64% in the East must be classified as poor according to EC standards. Every seventh child in the whole of Germany belongs, at least temporarily, to a household living on social security. Of single adults, 16% are considered poor in the West, most of them single women. Three times as many foreign residents as Germans are reduced to social security. More than 900,000 people are homeless, 35,000 of them permanently; last winter, eight people died from exposure.

The German Unemployed Workers Federation stated that since 1990 1,150 people lost their jobs every day. Every day 560 people drop into insecure jobs, 505 become long-term unemployed, 1,100 become poor and 220 homeless. The elderly, women, youth, foreigners and the handicapped are particularly affected. In 1993, 180,000 handicapped unemployed fully capable of working in normal workshops had no option but to take jobs in special publicly or privately run workshops. They are deprived of social and trade union rights and paid no more than a miserly amount of pocket money. They are employed on simple mechanical jobs, but since their workshops subcontract for big firms (70% of all handicapped workshops' products are supplied under contract to Volkswagen, Ford or Hoechst), their work provides those firms with a total turnover of 4 billion DM. Added to which, the firms save on the penalties they would have to pay for not employing any handicapped staff.

While taxation on wages and salaries rose from 15.8% in 1980 to 20.6 in 1995, taxes on business dropped from 21.2% to 13.9% during that period. With the rise of unemployment and legislation enabling multinationals to avoid taxation, the public authorities on all levels are less and less able to meet their liabilities. The national debt and the interest thereon escalates to the benefit of the banks and major bond holders, while it cripples the budgets of the federal, state and regional administrations which have, therefore, taken to privatizing vital public services, such as posts and telecommunications, railways and buses. Higher rates and fares, reduced range and poorer quality service (e.g. less attention to passenger safety) are the results, largely because of massive staff cuts. The local and state governments' restricted means curtails the construction of public housing; this, in turn, leaves the building industry to provide chiefly unsubsidized residential and business premises, which often find no tenants. Smaller construction companies unable to compete go bankrupt while large firms avail themselves of cheap, illegally imported labor, undercutting even the low minimum wages won after protracted struggle. In 1995 Germany, along with Greece and Italy, had the greatest number of bankruptcies in Europe, chiefly of small and middle-sized enterprises.

The "Alliance for Creating Jobs"

According to investigations by the German Unemployed Workers Federation, the country is short of 9.4 million permanent jobs. Providing them would require radical cuts in working hours without loss of pay and granting basic incomes to everyone. To cope with the present crisis, a number of left-wing theoreticians, many of them feminists, also call for a complete restructuring of the patriarchal and capitalist concept of gainful employment to include work hitherto considered nonprofitable. They suggest cutting working hours to a permitted maximum flexible time per year or over an employed person's lifetime with optional periods for parenthood, professional development or retraining; banning overtime and transforming it into new jobs instead; and providing part-time work for senior employees. Feminist critics especially insist on an adequate subsistence allowance for those temporarily or permanently without an income of their own, which, they claim, would allow people to volunteer for work in the social, health, and caring fields that, for lack of funds, is left undone.

While none of these ideas was seriously considered by the government or leaders of the major opposition parties, the "Alliance for Creating Jobs," initiated by trade union leader Klaus Zwickel, did so. His proposals are fully in accord with the dominant view, which takes it for granted that only higher profits as a result of abstention from wage demands and acceptance of poorer working conditions create new jobs. Zwickel, on behalf of the unions, offered employers moderate wage demands, approval of local undercutting of national wage and salary agreements, and cuts in social provisions in return for a promise by the employers to create new jobs. He appealed to the government to support the initiative. Kohl himself then formed a 14-member commission and promised to create two million new jobs by the year 2000, an undertaking that the Institute for Industrial Research in Halle derided as wishful thinking.

In a massive barrage, the employers' spokespersons put forward their interpretation of the trade unions' Alliance venture. The former vice president of the Employers Federation (BDI), Necker, was all in favor of it as far as the acceptance of real wage and other cuts was concerned but rejected the idea that employers could actually create new jobs; only the market could do that. Jobs would be plentiful, he claimed, if German industry were relieved of excessive social liabilities and thus enabled to produce globally competitive commodities. In a joint statement issued in December 1995, the BDI, the Federation of German Employers Associations, the German Chamber of Industry and Commerce, and the Central Association of German Trades demanded cuts in the cost of labor and a "reform of the welfare state." They called for further tax reductions on industrial capital, profits and estates; according to them, the special subsidies granted to East Germany (*Solidarzuschlag*) and, incidently, paid for by all East and West German taxpayers, should subside in 1997; no new ecological tax should be imposed. Instead, they suggested, the quota of public expenditure should drop from more than 50% of the gross national product to 46% by the year 2000. To reduce mass unemployment they offered to invest profits from surplus productivity in new jobs, provided the unions agreed to a wage freeze for a number of years and to cuts in holiday and Christmas bonuses, to less sickpay and further inroads into rehabilitation measures, cures, etc. The erosion of sickpay regulations has recently been accepted by several prominent trade union leaders as perfectly legitimate. Spokesperson for the SPD parliamentary party, Gerd Andres, also came out in favor of such a "reform." This, however, went too far for SPD leader Oskar Lafontaine, who declared on April 12, 1996, that his party was determined to combat the dismantling of the welfare state and would never agree to the scrapping of sickpay.

In an interview, Erich Gerard, president of the Federation of Employers' Associations in Berlin and Brandenburg and the boss of Siemens, also clamored for long term wage freezes and cuts in social expenditure. Although 80 million hours overtime per year are worked in Berlin and Brandenburg, Gerard rejected the idea of transforming them into new jobs as "technically impossible." Other prominent industrialists, bankers, managers and business advisers followed suit, arguing that unless German workers accepted a deterioration of their living standards, investment capital would migrate to low wage countries. Investigations into German investment abroad, however, reveal that more than 90% of capital investments in the first half of 1995 went into the EC countries, Japan, and the United States, and not to low wage countries. According to a metal workers union investigation, surplus from German metalware exports from 1991 to 1994 amounted to 122 billion DM, which would be sufficient to create 513,000 new jobs.

In their 1995 autumn statement, the six major economic institutes forecast a 2.5% rise in the gross domestic income which inspired them to join the faction of those clamoring for "moderate wage demands." The BDI immediately declared this forecast over-optimistic and stressed not only the need for moderation in wage agreements but also the indispensability of further delays in adapting the East German wages to the West German standard.

This campaign goes on, unmoved by the fact that net capital returns have risen by 177% since 1977; profits have doubled since 1982/83, when Kohl came to power. The leading chemical firm of BASF (the successor to IG Farben) had a turnover of 49.4 billion DM in 1995 and was able to double its annual surplus to 2.47 billion DM. Hoechst and Beyer were no less successful. Banks, too, made record profits; the Commerzbank had a record-breaking year in 1995, doubling its returns to 1.45 billion DM with an 18.2% rise in the bank's balance. Since this surplus was largely made abroad, no taxes were paid on it.

In the early 1980s, the share of taxes paid on profit from industrial enterprises and capital levies stood at 37%; it has since dropped to a mere 25%. According to an uncontested report by the magazine *Stern*, multinational industrial and financial enterprises are paying less and less taxes. The Deutsche Bank's profits prior to tax deduction rose by 77% in 1993; the DB, however, paid 9% less taxes on its 1993 profits than in 1990.

The incongruity of higher profits and lower taxes on the one hand, and soaring unemployment on the other is also due to the increasing refusal of major enterprises to reinvest profits. They prefer to invest their surplus in national and foreign bonds rather than in riskier industrial production. Only 32 billion DM were invested in Germany in the course of the last ten years. Productive capital investment rose by an average of 2% while investment in bonds has leapt to 12.2% since 1989.

The Neoliberal Backlash in Action

According to the neoliberal defenders of the "Standort Deutschland" (preserving Germany's status as a leading industrial power), competitiveness of the German trusts is the indispensable precondition of "national wealth and welfare." It is to be achieved exclusively at the expense of the working class. Experience has shown that the capitalist market is blind to the social needs of the people and that yielding to the demands of the employers never creates jobs but rather destroys them. Nevertheless, the neoliberal approach is supported by the heads of the trade unions and large sections of the SPD leadership. The SPD's policy of broadly accepting the government's dismantling of the welfare state was largely responsible for its loss of popularity. This became particularly evident in the Berlin elections of October 1995 when the SPD vote fell to a mere 23.5%—thus prompting much of the Berlin membership to demand that the party stop aping the CDU, which had lost far fewer votes.

Only in January 1996 did the SPD issue a ten-point program calling on the government to offer foreign investors three tax-free years if they created jobs in Germany; it demanded state support for the promotion of ecological industries; generous loans for people prepared to start up businesses; temporary subsidies to employers in the service industries willing to provide jobs to the long-term unemployed; and 20% tax reductions for private homeowners who employ registered craftspeople rather than cheap undeclared labor.

Though there has been some protest against the alignment of the German trade unions with neoliberalism, notably from a group of about 180 shop stewards, the leadership of the German Trade Union Federation (DGB) has stuck to its policy. The head of the DGB, Dieter Schulte, agreed with the employers that new jobs depended on lowering the cost of labor. Instead of insisting on legally binding agreements he was satisfied with the employers' promises of new jobs. Agreeing to wage freezes and cuts and other measures of social deregulation cost the trade unions 520,000 members in 1994.

With union approval, Volkswagen introduced the four-day work week in November 1993, which spelled wage cuts, fewer paid holidays and longer working hours as a result of the flexible time model. Consequently, the average VW worker now earns 3,300 DM per month instead of 4,100 DM, as formerly. These and other sacrifices made by workers have not, so far, stopped the big firms from destroying jobs, dismantling production sites, or shifting production abroad. But they enabled VW to increase productivity by 13% in 1995 and save a total of 1.6 billion DM. From 1992 to 1995 Mercedes Benz has slashed 40,000 jobs, which contributed to a 6 billion DM rise in profits. By introducing work teams, the firm was able to dispense with yet another 4,000 jobs.

The conservative-liberal coalition government's budget for 1996 contributes to the dismantling of the welfare state by helping the rich to rob the poor. The budget of the Ministry of Labor will be cut by 7.8%, thus slashing job creation and retraining programs. Unemployment assistance is to be reduced; workers not eligible for unemployment benefits will have to go on social security when they lose their jobs. Benefit and assistance claims, in the future, will be subject to intensified means testing. Moreover, legislation is being prepared to force the unemployed to accept jobs paying up to 30% less than their previous earnings. Periods of unemployment benefits are to be shortened, even for the elderly. The level of savings allowed by the means test will be lowered from 8,000 to 2,500 DM. Unemployment assistance is to be cut by an average of 60 DM per month. Well-off people offering domestic service jobs will receive substantial tax breaks.

The 1996 budget provides for total cuts of almost 60% for the support of families, senior citizens, women and youth. The right of every three-year old to admission to a kindergarten, promised in 1993 to discourage abortions, has been reduced to an offer of merely half-a-day care. Spending on the health service, environment and public transportation is also subjected to serious cutbacks. Student grants, which, unlike in the GDR, always had to be repaid, were cut in 1994. Now, students will also have to pay interest on the capital. For the first time since 1945, students will pay college fees. This will increasingly restrict higher education to the children of the moneyed elite.

Increased funds will be made available chiefly to industry

(an additional 48.8%), research, technology, development aid, foreign affairs, and, of course, defense. As far as development aid is concerned, there will be a slight rise, overdue in view of the fact that Germany's contribution in 1994 was a modest 0.33% of GNP, while the Netherlands and the Scandinavian countries allotted 0.7%. The budget will bring the national debt to approximately 60 billion DM.

Uneasiness, but No Resistance

The media provide an invaluable service to Germany's elite by constantly warning workers that "immoderate demands" will "jeopardize Germany's status as a leading industrial power." People are forever having dinned into them that the "state" can no longer afford the "explosion" of social benefits because of international competition. "We must all tighten our belts," they proclaim, and large sections of the population, especially in West Germany, believe them—particularly the poorest and often most uneducated and helpless, who are hardest hit by deregulation and cuts. The trade unions are told to "act responsibly" in the face of this challenge to the German *Standort*, and their leaders hasten to show their willingness to do so. Resistance to this campaign is not considered "politically correct." None of this, of course, applies to the wealthy, whose fortunes constantly increase, and the mighty, who continue to thrive. Thus, parliamentary allowances have continued to rise, as have the salaries of members of federal and state cabinets and of the top echelons of the civil service and business. There have been many warnings of impending social unrest by the churches and welfare organizations, the Unemployed Workers' Federation, the odd trade unionist and politician, and research institutions if mass unemployment and the policy of dismantling the welfare state continue. Yet the response of the majority of the people to the decline in the general quality of life, marred by increasing traffic jams and noise, by air and water pollution, rising crime and violence, by low-quality entertainment replacing valuable cultural achievements, is to deplore it in private but refrain from public protest.

A factor which paralyzes such protest is the tremendous segmentation of those affected by the dismantling of the welfare state and the employers' offensive. There is no mutual assistance given by East German to West German workers and vice versa, or by those who still hold safe jobs to those in precarious temporary or part-time employment. Male workers observe women workers being fired with total indifference. German workers resent the immigrants and foreign residents as competitors for jobs. A highly skilled male worker cares little about what happens to his elderly colleague pushed into early retirement or part-time work and is even less interested in the apprentice dismissed after completion of his training. Students know nothing about the situation of trainees or apprentices, and vice versa. The fierce competition between these different segments of the labor market is at the root of their atomization. They consider their interests to be incompatible. The fear of losing one's job rules supreme, unchecked by solidarity. As a result, a growing

number of people from previously stable sectors of society are gradually and silently being pauperized.

Though there is little public evidence of this, large numbers of people are very worried about the future and quite able to perceive the symptoms of a growing crisis. But they do not know what they can do about it. The failure in the past of political or trade union activities to force the government to change its policies has discouraged many former activists and whittled away mass support for even the most deserving issues. There are the rarely successful local or, at best, regional token strikes and demonstrations of workers threatened by mass job destruction. There are the Easter Marches and other events of public protest attended by a decreasing number of people. The general public's response to the crisis seems restricted to growing abstention from voting or, on a gradually increasing scale, by turning away from the established parties.

The turnout in Berlin's October elections hit bottom with under 65% of the voters going to the polls. As for those who do vote, the majority, particularly in the West, as three recent *land* elections showed, still put more trust in the conservatives than their competitors—largely for fear things might become worse if there were a change, since they consider other parties even less competent to stave off impending disaster and guide the country safely through the present crisis. The increasing popularity of the Greens in the West and the Party of Democratic Socialism (PDS)— the successor to the Communists— in the East continues the trend already evident in last year's gen-

eral elections. The fact that the SPD has so low an alternative profile and shows no apparent inclination to form an anti-conservative alliance strengthens the vote for the CDU and Free Democratic Party (FDP).

The present political stalemate is thus the result of a number of complex factors. There is tremendous fragmentation among those victimized by the changes, which engenders fear and distrust. The disintegration of the Left prevents it from playing a more active role, putting pressure on the trade unions and the SPD. This, in turn, hinders the ability of those who have traditionally led social and political struggles in West Germany to elaborate an effective and convincing strategy, and leaves the right-wing leaders in complete command. Last but not least, there is the tremendous pressure exercised by the government, the employers, and the media to convince people that there is no option to the neoliberal line of scuttling the welfare state. This is all the more effective because socialist and Green alternatives have been popularly experienced as failures, as have even the restricted industrial and political actions of recent years. This impedes the emergence of any effective resistance movement. While it would be a mistake to believe that the silent majority are content and optimistic, it is also true that unless they begin to overcome fragmentation and find a way to cooperate without any group trying to subordinate the others, the establishment will continue to handle the structural crisis exclusively in the interest of big business and finance and entirely at the expense of the majority of the German people.

Postscript

On April 25, 1996 the CDU-FDP coalition announced its "Programme to Promote Economic Growth and Create Jobs," surpassing by far the anti-welfare state measures hitherto implemented. Below is a selection characteristic of the kind of decisions made none of which is likely to create a single new job: abolition of capital levy, reduction of trade and sales taxes, more favorable conditions for deducting items from taxable income, increase of the death duties allowance from 250,000 DM to one million DM; tax allowances for employing domestic staff.

As against these measures, clearly benefitting the employers and those who enjoy unearned incomes, the gainfully employed will suffer from the deregulation of protective legislation against dismissal; payment of wages/salaries in case of sickness will be restricted to 80%, vacation pay will no longer include overtime. Pensioners will incur further losses of income; the retirement age for women will be raised from 60 to 63 by 1997, with a 3.6% cut per annum for early retirement. Unemployment pay for the first week of redundancy will be halved. Starting 1997 the Federal Labor Office will no longer be subsidized by federal funds. Health care contributions by the insured will increase. Child benefit increases are postponed for another year, as are child allowances. The social security increase scheduled for July 1, 1997 will be scrapped. Further cuts are proposed in job creation programs, and in various other areas of social benefits.

While the employers' federations welcomed the program, it was unanimously rejected by the opposition: DGB (German Trade Unions) Chairman Schulte called it a program of early capitalism incompatible with the creation of jobs. SPD Chairman Lafontaine considered it an election fraud; Fischer of Bundnis 90/The Greens Party censured the dismantling of the welfare state; Gysi, PDS Chairman, said that it was not the budget but society that was in a crisis. Whether the first general outcry against this "program of horrors" will lead to a determined and effective opposition to it, remains to be seen.

If, however, the opposition allows the government and the employers' lobby to get away with this program, it will definitely spell the end of the welfare state period in the history of the Federal Republic of Germany. Germany will become a country where the wealthy and powerful are unchallenged in the pursuance of a policy ruthlessly depriving the majority of the people of the social and political achievements won in the course of almost half a century of struggle. Who knows but that those who sowed the wind may not then reap the whirlwind?

May 1, 1996

Notes

1. On the Treuhand-Anstalt (Trust Fund Society) see my article, "Germany: The Stage is Reset" in *New Politics*, No. 14, Winter 1993.

2. There were spectacular instances of West German buyers illegally transferring the state subsidies they had been granted to modernize their East German acquisitions to West German sites. One concerned East German shipyards bought by the Bremen Vulkan Trust. The embezzlement of subsidies, of which the authorities were well aware, failed, however, to save the tottering Trust. Eventually it was decided to rescue the shipyards with more public money, thus forcing German taxpayers to subsidize endangered East German firms once more.

 Article Review Form at end of book.

The "Late Blooming" of the South Korean Labor Movement

Hochul Sonn

South Korea is generally known as an economic success story, according to which, once a hopeless "aid-junkie," it has emerged as one of the most successful NICs.[1] But few commentators pay attention to the fact that this success has been made possible mainly by the ruthless superexploitation of the Korean working class, exemplified by, among other things, the longest working hours and the highest industrial accident rate in the world. "Weak labor" and the absence of class politics in Korea enabled this superexploitation.

Since the 1980s, however, the South Korean labor movement has grown rapidly. In 1995 it finally established the Korean Confederation of Trade Unions (KCTU), the long-awaited national federation of independent and progressive but illegal trade unions, despite vicious repression by the state and capital. As reported throughout the world, the clash between this newly strengthened movement and the "neo-liberal" policy of the government resulted in the first general strike in Korean history, which brought about a de facto defeat of the government.

The Historical Background

There is a kind of "Korean exceptionalism" in relation to progressive movements in general and labor movements in particular. South Korea is exceptional in a dual sense: in the "early absence" of such movements and in their "late blooming."

Even by the standards of the third world, the South Korean labor movement was, until the 1980s, exceptionally weak. Labor movements were identified with communism, and the word "class" was until recently prohibited even in the academic world. This is due to several factors: 1) the exceptionally narrow ideological terrain resulting from the Korean War and the division of the nation which followed from it[2]; 2) state repression and "state corporatist" control of trade unions[3]; 3) the decentralization of the working class by the organization of industry predominantly in small factories, 4) high social mobility owing to the strong nation-wide passion for education and the consequent individualization of the working class.

But things started to change in the early 1980s. The Kwangju massacre in 1980, in which the military massacred officially about two hundred but allegedly about two thousand civilians in its multi-stage coup d'état after the assassination of President Park, revived the radical movements in South Korea for the first time since the Korean War.[4] The result was a sudden "explosion of Marxism" and radical movements, particularly among students.

These movements slowly penetrated the newly emerging working class produced by the heavy industrialization of the 1970s. In contrast to the fragmented working class of the period dominated by small factories, in the new industrial conditions there had emerged a class of highly concentrated workers with strategic power which could paralyze the whole economy but suffered from "premodern" labor relations and conditions.

So while Marxism, particularly after the fall of the Soviet Bloc, was undergoing an unprecedented crisis in most of the world, Marxism as well as the labor movement experienced an unprecedented "explosion" and "blooming" in South Korea. In particular, "democratization," achieved by the June People's Struggle in 1987, which thwarted the military government's plan to continue its rule, accelerated this tendency. The weakening of the repressive state apparatus kindled the historic Great July and August Workers' Struggle, in which the Korean working class broke its long silence and took to the streets all over the country.

This struggle was defeated partly because of the hostile attitude of the middle class whose main concerns were "order" and "economy." But a major factor in the defeat was the absence of a central organization and leadership in the labor movement. The struggle itself gave rise to a new union leadership. The new leaders adopted what they called a "militant unionism," which would struggle against inhumane labor conditions even if it meant breaking the law and sometimes employing violent means of self-defense. This new militancy represented a sharp contrast to the conciliatory and subordinate attitudes of the Federation of Korean Trade Unions (FKTU), which the American Military Government had organized simply in order to neutralize grass-roots leftist trade unions after the liberation from Japanese colonialism and which has not only been controlled by the government but has also sided with the dictatorship throughout its history.

"Militant unionism," for instance, produced annual strikes at Hyundai Heavy Industry, one of the biggest factories in Korea, against vicious repression by the

state. Each time, the state responded with a typical multidimensional and massive military operation, deploying more than ten thousand special task force police and mobilizing not only ground forces but also naval power and helicopters.

In 1989, recognizing that regional cooperation among unions would be much more effective than cooperation only among unions in the same industry, the leadership of the illegal democratic unions founded the Council of National Democratic Unions, a region-based organization established to fight police repression. It was from this Council that the KCTU would emerge.

Radical movements everywhere, of course, suffered serious set-backs as the Soviet bloc began to crumble in 1987, but in South Korea, the effects were somewhat delayed. Before 1990, many activists and progressive intellectuals believed that *perestroika* was strengthening socialism. But the failed coup and the collapse of the Soviet Union in 1991 finally poured cold water on the infant flames of Korean radical movements, at least radical *political* movements which had tried to build an underground Marxist party as well as an open socialist party. Many leaders, particularly intellectuals, left the movements with open denunciations.

The labor movement, however, was different. The collapse of the Soviet Union did not suppress the new union militancy, because what sustained the labor movement was not the existence of the Soviet Union nor dogmatic Marx-Leninism but the cold reality of Korean capitalism.

In spite of brutal repression by monopoly capital and the so-called "democratic" and "civilian"

government, this new labor movement successfully organized a number of heroic struggles and expanded its influence in key industries. In 1995, with a platform to build not only democratic labor movements but also "a truly democratic society," Korean workers finally founded the historically unprecedented KCTU in opposition to the FKTU. For the first time, Korea had an independent trade union federation.

At the time of the strike, the new KCTU had about half a million members from almost a thousand trade unions, whereas the older FKTU had 1.2 million members. The KCTU, however, had total control over the three vital industries in Korea: automobile, shipbuilding, and heavy industry, as well as over public transportation and key white collar workers such as those in hospitals, massmedia, and research institutes.

What Caused the Historic General Strike?

To understand the recent general strike in Korea, it is essential to have a basic knowledge of South Korean labor relations. The Korean labor acts have had many premodern, anti-democratic clauses which restrict the basic rights of workers. Typical examples are the so-called "four prohibitions": 1) prohibition of "third party intervention" in labor disputes; 2) prohibition of multiple trade unions, which has given monopolistic power to the government-controlled and undemocratic FKTU; 3) prohibition of the right of civil servants and teachers to organize; 4) prohibition of political activities by trade unions.

The Korean working class led by the KCTU launched numerous struggles to democratize this inhumane system. The government suppressed these struggles by utilizing not only the anti-democratic labor acts but also other laws such as the notorious national security act. This is dramatically illustrated by the fact that workers comprise the largest proportion of political prisoners under the current regime.

But the economic and social costs of these labor disputes increased drastically, to the point where the regime could no longer sustain them. To solve this problem, the present civilian government in its early period, in 1993, tried labor reform as part of an ambitious total reform project. Capital, particularly the *chaebols*, the family-owned conglomerates in Korea, responded with "capital strikes," a refusal to invest. As a consequence, the economy weakened and the government gave up reform to return to the old labor practices.[5]

As is well known, up to the mid 1980s South Korea was one of the most successful examples of rapid economic growth achieved through export-oriented industrialization on the basis of cheap and highly disciplined labor. But in the late 1980s things started to change. Korea's "international competitiveness" began to decline, with a rapid rise of wages resulting from the growth of labor movements and with competition from the emerging second generation NICs in Southeast Asia and China. At the same time, its two motors of economic growth, state-initiated industrialization and the *chaebol* structure, began to lose their magic. Excessive state intervention and regulation became dysfunctional. The economy, based on the competitiveness of overgrown *chaebol* groups rather than that of individual companies, became more and more ineffi-

cient. Finally, the acceleration of globalization exemplified by the Uruguay Round caused a new crisis in a Korean economy heavily dependent on export.

To solve this structural crisis, Korean capitalists introduced the "new management strategy" which would enable flexible accumulation, a kind of "dependent post-Fordist accumulation regime"; and the state introduced *Sekehwa* (the total globalization policy), a Korean version of global neo-liberalism, proclaiming its principal task to be the enhancement of international competitiveness.[6] So the state became more and more a kind of "civilian developmental dictatorship," or, to put it more precisely, an "international competitiveness dictatorship," armed with the slogan "international competitiveness first, democracy and distribution later."[7]

These attempts, however, encountered strong resistance from the working class. Capital was therefore obliged to change the labor acts to facilitate its flexible accumulation strategy. Finally, the decision to join the OECD in order to implement its globalization policy forced the government to "modernize" out-dated laws so as to meet the minimum international norm.

Under cross-fire from these pressures, in the summer of 1996, the Kim regime decided to amend labor laws in two contradictory directions. To meet international demands as well as those of labor, it intended to reform "collective labor relations" by eliminating the "four prohibitions," except the right of civil servants and teachers to organize. At the same time, it decided to permit capital to worsen "individual labor relations" by loosening the conditions of lay-off, allowing the employment of irregular workers, etc.

The government was persuaded by the capitalists' complaints that Korean individual labor relations, such as the conditions for layoff, were more "advanced" than those of the advanced countries, without paying attention to the difference between Korea and the West, namely that there is little social welfare in Korea. The ratio of welfare spending to the total governmental budget ranks a shameful 132 in the world. The state also hoped to introduce a Western-style "democratic societal corporatism" in labor relations by formulating the new labor law with the participation and consensus of labor and capital.[8]

But the KCTU replied that it could not accept the new individual labor relations, while capital rejected the new collective relations. The new labor act became the battleground of a total class war.

What Happened in the General Strike?

Failing to obtain consent from both labor and capital, the state decided to amend the law without their consent. In the meantime, the economic crisis worsened. Economic growth slowed down, and many companies, particularly medium and small firms, went bankrupt on a massive scale. At the same time, exports slowed down and the trade deficit increased dramatically. The Korean miracle seemed to have evaporated.

At this point, the Kim Young-Sam government made two key, and disastrous, strategic decisions. The bad economic situation and the outcry of the *chaebols* strengthened the voice of the neo-liberal "economy-firsters" against the reformists in the ruling bloc. The result was a decision to postpone the reform of the key prohibitions while satisfying the demands of capital. The new act represented a deterioration of already undemocratic labor relations and a brutal total offensive by capital against the Korean working class with the help of the state.

The second decision was no less important. The government decided to pass the law before the end of 1996 by any means possible, for fear that otherwise it might not be able to amend the law in the near future because of the upcoming presidential election and annual spring labor disputes related to annual wage negotiations. Furthermore, in order to utilize the National Security Planning Agency (a new name for the KCIA) during the coming presidential election, despite strong opposition, President Kim Young-Sam decided to pass, as a package with the new labor act, the National Security Planning Agency Act. This would restore to that secret agency, notorious for violation of human rights, powers which Kim had taken away during the political reform of his early years in office.

Fearing resistance from labor, the government kept the content of the final draft of the new labor acts secret even from its own National Assemblymen. Furthermore, the opposition parties, which had previously shown little opposition to the government's draft because of their political conservatism and their fear of the power of the *chaebols* in the coming election, suddenly changed their attitude and opposed the passing of the law before 1997 as a token gesture to the working class and in an attempt to seize the political initiative. This change forced the government to pass

these two undemocratic acts through the "snatching session" carried out in the early hours of December 26, orchestrated by secret military-like operations without even giving advance notice to the opposition parties or the press.

This arrogant action by the government set off a powder keg just waiting to explode. The result is history. The KCTU, which had previously threatened a general strike repeatedly, announced that it was now going to launch one. Many people worried about the result for many reasons. The leadership of the KCTU over the rank-and-file had never been tested. In particular, the timing was disadvantageous because of the holiday season. In view of the bad economic situation, the possibility that public opinion would turn against labor was worrying. The incumbent leadership of the KCTU therefore decided to adopt a "flexible strategy," that is, a protracted multi-stage general strike instead of total war—a kind of hit and run strategy.

Yet the response was far more successful than expected. The rank-and-file responded immediately. In fact, angry workers harshly criticized the flexible strategy for being too conciliatory. In that sense, it was the rank-and-file that pushed the leadership into the strike at the last moment, a leadership which had been hesitant about the actual execution of the strike for fear that it might lead to the total destruction of the young KCTU by state repression. Furthermore, even the FKTU joined the strike by initiating its own general strike in order not to be isolated from the rank-and-file. And the popular movements, which had been in decline under the Kim regime, were rapidly revitalized.

A national front to abolish the two undemocratic acts was organized, and not only the popular sector but also "civil organizations" (a Korean version of middle-class oriented new social movements) joined the front. "Common citizens," particularly the generally conservative "new middle class," which had been hostile to strikes, supported this one because of the job insecurity which the new labor acts would introduce. Big rallies were held every day all over the country to denounce the government, despite forceful interventions by the police. Major industries were brought to a halt. The authority of the state was nearly paralyzed, and public opinion abandoned the government. International support poured in from many foreign labor and democratic movements. So despite repeated warnings of punishment for violating the law, the government could not arrest the leaders of the KCTU who commanded the strike while on a hunger strike in a public place.

During the three stages of the strike, which lasted for twenty days with a stop-and-go pattern, under the leadership of the KCTU more than four hundred thousand workers from 528 unions participated more than once, and on an average about 190 thousand workers from 168 unions participated per day. The total cumulative numbers of the participants in the strikes and the public rallies amounted to respectively 3.6 million and 1.1 million. If the numbers of the FKTU are added to these figures, the total numbers could be doubled, though no one but the FKTU is sure of the exact numbers since they seem to have exaggerated the official number in order to compete with the KCTU. There were also supporting rallies in twenty-two nations and 223 letters of support from various foreign labor organizations and workers.

In the end, just before the announced fourth stage of the strike, the President was forced to make an announcement to admit his mistake with a humiliating apology and promises to re-amend the labor act. It was a de facto surrender to the working class.

The Aftermath of the Strike

There still remain live sparks, and the KCTU promises that the battle is not over. But now that the smoke has cleared, the battle has virtually ended. It is time to draw up a tentative, if not the final, balance sheet. As promised, the government re-amended the labor act in negotiation with the opposition parties. The final product resembles the government's original draft. It abolishes the four prohibitions except the right of the civil servants and teachers to organize. The KCTU has thus become not only the de facto but also the de jure representative of the Korean working class. And the exodus of the unions from the FKTU to the KCTU has already started. At the same time, most of capital's demands were also met with minor restrictions. Many in the democratic camp believe that the result is too little gain for the intensity of the fight.

The leaders of the KCTU halted their sit-in strike and withdrew the plan for continuing strike action after the President promised to re-amend the labor acts in negotiation with the opposition parties. But they also held

out the threat of another strike if the re-amended acts failed to satisfy the workers and worsened individual labor relations, as planned. The final product legislated by the political parties after a month of negotiation was, as expected, disappointing. The KCTU promised a fourth general strike if the National Assembly passed this draft. But a new political conjuncture, shaped by unexpected events such as the bankruptcy of a major *chaebol* and a related financial scandal of astronomical proportions, together with the political defection of a top-ranking North Korean official, compelled the KCTU to withdraw its promise once again. Instead, it decided to fight for the re-amendment of the new labor act during the annual wage negotiations in the summer.

The momentum and the golden opportunity appear to have been lost. The decision to postpone the strike after the president's promise to re-amend the act has proved to be a vital tactical mistake. In the month that followed the KCTU's first withdrawal of the threat to enter the fourth stage of the strike, the conjuncture changed in such a way as to force its second withdrawal. Had the KCTU pushed its advantage without suspending the strike in the first place, the result could have been the total surrender of the government and capital. Failing that, a "splendid heroic ending" by brutal force would almost certainly have resulted in a far stronger rebuilding of the movement in the near future, probably during the coming presidential election in the form of a working class candidate. Forgetting the simple truism that one should "strike while the iron is hot," the KCTU leadership

failed to deliver the final blow when it still had the chance.

Nevertheless, this does not diminish the historic significance of the strike. The fact that it was the first general strike in Korean history, especially a political general strike, is historically very important. In addition, for the first time in Korean history, the Korean working class succeeded in defeating a total offensive by capital and the state. This victory is even more significant when we consider that it was achieved in a country whose labor movement has until now been exceptionally weak. This is also a country which, because of its outward-looking economic structure, is highly vulnerable to globalization, the strategy adopted by capital, particularly in the metropolitan centers, to deal with its structural crises. The Korean class struggle, then, has challenged the conventional wisdom that national struggles are ineffective or even irrelevant in the age of globalization.

The strike hastened by at least ten years the "full blooming" of the labor movement and the formation of a working class party in South Korea by making the working class disillusioned with bourgeois politics and compelling it to recognize the urgent need to organize itself politically. Furthermore, by exercising its national leadership over other popular forces in democratic struggles, the Korean working class for the first time went beyond the expression of narrow "corporate" interests and began to function as a kind of "hegemonic" class, whose class interests were perceived as representing the interests of the people in general. As a consequence, according to a recent national survey of eligible voters, more than 40 percent of the respondents said that they would vote for the president of the KCTU in the coming presidential election in December. Finally, the strike is an important stepping stone for an international alliance of the working class, i.e., "globalization from below," to fight against the globalization of capital and global neo-liberalism.[9]

At the same time, many dangers face the South Korean labor movement, and we have to beware of too much optimism. There is a danger of the KCTU becoming another CIO, trapped in "industrial corporatism" or "business unionism."[10] The Korean working class is in danger of individualization because of job insecurity introduced by the new labor act. Pressures from globalization and a weakened economy may push the workers into subscribing to the propaganda of "economic revitalization first" or "saving the company first." Furthermore, Korean workers have to overcome the "red complex" and the "North Korean factor," particularly taking into consideration the bad economic conditions of North Korea. The working class must also overcome regionalism, the dominant political cleavage in Korea after democratization, in order to organize themselves politically. And even if political organization succeeds, the danger of cooptation into bourgeois politics as in Western social democracy is lurking nearby.

The Korean working class, as a late-starter, has five major difficult tasks, under particularly disadvantageous conditions in this age of unlimited global competition. First, it has to democratize the work place, that is, the pre-modern factory despotism. The second task is to create a united working class at the level of "civil society" and build its hegemony in it. For this, the KCTU and the FKTU have to merge into a single national organization under the leadership of the KCTU. And considering the low percentage of organized workers, it must organize the unorganized while organizing itself. It must overcome a variety of divisions within the working class: fragmentation by region, industry, company, big company versus small company etc. Thirdly, the Korean working class must organize politically. Fourthly, like labor movements elsewhere, it must find a way of maintaining the difficult balance between developing a more radical, socialist consciousness while keeping in touch with the masses. Finally, it must work hard for international alliances to compete with the globalization of capital.

The South Korean working class, even though a late-starter, is making, and must continue to make, painful but steady steps toward a humane society free from the oppression of capital.

Notes

1. See for instance Edward Mason *et al.*, *Economic and Social Modernization in the Republic of Korea* (Cambridge: Harvard University Press, 1980).
2. For the effect of the division, see Paik Nak-chung, "South Korea: Unification and the Democratic Challenge," *New Left Review*, no. 197 (Jan./Feb. 1993).
3. Choi Jang-Jip, *Interest Conflict and Political Control in South Korea*, Ph.D. Dissertation, University of Chicago (1983); Frederic Deyo, "State and Labor: Modes of Political Exclusion in East Asian Development," in F. Deyo ed. *The Political Economy of the New Asian Industrialism* (Ithaca: Cornell University Press, 1987).
4. On the Kwangju events, see Donald Clark ed., *The Kwangju Uprisings* (Boulder: Westview, 1988).
5. I have discussed the failure of this labor reform in a paper entitled "State and Civil Society in Korea: A Reappraisal," presented at the Georgetown Conference on Korea II, May 1995.
6. For the model of "dependent fordism" (though not "dependent post-fordism"), see Alan Lipietz, *Mirages and Miracles* (London: Verso, 1987). These models have some descriptive value, although there is a substantial body of literature critical of the "Regulation School" from which the concept of "dependent fordism" derives. See, for example, Daniel Cataife, "Fordism and the French Regulation School," *Monthly Review*, May 1989; Robert Brenner, "The Regulation Approach: Theory and History," *New Left Review*, July/August 1991; Richard Gunn, "Marxism, Metatheory and Critique," in W. Bonefeld et al., eds., *Post-fordism and Social Form* (London: Macmillan, 1991). I have critically examined the applicability of "fordism" and "post-fordism" to the Third World, including South Korea, in "A Critical Assessment of Strategic-Relational Theory of the State," in a paper delivered (in Korean) at the Conference on "The Achievements and Tasks of Modern State Theories," Korean Political Science Association, 1994.
7. I discuss this at greater length in the paper cited in note 5.
8. For the difference between state corporatism and societal corporatism, see Philippe Schmitter, "Still the Century of Corporatism?," in F. Pike *et al.* eds., *The New Corporatism* (Notre Dame: University of Notre Dame Press, 1974).
9. Richard Falk, "The Making of Global Citizenship," in John Brechter *et al.* eds., *Global Visions* (Boston: Southend Press, 1993).
10. See for instance Kim Moody, *An Injury to All: The Decline of American Unionism* (London: Verso, 1988).

 Article Review Form at end of book.

Islamic Financial Systems

Islamic finance is emerging as a rapidly growing part of the financial sector in the Islamic world. Islamic finance is not restricted to Islamic countries, but is spreading wherever there is a sizable Muslim community.

Zamir Iqbal

Zamir Iqbal, a national of Pakistan, is an Information Officer in the World Bank's Treasury Information Services Department.

According to some estimates, more than 100 financial institutions in over 45 countries practice some form of Islamic finance, and the industry has been growing at a rate of more than 15 percent annually for the past five years. The market's current annual turnover is estimated to be $70 billion, compared with a mere $5 billion in 1985, and is projected to hit the $100 billion mark by the turn of the century.

The growth in Islamic finance initially coincided with the current account surpluses of oil-exporting Islamic countries. But its continued growth in the face of eroding oil revenues reflects the influence of other factors, such as the desire for sociopolitical and economic systems based on Islamic principles and a stronger Islamic identity. In addition, the introduction of broad macroeconomic and structural reforms— in financial systems, the liberalization of capital movements, privatization, and the global integration of financial markets—have paved the way for the expansion of Islamic finance.

What Is Islamic Finance?

Islamic finance was practiced predominantly in the Muslim world throughout the Middle Ages, fostering trade and business activities with the development of credit. In Spain and the Mediterranean and Baltic states, Islamic merchants became indispensable middlemen for trading activities. In fact, many concepts, techniques, and instruments of Islamic finance were later adopted by European financiers and businessmen.

In contrast, the term "Islamic financial system" is relatively new, appearing only in the mid-1980s. In fact, all the earlier references to commercial or mercantile activities conforming to Islamic principles were made under the umbrella of either "interest-free" or "Islamic" banking. However, describing the Islamic financial system simply as "interest-free" does not provide a true picture of the system as a whole.

Undoubtedly, prohibiting the receipt and payment of interest is the nucleus of the system, but it is supported by other principles of Islamic doctrine advocating risk sharing, individuals' rights and duties, property rights, and the sanctity of contracts. Similarly, the Islamic financial system is not limited to banking but covers capital formation, capital markets, and all types of financial intermediation.

Interpreting the system as "interest-free" tends to create confusion. The philosophical foundation of an Islamic financial system goes beyond the interaction of factors of production and economic behavior. Whereas the conventional financial system focuses primarily on the economic and financial aspects of transactions, the Islamic system places equal emphasis on the ethical, moral, social, and religious dimensions, to enhance equality and fairness for the good of society as a whole. The system can be fully appreciated only in the context of Islam's teachings on the work ethic, wealth distribution, social and economic justice, and the role of the state.

The Islamic financial system is founded on the absolute prohibi-

Zamir Iqbal, "Islamic Financial Systems," FINANCE AND DEVELOPMENT, June 1997. Reprinted by permission.

tion of the payment or receipt of any predetermined, guaranteed rate of return. This closes the door to the concept of interest and precludes the use of debt-based instruments. The system encourages risk-sharing, promotes entrepreneurship, discourages speculative behavior, and emphasizes the sanctity of contracts (Box 1).

An Islamic financial system can be expected to be stable owing to the elimination of debt-financing and enhanced allocation efficiency. A "two-windows" model for Islamic financial intermediaries has been suggested in which demand deposits are backed 100 percent by reserves, and investment deposits are accepted purely on an equity-sharing basis. Analytical models demonstrate that such a system will be stable since the term and structure of the liabilities and the assets are symmetrically matched through profit-sharing arrangements, no fixed interest cost accrues, and refinancing through debt is not possible. Allocation efficiency occurs because investment alternatives are strictly selected based on their productivity and the expected rate of return. Finally, entrepreneurship is encouraged as entrepreneurs compete to become the agents for the suppliers of financial capital who, in turn, will closely scrutinize projects and management teams.

Basic Instruments

Islamic markets offer different instruments to satisfy providers and users of funds in a variety of ways: sales, trade financing, and investment (Box 2). Basic instruments include cost-plus financing (*murabaha*), profit-sharing (*mudaraba*), leasing (*ijara*), partnership (*musharaka*), and for-

The basic framework for an Islamic financial system is a set of rules and laws, collectively referred to as *shariah*, governing economic, social, political, and cultural aspects of Islamic societies. *Shariah* originates from the rules dictated by the *Quran* and its practices, and explanations rendered (more commonly known as *Sunnah*) by the Prophet Muhammad. Further elaboration of the rules is provided by scholars in Islamic jurisprudence within the framework of the *Quran* and *Sunnah*. The basic principles of an Islamic financial system can be summarized as follows:

Prohibition of interest. Prohibition of *riba*, a term literally meaning "an excess" and interpreted as "any unjustifiable increase of capital whether in loans or sales" is the central tenet of the system. More precisely, any positive, fixed, predetermined rate tied to the maturity and the amount of principal (i.e., guaranteed regardless of the performance of the investment) is considered *riba* and is prohibited. The general consensus among Islamic scholars is that *riba* covers not only usury but also the charging of the "interest" as widely practiced. This prohibition is based on arguments of social justice, equality, and property rights. Islam encourages the earning of profits but forbids the charging of interest because profits, determined ex post, symbolize successful entrepreneurship and creation of additional wealth whereas interest,

determined ex ante, is a cost that is accrued irrespective of the outcome of business operations and may not create wealth if there are business losses. Social justice demands that borrowers and lenders share rewards as well as losses in an equitable fashion and that the process of wealth accumulation and distribution in the economy be fair and representative of true productivity.

Risk sharing. Because interest is prohibited, suppliers of funds become investors instead of creditors. The provider of financial capital and the entrepreneur share business risks in return for shares of the profit.

Money as "potential" capital. Money is treated as "potential" capital—that is, it becomes actual capital only when it joins hands with other resources to undertake a productive activity. Islam recognizes the time value of money, but only when it acts as capital, not when it is "potential" capital.

Prohibition of speculative behavior. An Islamic financial system discourages hoarding and prohibits transactions featuring extreme uncertainties, gambling, and risks.

Shariah-approved activities. Only those business activities that do not violate the rules of *shariah* qualify for investment. For example, any investment in business dealing with alcohol, gambling, and casinos would be prohibited.

ward sale (*bay' salam*). These instruments serve as the basic building blocks for developing a wide array of more complex financial instruments, suggesting that there is great potential for financial innovation and expansion in Islamic financial markets.

Market Trends

Banking is the most developed part of the Islamic financial system. The state constitutions of Iran and Pakistan, for example, require their banking systems to be fully compatible with

Islamic law. In Egypt, Indonesia, Malaysia, Sudan, and the Gulf Cooperation Council (GCC) countries, Islamic banking exists alongside conventional banking. Islamic banking is currently practiced through two channels: "specialized" Islamic banks and "Islamic windows." Specialized Islamic banks are commercial and investment banks, structured wholly on Islamic principles, and they deal only with Islamic instruments. Islamic windows are special facilities offered by conventional banks to provide services to Muslims who wish to engage in

Some of the more popular instruments in Islamic financial markets are:

Trade with markup or cost-plus sale (murabaha). One of the most widely used instruments for short-term financing is based on the traditional notion of purchase finance. The investor undertakes to supply specific goods or commodities, incorporating a mutually agreed contract for resale to the client and a mutually negotiated margin. Around 75 percent of Islamic financial transactions are cost-plus sales.

Leasing (ijara). Another popular instrument, accounting for about 10 percent of Islamic financial transactions, is leasing. Leasing is designed for financing vehicles, machinery, equipment, and aircraft. Different forms of leasing are permissible, including leases where a portion of the installment payment goes toward the final purchase (with the transfer of ownership to the lessee).

Profit-sharing agreement (mudaraba). This is identical to an investment fund in which managers handle a pool of funds. The agent-manager has relatively limited liability while having sufficient incentives to perform. The capital is invested in broadly defined activities, and the terms of profit and risk sharing are customized for each investment. The maturity structure ranges from short to medium term and is more suitable for trade activities.

Equity participation (musharaka). This is analogous to a classical joint venture. Both entrepreneur and investor contribute to the capital (assets, technical and managerial expertise, working capital, etc.). Of the operation in varying degrees and agree to share the returns (as well as the risks) in proportions agreed to in advance. Traditionally, this form of transaction has been used for financing fixed assets and working capital of medium- and long-term duration.

Sales contracts. Deferred-payment sale (bay'mu'ajjal) and deferred-delivery sale (bay'salam) contracts, in addition to spot sales, are used for conducting credit sales. In a deferred-payment sale, delivery of the product is taken on the spot but deliver of the payment is delayed for an agreed period. Payment can be made in a lump sum or in installments, provided there is no extra charge for the delay. A deferred-delivery sale is similar to a forward contract where delivery of the product is in the future in exchange for payment on the spot market.

Islamic banking. Both Western banks and banks headquartered in Islamic countries provide Islamic windows.

Traditionally, specialized Islamic banks have been well positioned to attract deposits from Muslims, but these institutions have generally lacked the technical ability to invest efficiently. This gap has been bridged by the services of Western banks that swiftly and efficiently deploy funds into Islamically acceptable channels. But this has often meant lower returns for Islamic investors owing to the second layer of intermediation. This trend is changing. Islamic banks are becoming resourceful and are going global, in part owing to their increased integration with international markets. At the same time, aware of the potential of Islamic markets, Western banks are reaching out to investors directly and eliminating the middleman—the Islamic banks or Islamic windows of banks in Muslim countries. For example, Citibank opened its first Islamic bank subsidiary in Bahrain in 1996.

Historically, Islamic financial markets have lacked liquidity-enhancing instruments, thus eliminating a large segment of potential investors. However, more liquid instruments are emerging through securitization; Islamic funds, with a current market size of $1 billion, represent the initial application of securitization (see table). There are three types of Islamic funds: equity, commodity, and leasing. Equity funds, the largest share of the Islamic funds: equity, commodity, leasing. Equity funds market, are the same as conventional mutual funds but with an Islamic touch that requires a unique "filtration" process to select appropriate shares. The filtration process ensures that the mode, operation, and capital structure of each business the fund invests in are compatible with Islamic law, eliminating companies engaged in prohibited activities and those whose capital structure relies heavily on debt financing (to avoid dealing with interest). For this reason, companies with a negligible level of debt financing (10 percent or less) may be selected, provided that the debt does not remain a permanent feature of the capital structure. The future of Islamic equity funds is bright in part because of a new wave of privatization under way in Muslim countries such as Egypt and Jordan, and in high-growth Islamic countries such as Indonesia and Malaysia, where the demand for Islamic financial products is growing rapidly. Commodity and leasing funds are other forms of Islamic funds. Commodity funds invest in base metals. Leasing funds pool auto, equipment, and aircraft leases and issue tradable certificates backed by the leases.

International and regional institutions are working with Islamic finance and are contemplating the introduction of derivative products and syndication to enhance project finance. The International Finance Corporation (IFC) has successfully executed several transactions in the Middle East and Pakistan that conform to Islamic principles. While the introduction of derivative products is being cautiously studied, it

Emerging Islamic Funds

Fund	Type	Year Launched	Financial Institution	Size (million dollars)
IIBU Fund II Plc	Leasing	1994	United Bank of Kuwait	51.5
Faysal Saudi Real Estate Fund		1995	Faysal Islamic Bank of Bahrain	27.0
GCC Trading Fund		1996	Faysal Islamic Bank of Bahrain	10.0
Oasis International Equity Fund	Equity	1996	Robert Fleming & Co. (United Kingdom)	16.6
Faisal Finance Real Estate Income Fund II	Real estate	1996	Faisal Finance (Switzerland) S.A.	100.0
Unit Investment Fund (all tranches)	Income/*mudaraba* syndication	1996	Islamic Development Bank (Saudi Arabia)	500.0
Al Safwa International Equity Fund	Equity unit trust	1996	Al-Tawfeed Company for Investment Funds Ltd.	27.0
Ibn Khaldun International Equity Fund	Equity	1996	PFM Group (United Kingdom)	25.0
Adil Islamic Growth Fund	Equity	1996	Faisal Finance (Switzerland) S.A.	10.0

Source: *Islamic Banker*, 1995–96, various issues.

is suspected that these incorporate interest and may also support speculative activities. Simple derivatives, such as forward contracts, are being examined because their basic elements are similar to those of the Islamic instrument of deferred sale. Project finance, which puts emphasis on equity participation, is another natural fit for Islamic finance. The successful experimentation with long-term project financing in the construction industry in Malaysia is a positive development in this area.

Issues and Challenges

Islamic financial markets are operating far below their potential because Islamic banking by itself cannot take root in the absence of the other necessary components of an Islamic financial system. A number of limitations will have to be addressed before any long-term strategy can be formulated:

- A uniform regulatory and legal framework supportive of an Islamic financial system has not yet been developed. Existing banking regulations in Islamic countries are based on the Western banking model. Similarly, Islamic financial institutions face difficulties operating in non-Islamic countries owing to the absence of a regulatory body that operates in accordance with Islamic principles. The development of a regulatory and supervisory framework that would address the issues specific to Islamic institutions would further enhance the integration of Islamic markets and international financial markets.

- There is no single, sizable, and organized financial center that can claim to be functioning in accordance with Islamic principles. Although stock markets in emerging Islamic countries such as Egypt, Jordan, and Pakistan are active, they are not fully compatible with Islamic principles. The stock markets in Iran and Sudan may come closest to operating in compliance with Islamic principles. Moreover, the secondary market for Islamic products is extremely shallow and illiquid, and money markets are almost nonexistent, since viable instruments are not currently available. The development of an interbank market is another challenge.

- The pace of innovation is slow. For years, the market has offered the same traditional instruments geared toward short- and medium-term maturities, but it has not yet come up with the necessary instruments to handle maturities at the extremes. There is a need for risk-management tools to equip clients with instruments to hedge against the high volatility in currency and commodities markets. In addition, the market lacks the necessary instruments to provide viable alternatives for public debt financing.

- An Islamic financial system needs sound accounting procedures and standards. Western accounting procedures are not adequate because of the different nature and treatment of financial instruments. Well-defined procedures and standards are crucial for information disclosure, building investors' confidence, and monitoring and surveillance. Proper standards will also help the integration of Islamic financial markets with international markets.

Islamic institutions have a shortage of trained personnel who can analyze and manage portfolios, and develop innovative products according to Islamic financial principles. Only a limited number of Islamic institutions can afford to train their staffs and deploy resources in product development.

- There is lack of uniformity in the religious principles applied in Islamic countries. In the absence of a universally accepted central religious authority, Islamic banks have formed their own religious boards for guidance. Islamic banks have to consult their respective religious boards, or *shariah* advisors, to seek approval for each new instrument. Differences in interpretation of Islamic principles by different schools of thought may mean that identical financial instruments are rejected by one board but accepted by another. Thus, the same instrument may not be acceptable in all countries. This problem can be addressed by forming a uniform council representing different schools of thought to define cohesive rules and to expedite the process of introducing new products.

Future Directions

The further growth and development of the Islamic financial system will depend largely on the nature of innovations introduced in the market. The immediate need is to deploy human and financial resources to develop instruments to enhance liquidity; develop secondary, money, and interbank markets; perform asset/liability and risk management; and introduce public finance instruments. The Islamic financial system can also offer alternatives at the microfinance level.

Securitization is a step in the right direction but even this requires more sophistication. The scope of securitization—the process of unbundling and repackaging a financial asset to enhance its marketability, negotiability, and liquidity—in Islamic financial markets is very promising, because current market operations are restricted by the dearth of liquidity-enhancing products; secondary markets lack depth and breadth; and, more important, instruments for asset/liability management are simply nonexistent. With the expansion of securitization, the customer base of Islamic financial systems will grow as institutional investors, who have access to broader maturity structures, are attracted to the market; the secondary market will develop; and asset/liability management will become a reality. Other strong candidates for securitization include real estate, leasing, and trade receivables because of the collateralized nature of their cash flows.

Microfinance is another candidate for the application of Islamic finance. Islamic finance promotes entrepreneurship and risk sharing, and its expansion to the poor could be an effective development tool. The social benefits are obvious, since the poor currently are often exploited by lenders charging usurious rates.

An Islamic financial system can play a vital role in the economic development of Islamic countries by mobilizing dormant savings that are being intentionally kept out of interest-based financial channels and by facilitating the development of capital markets. At the same time, the development of such systems would enable savers and borrowers to choose financial instruments compatible with their business needs, social values, and religious beliefs.

 Article Review Form at end of book.

WiseGuide Wrap-Up

Following World War II, government leaders worried that if they did not institute economic supports for their working citizens, authoritarian leaders might convince citizens to abandon democracy and choose a nondemocratic form of leadership. Hence, democratic leaders created a welfare state that provided free or low-cost health care, education, decent wages, and a secure retirement package. As more countries increased their industrialization abilities and production and sales competition became more keen among states, businesses argued that they could no longer pay workers the benefits the state had decreed, and working citizens argued that they did not want to pay high taxes to support state programs for low-cost education, health care, and so on. In the 1980s, state leaders dismantled the welfare state, and business tried to take away benefits and reduce workers' wages. Workers' living standards dropped, and workers lost faith in their unions. As business ventures became risky, interest rates increased to protect bank loans to businesses and to earn a good return on business loans. This increased pressure on businesses to cut labor costs. Union members, like those in Reading 46 about Korea, either despaired and abandoned their unions or became more militant, more disruptive, and more political in their efforts to maintain a decent standard of living.

Western theorists argue that the market must be left to operate unregulated, even if it causes hardship. In the long run, they say, an unregulated market creates efficient business, and suffering workers and owners can switch to more profitable production sectors. Islamic theorists, on the other hand, argue that different values should govern business, state, and labor relations. Islamic citizens should practice Islamic finance, which includes interest-free loans that do not force high repayment costs onto owners, who then have to pass cost-cutting onto their workers.

R.E.A.L. Sites

This list provides a print preview of typical **coursewise** R.E.A.L. sites. There are over 100 such sites at the **courselinks**™ site. The danger in printing URLs is that web sites can change overnight. As we went to press, these sites were functional using the URLs provided. If you come across one that isn't, please let us know via email to: webmaster@coursewise.com. Use your Passport to access the most current list of R.E.A.L. sites at the **courselinks**™ site.

Site name: New Health Care Study Shows Employer-Based Health Coverage Is Declining Because Employers Are Shifting Rising Premium Costs to Workers
URL: http://www.aflcio.org/publ/press98/pr0219.htm
Why is it R.E.A.L.? This site contains information that shows that the data in the readings in this section are critically important to U.S. workers today, as well as to welfare state citizens.
Key topics: health insurance premiums, AFL-CIO

Site name: European Trade Union Confederation (ETUC)
URL: http://www.etuc.org/
Why is it R.E.A.L.? This site demonstrates the concerns of European workers to "counterbalance the economic forces" that are creating today's new labor-business relations context.
Key topics: European Trade Union Confederation (ETUC)

Site name: ICFTU-APRO 69th Regional Executive Board Meeting, Singapore, Omnibus Resolution
URL: http://sunflower.singnet.com.sg/~icftu/archives/ar-eb69.htm
Why is it R.E.A.L.? This document was issued at the International Conference Federation of Trade Unions Asian and Pacific Regional Organization meeting in Singapore in October 1997. It calls on governments to protect union workers from unfair business practices and to create legislation that allows Asian workers to organize to improve their standard of living.
Key topics: bargain collectively, occupational safety

section 5

Key Points

- Most people in the world are peasant farmers or earn their living from rural agriculture.

- Few governments spend much time or many resources to address the needs of peasants and rural farmers.

- When concerns are raised about the rural sector, these concerns often involve debates about land reform.

- Some people believe that the modern world requires increasing urbanization and that rural citizens are an anachronism and should be allowed to die off.

❓ Questions ❓

1. If you are going to study comparative politics, why should you have some understanding of peasants and rural farmers?

2. What are some of the contentious issues in land reform debates?

3. Why can't present countries do as the British did in the 1800s and just let their rural peasants be miserable and die off?

Peasants in Comparative Perspective

 **WiseGuide Intro**

The World Bank estimates that the primary occupation of 60 percent of the world's population is rural agriculture. In Africa, that percentage is even greater, reaching 70 and in some countries 80 percent. Under previous authoritarian governments, rural workers had few means by which to make their needs noticed. Even those who live now in newly democratizing states have trouble holding national officials accountable for their agricultural policies. Peasants generally have low levels of education, often work on private property for wealthy landlords, and have few modern means of communication, except government-controlled national radio stations. Finally, the rural population of most countries is spread across a vast geographic territory, making it difficult for organizers to effectively mobilize peasants on national issues.

National officials often spend their scarce resources on addressing the concerns of urban areas, where foreign visitors form impressions of the country and where political protests are easily seen and heard by national, urban-based policy makers. Economist Ann Seidman says that the rural-urban distinction is false. She argues that the prospects of citizens in both rural and urban areas are intertwined and that urban as well as rural areas benefit when improvements are made in the rural areas.*

Since World War II, much of the debate about peasants and development has centered on land reform. But as Ricardo Tavares argues, in Reading 48, in places like Brazil, land reform is unlikely to find its way onto the national policy agenda. Instead, peasant advocates are now hoping to make the living conditions of rural wage earners the focus for political mobilization.

When peasants have little that is their own, are allowed mobility, and believe that they can find economic success elsewhere, they migrate generally to already overcrowded cities. In China, as Chen argues in Reading 49, the state has attempted to empower peasants in the rural areas, undertaking reforms throughout the 1980s and 1990s. The political and economic consequences are crucial to China's future. How to modernize the peasantry without creating a politically and economically unmanageable social group is a question that is central not only to China but to most countries throughout Latin America, Africa, and the Middle East.

* Ann Seidman, *The Roots of Crisis in Southern Africa* (Trenton: Africa World Press, 1985).

Land and Democracy

Reconsidering the agrarian question

Instead of isolating the question of land redistribution as many had in the past, those working in support of the rural poor are seeking to situate the agrarian-reform issue within the broader struggle against poverty and hunger.

Ricardo Tavares

The period from the election of Fernando Henrique Cardoso as president of Brazil on October 3, 1994, to his inauguration two months later spawned surprising changes in the agrarian-reform debate in Brazil. First, the Rural Democratic Union (UDR), the landowners group which had become the leading opponent of agrarian reform, decided to close its doors, announcing that its work was done. 1994 also ended with one of Brazil's leading intellectual and political supporters of agrarian reform questioning whether it makes sense to use the term "agrarian reform" in the 1990s. "The expression 'agrarian reform' gives rise to ideological confrontation," said Herbert "Betinho" de Souza, coordinator of the Citizens' Action against Hunger and Misery. "What is important is to seek consensus and results." The Campaign against

Hunger decided that henceforth it would use the concept "democratization of the land."[1]

The two actions seem to suggest that agrarian reform—in this country with the hemisphere's most uneven distribution of land—is off the political agenda for the foreseeable future. The reality, however, is more complex. While Brazil's large landowners appear to be at ease, with no "threats" in sight, the social movements, the Catholic Church, and non-governmental organizations (NGOs)—the key sectors working in support of the rural poor—have not given up the struggle. Rather, they have decided to rethink their strategy. Instead of isolating the question of land redistribution as many had in the past, pro-agrarian reform groups today are seeking to situate the agrarian-reform issue within the broader movement to consolidate and further the democratic regime. They associate this movement with the more general goal of fighting poverty and

hunger in a country rife with social inequalities.

The agrarian question has deep roots in Brazilian history, dating back to the Portuguese colonizers, who gave immense land tracts (*capitanias hereditárias*) to a small group of settlers (*donatários*) to establish plantations based on slave labor. Up to the late 1950s, rural workers faced obstacles to organizing in the form of legal constraints and landowner violence. Nonetheless, in the late 1950s and early 1960s peasants struggled against traditional forms of political domination by claiming the right to remain on the rural properties where they lived, and legal title to the land. The rural landowners were losing the traditional mechanisms of social control which had operated up until that time. President João Goulart, who assumed power in 1961, sought to carry out agrarian reform as part of his broad-based program of "grassroots reforms" (*reformas de base*).

Ricardo Tavares, "Land and Democracy, Reconsidering the Agrarian Question," NACLA REPORT ON THE AMERICAS; Vol. 28:6, pp. 23-30. Copyright 1997 by the North American Congress on Latin America, 475 Riverside Dr., #454, New York, NY 10155-0122.

The military overthrew Goulart in 1964, claiming the need to "re-establish order" and put a halt to the "Communist threat." During the ensuing 26-year dictatorship, peasant movements were severely repressed. Nonetheless, the military had to respond to the social pressures in rural areas. It drafted the most radical agrarian-reform legislation in the country's history, but then failed to implement it. The key element of this legislation was the 1964 Land Statute, an ambiguous law which sought to modernize agriculture, with land reform as one of its instruments. The Land Statute established a legal framework for later government subsidizing of the overhaul of traditional *latifúndios,* which became more capital-intensive as they developed into agroindustrial complexes.[2] Tenant farmers (*moradores)* were expelled from these properties. Millions became rural wage workers, and millions more migrated to the industrial cities, transforming part of rural poverty into urban poverty.

At the same time, the Land Statute defined rules for the expropriation of large idle rural properties and others not efficiently exploited. This expropriation of land did not take place, largely because of the clout of large landowners in the Brazilian political system. This influence stems from the fact that rural states in North—mainly the Northeast—elect proportionally more members of the National Congress than the industrial and more populous states of the South and Southeast, perverting the principle of "one person, one vote." This distortion in the Brazilian political system, which has been in place since 1930, allowed the military to rely on the landed oligarchy as one of its main bases of support.

Over the course of the military regime, three important actors in the Brazilian rural scene de-veloped national policies to support the demands of peasants and rural workers: the Catholic Church, the National Confederation of Agricultural Workers (CONTAG), and the social movements associated with the Workers' Party (PT). With the "political opening"—the "slow, gradual and steady" political easing of tensions begun under General Ernesto Geisel (1974–1979)—opportunities appeared for waging open struggles for social rights in the countryside. Thousands of groups including rural unions, opposition trade unions, movements of the landless, associations of small rural producers, and NGOs organized across the country.

The Church chose agrarian reform as a key issue in its pastoral work nationwide, setting up the Pastoral Land Commission (CPT) in 1975. In agricultural frontier areas, priests and bishops sided with the *posseiros* (squatters who work the land but have no legal title) against the *grileiros* (colonists with fraudulent title) and large landowners, in a struggle which often became bloody.

Another fundamental actor in the democratic transition was CONTAG. Formed in 1963, just before the April 1964 military coup, CONTAG had a reformist, not radical spirit. It had opposed radicalization of the Peasant Leagues prior to the coup, devoting its energies to forming rural wage-workers unions. At first, it suffered harassment by the military regime. By 1968, however, when a group of unionized rural wage workers from the Northeast assumed leadership of the confederation, CONTAG came to be tolerated by the military, which wanted to maintain relative independence from the large landowners in rural-policy matters. The CONTAG unionists navigated in turbulent waters, exploring "the politics of the possible."[3] Defending an agrarian reform negotiated with the democratic transition government which took power in 1985, the confederation focused its efforts on mobilizing rural wage workers on sugarcane plantations, especially in the Northeast.

In the first half of the 1980s, the Movement of Landless Rural Workers (Movimento dos Trabalhadores Rurais Sem Terra, MST) and the National Department for Rural Workers of the Unified Workers Central (DNTR-CUT) were both formed. The MST began a new form of struggle for land based on setting up *acampamentos,* or makeshift encampments, on roads alongside large estates, and occupying lands considered unproductive, mainly in the three states of southern Brazil (Rio Grande do Sul, Santa Catarina and Paraná). The CUT and MST adopted a strategy of confrontation with the state, as they pressured for social reforms by taking mass actions in the countryside. The two groups played a decisive role in building a rural political base for the PT.

All these organizations helped build up public opinion in support of agrarian reform. As a consequence, agrarian reform was prominently featured in the political program of the democratic transition, when the oppostion to and dissidence within the military regime came together to elect Tancredo Neves, the candidate of the reformist alliance between the

Party of the Brazilian Democratic Movement (PMBD) and the Liberal Front Party (PFL), in the 1985 indirect presidential elections. While CONTAG decided to participate in the coalition that elected Tancredo Neves, the CUT, MST and PT denounced the indirect election as little more than a pact among elites. The MST was particularly distrustful of Vice-President José Sarney, who was a traditional politician associated with the civilian base of support of the military regime, and a member of the Northeast rural oligarchy.

Tancredo Neves sought to transform the alliance that had come together to support populist Getúlio Vargas from 1930 to 1954. Vargas allied with the industrial sectors and urban workers to promote import-substitution industrialization, and gave the rural oligarchies the right to savagely exploit the peasantry.[4] By contrast, Tancredo Neves' objective was to promote an austere economic policy so as to tame the industrial sector and urban trade unions, while also undertaking a bold agrarian-reform plan aimed at eradicating rural poverty.[5]

Neves did not live long enough to carry out this project. He died one month after taking office, and Vice-President Sarney assumed the presidency. In the first year of his administration, Sarney kept intact the alliances that had come together to support Neves. A Ministry of Agrarian Reform (MIRAD) was formed, and Nelson Ribeiro, a lawyer with ties to the Church and the PMDB, was named agriculture minister. The former president of the Brazilian Association for Agrarian Reform (ABRA), José Gomes da Silva, was appointed president of the National Institute for Colonization and Agrarian

Reform (INCRA). The ministries of agriculture and justice, which are extremely important for carrying out agrarian reform, included representatives of the left wing of the PMDB. In May, 1985, Sarney addressed the IV Congress of CONTAG to announce the "proposal" for the First National Agrarian Reform Plan (PNRA), with the goal of expropriating 43 million hectares of land to eradicate rural poverty in 20 years.

In 1985 agrarian reform became the key issue in national politics, achieving even more prominence than the challenge of controlling inflation. The MST multiplied the number of its occupations of large estates to pressure the government to carry out the reform. The PNRA's audacious program met, however, with the violent opposition of large landowners. The Rural Democratic Union (UDR), created in December, 1984 by cattle ranchers and landowners, became the central force of the anti-PNRA campaign. The UDR organized "auctions" of cows and horses nationwide to raise money for the campaign to stop the agrarian reform. Part of the money was used to purchase weapons, while another share went to purchase advertising in the mass media, mainly television and radio. The UDR's media campaign denounced the seizure of private property by the federal government, and tried to improve the image of the large rural landowners by calling them "rural producers" instead of *latifundiários*. The landowners filed suits in the courts to obstruct the government's first efforts to expropriate large holdings. Assassinations of peasant and religious leaders increased.

The National Constituent Assembly (1987–1988), which gathered to draft a new

Constitution, provided a rare opportunity to the rural oligarchy to derail the agrarian-reform process. The industrial and financial groups of São Paulo, the center of Brazilian capitalism, threw their support behind the UDR's anti-agrarian reform campaign. This alliance was in their own interest since rural landowners and other business interests in the state of São Paulo own more than half of all land in the country, having invested heavily in agricultural frontier areas over the last 30 years. Reflecting the power of the large landowners, the new Constitution, adopted in 1988, contains a ban on the expropriation of "productive lands."

In spite of the fact that the PNRA did not expropriate the 43 million hectares originally proposed, it did succeed in expropriating some areas, and in many micro-regions of the Brazilian interior, important opportunities for social change were created. On the other hand, countless mistakes were made in the plan's design and political direction.[6]

The first problem worth mentioning resides in the very conception of agrarian reform in the PNRA: it focused exclusively on land ownership, dissociating land policy from agricultural policy (credit, infrastructure, market access, technical assistance, and a broader view of rural development). Exacerbating the problem, the PNRA sought to benefit only the *sem terra*. The main result of this logic was to facilitate the strategy of alliances of the large landowners who sought to block the reform. Small producers, many living close to the poverty line, were totally excluded from the benefits of the reform, despite rhetoric to the contrary. They felt threatened by the landless rural workers in many parts of the country, making them receptive to the anti-agrarian reform demagogy of the landowners.

While the faltering Brazilian economy during the Sarney years contributed to the landowners' success in burying the PNRA, the plan also lacked a broad base of political support. To carry out agrarian reform in Brazil, backing must necessarily come from the key offices of the executive branch: the office of the president, the federal government's agrarian-reform agencies, the ministries of agriculture and justice, and the state-owned Banco do Brasil. President Sarney did not stake a great deal of his political capital in the PNRA, since he never really saw the program as his own, but as a creation of Tancredo Neves. The fundamental challenge, however, was to win the political support of the National Congress, which had never endorsed an agrarian-reform program in Brazilian history. The PNRA failed on that count as well. The Brazilian judiciary also became an obstacle bringing PNRA reforms to a standstill in several states.

The left was also in part responsible for the plan's failure. Coming from an anti-state strategy during the military regime, the social movements linked to the PT, the CUT and the MST defined themselves together as the opposition to the Sarney administration. Only when Sarney completely withdrew his support for the PNRA, at the end of his term in office, did the PT make a clear show of support for the plan. By then, it was too late.

In the 1989 campaign for the first direct presidential elections since 1961, agrarian reform was an important political issue, though not the central one. The then-president of the UDR, Ronaldo Caiado, ran for presi-

dent, but garnered an insignificant number of votes. Luis Inácio "Lula" de Silva, of the Workers Party, made agrarian reform one of the key points in his proposed reform package. Lula's program, however, emphasized the land question, giving short shrift to agricultural policies and rural development. The triumphant candidate, Fernando Collor de Mello, pledged to settle 500,000 families in agrarian-reform projects, a promise he did not fulfill. Once elected, Collor shut down the MIRAD created under Sarney, transferring its functions to the Ministry of Agriculture.

The agrarian-reform issue was not prominent in the 1994 election campaign. The "Real Plan," implemented on July 1, 1994, made economic stabilization and control of inflation the almost exclusive focus of the presidential campaign, limiting opportunities to debate other issues.

Only Lula, running again as the Workers Party candidate, visited settlements of landless rural workers on agrarian-reform projects as part of the campaign activities.[7] The MST openly supported Lula, as did the CUT and most of the national leaders of CONTAG (except its president, Francisco Urbano, who is a member of Fernando Henrique Cardoso's Brazilian Social Democratic Party).

Even if the issue was not talked about much in the campaign, agrarian reform was de rigeur in the candidates' programs. Lula set the goal of settling 800,000 families in plots of about 30 hectares each in the span of four years, the same number of families settled by Lázaro Cárdenas in Mexico from 1934 to 1940.[8] To achieve this, the PT planned to expropriate 24 million hectares of land, at a likely cost of

$8 billion, excluding the price of land.[9] The PT's program sought to do a better job of balancing the land question and agricultural policy than it had in 1989. Yet the vote for Lula in rural areas was once again very low.

Cardoso's goals were much more modest: "To adopt a realistic and responsible agrarian policy with the settlement of 40,000 families in the first year; 60,000 the second year; 80,000 the third year; and 100,000 families the fourth year."[10] PSDB advisers never gave details during the campaign about how these goals would be achieved.

The June 13, 1994 issue of *Jornal do Brasil* covered the candidates' views on agrarian reform. Cardoso took the opportunity to attack the PT: "Agrarian reform is an important point in addressing the priorities of employment and agriculture. Indeed, it is time that we move from words to action. The workers are victims, first, of the unjust concentration of landed property; second, they are victims of the PT which, with its radicalism, blocked the adoption of a modern and just agrarian reform in the Constituent Assembly. The PT refused to enter into an agreement with the other parties. The result is this: we went back to a situation prior to the Land Statute enacted by President Castelo Branco, which would be considered radical in the current situation."

Lula, in turn, defended the paradigm of European agriculture: "If we had an agrarian-reform policy made to order, there would be no occupations or land invasions. It is necessary to make a survey of the unproductive lands in each municipality. From there, it is possible to determine who is in the countryside and wants to continue there. Most fundamental is undertaking an agrarian reform with subsidized credit, technical assistance, facilities for getting output to market, and a guaranteed minimum price, as is done in any decent and democratic country in the world. If we take the European countries as an example, we note that there, small and medium rural properties are the mainstay of production."

In his inaugural speech of January 1, 1995, President Fernando Henrique Cardoso said: "We once again have freedom . . . . And we will have development. There is no social justice. And this is the great challenge in Brazil as the century draws to a close. This will be my administration's number-one objective." Nonetheless, Cardoso has not offered any substantive ideas about the agrarian reform he may seek to carry out. In fact, the intellectuals of the PSDB, including some of President Cardoso's close advisers, have three main criticisms of agrarian reform:

1. *It is false that Brazil needs a wide-ranging agrarian reform.* According to Franciso Graziano Neto, agronomist and personal adviser to Cardoso, demand for land in Brazil is much less than what the PNRA wanted to redistribute and the peasant movements demanded. "To think," he writes, "that all rural workers have as their main concern the struggle for land is to interpret Brazilian reality in a skewed fashion, twisting the facts so as to bring them into line with the old theories of the European peasantry at the time of the transition from feudalism."[11] In his view, the only true mass movement in the countryside is made up of rural wage workers, who are demanding better living conditions and

wages, not land. Sharecroppers and tenant farmers, according to Graziano Neto, have no intrinsic right to the land: "There's no reason to think that a tenant farmer growing rice in Rio Grande do Sul should receive a piece of land from the authorities."

2. *It is difficult to make an agrarian reform viable in the framework of international competition for technology, capital and modern agricultural markets.* Guilherme Leite da Silva Dias, professor at the University of São Paulo (USP) and PSDB adviser, considers urban supply the key issue. In his view, in the context of Brazil's growing insertion into the world economy, food imports may continue to be the cheapest solution. "An endless number of options will appear," he writes, "the cheapest being to feed the city through food imports. Everyone is figuring out how to import. It takes 20 days between making the decision and having the corn 500 kilometers inland from port."[12] Silva Dias believes that to ensure that agrarian reform is technically in order, it should introduce the modern technological set-up in the new properties, and it should involve intense training and education of the settled workers.

3. *It is not politically viable to implement a massive agrarian reform centralized in the federal government.* "It is simply impossible," writes Graziano Neto, "to work with the Brazilian agrarian question in an aggregate manner. The diversity of relations of production requires varied forms of intervention that respect the predominant characteristics of agriculture as it is organized in the different

regions. . . . Taxation, expropriation, legalization and colonization, among others, are also important land-policy actions, depending on where they are to be used."[13] Silva Dias adds: "In the context of this path of democratization that we are experiencing, power is highly diluted in the Brazilian federation. So the ability of the national state, of the central state, to impose solutions, to try to impose a direction, is extremely limited."

What unites these PSDB intellectuals is their concern for increasing the productivity of Brazilian agriculture, not for finding work or land for the country's rural poor. In a typical framing of the issue, economist Geraldo Muller writes: "There is no point distributing land and creating new rural landowners. What is fundamental for increasing, diversifying, and improving the quality of the agrarian surplus is not bringing more people or land into the productive process, but having a financial arrangement that makes it possible to intensify exploitation of labor and land, and incorporating technical advances.[14]

If the PSDB is so critical of the agrarian reform, why did the party include in its program the goal of settling 280,000 families in agrarian-reform projects over four years? The answer lies in the particular character of Brazilian politics. Agrarian reform draws the line between the right and left in Brazil. Having forged alliances with the conservative parties in order to win the election, Cardoso did not want to serve up evidence on a silver platter that would support the PT's accusations that he had moved sharply to the right. In addition, concentration of land ownership in Brazil is so great that any party that contemplates confronting social problems has to address the issue. In 1985, less than 0.9% of landowners occupied 44% of all arable land, while the poorest 90%, in terms of land ownership, occupied only 21% of all land.[15]

Agrarian reform, however, is far from being a really important policy matter for Cardoso. In his first year of government, the President's absolute priority is to pass neoliberal economic reforms. He will not risk undertaking any social reforms that may upset his conservative allies in the National Congress, who are key to the success of his economic agenda.

One sign of this approach was the choice of banker Andrade Vieira for minister of agriculture, supply and agrarian reform. A long-standing opponent of agrarian reform. Vieira was given the ministry in order to satisfy the Partido Trabalhista Brasileiro (PTB), one of the parties in the Congress that backs Cardoso. Vieira favors replacing an agrarian-reform plan with a lease system. Some analysts argue that the structure of agricultural production is less concentrated than the size of rural landholdings suggest, since most of the large properties produce nothing. Instead of being expropriated "for the social interest," they say, this land can be leased to small producers seeking larger production areas.

In some regions of the country, with support from official banks such as the Banco do Brasil, large landowners have begun leasing lands to small rural producers in order to make their lands "productive." The government provides credit to the small producers. Today, this leasing arrangement is the best-articulated project of the sectors opposed to agrarian reform. The problem with lease policies is the opposite of the flaw in the PNRA: it tends to benefit mostly small producers interested in obtaining larger areas for planting, while it excludes landless farmers.

Once the main neoliberal economic reforms that require constitutional amendments are concluded, President Cardoso will have to turn to his social-reform strategy. His economic program is clear, and is the basis of the center-right alliance that supported him in the campaign and is the basis of his administration. The social program, however, has not been spelled out so far. Cardoso will have to make advances on this front if he is going to have the popular support he will need to reform the Constitution to permit his re-election to a second four-year term. The alliances needed to carry out social reforms may not be the same as those required to carry out the economic reforms.

In Brazil today, in large parts of the interior, the limited presence of the state has enabled rural oligarchies, both old and new, to exercise private discretionary control over labor relations. In 1992 alone, 16,442 people toiled as slave labor in the states of Bahia, Minas Gerais, Rio de Janeiro, Pará, Mato Grosso, Mato Grosso do Sul and Rio Grande do Sul. The rural oligarchies, the social base for many of Brazil's past authoritarian regimes, still violate human rights with impunity.

The slogan of the rural social movements during the democratic transition was "without land, there is no democracy." Today, the situation seems to have been inverted: "without democracy, there is no land." The maintenance of the democratic regime appears to be the only way of challenging the private power of the large landowners and of pressuring the state to redirect its resources. The presence of "authoritarian enclaves" in Brazilian territory, however, is a significant obstacle to the consolidation and expansion of democracy.[16]

The rural social movements have chosen this year to launch a national campaign for "democratization of land" and generation of rural employment. Over the past 15 years, Brazil's social movements have won some political battles for agrarian reform, but have lost the head-on war against the large landholdings. They have learned that reducing all rural conflict in Brazil to the contradiction between the *sem terra* and the large estates will only lead to failure. Nevertheless, as broad sectors of the Brazilian public come together in the struggle to democratize access to the many fruits of this economically robust nation, part of that struggle must be directed to the democratization of access to land.

Notes

1. Aziz Filho, "Terra passa a ser alvo da campanha de Betinho," *Folha de São Paulo*, December 25, 1994.
2. The Land Statute (Law 4504/64) provided the first conceptual definition of the *latifúndio* in a legal document, creating a legal distinction between a *latifúndio*, or traditional large landed estate, and a rural enterprise. See *Reforma Agrária e Estatuto da Terra* (Rio de Janeiro: Gráfica Auriverde, 1987), pp. 66 and 80.
3. In this regard see Alan Biorn H. Maybury-Lewis, "The Politics of the Possible: the Growth and Political Development of the Brazilian Rural Workers' Trade Union Movement, 1964–1985," Ph.D. dissertation, Columbia University, 1991. See also

Ricardo Tavares, "CONTAG, da
ditadura à transiçao—memória
social e construçao política do
'campesinato,'" Masters
dissertation, IUPERJ, 1992.
4. See Elisa Reis, "State Penetration
and Citizenship in the Brazilian
Countryside," IUPERJ, *Série Estudos*,
No. 7 (September, 1992).
5. Francisco Dornelles, federal deputy
for the PFL from Rio de Janeiro,
relative of Tancredo Neves and
Minister of the Treasury for the first
six months of the transition
government, interview in *Jornal do
Brasil*, in 1985.
6. I fully endorse the words of Solon L.
Barraclough in his broad assessment
of agrarian reforms in Latin
America: "Like all quests for greater
social justice, struggles for land
reform have brought
disappointments and tragic
perversions as well as limited

successes."See Solon L. Barraclough,
"The Legacy of Latin American
Land Reform," *NACLA Report on the
Americas*, Vol. XXVIII, No. 3
(Nov/Dec 1994), p. 21.
7. "Lula Prega Cidadania com
Reforma Agrária," *Jornal dos
Trabalhadores Rurais Sem Terra*, Year
XIII, No. 134, p.5.
8. Workers Party, 13 *Propostas do
Governo Lula para o Campo*, São
Paulo, 1994, p. 3.
9. Wilson Cano, "Ensaios e Debates,"
Reforma Agrária, Journal of the
Brazilian Agrarian Reform
Association, May–August, 1994.
10. Fernando Henrique Cardoso, *Maos à
Obra, Brasil–Proposta de Governo*,
Brasilia, 1994, p. 103.
11. Francisco Graziano Neto,
"Recolocando a Questao Agrária,"
in *A Questao Agrária Hoje* (Porto
Alegre: Editora da Universidade
Federal do Rio Grande do Sul,
1994), p. 245.

12. Guilherme Leite da Silva Dias,
"Ensaios e Debates," *Reforma
Agrária*, Journal of the Brazilian
Agrarian Reform Association,
May–August, 1994.
13. Francisco Graziano Neto,
"Recolocando a Questao Agrária,"
p. 251.
14. Geraldo Muller, "São Paulo—
o núcleo do padrao agrário
moderno," in *A Questao Agrária
Hoje*, pp. 235–236.
15. See Jacob Gorender, "Gênese e
Desenvolvimento do Capitalismo
no Campo Brasileiro," in *A Questao
Agrária Hoje*, pp. 56–57.
16. See Jonathan Fox, "Latin America's
Emerging Local Politics," *Journal of
Democracy*, Vol. 5, No. 2 (April, 1994).

**Article Review
Form at end of
book.**

R E A D I N G 4 9

Peasant Challenge in Post-Communist China

Weixing Chen

*Peasants constitute about 73% of
China's population. To a large extent,
the success of China's modernization
program and transition depends on
where peasants are heading. Peasants
have posed new challenges for the
Chinese Communist Party (CCP) in*
*the 1990s after 17-year economic re-
form. This article argues that these
challenges derive from the empowerment of the peasants since the mid-
1980s. How well the CCP could deal
with these challenges directly concerns China's political stability and
reform. Through the examination of
the evolution of the peasant–CCP relations and of the implications of the*
*challenges for China in the 1990s
and beyond, this article raises an
open question for China scholars to
address.*

Peasant challenge[1] has always been one of the most crucial
issues to address in China, as
China was and still is an agrarian
society. China's peasant population in 1992 constituted about 73%

Weixing Chen, "Peasant Challenge in Post-Communist China," JOURNAL OF CONTEMPORARY CHINA (1997) 6 (14), 101-115. Reprinted by
permission of Carfax Publishing Limited, PO Box 25, Abingdon, Oxfordshire OX 14 3UE, United Kingdom.

of China's total population.[2] Historically, Chinese revolution succeeded largely because the Chinese Communist Party (CCP) was able to build a revolutionary movement on peasant discontent through careful, pains-taking organization. The Maoist model of development from 1958 to 1976 failed because it built peasant discontent by binding peasants physically on land and politically under the people's commune system. Responding to the need for economic development and peasants desire and demand for a better life, the CCP launched a modernization program in the late 1970s. Unlike the military and political campaign before 1949 and the political and economic program under the Maoist model of development, the modernization program is primarily an economic drive and its success requires the empowerment of the peasants through demobilization rather than mobilization.

The empowerment of the peasants has thus posed new challenges for the CCP in the 1990s. The seriousness of the peasant challenge, as Jiang Zemin (chairman of the CCP and president of the People's Republic of China) pointed out at a national work conference (26–31 October 1994) convened by the CCP Central Committee and participated by all provincial governors and heads of party and government departments concerned, directly concerns China's stability, the CCP's position as a party in power, and the success of China's modernization program.[3] As such, a study of the peasant challenge has significant theoretical and practical implications for China's transition.

This article examines the evolution of peasant–CCP relations, discusses the empowerment

of the peasants and outlines the consequences of the empowerment of the peasants and their implications for China in the 1990s and beyond.

Peasant–CCP Relations in Historical Perspective

The peasant–CCP relations have undergone three distinctive phases of development since the 1920s. The peasant–CCP relations, before the CCP became a party in power in 1949, has been described by the CCP as water–fish relations (the CCP is the fish and the masses, primarily peasants are the water). The fish–water relationship was largely determined by the hostile environment in which the CCP was placed. To survive and succeed, the CCP, as a weak side in its competition with the Nationalist Party (Kuomintang), must seek masses' especially peasants' support as the peasants was the CCP's power base. Since the CCP's policy and success were contingent on peasants' response and acceptance, the CCP had to take peasants interests and response seriously. The politically and militarily competitive environment of the revolutionary period, as Womack points out, constrained the CCP to be 'mass-regarding' in policy and behavior despite their authoritarian internal structures.[4]

The fish–water relationship, based on perceived common interest, was one of mutual dependence. Such a relationship was organizational and personal. It was personal, because the CCP members and cadres sacrificed their lives to fight for the peasants, while the peasants supported and protected the CCP members and cadres in their fight. The role played by the peasants

under such circumstances was direct and clear-cut. If the CCP members and cadres separated themselves from the peasants they found it difficult to accomplish anything, and their very safety and livelihood were jeopardized. It was organizational, because Chinese revolution was a rural revolution and the CCP's political strategy was to mobilize the peasants. To liberate and mobilize the peasants was both the means and the immediate end of the revolution.

The CCP's victory in 1949, however, changed the context of the peasant–CCP relationship. The CCP became a party in power in 1949, and with the establishment of a monopoly of state power by the CCP, the CCP also became the state. Under the new circumstances, peasants lost the clout with the party-state and peasants could, by no means, compel state leaders to change policy. If what the CCP fought for was also what the peasants wanted before, what the CCP wanted to accomplish after 1949 was not necessarily what the peasants wanted even though, programmatically, the interests of the masses still provided policy goals of the party-state. The relationship between the peasants and the party-state became organizational and impersonal.

It was no longer personal, because, as a *Renmin Ribao* editorial pointed out, 'our party became the ruling party and the cadres became leading personnel in the government at all levels. In this new context, it became possible for them to entertain the illusion that they had become government officials while the masses were the common people under their jurisdiction'.[5] It was still organizational, because it was still necessary, at least to the CCP leaders, to involve the peasants in the CCP's effort to build a utopia in rural China. Different from the previous phase, however, mobilization of the peasants became the means for ideological ends this time.

To Maoists, the historic mission of the CCP in post-1949 China was to transform the Chinese society into a prosperous socialist one, materially and spiritually, in which productivity was advanced and people had high political consciousness. Ideological purity and economic development were thus the two facets of the same coin of development. The difficult doctrinal problem that the CCP had to face, however, was to create a socialist revolution and build a socialist society in an agrarian country close to its feudal past. How could the CCP create a socialist civilization without ties to private property in the search for utopia and achieve economic development at the same time in China? To Maoists, continuous socio-economic and political changes would enable them to fulfill these purposes.

The development strategy developed for this purpose was embodied in the 'three red banners' of (1) the 'General Line for Socialist Construction' (namely, go all out, aim high, and achieve greater, faster, better, and more economical results in building socialism), (2) the Great Leap Forward and (3) the People's Commune. Mao believed that communization with the integration of xiang (township today) with the commune was the embryonic form of future society.[6] The People's Communes were to combine industry and agriculture, civilian and military affairs, and political leadership and economic management. It was hoped that a larger communist commune con-

sisting of many people's communes surrounding cities would emerge through the establishment of the people's commune system in rural China.

It was also believed that communization through control over economic activity and the ownership of the means of production to higher levels in the structural hierarchy would enable a structural change in the form of collectivity and integrate vertically the rural organization, merge production teams and transfer control over supply and marketing cooperatives from individual peasants to the commune. Collectivization would not only bridge a backward agrarian China to a modern China, but also set the stage for the transition from socialism to communism by destroying the peasants' tie to private property and making them rural proletarians.

The Great Leap was regarded as a great revolutionary movement that involved millions and millions of people. Implicitly, the people's commune and the Great Leap became the Maoist instrument for carrying out the socially revolutionary measures of the transitional period in China.

Participation in the people's commune was basically mandatory. The collective directly managed the land and labor of the producers living on that land within the parameters of tight state control. Individual peasants must participate in collective production and activities. If they didn't, they would be penalized economically and politically. The collective produced what the state specified, purchased quantities of agricultural producer goods at state prices, and sold designed quantities of its produce to the state at low official prices.

According to the household registration and control system (implemented in 1955), collective members were bound to the village of their birth not only in the sense that they were barred from migrating elsewhere but also in that they were legally obligated to labor for, and on terms set by, the collective. State and collective closely restricted the movement of rural residents not only between town and countryside but also among different rural areas. As Mark Selden correctly stated, 'the integration of peasants and land was so tight that one is almost tempted to say that the land owned the people'.[7]

The framework of the people's commune and the household registration and control thus bound the peasant legally and substantively to the land. As a result, peasants' status under the people's commune changed from that of 'water' to that of 'slave'. Under such circumstances, peasants' power was, at most, residual. Peasants had to and did occasionally employ 'the weapons of the weak', such as cheating, lying, and stealing to squeeze unintended results out of state policy.[8] Daniel Kelliher in his study discussed various ways in which peasants tried to change political outcomes. In each case, what power the peasants could bring to bear was unsanctioned; it intruded on state policy deliberations surreptitiously, covertly, illegally.[9]

The ideal world that Maoists had been trying to build fell short of their dreams. Instead, Maoist effort produced three undesirable outcomes: the permanent sacrifice of the peasants to the state and the consequent economic stagnation in rural China; deep grievances against the political chaos and economic losses that alienated peasants and large segments of the society from the CCP; and the questioning of the CCP's legitimacy. A regime whose legitimacy was based on future promises was legitimate only if its policy was successful and its promises were fulfilled. The situation in which the CCP was by 1978 was so difficult that a reevaluation of policies, values, and goals was inevitable. The serious situation, blessed by the death of Mao himself in 1976, created an unprecedented opportunity for change. The reform that was started in the late 1970s implied a new era of peasant–CCP relationship. The major feature of the new relationship was the empowerment of the peasants in the CCP-sponsored modernization drive.

The Empowerment of the Peasants in Post-Mao China

In the previous two phases, peasant power was mobilized through organizational means to serve the CCP's political and military purposes. Unlike the previous two phases, the CCP must demobilize the peasants through organizational means in its modernization drive. The empowerment of the peasants can be seen as a result of three factors: the CCP's effort to demobilize the peasants, the unintentional aggregation of peasants' interest and the necessity for economic development.

Four major changes had occurred by the 1990s: the CCP was being changed from a party of politics to a party of economics with the change of its developmental goal and the rejection of class struggle and political and ideological campaigns; a planned economy has been replaced by a semi-planned, semi-market economy; the state–society relationship has changed; and all societal institutions are now exposed to market competition. As a result of these changes, peasants have gained greater freedom and autonomy, which is reflected in five respects.

First of all, with the rejection of the ideological and political campaign, the state has lost a familiar vehicle for direct political control over peasants.

From the 1960s to the 1980s, ideological and political campaigns were a regular occurrence in China.[10] Ideological and political campaigns had enabled the state to penetrate the village. Before 1978, economic goals were never considered on a par with ideological goals, and peasants' involvement and participation in ideological and political campaigns was a matter of mandate, as politics directly affected peasants' material interests. Ideological goals are unlikely to come to the fore again in the 1990s unless the CCP wants to reverse the economic reform, which would be enormously difficult after 15-year reform even if the CCP was capable of doing it. This is because the downward transfer of authority since the reform has made ideological and political campaign an ineffective instrument of penetration and control, as the implementation of the household responsibility system characterized by the assignment of land to individual peasants, division of village collective properties, and lease of the village enterprise by individual peasants and the dismantlement of the people's commune in 1984 have greatly weakened the organizational and institutional linkage between the state and the peasants. As a result, the CCP has lost its material and

organizational basis for political leadership in the countryside.

Secondly, the planned economy has been replaced by a semi-planned, semi-market economy. The state's power and control today are largely imposed indirectly on peasants through its guidance planning, finance, price and tax policy, and its control over resource allocation.

The former village brigade[11] was under the influence and control of a centralized command planning. The village's income and benefits were directly tied to their economic performance but the village had little freedom for its own production and economic activity. Teams and brigades could not sell, transfer, or rent their land, except as directed by the state. Nor could they autonomously decide what to grow, or even not to cultivate unproductive land. Peasants had no right to sell, rent, or leave the land and were even heavily restricted in the use of their private plots. Peasants were forced to depend on the collective economy for the satisfaction of their various needs.[12]

Today, Chinese peasants are still under the influence of the state's guidance planning but they are more autonomous in their production and economic activity. They have the freedom to determine their own economic activity and to develop their own strength of production in response to the market. They also have control over their own labor and products.

The economic model under the people's commune placed extreme emphasis on maximizing grain production throughout China. Peasants today are engaged in diversified economic activities. The share of rural output value contributed by agriculture has declined dramatically since the mid-1980s. For instance, 70%

of China's total rural social output value in 1993 was from rural enterprise, and 60% of nine hundred million Chinese peasants' net income was from the rural enterprise.[13]

Thirdly, peasants used to be bound on the land which they neither owned nor had control over by a strict registration system under the people's commune. They were unable to move freely, because the strict residential registration system coupled with a strict rationing system in an environment of scarcity made it impossible for peasants to make a living in areas other than their own registered residential area. Since the land on which they were bound was publicly owned and managed, peasants were virtually reduced to the slave of the land in the locality. With the dismantlement of the people's commune, the change of public ownership and management of land to public ownership and private management, the relaxation of ration system and the abolishment of the ration coupon system, peasants are no longer bound on the land. Thanks to these changes, the household registration system, though still intact, was no longer binding on peasants. Peasants are free to leave their land as they wish and go wherever they want to.

Fourthly, peasants have always been the third-rate citizens in China. On one hand, peasants were forced to sacrifice their own interests to support industry and urban residents. They were forced to sell goods and products to the state at discount prices, to plant grain instead of profitable economic crops; and to submit to a set of exchanges that built relative prosperity in the cities while confining peasants to the penurious

countryside. On the other hand, the socialist state had never intended to guarantee benefits and services for its peasants beyond disaster relief, and Chinese peasants never enjoyed the same kind of services and benefits provided by the state as urban residents and state employees, such as health insurance, pensions, subsidies, housing, and other state-provided services.

Chinese peasants are in a much better position today despite the fact that they are still discriminated against in certain areas. For the first time since 1949, their third-rate citizen status has really been improved. They do not have to sacrifice as much interest as before to the state and urban residents They are able to make full use of their advantages and enjoy a larger share of their own economic success.

Finally, with more freedom and better opportunities for individual peasants and with the rise of the rural enterprise and the development of cross-region, cross-province and multinational corporations, peasants today are able to and are better equipped to rebel against local governments and escape from various government constraints.

Peasants today are still vulnerable to the depredations of local officials in the form of ad hoc taxes and fees. But peasants do not have to employ the 'weapons of the weak' to deal with these depredations. They could openly rebel against local authorities. According to Chinese press reports, at least 830 incidents of rural rebellion involving more than 500 people each were recorded in 1993, including 21 cases involving crowds of more than 5,000.[14]

Today, peasants are also in a much better position to maximize

their economic opportunity by evading government regulations, insulating themselves from the government's political penetration and taking advantage of the gray area between legal and illegal, and are more flexible in allocating their own resources for whatever purposes.

Peasants are empowered also because of the unintentional interest aggregation of the peasants' interests.

The CCP's effort to demobilize peasants was made through mobilization. Despite the tendency of decentralizing policy, China's economic reform is after all a state-sponsored project. Peasants throughout China have been guided or misguided by projects such as the household responsibility system in the late 1970s and early 1980s, the dismantlement of the people's commune in the mid-1980s, and privatization in the late 1980s and in the 1990s. The consequence, as Daniel Kelliher points out, is that 'they may unintentionally react to openings for change with overwhelming unity and in overwhelming numbers.[15] Peasants' interest, aggregated this way unintentionally, exerts great influence on the government. The government has to always pay special attention to peasant's move and respond to peasants' demand. Such peasant power has become more significant since the reform because peasant power aggregated this way can not be easily channeled into organizational action for the CCP's purpose and the CCP can no longer take order and stability for granted as they did before.

Finally, the empowerment of the peasants derives from the necessity for the success of China's economic reform.

Rural development is essentially important in China, because peasants constitute about 73% of China's population and the success of China's modernization program depends largely on rural development. Unlike other developing and post-communist countries, China could not possibly absorb its large rural population into its urban areas. In its drive for modernization, China has to develop rural areas and turn rural areas into urban areas through industrialization. To promote rural development and industrialization in the rural area, the CCP not only must conscientiously protect peasants' interest and encourage and endorse peasants' initiatives in rural development but also must conscientiously empower peasants by all means. The empowerment of the peasants is, after all, the key to the success of rural development.

For centuries, Chinese peasants have been engaged in a fight against nature for subsistence. Agricultural production, though constrained by the rigid central policy before 1978, had managed to grow over the years. By 1980, two decades of effort by peasants had paid off, and most peasants were no longer troubled by subsistence. The mentality of 'moral peasants' is being replaced by that of 'rational peasants'. Blessed by the new policy environment and countered by large surplus of labor, Chinese peasants, freed to leave agriculture and eager to seek better economic opportunities, turned to handicrafts, transportation, service trades, rural enterprise, and commercial activities and were starting to explore all kinds of possibilities and opportunities for profit. The mid-1980s thus witnessed the beginning of the third wave of rural development in China.[16]

The empowerment of the peasants have been a mixed blessing so far. On the positive side, China became the fastest growing economy in the world in the 1980s, and peasants have contributed enormously to China's economic growth. About 30% of China's general social output value increase, 35% of national industrial output value increase and 45% of China's total export have been contributed by rural enterprise alone for the last fifteen years.[17] On the negative side, the empowerment of the peasants has created serious social and political problems. These problems have posed new challenges for the CCP in the 1990s and beyond.

Peasant Challenge in the 1990s

The empowerment of the peasants has resulted in the reinforced old Chinese traditions and customs (which were weakened if not destroyed in Mao's era), the emergence of unprecedented diversification of economic activity, the widening gap between the rich and the poor and between the developed areas and underdeveloped areas, the diminishing arable land, the dramatic decline of agricultural production, and large surplus of labor in the rural area. The direct consequences of all these are: first, the wealthy and developed regions and villages have developed a tendency toward localism; second, large numbers of temporary rural—urban migrants from poor and undeveloped areas have emerged, which have created various social, political and policy problems; third, with the reemergence of old traditions and customs has emerged a new form of politics—guanxi (connection) politics, which has contributed to the rampancy of corruption throughout the society; and fourth, China is heading for an ecological nightmare.

Localism

Localism could be described at several levels. Provinces have always been the traditional and powerful level of government in China. Some people worry that the center could no longer regain the control over the provinces it had just a decade ago without severe economic consequences and that the center is in danger of losing its general regulative capacity. The provinces, however, are facing the same rising demands from their localities and citizens within their provinces. As the question of where is all this heading? is too big to be dealt with comprehensively, this paper concentrates on one facet of these developments, namely, the development of localism for the successful villages—the most basic-level societal institution in rural China.

Parallel to the process of privatization (the implementation of the household responsibility system) described above was the transformation into today's village conglomerates (VC) of the villages that did not undergo the process of privatization. The VC that has evolved from the former village brigade is a natural village-based communal collective with considerable diversification in agricultural production, industrial production and commercial activities. It is a collective because land, property and enterprises are owned by the VC, and various activities are conducted under the unified leadership of the VC party organization and under the management of the village committee.

VC membership is primarily limited to the natural village residents. Unlike state-run enterprises, the VC is responsible for its own success and for providing services and benefits for its own members.

The VC, in many respects, has been the pioneer in the third wave of rural development. The ten most wealthy villages (with income of over 1 billion yuan renminbi) nationwide in 1993 were all VCs. In Shandong Province's Yantai district, the 84 most developed villages (with income of over 100,000,000 yuan) in 1993 were also VCs.[18] Thanks to their success, many VCs have developed a tendency toward localism, and some of them have become 'local empires' that are independent of local, municipal, as well as provincial governments and bully and oppress their neighbor villages. Many VCs are able to establish their own 'empires', both because of their wealth and economic strength, established ties and connections, and their monopoly of the local market and economy and because of their political influence. In some extreme cases, they developed their own security forces. With the emergence of these VCs have also risen the new rural elites. Mary B. Rankin, in her study of the commercial expansion in late imperial China, used a tripartite division of state, public, and private to delineate the growth of 'elite activism' that emerged in the gray area between state and society. In traditional China, a ruling elite of gentry-scholar-bureaucrats was always able to dominate political, economic, and cultural life. The new rural elites that have emerged with the rise of the VC are both party secretaries and entrepreneurs who represent both the state and the society. They are not only 'red and expert' but also wealthy. One case in point is the well-publicized Daqiu VC in suburban Tianjin.

Daqiu VC has become one of the most wealthy villages in China since the reform. In 1992, its agricultural and industrial output value reached 4 billion yuan, and its per capita output value was about one million yuan. Under it were hundreds of factories and enterprises and 28 joint ventures. It hired thousands of employees, many of whom were professionals from urban areas throughout the nation. There were more than six hundred private cars in Daqiu VC, about thirty of which were Mercedes Benz. All villagers are now living in contemporary spacious houses. Yu Zuomin, president and party secretary of the Daqiu VC, won the title of national peasant entrepreneur and became a national model worker in 1989. He was also a deputy to the National People's Congress. With the accumulation of economic wealth and political influence, Yu began to build his own empire, developed his own security force, and became the 'king' of his kingdom. Neither the local government nor the local public security bureau could penetrate his empire. This case was first exposed because of homicide committed by the executive board of Daqiu VC.

Wei Fuhe, a non-resident of Daqiu, was hired by Daqiu VC in 1990. As an outsider, Wei was suspected of graft and embezzlement and was brought to trial by the Daqiu executive board. When Wei denied the charges, he was tortured to death. When public security officers from Tianjin public security bureau came to investigate this case, they were held in custody by the Daqiu security force. These officers were not released until the direct intervention by the Tianjin Municipal government. The Tianjin Municipal government then organized a special committee to investigate this case and sent four hundred armed police to blockade Daqiu village. Yu Zuomin and many others were eventually arrested and sentenced for murder, but only after frustrated pressure from national media, party and government, Yu was sentenced to 20 years' imprisonment.[19]

Daqiu VC is an exception only in that it was exposed and reported. There are many other empires like Daqiu throughout China today. To a certain degree, Daqiu can be seen as a microcosm of a national pattern.

Peasant Mobility

The great success story of the richer areas has been the growth of enterprises. About 120 million peasants are now employed by various rural enterprises. But the overall picture of rural China is not as encouraging. Peasants' incomes in the poor areas have been stagnant for the past decade while inflation has been in double digits. The income correlation shows that the more dependent a province or an area is on farming, the more poor its people. As a result, investment in agriculture has been at a low ebb, having fallen from 6% of all national investment in 1981 to 1% in 1993. At the same time, rising farm productivity has left perhaps more than 110 million peasants without regular work. Under these circumstances and thanks to the freedom and autonomy that peasants have gained, a large 'floating' population of temporary rural—urban migrants has emerged. The number of temporary rural—urban migrants has increased dramatically in recent years. Approximately 130 million rural Chinese have migrated to cities in search of better lives, and in the next decade, millions more are expected to leave the countryside.[20]

In China, temporary migration is not defined in terms of its duration but in terms of the official household registration at the time of the move. Large numbers of temporary rural—urban migrants have been a mixed blessing for China. On the positive side, these migrants have contributed to China'a economic growth in general by providing needed cheap labor for the urban area, and to rural development in particular by bringing capital, information, technology and know-how from the developed coastal urban areas such as Guangzhou and Fujian to rural areas. But on the negative side, these migrants have created serious social, political and policy problems. The problems produced by this large 'floating' population include but are not limited to crimes, pressure on infrastructure, tensions between migrants and urban residents, birth control, pollution, education, and potential political instability. As temporary rural—urban migrants are a 'floating' population that is under nobody's jurisdiction, they have become a tough problem for the CCP to tackle.

The dramatic increase in crime rate for the last ten years can be attributed partly to this 'floating' population. Crimes such as drug-dealings, prostitution, robbery, trade in human beings and stealing, are largely associated with these temporary rural—urban migrants.[21] In an environment of 'money worship', many of the temporary migrants would do whatever necessary to make money. Illegal activities turned out to be one of the quickest ways to make big money for many of them. The majority of the prostitutes in Guangzhou, Shenzhen, and other major cities today belong to this population. Most drug-related crimes, robbery and trading in human beings are also associated with this large 'floating' population.

Given the limited resources and lack of space in the already crowded cities, this 'floating' population has also created enormous pressure on communication, transportation and service facilities in the urban areas. Numerous villages such as Sichuan village, Anhui village, etc. (migrant 'slums' for peasants from the same province) have emerged in the inner corners of big cities in recent years throughout China. These 'city villages' have caused serious environmental problems such as pollution and epidemics. All these have created tensions between urban residents and these temporary migrants, which may result in riots any time.

This large 'floating' population has also brought about many policy problems such as education and birth control. Thousands upon thousands of migrants' children would not have opportunities to go to school both due to the limited school facilities and high tuition for these non-urban residents and due to their illegal status and discriminating admission policies. Given the fact that this population is under nobody's jurisdiction, it seems impossible to control the births of this population.

Politically, such a large 'floating' population is itself a source of instability. The real nightmare to the central government is that if this large 'floating' population, no matter for whatever purpose or reason, is allied with radicalized urban groups or students, order would be out of control.

Guanxi Politics and Corruption

There has been a popular saying in China: nothing could be accomplished without guanxi. Guanxi politics today is the key to understanding the human realities of life, society and politics. Guanxi politics is a complicated social, cultural and political phenomenon, and the patterns of guanxi are complex and variegated. In general, it refers to interpersonal connections and relations. Often it involves behind-scene deals, transactions and politics. Connection-building, deal-making, haggling and shiedling of all with and against all at every level of society have become a way of life in China today. At a higher level, peasants and basic-level societal entities are networked through interpersonal connections with the state and with each other. At a lower level, guanxi politics concerns interpersonal relations and connections within a community and in the society. The sources of guanxi include but are not limited to kinship, social and cultural ties, exchange relationships, connections with the party and government apparatus and connections based on the transaction of goods, service and money.

Guanxi politics can be attributed to several factors. Traditionally, Chinese society has always been a group-oriented society which the economic reform of the last fifteen years has not been able to change. Living so closely involved with family members, neighbors and other people has accustomed the Chinese people to group-oriented collective life that gives the high priority to interpersonal connections and community life. Empowered and enriched, peasants thus have become the most bold practitioners of guanxi politics.

Politically, if the relationship between peasants and the state in the context of an official ideology and a command economy is impersonal, guanxi politics, which is based on interpersonal relations and connections, is naturally becoming more important after the general failure of communist ideology, the rejection of political campaigns, and the transformation of the command economy. The institutional and organizational linkage between the state and the peasant has always been weaker, even under the people's commune in Mao's era. Vivienne Shue discussed this weak linkage by describing the village communal solidarity and the impotence of the center at the village level in Mao's era.[22] The weak organizational and institutional linkages between the state and the peasants have collapsed in the countryside since 1984. According to a *Renmin Ribao* report, the more than 800,000 basic-level organizations in the countryside throughout China must be rebuilt soon,[23] because they are not functioning.

Socially and economically, under the current framework of 'socialism with competitive capitalism', guanxi politics has proven to be indispensable to the function and operation of the economy and society due to its role in adjusting the circulation of resources in the society and the demand—supply relationship on the market. Guanxi politics enables everybody to get what they deserve and what they could afford. After 15-year practice of guanxi politics, it has been institutionalized and life would stop without guanxi.

Starting in the late 1970s, peasants started exercising, without much restraint, the century-old tradition of 'paying tribute' to high-ranking officials in the central, provincial and local governments. In return, peasants got what they paid for, such as loans, contract, scarce resources, etc. Given the high inflation rate and relatively low income for majority of government officials and employees and the appeal of 'money worship' in a market environment, extra income is not only attractive but also of necessity for government officials and employees to make a decent living. Since guanxi politics often involves behind-scene dealings and transactions on an individual basis that involve the use of power and state and collective resources for personal gains, guanxi politics and corruption are two sides of one coin. With its 'institutionalization', guanxi politics has contributed to the rampancy of corruption in the society.

This author visited several very successful VCs in Shandong Province in 1992. In describing their successful stories, all the VC leaders claimed that one of the most important reasons why they succeeded was that they could freely use their resources to build guanxi networks. Large sums of money were spent every year for this purpose in each and every one of these successful VCs. Guanxi networks have enabled them to get low-interest loans, important information, contracts, scarce resources, and special favorable policies. The department of 'public relations' or guanxi has proven to be indispensable to their competitive edge and success.

Andrew Walder and Jean Oi studied 'the patron—client' relationship in the context of a Communist ideology and planned economy. The essential difference between the patron—client relationship described by Walder and Oi and guanxi politics is that the former provides a structural and institutional explanation while the latter focuses on interpersonal relations and connections in the absence of an institutional structure. The old structures that created clientelist politics have broken down in the countryside.

Guanxi politics should also be distinguished from clientelist politics in a corporate state. Clientelist politics emphasizes organized interest and representation in the policy-making process, whereas guanxi politics, as emphasized time and again in this article, focuses on interpersonal connections and relations.

An Ecological Nightmare

The transformation of rural China from centralized agriculture to decentralized agriculture has also significant ecological implications.

China's cultivated land per head is about 800 square meters, well below the world average. China has to manage to feed about 24% of the world's population from about 7% of the world's arable land. China has continuously been losing agricultural land.

China has already lost about a third of its cropland over the past 40 years to soil erosion, desertification, energy projects, and, at an accelerating rate since the economic reform, to deforestation and industrial and housing development. The central government had primarily concentrated on industrial development despite its lip service to the importance of agriculture since the mid-1990s.

The open space for industrial and housing developing is in the rural area. Regulations that prohibit the use of arable land for purposes other than agriculture have not been well and effectively enforced due to guanxi politics and corruption. Peasants with money also preferred to build new houses, or to look for a higher return by investing in the development of rural industry. Peasants' effort and activity have never been well coordinated since the mid-1980s. At the same time, population control in rural China has been made more difficult since the mid-1980s. Besides, growth of a predominantly young population with an increasing life expectancy cannot be throttled down for decades to come. China is projected to add at least 490 million people in the four decades from 1990 to 2030, swelling the population to close to 1.7 billion. A soaring population would become ever growing strains on the ability of the Chinese to feed themselves unless population could be controlled and the continuing loss of agricultural land could be curbed.

China today is already one of the very few countries in the world that has been using agricultural land so intensively. The pursuit of ever larger harvests has made China the world's biggest producer of fertilizer, but the use of fertilizer is subject to diminishing returns. Unsupervised use of chemicals and industrial effluents is polluting the water, while use of unwashed soft coal for energy is polluting the air. What are the implications for China and the world if China will have to raise substantially its reliance on imported food? According to *The Economist*, a China with the same fish consumption per head as Japan, for instance, would alone consume more fish than are at present caught in the world's oceans, and a China of the early twenty-first century with the eating habits of South Korea today would need 600 million tonnes of grain—implying, if China's harvest remained at its current level, a demand for imported grain roughly equivalent to all the world's grain shipments of 1994.[24]

China is heading for an ecological nightmare unless collective effort could be made by the governments and the peasants to overcome it.

If the CCP could not effectively deal with localism, a large 'floating' population and corruption, the prospect of a radical, possibly violent, political rupture would become more likely. If the ecological nightmare could not be overcome, China is ruined.

Conclusion

Faced with the peasant challenge, the CCP is determined to strengthen its political leadership in the countryside on one hand and devote more resources to agriculture and develop more policy incentives for agricultural production on the other hand. According to a *Renmin Ribao* editorial, the CCP will make serious effort in the coming three years to rebuild basic-level party and social organizations in the countryside, improve the quality of peasant party members and make them play a leading role in the economic reform. At the same time, the CCP will increase general investment in agriculture and establish more incentives for agricultural production, such as low interest or no interest loan, higher price for grain, etc.[25] What this reveals is that the CCP has realized the seriousness of the peasant challenge, but the question is: could the CCP effectively deal with the peasant challenge in the 1990s after a 17-year economic reform? Perhaps it is appropriate to rethink the peasant challenge that Mao Zedong posed at the very beginning of the Chinese rural revolution: 'There are three alternatives. To march at their head and lead them? To trail behind them, gesticulating and criticizing? Or to stand in their way and oppose them?'[26] From the 1920s to 1949, the CCP was able to lead peasants where peasants wanted to go, and the peasant—CCP relationship was one of fish and water. The successful handling of the peasant challenge enabled the CCP to gain control of China. From the late 1950s to 1979, the CCP was forcing peasants to go where they did not want to go, and the peasant—CCP relationship was one of master and slave. But the CCP's effort to build a utopia in rural China failed. The fish-water relationship is one of mutual dependence, whereas the master–slave relationship is one of control and oppression. From 1979 to the present, the CCP has tried to lead peasants where they wanted to go by sponsoring a modernization program and relaxing its control over the peasants, but the CCP has created a dilemma for itself. To promote economic growth, the CCP has to relax its control over the peasants and reject one of the CCP's most familiar political vehicles—mobilization. But the CCP might well be overwhelmed by the consequences of the empowerment of the peasants.

What alternatives does the CCP have this time? This is an important, complex, open question that demands more research from China scholars.

Notes

1. 'Peasant' is used here to refer to the 75% of China's population that are not registered urban residents.
2. *Statistical Yearbook of China*, (1993), p. 81.
3. Jiang Zemin's Speech, *People's Daily* overseas edition, (31 October 1994), p. 1.
4. Brantly Womack, 'The Party and the People: revolutionary and postrevolutionary politics in China and Vietnam', *World Politics* XXXIX(4), (July 1987), p. 480.
5. 'Do not forget the fish-water relationship', special commentator, *Renmin Ribao*, (19 August 1978).
6. Li Rui, *A True Account of Lushan Meeting* (Wuhan: Chunqiu Press and Hunan Education Press, 1988), p. 363.
7. Mark Selden, *The Political Economy of Chinese Development* (Armonk, New York: M.E. Sharpe, 1993), p. 190.
8. James C. Scott's *Weapons of the Weak* is a pioneering study of the ways peasants assert themselves through illegitimate means. Scott's study is based on Southeast Asia rural society. See James C. Scott, *Weapons of the Weak: Everyday Forms of Peasant Resistance* (New Haven: Yale University Press, 1985).
9. Daniel Kelliher, *Peasant Power in China* (New Haven: Yale University Press, 1992), pp. 239–242.
10. See Weixing Chen, 'The CCP's socialist ideology education campaign of 1990–92: a funeral for ideology?', *Issues & Studies* 29(5), (May 1993), pp. 70–88.
11. The natural village became the village brigade in the people's commune, which was the intermediate level between the commune (township today) and the production team within the village.
12. Detailed discussions of peasant situation under the people's commune were provided in Sulamith H. Potter/Jack M. Potter, *China's Peasant* (Cambridge: Cambridge University Press, 1990); and Mark Selden, *The Political Economy of Chinese Development* (Armonk, New York: M.E. Sharpe, 1993).
13. *Renmin Ribao (People's Daily)* overseas edition, (8 January 1994), p. 1.
14. Given the nature of controlled media and press in China, there should be more incidents of this kind that were not reported. The figures presented here are from 'A survey of China', *The Economist*, (18 March 1995), p. 19.
15. Daniel Kelliher, *Peasant Power in China* (New Haven: Yale University Press, 1992), p. 31.
16. Rural China has undergone three waves of development, namely, communization from 1957 to 1978, the implementation of the household responsibility system from 1978 to 1984, and the rise of rural enterprise and commercial activities from 1985 to the present.
17. *Renmin Ribao (People's Daily)* overseas edition, (27 December 1994), p. 1.
18. *Renmin Ribao* overseas edition, (14 May 1994), p. 9.
19. For a detailed description of this case, see *Renmin Ribao* overseas edition, (28 August 1993), pp. 1, 3.
20. Joseph R. Gregory, 'China, Taiwan, and Hong Kong: US challenges', *Great Decisions 1995* (Foreign Policy Association, 1995), p. 61.
21. Official data for these 'negative things' are not available.
22. See Vivienne Shue, *The Reach of the State: Sketches of the Chinese Body Politic* (Stanford: Stanford University Press, 1988).
23. *Renmin Ribao* overseas edition, (31 October 1994), p. 1.
24. 'A Survey of China', *The Economist*, (18 March 1995), p. 2l.
25. Editorial, *Renmin Ribao* overseas edition, (31 October 1994), p. 1.
26. Mao Zedong, 'Report on an investigation of the peasant movement in Hunan', *Selected Works of Mao Zedong* l (Beijing: Foreign Languages Press, 1967), p. 24.

 Article Review Form at end of book.

WiseGuide Wrap-Up

Anyone who wants to understand countries in a comparative way cannot ignore rural workers, who comprise the bulk of the world's population.

Most rural workers want their own (or more) land, land that usually already belongs to someone else. Additionally, many peasants, as those in China, want some control over the decisions that affect their lives. Some government officials fear that peasants' land practices create environmental damage. Property rights, historic injustices, and environmental degradation are some of the contentious issues that arise when discussing land reform.

Few resources have been invested in the rural areas of countries, and many government policy makers believe that only urban industrial projects are a real mark of development. Under authoritarian governments, political leaders could ignore peasants' concerns. Today, however, with free elections held in many countries, political leaders must address rural workers' concerns or risk losing an election and the benefits of holding office.

R.E.A.L. Sites

This list provides a print preview of typical **courswise** R.E.A.L. sites. There are over 100 such sites at the **courselinks**™ site. The danger in printing URLs is that web sites can change overnight. As we went to press, these sites were functional using the URLs provided. If you come across one that isn't, please let us know via email to: webmaster@coursewise.com. Use your Passport to access the most current list of R.E.A.L. sites at the **courselinks**™ site.

Site name: Time to Help Us, Say Poor Peasants—Gemini News Service

URL: http://www.oneworld.org/gemini/mar96_china.html

Why is it R.E.A.L.? Gemini is a London-based news service. In this article by author Fans Tuinstra, identify five of the grievances that Chinese peasants raise about their lives in contemporary China.

Key topics: China, peasants, prices

Site name: Plight of Mexican Farmers/Peasants (*Chiapas News,* September 13, 1994)

URL: http://bioc09.uthscsa.edu/natnet/archive/nl/9409/0101.html

Why is it R.E.A.L.? The information at this site presents the point of view of the Mayan Indians and why they believed that their only recourse against the Mexican government's policies was to take up arms. Identify and discuss the important issues from the Mayan Indian point of view.

Key topics: land, credit

Site name: Tje USAID FY 1998 Congressional Presentation Tanzania

URL: http://www.info.usaid.gov/pubs/cp98/afr/countries/tz.htm

Why is it R.E.A.L.? The information at this site provides a pro-market, anti-cooperative, and anti-President Nyerere view of current conditions in Tanzania. It also provides some data. For example, you will notice that in 1979–80, when President Nyerere was in office, primary school enrollment was nearly 100 percent. Today, under free-market conditions in which families have to pay for schooling and need their children to help earn a living, enrollment is under 70 percent.

Key topics: primary education

section 6

Key Points

- To understand politics comparatively, you must understand the differential responses of state leaders to common outside pressures.

- States rarely adopt policies without consulting outside powers, be those powers military neighbors, international organizations, multinational corporations, regional organizations, or international conference negotiators.

The International System Constrains State Choice

 **WiseGuide Intro**

Although "Think globally and act locally" was an activist slogan of the 1970s, in the 1990s, it is even easier to see how global affairs are influencing local politics. Globalizing trends in which flows of capital, goods, and services rapidly cross national boundaries and in which international telecommunications networks transmit data and information to people worldwide are constraining state choices and affecting the internal politics of once-sovereign states, and in turn, the lives of citizens living within each state.

For example, in Reading 52, Helen Safa has documented the consequences for women wage earners when the global market constrains national economic choices and forces countries to keep export zone wages low to attract foreign investment. Women who are recruited to work in factories located in export zones have little political leverage with which to bargain for a living wage.

In analyzing the South African case, in Reading 50, Audie Klotz reveals how the consequences of international geopolitics, especially Cold War diplomacy and military engagements, have affected competing political actors in South Africa and the outcomes of their conflicts. Likewise, political leaders in countries in the Americas have long felt constrained in their actions because of their geographical proximity to the United States, the superpower to their north. East European state politicians also have felt constrained as the former Soviet Union restricted their freedom of action in various issue areas.

Economic and military activities at the global level affect and constrain domestic politics, but even nonmilitary and nonpolitical international conferences of "experts" can have an impact on domestic politics. In Reading 53, U.S. Secretary of State Madeline K. Albright (former U.S. Ambassador to the United Nations) makes the case that by identifying internationally agreed-upon principles, as was accomplished at the Beijing conference on women, the conference affects and benefits women in all countries because governments are encouraged or pressured to address conference concerns. Finally, as European Union President Jacques Santer argues in Reading 55, regional organizations have to pressure individual states to act together for the common good of the group of states.

What is clear from the information presented in this section is that states are being forced to react to the forces of globalization and to the actions of nonstate actors, such as multinational corporate investors and/or regional organizations. How state leaders manage their policy responses and the ways in which outside organizations and powers constrain those responses are critical to an understanding of comparative politics.

Questions

1. According to Klotz, how did international pressure help end human rights abuses against black Africans in South Africa?

2. To improve their lives, why might women in Mexico have to strategize about responding to foreign political actors?

3. What evidence do Dunlop, Kyte, and MacDonald offer to suggest that women from Southern rather than Northern countries at the Beijing conference were critical to establishing the internationally adopted standards for governments' treatment of women?

4. European Union President Jacques Santer argues that European states should be constrained in creating individual policies and instead should band together and integrate their policies. Why?

Transforming a Pariah State

International dimensions of the South African transition

Audie Klotz

South Africa's transition to majority rule in April 1994 presents a special case in recent trends of liberalization and democratization. Many of the factors noted by comparative politics analysts, including pressures of globalizing market forces and cross-national demonstration effects, are certainly salient.[1] But in addition, a wide range of international military, economic, cultural and diplomatic sanctions influenced South African reform. Unlike most other states, South Africa became a pariah because its racial repression appeared more extraordinary than other governments' similar militarization, bureaucratic control and use of torture.

In the aftermath of universal suffrage elections, however, South Africa's uniqueness fades. By understanding the extent to which these sanctions affected South Africa, one can explore the extent to which outside actors and international pressures can, and cannot, influence the prospects for democracy both in South Africa and elsewhere. Economic and cultural dimensions of international

pressure against South Africa had important, and generally underestimated, consequences for both the ruling National Party and its critics.

As a prelude to evaluating these non-coercive influences, I briefly discuss South Africa's internal and external militarization during the Cold War. In analyzing some of the effects of international sanctions on the South African transition to majority rule, I then focus on two targets, the apartheid state and the anti-apartheid opposition. The lessons from this sanctions case have general implications both for consolidating democracy in South Africa and for those interested in the relationship between international and internal politics of other countries.

Cold War Militarization

If sanctions can positively influence the democratization process, as initially appears to be the case in South Africa, it would be helpful to improve understanding of the relationship between international and internal politics. However, the study of international relations has traditionally concentrated on states as au-

tonomous actors. International context, consequently, would simply limit a state's foreign policy choices because its domestic structures and internal coalitions presumably remain insulated from international influences. Sanctions, as a form of quasi-military coercion in this conventional view, would only alter foreign policy, not internal racial discrimination. Sovereignty reigns in realist theory, even if it remains a myth in practice.

For South Africa, this traditional emphasis on coercive power led to a focus, both in analysis and in practice, on military resources in the southern African region and its importance to broader super-power political agendas. South Africa's all-encompassing definition of enemies as communists and terrorists, evident in the "total onslaught" and its "total strategy" in the 1980s, mirrored the super-power military and ideological conflict. And as we have seen in practice, international criticism of apartheid often provoked South African military retaliation, especially in the region.[2] At first glance, therefore, threats of sanctions appear to have been ineffec-

Audie Klotz, "Transforming a Pariah State: International Dimensions of the South African Transition," AFRICA TODAY, Vol. 42, nos. 1-2, 1995. Reprinted by permission of AFRICA TODAY.

tive or counter-productive at the inter-state level.

The Cold War, however, undermined democracy by strengthening the role of the military within the state and society. An increasingly strong external role for the South African military was one result. Previously, the armed forces remained relatively small as post-World War II demobilization was rapid, and the National Party, elected in 1948, remained skeptical of standing armies.[3] Even as decolonization progressed throughout most of Africa in the 1960s and early 1970s, and international criticism of apartheid escalated, South Africa's defense forces remained more than sufficient for any conventional warfare in the region. Following Portuguese decolonization of Mozambique and Angola in 1975, and escalating guerrilla war in Rhodesia, South Africa's military role in the region expanded substantially by the late 1970s. Regional conflict, including covert actions against neighboring Frontline States, culminated in undeclared war against Angola in the 1980s.

The effects of global conflict also reached deeper than this expanding external role for the South African defense forces. Military and political leaders could dismiss internal discontent as the result of external agitation, rather than recognizing it as a legitimate political demand for representation by the black majority. While global criticism of its institutionalized racism escalated and demands for sanctions reached increasingly sympathetic ears even in Western Europe and the United States, the National Party continued trumpeting its role in the defense of southern Africa from communism. After 1979, under Prime Minister (and former Defense Minister) P. W. Botha, the military attained unsurpassed influence in policy-making through what came to be known as the National Security Management System.[4]

Escalating township unrest in the 1980s also reinforced the National Party's reliance on the internal use of force and, consequently, the military's position within the decision-making circles of government. While the line between defense and police blurred, so too did the line between military and civilian within society and the economy at large. Paramilitary training began within white educational institutions. Conscription needs expanded as well, bringing more whites and blacks into the armed forces. Industries acquired unprecedented strategic importance.[5]

Combined with the paternalism of its leaders' racial views, pervasive militarization reinforced the South African government's reliance on coercion, internally and externally, to retain white political power. Based on this Cold War framework, the lack of support from the white minority for non-racial democracy is no surprise, but reform is. Was the South African transition, therefore, primarily the result of the end of the Cold War?

Certainly global political changes had an impact on National Party leaders' perceptions. Numerous reports indicate their awareness of the decline of the Soviet threat, including the African National Congress's (ANC) loss of its traditional source of military support.[6] F. W. de Klerk's ascension to the presidency also led to the demotion of the military within government decision-making as part of the demise of P.W. Botha's power, perhaps bringing forth new attitudes. But the direction of that change remained unpredictable. The end of the Cold War did not cause reform, although it created a context conducive to political change.

The collapse of the Soviet Union did not necessarily mean that Afrikaners would or should negotiate with the ANC for a new, non-racial constitution. Indeed, if the National Party had feared the ANC in the past, the latter's substantially weakened position should have enabled the white minority regime to strengthen its domestic position by eliminating the ANC threat.[7] South Africa remained a highly militarized state and society, despite changes in Europe, and the National Party viewed itself as firmly in control, not a vulnerable government on the brink of collapse.[8]

In order to understand the dynamics of South African reform, therefore, it is necessary to consider additional non-military dimensions of international and internal politics. This brings us to the question of international sanctions. What effect did sanctions have on South Africa? In the following two sections, I argue that sanctions had substantial consequences for the National Party and for the anti-apartheid movement. Although not the sole cause of the South African transition, sanctions enhanced pressure on the government both directly and indirectly.

Sanctions and the South African State

If sanctions affect more than a state's foreign policy, and can perhaps even reach down to the level of domestic society, we need to understand the mechanisms for such influence. One view is that international sanctions change the external incentives that actors face. Assuming states are rational, sanctions alter the costs and benefits which determine policy choices.[9] A second conceptualization emphasizes that sanctioners seek to enforce certain global norms which can legitimate government policies and domestic actors.[10] A combination of both these incentive and legitimation effects explains crucial elements of the South African transition to majority rule, particularly why F.W. de Klerk and the National Party adopted some reforms but not others.

One effect of international sanctions was to guide the South African government's initial reforms which opened the political system in 1990–91. At the peak of the international momentum for global sanctions in the mid-1980s, numerous international organizations and states had adopted partial economic sanctions against South Africa, supplementing existing diplomatic restrictions, arms embargoes, and other voluntary measures. The Commonwealth, despite British objections, strengthened their measures from 1985 to 1987. Even the U.S., steadfastly opposed to economic sanctions for thirty years, adopted substantial restrictions in 1986 despite the objections of the Reagan administration. The European Community followed suit, even forcing the Thatcher government to abide by collective restrictions.

Various agreements and legislation, including the Commonwealth accords and the U.S. Comprehensive Anti-Apartheid Act, contained a list of conditions for the lifting of sanctions. These included ending the state of emergency and releasing political prisoners. The liberation movements, including the ANC,

Pan African Congress (PAC) and Communist Party, needed to be unbanned. The fundamental legal basis for apartheid, including the Population Registration Act, the Land Acts and the Group Areas Act, had to be eliminated. The South African government also had to enter preliminary negotiations, "talks about talks," with legitimate representatives of the majority population.[11]

De Klerk's initial reforms satisfied these conditions—no more and no less—in short order. Sanctions were lifted almost immediately, despite ANC objections. Many international sanctioners, especially South Africa's long standing allies including Britain and the U.S., sought to reward the National Party for its reforms. De Klerk indicated that he expected this amelioration of isolation, although he denied that he was responding to sanctions pressure.[12] Even if de Klerk wanted to deny foreign influence in order to retain his domestic credibility, the government's behavior corresponded to international demands. Future benefits, specifically the lifting of sanctions, apparently outweighed both the costs of maintaining the status quo and white fears of the future under majority rule.

The threat of the reimposition of sanctions, furthermore, fostered support for the National Party's reforms, in the face of vehement Conservative Party opposition in the early 1990s. These conservatives had been resisting reform since the era of P. W. Botha. In 1982 they split from the National Party and soon established themselves as the main opposition within Parliament. Relying upon their relatively strong electoral support, Conservative Party leaders accused de Klerk of betraying the mandate of

the 1989 elections. Hoping to refute his reforms, they demanded that he hold another election, one they confidently expected to win.

In response to conservative criticism, de Klerk called for a whites-only referendum on his reforms but not another election. It asked specifically, "Do you support continuation of the reform process which the State President began on February 2, 1990 and which is aimed at a new constitution through negotiation?" Conservatives even challenged the wording of this ballot.[13] Sanctions, particularly the implicit threat of renewed economic and cultural isolation should the reform effort be repudiated, figured prominently in the debates leading up to the 17 March 1992 vote.

Many whites feared the renewal of economic sanctions; they predicted increased unemployment and a general decline in prosperity should de Klerk's referendum fail. Businesses went so far as to launch an expensive advertising campaign advocating a yes-vote.[14] Sports enthusiasts, furthermore, dreaded a return to isolation just as South Africa entered its first world cricket match in years and hoped for an Olympic appearance in Barcelona.[15] Conservatives, in contrast, stressed South Africa's ability to survive, indeed thrive upon, international isolation.

By gaining a substantial majority of the white vote, 68.7 per cent overall, de Klerk successfully outmaneuvered his opponents. Only the most conservative districts of the Transvaal sided against the reforms, and even there de Klerk gained 38 per cent of the vote.[16] In the aftermath, the conservatives splintered even more amongst themselves, between those who accepted the inevitability of negotiations and those who threatened violent opposition.[17] Some recognized a need to bargain for the best possible outcome within a negotiated new constitutional system—still a far cry from accepting majority rule. More extreme conservative whites called for a separate state, in effect the dismemberment of a unitary South Africa. The concept of apartheid in its Verwoerdian sense had become obsolete, although conservatives still demanded white self-determination.[18] With the conservatives unable to offer a credible alternative, the National Party's commitment to reform became the uncontested direction for South Africa's future.

Thus international economic and social sanctions offered prospects of benefits if reforms should be implemented and increased costs if they were not. The National Party government and white South Africans generally responded to these incentives. Sanctions induced, rather than coerced, reforms and reinforced the legitimacy of government policy. The specific contours of reform, however, remained to be negotiated with the ANC and other parties.

Sanctions and the Anti-Apartheid Opposition

The effect of sanctions on state policy is only half the story of South Africa's transition to majority rule. Moving even further away from the traditional state-centric view of international relations shifts our attention to direct connections between international and domestic politics. Again, one can analyze the means of international influence through cost-benefit analysis and legitimation effects on domestic actors. Sanctioners supported apartheid opponents' demands for majority rule both materially and morally.

When the South African government signalled its commitment to reforms, the question remained with whom they would negotiate. Clearly the National Party preferred not to deal with the ANC, but rather cooperate with groups which supported its preference for power sharing and minority rights. The primary challenge to the ANC came from Buthelezi's Inkatha Freedom Party. Sanctions reinforced the ANC's legitimacy and primacy over Inkatha by undermining the homelands as a legitimate concept and reinforcing the principle of universal suffrage rather than minority rights. In effect, international pressures, and not solely domestic bargaining, defined legitimate actors, principles and state boundaries.

Buthelezi's standing and Inkatha's claims of cultural rights cannot be separated from the apartheid concept of homelands. Initially, Buthelezi emerged through the ANC as an opponent to apartheid but shifted to a Zulu cultural base after most political opposition groups were banned in the early 1960s. At the same time, the South African government sought to legitimate its policy of separate development by creating ethnically based black states that mimicked newly independent states throughout Africa, especially neighboring Botswana, Swaziland and Lesotho.[19] While using the homelands apparatus as a political (and patronage) base, Buthelezi augmented his power within South Africa at the same time that he attempted to challenge the government's policy of granting independence to the homelands. Internationally, no one acknowledged the legitimacy of the homelands as independent nation-states. Diplomatic sanctions, consequently, strengthened Buthelezi's position against independence, enabling him to work within the very system he claimed to reject.

The homelands legacy lasted into the 1980s and early 1990s, demarcating the boundaries of dispute between rival opposition movements. From his position as leader of the non-independent homeland of KwaZulu, Buthelezi strengthened Inkatha's standing domestically while the ANC remained in exile. As a black leader with a substantial following, Buthelezi well suited the needs of both the South African government and its conservative allies who sought to prevent the imposition of economic sanctions. During the peak of the global sanctions debate in the 1980s, Buthelezi positioned himself as the primary advocate of capital investment.

Presenting Inkatha as a legitimate representative of black opinion that rejected the ANC as a tool of communists, opponents of sanctions bolstered Buthelezi's importance. In effect, Inkatha had become a construction of the South African government, through both indirect and direct financial support. As the Inkathagate" scandal of 1991 revealed, the government had channeled money to Buthelezi's group in order to undermine the popularity of the ANC.[20] According to Foreign Minister Pik Botha, the government redirected funds to Inkatha from a secret account used to fight sanctions.[21] In the long term, government support for Inkatha undermined its standing internationally and domestically, helping the ANC emerge as the primary negotiating force.

By the time constitutional negotiations began, Buthelezi was uncomfortably situated between the ANC demands for universal suffrage and a unitary state on the one side, and the National Party's emphasis on minority protection under federalism on the other.[22] International rejection of the homelands, UN and other international support for the ANC, as well as the precedent of universal suffrage in transition from Rhodesia to Zimbabwe, reinforced ANC demands. Nothing less than one person, one vote would likely satisfy international critics. Certainly white conservatives talking of secession, later echoed in Buthelezi's threats of the same for KwaZulu, had little hope of attaining the requisite international recognition, without which their fledgling states could not hope to survive.

A Zulu state, based on a monarchy and no elections, had no hope of attaining independence, leaving Buthelezi with only the threat of civil war to increase his bargaining power with the government and the ANC. Furthermore, his loss of political resources after homelands were eliminated following the 1994 elections highlights his inability to transform Inkatha from a Zulu based movement into a full-fledged national party as the political process opened in the early 1990s.

Sanctions were certainly not the only factor which undermined Inkatha and bolstered the ANC's position. They were, however, a significant influence on the rise and fall of Buthelezi, illustrating that international pressures can successfully legitimate group identity and behavior. Neither international nor domestic pressures for majority rule were alone responsible for the National Party's turn to multiparty elections. Combined pressure, however, successfully transformed South Africa from a pariah into a non-racial democracy.

South Africa's Future

South Africa's transition to majority rule is a remarkable example of the success of a global human rights movement which generated a complex array of domestic and international pressures for reform. South Africa represents an extreme example where global pressures converged to an unprecedented extent, because racial discrimination through the apartheid system abrogated international norms to such an extraordinary extent. Yet the two processes of inducement and legitimation are not unique to the experiences of a pariah state; they operate in more subtle forms on all states in the international system. Thus one can expect that milder forms of international pressures will continue to influence domestic South African politics as the new government of national unity attempts to consolidate democracy.

From a comparative perspective, we are reminded that South African democracy will be fragile, haunted by the possibility of military intervention (e.g., Nigeria, Argentina, Brazil) or internal strife (e.g., Angola, Somalia, the former Soviet Union). The ways in which international pressures might influence South Africa in the future depend in part on what types of challenges to democratic principles remain. In 1995, the government faces two types of extra-parliamentary opponents: radical elements within the armed forces and disenchanted losers in the transition from both the right and left.

Given the history of military coups throughout Africa and Latin America, as well as the importance of the military in policy-making in South Africa in the 1980s, it is natural to wonder whether the armed forces will seek an indirect or direct role in politics in the future and to ask how international influences might reinforce, or limit, the role of the military.

Confronted with the task of integrating the former guerrilla armies within the South African defence (SADF) and police forces (SAP), the government is likely to sustain and expand its military, as did Zimbabwe. Substantial right wing support within the former SADF and SAP increases the incentives for the government to expand the multiracial forces as one way to dilute white influence. Any expansion of the defense forces, however, remains an expensive proposition. International factors will influence whether the maintenance of a large military is a viable option for South Africa. With peace in the region, no external military threat exists to justify such expenditure, nor are international lenders likely to tolerate it as an alternative state employment program. Conditions may be placed on trade and aid that are linked to demilitarization.

The second plausible threat to South African democracy would be secessionist pressures, either from the white right or a disenchanted Buthelezi. Rather than being a direct threat of civil war, however, these pressures are more likely to produce a conservative land reform policy, one which will not disturb rural white radicals (who are well-armed). South Africa does not have the Zimbabwe option; the most dissatisfied whites cannot simply flee south of the border. Indeed, doubly displaced Rhodesians are among the armed discontents. Demands for decentralized government will continue long into the future, but no secessionist state is likely to receive international recognition, thus belying hasty comparisons to Yugoslavia.

Dissatisfied progressives represent a third source of potential instability if the government does not provide acceptable redistributive policies within the next five to ten years. Currently speculation about Winnie Mandela as the next president may be presented as a joke—or for some their worst fear—but the basic needs of the majority of the South Africa population remain high. The distributive implications of trade and aid policies need to be considered, particularly for understanding whether they produce domestic socio-economic conditions that would provoke a military coup.

As the pariah reintegrates into the international system, renewed ties can play both a positive and negative role in the new South Africa. These diverse speculative examples of ways in which international factors might influence democratic consolidation within South Africa highlight the need to understand better the role of international politics in the global democratization process.

Sanctions for Democracy?

Although sanctions were not the single causal factor in the transition in South Africa, they were an important one, illustrating that international influence means more than direct military control or coercion by one state over another. Sanctions can offer considerable incentives for domestic actors to change their views, behavior, and state policies. By reinforcing international norms, sanctions also serve to legitimate certain do-

mestic actors and institutional structures.

Yet to the extent that people continue to focus on the coercive power of states such as the U.S. to influence domestic political change in countries around the world, they overlook a crucial lesson from the anti-apartheid experience. The National Party did not reform primarily in response to coercive threats. Rather, a combination of economic and social threats demonstrated to elites that racial discrimination abrogated international norms at significant material and symbolic costs. Similarly, leaders in other countries are unlikely to forego military rule in the absence of substantial social and economic costs.

As realists and cynics frequently argue, the major powers have other compelling interests which will prevent them from making a sustained commitment to democratization. A second lesson from the anti-apartheid experience, consequently, becomes even more important. The anti-apartheid movement was particularly noteworthy for its transnational character and its ability to circumvent state boundaries. Transnational influence on state policies, not simply the interests of U.S. leaders, transformed foreign policies toward South Africa. Lobbying groups such as TransAfrica continue to influence U.S. government policy toward countries such as Haiti, and have recently turned their attention to military rule in Nigeria as well. Thus international pressures for democracy operate in part because of the lessons learned and influence gained from the anti-apartheid movement.

Those who care about global democratization would do well to replicate the methods of the anti-

apartheid movement: establish global normative standards and manipulate market forces to these ends. The major powers may not applaud at first, but they will eventually hop on the bandwagon. Since coercing democracy remains an oxymoron, sanctions remain a useful means of inducing and legitimating domestic political change.

Notes

1. For an overview of the relationship between liberalization and democratization, see Leslie Elliott Armijo, Thomas J. Biersteker, and Abraham F. Lowenthal, "The Problems of Simultaneous Transitions," *Journal of Democracy* vol. 5, no. 4 (October 1994), pp. 161–75.
2. James Barber and John Barratt, *South Africa's Foreign Policy: The Search for Status and Security 1945–1988* (Cambridge: Cambridge University Press, 1990).
3. Kenneth W. Grundy, *The Militarization of South African Politics* (Bloomington: Indiana Universtiy Press, 1986), pp. 7–9.
4. Annette Seegers, "South Africa's National Security Management System, 1972–90," *Journal of Modern African Studies*, vol. 29, no. 2 (1 June 1991), pp. 253–73; Grundy, *op. cit.,* pp. 34–57.
5. See Neta Crawford's contribution to this volume, as well as: Jacklyn Cock and Laurie Nathan, eds., *War and Society: The Militarisation of South Africa* (Cape Town: David Philip, 1989); Grundy, *op. cit.,* pp. 58–70; Nancy L. Clark, *Manufacturing Apartheid: State Corporations in South Africa* (New Haven: Yale University Press, 1994).
6. Heribert Adam and Kogila Moodley, *The Opening of the Apartheid Mind* (Berkeley: University of California Press, 1993).
7. Afrikaners continued to see communism, still synonymous with the ANC, as a major threat even after glasnost and perestroika took hold. See Kate Manzo and Pat McGowan, "Afrikaner Fear and the Politics of Despair: Understanding Change in South Africa," *International Studies Quarterly*, vol. 36, no. 1 (March 1992), pp. 1–24.
8. Adam and Moodley, *op. cit.,* pp. 39–58.

9. This rationalist framework underpins the neoliberal institutionalist perspective in international relations theory. For its application to sanctions, see Lisa L. Martin, *Coercive Cooperation: Explaining Multilateral Economic Sanctions* (Princeton: Princeton University Press, 1992).

10. This focus derives from an interpretive, "social construction" perspective in international relations theory. See Audie Klotz, *Norms in International Relations: The Struggle against Apartheid* (Ithaca: Cornell University Press, forthcoming 1995).

11. Commonwealth Secretariat, *The Commonwealth at the Summit: Communiques of Commonwealth Heads of Government Meetings, 1944–1986* (London: Commonwealth Secretariat, 1987); United States, 99th Congress, "The Comprehensive Anti-Apartheid Act of 1986: PL 99-440, 2 October 1986," *Statutes at Large*, vol. 100, pp. 1086–116.

12. Christopher Wren, "South Africa Ends Race Registration," *New York Times* (New York) (18 June 1991), p. A8.

13. Christopher Wren, "Turnout Heavy as South Africans Vote on Change," *New York Times* (New York) (18 March 1992), p. A8.

14. Christopher Wren, "A Mandate for Change," *New York Times* (New York) (20 March 1992), pp. A1, A7.

15. Rob Nixon, *Homelands, Harlem and Hollywood: South African Culture and the World Beyond* (New York: Routledge, 1994), pp. 152–53.

16. Christopher Wren, "Practical, Not a Gambler, De Klerk Tells His Story," *New York Times* (New York) (26 March 1992), p. A6.

17. Johann van Rooyen, *Hard Right: The New White Power in South Africa* (London: I.B. Taurus, 1994), pp. 187–200.

18. *Ibid.*, pp. 156–70.

19. For an overview of the homelands policy, see Jeffrey Butler, Robert I. Rotberg, and John Adams, *The Black Homelands of South Africa: The Political and Economic Development of Bophuthatswana and KwaZula* (Berkeley: University of California, 1977); and Adam Ashforth, *The Politics of Official Discourse in Twentieth-Century South Africa* (Oxford: Clarendon, 1990).

20. Heribert and Moodley, *op. cit.*, pp. 125–33.

21. Christoper Wren, "Pretoria Admits More Secret Payments," *New York Times* (New York) (22 July 1991), p. A3.

22. Steven Friedman, ed., *Long Journey: South Africa's Quest for a Negotiated Settlement* (Johannesburg: Ravan, 1993).

Article Review Form at end of book.

R E A D I N G 5 1

Mexico Foreign Policy in Focus

David Brooks

Mexico-U.S. Dialogos

Since the early 1980s Washington has sought to break down all barriers to U.S. trade and investment in Mexico. It has done this through bilateral "framework agreements," debt-management negotiations, support for the structural adjustment-programs imposed by the international financial institutions (IFIs), and the inclusion of Mexico in the 1993 North American Free Trade Agreement (NAFTA).

As part of this economic-liberalization agenda, the U.S. has also supported policies to ensure stability in this country with which it shares a 2,000-mile border. Widespread instability would not only threaten U.S. economic interests in Mexico but would also put the U.S. free trade agenda at

Key Points

- U.S. policy is dominated by economic considerations, although maintaining social and political stability is an ever-present concern.

- The prominent U.S. role in the financial bailout following the late-1994 peso crisis reflected U.S. concerns about the repercussions of a collapsing free market model on the policies of other emerging markets.

- U.S. concerns about Mexico's commitment to democratization and respect for human rights are generally framed by the more fundamental interest in maintaining the economic opening and controlling its destabilizing consequences.

risk throughout the hemisphere. In addition, Washington policymakers fear that economic and political instability in Mexico would aggravate immigration and drug flows into the U.S.

Recent U.S. policy reflects this dual agenda of keeping Mexico open to U.S. business and sustaining stability. Although in 1988 Washington chose to endorse a fraudulent presidential election that guaranteed to keep the free trade/free market agenda on track, more recently U.S. policymakers have increasingly promoted political modernization as the means necessary to maintain social stability and ensure the long-term viability of neoliberal economic policies.

For the same reasons, the Clinton administration orchestrated a $50 billion financial bailout—including U.S. Treasury bonds, credit guarantees, and IFI loans—to keep the neoliberal model from collapsing in Mexico under the impact of the 1994 peso crisis. Justifying the unprecedented "rescue package," U.S. Treasury Secretary Robert Rubin explained that any escalation of the crisis in Mexico would consti-

tute a "long-term threat to U.S. exports and jobs that depend on bilateral trade."

What is more, Federal Reserve Chairman Alan Greenspan declared that "any reversal of Mexico's economic reforms and a spread of Mexico's financial difficulties to other emerging markets could halt or even reverse the global trend toward market-oriented reform and democratization."

In their campaign to install a new wave of "free market democracies" throughout the South, U.S. policymakers have increasingly confronted the social costs of market-oriented structural adjustment and its threats to stability. The U.S. Embassy in Mexico has established a "working group" to examine the social and political repercussions of the deepening economic crisis. Treasure Department officials and their colleagues at the IFIs have increasingly raised the concern of income disparity and poverty as "regime-threatening" factors. The Pentagon's Mexico contingency plans focus on potential internal unrest and its consequences resulting from economic polarization and social disintegration associated with the neoliberal model of globalization as the primary "security" concern.

Although a priority of U.S. policy in Mexico is promoting and sustaining a neoliberal structure of economic relations, other policy considerations also come into play, most prominently immigration control, drug control, human rights practices, and political modernization. But all are evaluated within the context of continuing economic liberalization policies and managing their potentially destabilizing effects.

The issues of immigration control and drug control are dri-

ven more by U.S. domestic politics than by concerns about bilateral relations. In the U.S., state and national lawmakers have passed extreme anti-immigrant measures and frame drug control as a national security concern. Both approaches have resulted in the militarization of the U.S.-Mexico border. In Mexico, U.S. drug-control programs have expanded the U.S.-Mexico military and law-enforcement relations, thereby lending support for increased militarization in the country's interior.

Problems with Current U.S. Policy

Those in U.S. policy circles generally agree that U.S. policy toward Mexico has been successful and continues on an appropriate track. U.S. transnational corporate interests are served by these policies that have helped install a "free market democracy" in Mexico and have created lucrative openings in sectors. The free fall of the Mexican economy in 1994 is regarded as a temporary setback but one that would have been much worse without the economic liberalization policies cemented by the NAFTA accord. Despite some tensions, cooperation is high between the U.S. and Mexican governments. And these officials commonly agree that the prescriptions put in place to address the 1994 crisis are working. Since the early 1980s when economic liberalization began in earnest, overall U.S.-Mexico trade has increased dramatically, from $30 billion to $107 billion in 1995.

The U.S. commitment to the principles of economic liberalization abroad has not wavered despite increasing evidence of the severe social consequences of neoliberal restructuring and the

Key Problems

- Those shaping economic integration policy have rejected appeals for a program that prioritized equitable development, choosing instead to rely almost exclusively on a corporate-driven agenda to direct the course of globalization.

- An unusual level of diplomatic and business consensus on current U.S.-Mexico relations coexists with high levels of social dissidence on current bilateral policies in both countries.

- Protectionists from both the left and the right, together with representatives from vulnerable U.S. business sectors, color the U.S. debate about NAFTA and relations with Mexico.

free trade system that Washington manages.

In the heat of the NAFTA debate in the early 1990s, Presidents Bush and Clinton praised Mexico for opening up its markets to foreign capital. Yet it was precisely the manner in which this opening took place, with its extreme dependence on speculative capital, that led to the financial collapse at the end of 1994. The financial speculators, both national and foreign, who had taken advantage of the opening used that same open door to take their "hot money" out of Mexico—thereby precipitating the peso crisis and the continuing disinvestment in Mexico's productive sector.

The precipitous nature of that economic opening and the privatization strategy have devastated entire sectors, most notably subsistence agriculture and the small and medium-size industries that produce for the shrinking domestic market and that have generated the most jobs for Mexicans. The result of the U.S.-touted policy intensified other key problems in the bilateral relation in direct contradiction to U.S. stated objectives: immigration and narcotrafficking. Increased immigration, or the perception of it, was met in the U.S. with stepped-up measures to stop Mexicans at the border. Similarly, U.S. economic policy has advocated the extensive privatization of state enterprises and the dismantling of government service programs, especially in rural areas. Marginalized within a rural economy increasingly dominated by agribusiness, many campesinos have turned to drug production as a survival option.

Such concerns about the socioeconomic impact of integration between two such economically disparate nations were raised during the NAFTA debate. However, with the exception of the founding of the largely symbolic North American Development Bank, policymakers rejected appeals for an economic integration program model that made equitable development a priority, choosing instead to rely exclusively on the market to direct the course of globalization.

U.S. policy toward Mexico today occurs within a bilateral context in which the governing elites of both countries are more explicitly in agreement on their shared interests than perhaps at any time since the turn of the century. Yet the very nature of the economic integration process favored by Washington has provoked one of the fiercest public political debates on U.S. international economic relations in recent history and continues to generate rifts among diverse interests at the elite and grassroots levels within the United States. NAFTA, the highly politicized debates on immigration and drugs, and the financial bailout of Mexico all highlighted sharp differences in the U.S.—within both the right and left—regarding the appropriate U.S. approach to globalizing trade and production.

Unfortunately, this debate focuses on narrow definitions about what serves U.S. national interests. NAFTA supporters were led by corporate interests that regard free trade as the best vehicle to increase profits, all the while arguing that the benefits of new trading opportunities would eventually be shared by all. Most U.S. groups opposed to NAFTA—whether on the left or the right—were largely responding to constituencies who believed that they would be harmed by further economic integration. Consequently, the arguments against NAFTA on both sides of the political spectrum were quite similar. During the trade negotiations, U.S. domestic producers, consumer groups, labor unions, and environmentalists all sought to impose regulations on Mexico to ensure that their constituencies were protected.

Rather than identify NAFTA as simply the formalization of the ongoing economic integration process between both countries, guided primarily by transnational corporations, opponents scapegoated Mexico for undermining U.S. living standards through runaway jobs, pollution, drugs, and "illegal" immigrants. This protectionist and unilateral perspective continues to dominate the debate on relations with Mexico. At one point, liberal legislators together with progressive citizen groups opposed to NAFTA drafted legislation that stipulated a permanent U.S. trade surplus with Mexico as a condition for keeping NAFTA, in effect mandating a permanent economic subordination of Mexico.

Toward a New Foreign Policy

Currently, in both countries—one relatively rich and one relatively poor—the economic agenda that guides the bilateral relationship is not working for the interests of the majorities. In both countries, 80 percent of the population is suffering a loss of its share of national income while the wealthier 20 percent is gaining at the expense of the poor. The promised benefits of this model for the vast majority in both countries are not in evidence, all to the contrary.

Thus, a new U.S. foreign policy toward Mexico can only be articulated if U.S. domestic social and economic policies are redefined. A new U.S. policy must consider two issues: the need to replace economic growth as an objective with a bilaterally defined notion of development and the need to democratize control of the globalization process.

To define new policy objectives for integration with Mexico, the U.S. policy debate must first redefine the purpose of its own economic development model. Only through this process can policymakers identify the premise for a binational debate on the nature of trade, investment, and economic cooperation. Without this process, policy recommendations are limited to piecemeal proposals that do not ultimately generate a new policy paradigm for bilateral relations.

Without a serious attempt to define a development policy in the U.S., alternative policy proposals regarding NAFTA or other aspects of bilateral relations inevitably degenerate into calls for unilateral, protectionist measures that are a poor foundation for establishing viable, constructive approaches to mutual development.

Key Recommendations

- A new policy toward Mexico must incorporate the interests of grassroots social actors such as trade unions, agricultural workers, community groups, and small producers in both countries.

- No discussion of the premise of a new policy toward Mexico is possible without a consensus in the U.S. on the appropriate development model for this country and the democratization of the policy-making process regarding economic globalization.

Any new policy process on Mexico must ensure first that it is defined in a democratic fashion, where U.S. policymakers incorporate the representatives of broad social constituencies directly affected by the bilateral relationship into the discussion at the domestic level.

In its foreign policy decisions, the U.S. government routinely includes representatives from the Fortune 500 firms. More democratic policies that reflect a broader social consensus would result if a similar effort were made to incorporate representatives of unions, farmer organizations, constituency-based environmental organizations, and other affected communities.

A new U.S. foreign policy toward Mexico must emerge from a binational process to design and implement truly bilaterally defined policies that recognize interdependence, self-determination, and the disparity of power relations.

If economic integration is to work—meaning that the 80% majority in both countries see their proportion of national income rise—then new bilateral agreements are needed to protect disadvantaged workers and small producers, aid adversely affected communities, retrain workers on both sides of the border, and otherwise decrease the disparity be-

tween the two countries. Part of this new approach to development must include serious debt relief since Mexico's debt burden denies funds for domestic development programs to increase productivity and employment.

Bilateral economic integration will continue to be contrary to the interests of working people on both sides of the border if it only promotes trade and investment and does not address the need to ensure that the work force of each nation has productive employment and full labor rights for all, especially immigrants wherever they work. Similarly, the drug issue cannot be properly addressed without considering economic development. The drug war will not stop the flow of drugs to U.S. consumers. Increasing drug use and related crime should be considered as mutual problems, while recognizing that the U.S. narcomarket spurs production and trafficking in Mexico. U.S. financial support would be better spent on supporting NGO and government programs to create alternative economic opportunities.

The Mexico-U.S. relationship poses the fundamental challenge to all who wish to devise a new North-South relationship: the entire spectrum of problems between the developed and the developing worlds are concretely manifested here. The process required to evolve a new U.S. foreign policy toward Mexico will serve as a framework for defining a new U.S. foreign policy agenda that addresses global inequities and the problems created by economic globalization both in the U.S. and abroad.

 Article Review Form at end of book.

Where the Big Fish Eat the Little Fish

Women's work in the free-trade zones

In the new world economic order, small countries must compete against each other by offering lower wages to attract transnational investment. In this "race to the bottom," women workers pay dearest.

Helen I. Safa

"When I started to work in the free-trade zone," says Esperanza, who worked in a garment factory for ten years, "I earned 15 pesos a week. With those 15 pesos I did many things. I went to the market and bought groceries. I even bought toilet soap, which I can't afford now." Like other women who work in the Dominican Republic's sprawling free-trade zones, Esperanza complains about how much more difficult it is to manage on the low wages factory work pays today. Despite wage increases, inflation has decimated the buying power of Dominican workers. "Now a worker earns 200 pesos or more," she says, "but it's still not enough to make ends meet."

Esperanza is one of thousands of women who began working in the free-trade zones in the 1980s. Although free-trade zones have existed in the Dominican Republic since the 1960s, export manufacturing has boomed over the last decade, largely due to structural-adjustment measures implemented after 1982 in response to growing public debt and general economic crisis. Structural adjustment meant currency devaluations, which forced the basic cost of labor in the free-trade zones down from $1.33 an hour in 1984 to $.56 an hour in 1990.[1] With one of the lowest wage levels in the Caribbean, foreign investors flocked to the Dominican Republic to set up shop in its growing free-trade zones. Tariff benefits provided by the U.S. government to offshore garment producers under the Caribbean Basin Initiative and other special programs also helped stimulate textile production, and garments are now the country's primary export. The free-trade zones constitute the third-largest source of employ-ment, following the public sector and the sugar industry.[2] While the free-trade zones employed 20,000 Dominican workers in 1982, today, 180,000 Dominicans, most of them women, work in this sector.

While women continue to enter the workforce in droves, life is increasingly precarious, especially for women workers. Under the rubric of structural adjustment, government programs have been cut drastically, undermining gains in women's health, education and occupational mobility won in previous decades. Growing poverty has pushed an increasing number of women into the labor force to meet the rising cost of living and the decreased wage-earning capacity of men. While this has helped increase the importance and visibility of women's contribution to the household economy, it is also a reflection of the desperate conditions facing Dominican workers.

Helen Safa, "Where the Big Fish Eat the Little Fish: Women's Work in the Free Trade Zones," NACLA REPORT ON THE AMERICAS; Vol. 30:5, pp. 31-37. Copyright 1997 by the North American Congress on Latin America, 475 Riverside Dr., #454, New York, NY 10115-0122.

José, who has worked in the free-trade zone for eight years, complains bitterly about wages and working conditions. He already had to switch jobs because of difficulties with his supervisors, and says he is only working out of desperation: "Work in the free-trade zone is no good. You work because you have to and because there is no other source of income. The policies of managers are always to suppress the workers, to squeeze us dry." He sums his feelings up with a phrase common to the Dominican working class: "The big fish eat the little fish." Though Dominican workers are referring to the relationship between capital and labor, the phrase also aptly characterizes the relationship between multinational corporations and the Dominican state, and between big, powerful countries like the United States and small, vulnerable countries like the Dominican Republic.

Over the past few decades, the Dominican economy has undergone a sharp transformation. A largely rural economy based on sugar exports and import-substitution industrialization in the 1960s, the Dominican Republic today is a service economy dependent on tourism, export manufacturing and agribusiness. Unlike import-substitution industrialization, export promotion does not require the development of an internal market, but the reduction of labor costs in order to compete effectively in the so-called new international economic order. Working conditions have consequently deteriorated, as workers' wages are continuously driven lower and their labor rights are minimized.

These shifts in the economy have had dramatic consequences for the makeup of the Dominican labor force. As import-substitution manufacturing was scaled back and the U.S. government cut the country's sugar quota, male wage labor deteriorated, forcing increasing numbers of men to seek refuge in the informal sector. Export promotion, on the other hand, has favored the employment of women—the preferred labor force in garment production, the predominant industry in the free-trade zones. By 1992, when the Dominican Republic became the leading source of apparel exports to the United States in the Caribbean Basin, surpassing even Mexico, two of every three firms in the free-trade zone produced garments.[3]

Declining employment opportunities has forced many Dominican men to take jobs in the free-trade zones. Today, about 30% of the workers in the free-trade zones are men. Many men like José work on heavier garments like pants and coats, where women's "nimble fingers" are less advantageous, and where men apparently feel they are not doing "women's work."

Several of the women I interviewed say they feel sorry for men who have to work in the free-trade zones, mainly because of the low salary. "Men don't like to work in the zone," says Teresa, a former free-trade zone worker. "Just imagine! The wage they pay in the zone is not a wage for men." While Teresa said the wages were also inadequate for women, she thought that women should stay home, as she now does, and work in the informal sector. "Women can earn more money by working out of their home than in the zone," she says, "even if it's just making johnny cakes, selling ice cream—whatever."

The rise in work for women in the free-trade zones has resulted in a four-fold increase in female employment between 1960 and 1990, from 9.3% to 38%. At the same time, however, female unemployment remains much higher than for men, reaching 46.7% in 1991.[4] This cannot be explained by educational levels—in 1991, 63% of women in the free-trade zones had completed secondary school, compared to 47% of the men, reflecting a nationwide trend of higher educational levels for women. Despite these gains in education, women are employed primarily as unskilled production workers while men are still preferred for higher-paid managerial, professional or supervisory positions.[5] Overall, women also receive lower salaries than men. The persistence of gender hierarchies, even within a predominantly female labor force like that in the free-trade zones, seems to be accepted by women workers, who are accustomed to having men in charge at the workplace.

Women who have worked a long time and demonstrated skill in the garment industry may rise to become supervisors, but to my knowledge, all the plant managers are men. Supervisors are paid more and often receive special benefits from the company, like Mariá, who has worked for the same plant for 17 years. Though she earns over 3,600 pesos a month plus extras—about $280, triple the salary of a regular factory worker—Mariá still complains that she can't make ends meet. Yet certain benefits, like a company scholarship which allows her six-year-old daughter to attend a private Catholic school, make Mariá feel lucky to have her job. Like many long-term employees—she recently received a plaque noting her 15 years with the company—Mariá identifies strongly with the company and its recent growth. "The company has progressed a lot," she says. "It grows and grows; they give us more work; they show that they have more confidence in us. As the company grows, we grow also because we develop. The company is our school because we learn there." The sense of pride and self-worth Mariá derives from her work is not matched by most workers, even long-term employees, who often feel there is no future for them in the free-trade zones. Yet by fostering employee identification with the company, employers help dampen the development of worker consciousness.

In 1992, the government, under pressure from labor in the Dominican Republic and in the United States, passed a new Labor Code which protects the right of collective bargaining for all workers. Prior to the passage of this law, there was an informal prohibition on union activity in the free-trade zones for years. Workers who were involved in union activity lost their jobs and were blacklisted from employment with other firms in the zone. Hilda lost her job several years ago because she was involved in an attempt to form a union. She says that management told the workers that "the big fish eat the little fish, and you need us more than we need you." They were right, she says, "because even if you don't want to work in such conditions, you have to, out of necessity and poverty." Today, she regrets her activism because it cost her her job.

Women workers, while aware of the new labor code, were not well informed as to its contents. Several women, for example, believed that the new labor

code forced companies to pay workers severance pay at the end of each year, in effect firing each worker and rehiring them as "new" workers the following year. The women approved of this practice because of the extra income it provided them at the end of the year. This is not a mandate of the labor code, but a practice instituted by some companies to retain workers, which may in fact deprive them of severance-pay benefits that would accumulate if they were not paid out yearly. Several companies are known for never paying severance pay, even for workers with many years on the job.

After the new code was passed, the newly formed National Federation of Free-Trade Zone Workers (FENATRAZONAS) helped organize nearly a hundred new unions. FENATRAZONAS is an affiliate of the National Confederation of Dominican Workers (CNTD), the largest of the three major Dominican labor confederations, which has the support of the American Institute for Free Labor Development (AIFLD). The Dominican Ministry of Labor also brought sanctions against several firms for code violations—a notable departure from the past, when worker complaints of mistreatment or unjust dismissal were generally rejected in favor of management.[6] In response, ADO-ZONA, the Dominican free-trade company association, led a barrage of criticism against the government for its supposed bias in favor of organized labor. After protracted struggles in which several hundred workers lost their jobs and the Dominican Republic faced a possible retraction of tariff benefits under the Generalized System of Preferences (GSP) because of AIFLD's complaint of Dominican workers' rights viola-

tions, four companies in the free-trade zones finally signed collective-bargaining agreements with unions in 1994.[7]

Despite these seeming gains in workers' rights, Dominican workers remain skeptical about the viability of the incipient union movement in the free-trade zones, and most continue to express their dissatisfaction through turnover and withdrawal rather than through union organizing. Unions have always been weak in the Dominican Republic, partly because of their fragmentation and ties to political parties, and have never represented more than 10 to 15% of the labor force.[8]

The only factor Dominican workers have in their favor is the high demand for labor, and company demand for cheap labor has spurred the creation of additional free-trade zones in the interior of the country, where labor is still abundant. But the Dominican Republic's drawing power may soon decline, as export manufacturing proliferates in other countries that offer ever-cheaper production costs—and hence more profits. After the 1995 peso debacle in Mexico, many export manufacturers moved production to that country. As a result, Mexico has since surpassed the Dominican Republic as the largest supplier of apparel to the U.S. market.

Low wages combined with a rising cost of living have increased the desperation of workers in the free-trade zones and forced them to look for alternate and supplementary sources of income. In 1992, a family of five needed an estimated 7,580 pesos, about $600, to cover monthly expenses for basic necessities, but free-trade zone workers at that time were earning a monthly minimum wage of 1,269 pesos, about

$100.[9] Even when both husband and wife are working in the zone, it is very difficult for young families to survive on such low salaries. Despite several increases in the minimum wage in the free-trade zones, the cost of living has increased so much that workers are barely able to feed their families and never have money to save, to educate their children, to buy a house or simply to enjoy themselves.

Families with young children have the most difficult time, because unlike single women or elderly workers, they have additional costs of food, housing and child care. Linda and her husband Pedro, who earn higher salaries because they both hold higher-level positions in the free-trade zone, are barely able to manage with two small children. They pay 600 pesos a month to her younger cousin, who lives with them and watches the children while they work, and 400 pesos a month for a small three-room house. The couple shares the bedroom with the children, while Linda's cousin sleeps in the kitchen. "We can't save anything," says Linda. "We spend all our money on rent, food and a few other basic items. We can't afford any kind of recreational activities, like going to a dance or to the movies. We hardly ever go out."

Female heads of household with young children to support often rely on the assistance of extended kin for child care and/or financial support. Mariá, a single mother who works in the free-trade zone, just moved into a separate unit in her father's house to be closer to work, and her father's wife takes care of her daughter while she works. Mariá and women like her who head secondary households would probably be considered by census-takers as part of an extended family headed by her father, even though she pays him rent and maintains an independent budget for her child and herself. Over 10% of all households surveyed by the Institute for the Study of Population and Development (IEPD) in 1991 were secondary households headed by women like Mariá, which suggests that the percentage of female-headed households in the Dominican Republic, which officially rose from 21.7% in 1981 to 29.1% in 1991, is actually much higher.

Structural adjustment, by forcing women to assume more economic responsibility and reducing employment opportunities for men, seems to be contributing to this increase in female-headed households. Women are resisting marriage because the "marriage market" of eligible men willing and able to support a family has shrunk.[10] Many Dominican women complain of male irresponsibility and, like Mariá, they refuse to live with a man who cannot offer financial support. "I won't allow anyone to live with me unless he is able to contribute to the household," she says. "I know many women who make life very easy for men. The woman goes to work while the man stays home resting. If women demanded that men assume responsibility for the home, like our mothers used to, things would be different." The father of Mariá's six-year-old daughter left for the United States shortly after she was born. He has never supported the child, except for 500 pesos, about $40, he gave Mariá on a return visit.

The IEPD survey also suggests that the profile of women heading secondary households, or sub-heads differs considerably from that of women who head their own household. In comparison to female heads, subheads are younger (85% are under 35), have higher educational levels, and higher labor force participation—all of which contribute to their higher incomes. Nearly three-quarters of these female sub-heads live with a parent, usually their mother, and over half have only one child. Two-thirds have no resident male partner, about half are separated, and a third are married or living in consensual unions.[11]

In 1991, 40% of all Dominican households were considered extended families—a high figure for an urban society. Even more notable is that extended families are far more prevalent in urban than in rural areas. Female sub-heads help raise incomes in these extended households to the point that they compare favorably with male-headed households, and are considerably higher than female-headed households with no secondary households.[12] This suggests that extended families—most of which are headed by women—represent an advantage not only to single mothers, but also to the households in which they live.

The need for alternative sources of income to supplement or substitute for wages under structural adjustment has contributed to the growth of the informal sector in the Dominican Republic. La Romana, the town where the free-trade zone I studied is located, now has numerous informal garment workshops run by women. The women collect the excess cloth from the factories to make garments which are sold in boutiques in the capital, despite laws against the sale of imported, duty-free cloth for domestic consumption. Women with some higher education have also started up private elementary schools in La Romana. Despite the high cost of 100 pesos or more a month, many women prefer to send their children to these private schools because the public-education system has deteriorated so badly.

More men than women are employed in the informal sector (excluding domestic service). In 1991, 24% of the economically active women in the Dominican Republic were self-employed compared to 38% of the men.[13] Incomes are generally lower in the informal sector, but some men engaged in illegal activities, such as money lending, have done quite well. Teresa's husband, Jorge, left the police force several years ago to become a money lender, and his family lives comfortably. They now own the home they live in, plus two others which they rent out, and they bought a car. Their children study at a private school and they go to a private clinic for health care. Teresa quit her job in the free-trade zone at Jorge's insistence—he wanted her to stay home with the children and avoid the stress of factory work, which was taking its toll on her health. Today, Teresa helps Jorge with his business. Jorge does the shopping and administers all the household expenses, and is clearly the dominant figure in the household.

Desperate working and living conditions in the Dominican Republic are fueling a riskier survival strategy: illegal migration. "People are willing to risk their lives," says Hilda, "in order to leave." Almost all of the women interviewed spoke of leaving the country, and are deterred only by their responsibility for young children and their fear of the dangerous trip by raft across the straits to Puerto Rico, a cheaper way to emigrate illegally. Most women have siblings abroad, and remit-

tances are the primary source of foreign exchange in the Dominican Republic. In the 1991 IEPD survey, the percentage of families with members who presently or previously resided abroad increased from 15% in the early 1980s to over 35% in the late 1980s. Most migrants are young urban residents under 30 with professional and clerical skills, and about half are women.[14]

Migrants leave because they see no future working for wages in the Dominican Republic. Hilda has now been living in St. Thomas for eight years, where she works as a hotel housekeeper for $7 an hour. The first two years were very difficult, she says, because her youngest daughter was only four, and it was dangerous to visit her family because she had migrated illegally. She has since managed to obtain legal residence not only for herself, but for two of her younger children, and hopes to do the same for the other two. She bought a nice home in La Romana where her children live, and she rents out her former house. Hilda's oldest son is completing his studies in civil engineering. She wanted her daughters to study also, but they did not want to, and the oldest works intermittently in the free-trade zone. Hilda lives sparsely in St. Thomas. "I am not going to tell you that I live well or comfortably," says Hilda, "because for me to live comfortably in St. Thomas, my family would have to live uncomfortably here. My wages don't stretch that far."

Hilda is a good example of a once-militant worker who has displaced all her energy into the struggle for survival, renouncing collective action in favor of individual gain. Dominican women workers are increasingly opting for individualistic solutions, try-

ing to win the favor of management, migrating or setting up a business of their own. Union organizing seems to be largely irrelevant to women who feel little pride in their work, and who rarely identify themselves as workers in the first place.

Since cheap labor is the prime determinant for investment, especially in small countries lacking other resources or infrastructure like the Dominican Republic, the chances for improvement are slim. As one plant manager said, in order to remain competitive in the new world economic order, small countries like the Dominican Republic will have to follow the large powers in order to survive—what some economists have called a "race to the bottom."[15] Workers—especially women—continue to pay the price in terms of increasing poverty, subordination and despair.

Notes

This article draws on research on Dominican women workers carried out in 1986 as part of a comparative study of women workers in the Hispanic Caribbean, and on a series of follow-up interviews conducted in 1994 in the Dominican Republic to examine the impact of structural adjustment on working conditons, survival strategies and gender relations. The author gratefully acknowledges research support provided by the North/South Center at the University of Miami.

1. David Jessup, "Workers Rights and Trade: Democracy's New Frontier," paper presented at a conference on U.S.-Latin American Trade and Women at the University of Texas at San Antonio, 1994.

2. U.S. Department of Labor, *Foreign Labor Trends: Dominican Republic*, 1992–93 (Washington, D.C., 1993), p. 10.

3. Consejo Nacional de Zonas Francas de Exportación, "Evaluación de Zonas Francas Industriales" (Santo Domingo, 1993), p. 4.

4. Nelson Ramírez, *La Fuerza de Trabajo en la República Dominicana* (Santo Domingo: Instituto de Estudio de Población y Desarrollo, 1993), p. 10.

5. Fundación APEC de Crédito Educativo (FUNDAPEC), Encuesta Nacional de Mano de Obra (A report prepared for the Inter-American Development Bank) (Santo Domingo: FUNDAPEC, 1992), p. 28.

6. Helen I. Safa, *The Myth of the Male Breadwinner: Women and Industrialization in the Caribbean* (Boulder: Westview Press, 1995).

7. U.S. Department of Labor, *Foreign Labor Trends: Dominican Republic, 1994–95* (Washington, D.C., 1995).

8. Rosario Espinal, "Between Authoritarianism and Crisis-Prone Democracy: The Dominican Republic After Trujillo," in Colin Clarke, ed., *Society and Politics in the Caribbean* (Oxford: Macmillan Press, 1991).

9. U.S. Department of Labor, *Foreign Labor Trends: Dominican Republic, 1992–93*, p. 12.

10. Helen Safa, *The Myth of the Male Breadwinner.*

11. Isis Duarte, "The Impact of Structural Adjustment on Women in the Free Zones of the Dominican Republic" (Santo Domingo: The Institute for the Study of Population and Development, 1994).

12. Isis Duarte, "The Impact of Structural Adjustment on Women."

13. Nelson Ramírez, "Nuevos hallazgos sobre fuerza laboral y migraciones: Análisis preliminar de los datos del cuestionario de hogar ampliado de la ENDESA 1991," in *Población y Desarrollo*, No. 2 (Santo Domingo: Profamilia, 1992), p. 110.

14. Nelson Ramírez, *La Fuerza de Trabajo*, p. 19.

15. David Jessup, "Workers Rights and Trade."

Article Review Form at end of book.

The Fourth World Conference on Women

Ambassador Madeleine K. Albright

Last September, representatives from governments around the globe assembled in Beijing, China for the Fourth World Conference on Women. They approved a Platform for Action that will serve as a blueprint for efforts to enable women to participate fully as citizens in societies everywhere. The focus now shifts to the implementation of the platform, and to removing or ameliorating the obstacles to its success that exist in each country.

The conference agenda was expansive, including many aspects of women's lives and addressing the varied family, social, political and professional roles of women. Although those attending represented virtually every cultural and political system on earth, a remarkable consensus emerged around a number of basic principles, including the following:

• Violence against women must stop;

• Girls must be valued equally with boys;

Madeleine K. Albright, "The Fourth World Conference on Women." This article originally appeared in the Winter-Spring 1996 issue of SAIS Review, The Journal of International Affairs of the Paul H. Nitze School of Advanced International Studies.

- Women must have equal access to education, health care and the levers of economic and political power;
- Family responsibilities should be shared; and
- Freedom of expression is a prerequisite to human rights, which include women's rights.

A half century ago, a great First Lady of the United States, Eleanor Roosevelt, was the driving force behind the Universal Declaration of Human Rights. This year, another courageous First Lady, Hillary Rodham Clinton, provided the dramatic high point to the Beijing Conference when she eloquently reaffirmed America's commitment to that Declaration and its application to all people:

> On the eve of a new millennium, it is time to break our silence. It is time for us to say here in Beijing, and for the world to hear, that it is no longer acceptable to discuss women's rights as separate from human rights. . . . If there is one message that echoes forth from this conference, it is that human rights are women's rights . . . and women's rights are human rights.

Throughout the Conference, the United States delegation stressed the fact that the Universal Declaration reflects spiritual and moral roots that are central to all cultures. It obliges each government to strive in law and practice to protect the rights of those under its jurisdiction. Whether a government fulfills that obligation is a matter of concern to all.

At the heart of the Universal Declaration is a fundamental distinction between coercion and freedom. No mother should feel compelled to abandon her daughter because of a societal preference for males. No woman should be forced to undergo genital mutilation, or to engage in prostitution, or to enter into marriage or to have sex. No woman should be forced to remain silent for fear of political prosecution, detention, abuse or torture. And all women should have the right to help shape the destiny of their communities and countries.

These are simple principles, but if they were observed around the world, they would have astonishing results.

Despite recent gains, women remain an undervalued and underdeveloped human resource. This is not to say that women have trouble finding work. In many societies, they do most of the work. But often they are barred from owning land, excluded from schools, denied financial credit and permitted little or no voice in government.

It is no accident that most of those in the world who are abjectly poor are women. Frequently, they are left to care for children without the help of the children's father. Many are trapped at a young age in a web of ignorance, powerlessness and abuse.

Consider that more than half the murders of women in countries as diverse as Bangladesh, Brazil, Kenya, Papua New Guinea and the United States are committed by present or former spouses or partners.

In a number of countries, child prostitution is growing because clients believe older prostitutes are more likely to be infected by HIV.

In many rural societies, women perform much of the farming and all of the child rearing, but are denied a role in financial decisions.

And almost everywhere, women are hurt by discrimination and by social and economic structures that are unjust.

No one could expect the Women's Conference to solve these problems, but it has outlined a plan for addressing them. This matters not only to women, but to everyone. Releasing the productive capacity of women is one key to breaking the cycle of poverty and improving standards of life everywhere. When women are empowered, families are strengthened, socially-constructive values are taught, sexually-transmitted disease is slowed and truly sustainable development becomes possible.

That is why the Women's Conference Platform for Action went far beyond its core commitment to the fundamental human rights of women to explore the linkages that exist between those rights and the varied expression of women's lives.

For example, the Platform joins the issues of rights and economic empowerment by committing governments to take steps to enable women to engage on an equal basis in economic activity, including owning property, having the right to inherit, running businesses and obtaining access to credit.

The Platform recognizes the importance of sharing family responsibilities. It encourages flexible work arrangements and the opportunity for both women and men to take temporary leave from employment to deal with family emergencies.

The Platform calls for a comprehensive approach and improved access to health care and education for women of all ages. The U.S. delegation, in particular, played a leading role in encouraging a life span approach to health. Specific issues addressed included breast and ovarian cancer, reproductive health; substance abuse; sexually transmitted diseases; and environmental and occupational health.

The Platform also makes an explicit link between improving the status of women and increasing their participation in political and economic decision-making.

In the months leading up to the Conference, there were those who suggested that its agenda would be controlled by a radical and unrepresentative minority. As the final Platform for Action attests, this was not the case. The United States prepared for the conference through a series of regional meetings designed to gain input from citizens reflecting a wide range of social and political views. The U.S. delegation included members from both genders and both parties, with experts in everything from health care to the environment to education to micro-enterprise.

The Women's Conference was a success despite inclement weather and a number of well-publicized logistical difficulties. These difficulties were particularly acute at the companion non-governmental forum, in which more than 7,000 Americans participated, and which took place in the city of Huairou, about an hour's drive from the main Conference center in Beijing.

The United States worked hard to ensure the broadest possible participation in the Conference and Forum by non-governmental organizations with a legitimate interest in women's issues. Despite this, a number of problems and inequities did arise with respect to the credentialing and issuance of visas to NGO representatives. The Clinton Administration protested at the time, and has since asked the United Nations Secretariat to de-

velop procedures to guarantee that similar problems do not arise in connection with future events.

Notwithstanding the difficulties, visitors to the NGO Forum in Huairou were treated to a kaleidoscopic display of seminars, workshops, demonstrations, artistic and cultural expression, and networking. Although some had debated in advance the question of whether it would be worthwhile or appropriate to attend a human rights conference in China, it was clear from day one that, for those who care about advancing the status of women, the decision to attend was the right one. As I told an audience assembled in the Disabilities Tent in Huairou:

> Since the first Women's Conference 20 years ago, opportunities for women have expanded around the world. This is no accident. It is because women did not wait for governments to act on their own. It is because you—the NGO's—created a global network that shares information, provides counseling, lobbies for change, and reaches out to women who need help or who are abused.

If measured by the degree of consensus in Beijing, and by the core principles affirmed in the Platform for Action, the Fourth World Conference was a major step forward. But the true measure of its accomplishments will be found not in what happened there, but in what happens now—in the actions taken to fulfill the commitments made there.

Although the United States has long been an international leader in efforts to promote equal rights for women, leaders cannot stand still. Barriers to the equal participation of women persist in our country. The Clinton

Administration is determined to bring those barriers down.

Even before the Conference ended, the President announced the formation of the President's Interagency Council on Women. This interagency group will coordinate the U.S. response to the commitments contained in the Platform for Action.

Among the concrete steps planned or underway are the following:

1. The Justice Department's Office on Violence Against Women is leading a comprehensive effort to fight domestic and other forms of violence against women. They are doing this by combining tough new federal laws with assistance to states in law enforcement, victim assistance, prosecutions and crime prevention.

2. The Department of Labor has launched a year-long campaign to solicit pledges from employers related to job security, work and family responsibilities that will benefit women and their families.

3. The Department of Health and Human Services has embarked upon a series of programs related to the well-being of women and girls, with goals that include reducing smoking among children and adolescents by 50 percent; a reduction in teen pregnancy; increased education about AIDS; and new initiatives on cervical and breast cancer.

4. The Department of the Treasury will take the lead in improving coordination of federal efforts to support the growth and development of the micro-enterprise field in the United States and women's involvement in it.

5. The Agency for International Development will continue to lead in promoting and recognizing the vital role of women in development, including new efforts to increase women's participation in political processes and to promote the enforcement of women's legal rights.

In recent decades, in the United States and around the world, opportunities for women have expanded. It is no longer a question of whether women from all countries will have a strong voice in controlling their destinies, but only when and how that goal will be achieved.

But building inclusive societies is still a work in progress. The United States has been working on it for two centuries. For more than half our nation's history, until 75 years ago this past August, American women could not even vote. Many traditional or authoritarian societies still have a very long way to go. The Fourth Women's Conference offers a roadmap every country can use to move forward, whatever current practices and policies may be.

It also provides NGO's and other grassroots organizations with an internationally-approved statement of principles and goals to be used as Leverage in pursuit of further positive change. In so doing, it will lend momentum to actions undertaken in households, village squares, markets, classrooms, courtrooms, board rooms and legislatures to translate promises into reality, and the idea of equality into the reality of people's lives.

The Fourth World Conference on Women is part of a centuries long process of adjustment to a changing technological, social and cultural environment. It is part, also, of an historic struggle to build societies based on law, decency and respect for the dignity of every human being.

In preparing for the conference, I came across an old Chinese poem in which a father says to his young daughter:

We keep a dog to watch the house;
A pig is useful, too;
We keep a cat to catch a mouse;
But what can we do with a girl
    like you?

For me, the Women's Conference will be a success if it brings us even a little closer to the day when girls all over the world will be able to look ahead with confidence that their lives will be valued, their individuality respected, their rights protected, and their futures determined by their own abilities and character.

In such a world, the lives of all of us—men and women, boys and girls—will be enriched.

It is to make progress towards such a world that the United States went to Beijing and participated, actively, forcefully, and proudly in shaping an agenda for action that will—when implemented—bring us all far closer to that goal.

 Article Review Form at end of book.

Women Redrawing the Map

The world after the Beijing and Cairo conferences

Joan Dunlop, Rachel Kyte, and Mia MacDonald

In Beijing at the United Nations Fourth World Conference on Women, governments reaffirmed and moved beyond what they had agreed at recent global conferences on the environment (Rio 1992), human rights (Vienna 1993), population and development (Cairo 1994) and social development (Copenhagen 1995). Indeed, this series of conferences made the achievements in Beijing possible.

The Beijing Conference was a turning point in the world's understanding; an acknowledgment that women's issues are the world's issues, and vice versa. It provided a clear indication of global priorities for the next century, and of women's centrality to them. The Conference's final document, the Platform for Action, demonstrates that the agreements reached in Cairo at the International Conference on Population and Development (ICPD) is accepted global policy. And for the second time in 12 months, countries of the world reaffirmed the human rights of women and the critical importance of reproductive and sexual health and rights to women's empowerment and to development.

Beijing marked the first time a United Nations women's conference had as its central focus the human rights of women—economic, social, cultural, civil and political. Beijing also represents the coming of age of the international women's movement, with women playing key roles in the inter-governmental negotiations as delegates, advisors, and advocates. Since the 1985 UN World Conference on Women in Nairobi, women around the world have mobilized in their communities, countries and internationally to gain access, successfully, to the arenas where policies are made and implemented.

Billed as a conference on equality, peace, and development, the Beijing meeting, at its core, was about eliminating coercion, discrimination, and violence in the public and private lives of women. Governments urged that: economic and employment policies recognize women's unpaid contributions to the economy; eliminate differentials in pay between men and women for equal work; and women be guaranteed equal access to public office, education, basic health care, and all other aspects of public and private life. In addition, they called for elimination of violence in the home and in public, where rape is not only a crime against the individual, but is still used as a weapon of war. Finally, the governments represented in Beijing reaffirmed what they had agreed in Vienna in 1993, that international human rights laws and standards must not be diluted by religious practices, or tradition when applied to women.

Joan Dunlop, Rachel Kyte, and Mia MacDonald, "Women Redrawing the Map: the World After the Beijing and Cairo Conferences." This article originally appeared in the Winter-Spring 1996 issue of SAIS Review, The Journal of International Affairs of the Paul H. Nitze School of Advanced International Studies.

The conference opened with 35 percent of its Platform in "square brackets" because governments could not agree to terms. [Square brackets are placed around language that has not been accepted by consensus, pending further negotiation or, ultimately, reservation by a delegation at the end of the conference. All brackets must be removed by the conference's end; reservations are the means for countries to state on the record that they do not agree with particular sections or words of the final agreement.] Yet, by its final session, the conference had, as Norwegian Prime Minister Gro Harlem Brundtland said in her closing speech, "unbracket[ed] the lives of girls and women." When the negotiations ended, just before dawn on the morning of September 15, governments had agreed to the strongest international document ever detailing the reality of women's lives and which called for sustained and precise action.

In this article, we will analyze how the Fourth World Conference on Women took the global community beyond the achievements of the recent series of global conferences in critical ways. In particular, we discuss the importance of the conference's strong reaffirmation of the new conceptualization of population-related health and development policies agreed on at the ICPD in 1994 which centered on women's reproductive health and rights. We also compare and contrast key dimensions of the process and outcomes of the ICPD and the Fourth World Conference on Women, including the genesis of leadership, political actors—not only government delegations but also non-governmental women's

organizations—and the pattern and content of the diplomatic negotiations. We provide details of the most important points governments agreed in Beijing, many of which are unprecedented. A concluding section summarizes what the Beijing Platform for Action means for women's lives around the world, what it shows about the process of negotiating global agreements, and how real change can take place.

A Global Shift

The Fourth World Conference on Women was the culmination of a series of global conferences that caused a re-examination and re-shaping of governments' understanding of the role of the international community, as well as the global understanding of development. The agreements reached at the Earth Summit in 1992 and the World Conference on Human Rights in 1993 created momentum for the breakthrough agreements reached at the International Conference on Population and Development (ICPD) in Cairo. There, 184 governments reached an unprecedented consensus on a twenty-year Programme of Action to balance the world's peoples with its resources. The Programme puts women's equality, empowerment, reproductive rights, and sexual health at the center of population and development policies.

Previous international agreements on population have set demographic targets for limiting population growth and have focused on contraceptive services as the method to achieve these goals. By contrast, in Cairo the international community recognized the interrelationships between con-

sumption and production patterns, economic development, population growth and structure, and environmental degradation. Also in Cairo, the understanding of the term "population" was broadened significantly, in large part due to the influence of non-governmental organizations (NGOs), especially women's groups from all over the world.

Impact of the Women's Movement and Southern Leadership

The outcome of the ICPD provoked some conservative delegations to threaten to use the Beijing conference to turn back agreements women had achieved in Cairo. Most of the opposition came from delegations that had not fully accepted the Cairo accord, specifically its provisions on reproductive health and reproductive rights. Such groups included the Holy See, conservative Islamic countries, and several states in Latin America. Despite this challenge, governments of the world were able to achieve a consensus on a Platform for Action that included verbatim language from Cairo (including reproductive and sexual health and reproductive rights), as well as language that extends and operationalizes the Cairo Programme of Action in key areas.

As in Cairo, much of the progress achieved in Beijing was due to the capacity, skill, and tenacity of women's NGOs from all over the world, who worked at regional conferences, preparatory meetings and at the Beijing conference itself to move government delegations towards consensus. Rooted in the experience of domestic campaigns over the last 20 years, the series of international women's conferences (Mexico City, 1975; Copenhagen, 1980; Nairobi, 1985), and the force of women's organizations at the recent global conferences, women had refined an inside-outside lobbying strategy. They gave priority to ensuring that feminists were made members of government delegations, worked with delegations at preparatory meetings, and had crafted specific language for negotiation. Many of the over 7,000 women from NGOs who were accredited to the conference worked as a pressure group, and interpreted the complexity of issues and negotiations to the international media.

Contrary to assertions in the press and by opposition delegations, the bulk of the progress came not from Northern radical feminists, but from women of the South. It was clear, the political fulcrum had shifted from Northern to Southern countries, and from men to women. Consensus on sexual rights, abortion, adolescent access to services, the right to inheritance and succession, and most other issues covered by the Platform for Action were forged primarily by delegates who were neither white, nor liberal, nor necessarily feminist. What really happened is that governments of the world, represented by women delegates, stepped forward to acknowledge the realities of women's lives. Delegates wanted to leave Beijing with a document that reflected those realities and that committed the world's governments to take concrete and effective action to end coercion, discrimination, and violence against women of all forms.

Central to this process was the leadership of Africa which had been given focus and energy by the moral authority of South Africa; the courage of many Latin American countries in breaking free of the influence of the Vatican hierarchy; and the steadfastness of the Caribbean. These countries placed women in key positions in their delegations who were not swayed from progressive language on human rights, sexuality, and inheritance among other contentious issues.

The Preparatory Process

The Conference in Beijing was prefaced by a preparatory process that gained momentum over a two year period. Part of the planning for Beijing took place in the context of the ongoing review of implementation of the recommendations of the last women's conference in Nairobi. Unlike other world conferences held in the 1990s, the focus of preparations for Beijing was at the regional level. Five regional conferences were held, in Indonesia, Argentina, Austria, Senegal, and Jordan, focusing on the specific priorities in each region. This process helped Africa, Latin America and the Caribbean, in particular, to work as strong regional groups in Beijing.

In March, 1995, at the annual session of the United Nations Commission on the Status of Women, the draft Platform for Action, compiled by the Con-ference Secretariat from the five regional conferences, was negotiated for the first time. With only this one chance to negotiate a document never seen in its entirety, the deliberations were tense. This mood was exacerbated by what were widely understood to be de-

liberate "blocking" tactics by delegations opposed to a constructive agreement on women's equality. Furthermore, many delegations were ill-prepared to negotiate and the Conference Secretariat was afraid of potential controversy. As a result, the draft Platform for Action emerged from the four week preparatory committee process with more than a third of its text unresolved. Among the concepts bracketed were "gender" and the "human rights of women."

Over the summer, a contact group convened to resolve the use of the word "gender" and informal negotiations were held in early August to remove some of the more redundant brackets. Apparently unsettled by the chaos of the preparatory process during the Commission on the Status of Women, diplomats in August tried to bring some order to negotiations, both in terms of process and tone. They were successful.

Indications of a Tide Turned

In the first few days of the official conference, which opened on September 4, events indicated that the negotiations would be painstakingly slow. But given the fact that most delegations were resolved not to reopen agreements reached in the recent past, it seemed likely that agreements made in Cairo would be fully reaffirmed. The first positive sign was the appointment of an experienced diplomat and skilled negotiator, Merwat Tallawy, Egypt's ambassador to Japan, as chair of the contact group on the health chapter. This task would not be easy. Achieving consensus on health, which included concepts of sexual and reproductive health and rights was expected to be a difficult and intricate process in itself. It was made even more difficult by the need to reconcile relevant language in the other sections of the document on poverty, the girl child, and human rights, as well as the preamble. Tallawy, who had led the Egyptian negotiating team at the ICPD, has years of experience regarding UN rules and procedures from her work on the Committee of the Convention on the Elimination of All Forms of Discrimination Against Women (CEDAW) and the Commission for the Status of Women. Tallaway steered the delegations through the most contentious issues, constantly reminding them that the conference was to achieve consensus by finding language acceptable to the majority of delegations.

After an effort by the Holy See and its few allies to unseat Tallawy had failed, and interventions by some delegations to slow the negotiations down were met with vocal derision by the other delegations, a consensus emerged by the end of the first week. As a result, the Holy See quietly announced that they would not challenge Cairo language. But the tide had not fully turned. Concepts outside, but related to, the specific language agreed in Cairo were challenged repeatedly not only by the Holy See but also by conservative delegations from Islamic states. Nonetheless, when language was agreed upon stating that "the right of all women to control all aspects of their health, in particular their own fertility, is basic to their empowerment," (Platform, Para. 94), it seemed clear that moving beyond Cairo was possible. That such a controversial statement, unattainable one year earlier, was possible in the first week suggested that the majority of delegates to Beijing were determined to secure agreements on women's empowerment. In essence, the mood in Beijing conference rooms was much different from the mood in the conference rooms in Cairo.

The Pattern of Diplomacy

Some threads of the pattern of diplomacy in Beijing were recognizable from Cairo, but they were overlaid with a more balanced global interplay with all regions of the world taking a significant role.

In Cairo, the negotiations were marked by the new assertiveness of the US under the Clinton Administration, a much hyped Holy axis of the Holy See and Iran, South Africa's first UN conference since its re-emergence onto the international scene, the decision by the Group of 77 to only operate as a block on economic issues—the group's original mandate—and the tentacles of the Holy See stretching from Malta to a rump of countries in Central and Latin America and West Africa.

In Beijing, the pattern of diplomacy included the emergence of Africa as a coordinated region and the strong voices of Senegal, Namibia, and Zambia, as well as South Africa. This was essential in reaching consensus on the sections on health, poverty, the girl child, and human rights. This coordinated African voice had been strengthened through the process of regional preparations which included a regional preparatory conference, regional ministerial meetings, sub-regional meetings, and a meeting sponsored by the Organization of African Unity. Also for the first time, representatives of African women's movements were represented on multiple delegations, and delegations spoke out with confidence on issues from which their diplomats had previously shied away.

Northern countries paid a price for approaching the conference as if it were only about the quality of women's lives in the South, and about the responsibility—or lack of responsibility—of the North for that quality of life. Most Northern delegations did not wish to discuss situations of inequality in their own countries, between women and men or between the wealthy and the poor.

The European Union (EU), now with a common position of 15 countries, did create political space for consensus by staking out strong positions in many areas, including sexual rights. However, other delegations and NGOs expressed frustration as the EU failed to develop a strategy to negotiate its positions, even as consensus was being built around language on women's rights to control their sexuality that was included in the Platform for Action. The fragile consensus on sexual rights that stretched from Iran to Norway nearly broke under the strain of the pressure within the EU for inclusion of the phrase "sexual rights." The same lack of negotiating skill held up other debates. But, Canada, New Zealand, Norway and Australia often found a way out, toward consensus, as the core of the JUSCANZ alliance.

In contrast to Cairo, at Beijing the US delegation played a low-key role in the negotiations. Silent at critical moments due to fear of domestic lobbies of the Christian right, the US delegation was uncomfortable being visibly in the lead on issues central to the Cairo consensus. However, echoing the First Lady's adoption of the women's rights community's phrase "women's rights are human rights," the US fought to defend the language of the 1993 Vienna conference in the human rights section.

Much has been said about the "unholy alliance" forged in both Cairo and Beijing between conservative forces of different fundamentalist religious standpoints. In Cairo, the alliance broke down as it became apparent that the motivations and concerns of each side of the alliance were different, and as the Holy See and Iran shrank from public association. In Beijing, a smaller core of countries associated themselves with each other much more visibly. Scripted and coordinated as a grouping that was fundamentalist in its approach, Sudan, Yemen, Malta and the Holy See were the only reliable members of such an alliance.

Opposition to the empowerment of women, expressed most vocally in negotiations on equal inheritance rights, sexual rights, and reproductive and sexual health, came from a diminished Catholic conservative bloc (much smaller and less united than in Cairo), and from conservative Islamic countries that were more vociferous than in Cairo. At times, these two blocs worked together, but were countered by the unfettered voices of many Latin American countries, including Brazil, Colombia and Mexico. For the first time in such a conference, the Organization of Islamic States acted as a country grouping to coordinate positions. This task proved difficult as secular Muslim countries, like Bangladesh and Indonesia, conservative fundamentalist states, including Sudan and Yemen, and dealmakers, such as Iran and Egypt, struggled to reach and maintain unified positions.

What Was Achieved

The key tenets established in the Beijing Platform for Action are:

- *The primacy of women's rights:* Human rights standards and international laws cannot be applied differently to women than to men, even if culture and tradition may seem to sanction restrictions on women's rights. This is an unequivocal statement, like the stance taken at the Vienna World Conference on Human Rights. By comparison, the chapter on reproductive health and rights in the ICPD Programme of Action refers to culture specificity and national sovereignty in these matters. No such equivocation exists in the Beijing Platform.

- *Action to ensure reproductive and sexual rights:* The Platform reaffirms the human rights of women, including their reproductive rights and the right to control matters related to their sexuality, and directs governments to ensure that these rights are fully respected and protected. This paragraph (Platform for Action, Paragraph. 232f) operationalizes the agreements made in Cairo, where reproductive rights were defined. In Beijing, governments agreed to take action to ensure these rights and sexual rights were treated as human rights.

- *Abortion law review:* Included in the Platform for Action is a call for all countries to consider reviewing laws containing punitive measures against women who have undergone illegal abortions. (Platform, Para. 106k). In countries where abortion is legally restricted and women resort to clandestine or self-induced abortion, this agreement means that when a woman seeks treatment from a health clinic for an infection or hemorrhage caused by a botched abortion, she should be treated—not interrogated and arrested. This directive is a step toward decriminalizing abortion. It also keeps the focus, first recognized internationally in Cairo, on the number of women who die or are seriously injured from unsafe abortions worldwide.

- *Adolescent rights recognized:* An avalanche of conditional language asserting parental rights in sections of the Platform relating to reproductive and sexual health education, information and services for children and adolescents was streamlined. The final agreement recognized the primacy of adolescent rights, over the duties, rights and responsibilities of parents, thereby taking into account the evolving capacity of the child. This language is true to the basic premise that the needs of the child come first, as expressed by the international community in the 1990 Convention on the Rights of the Child.

- *Women's control over their sexuality:* Beijing established that the rights of women include the right to control their own sexuality, free from coercion, discrimination, or violence (Platform, Para. 96). This is much more than the right to say no to sex. It gives women the basis to be free from multiple abuses of their sexual rights, including trafficking, rape, battering, and female genital mutilation.

In the Conference's last negotiating session, an impassioned and unprecedented debate on sexual orientation took place. This debate ranged from outright denunciations of homosexuals and lesbians as deviant, to strong pleas to end discrimination in all its forms. A particularly eloquent and resonant statement was made by South African Health Minister Nkosazana Zuma when she assured the world that South Africa would not discriminate against anyone, no matter what his or her sexual orientation, and that the nation supported retaining the language on sexual orientation to show that South Africa has no short memory on how it feels to be discriminated against. However, despite the support of the majority of the delegations who took the floor to retain specific references to disallowing discrimination on the basis of "sexual orientation," it was ultimately stricken from the Platform for Action as part of an intricate bargain to achieve consensus on the document as a whole.

At the final plenary session of the Conference, more than 40 countries added interpretive statements or expressed reservations to specific passages of the Platform. Many other countries took the floor to express their "unqualified support" for the Platform, including Bolivia, El Salvador, Panama, India, and South Africa. In Cairo, 17 reservations and interpretive statements were made on multiple sections of the Programme of Action. By contrast, in Beijing, the majority of the 28 reservations and interpretive statements focused specifically on two of the 362 paragraphs

comprising the Platform for Action: paragraph 96 (which establishes a woman's right to control her own sexuality) and paragraph 106k (which calls for countries to consider reviewing abortion laws that punish women who have had illegal abortions). The Holy See, as expected, expressed a reservation on the entire health chapter and additional paragraphs, but eventually joined the overall consensus. The reservations expressed were narrowly defined and, as such, do not undermine the value of the 125-page long Platform.

What It Means

To a great extent, the final consensus was due to the new dialogue witnessed in the negotiating rooms. More countries were represented than at previous conferences by women. As was not often the case in the past, these women were not tokens—there because of whom they married. In Beijing, women served as delegates because they were professionals, experts, elected officials, activists, and leaders of women's organizations. Many of them have backgrounds in women's movements, nurtured by the UN Decade for Women (1975–85), and the three previous women's conferences. Many of these women had participated, as government delegates or NGO observers in previous global conferences, and therefore were skilled in the process and substance of U.N. negotiations. Without question, their expertise and experience were critical to the outcomes of the conference.

The overall messages from this conference to the world are: First, equality is not for debate; it is desired, essential, and will come about. Second, coercion, discrimination, and violence must be eradicated from the lives of women, wherever they occur—in economics, politics, health care and within communities and families. Third, the vision of population and development adopted in Cairo is truly global policy. And fourth, women's rights are human rights. Governments and nongovernmental organizations must now deliver, and the women of the world, working in partnership with men, will hold them accountable.

What Beijing showed is that change can come about through intense collaboration, discipline, and a shared purpose. That change may not be immediately visible, especially heroic, or particularly sweeping. Still, it is hard to believe that the Beijing agreements will not have an impact. Such a diverse assembly *will* effect change, large and small, in public and private arenas. Positive energy pervaded the negotiations in Beijing—an intensely political conference about women's lives— and the first of the women's conferences not to be mired in other geo-political struggles. This energy will be kept alive by NGOs, as they press for realization of the commitments made not just in Rio, Vienna, Cairo, and Copenhagen, but those remade and extended in Beijing.

 Article Review Form at end of book.

'I Cannot Accept an 'a La Carte Europe'

While President Santer wants the Commission to do less, but better, he is against pick 'n' mix, describing it as an unacceptable dilution of the Union.

When he took office as European Commission president, Jacques Santer promised to do less, but better. That remains his proud motto. But as he approaches the mid-point of his five-year term, how does his record measure up?

He has staunched the flow of EU legislation, it is now a trickle compared with the flood under his predecessor. Yet, during his time in Brussels, Europe's unemployment has soared beyond people's worst expectations. More than 18 million Europeans now find themselves condemned to dole queues. And, though still just about on track, the daring march towards a single currency remains beset by pitfalls. Europe, clearly, is entering a nail-biting new phase. The genial and mild-mannered Santer is oddly cast to preside over such a period of nerve-wracking transition.

To combat popular disenchantment with Europe he has launched the ambitious Citizens First campaign, part of an effort to bring Europe "closer to the people". This attempts to spell out to citizens hoping to get work in another EU state, for example, what their rights would be and what their obligations are. Citizens First has proved a winner everywhere apart from Britain, where, in the run-up to a bitterly-contested general election, the idea of an EU-sponsored advertising campaign was promptly squashed.

Sober-suited with a modest silk tie and restrained shirt, Santer lacks the smallest trace of theatricality. His words are similarly measured. Yet he does allow himself one exuberance. In conversation his hands are mobile and remarkably expressive. Scarcely a word passes without him cupping his hands, sweeping them through the air or bringing them down emphatically on his desk in an accompanying gesture.

Overall, President Santer exudes a relaxed, if low-key, charm. His message is one of reassurance. This is no visionary technocrat in the mould of the overly bold Jacques Delors.

In an interview with *The European's* Editor in Chief Charles Garside and Political Editor Victor Smart, President Santer sets out his reasons for believing that European integration is moving ahead as planned. And he outlines the two great prizes that Europe still has within its grasp: a prosperous single market and a historic 21st-century enlargement of the European Union healing the scar of the Iron Curtain.

Is the Citizens First campaign living up to your expectations?

It is an information campaign, not a propaganda exercise, of course, explaining to people their rights—what requirements they need to meet if they move to a job in another EU country, what healthcare entitlements are, and so on.

The results have been very encouraging in all member states, with the possible exception of the United Kingdom. It has satisfied a real need at the level of the ordinary citizen.

Latest figures show the number of people per 100,000 households using the phone lines ranges from 32 in Germany to 361 in Ireland.

Even taking into account the poor British response, the average around the Union is 116. A similar number of Europeans are accessing us through the Internet. It is all part of bringing Europe closer to the citizen.

Has much real progress been made on making the EU machinery open and transparent to outsiders?

I am delighted that the European ombudsman has helped make this an issue. Ninety per cent of all requests coming from citizens for documents are fulfilled now. That is a huge amount of requests successfully met. Environmental issues are prominent. It's an excellent opportunity to test what issues actually concern ordinary people.

You are approaching the midpoint of your five-year term. How well has your vision of the Commission's role been fulfilled?

I stick to my slogan that I want the Commission to do less, but better. I am very committed to the principle of subsidiarity. We must not meddle in everything. We must always focus on initiatives which are important and necessary, say, to bolster the single market.

We withdrew in one year 47 directives that had been tabled. We are also consulting people—employers' organisations, green groups and so on—much more thoroughly through green papers. We can do still better, but there is real progress.

Is the single market proving a dynamic force?

We created a single market, but it does not yet function as a single market. We have to improve that, to deepen the market, for the sake of our industry's competitiveness.

We are framing an action plan with Mario Monti [the European commissioner responsible for the single market and taxation] with deadlines. We want the remaining fields of the single market to be achieved on 1 January 1999. That will mean there is a clear parallel with the first entry by currencies into monetary union and the completion of the single market.

Surely, the failure to complete the single market is heightening the disenchantment with Europe resulting from the tight monetary union deadline?

The single currency is one key element in making the single market a reality. I don't know of a single market elsewhere which functions smoothly with 14 distinct national currencies.

So many different currencies produce distortions. The euro will help our businesses to captalise on all the opportunities presented by the single market. Remember, 92 per cent of European Union trade takes place within the EU states themselves.

Because we have grasped the importance of all this we have pushed hard with liberalisation in areas such as telecoms and gas.

Business will become even keener on the single market once the benefits of the single market are realised.

The single market obviously benefits the consumer, too.

Don't the political shock waves resulting from the unemploy-

ment crisis in Germany suggest that the 1999 deadline for economic and monetary union may be unattainable?

I am quite confident that we will meet this deadline on the basis of the convergence criteria and with a significant number of member states participating.

Without any fudging?

Yes, without a fudge. I'm in favour of very strict rules because we need a strong currency. The euro must be strong, and that means it must be credible to the financial markets.

It is not just an issue decided by governments: the markets must view the euro in a very positive light. I am quite confident that in Germany the determination of Chancellor Helmut Kohl and also his Finance Minister Theo Waigel to meet the criteria will succeed.

Yet aren't you uncomfortable that the future of European integration hangs so much on the political survival of a single individual, that is Chancellor Kohl?

It's not just one person. Certainly, the chancellor is strongly committed to achieve the European project in all its aspects. But the younger generation in his party, the CDU, is also very much dedicated to the European Union. A few days ago the president of the German trade unions said he was also wedded to the single currency, and business feels the same. Companies like Nestlé believe in it very strongly.

If industrialists are so much in favour of the idea, it must be because they believe they will thrive with it. In Germany, attempts to mobilise voters against the euro have been a flop.

Unemployment is now worse in Europe than it was when you became head of the Commission. That is surely a dismal record?

Joblessness is undeniably the overriding priority. If you have a gap between ordinary citizens and politicians in EU institutions, it is because people feel insecure. It affects their daily life. They cannot fathom how Europe, an entity of 370 million people, the world's biggest trading power, cannot make inroads into unemployment.

Unemployment is first and foremost the responsibility of each member state. But the confidence pact that I launched a year ago set out to co-ordinate the strategies of the individual countries, thereby setting up a multiplier effect, to enhance the national efforts.

But doesn't the agonised struggle to meet the tough single currency convergence criteria further lengthen the dole queues?

In my view, monetary union will lower interest rates, stimulate investment and create new jobs in the future. It is not an end to pursue on its own. We pursue it because of its economic benefits.

Some say that the social chapter is stifling job creation.

The social chapter has done nothing to erode competitiveness. After all, it is not an agenda in itself. It is only a legislative mechanism.

Many countries which have adopted it—including Denmark, Ireland, the Netherlands and Portugal—are doing very well on the job front.

The challenge is to increase the competitive edge of business through making the single market work, creating new markets for our companies.

We have millions of small and medium-sized businesses which are crucial. We need a stock market for these budding companies and so on.

Overall, good industrial relations improve competitiveness. Recently, we have raised our productivity more than the United States.

But we have to ask how we can capitalise on our assets even more. How can we compete with other parts of the world? How can we gain access to the information technologies? How can we match Southeast Asia's success.

Isn't it inevitable now that the new intergovernmental treaty (IGC) will contain a so-called "flexibility" clause which will allow states to veer off on their own chosen course?

We have to succeed in the IGC, otherwise I don't see how we can succeed in the enlargement process. And that is the biggest challenge that we face for the next century.

But bear in mind that in the past the European Union has always developed at different speeds. You see that today with monetary union and before that many derogations existed.

What I cannot accept is an `a la carte Europe, a pick 'n' mix Europe where people choose the single market, enlargement of the European Union to east, the single currency or whatever they fancy. That would be an unacceptable dilution.

What we are happy with is that several countries, a majority of countries that is, can go ahead faster in the integration process, so long as they accept the same destination as everyone else.

The final port must be the same for all the ships in the convoy. The target must be the same.

If there are different speeds that is OK. But these countries that are speeding ahead cannot be permitted to form an exclusive inner core. They must be open to newcomers. They must be a magnet to other members states which cannot follow quite yet.

Shouldn't states be allowed to choose their own destination?

I think that would be deviation from the European goal that we have. The European project has always been no ordinary project, but a political project, a project of peace.

You are saying that you can only be a member of the European Union if you agree that you want to go the ultimate destination agreed by the inner grouping?

Yes. You have to accept the targets. You have to accept the objectives. You have to accept the *acquis communautaive* [body of European Union law]. But you shouldn't imagine that we are building a superstate.

Europe would never create itself in the image of the United States of America. We have to take account of our national identities, our cultural identities and so on.

Somewhere between a partnership of nations and a United States of Europe?

Yes, quite right. It's not a federal state. Some elements of a decentralised organisation and intergovernmental function are combined.

It's a quite new model. Incidentally, I much prefer the term Community to Union. We can harmonise rules to enhance the single market. But we can never harmonise our own nations. That is unthinkable. We always have to take account of our national identity.

But haven't people in the Commission encouraged us to be Europeans first and put our nationality second?

No, no, no. Coming from a smaller state, I have always seen federalism as decentralisation. If we are creating a federal state, it's a federal state of nations.

That might sound like a contradiction in terms, but that's the evolution we have made. In our view, we always take into account our national and cultural identity—this is something that makes our EU so strong through its diversity, the histories and traditions. That's my view for Europe of the 21st century.

If a country is unhappy about the direction the European Union's vanguard states are taking would it do best to leave the Union?

That's not my view, of course. Each member state has special sensitivities and brings separate things to negotiations.

Though it can sometimes be maddening, that is a plus. We should not exaggerate our differences.

On 19 February the European Parliament is to demand that the Commission block payments from Brussels to United Kingdom farmers in protest over Britain's handling of the BSE crisis.

In this case we have to have solidarity with the British farmers. They are not to blame for the problem.

We have to be cautious in our own judgment. Perhaps our predecessors would have acted differently if they had the scientific information we have now.

But at the beginning, the crisis was related to animal health. We have to have some solidarity with British farmers.

Personally, I believe that we must offer support to overcome this crisis.

After all, that is the spirit of a community based on the principle of solidarity. The European Council in Florence has already dealt with this matter and agreed that this should be how we proceed. And that means the farmers are benefiting quite rightly from the Community's finances.

If you had to give a single positive message for the people of Europe for the new millennium, what would it be?

My message would simply be that we should build a very strong Europe that is both an international and economic power but can also play a part in world affairs.

We have the opportunity, especially, to achieve for the first time in 500 years—since before the time of the Renaissance—a reconciliation of the continent with itself.

We have achieved peace in the past decades. My family suffered badly in the war and I know what an achievement this peace is. The challenge now is the enlargement process, healing the scar of the Iron Curtain.

That should now be the motivation of our children, just as the reconciliation of France and Germany was for an earlier generation.

 Article Review Form at end of book.

WiseGuide Wrap-Up

Governments, like businesses, respond to pressures that constrain their choices. For example, understanding the ways in which international pressure can affect government choices was helpful to the international antiapartheid movement when it worked to introduce economic sanctions against South Africa. The sanctions, in turn, pressured the white-led South African government to allow black Africans to enjoy the same rights and privileges as white citizens. Constraining the policy choices of white South African leaders at the same time that black South Africans fighting for change saw their support from the Soviet Union diminishing helped begin negotiations to end human rights abuses in South Africa.

Women working for export firms in any country have heard their bosses claim that international competition forces them to cut costs to sell at competitively low prices; this translates into cuts in the women's salaries. To understand their own situations and how they might respond effectively to such claims, women first must understand the nature of the international market and their role in that market.

Often, Northern states and Northern citizens are accused of imposing rules on citizens from Southern countries. In Reading 54, Dunlop, Kyte, and MacDonald demonstrate that the large numbers of women from Southern states who participated (through their nongovernmental organization affiliation) in the United Nations' Beijing conference on women helped to determine the policy outcomes of the Beijing conference.

President Jacques Santer of the European Union argues in Reading 55 that regional constraints on European states' choices are important to integrating the policies of European states and to creating a political and economic block that benefits from economies of scale and standardization of parts. Integration also lowers the transaction costs of crossing European borders for business or pleasure, and makes it easier for people to do what they like to do in neighboring states. Santer argues that only through integration can Europe successfully compete in the world.

R.E.A.L. Sites

This list provides a print preview of typical **coursewise** R.E.A.L. sites. There are over 100 such sites at the **courselinks**™ site. The danger in printing URLs is that web sites can change overnight. As we went to press, these sites were functional using the URLs provided. If you come across one that isn't, please let us know via email to: webmaster@coursewise.com. Use your Passport to access the most current list of R.E.A.L. sites at the **courselinks**™ site.

Site name: The United Nations Fourth World Conference on Women

URL: http://www.undp.org.fwcf/

Why is it R.E.A.L.? This site lists the concerns of women around the world. It offers regional documents on concerns of women from Asia and the Pacific, Latin America, Africa, Europe, and Arab countries.

Key topics: women's equality, women's property rights

Site name: Ben and Jerry's Ice Cream

URL: http://www.BenJerry.com

Why is it R.E.A.L.? The Ben and Jerry Ice Cream Company recognizes that international pressures restrict states' choices and also help citizens in foreign countries who want outside forces to constrain the policy choices of their governments so that those governments adopt policies that benefit all their citizens. This site includes information about international boycotts and pressure campaigns on governments and large companies to preserve the environment and to observe international human rights standards.

Key topics: rain forest, ice cream

section 7

Key Points

- Environmental tourism may provide jobs, but it also damages the environment and citizens' health and long-term well being.

- Many domestic pressure groups have alternative views on how their country should use its natural resources and which policies their politicians should support.

- Environmental problems are not just technical problems that require scientific solutions; they also require political choices—choices in which some groups will win and others will lose.

? Questions ?

1. If tourism results in money and jobs, why do some citizens oppose expanding the tourist sectors in their countries?

2. According to Vandermeer and Perfecto in Reading 57, what three modes of production are creating deforestation in Central America?

3. Why is it important to study the comparative politics of environmentalism?

Environment and Development

The tradeoffs between damaging the environment and providing jobs and affordable consumer goods are frequently debated. In Reading 56 on tourism in Indonesia, Cohen highlights some of the important arguments in this debate. In Reading 57, Vandermeer and Perfecto analyze how national governments in late industrializing countries in Latin America have tried to manage the use of their rain forests and look at the pressures those governments face from interest groups who want access to the rain forests to advance their own, and their nation's, economic goals.

Third World leaders argue that their states should be compensated for any losses they suffer from not exploiting their natural resources, as global environmentalists request of them. These leaders note that the Northern states exploited their natural resources without external interference throughout the years of Northern industrialization. Yet now, the Northern states expect Southern states (late industrializers) to forgo the important economic gains and security derived from the mining, agriculture, and animal herding that could be undertaken within their states. Additionally, economic activities in rural or undeveloped areas also provide a steam valve for Third World urban overpopulation by offering the nonworking poor of the urban areas lucrative economic employment in return for migration to newly opened national territories.

Global environmentalists counter that if Third World states destroy the last remaining habitats of natural life on the planet, the human species will not likely sustain itself on planet earth. The earth's fragile ecosystem is already so disturbed that world governments must take swift international action if we are not to destroy ourselves. International action is required to prevent additional degradation of Third World state environments and also to undo the damage that Northern industrial states have caused. Undoing the North's environmental degradation will incur both financial and opportunity costs for Northern citizens and states, just as effectively managing conservation efforts in the South bears a cost.

In Reading 57, Vandermeer and Perfecto argue that technical solutions and programs to protect the earth's ecosystem cannot take the place of the necessary political solutions that must be negotiated if we are to successfully protect our internationally fragile environment.

Tourism
Think and think again

Margot Cohen

In Parangtritis, central Java

When in doubt, meditate. That's the practice on Parangtritis beach, where Javanese believers regularly commune with Nyai Roro Kidul, the mystical goddess of the South Seas. So it seemed only natural to seek divine guidance recently on a controversial 100-billion-rupiah ($41.2 million) Parangtritis tourism project, spearheaded by the Jakarta-based firm PT Awani Modern Indonesia.

Apparently, however, even the spirits could not reach consensus over the proposed luxury resort, golf course and recreation area, to be located 27 kilometres from the city of Jogjakarta. After a night filled with incense and solemn incantation, a team of mystics announced the Nyai Roro Kidul had given the project a green light. Sure enough, another team of mystics had a very different revelation: the spirit of an ancient Javanese king warned that the project could trigger catastrophe.

It took the charisma of the reigning Sultan of Jogjakarta, Hamengku Buwono X, to settle the matter—at least temporarily. Citing a host of objections to the project on cultural, environmental and economic grounds, the sultan made it clear in March that the proposed resort would have to be relocated. "The Jogjakarta palace does not need big investors who think only of their own best interests," explains palace Executive Secretary Joyokusumo, a Javanese aristocrat who is the sultan's younger brother. "What we need are investors who show understanding and wish to promote the economic development of the people, even if their investment is small scale."

This is no small thing in the history of Indonesia's tourism development. Major tourism projects are usually pushed forward, no matter how many complaints are lodged over the anticipated impact on local culture and environmental resources. In the enthusiasm to create new jobs and boost tax revenues, local officials across the archipelago often show little patience for community concerns.

The fate of the Parangtritis project may reflect a growing sensitivity towards sustainable development. A March report from the Department of Tourism, Post and Telecommunications called for "an increase in tourism with an environmental outlook, and environmental preservation with a tourism outlook." Complaints that the Parangtritis resort could damage unique 20-metre-high sand dunes were taken seriously by central government officials, who support the sultan's stance. "Our concept of tourism is not only based on economics, but also social, cultural and environmental factors," maintains Syamsul Lussa, public-relations officer for the director general of tourism.

The economic factors in the Parangtritis case are common to many other proposed projects throughout Indonesia. The resort was slated to occupy 200 hectares of government land. Some of that land is currently occupied by small vendors and other poorly educated Indonesians who would have difficulty landing jobs in a posh resort.

And like many other places in a country where land and religion are closely linked, Parangtritis boasts a special cultural tradition. Just 700 metres from the resort's proposed boundary lies Parangkusumo, a complex of open-air pavilions and elaborate fences guarding the holy spot where Nyai Roro Kidul is believed to have met with the first ruler of the Mataram kingdom.

On Thursday evenings, the pavilions overflow with supplicants. Convinced that their dreams will produce revelations, some of them bed down on cardboard for the night amid thermoses and radios playing soft tunes on Indonesian traditional instruments. Others cast flower petals and jewellery into the sea, in thanks to the goddess. The palace also holds special rituals here, attracting Javanese from miles around.

Some feared that the resort would eventually include a discotheque, attracting the wrong kind of crowds. "If the atmosphere becomes too raucous, this place will no longer be sacred," declared Ngabehi Sukarso Rejo, one of 15 keepers of the keys to Parangkusumo. In devoted service to the palace, he has laboured here since 1957 for the less-than-princely sum of 5,000 rupiah a month. He is confident that the sultan's wishes to relocate the project will be respected. "The sultan is in control here, not the government," he says firmly.

Indeed, some observers are convinced that royal power is far more important a factor in this case than any sudden official enlightenment on environmental issues—which suggests that Parangtritis may prove the exception rather than a precedent. In a country where most regional royalty has been rendered politically feeble and economically weak, Hamengku Buwono X still enjoys an enormous amount of authority and popular support.

This may partly stem from the fact that President Suharto and many other top figures in the government and the military hail from central Java, and were reared in the aura of the palace. The sultan's leadership in the Parangtritis

case has buttressed the palace's reputation for protecting its constituency.

Lately, the Indonesian government has made renewed efforts to milk royal splendour for tourism dollars. In July, for example, a palace festival will be held in the West Java city of Cirebon, drawing elaborately costumed royals from around the country. The lavish spectacle, however, will hardly confer clout in shaping tourism policies.

The weakness of the system is evident. More than a year-and-a-half ago, the sultan made his disapproval clear to the Bantul regent, Sri Roso Sudarmo. But the regent remained an enthusiastic proponent of the Parangtritis resort, and even encouraged PT Awani Modern Indonesia to fund a 350-million-rupiah market for the community living 10 kilometres away from the proposed site. It remains unclear whether this represented partial payment for the 50-year lease of government land, or was simply a show of good will on the part of the company. The episode does, however, broadcast a warning to other potential investors that preliminary pay-offs may not guarantee a project's completion.

For some observers, the Parangtritis case also illustrates the perils of decentralization without adequate supervision by the national government. "We hope that decentralization will not mean distributing the arrogance of power to the countryside," says Joyokusumo.

For the moment, PT Awani Modern Indonesia prefers to remain silent. "Currently we are still in discussions with the authorities and would not...wish to make any comments or forecasts until the situation has been clarified," wrote general manager

Lucia Engelina, in response to a REVIEW query.

Meanwhile, the small vendors on Parangtritis beach are struggling to reap their own profits. Swimming is forbidden, due to the perilous undertow, but those anxious for sport can hop on a horse and cantor across the sand. Brightly painted horse buggies are available for the less adventurous. It's a relaxed, humble scene, with nary a fancy hotel in sight.

That might explain the scarcity of foreign tourists sunning themselves immodestly. A 1996 report by the local tourism authorities in Jogjakarta noted that only 3% of the city's 351,542 foreign visitors last year opted for an excursion to Parangtritis.

According to Tazbir, a government official involved in tourism marketing, the availability of a beach resort would allow Jogjakarta to increase tourists' average length of stay, which is currently only 1.7 days. Many visitors simply rush over to the famed Borobudur and Prambanan temples, and then rush off again, without sampling the rest of the city's incredibly rich cultural fare.

The government says that 5,034,472 tourists visited Indonesia last year, a 16.4% gain over the 1995 figure. Those numbers should be taken with a grain of salt, since the category of "tourist" includes businessmen with tourist visas on a quick trip to Jakarta. But whatever the true volume of tourists, Jogjakarta wants more of them—and a greater share of the $6.1 billion in foreign exchange they bring in.

Local tourism officials and hotel managers have good reason to be optimistic. A new international airport was opened in April in the neighbouring city of Solo, and a new toll road will be built soon to whisk visitors to Jogjakarta. Direct air links are planned with Medan in North Sumatra and the island of Batam, two additional international gateways. Tour operators from Japan and the United States have been invited recently for grand tours of Jogjakarta, and the city is being pitched abroad as a lively convention site.

All of these initiatives should help boost the current average 48% hotel-occupancy rate, partially the result of overexpansion in connection with "Visit Indonesia Decade." If not, competition looks to become even fiercer. A Hyatt, a Novotel and an Ibis hotel are planning Jogjakarta openings this year.

Article Review Form at end of book.

R E A D I N G   5 7

Rain Forest Conservation

The direct or indirect approach?

**John Vandermeer
and Ivette Perfecto**

In 1990 when World Resources reported on deforestation rates for most countries in the world, some new and surprising data became available to environmentalists. In its rush to free its terrain of trees, Costa Rica claimed the dubious prize for First Place. For almost a decade Costa Rica, partly because of its proximity to revolutionary Nicaragua, had received the bountiful largesse of the Reagan administration. Development aid for Costa Rica was enormous, part of the same overall strategy that brought war to Nicaragua.[1] Concomitant with this influx of U.S. dollars was a conservation movement, strongly influenced by North Americans, and with few parallels in the Third World. Combine this conservation movement with an enormous amount of money and one would expect spectacular results. Indeed Costa Rica's conservation policies suggest exactly that: approximately 27% of its national territory lies under some sort of protected status; it has arguably the most impressive national park system in the Third World (12% of its total land area[2]); and boasts some of the most progressive forestry laws in the world.[3]

Conservation policies in Costa Rica were based on the assumption that rain forest destruction could be curbed by 1) buying up and protecting large tracts of land; 2) passing legislation; 3) securing large sums of project money from foreigners; and 4) mounting a massive public relations campaign. Alas, all this was done with little concern about the impact of some crucial socioeconomic factors, such as one of the most uneven land distribution patterns in Central America.[4] The cherished belief was that these policies were working. But the

John Vandermeer and Ivette Perfecto, "Rain Forest Conservation, the Direct or Indirect Approach" in BREAKFAST FOR BIODIVERSITY: THE TRUTH ABOUT RAIN FOREST DESTRUCTION (Oakland, CA: Institute for Food and Development, 1995), pp. 105-123. Reprinted by permission.

World Resources figures reported in the summer of 1990 showed otherwise. Despite Costa Rica's policies, during the 1980's their forests came down at an alarming rate of 7.6% per annum.[5] Such destruction certainly represents a reality check for all rain forest preservation advocates. Not only was deforestation higher than anyone had anticipated, it was the highest in the world!

Preserving the world's rain forest has become *de rigueur* in the developed world. While it has been difficult to ignore such readily available facts as the militant socialist agenda advocated by Chico Méndez,[6] the western rain forest conservation movement has nevertheless remained largely a bourgeois business. While we should perhaps have been asking questions about the Indonesian military government and its transmigration program to Kalimantan, or the Guatemala military's reported use of herbicides to clear vegetation in areas where guerrillas were suspected to be hiding, or Nicaragua's progressive land reform program, Costa Rica, for the insiders in the rain forest preservation movement, represented a far cleaner story. In Costa Rica, no military intervention, no socialism, no revolution, no anti-U.S. sentiment clouded the picture. Bird watching and nature appreciation tours were touted in the travel sections of all major U.S. papers. In addition, Costa Rican authorities were amenable to advocating all the goals and programs of the mainstream rain forest conservation movement. Consequently the past twenty years have seen the truly remarkable growth of a conservation program, but one whose aims and advocacies have remained almost totally isolated from some major socio-political questions

plaguing Costa Rica. And this isolation is precisely the problem.

There has been, we believe, a general failure to address the underlying causes of rain forest destruction. Our purpose—hopefully obvious by now—in writing this book, is to note and acknowledge those root causes. We are well aware that our analysis is at odds with much of the international community that seeks to preserve rain forests. We do not despair at this incongruity. The problem of rain forest destruction is far too important to leave to misguided proposals and ineffective solutions.[7] It is an unfortunate truth that "empire building," careerism, and even economic self-interest, sometimes drive conservation programs, and foster "analyses" which systematically exclude a search for the real root causes. Perhaps this is because these root causes create conditions in other spheres of life, which the conservationists would not like to see challenged. Perhaps the same political arrangements, which provide conservationists with the privilege to ponder such weighty questions as, for example, biodiversity, also create the impoverishment that forces peasants to cut down rain forests. If so, it would be prudent to keep those political arrangements out of the spotlight—for the mainstream conservationists, that is. But we, as the Lorax,[8] seek to speak for the forest. For that reason we intend to focus the spotlight on exactly those underlying causes.

In this chapter we draw attention to these political issues in the hopes of challenging what seems to have become a myopic and elitist view of rain forest destruction—a view often, unfortunately, tailored more to careers in conservation biology and the maintenance of good relations

with potential funders, than to a sincere desire to stop the progressive loss of the world's rain forests. We first revisit the *Sarapiquí* region of Costa Rica as described in Chapter 1,* and detail some of the complexities that exist there. We then compare that site with a similar one in Nicaragua, elaborating patterns that existed there mainly during the 1980's. Our intent is to demonstrate first, that the main stream rain forest preservationist view of the issue is hopelessly superficial, and second, that an analysis of the entire matrix of socio-political-ecological forces is essential to understanding what in fact causes, in these cases, the destruction of rain forests.

The *Sarapiquí* Revisited

This book began with the example of the banana expansion in the *Sarapiquí* region of Costa Rica. It is fitting now that we return to that example (refer to the map in figure 1.2).* As anticipated, the situation is deteriorating rapidly. The current players are an international tourism company, a well-connected conservation research organization, two local political groups, several absentee landlords, and some fruit companies (figure 7.1).

The first local political group is a large, highly organized group of homesteaders in a community they call *El Progreso*. Their story began some fifteen years ago when a North American who owned a very large ranch in the area, was indicted on drug trafficking charges.[9] He fled the country. According to Costa Rican law, an absentee landlord can have his land expropriated if Costa Rican nationals establish a homestead thereon, which is exactly what

*Does not appear in this publication.

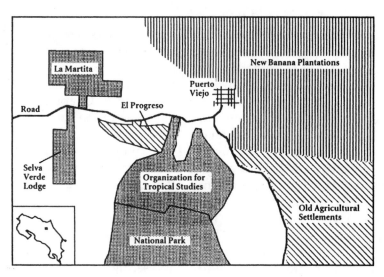

Figure 7.1 Sketch map of the region surrounding the town of Puerto Viejo in the *Sarapiquí* county of northern Costa Rica (inset shows location of area of detail), showing approximate locations of sites mentioned in text.

happened. A Costa Rican couple who had worked for the North American, established themselves as homesteaders and petitioned the appropriate government agency for title to the land. Meanwhile the North American got wind of what was happening and solicited the aid of a lawyer friend in Costa Rica. The lawyer apparently filed papers aimed at incorporating the ranch into a group of farms he already owned. At the same time the Costa Rican couple renamed the farm *Gerika*.

This the farm, now known as *Gerika*, came to have two or three owners: the indicted North American who left the country, his lawyer friend, and the Costa Rican couple. Then in August of 1993 tragedy struck the Costa Rican couple. The wife murdered the husband and then killed herself. In such circumstances Costa Rican law and tradition says that if there is a known long-term caretaker of the farm, ownership passes on to him or her. In this case a woman had been the caretaker, and she quickly laid claim

to the farm. But there is another Costa Rican law that allows for homesteaders to occupy unused land. With the bizarre death of the Costa Rican couple, whom most locals had assumed were the owners, homesteaders saw the opportunity to seize what had been for quite some time unused land. Only weeks after the couple had passed away, homesteaders invaded part of *Gerika*, calling their new community *El Progreso*.

The invasion was not without violence, and the combination of angry homesteaders, private guards, and Costa Rican security forces produced some ugly incidents, including one death.[10] But a year after the establishment of the homesteading site, *El Progreso* was home to 350 families who had obtained legal "right to possession," the first step towards getting official title to the land under the Costa Rican homesteading act.

Several interesting facts highlight the *El Progreso* affair. First, some unknown number of the homesteading families are

Nicaraguan (local estimates range from "not many" to "almost all"), most having been attracted to the area by the promise of employment in local banana companies. Second, the back border of the farmable land claimed by the homesteaders abuts directly on property claimed by the Organization for Tropical Studies, one of the major conservation players in the area. Third, many in *El Progreso* are currently employed by the banana companies, which send busses to the community each morning to pick them up, and many others are ex-employees of the banana companies. Finally, evidently the real estate they have occupied is fairly rotten. While the members of the community are optimistic about their dreamed-of farms, we doubt much will come of their agricultural activities. The soils seem to be old alluvium, but are probably very acid and lacking in nutrients.

The second major local political group is the Sarapiquí Association for Forests and Wildlife. Their goal is to "promote the conservation and sustainable development of the natural and human resources in the county of *Sarapiquí*."[11] The association was formed by local residents with the help of a non-governmental organization that provides legal assistance to local grass-roots groups seeking to develop conservation projects.[12] The Sarapiquí Association's immediate objective is to purchase a piece of land called *La Martita*, whose Colombian owner has applied for a logging permit from the government. As the association points out, several biological reserves and stands of old-growth forest exist in the *Sarapiquí*, but all are owned by foreigners. With the development of the ecotourism industry, local residents have garnered some benefit as employees of ecotourism entrepreneurs, but there seems to be no example of a local resident who is owner of a successful ecotourism establishment. The goal of the Sarapiquí Association is to use *La Martita* as a community biological preserve where locals can begin developing their own ecotourism operations (see figure 7.1).

Much of the *Sarapiquí* is still owned by absentee landlords, both Costa Rican and foreign. Excluding the banana companies, the main activity on these lands is cattle ranching, although many still contain substantial tracts of rain forest. Cattle produce very poorly in the region, and it has been suggested that the only reason they are kept on the land is to claim that the land is in "use" so it is not subject to invasion by homesteaders. *La Martita* is one such operation. The part of the property that connects with the main road is in cattle pasture and boasts a sign in front that reads "Warning, vicious dogs." The back of the property, the forested part, is not accessible from the main road, so it has not yet been a target of homesteaders. That is likely to change if the current owner sells the timber on the land and a logging company constructs logging roads into the area. It is not out of the question to envision another group of ex-banana workers establishing a homesteading community here, if the opportunity arises. If the association is successful in purchasing the land and preserving the forest, such an invasion is far less likely.

The international tourism company is Holbrook Travel Inc., and they own the Selva Verde Lodge (see figure 7.1). Styled after the highly successful nature tourism industry of Kenya, this lodge has up-scale facilities that shield the tourists from the local people, except for those who work as cooks, maids, or maintenance workers. This impressive facility includes the largest privately-owned nature reserve in the area, and is one of the largest employers in the local ecotourism business. Local people most frequently cite the Selva Verde Lodge when they speak about foreign ownership of the local ecotourism business.

The other large ecotourism operation is the Organization for Tropical Studies, OTS, a consortium of universities in the U.S. and Latin America, with some fifty members. Its goals are research and education in tropical biology, and it is one of the most famous organizations of its kind in the world. Because OTS attracts rich foreign ecotourists and is owned mainly by non-Costa Ricans, the organization has come to be viewed by many local people as similar to Selva Verde. Such a perception is natural.

Finally, and still the predominant feature of the area, are the banana companies, dominated by the multinationals Chiquita, Dole, and Geest. As we predicted in Chapter 1, the expansive phase of their operation has ceased, and many workers have been laid off. These workers and their families are now living in homesteading communities like *El Progreso,* homesteading individually in various corners of the landscape, seeking employment wherever they can get it (not much in the area other than the banana plantations), and increasingly migrating to San Jose, the capital. Most recently the situation of the workers has gotten so bad that the all but defunct banana unions have reappeared on the scene, and in May 1994 a short strike against the Geest plantations shocked the country.

This then is the current landscape. Ecotourism and international conservation groups rapidly losing credibility among the local population; banana companies attracting workers to the region and dumping them onto the landscape; absentee ranchers hiring armed thugs to protect their land from homesteaders; international tourists who can spot the rarest of birds through their binoculars yet cannot see the desperate and hungry people just across the road; 350 hopeful and optimistic families in a new community with a utopian plan to turn acid soils into productive agriculture; and a weak, largely-ignored local conservation group trying to get something for Costa Ricans out of ecotourism.

The current landscape would seem to leave little reason for optimism. The dilemma, we believe, is that analysis of the problem has been made in a fragmented fashion by the various interest groups. Local conservationists are concerned with preserving whatever forest remains and see the homesteaders as conniving ne'er-do-wells. Some conservationists even attribute rain forest destruction to overpopulation. Foreign ecotourism companies pay lip service to conservation, but cease even that when their profits are threatened. Homesteaders see large tracts of land unused by foreigner owners and view their own landless situation as unfair. Gaining property title to a piece of logged-over forest seems logical and fair to them. The central government continues its policy of promoting the expansion of bananas, even while promoting conservation programs in other areas of the country. And lastly, the banana companies see the conservationists as romantic idealists who simply do not understand the nature of business, which is to make profits; nor the need of the country, which is to generate revenues to pay off their international debt.

If, however, the problem is viewed in all of its complexity, and a plan devised that takes all parties into consideration, there is much that can be done. We envision, tentatively, a three-part program. First, local people need jobs. We regard the question of food security as the underlying basis of any sound conservation policy. To this end, the labor practices of the banana companies must be regulated. No longer should they be allowed to hire workers for eighty-nine days and then fire them, because the companies become liable for various social security benefits after ninety days. Working conditions must be improved, and above all job security must be instituted. While there is little that can be done about the banana plantations already in existence, a moratorium should be immediately announced concerning the further expansion of such production technology.

Second, there are clearly not enough jobs in the banana industry to employ everyone in the region. It should be noted that during the banana expansion of the early 1990's, the banana companies asserted there were not enough workers in the region, and in coordination with the Costa Rican government, brought in Nicaraguan workers. Rumors of available jobs attracted people from all over Costa Rica and Nicaragua, dramatically increasing the region's population. The only obvious beneficiary of this chaotic migration process has been the banana companies, which now enjoy a surplus of workers.

The reality remains that not everyone will get a job in the banana industry. Existing homesteader communities, beginning with *El Progreso*, need technical aid and bank credit to make their farming operations as viable as possible. It should be noted that viability may not, in fact, be technically feasible. Despite twenty-five years of active biological inquiry in the area, only a tiny fraction of that research is even theoretically relevant to finding solutions to the many problems faced by farmers in the region. Indeed, if the current agricultural areas of *El Progreso* turn out to be difficult to farm on a continuous basis, *El Progreso's* farmers may expand their agricultural activities into the forested areas that border their farms. This includes some of the forested land claimed by the National Park, the Organization for Tropical Studies, and the Selva Verde Lodge. It would seem that making *El Progreso's* agriculture successful should be an obvious priority, even for the ecotourism ventures.

Third, local people must directly benefit from the increase in ecotourism in the region, not just as janitors, cooks, and badly paid tour guides, but as entrepreneurs and owners of lodges and reserves. This probably means support for the Sarapiquí Association for Forests and Wildlife, especially with their current efforts to purchase *La Martita* and turn it into a community-owned forest reserve. Part of this general goal can be easily coupled with the agricultural imperatives for the region. Ecotourists are often interested in seeing alternatives to destructive agriculture and the people of *El Progreso* already have an impressive conservation ethic. Several homesteaders independently offered the opinion that deforestation was the country's biggest problem right now, and that ecotourism should be promoted. They see potential jobs for themselves in ecotourism. And, if they begin an experimental program of sustainable agriculture/agroforestry, their land might produce more than just corn and beans, it might produce tourist dollars.

What chance does this three-part program have for success? Given the constraints of the real world, probably very close to zero. But each component is worth pursuing. The alternative, foreign conservation organizations and ecotourism companies dominating all the forested land, banana companies dominating the remainder and hiring and firing workers chaotically, will certainly not work in the long run. Poor people need to feed themselves and their families. They need steady jobs or access to good agricultural land and technology. If they have no job and no hope of getting one, if they are excluded from the promise of the bright future they can see the foreigners already have, if their crops continue to fail on the small piece of rotten land they have grudgingly been allocated, they will do whatever they deem necessary to survive. Even if that means cutting and burning primary forest on preserved land.

By Contrast, the RAAS of Nicaragua[13]

The story in Nicaragua is quite different from Costa Rica, although it also illustrates features of the general pattern we have described. The Atlantic coast of Nicaragua contains the largest remaining tract of lowland rain forest in Central America,[14] with significant closed-canopy forest, or at least patches of it, extending from the border of Honduras all the way south to the border of Costa Rica (see map in figure 1.2).* There are, however, several foci of agricultural expansion. For the past few decades the largest of these agricultural frontiers has diffused eastward toward the area surrounding Bluefields on the Atlantic coast. Since 1990, the rate of expansion has increased dramatically, perhaps aided by the devastating effects of the hurricane of 1988 and the elections of 1989. The agricultural frontier has effectively cut the Atlantic coast rain forest into a northern and southern section, and is now expanding northward and southward (see figure 1.2).* If this pattern continues we can expect the destruction of all but small islands of protected forest, with little potential for stable economic activity for the local population.

The majority of the upland area surrounding Bluefields (about 400,000 hectares) was originally covered with lowland tropical rain forest, almost all of which was severely damaged in 1988 by Hurricane Joan. The forest is now in various stages of ecological succession. Despite the severe destruction, our studies indicate that natural resprouting and direct regeneration have resulted in a habitat well on the way to mending itself. Small peasant farms dot the area and continue expansion into formerly forested land. A large sugar plantation is located north of Bluefields, and an old extensive cattle operation covers an upland area known as *Loma de Mico*. For the past decade the sugar operation has rarely been profitable, and the cattle operation was virtually abandoned in the mid 1980's. Finally, a large African oil-palm plantation was planted in the mid 1980's and is producing at approximately 25% productive capacity.

The human cultural history of the Atlantic coastal area is extremely complex. The bulk of the population is about evenly divided between African Americans brought from Jamaica as slave laborers in the 1800's, and Mestizos who migrated from the Pacific coast during the past century. Additionally, three small Native American groups inhabit the area: the Rama; the Sumos who have small communities north of Bluefields; and the Miskitos, most of whom live in the North Atlantic zone, with small numbers in the South Atlantic zone, living in either small villages or as individuals among the other cultural groups. Another ethnic group, the Garifuna, originally derives from escaped African slaves. While all groups maintain strong cultural identities, they are also united in a coast culture and regard themselves as *costeños* (coast people).

The political panorama is as complex as the cultural. The well-known friction between the Sandinista party and the UNO (United Nicaraguan Opposition) is complicated by the presence of YATAMA (another political party representing mainly the Miskitos), and the entire political framework is permeated with the question of autonomy. Historically isolated from the Nicaraguan mainstream, the Atlantic coastal region has always been fiercely independent in politics and economics. In 1989 the first autonomous administration was elected, and—at least on paper—the RAAS (South Autonomous Atlantic Region) is supposed to be independent of the central government administration. This formal independence extends to decisions on all natural resources, including rain forests.

The RAAS encompasses the southern half of the Atlantic coast of Nicaragua (see map in figure 1.2).* Economically, it is something of a disaster. While Nicaragua is second only to Haiti in poverty in this hemisphere,[15] the Atlantic Coast is the most underdeveloped region of Nicaragua. Local government officials claim an unemployment rate of over 90% in Bluefields, and a short visit to the area convinces even a casual observer that this is indeed the poorest region of Central America.

During the Somoza years (1930–1979) the area was relatively isolated, and while Nicaragua as a whole has been reported to have experienced massive deforestation during that time, little evidence exists for such deforestation in the RAAS in particular. During those decades, the agricultural frontier slowly expanded towards Bluefields, the large sugar plantation and cattle operation opened up, and timber extraction, primarily by North American companies, was more-or-less continuous. Though it is not known for certain, it is probable that, as elaborated above, the local logging operations were followed by peasant agriculture.

Following the Sandinista Revolution of 1979, two major forces relevant to tropical forests came into being. First, the contra

*Does not appear in this publication.

*Does not appear in this publication.

war waged by the Reagan administration made it especially difficult to engage in large forestry operations. The contra war also made it difficult, in areas constantly threatened by fighting, for peasants to homestead or create new agricultural plots. However, casual interviews with people in Bluefields do not suggest that large numbers of landless peasants were chomping at the bit waiting for the war to end so they could carve out a homestead from the remaining forest. To the contrary, the landless peasantry seems to have largely disappeared due to the second relevant force: the Sandinista administration's agrarian reform program. The rate of deforestation in the region was relatively low during the eighties.[16]

The elections of 1989 changed everything. The progressive agrarian reform of the Sandinistas was reversed, and once again landless peasants were forced to seek new homesteads, frequently after having been forcibly removed from land acquired under the Sandinista reforms. As part of a deal with the new government, so-called "poles of development" formed new bases of agricultural expansion. Former contra rebels were given forested land to distribute among their "soldiers" and their families to establish agricultural communities. A typical pattern consists of two or three years of cultivation after cutting a piece of forest, followed by a ten-year fallow period, followed by a single year of cultivation, and a strong desire to move on in hopes of a better piece of real estate under the next parcel of forest.

The relative stability the Sandinista agrarian reforms provided now seems to have been destroyed. We have been traveling in this area since 1982, and the changes since 1989 have been frightening. Before the 1989 elections there was a great deal of debate on questions like: use of the natural resources of the area; the role of the state in regulating chain saws; how the state logging company (the only logging company operating) should be responsible to local communities; and how agrarian reform must extend into the technical sphere to provide peasants an alternative to burning for land preparation. By 1993, the constant drone of chain saws could be heard anywhere there was forest. Three lumber companies were actively engaged in cutting trees (openly flaunting a ban on cutting), and central government figures were accepting bribes for allowing logging concessions.[17] Fires were everywhere as landless peasants burned yet another piece of forest, and former contra bands, apparently frustrated with their inability to produce anything on the poor soils of the region, engaged in robbing passing boats and fighting with one another.

In addition, the economic situation has deteriorated significantly. The peasantry, which in the past could hope that the government would help in times of crisis (e.g. if the crops failed there was reasonable expectation that the government would supply the community with basic grains), has become despondent and is often forced to do anything possible to eke out a living, usually with little success. A typical story was related to us by the residents of a peasant community on the Patchy River, north of Bluefields. The community, a group of ex-contra rebels, had been resettled in the area under the leadership of their former commander, whose *nom de guerre* was Ranger. Ranger contracted with outside contractors to purchase the mahogany and rosewood from the forest behind their small settlement. The community had neither beasts of burden, nor tractors, so Ranger paid the peasants the equivalent of $3.50 per trunk (which would retail for at least $1000 on the world market), to haul them down to the river dock by hand. In the end, to add insult to injury, Ranger disappeared with the logs and didn't even pay his men the $3.50 per trunk he had promised.

The Lessons of the Costa Rica/Nicaragua Comparison

That the rain forests of Central America are being destroyed is a point on which there is no debate. The causes of their destruction are considerably more debatable. Many biologically-oriented analysts tend to tie the destruction to the simple metaphor of the rain forest as a commons, and overpopulation the driving force. This might lead to the (erroneous) conclusion, for example, that the development of effective birth-control programs in the *Sarapiquí* would stop small farmers from seeking farms in the area. The reality is different. Since workers are actively recruited into the area by the banana companies, condoms are unlikely to solve the problem of rain forest destruction. Indeed, as far as the banana producers are concerned the area remains underpopulated.

The alternative explanation, more complicated and nuanced than overpopulation, has been presented above and in Chapter 1.* It takes its framework from a

---

*Does not appear in this publication.

variety of classic ideas, and sees rain forest destruction as the consequence of the interaction among several forces operating within a particular world system. Three modes of production (forestry, peasant agriculture, and modern agriculture), interact with two socioeconomic groups (export agriculture bourgeoisie, and rural peasant or proletariat) in the context of a national and international political structure in an ecological matrix. It is impossible to understand deforestation if one remains at only one or another of these levels, since the cause is located in the overall structure.

A comparison between Nicaragua and Costa Rica during the early 1980's is illuminating. Both countries had significant areas of rain forest remaining, but Costa Rica lost rain forest areas at an extremely rapid rate during the 1980's, while the rate of deforestation in Nicaragua was much lower.

Nicaragua was distinct from the other Central American countries during the 1980's. For one thing, the contra war mitigated against significant lumber operations, hence extensive access roads were not built. The war, while sometimes intense in places along the northern border, was a more low-intensity conflict where the rain forests were concentrated on the Atlantic coast. Small bands of counterrevolutionaries were scattered throughout the Atlantic lowlands, especially in heavily-forested areas. Thus the region was not likely to be subjected to intense commercial logging, or even small peasant clearings during the war.

However, there was an even more important factor. The massive agrarian reform program initiated after the 1979 revolution all but eliminated land-hungry peas-

ants in Nicaragua. In 1978 36% of the land was in farms larger than 850 acres. By 1985 that fraction had dwindled to 11%. In 1978 there were no production cooperatives. By 1985, 9% of the land and 50,000 families were integrated into the cooperative sector. By 1985, over 127,000 families had received title to their own land.[18] This was an agrarian reform without precedent in the history of Latin America.

Costa Rica's agrarian reform program was entirely different, bearing the recognizable fingerprint of similar programs in El Sálvador, and—years before that—in Vietnam. Organized by the state agency IDA (Instituto de Desarrollo Agrario), landless peasants were located on or near undeveloped areas, only occasionally on the lands of large landowners. Expropriation of large inefficient enterprises was totally absent from the system, and land titles were given with twenty- or thirty-year mortgages, forcing farmers into cash-crop production. Traditional farmers who sought a plot of land, if they got anything at all, acquired a piece of marginal, undeveloped land and, for the first time in their lives, a bank debt.

Interviews with small farmers in Nicaragua and Costa Rica reflected the basic differences in agrarian reform programs. Costa Ricans emphasized the land tenure issue, voiced disquietude over their lack of land title, or their inability to pay recently acquired mortgages (many were quite surprised at their new debt), and focussed their economic concerns on the attainment of land security. Nicaraguans were the opposite, at least before the 1989 elections. While they had many legitimate gripes, lack of land was not one of them, and rarely did a

Nicaraguan small farmer talk about needing a piece of land to call his own. The consequences with regard to pressure on rain forests are obvious.

With this model of land tenure in Nicaragua, one could have predicted that the pattern, so common in Costa Rica, of land-hungry peasants following logging roads into the forest, would not be a problem in Nicaragua. Recent electoral changes in Nicaragua have put this model to the test, since the new government made the rollback of much of the agrarian reform program part of its electoral platform. As expected, and as detailed above, the new class of landless peasants is busy following new logging roads, and clearing forests in southeastern Nicaragua, conforming quite well with our overall interpretation.

One point of comparison outside of Central America is worth making. The Caribbean nations of Puerto Rico and Cuba are the only tropical countries in the world to have experienced an increase in the area covered by forest in the past few decades,[19] though for different reasons. Because of the development program imposed by the colonial administration in the 1940's, Puerto Rico can hardly be categorized as an agrarian economy; and in view of its peculiar articulation with the United States (not of its own accord), Puerto Rico has become an industrial colony. In a grotesque parody of real development, Puerto Ricans have been converted into classical proletarians by massive federal money transfers. Consequently, to speak of a rural peasantry in Puerto Rico is anachronistic, and any notion of a movement of landless peasants into forested lands is ludicrous. Industrial development—however artificial and imposed from afar without the democratic participation of the Puerto Rican people themselves—has transformed the class structure of Puerto Rican society to such an extent that the basic structure, which we assert causes deforestation, simply no longer exists there.

Cuba's development has been along a different line than Puerto Rico's, emphasizing socialist goals. The successes and failures of this line of development are obviously hot topics for debate, but a single feature of Cuban developmental strategy is relevant to the present discussion. Cuban peasants are not land-hungry. Because of the basic philosophical commitment to a secure economic environment for all members of society, the Cuban peasantry has either been absorbed into the urban sector, or has received land security on state farms, cooperatives, or private farms. Cuba simply has no landless peasants. It is worth noting the obvious at this point. The probability that either the Cuban socialist solution, or the Puerto Rican federal-subsidy solution will occur in Nicaragua, Costa Rica, or in any other tropical country, is vanishingly small. So what might we realistically expect in Central America? Indeed prospects for the future do not seem sanguine. If general world trends continue, and especially if the relationship between the developed and underdeveloped worlds evolves along the lines anticipated by the so-called "New World Order," we can only expect more of the same. The class conflicts that raged in Guatemala, El Salvador, and Nicaragua during the past twenty years are not likely to subside, although their specific form will change. With the threat of U.S. military adven-

ture constantly on the horizon, and no longer balanced by the Soviet Union, we can expect continual increase in the power of bourgeois elements, and consequent further erosion of the land base of the peasantry.

Everything seems to be in place for the continued growth of landlessness and poverty. If industrialization cannot absorb the expanding landless peasantry, then a replay of past deforestation patterns seems unavoidable. And with the current international debt situation, and continuing political conflict, the prospects for significant anti-industrialization do not seem very bright. The vision of agrarian reform programs like Nicaragua had in the 1980's has all but disappeared in its country of birth, and is hardly a serious proposition in the other countries of the region. Therefore, the basic rural program that would help stem the tide of deforestation, agrarian reform, is not realistically on the horizon. Industrialization, the only other option, seems just as far off.

This puts conservationists in a holding pattern dividing along the same lines we introduced in Chapter 1. Mainstream environmentalists have been concerned with accumulating large sums of money to purchase and protect islands of pristine rain forest, with little concern for what happens to either the ecosystem or the human societies located between those islands. As we indicated previously, we do not imagine this strategy has much chance of working in the long run. The landscape will be converted into isolated islands of tropical rain forest, drowning in a sea of pesticide-drenched modern agriculture, with masses of landless peasants looking for some way to support their families. Unless the pace of industrial-

ization increases dramatically (something few observers expect), these peasants are unlikely to be absorbed into the industrial work force. Instead, they are very likely to begin homesteading in those islands of protected forests.

The alternative strategy emphasizes that land *between* the islands of protected forest, and acknowledges the interconnections in this complicated system. This sustainable development point of view conceives the ecological side of the dilemma as a landscape problem with forests, forestry, agroforestry, and agriculture as interrelated land-use systems, and seeks to develop those land-use systems to maintain conditions of production. The idea has seen much recent analysis,[20] and is perhaps our best hope.

Past historical contingencies and current economic realities place the Third World in a disadvantaged position for economic development under the world system. Development specialists from all spheres of political and economic influence have attempted to deal with the Third World problem ever since it was recognized, and "development," irrespective of its sustainability, has not been common. The imposition of restrictions like sustainability only heighten that disadvantage. Quite the contrary, an advantage will accrue to those regions and countries that do not impose constraints on their development. Sustainability is just such a constraint.

So we end this chapter, first with a paradox and finally, with a note of pessimism. Stemming the tide of rain forest destruction requires not only development, but development that is sustainable. Obviously sustainability is not sufficient, but is a necessary requirement. In the New World

Order rational planning is not anticipated at either national or international levels, while development will proceed fastest for those able to ignore constraints others either cannot or will not ignore. Sustainability is precisely such a constraint. Thus, although sustainability is required to save the rain forests, it seems unacceptable as a constraint on development, at least under conditions of the current world order.

Our note of pessimism, if the above paradox is not sufficiently pessimistic, is that the structures to which we lay blame for the destruction of rain forests are still in place, probably more solidly than ten years ago. The same modes of production (forestry, peasant agriculture, modern agriculture) interact with the same socioeconomic groups (export bourgeoisie, peasantry) in the same national and international political arena within the same ecological matrix. Forces in the national and international political arena have constructed an ideology in which the rain forest is assumed to be an externality that fits into and fortifies the overall political structure, thus creating an inexorable dynamic in which deforestation is an inevitable consequence. As long as present political arrangements survive, a solution simply does not seem possible. To the extent that conservationists and the conservation movement are part and parcel of those political arrangements, they remain part of the problem.

Notes

1. The history of the 1980's in Central America has been covered in many volumes. For example, Rosset and Vandermeer, 1986; Barry, 1987; and Edelmen and Kenen, 1989, are excellent sources.
2. Boza, 1993; Tangley, 1990.
3. For a critique of these forestry laws see Thrupp, 1990.
4. Seligson, 1980.
5. World Resources Institute, 1990.
6. Chico Méndez was the militant organizer of the rubber tappers in Brazil. His death at the hands of thugs hired by the cattle ranchers has galvanized much of the rain forest preservation movement. In addition to his well-known activities on behalf of the rubber tappers, Méndez was a leader in Brazil's Workers Party, and an advocate of socialism as the only ultimate solution to the problems of environmental deterioration and social injustice (Méndez, 1989).
7. A similar point of view, associated with African wildlife, was presented by Bonner (1993).
8. Children's author Dr. Seuss' mythical creature who spoke out against the ruthless exploitation of the trufula trees.
9. This and the rest of the story of *El Progreso* comes from interviews with several residents of the community conducted in the summer of 1994.
10. *Tico Times,* July 9, 1993.
11. Document prepared by the Sarpiquí Association for Forests and Wildlife (undated).
12. There is some debate as to how strong the influence of foreigners is in the association (personal interviews with local residents, 1994).
13. Most of this section is taken from Vandermeer, 1991, and Perfecto et al., 1994.
14. In 1990 the FAO reported the following figures for rain forest extent in Central America (in 1,000 hectares): Costa Rica - 625; El Salvador - 33; Guatemala - 2,542; Honduras - 1,286; Nicaragua - 3,712; Panama - 1,802 (World Resources Institute, 1994).
15. In 1986, Haiti's per capita GNP stood at $330, while that of Nicaragua was $790. For comparison, the Dominican Republic was $710 and Honduras was $740. All other Central American and Caribbean countries had GNP's larger than Nicaragua. By 1991, Nicaragua's GNP stood at $283, the worst in the hemisphere (Haiti stood at $375 at that point). We do not have more recent figures in Haiti, but subsequent to the ouster of Aristide and the economic blockade, we strongly suspect Haiti has returned to its unfortunate position as the poorest country in the hemisphere. Nicaragua is a close second.
16. Vandermeer et al., 1991.
17. This was a widespread claim in both the Atlantic coast and Managua. Obviously its strict verification is hardly possible under current political circumstances.
18. Kaimowitz, 1986.
19. Current estimates suggest that about 18% of Cuba is covered in forest, which clearly represents an increase from the figures of 1959 (Rosset and Benjamin, 1994). Some of that area is clearly under plantations of trees and thus does not represent true tropical forest, but we are unable to determine how much. The FAO reports an annual deforestation rate in Cuba of 0.9% during the decade of the 1980s. We are, nevertheless, convinced that the forest cover has indeed increased since 1959. In the case of Puerto Rico, the island was almost completely deforested by the 1930's, where 99% of its primary forests were gone by that time and with an estimated cover of secondary forest of 10–15% (Lugo, 1988). It had increased its forested areas to 31% (284,000 Ha) by the late 1970s, (Birdsey and Weaver, 1982).
20. Unfortunately terms such as sustainable development or ecological development, or ecodevelopment and a variety of others have now been adopted and coopted by the very agencies that have been promoting ecologically damaging development in the past, changing only the name of what they do.

 Article Review Form at end of book.

WiseGuide Wrap-Up

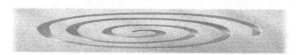

Despite the wealth that an expanding tourist industry often provides to a local economy in a late industrializing country, some citizens oppose expanding the tourist sector in their countries. These citizens may dislike the lifestyle that tourism introduces, but also often worry that the water and land degradation that results from tourism will cause long-term damage to their community's fragile ecostructure. Polluted water and increased numbers of, or expanded, waste disposal sites could then, in turn, pose health hazards to citizens.

In Reading 57, Vandermeer and Perfecto investigate how environmental degradation in the form of deforestation results when citizens in developing countries try to make a living by using the resources available to them. Three modes of production in Central America cause deforestation. Peasant agriculture that involves chopping down trees to clear land for planting, the forestry companies that chop and export trees, and the large exporting agricultural firms that clear huge estates all contribute to deforestation.

Unless we understand the causes and motivations of environmental degradation, we cannot create policies to avoid environmental ruin. Study of comparative political models of success and failure in the environmental arena allows for better decisions regarding alternative development strategies.

R.E.A.L. Sites

This list provides a print preview of typical **coursewise** R.E.A.L. sites. There are over 100 such sites at the **courselinks™** site. The danger in printing URLs is that web sites can change overnight. As we went to press, these sites were functional using the URLs provided. If you come across one that isn't, please let us know via email to: webmaster@coursewise.com. Use your Passport to access the most current list of R.E.A.L. sites at the **courselinks™** site.

Site name: Friends of the Earth

URL: http://www.foe.co.uk

Why is it R.E.A.L.? This site presents the Friends of the Earth agenda and explains why this group has chosen to take action on particular issues. For each problem reviewed, Friends of the Earth proposes some action or solution.

Key topic: Friends of the Earth

section

8

Key Points

- Structural adjustment programs are designed to help the state avoid bankruptcy, not advance the short-term well-being of citizens.

- Structural adjustment programs are sometimes referred to as "economic shock" programs because after these policies are enacted, citizens are shocked by the loss of value of their earnings and savings.

- As of June 30, 1997, fifty-seven countries were administering some form of structural adjustment program, and many others were negotiating to initiate a program. To comparatively understand the political economies of states around the world, we have to understand these wide-reaching policies. (Source: *IMF Survey*, July 21, 1997)

Structural Adjustment in Comparative Perspective

WiseGuide Intro

In the 1980s and 1990s, indebted countries realized that to compete in today's global economy, they would have to adjust their economically productive sectors. To obtain debt relief and begin an effort to restructure their economies, indebted countries borrowed money from international financial institutions, such as the International Monetary Fund (IMF) and the World Bank (International Bank for Reconstruction and Development [IBRD]). But these international institutions do not lend money or provide requested technical assistance unless a state pledges to meet both the economic and political conditions that these lending institutions impose. The conditions required for obtaining a loan include the adoption of a structural adjustment program (SAP) that includes policy alterations in the state's provision and amount of domestic credit, public sector deficit spending practices, national financial reserves, schemes for managing external debt levels, payout procedures, exchange rates, interest rates, and the prices of commodities. Adoption of a structural adjustment program also affects employment policies, tax and subsidy measures, export promotion, the provision of social services, and government record-keeping practices.

By instituting the changes that foreign lending institutions require, states impose what have been referred to as "economic shocks" on their populations. Inflation soars as countries devalue their currencies to market levels. Interest rates soar just when citizens are short of cash due to inflation. Despite the increased costs of living, wages are kept low, and usually, thousands or tens of thousands of workers lose their jobs through efficiency initiatives in the corporate and state sectors of the economy. Thus, while the state pulls itself out of bankruptcy, many of its citizens become impoverished overnight.

Acceptance of a structural adjustment program is generally a prerequisite for assistance from bilateral donor countries, such as the United States, the United Kingdom, and Japan. Loans from commercial banks and regional financial institutions generally also are contingent on the adoption of an IMF and World Bank structural adjustment program.

The readings in this section offer perspectives from defenders and critics of structural adjustment policies.

Questions

1. Why does the IMF argue in its own publication, *Finance and Development* (see Reading 58), that its policies are working?

2. In Reading 59, what does Richard Jolly mean by "adjustment with a human face"?

3. According to Sandberg and Ault in Reading 60, why do the wealthy Northern countries set the conditions for obtaining a loan from the IMF?

4. According to Sandberg and Ault in Reading 60, in the Zambia case, in what ways did the new structural adjustment policies particularly affect women?

5. What are Steve Hanke's financial concerns in Reading 61 about the IMF's overseas policies?

Experience Under the IMF's Enhanced Structural Adjustment Facility

The IMF supports reform in poor countries through its Enhanced Structural Adjustment Facility (ESAF). An IMF study found that policy gains under ESAF have helped improve growth and living standards and progress toward external viability.

IMF Policy Development and Review Department

ESAF and its precursor, the Structural Adjustment Facility (SAF), were set up to assist low-income countries address deep-seated and persistent economic problems, as part of a broader effort involving support from the World Bank and other agencies and donors in the international community (Box 1). When they applied for SAF or ESAF assistance, many of these countries were struggling with the legacy of development strategies based on state intervention, public ownership, and protectionism. These policies had stifled entrepreneur-ship, promoted waste and corruption, and exacerbated their economies' vulnerability to economic shocks. In many countries weaknesses had been masked during the 1970s by heavy foreign borrowing and improving terms of trade. But when world commodity prices plummeted and interest rates rose in the early 1980s, both the debts and policies they had financed became unsustainable.

The immediate need in most of these countries was to bring some order to external cash flow positions, through a combination of debt relief or rescheduling and new resource flows. Even though many countries had already begun reform programs supported by IMF stand-by arrangements, their external situations were precari-ous—current account deficits (excluding transfers) averaged 12–14 percent of GDP; scheduled debt service was typically 35–40 percent of exports; and official reserves were uncomfortably low.

These countries were suffering from more than a temporary liquidity problem. Stuck in a cycle of low saving, weak external positions, and slow growth, they were falling behind other developing countries in terms of per capita income; their saving rates were half the average of other developing countries; they had larger budget deficits, higher inflation, heavier external debt burdens, more distorted exchange systems; and their fast-growing populations were worse off in terms of education, health, and life expectancy.

IMF Policy Development and Review Department, "Experience under the IMF's Enhanced Structural Adjustment Facility," FINANCE AND DEVELOPMENT, Sept. 1997, pp. 32–35. Reprinted by permission.

The Adjustment Strategy

Programs supported by SAF and ESAF arrangements, while tailored to the diverse needs of individual countries, share core objectives:

- raising saving rates,

- securing financial stability,

- liberalizing and opening economies to foreign trade,

- reducing state intervention and making markets more efficient,

- reorienting government spending and improving revenue collection, and

- mobilizing external resources.

Reforms to achieve these objectives would have been challenging to implement in the best of times, but the global environment during the past decade—falling commodity prices in the late 1980s and early 1990s, and the industrial country recession of 1991–93—made the challenge harder still. One-fourth of ESAF countries experienced war or civil strife during this period, making it difficult to formulate, much less to implement, policies. Natural disasters such as drought and cyclones also took their toll in some countries. ESAF countries suffered throughout the past decade from restricted access to key export markets in the industrial world, particularly in agriculture, textiles, and clothing. However, market conditions improved after 1993, when global demand and nonfuel commodity prices rebounded, while world energy prices remained subdued. Civil conflicts—with some exceptions— subsided. This generally more favorable climate probably contributed to the widespread improvement in growth rates in

| Box 1 | The Enhanced Structural Adjustment Facility |

In the mid-1980s, the IMF recognized that some of its low-income member countries needed highly concessional financial support on a longer-term basis than it was able to provide through its existing financing mechanisms. It therefore set up the Structural Adjustment Facility (SAF) in 1986, and the Enhanced Structural Adjustment Facility (ESAF) one year later. Under ESAF arrangements, the IMF extends support for 3-year structural adjustment programs aimed at fostering sustainable growth and strengthening the country's external position. Based on their per capita incomes, 79 IMF member countries are now eligible for ESAF assistance, and the IMF is currently supporting ESAF programs in 34 countries. As of the end of June 1997, cumulative commitments and disbursements totaled $10.9 billion and $7.7 billion, respectively. ESAF loans carry an annual interest rate of 0.5 percent; repayments are made semiannually, beginning 5-1/2 years and ending 10 years after disbursement.

Recognizing its usefulness, the IMF's Interim Committee agreed in September 1996 to continue to support ESAF as a financially self-sustaining facility that would continue to be the centerpiece of the IMF's strategy to help low-income countries.

ESAF countries during the last three years.

What Has Been Accomplished?

The IMF study reviews the experience of 36 countries that received support under the SAF/ESAF in the context of 68 multi-year adjustment programs over 1986–94. (Box 2). The study found that these countries now had economies that were materially stronger and more market-oriented than a decade ago. Substantial policy gains, where achieved, had contributed to growth and living standards and to progress in most countries toward external viability. At the same time, progress was uneven, reflecting in large part policy weaknesses. Most countries continued to fall short of their potential.

Fiscal Consolidation

The programs' goal was to cut budget deficits (excluding grants and interest payments) by a little under half over a three-year period or by about 3 percentage points of GDP, on average. Whether this adjustment was to be achieved by cutting expenditures or increasing

revenues varied from country to country, but most programs were designed to boost capital spending while selectively cutting current spending in relation to GDP. Of the savings sought in current spending, roughly half was to come from the wage bill and half from subsidies and transfers (through, for instance, reduced support for public enterprises and better targeting of consumer subsidies). Many programs included pledges to strengthen health and education spending and incorporated safety net measures for vulnerable groups. On the revenue side, programs aimed to shift the burden from nontax to tax revenues and from direct to indirect taxation (especially to broad-based consumption taxes), and to improve revenue from tax and customs administration reforms.

The shift from current to capital expenditure did occur, albeit to a lesser extent than hoped. More encouragingly, the available data suggest that roughly three-fourths of the ESAF countries increased spending on health and education. Many countries also cut military spending. Nevertheless, on average, only about half of the targeted reduction in budget deficits was

Box 2 ESAF Countries Covered in the Study

The study divided the 36 countries under review into five regional groupings, as follows:

CFA Africa	Other Africa	Asia	Latin America and Caribbean	Transition Economies
Benin	Burundi	Bangladesh	Bolivia	Albania
Burkina Faso	The Gambia	Nepal	Guyana	Cambodia
Côte d'Ivoire	Ghana	Pakistan	Honduras	Kyrgyz Republic
Equatorial Guinea	Guinea	Sri Lanka	Nicaragua	Lao P.D.R.
Mali	Kenya			Mongolia
Niger	Lesotho			Vietnam
Senegal	Madagascar			
Togo	Malawi			
	Mauritania			
	Mozambique			
	Sierra Leone			
	Tanzania			
	Uganda			
	Zimbabwe			

achieved. Performance varied widely, and almost half of the programs produced no improvement.

The reasons for these shortcomings were complex. Revenues fell short of targets in two-thirds of the programs and, on average, were barely changed from pre-program levels. Missed deficit targets were more closely associated with expenditure overruns, however, as governments failed to cut civil service staffing levels or trim subsidies, including to public enterprises. Other factors included the weakness of budgetary institutions and difficulties in broadening tax bases.

Inflation Reduction

Programs succeeded in reducing high inflation rates. However, with a few exceptions (notably, the CFA franc countries), they failed to bring inflation rates down to single digits on a sustained basis. Inflation remained high in most of non-CFA franc Africa. Inflation in Asian ESAF countries was generally stable, at around 10 percent.

Structural Reform

Progress in structural economic reform among ESAF countries was profound but uneven (Chart 1).* With advice and support from the World Bank and other agencies as well as from the IMF, significant advances were made in deregulating the pricing and marketing of goods, and price-setting mechanisms for products still subject to controls became more rational. Many countries eliminated distortions in their foreign exchange systems, although foreign exchange markets commonly remain subject to restrictions on capital transactions. The easing of trade barriers got off to a slow start but accelerated in the 1990s.

Reforms of public enterprises were an important component of programs in two-thirds of the ESAF countries, but progress was slow and protracted. The biggest problems were typically in the strategic sectors, where attempts to restructure large en-

*Does not appear in this publication.

terprises were disappointing. Managers did not change their ways, despite the introduction of performance contracts, and governments tended to replace direct budgetary support with quasi-fiscal assistance such as tax concessions and loan guarantees.

Reforms of financial systems had mixed results. Most countries liberalized interest rates, eliminating negative real interest rates in many cases, and began to develop financial markets and to move to indirect instruments of monetary control. However, weaknesses in countries' banking systems remained pervasive, impairing their ability to mobilize and allocate resources efficiently. While reforms sought to strengthen banks' financial positions, improve decision making, and strengthen supervision, progress was hesitant. Banking reform seems to have been hindered by the dearth of local banking skills, a failure to expand competition, and the unwillingness of governments to stop pressuring banks to lend to uncreditworthy public enterprises.

Programs were designed to make a positive contribution to strengthening property rights and improving economic aspects of governance, directly, for example, by promoting reform of land tenure systems and the adoption of more liberal and transparent foreign investment codes, and indirectly, by reducing the distortions and regulations that feed corruption. Assessing overall progress in this area is particularly difficult, but the evidence suggests that property rights improved in roughly two-thirds of ESAF countries (mainly in Asia and Latin America and the Caribbean, but also in some African countries) and deteriorated in one-third.

Openness

ESAF countries made modest progress toward increasing the outward orientation of their economies. Liberalization of exchange and trade regimes, nominal depreciation, and fiscal adjustment led to a steady depreciation of the real exchange rate in all regions after 1985, which contributed to the growth of foreign trade as a share of GDP in almost all regions. However, ESAF countries in Africa and Latin America and the Caribbean suffered major losses in export market share throughout the 1980s (although these losses were stemmed or even reversed in the early 1990s), while Asian ESAF countries' share of export markets rose steadily from 1985 to 1995.

Economic Growth

Growth in most countries improved over the adjustment period. In the early 1980s, real per capita GDP in nontransition ESAF countries was declining annually by almost 1.5 percent, on average. But it rose at a positive annual rate of about 0.3 percent in the early 1990s (Chart 2)* and to 1 percent during 1994–95.

Important as these gains are, however, there are other, less sanguine perspectives. First, since output expanded less rapidly in ESAF countries than in the rest of the developing world over the past decade, per capita incomes fell further behind. Living standards and social indicators improved in ESAF countries, but more slowly than in the rest of the developing world. Second, not all ESAF countries shared equally in the recovery. The turnaround in economic growth was most pronounced in some of the ESAF

*Does not appear in this publication.

countries in Latin America and the Caribbean. Although per capita GDP growth rates in 8 of the 22 African ESAF countries were higher than the average for all developing countries during 1986–95, other African countries saw only a small degree of convergence toward the average growth rate of the developing world.

External Viability

The IMF study measured progress toward external viability—a situation in which the external current account can be financed by normal and sustainable capital flows—based on three ratios: debt-service burden to exports, debt-service burden to GDP, and reliance on exceptional financing. Of 27 nontransition countries where data permit an assessment, 12 can be said to have made "clear" progress toward external viability, meaning all 3 ratios showed improvement or remained stable, and 9 made "limited" progress, meaning that only 1 of the ratios had deteriorated. Six countries made no apparent progress toward external viability. The decisive factor appears to have been economic growth— export growth, in particular. In countries that made "clear" progress, annual growth rates for real GDP and export volumes were 3 to 6 percentage points higher, on average, than in countries that made no progress.

Lessons for Program Design

Countries undertaking SAF and ESAF-supported programs have clearly brought their economies a long way from the doldrums of the early 1980s. Developments in the last 1–2 years have been especially encouraging. While this

may owe something to the favorable global environment, the liberalization and restructuring over the past decade give grounds for believing that durable gains in economic potential have been achieved in these countries. Nonetheless, ESAF countries are still among the world's poorest and must therefore aim for faster economic growth than other developing countries on a sustained basis if they are to close the large gap in living standards. This is not in prospect so long as their investment and domestic saving rates continue to fall so far short of those in the rest of the developing world. The mutually reinforcing objectives of growth and external viability call for ambitious strategies that are resolutely implemented.

In their discussion of the report, the IMF's Executive Board agreed that achieving greater success in cutting government budget deficits must be at the heart of the strategy for ESAF countries. While greater attention needs to be paid to factors that could increase incentives for private saving, numerous empirical studies have concluded that public saving is the quickest and surest way to raise national saving. Weak fiscal discipline inhibits growth through other channels, too—by contributing to chronic inflation, weak external positions, and stop-go policy implementation. With these interrelationships in mind, the IMF study's proposals for strengthening ESAF-supported programs focused on a stronger and reoriented fiscal adjustment effort; a more resolute approach to reducing inflation; a more focused, concerted push on crucial structural reforms; and steps to encourage sustained policy implementation.

Growth-Enhancing Fiscal Adjustment

By and large, fiscal adjustment thus far in ESAF-supported programs has been modest. For many countries, simply meeting targets more or less as ambitious as those set in the past would represent a significant advance, while for others the objectives themselves should be more ambitious. A general aim in most countries should be to raise national saving rates significantly over the course of an ESAF-supported program. The means to achieve the required additional adjustment, however, may have implications for economic growth, as well as for the path of adjustment itself. Although there was scope for increased revenue in some cases, significant deficit reduction will have to come from structural reform on the expenditure side, in the civil service and public enterprises in particular. Such reforms can be costly in the short term (requiring redundancy payments, for instance); where necessary, deficit targets should accommodate these costs, provided that the medium-term savings are reasonably assured.

How government spending is cut is important, and expenditure that is growth-enhancing should be protected. This would include productive capital spending for key infrastructure and high-priority spending on health and education. Social spending is of considerable importance, given that rapid population growth and inadequate investment in human capital appear to be the dominant factors behind Africa's relatively sluggish growth rates. The quality of social spending is as important as its quantity, however. Hence, devices such as "core" budgets to protect such spending, while helpful in some circumstances, cannot be a substitute for careful monitoring of the delivery of social services. Improvements are needed in the quality and availability of expenditure data to ensure the adequacy and efficiency of spending on priorities such as these, as well as to monitor more closely the effectiveness of social safety nets. Efforts to reduce the civil service wage bill, reform public enterprises, and reduce unproductive spending should also be intensified. Finally, improved and more transparent budgeting and expenditure control systems are needed.

Inflation Reduction

The evidence suggests that those countries with inflation rates stuck in double digits are sacrificing growth. The potential gains from achieving and maintaining inflation in the single-digit range appear to be substantial, not only for increasing output growth but also for improving income distribution. Growth may benefit from low inflation directly, through improved resource allocation and higher investment, or indirectly, as a result of the broad-based reforms that are typically needed to sustain low inflation. Thus the full benefits are likely to accrue only in response to an anti-inflation strategy that is comprehensive and consistent.

SAF and ESAF-supported programs have in fact consistently targeted single-digit inflation. Yet they have also frequently failed to achieve this goal. One possible reason for this is that the extent of fiscal adjustment needed may have been underestimated. Another is that most programs (excluding, of course, the CFA franc countries) lacked an effective nominal anchor, possibly because the likely fiscal stance was thought to be incompatible with such an anchor, particularly in light of concerns about competitiveness.

Strong and durable adjustments of public sector imbalances will be critical to greater success in reducing inflation. In some cases where the exacting prerequisites of a formal nominal anchor—staunch adherence to fiscal discipline and minimal indexation—are feasible, an announced commitment to targets for the nominal exchange rate, monetary growth, or the inflation rate itself could facilitate the move to low inflation. The potential risks associated with nominal anchors would need to be carefully considered in each case, however, and exchange rate pegs would need to be accompanied by a clearly articulated exit strategy.

Structural Reforms

The supply response to macroeconomic adjustment will be quicker and stronger if accompanied by structural reforms that stimulate private investment and entrepreneurship. Many ESAF countries have achieved a great deal already. The challenge now is to move forward with the "second generation " of reforms—those where progress has lagged, or where more can be done to raise countries' economic potential. These areas would include: foreign trade and investment liberalization, public enterprise reform, bank restructuring, and strengthened property rights. Many aspects of these reforms lie within the domain of the World Bank, and strengthening policies and their implementation would involve continued close coordination and collaboration with the World Bank. Technical assistance to improve institutional capacity would also be important.

Sustaining Programs

As many as 28 of the 36 countries covered in the study experienced significant interruptions during or between SAF/ESAF-supported programs, in most cases as a result of poor policy implementation. Policy slippages undermine economic performance, both directly and through their effects on investors' and market sentiment. The resulting loss of credibility is costly even when policy adjustments are subsequently made to retrieve the ground lost.

The reasons for program interruptions were complex. Political factors were frequently at play, including lack of public support for adjustment policies, governments' reluctance to confront special interest groups, poor organization, and governance-related problems. In some cases, political disruption was so severe as to preclude effective formulation or implementation of policies. In less extreme cases where policy slippages were a dominant factor, the IMF study found that the likelihood of interruptions might have been reduced by more intensive program monitoring and more proactive technical assistance. More consistent contingency planning against shocks beyond the government's control (e.g., terms of trade or weather-related shocks) might also have helped.

Differing views were expressed by the Executive Board on whether the IMF should go beyond these steps, and be more cautious and selective in supporting countries' programs where the government's ability to commit to the program was in question. Some Executive Directors favored remaining engaged, if necessary with a slower pace of adjustment and reform, while others suggested that greater selectivity would be helpful in motivating strong reform programs.

Article Review Form at end of book.

Adjustment with a Human Face

Richard Jolly

The Urgent Need for a Broader Approach to Adjustment Policy

There is no need to describe at length the tragic and deteriorating human situation in many parts of the world today—of rising malnutrition, increasing poverty and a general slow-down and often reversal in the human indicators of development. Already, it is clear that historians of the future will document the early 1980s as a period when nutrition levels in many parts of the world started to deteriorate sharply. The most obvious and the most extreme situation is that in Africa, where the disaster of drought follows a decade or more of misdirected development, national and international, and has pushed some thirty million persons to the extremes of

This article was first published in 1985 in *Development: Seeds of change*.
Reprinted by permission of Sage Publications Ltd. from Richard Jolly, "Adjustment with a Human Face," DEVELOPMENT, Vol. 40 (1997), 97-105. Copyright © 1997 The Society for International Development.

hunger, starvation and often death.[1] But this is only the visible tragedy. There is a much broader crisis of growing malnutrition, which too often remains hidden elsewhere, through lack of visual and statistical evidence. The World Bank estimates that the number of persons malnourished in Africa has risen from eighty million to one hundred million since 1980 (World Bank, 1984). UNICEF has been documenting the evidence of child malnutrition from a number of countries, the majority of which show rising levels of both moderate and severe degree malnutrition, among the 0–5 age group, the most vulnerable of all (UNICEF, 1985).

In Ghana, for example, not a drought country, the rate of malnutrition among children six months to three and a half years doubled from 1980 to 1983 (UNICEF, 1984). Evidence from Botswana, Malawi and Kenya shows a similar picture. In Zambia, comparison between surveys of the early 1970s and early 1980s show an increase in stunting and a decrease in weight for age among all age groups and for both sexes of the under-fifteen years old (UNICEF, 1984).

In Latin America, starting from levels of nutrition and welfare much higher than in Africa, there is evidence from a number of countries of rising levels of malnutrition, increases in morbidity and a slow down in the long-term downward trend in infant mortality—and as in the case of Costa Rica, even some increase in infant mortality. In Asia, where economic growth and dynamism has been better maintained, the picture appears to show continuing progress. But even in the industrialized countries, the tougher economic policies adopted are probably having a

deleterious effect on the poor. In the United States, for example, the percentage of households nationwide below the poverty line has started rising again. In New York City, for example, the proportion of children in poverty is reported to have increased from 15 percent to 40 percent.

These reversals are the result of both national and international factors—and in no way should one pretend that the causes are always, or in most cases, even mainly international. In most cases, international and national factors are inextricably linked in ways that are causing severe downward pressures on living standard and welfare services, particularly for the poor. UNICEF, two years ago, undertook a survey on the impact of world recession on children which analysed the process in a diversity of a dozen countries, rich and poor, left wing and right wing, around the world. This revealed that a multiplier mechanism was at work—transmitting the impact of recession in the industrial countries to the developing countries, and within the developing countries, from urban to rural and to different income groups and classes. At each stage, the linkages mostly served to multiply the impact rather than diminish it, as one moved further along the chain, from rich to poor. We termed this 'a reverse shock absorber effect', in which the impact on poverty and vulnerability was increased rather than absorbed.

But none of this was inevitable. The reverse shock absorber reflects the ways policies and institutional mechanisms, national and international, are allowed to work. It would be possible to arrange them to work in a different way, like a normal shock absorber.

Conventional adjustment policy is a crucial part of this mechanism. As it mostly operates at the moment, adjustment policy, national and international, transmits and usually multiplies the impact on the poor and the vulnerable. The result as shown in many countries, is rising malnutrition in the short run—and in the long run, reinforcement of a style of development which will primarily rely on accelerated growth and trickle down, if it works at all, to modify malnutrition in the future.

Yet this form of adjustment is no more than the form of adjustment conventionally adopted at present. There are alternatives. It would be possible consciously to recognize that the human consequences of adjustment should not be left as an inevitable and unfortunate by-product—but treated as an essential concern. The protection of minimum levels of nutritional status and other basic human needs could be monitored and made as much a part of the objectives of adjustment as the balance of payments, inflation and economic growth.

Such a broader approach to adjustment is not only a matter of human welfare. To miss out on the human dimension of adjustment is not only a human tragedy. It is an economic error of the most fundamental sort. Much evidence already exists of the economic returns to investment in human resources (UNICEF, 1984). To fail to protect young children at the critical stages of their growth and development is to wreak lasting damage on a whole generation, the results of which may well have effects on economic development and welfare for decades ahead. Moreover, in the short run, it is plainly absurd to imagine that economic dynamism can be fully restored when an important fraction of a country's workers remain malnourished—or even remains, as among small-holder peasants in many African countries today, with too few basic goods to buy to provide incentives for extra effort. Consumption needs are a matter of proportion and degree. Not every cut-back on consumer expenditure is wrong or counter-productive. But there comes a point beyond—or rather below—which the cut-backs and reductions of an adjustment process become absurdly counter-productive to the economic process, let alone to the political and human viability of a country.

Let me also add here a particular word on giving special concern for women in the adjustment process. In part because many of the important activities of women are not counted in the conventional economic statistics, their vital economic contribution is often underestimated. This is likely to be even more the case with adjustment, where many forms of cut-backs impinge especially hard on women, especially those engaged in small scale and informal sector activities. Yet, there is much evidence to show that in terms of economic contribution, use of local resources in place of imports, returns to investment and employment creation, many women engaged in household and informal sector activities make a disproportionately large contribution to the economic welfare of the poorer sections of the population.[2] Their contribution should, therefore, be especially encouraged in the adjustment process—not ignored, let alone cut back.

The Elements of a More Human-Focused Approach to Adjustment

A broader approach to adjustment, 'adjustment with a human face' as one might call it, would involve three things:

- first, a clear acknowledgement in the goals of adjustment policy, of concern for basic human welfare and a commitment to protect the minimum nutrition levels of children and other specially vulnerable groups of a country's population.

- second, the implementation of a broader approach to the adjustment process itself, comprising four components:

  (a)   actions to maintain a minimum floor for nutrition and other basic human needs, related to what the country can in the long term sustain;

  (b)   restructuring within the productive sectors—agriculture, service, industry—to rely more upon the small-scale, informal sector producers and to ensure their greater access to credit, internal markets and other measures which will stimulate growth in their incomes;

  (c)   restructuring within health, education and other social sectors, to restore momentum and ensure maximum coverage and benefits from constrained and usually reduced resources. Already, there are important examples of what can be done to reach all of a country's population, but still at relatively low cost;

  (d)   more international support for these aspects of adjustment, including the provision of more finance, flexibly-provided and with longer-term commitments. The extremes of the present situation will often require a ceiling on outflows of interest and debt amortization if the protection of human needs is to be feasible in the short run;

- third, a system is needed for monitoring nutrition levels and the human situation during the process of adjustment.

We should be concerned not only with inflation, balance of payments and GNP growth—but also with nutrition, food balances and human growth. The proportion of a nation's households falling below some basic poverty line should be monitored—and treated as one of the relevant statistics for assessing adjustment.

Let me note in passing that in respect of disasters, a number of countries (with the support of international and national agencies), have already made a start with early warning systems for famine which focus, in part, on household food security and nutritional indicators. We now need to apply the same concerns, not merely to natural disasters, but to the man-made consequences of adjustment, and not merely to warn but also to avert the human consequences which often follow.

I have stressed the need for restructuring *within* the social sectors, in addition to the continued concern with restructuring the economic sectors. Here I must make a general point of fundamental importance. Adjustment policy with a human face will remain a sham—'an attempt to paint a smile on a face with tears'—if it is seen only as a matter of a change in the macro-economic policy of government. Instead it must involve a move towards a more people-focused adjustment, a more-fundamental restructuring—a shift to much greater self-reliance, to decentralization, small-scale production and community action, empowerment of people and households. These are the groups and approaches which in fact provide the goods and services and which generate the incomes for low income sections of most populations. These are also the sectors which more often than not are squeezed by adjustment approaches, as conventionally implemented. Yet for sheer cost effectiveness as well as protection for the poor, they are the approaches that matter.

Let me give an example of the type of approach required. Over the last year or two, numerous examples have demonstrated how infant mortality can be reduced and child health and welfare can be improved, at a fraction of the cost and a multiplier of effectiveness, if people's action and social mobilization are used to apply new technologies on a national scale, using the media and enlightened government leadership. As many will know—as I hope all will soon know—this is leading to a dramatic increase in immunization coverage and largely home treatment of diarrhoea by oral rehydration therapy (ORT). It has already led in 1984 to an estimated reduction in child deaths by a million a year (UNICEF, 1984). This is already moving the 1990 goal of universal immunization to becoming a feasible reality and not only a Utopian dream.

This example illustrates the potential and opportunities available, but also some vital points about adjustment with a human face. It must get down to specifics, both to mobilize public interest and awareness and to make the case with Ministers of Finance and visiting missions—and to carry this through to planning implementation when the case is accepted. Macro-economics can provide a supporting frame. But only when community leaders, sector specialists and a host of others are involved will such an approach work. There are many other areas of alternative approaches to draw upon. They include many of those advocated by basic needs proponents, appropriate technology enthusiasts and community activists in health, housing, small-scale agriculture, water, local manufacture of clothing and transport. Relevant low-cost approaches exist across virtually the whole field of basic needs.

I would stress the need for these groups, including community leaders and sector specialists, to present their case in ways which show its importance for the goals of adjustment. At the moment the tough, people-oppressing features of many adjustment policies are often supported because the policy-makers involved see little alternative. If alternatives are made clear in specific terms, and with cost tags attached, they may often prove more acceptable, even desirable. There is, after all, a political pay-off from action which visibly benefits the majority—and this can be an important force for change, especially at times of severe constraints.

To show the possibility for doing more is the first step to winning political support. There is

also a critical need to restructure expenditure in a more difficult and continual area: to reduce the resources flowing to armaments and the military. Armaments and military expenditures are probably the greatest single area of neglect in adjustment policy, as in economic development analysis. In spite of the constraints of foreign exchange and the tough cut-backs forced by adjustment, in the majority of countries military expenditure has been rising, at least until 1984. In some cases, the increase in military expenditure has been greater than the financial cut-backs in health and education. Moreover, as Barbara Ward so eloquently and so frequently pointed out, military expenditure is the greatest inflationary factor in the modern world. Military expenditure thus adds to the difficulties of adjustment and often defeats its purpose. Its enormous use of national resources, especially foreign exchange, for producing a product which is neither bought nor sold makes it a prime force for increasing taxation, inflation or debt, and usually all of them. And the impact of growing armaments is not only on increasing risk and insecurity but in adding to domestic repression and violence.

There are some particular reasons at this time for reviewing the links between adjustment policy and rising military expenditures, most clearly shown in Latin America. Over the last few years, most Latin American countries have moved dramatically and mostly democratically to elections and elected governments. These changes still rest on a fragile base, with a new need for those in power to maintain support from the electorate, often with the military still waiting in the wings. The cut-backs and constraints of adjustment on incomes and social expenditures on basic services for the majority hardly makes this an easy task, as a number of recent examples make it only too clear. Nevertheless, in this world of tight economic constraints, the choice between cutting military expenditure and cutting health, education and other basic services becomes an increasingly direct and evident trade-off, attracting attention from many parts of the electorate. Combined with measures of collective action (regional or global) towards greater security, these conflicting interests might even be turned to encourage some measure of reductions in military spending.

An Example of Human-Focused Adjustment—Britain during World War II

British experience during World War II provides an example of incorporating nutritional concern in an adjustment programme and of the fact that it can be done even in extreme circumstances and concurrently and successfully with adjustment measures.

The adjustment problem, faced by Britain during the war, was to reduce imports very drastically, restructure industry and the economy for the war effort. All had to be done very rapidly, for a war originally thought to last no more than eighteen months. But in contrast to World War I and earlier, protection of the nutritional status of the whole of the British population was made an integral and conscious part of the adjustment process (as it was also in a number of other countries). Nutritional needs were defined for each group of the population: babies, young children, older chil-

dren and adults, pregnant and lactating mothers and so forth. At Churchill's direction, no distinctions were made between different groups of the population, except on the basis of physiological needs. Churchill indeed at times explained and defended the programme in Parliament, summing it all up on one occasion with the memorable phrase: 'There is no finer investment than putting milk in babies'—an early and eloquent example of the human capital argument. (If UNICEF had had a hand in the drafting, we would no doubt have pointed out that milk from mothers is always preferable to milk from bottles.)

Before leaving this example, let me make three points about these experiences:

- first, it shows there is nothing theoretically or operationally impossible in combining an adjustment programme with the objectives and measures required to protect the nutritional status and basic consumption needs of a country's population. This is not to say that other countries can or should do it the same way. But there are sound reasons in all countries to ask how it might be done, in their particular circumstances;

- second, the British experience was remarkably successful in nutritional terms. By the end of World War II, in spite of all the hardships and constraints, the nutritional status of the British population was better than ever before in British history and probably as good as or just possibly even better than today;

- third, and this is a point Barbara herself would surely have stressed, it provides a

superb example of what the vision and practical leadership of a few people can achieve.

One key figure in this case was Jack Drummond, a professor, scientist and expert in nutrition, who was appointed a month or two after the war had begun to be responsible for de-contamination of food from poisonous gas—a hark-back to the gas fears of World War I. Within three months, Drummond had, however, redefined his job to be concerned with protecting the nutritional status of the whole of the British population—a much bolder and more fundamental task. That, as Barbara might have said, was an example of real vision and scientific initiative.

Another key figure was Lord Woolton, the Minister of Food, who provided the political leadership and advocacy, in Parliament and outside. Later to become Chairman of the Conservative Party, his inspiration and human concerns had grown out of earlier experiences working in the Liverpool slums. The professionalism of the whole programme was heavily influenced by Woolton's scientific background and the small circle of top professional scientists he gathered around him.[3]

Indeed, the whole programme was built on a framework of professionalism and science, turned to the protection of basic needs. Keynes in the background provided the macro-framework for combining a policy for maintaining minimum consumption needs with the pressing claims on resources and government expenditure for the war effort—and setting all within a pragmatic combination of government planning and the use of market forces. Those with an admiration for creative journalism might note that the essential elements of all these were originally set out in three articles by Keynes in the London *Times*, and then published in early 1940; under the title 'How to pay for the War'. Keynes also introduced two other ideas: the child allowance, initially of five shillings per week, designed to provide *additional* financial support to a family in relation to children's needs; and, secondly, the idea of constructing what might today be called a 'basic needs price index' to monitor the changes in the price of the goods required to meet minimum consumption needs.

Before leaving the lessons of history, let me jump ten years forward to the early 1950s and the formative years of the United Nations. As during the war, and in the early years of the UN, one is struck by the creativity and professionalism of so much of the work undertaken. In the UN, it was applied for peace, international economic relations and the early post-war efforts to tackle economic and social development problems. The names of those involved on the economic side conjure up some sense of the quality of their contributions, though, of course, at the time the reputations of many of these persons had yet to be made.

It is not the names I emphasize but the fact that from this group of people, and others, poured forth a stream of ideas, analyses and proposals which influenced both the international debate and, in time, led in a number of important cases to practical and specific action—World Bank's IDA and the compensatory export finance facility of the IMF, both proposals made in the UN itself during the 1950s; and, of course, this work led to the creation of UNCTAD.

New Roles for the United Nations and the International Community

This brings me back to today—and to the greater role which I believe the UN itself could and should play in supporting a broader approach to adjustment as I have earlier outlined it. The UN, in the sense of the core of agencies directly under the Secretary General, has some very natural advantages—one could say comparative advantages, in fulfilling such a role. The technical agencies of the UN are multidisciplinary and already concerned with a variety of the broader but often neglected areas of development—women's concerns, children's needs, urban problems, environment, etc. They include the commissions with their special knowledge and focus on the main regions of the world. They also include four major agencies with resources to support development: UNDP, WFP, UNICEF, UNFPA, which together provide some $2.5 billion of grant support to developing countries each year. And outside this circle are the specialized agencies of ILO, WHO, FAO and UNESCO.

The common element of this core of agencies and the four outside is their human focus and concern—a human focus which is by no means absent from the programmes of the World Bank, but certainly less marked in the World Bank and the IMF than in these other agencies. It would be a natural approach to bring the UN agencies together in support of some form of special and coherent commitment to the human dimension of adjustment, not merely as a short-term stop-gap arrange-

ment but as a means for strengthening long-term revival and development on a new basis.

There would need to be, of course, close links, *closer links*, with the World Bank—but not so close as to merge identities. There are, in my view, great advantages in approaching the human dimensions of development with the human concerns and human-centred objective uppermost in one's mind, rather than approaching them from the viewpoint of people seen primarily as human capital or an input into some abstract process of development. Closer links between development agencies of the UN and the World Bank, and a clearer definition of their respective roles would greatly help, but a merger would be unfortunate.

The IMF raises different issues. Although some of us passionately believe that the IMF needs to take more conscious account of malnutrition and other indicators of human welfare, there will be, I suspect, a strong consensus for keeping its *operations* limited to the economic and financial mechanisms of adjustment.

The IMF view, as I understand it, is that it has neither the staff, nor the mandate nor the technical capacity to extend their analysis and actions much beyond the existing frame. This need not matter, *provided* the IMF consciously accepts that the human impact of adjustment in the short run, and not only in the long run, is a matter of vital concern.

It also needs to ensure that its own guidelines and approaches are broad enough to permit governments and others to take positive actions to protect the nutritional status of vulnerable groups with whatever priority a country chooses. Note that such concerns are already in principle provided for in the IMF Articles which identify multiple objectives for the Funds actions, including providing and maintaining high levels of employment, incomes and economic development as *primary objectives.*

Indeed, there already are precedents for the IMF to look at the nutritional effectiveness of food subsidies and food arrangements. The critical change will require not so much an alteration in the IMF terms of reference but in its willingness to be more responsive to specific welfare measures when a government proposes them and the acceptance of a more flexible and pragmatic approach to the use of policy instruments such as targeted subsidies.

In this sense, the macro-frame for adjustment must be adapted to measures to protect nutrition and improve the incomes of the poorest in two senses. Micro rules must also permit sectorial efficiency in protecting human needs with the resources available and in ways in keeping with the economic, social and cultural context of each country. For instance, approaches to cost recovery of water, education, health services, etc. ought to be matters left to national strategy and political style, taking account of basic needs objectives.

The other requirement of macro-adjustment policy relates to the total flow of financial resources available to support countries undertaking adjustment. Almost certainly, the protection of minimum human standards as part of adjustment policy in a highly constrained economy will require some additional financial support from outside and for such support to be sustained over a longer period to permit adjustment to be more gradual. Already,

this is widely recognized in principle and provides the justification for the World Bank and other development institutions and donors to provide such support. There are two organizational problems which need to be tackled, however.

First, in most cases, the negotiations with the IMF on adjustment policy take place earlier and separately from the broader discussions of development policy. At the best, this leads to economic inefficiency, in the sense that the adjustment parts of the programme are not fully integrated with the long-term development parts and with the resources required and available to support them. But in the worst cases, demands for an adjustment process are set in motion and in an ad hoc and hap-hazard way, with different donors and voluntary agencies left *subsequently* to deal with the neglected human dimensions. A more coherent and integrated approach is primarily a matter institutionalizing a coherent discussion of the human and development issues, at the time of and as part of the original adjustment discussion. In practical terms, the Consultative Group Meetings called by the World Bank and the Round Table meetings organized by UNDP would be an appropriate forum especially if these meetings formally adopted a commitment to be concerned with the protection of minimum living standards as part of their agenda.

The second and major omission of macro-adjustment at the moment, is the inadequacy of the total flow of resources. In the case of Africa, the challenge is as much in decreasing the annual *outflows* of interest and amortization payments on debt as in increasing of the gross *in-flows* of development support. It is not my purpose to-

wards the close of this paper to enter into a full discussion of these issues. Much has been written and many proposals have been put forward. But I wish to underline the link between the minimum floor for nutritional and basic needs support needed within countries and the minimum flow of finance required from outside.

There comes a point beyond which no variations in adjustment policy can succeed in *both* protecting the nutritional and welfare needs of the population *and* in maintaining the out-flow of foreign exchange required for servicing very high levels of debt. At that point, a choice must be made.

As President Nyerere has said, the choice becomes one of repaying one's debt or starving one's children.

Yet, there are examples in history where the need for a ceiling on debt repayments has been recognized. In the case of reparation (the high levels of payments by Germany after World War I). Keynes argued eloquently but without success for a reduction. His failure to convince the authorities in time stimulated, as many have recognized, the rise of nazism and the inexorable moves to World War II. In the 1930s, a number of Latin American countries called *force majeure* on debt servicing and some repayments were never completed. An interesting African tradition, known at least in West Africa, is for victors in tribal warfare to take cattle and property from the vanquished but never so much as to leave women and children with too little to eat. How civilized compared with our present institutionalized international arrangements!

I do not propose how the issue of debt restructuring, retroactive terms of adjustment, increases in debt prices or increases in financial aid should best be tackled at the moment, especially for the poorest countries in Africa.[4] All I know is that for so long such issues have been debated and so little has been done. Must the efforts of countries to protect the nutritional standards of their population be abandoned through lack of international support?

There are, as Barbara eloquently reminded us, the benefits to the industrial countries, in terms of economic returns as well as of political stability, of concerted international action to increase support to the poor countries. She proposed a twenty-year Marshall Plan for the Third World, which the Brandt Report further elaborated. The fact that this idea is still not seriously on the international agenda reflects, not lack of need and inappropriateness, but the current economic ideology of the dominant and the lack of vision and international leadership. And for this reason, much of the Third World languishes. Yet the inadequacy of current inaction will in time be recognized, in the North as already in the South, and serious debate on forward movement will return. We, who are convinced of the need for change, should not falter in our convictions but be exploring how to turn vision into action.

I come finally to the last and most difficult part. What makes me imagine that any of those who would be involved have the slightest interest in a change in approach? Let us not make it seem too easy, but nor should we make change seem impossible. History shows endless examples of the citadels of power, and the wisdom of the day, resting on sand, sometimes shifting sand, sometimes sinking sand swallowing up all. The more uncertain the founda-

tions, the stronger the protestations that the base is solid rock.

Keynes put it that the power of vested interests was vastly exaggerated compared to the power of ideas. Barbara more poetically said:

'we learn from the visionaries, we do not learn from the practical men of affairs. They are marvellous, once the direction is set, but you will not find them in the forefront. They were not in the forefront in the 19th Century, they are not in the forefront in the 20th Century'.

Certainly there is today much questioning—sometimes rethinking—on adjustment policy among those directly involved in the international agencies and among the bankers.

It is not difficult to think of Third World leaders struggling to protect or implement a more human-focused approach. Not every Third World leader is concerned, but why should we withhold support from those who are?

And there are also industrial country supporters for a more human-focused approach: governments in a number of cases and probably a sizeable proportion of the population in many others, especially if they knew the facts. The outpouring of popular support for Africa followed when the ordinary television viewer saw what was happening. The dramatic change of *government* policies and support *followed after that*. Would donor country governments remain so unmoved on debt and adjustment issues if their populations realized what was really happening.

So stirrings are afoot in many quarters—but existing approaches, with only minor changes, remain in place. And the inefficiencies and

absurdities continue . . . . and the people suffer.

So what holds us back? Inadequate evidence? Weak arguments? The adequacy of the present situation, the radical nature of alternatives? Everyday I become more convinced it is none of these but the factors systematically ignored by social scientists and too many others; vision, values and leadership.

Here I must quote Barbara, again, for she makes the points so much more eloquently than others:

'Virtually everything that works began with a vision and with a group of idealists prepared to work for it. Things which would have seemed inconceivable in early days of history, began with as unlikely a group as the small Quaker movement dedicating itself to the abolition of slavery. Everyone assumed that slavery was part of nature. Yet we have lived through a period in which slavery was abolished. Or take the great events which started with the American revolution. Or who would have conceived in the 1880s that imperialism would be dissolved in another hundred years. . . . Our visionary perspective is the true realism and that is what we have got to pursue'.[5]

Notes

This paper was presented at the 18th World Conference of SID in Rome, on 2 July 1985. I have taken the chance to make some minor revisions and add some references for this version. The paper draws heavily on work thinking and action in UNICEF over the last year. I am especially grateful for close partnership in this with Paul Altesman, Andrea Cornia, Denis Caillaux, Farid Rahman, Gerry

Helleiner and Frances Stewart. Hans Singer, as so often, has provided useful comments and endless inspiration. The paper is, however, a personal statement, not a statement of UNICEF as such or of particular colleagues.

1. The documents prepared by African Ministers of Planning and submitted to the OAU meeting provide a sober overview.

2. See for example *The New Yorker*, April 1985 and also Arden Miller, 'Infant Mortality in the US,' *Scientific American*, July 1985. The Congressional Budget Office study, 'Reducing Poverty Among Children', May 1985, shows that 22 percent of all children in the US were classified as poor in 1983, the highest percentage since 1969 when it was 14 percent.

3. As he explains in *The Memoirs of the Rt. Hon. the Earl of Woolton* (1959). London: Cassell.

4. The report of SID's North South Roundtable provides some excellent analyses and specific proposals. See Khadija Haq (ed.) (1985) *The Lingering Debt Crisis*, Islamabad: SID.

5. These final quotations are from the last public address Barbara gave, at the SID North South Roundtable on the Brandt Report, held at IDS, Sussex in July 1980, *Beyond Brandt: Menace and Hope* and summarized in *Development, Volume XXII No. 4, 1980.*

References

UNICEF (1984) 'Situation Analysis of Children in Ghana', Accra mimeo.

UNICEF (1984) 'The Impact of Recession on Children'. Part IV, *State of the World's Children Report*, Oxford: OUP.

UNICEF (1985) 'Report on The Neglected Human Dimensions of African Development'. Oxford: OUP.

World Bank (1984) *Towards Sustained Development in Sub-Saharan Africa: A Joint Programme Of Action.* Washington, DC: World Bank.

 Article Review Form at end of book.

Our Policies, Their Consequences

Zambian women's lives under "Structural Adjustment"

Amber Ault and Eve Sandberg

Women around the globe share many concerns, including meeting basic subsistence needs, improving the prevention and treatment of diseases like AIDS, providing for reproductive health and freedom, reducing infant mortality and childhood illness, preventing violence against women, ensuring gender equity in labor, law, and education, and increasing women's ability to exercise sexual self-determination. Because wealthy countries and poor countries occupy very different positions in the global economic system, however, the social, economic, and political oppression experienced by women of poor countries differs in form from that experienced by women in wealthy countries. Furthermore, the oppression of women in Third World countries does not exist in a vacuum that begins and ends at national borders. Indeed, much of the poverty, discrimination, disease, and violence experienced by Third World women results from the exploitation of their countries

Amber Ault and Eve Sandberg, "Our Policies, Their Consequences: Zambian Women's Lives under 'Structural Adjustment,'" FEMINIST FRONTIERS: RETHINKING SEX, GENDER AND SOCIETY, eds. Laurel Richardson, Verta Taylor, Nancy Whittier, 4/e, New York: McGraw-Hill, 1997. Reprinted by permission of the authors.

by wealthier countries and the international organizations that they control. As feminist scholars and activists in wealthy Western countries, we must educate ourselves about our roles in supporting the systems of domination which perpetuate the exploitation of women elsewhere.

We do not argue that all women in industrialized nations enjoy vast, substantial advantages over all women in Third World countries. Indeed, many women in the United States live in extreme poverty, without decent housing, steady health care, stable employment, or any assurance of personal safety, while some women in poor nations enjoy relatively high standards of living. Nonetheless, because wealthy Western countries benefit from the labor of exploited Third World workers, Western feminists need to understand the roles their governments play in women's oppression in other countries.

In this brief report, we use a case study to demonstrate how the self-interested practices of wealthier countries in one international organization exacerbate and sometimes create the oppression of Third World women as women, citizens, and workers. To explicate the connections between the United States government, one powerful international organization, and the lives of women in Third World countries, we recount the impact of an International Monetary Fund (IMF) Structural Adjustment Program in the African country of Zambia.

The International Monetary Fund constitutes an international agency designed to promote a stable world economy. As part of its mission, it provides loans to countries with failing economies. Capital for such loans comes from deposits made by the countries

participating in the International Monetary Fund. The conditions each borrowing country must meet to secure a loan are contingent on the ultimate approval by the Board of Directors of the Fund, which includes representatives of the member states, whose votes are weighted relative to their countries' financial contributions; wealthy nations like the United States make large contributions and therefore enjoy great influence over the contingencies attached to loans the agency makes, as well as its policies and actions. Not surprisingly, the terms of loans to Third World countries reflect the economic and political interests and values of the world's wealthiest nations.

The "Structural Adjustment Program" constitutes one kind of loan package managed by this organization. The International Monetary Fund makes financial assistance to Third World countries contingent upon borrower countries' willingness to make significant adjustments in their economic systems. The adjustments required by the International Monetary Fund reflect Western capitalist economic ideologies. In addition, they often reflect a disregard for the structural, cultural, social, and technological features of the borrowing country. As a result, Structural Adjustment Programs administered by the International Monetary Fund frequently result in dramatic and devastating changes in the countries that adopt them. Nonetheless, because the International Monetary Fund constitutes one of the few sources of loan capital to which an indebted country can turn, countries suffering severe economic difficulty often accept the terms of Structural Adjustment Programs.

Such was the case of Zambia, a Black-governed country in

South-Central Africa that implemented an IMF Structural Adjustment Program in October, 1985 and wrestled with it in various forms until its termination in May, 1987. Before we describe the policies and outcomes of the Structural Adjustment Program in Zambia, we offer a brief description of some features of the country, so that readers may more fully grasp the ramifications of the program on the lives of citizens in general and women in particular.

At the time it instituted its IMF Structural Adjustment Program, Zambia reported that its population numbered about 6.7 million citizens. About 3.81 million Zambians over the age of 11 were working or actively seeking work, but only about 71% of these people could find jobs. While some urban Zambian women worked as teachers, nurses, secretaries, and waitresses, many more were self-employed as food sellers, street vendors, and charcoal producers, or in other jobs in the "informal sector"; in rural areas, women usually worked as farmers.

Then, as now, Zambia imported many goods. Government controls on foreign exchange rates held in check the cost to consumers of food and other goods imported by retailers before the implementation of the Structural Adjustment Program. Such controls helped to allow families in both urban and rural areas to meet their basic subsistence needs, and were especially beneficial for women upon whom rests most of the responsibility of supporting the family.

Other government policies and programs helped to make life in Zambia manageable for its citizens before the Structural Adjustment Program. For example, the Zambian government made heavily subsidized health care available to all citizens, and ensured access to basic education. Zambian governmental policies also kept domestic tensions in check by equitably distributing government-subsidized resources to the four separated geographic areas occupied by the country's four major ethnic groups.

Before it would disburse a loan to Zambia, the IMF required the Zambian government to promise to make major changes in the structure of its economy. According to the IMF, the required changes would allow the country to participate more successfully in the world market and, as a result, would allow it to repay its loan. Although many of the wealthy countries with controlling interests in the IMF do not have balanced national budgets, the IMF's Structural Adjustment Program packages are designed around the idea that Third World countries should achieve balanced budgets, and that they should do this in part by suspending support to domestic programs.

The International Monetary Fund required Zambia to devalue its currency, discontinue its subsidization of food, health, and education, suspend social welfare programs, lay-off federal employees, and turn its attention to both diversifying and increasing its exports for international markets. The result: a socio-economic nightmare for the country's people. The changes required by the IMF produced widespread unemployment; inflation of astronomical proportions; the suspension of the education of many people, especially girls; a dramatic decrease in access to health care; an increase in violence; conflict between the country's ethnic groups; and increased class stratification. While these problems affected most citizens, they made life especially arduous for women.

Over night, the devaluation of Zambian currency and the suspension of government subsidies on imported goods produced massive inflation. The consumer prices of domestically produced products and services, including health care, school fees, and transportation, rose by 50%; the prices of many imported goods doubled. Women and girls were especially hard-hit by inflation. For example, because women are primarily responsible for feeding and clothing their children, the dramatic increases in the cost of food and household goods took a great toll on their limited incomes; with the increase in household expenses, and the end of nationally subsidized health care and education, medicine and schooling became increasingly beyond the means of most families. As a result, families made difficult decisions about who would receive the benefit of increasingly limited resources, and those decisions reflected entrenched patriarchal values. In the case of education, for example, families often reverted to traditions that promoted the education of male children over that of girls.

Sudden, massive unemployment exacerbated the problems resulting from inflation. The IMF required the Zambian government to lay-off scores of government workers as a means of reducing expenditures. As a result of reduced consumer spending, private businesses and industry also let large numbers of workers go. In both spheres, women suffered great losses because their positions were frequently regarded as the most expendable. Joblessness, coupled with inflation, left Zambians destitute; sexist social structures disadvantaged women, even relative to men who were suffering greatly.

For example, while the inflated price of gasoline made the cost of public transportation beyond most citizens' means and forced those who retained jobs to walk long distances to and from work, after-work hours were very different for men and women. Because they are responsible for feeding their families, many women had to extend their days with either extra income-producing activities or by obtaining land on which to create family gardens. Women's "double burden" of work and child-care became even greater under the hardships of the Structural Adjustment Program.

Women also suffered directly at the hands of men as a result of the social stress the country experienced during the Structural Adjustment Program. Men, pressed to their limits, took advantage of women's resources and patriarchal social structures which allowed them to succeed in such efforts. For example, one woman farmer interviewed recounted how her brother had stolen from her: their father had willed them an ox to share, and every year she and her brother took turns using the animal to plough their fields; in the first year of the Structural Adjustment Program, the brother took the ox, refused to return it, and rented it to others for extra income, saying that his family could not survive if he did otherwise: the woman, in turn, could not plant enough to feed her family that year, and since customary law in the area did not recognize women's right to property, had no recourse. Such situations were not uncommon.

Nor was physical violence. In the years of the Structural Adjustment Program, the rate of violent crime in Zambia rose sharply. Women's increased activity away from home, as a result of their need to have extra income-generating activities, made them increasingly vulnerable to attack: women walking to and from work or their gardens, often distant from their homes, were fearful of being assaulted. At home, too, people were wary. One interviewee described how she and her husband took turns staying awake at night to protect themselves from prospective robbers.

These problems were further exacerbated by increasing conflict between groups in Zambia. As a result of IMF conditions, the government suspended its policy of distributing agricultural resources equitably throughout the country. Some areas of the country began to receive more and better supplies, setting the stage for conflicts between the ethnic groups living in different geographic regions. The Structural Adjustment Program also indirectly produced increased stratification among the country's women: those women farmers who happened to live along the country's supply roads received many more resources than those who lived in remote territories. While such women were among the few to benefit financially from the Structural Adjustment Program in Zambia, their prosperity rested on the deprivation of others.

Clearly, the imposition of the conditions of the IMF Structural Adjustment Program in Zambia wreaked havoc on the lives of the country's people. Similar IMF Structural Adjustment Programs throughout the Third World have produced equally devastating effects. We note that some IMF Structural Adjustment Programs in other impoverished countries have included a feature missing from the Zambian program: special encouragement for multinational corporations to promote exports. The mistreatment of women workers by such corporations has been well documented by other feminist scholars. (Nash and Fernandez-Kelly, 1983; Fuentes and Ehrenreich, 1983; Ward 1990)

A small number of women entrepreneurs benefit from the free-market conditions created by IMF adjustment programs, and some women find empowerment and forge coalitions with other women in their efforts to resist the hardships the programs impose. Generally, however, throughout the Third World, people suffer greatly as a result of the conditions their governments must accept in order to procure loans designed to relieve the economic instability of their countries.

As voting members in the IMF, western governments, including that of the United States, condone and encourage the policies that so disrupt the lives of so many millions in Third World states. The United Nations Economic Social and Cultural Organization (UNESCO) and the United Nations Africa Economic Committee (UNAEC) have criticized the extraordinary toll that citizens in Third World states, especially women, are paying for their governments' Structural Adjustment Programs. In the 1990s, other organizations and individual citizens in Western countries are also attempting to alter IMF policies. The Development Gap, for example, a Washington, D.C. based non-governmental organization concerned primarily with the environment, began a campaign in 1991 to urge the U.S. Congress to use the U.S. voting position in the International Monetary Fund to alter IMF Structural Adjustment Programs.

Western feminists can join or initiate efforts to alter the IMF's programs. Women from wealthy countries must recognize our collaboration in the global system that oppresses women. As citizens of the countries intimately involved with the implementation of international policies which foster the exploitation of women in the Third World, we can seek to change the system. Indeed, we must: to fail to act on behalf of the women suffering as a result of our government's involvement in the IMF is to perpetuate the oppression of others, even as we seek to relieve our own.

References

Fuentes, Annette and Ehrenreich, Barbara, eds.: *Women in the Global Factory.* Boston: South End Press, 1983.

Nash, June and Fernandez-Kelly, Patricia, eds.: *Women, Men, and the International Division of Labor.* Albany: State University of New York Press, 1983.

Ward, Kathryn, ed.: *Women Workers and Global Restructuring.* Ithaca: Cornell University Press, 1990.

 Article Review Form at end of book.

The IMF
Immune from (frequent) failure

Steve H. Hanke

Mr. Hanke is a professor of applied economics at The Johns Hopkins University

The International Monetary Fund failed to anticipate the Mexican peso fiasco of 1994–95. This proved to be a huge embarrassment. But never mind. The IMF rode to the rescue. Indeed, Managing Directory Michael Camdessus asserted at the time that "we must think big." And that he did. With the support of Treasury Secretary Robert Rubin, he engineered the biggest bailout in history.

But that was not enough. As has been the case with each financial crisis since the collapse of the Bretton Woods system in 1971, the ever-opportunistic IMF invented yet another raison d'être: It installed and early-warning system designed to supply more extensive and timely information to policy makers and market participants. The IMF was then supposed to keep a hawk-like lookout for signs of financial weakness and sound the alarm whenever a crisis was brewing.

How well has the IMF's new system worked? On July 2, Thailand devalued the baht, and shortly thereafter other currencies in Southeast Asia got hammered. Predictably, the IMF's early warning system remained deafeningly silent prior to the crisis. Indeed, the IMF's World Economic Outlook, issued in May, failed to flash red. The IMF flunked, again.

What has been the IMF's reaction? In addition to delivering yet another bailout, the IMF said that it knew the right answer all along and that it had the internal documents to prove it. Fine. But is secrecy the hallmark of an early-warning system?

The IMF's failing grade is inexcusable. The Thai baht was pegged to a basket of currencies heavily weighted in U.S. dollars. Unlike a devaluation-immune fixed exchange rate, such as Argentina's or Hong Kong's, a pegged exchange rate is not a free-market mechanism for international payments. A pegged regime is an interventionist system. It requires a central bank to manage its currency's exchange rate, the domestic liquidity and its capital account all at once. This is a tricky, if not impossible, task. Indeed, a pegged rate inevitably results in contradictory policies that invite a speculative attack.

When under siege, a peg cannot last unless interest rates are raised sky-high or foreign exchange controls are imposed. The landscape is littered with pegged regimes that have blown up and been followed by devaluations: the European Rate Mechanism (1992 and 1993), Mexico (1994), the Czech Republic (1997) and most recently Thailand, Indonesia, Malaysia and the Philippines. The IMF should have known that, as a matter of principle, the pegged systems in Southeast Asia were fatally flawed and vulnerable.

The new warning system should have set off loud warning bells in Thailand early in 1997: Its growth in domestic liquidity and inflation had been exceeding the rates of the countries to whose currencies the baht was linked. And the private sector was highly leveraged and burdened with mountains of debt denominated, in large part, in unhedged foreign currencies. The imbalances and contradictory policies were there for all to see, including the ever-vigilant speculators.

By February 1997, the speculators were starting to place large one-way bets against the baht.

Consequently, Thai interest rates shot up. The punishing interest rates hit the overblown property market, causing prices to slump. This had an immediate effect on the asset quality of the notoriously fragile banking system.

The speculators knew the game was up. The only ways the Thais could hold the baht peg were to allow interest rates to climb even higher, or to impose even tougher exchange controls. But this would have caused further damage to the property market, decimated the banking system and further squeezed the highly leveraged private sector.

All this information was available in the markets. But it failed to show up on the IMF's radar screens. This should not surprise anyone. Since the breakup of the Bretton Woods system, the IMF has been busy touting the glories of central banking and fine-tuning for less-developed countries. Just look at the results: Average annual inflation in less-developed countries has been 8.6 times higher and the variability of that inflation has been 106.8 times higher than the comparable figures in the developed countries.

Not surprisingly, the IMF's record for promoting sound banking is not any better. Since 1980, more than 50 developing countries have witnessed the complete loss of their banking systems' capital, and in some this has occurred more than once. In a dozen of these countries, more than 10% of annual gross domestic product has been used to clean up the accompanying banking crises. Just since 1980, the total cleanup cost in developing countries has been a staggering $250 billion.

With a record like this, it's time to pull the plug on the IMF.

In today's global economy, the private sector is able and willing to supply capital to the developing countries. Just five years ago, official capital flows to such countries exceeded private flows, but now private flows dwarf official flows. Who needs the IMF?

At the very least we should stop the policy of rewarding the IMF for failure by providing it with new jobs and more money after every crisis. Each time the IMF's early warning system fails, each member country should have its required capital contribution to the IMF cut by a fixed percentage, let's say 20%. With these incentives, either the early-warning system would start to function properly or the IMF would wither away.

 Article Review Form at end of book.

WiseGuide Wrap-Up

Reading 58 argues that the International Monetary Fund (IMF) has been successful in lowering inflation in some countries, especially those in Asia. Further, IMF programs have pressured inefficient governments to retreat from much of the economic activity in which they were previously involved and to allow individual private investors take the lead in economic affairs. In the long term, according to the IMF, this will create economic benefits that will eventually trickle down to the poor and middle classes, who currently suffer from the economic shocks that IMF policies cause.

Jolly's phrase "adjustment with a human face" in Reading 59 recalls the struggles of those who opposed the Communist regimes' top-down policy-making styles during the Cold War. At that time, people called for "socialism with a human face" and asked for policies to benefit people, not just the state. The capitalist policies that international organizations like the IMF require today are being implemented by state leaders with no consultation with their populations. The average citizen is suffering and wants the state to make the faceless state policies of adjustment palatable for the people who must live under them. Jolly calls for adjustment policies that consider human welfare, not just balanced budgets at the state level.

In Reading 60, Ault and Sandberg explain that the decision-making boards of organizations like the IMF and World Bank consist of representatives of wealthy Northern states who contribute substantial funding to these organizations and therefore want to determine the terms on which the organizations make loans. Ault and Sandberg's analysis of the effects of structural adjustment programs on women suggests that, because women must live according to sex-specific roles in many countries, they have additional workloads, are denied schooling when costs for attending schools are introduced, and must allow men to utilize the scarce resources that remain when structural adjustment programs are put into effect.

Hanke's objections in Reading 61 to structural adjustment programs seem to stem less from what might be considered a liberal's concern for the poor than from a conservative's concern that IMF programs are not working. He notes that IMF programs fail to curb inflation, promote sound banking, or provide early warning signals of impending economic catastrophe. Why then should Northern states continue to pour money into the IMF rather than let the private sector deal directly with private citizens in countries that are asking for loans to jump-start their development? Hanke argues that it is time to "pull the plug" on the IMF due to its record of economic failures.

R.E.A.L. Sites

This list provides a print preview of typical **coursewise** R.E.A.L. sites. There are over 100 such sites at the **courselinks™** site. The danger in printing URLs is that web sites can change overnight. As we went to press, these sites were functional using the URLs provided. If you come across one that isn't, please let us know via email to: webmaster@coursewise.com. Use your Passport to access the most current list of R.E.A.L. sites at the **courselinks™** site.

Site name: United Nations Development Fund for Women (UNIFEM)
URL: http://www.unifem.undp.org
Why is it R.E.A.L.? At this site, you can explore all manner of resources related to women and development worldwide.
Key topics: women, development

Site name: The World Bank Group
URL: http://worldbank.org/
Why is it R.E.A.L.? Like the International Monetary Fund, the World Bank requires states to adopt structural adjustment programs before it will lend to those states. Visit this site to determine why the World Bank believes these programs are necessary.
Key topic: structural adjustment programs

section 9

Many analysts warn that a resurgence of religious, ethnic, and national identity is creating intractable political problems and prolonging tragic civil wars. Martin Tyrrell's thesis in Reading 62 argues that the state is not an inevitable political form and that other identities can be mobilized to form other political affiliations. Tyrrell notes that, although capitalists and Marxists want to debate the role of the state and who should control it or what control it should have, we must focus on other units of analysis to understand modern political events.

Ethnic barriers are not just found within states; such prejudices cross oceans as well. In Reading 63, Africanist Michael Chege notes that Africans have long reported foreign Asian prejudice against blacks. Simultaneously, however, Africans have often been guilty of prejudice regarding their minority Asian communities. Now, in the late 1990s, in response to the challenges of global economic competition, Africans are looking eastward for models and making an effort to find common ground with Asians both abroad and at home.

In Reading 64, Samuel Huntington argues that, although communism has been defeated, new threats to the Western world have emerged as domestic revolutions spill over into the international arena. According to Huntington, Western, Judeo-Christian values and enlightenment principles are now in danger of being annihilated by a Confucian-Islamic alliance that is seeking to overpower Western states. For Huntington, this "clash of civilizations" will define the lives of future generations.

In Reading 65, AbuKhalil warns not to homogenize all Islamic political environments and documents. For example, the status of women varies greatly under different Islamic governments.

Key Points

- Ethnicity and nationalism are not the only bases on which people form solidarity, but to understand modern politics, we must analyze these bases for solidarity, instead of just looking at who controls the state and determines the state's economic program.

- Ethnic and racial prejudices are found around the world but may be overcome when people decide they can learn from one another, as is currently the case with some Africans and Asians.

- The values of competing civilizations, not just nationalities, may determine the politics with which our children must live.

- We must be careful to understand the differences among other groups of people. Each human being is an individual first and likely does not agree on all issues with any group of people.

Questions

1. Why does Tyrrell in Reading 62 believe that he has to defend his view that nationalism and ethnicity have important political consequences?

2. Despite years of prejudice against one another, what is causing Africans and Asians to look for ways to cooperate with and accept one another?

3. In Reading 64, between which groups does Huntington predict there will be a "clash of civilizations"?

Nation-States and States of Mind

Nationalism as psychology

Martin Tyrrell

Abstract: *The rise of nationalism parallels that of the state, suggesting that the relationship between the two is symbiotic and that nations are neither natural nor spontaneous but rather are political constructions. Ernest Gellner's economically determinist account of the rise of the nation-state, however, understates the emotive and psychological appeal of nationalist ideology. The Social Identity Theory of Henri Tajfel, by contrast, suggests that nationalism benefits from possibly innate human tendencies to affiliate in social groups and to act in furtherance of these groups, while Serge Moscovici's social psychology of popular belief elucidates the means by which such tendencies can take the shape of nationalism in mass publics.*

In the eighteenth century, it was still possible for a British subject to travel through France at a time when France and Britain were at war. A century later, however, a holiday through hostile territory would have been madness. And so it has remained. Between the 1700s and the 1900s came nationalism and with it, large numbers of people, usually unrelated in any way and frequently quite dis-similar, began to make common cause with one another and with the state, *their* state. It is nationalism, more than any other political ideology, that has made the personal the political, making even the most apolitical people identify with the polity. With nationalism, relations that were once local and interpersonal have become intergroup, and this intergroup context has become fundamental. If there is no "them," there is no "us."

Is nationalism inevitable, however? Many academic commentators would say that it is; that if it did not exist, it would be necessary to invent it. After all, once, when it did not exist, it *did* prove necessary to invent it. The necessity remains. Nationalism, once nowhere, is now everywhere. Today, "a man without a nation . . . provokes revulsion." So claims Ernest Gellner in *Nations and Nationalism* (1983), an almost a priori account of nationalism. In Gellner there is quite deliberately more historicism than history and scarcely a word about the likes of Herder, Fichte, and Mazzini. Nationalist ideologues, the author says, are too much a part of the phenomenon for their explanations to be trusted, and history is primarily an axe that they grind. In place of history and ideology, Gellner puts theory, a theory worth discussing. Central to Gellner's account is the phenomenon of the nation-state, which, to nationalists, represents the only legitimate form of political order. A nation-state is a state that includes all, or nearly all, of the members of a particular nation within its borders. In a nation-state, regardless of how greatly individual citizens might differ in terms of their wealth, power, or status, they will at least have their nationality—their national allegiance—in common. It is to this kind of state that all nationalists aspire and it is with deviations from this ideal that they take issue. To Gellner, the ubiquity of nationalism in modern times is no accident. It is the latest stage in a dynamic process of human social evolution whereby each in a succession of changing technologies—hunting and gathering, agriculture, industry—generates the need for a specific type of social and political order. Industry is the most recent of these technologies and nationalism is, he claims, the style of politics that suits it best. It is the nation-state that supplies the integrated, homogeneous society that industrialization demands.

Martin Tyrrell, "Nation-States and States of Mind: Nationalism as Psychology," in CRITICAL REVIEW, Vol. 10, no. 6, 1996, pp. 233-250.
Reprinted by permission of the author.

States and Nations

In Gellner's account, nationalism has more to do with the state-and nation-building policies of governments and political movements (aspirant governments) than with either "ethnic" culture or spontaneous collective aspiration. Nations begin in politics, either the politics of the state or the politics of a movement that is, however implausibly, a state in waiting. They do not emerge out of culture. Many people today feel a strong sense of personal attachment to a particular national culture, but this is not *why* they live in a nation-state; it is the *result* of the fact that they do. Any national culture and any widespread sense of national identity go through much of their development after, rather than before, the nation-state is in place. Seen in this way, nationalism, so natural to its ideologues, becomes a highly artificial state of affairs, a political construction. Without politics, it is nowhere. Its rise has paralleled that of the state. And just as the wider state is a thing of comparatively recent times, so too is nationalism.

As Eric Hobsbawm (1990) has argued, it was only from the mid- to late 1800s (and then only in Western Europe, North America and Australasia—the "West") that the state began to play a role in the daily lives of the mass of the people. Only from the 1850s onwards were its agents everywhere. They administered law and order, delineated and defended borders, staffed schools and hospitals, collected taxes, and stood for election. They even delivered the mail. In the nineteenth century, much that had been apolitical was politicized and this, together with growing literacy and the rise of mass political participa-tion, began to bring matters of state into every household. Every adult in Britain today knows the name of the prime minister; 200 years ago, many—perhaps most— would not have known what a prime minister was. It was in the context of the growing politiciza-tion of life that popular national-ism flourished. Gellner dates it from about 1800, but Hobsbawm (1983), Eugen Weber (1979), and Walker Connor (1990) all give good reasons for regarding it as a late-nineteenth- and early-twentieth-century phenomenon. Bastille Day, for example, became a regular French holiday only in 1880, at around the same time that the British royal family, hitherto a deeply unpopular institution, ac-quired its current range of public ceremonials. Only in the latter part of the century did the bur-geoning state began to celebrate itself with public holidays and a make-believe antiquity. The rise of the mass media (usually under the direct or indirect supervision of the state) in the twentieth cen-tury has provided nationalism with a further catalyst. Without radio and, later, television, heads of state could not have made their increasingly avuncular addresses to the nation; political careers like those of Churchill, Roosevelt, or Kennedy could not have been staged; the state could not have promoted and publicized itself; the national economy could not as effectively have been depicted as a natural unit to be compared with other national economies in terms of GDP, inflation, the rela-tive standing of the national currency and the balance of pay-ments, all rendered graphically; and the vivid dramatization of competing national identities that is international sport could never have taken place. Events like the Olympic Games and the World Cup, and the strong nationalist passions to which they give rise, are aspects of a specifically twentieth-century form of nation-alism. George Orwell, in his 1945 essay "The Sporting Spirit," wrote:

> At the international level sport is frankly mimic warfare. But the significant thing is not the behaviour of the players but the attitude of the spectators: and, behind the spectators, of the nations who work themselves into furies over these absurd contests and seriously believe—at any rate for short periods—that running, jumping and kicking a ball are tests of national virtue. . . . If you wanted to add to the vast fund of ill-will existing in the world at this moment, you could hardly do it better than by . . . sending forth a team of eleven men, labelled as national champions, to do battle against some rival team, and allowing it to be felt on all sides that whichever nation is defeated will "lose face." (Orwell 1970, 62–64)

If nationalism starts out as politics, then it soon becomes something else. Nationalism is politics with passion, a passion that other political creeds—communism, feminism, interna-tionalism, liberalism—do not con-sistently possess to anything like the same extent. In opting for an explanation based firmly on social and economic undercurrents, Gellner and others say too little of nationalism as an idea and too lit-tle of the emotive power of that idea. Yet, compared with national-ism, said Orwell, "Christianity and international socialism"— market liberalism, too, one might add—"are weak as straw."

Marx may have recognized the threat posed by nationalism; Roman Szporluk (1988) sees the German nationalist Friedrich List as the unnamed target of *The Communist Manifesto*. Marx held that free trade would eventually undermine traditional cultures and loyalties and in so doing, make more explicit the fundamentally class-based nature of society. In a global free market, he argued, the reality that the working class had no nationality but labor and no government but capital would be obvious. Nationalism was, in comparison, simply a new kind of false consciousness. But List, unlike many nationalists, was neither a romantic nor an antiquarian. His argument—influential still—was that "infant industries" in latecomer capitalist economies needed to be protected from competitors if they were to mature. Whereas Marx held that it would be better for backward Germany to be taken over by internationalism, List favored the development of a national German economy via a government-sponsored program of national industrialization. Market liberals (and their erstwhile Marxist allies) could preach comparative advantage all they might; this national economy was what the people wanted. And by the 1920s, it was what the Marxists wanted too. Nationalism, not internationalism, was what took over and stayed in charge. Not every prospective nineteenth-century nation got a state, but many did, and it was largely on the basis of these states that twentieth-century capitalism and socialism developed. In the world today, no state has withered away. You can have any "ism" you like so long as you have a functioning nationalism first.

Thus, it would seem that Gellner's claim that industrialization fosters nationhood is mistaken. Perhaps on the contrary, nationalism sets limits on industrialization. Nationalism is *not* the style of politics that suits an industrial economy best; *internationalism* is. The latter offers the possibility of a universal culture—the "Coca Cola culture" of nationalist demonology—and a homogeneous world market. In practice, however, nationalism is what exists, and it is on the basis of the nation that industry has developed. In times of war, nationalists have been willing to sacrifice long-term economic development for the achievement of national goals. In that sense, war is bad economics; but it is also the nationalist argument followed to where it is going. So nationalism is bad economics, too.

Gellner's historicism fails to fully explain why nationalism rather than either Marxism or free-market internationalism should be one of the more enduring passions of recent times. The processes underlying the nation-state are not just historical, political, or economic; they are also *psychological*. Nations are everywhere—in the media, in history—but they are also nowhere. Nobody has ever seen a nation and nobody would be quite sure even if they had. "What is a nation?" asked Ernest Renan in 1882, and many have asked that since. It is not for want of effort that we are no closer to an answer. Benedict Anderson (1991) has the makings of an answer but to a very different question: not *what*, but *where* is the nation? It is all in the mind. The nation is imagination, an imagined community: "The members of even the smallest nation will never know most of their fellow members, meet them, or even hear of them, yet in the minds of each lives the image of their communion" (Anderson 1991, 6).

Psychology and Nationalism

The social psychologist Serge Moscovici and such colleagues as Charlan Nemeth, Gabriel Mugny, and Stamos Papastamou have developed a model of the psychological processes underlying social influence, processes that explain the development of widespread systems of belief. Moscovici (1976; 1985) contends that popular beliefs originate in the activities of minorities opposed to the prevailing consensus. Such minorities, he argues, are a facet of any intergroup situation, and their actions—indeed their very existence—are evidence that no consensus can ever be total. There are official (majority) and unofficial (minority) "ways of seeing" and frequent exposure to the latter can undermine a person's confidence in the former. Gabriel Mugny (1982) has developed this position. He says that minorities and majorities cannot be defined in strictly numerical terms. Rather, a "minority" is any group opposed to the existing ideological consensus; a "majority," any group that supports it. Both majorities and minorities are, in fact, numerically small; these terms simply name the groups who compete for the minds of the wider population. At the bottom of any process of social influence there is a relatively small social group, and all social influence is ultimately a process of minority influence.

Moscovici's theory of social representation (1981; 1984) addresses the consequences of this process of influence for the popular imagination, helping to explain the appeal of doctrines like nationalism. The precise claims of Moscovici's theory are not always particularly obvious. Like all the best gurus, Moscovici seems incapable of resisting that extra dash of ambiguity. One possible reading of the theory—*my* reading of it—is that a social representation is a kind of vulgarization of some more arcane concept or proposition. Moscovici is more or less saying that distortion invariably accompanies the popularization of ideas; any theory that becomes widely known will also be misunderstood and misinterpreted. In effect, therefore, he is telling (most of) his readers in advance that they are unlikely fully to grasp the actual meaning of his words (or those of anyone else) and that, over time, they might well lose his thread completely. (Perhaps this explains the author's ambiguity. After all, why aim for precision if part of your argument is that the people who read you are going to misinterpret what you actually said?)

Moscovici proposes (or seems to propose) that ordinary people evolve social representations over time by using what they glean from the media or learn at school as "food for thought." In this way, relatively obscure ideas are rendered more everyday or "colloquial." It is in representations grounded in a bedrock of the familiar that political positions, scientific theories, and events from history are made accessible. Delacroix's "Liberty Leading the People" both encapsulates and perpetuates a particularly romanticized view of the French revolution of 1830; "The Spirit of 1776" does much the same for the American Revolution. In Northern Ireland, the many stylized murals of King William III (William of Orange) might not be realistic but they are, nonetheless, more real to many than anything to be found in a history book. Only in Northern Ireland, consequently, do people know William well enough to call him "King Billy." Everywhere else—even in Holland—he is all but forgotten.

"Anchoring" is an important aspect of social representation. Moscovici claims that things that are unfamiliar are often translated into more familiar terms through being "anchored" in something supposedly analogous but actually commonplace. Religion is one of the heaviest anchors conceivable. Connor Cruise O'Brien (1989) observes that nationalism benefited from the demise of religion by becoming, in a sense, a kind of religion. In the aftermath of the Enlightenment, fewer and fewer people were inclined to take religion proper seriously. Nationalism helped fill the gap in part because it was popularized in a manner similar to that of Christianity centuries before. Christianity could not have progressed by theology alone; such aspects of popular devotionalism as hymn singing, the veneration of saints and their relics, pilgimages to holy places, icons, and the appropriation of popular, pre-Christian festivals were crucial to its development as a mass movement. Likewise, all nationalisms have had their anthologies of patriotic songs, prose, and poetry; their national heroes; their monuments; and their borrowings.

Many national ceremonies incorporate religion more directly. Perhaps the key event in the mythos of Irish nationalism is the Easter Rising of 1916, the date of which was chosen with care: Nationalist insurgents decided that the national resurrection would happen on the anniversary of the Christian Resurrection. But Easter is a "movable feast" of the Catholic church and, as such, does not always fall on the same date every year, so the commemoration of the Rising also moves around. It is never celebrated on its secular anniversary (April 24). Even now, no one cares to upset the religious symbolism of the event. Polish nationalism has similar religious overtones. In Mickiewicz's poetry, for example, Poland is the suffering Christ awaiting resurrection, whilst the Black Madonna of Cziestochowa is as much a national as a religious icon.

Personification is one of the most common allegories by which something vague is anchored in the familiar, and it is a staple of nationalism. Most nationalist ideologies posit a very abstract ideal of the nation. O'Brien (1988; 1989) proposes that in the eighteenth century the state, which had hitherto been associated with the sovereign, began to be associated instead with the sovereign people or citizenry. Where once kings had ruled, now it was the turn of the people to do so through a republican state that embodied the Rousseauian "general will." But the general will is ultimately as abstract and unsatisfactory a concept as, say, Divine Right. It implies that a nation is some kind of popular consensus, something that no nation can ever be. The nation-state in practice is not what it is in theory. Government, however national, is not the general will but the will of some exercised over the wills of many. Ideally the state does what you will, but often in the end it wills what you do. The general will exists only as part of the ideological context in which this occurs. It represents the nation as a kind of thing-in-itself exists above and beyond, not to say before and after, the lives of any of its individual members.

Elie Kedourie (1993) suggests that this abstract aspect of nationalism derives largely from the works of such post-Kantian German philosophers as Fichte and Schelling. For them, the Kantian *noumenon*—the thing-in-itself that is outside the world of appearances and thus beyond time and space—becomes a kind of national essence, of which the individuals are the phenomenal manifestation. From this comes the rather nebulous idea of the nation as a somehow trans-historical entity, an enduring whole greater than the sum of its ephemeral parts.

The results of this kind of theorizing are never easy to visualize, even, I rather suspect, for the people most prone to it. If the nation is more than just the sum total of the men, women, and children who comprise it, if it is not merely a quantity but a quality as well, what is this quality? It appears to be too abstract and metaphysical for scientific or historical study, as inaccessible as a Platonic Form. Personification of the nation gets rid of the immediate problem or, at least, renders it more tolerable, if not more soluble. In this case, personification involves the anchoring of unfamiliar concepts drawn from nineteenth-century German Idealism in the most familiar thing of all—people. Nations are frequently personified as a kind of immortal parent, a "fatherland" or "motherland." Fatherlands and motherlands are born and reborn; they rise and they sleep; sometimes they swell with pride but, on other occasions, they shrink in humiliation. From time to time they die (only to be resurrected). Open almost any history book or newspaper and there they will be. "Sweden" was "mistress of the Baltic" in the seventeenth century; "France" was "humiliated" in the Seven Years War; "Turkey" was "the sick man of Europe"; "Italy," "reborn" in the 1500s, was resurrected in

the 1860s; "little Belgium" defied the bullying "Germany" in 1914. I particularly like this last representation because it involves two distinct "characters," anchored in a familiar and enduring story—David and Goliath; top dog and underdog, Tom and Jerry. This is how the event was represented in the famous (and politically influential) "Bravo Belgium!" cartoon from *Punch*—Belgium as a weedy-looking peasant boy guarding the gateway to a field, determinedly shaking a stick at Germany, a fierce, bloated old Junker with a cudgel.

The idea of the nation as a whole greater than any or all of its constituent parts is not the only aspect of nationalist ideology to generate social representations. One of the most important kinds of representation is that of history, not as an account of what actually happened, but as a more nationalistically satisfying myth. George Wells (1991) notes the minimal factual historical basis to the Swiss national myth of William Tell; similarly, little historical basis exists for English national myths such as those of King Arthur and Robin Hood. The Second World War has generated a plethora of historical myths that have yet to be really disestablished: the French Resistance; the Battle of Britain; Churchill as courageous war leader; the classless solidarity of Londoners during the Blitz. Increasingly, it would appear that all of these had their origins in British propaganda at a time (1941) when the war was all but lost (Charmley 1993; Ponting 1994).

Territory is another important strand in nationalist thought and in nationalist representations. Without territory, after all, there can be no nation, and often the very shape of a nation's national

territory comes to function as a powerful signifier of that nation. Anderson (1991) notes the importance of maps in nationalist iconography. With maps, the nation can be imagined as recognizable, "bounded territorial space" (173). Maps can even serve as a kind of logo:

> In the final form all explanatory glosses could be summarily removed: lines of longitude and latitude; place names, signs for rivers, seas and mountains, neighbours. Pure sign, no longer compass to the world. In this shape, the map entered an infinitely reproducible series, available for transfer to posters, official seals, letterheads. . . . Instantly recognisable, everywhere visible, the logo-map penetrated deep into the popular imagination forming a powerful emblem. (175)

The island of Cyprus features on the Cypriot flag, whilst the island of Ireland turned up on the first postage stamps issued by the Irish state after independence. Neither government controlled the entire emblematic territory. Both, however, aspired (and aspire) to do so.

It is precisely in these situations of disputed territory that the doctrine of national frontiers is most often invoked. This doctrine holds that national homelands have been somehow set apart from the rest of the world by a natural barrier. In this way, various geographical and agricultural accidents are invested with a deep ideological significance. It is easy to mock imaginings of this kind, but they are commonplaces of nationalism. Most nationalist ideologies are full of attempts to find these territorial markers; these efforts sometimes lead to the view that the landscape of the home territory is vastly superior to that of any other place. Finding a positive distinction somewhere—

anywhere—is an important way in which the collective identity of the national in-group can be asserted and the perceived superiority of "us" over "them" maintained among its members. Joshua Fishman (1963) demonstrates how nationalists, confronted with a range of national flags, will often assert that the flag of their own nation is superior to the others. The individual designs, because of what they signify, acquire a sentimental "charge" that leads people to adopt what Fishman calls an "ideologized position" towards them. Henri Tajfel (1981) reports similar ideologization among children presented with maps of different countries. Like the royal children in *The King and I*, they tended to overstate the size of their own national territory relative to others and took some persuading that this was not the case.

Social Identity Theory

Effects like those noted by Tajfel and Fishman have both a cognitive and a behavioral component. The cognitive element is the idea of the group in the minds of those individuals who feel that they are its members, together with its corollary, the idea that there are other, similar groups in the world. And though large groups like nations cannot be known in any literal sense—that is, "one member at a time"—Moscovici's Social Representations Theory suggests that a nation can be known in representational ways: as a kind of person with quasihuman characteristics; as an iconic territory; as myth; and as an imagined community. A group such as a nation only really matters, only really has life, when it is an idea or a representation in the minds of a great many individuals. Where

nationalism is concerned, the group is in the individual more than the other way around.

Muzafer Sherif (1956) was among the first social psychologists to investigate the phenomena of group identity and pro-in-group behavior. In Sherif's experiments, boys attending holiday camps were divided, on a purely random basis, into two distinct groups. By way of further differentiation, these groups were given names, colors, and emblems. They were then required to participate in various competitive games and tasks, and their attitudes and conduct were surreptitiously monitored and recorded. Typically, there was a gradual deterioration in intergroup relations, with attitudinal hostility progressing to outbreaks of verbal and even physical animosity.

Sherif's conclusion was that the competitive nature of the situations into which he had brought the groups was the source of all the subsequent antipathy. Others have also noted the ill effects of this kind of competition in intergroup contexts. However, Michael Billig (1976), in a comprehensive analysis of Sherif's findings, concludes that in several instances, the first stirrings of intergroup hostility could be identified well in advance of the start of any overtly competitive activities. In Billig's view, the mere fact that there were two distinct groups by itself seemed sufficient to cause animosity. Competition simply exacerbated the kind of mutual dislike already caused by the unambiguous intergroup context. Where there are groups, Billig argues, there is likely to be straightaway some degree of intergroup conflict, as individuals relate to each other, in the first instance, not as individuals at all, but as members of their respective col-

lectives, agents of social groups, or real-life representatives of imagined communities.[1] Billig comments that a "feeling of solidarity might, in its starkest form, be associated with the label of group membership rather than any significant social facts underlying that label" (Billig 1976, 334).

It is this kind of effect that Tajfel and his various students and coworkers have studied. Out of this research has come Social Identity Theory (SIT), probably the most important research paradigm in European social psychology today.[2]

SIT draws a distinction between personal and social identity. Social identities derive from membership in particular social collectives. This means that most people will have many social identities, deriving from the numerous groups of which they are members. Membership in a family, a church, or a club will confer a social identity, but it is the social identities deriving from racial or national groups that tend to be the most important. This is because these latter identities are less escapable than the others and there are relatively few social contexts in which they are not, to some extent, salient. The world in which we live is a world of nation-states and would-be nation-states. For this reason, it is difficult for people not to think nationalistically and to feel loyalties toward and affinities with their given (if "imagined") national community.

In SIT, social identity is an integral aspect of an overall sense of self. Moreover, just as people can feel good or bad about themselves at the personal level, so, too, can their social identities be a source of positive or negative self-esteem. The degree of esteem arising from membership in a group is proportional to the current standing of that group in the wider world. The nationals of a "second-league" nation-state, the argument runs, cannot possess as much self-esteem as those of a "first-division" nation-state; this should remain true however much and however often those nationals might succeed at the personal level.

However much I might dislike being seen as part of a particular group, though, there will always be those who insist on categorizing me among its members and dealing with me on the basis of this categorization. There are some social identities that, try as we might, we shall never be allowed to shake off. Their permanence limits our options in dealing with them. For some social identity theorists, the option most often pursued is to become *engagé* in the contest between our own and other social groups. Only by doing so can we enhance the standing of the in-group and thereby improve the sense of identity it affords us. But benefiting the in-group in this way can often entail undermining an out-group.

The rise of German nationalism in the nineteenth century offers a good historical example of this phenomenon. Late in the previous century, German intellectuals, influenced by Immanuel Kant's *Perpetual Peace* (1794), aspired to the creation of a universal republic and saw in Revolutionary France the first stirrings of such a state (Kedourie 1993). In the event, however, the political development of France took quite a different turn. Far from becoming a universal home for the disaffected radical—a "Vatican of Reason"—Revolutionary France proved to be merely a more efficient imperial power than its Bourbon prede-

cessor. It made the advancement of French culture and the French state, and the expansion of this state to fit generously defined "natural frontiers," its principal objectives. By the mid-1790s, Republican France was executing its foreign *admirers* on suspicion of treachery and exacting tribute from its so-called *républiques soeurs* (O'Brien 1989). By the early 1800s, France had abandoned even the pretense of being a republic.

It was the sight of its imperial army in Berlin that prompted Fichte's *Address to the German Nation.* Seeing what a self-styled *grande nation* could achieve, he and many others sought to reinvent Germany along the same lines as France. If the French had made citizenship dependent upon ethnic and linguistic criteria, then so, too, would the Germans. Herder's recommendation that Germans—previously francophile and francophone—speak German, not French ("Spew out the ugly green slime of the Seine; German, speak German!") began to be acted upon. If the German radicals could not have a homeland in France, they would have it in Germany. Ernest Mortiz Arndt, in *The German's Fatherland* (1813), gave Germany generous natural frontiers. German intellectuals' embrace of nationalism was, then, a reaction to the French volte-face of the 1790s. What sense could there be in Germans remaining loyal to universalist principles that had been abandoned by the state that had promulgated them? The defense of the German identity against the French required that Germany become itself a kind of France.

Other, more intriguing, support for SIT comes from the series of empirical studies carried out from the late 1960s onwards for

which SIT is known, if at all, beyond social psychology. Tajfel and others at Bristol University used these experiments to text the Minimal Group Paradigm (MGP). Tajfel had his volunteers assigned to groups either at random or on the basis of some trivial criterion. (In one experiment, assignment depended on whether the participant preferred a painting by Klee to one by Kandinsky.) This procedure ensured that the groups in the MGP experiments were genuinely "minimal." Having no historical or sociocultural significance, they could reasonably be expected to excite no loyalty or affinity among their members beyond that which occurs naturally (the independent variable).

Once a volunteer had been assigned to a minimal group, he was asked to allocate points between two anonymous people. These people were never seen and the participant was told nothing about them except that one was a member of the in-group, the other a member of the out-group. Points were allocated using a "distribution matrix" featuring various pairs of points. The participant selected a pair of points on the understanding that the first of the pair would go to the in-group member and the second to the out-group member. Each pair of points on the distribution matrix was designed to allow the participant the opportunity to adopt a particular allocation strategy. Various allocations were possible: "fairness" (an equitable distribution of points); "maximum joint profit" (the pair of points with the largest overall total, regardless of which recipient ended up with the most); "maximum in-group profit"; and "maximum difference" (the allocation that created the greatest possible relative superiority for the in-group).

The "fair" strategy and the maximum difference strategy were of particular importance in the MGP research. If participants adopted a strategy of fairness, the in-group recipient tended to receive *numerically* more points than if the maximum difference strategy were followed. Maximum difference merely established a *relative* advantage for the in-group, and the cost of this advantage was the extra points that would have been gained had a strategy of fairness been pursued. Hence, to discriminate was to incur a cost. Surprisingly, perhaps, successive MGP replications have generally shown that a majority of participants prefer a policy of maximum difference to one of fairness. In effect, most MGP volunteers have felt that the price of discrimination is one that is worth paying.

The implication of SIT is, then, that to have a social identity—whether a "real" social identity or one assigned in a laboratory experiment—is to act in furtherance of such an identity or of the group to which that identity refers, however unfair or even self-denying that action might be. When a person is conscious of belonging to a group, when a group is "in" that person, then there is strong motivation to behave in ways that benefit the group *at the expense of others*. If this tendency is not innate, it is at the very least one that is quickly and comprehensively acquired.

The Need for Psychological Explanations

Marxism aims ultimately for anarchy, whilst market liberalism looks forward to a future in which there will be, if not *no* govern-ment, then at least *less* government. Neither of these aspirations appears likely to be fulfilled. We live in a world in which the principal opposition to any particular state tends to come from some other state or some would-be state, and where politics dominates economics, not the other way around. Since the end of the last century, economies—*national* economies—have always taken shape within limits set by politics. This is why Gellner is mistaken in locating the source of nationalism in the economy. The source is the spread of the state into more and more areas of everyday life. The state politicizes, and nationalism is the result of that politicization. The economy is just one more area that gets "taken over" by nationalism.

Against the view of "modernist" scholars, such as Gellner and Hobsbawm, who hold that nationalism is recent and that national cultures are largely manufactured, "ethnicists" like John Armstrong (1982) and Anthony Smith (1991; 1994) view national communities as developing out of earlier, ethnic communities. In practice, however, there is little difference between these two positions. Even Gellner, seen by some ethnicists (Hutchinson 1994) as the most doctrinaire of the modernists, accepts the role of premodern communal affinities in the development of modern national societies. Similarly, all of the ethnicists would accept that nationalism necessarily entailed a break with the ethnic communities of the past. Nationality might draw upon ethnicity but it is not, itself, ethnicity. In fact, I would argue that nationalists, in their desire to create a homogeneous society, are frequently more destructive than preservative of earlier ethnic cultures.

At any rate, neither modernism nor ethnicism can, in the end, explain the enduring appeal of nationalism. This is not to say that some of its attraction cannot be attributed to the fact that it is, in part, old—although another part of its appeal is that it is, in part, new. But the power of nationalism cannot be mainly ascribed to primordial ethnic ties (too little of it is genuinely old) any more than to its novelty (other novelties have come and gone). A likely candidate for a deeper source is the psychology described by SIT and by Moscovici's Social Representations Theory. The tendency to align with an in-group and to acquire a social identity based upon that in-group is a plausible basis for national loyalty, while the tendency to conceptualize the unfamiliar in terms of the familiar explains why the concept of the nation as a transhistorical, suprahuman entity is digestible.

The implication of Tajfel's research is that people will affiliate with even the most trivial of social groups and will develop strong loyalties in favor of those groups. Because the fate of the group will have ramifications for its individual members' self-esteem, they are likely to discriminate against people whom they have never met and about whom they know nothing except that they are members of an out-group. In a context of in-groups and out-groups, the preservation of the social identity that the in-group affords its individual members will ensure that they behave in ways that benefit the in-group at the expense of others. And if this is what happens based on membership in *minimal* groups, how much more will it happen when the groups to which people belong have been promoted and popularized by culture and state all of people's lives? Nationalism is not the form of politics that suits industrialization best; it is the form of politics best placed to benefit from the tendencies uncovered by the minimal-group experiments.

The nation-state is ubiquitous. All of the many things it touches become politicized in the national interest: sport, the arts, language, even the food we eat and the currency—the *national* currency—we earn and spend. Airports, hospitals, and hydroelectric power stations operated by a nation-state cannot simply be utilities; they become sources of national pride (or embarrassment). Nationalists, and even ordinary nationals, are often able to tell foreign visitors that a particular airport or hospital or power plant is the largest or the busiest or the most advanced in the world. The other political ideologies are as indifferent to such comparisons as to the nationality of athletes. Socialists used to support the ideal of an international language, and by the universalist logic of both Marxism and liberalism neither language nor culture should have any national basis. But the logic of nationalism is precisely to confer significance on real and imagined particularity, beginning with place of birth and residence.

The implication of Tajfel's findings is that if language or banknotes or cuisine or styles of dress or architecture or football teams come to be seen as *our* language, *our* banknotes, and so forth, as distinct from *theirs*, then they are instantly engaged in the implicit competition that goes on wherever the context is one of us and them. And in a world of nations, that is always the context. Nations, once established, will not be so readily disestablished.

Notes

1. Similarly, Gellner argues that mass national identification exists after and not before the political creation of the nation as an idea, an ideal, and a polity.
2. My account of the research in this area is based on Hogg and Abrams 1988, which (in spite of possible normative weaknesses) provides a comprehensive summary of SIT research.

References

Anderson, Benedict. 1991. *Imagined Communities: Reflections on the Origins and Spread of Nationalism.* London: Verso.

Armstrong, John A. 1982. *Nations before Nationalism.* Chapel Hill: University of North Carolina Press.

Billig, Michael. 1976. *Social Psychology and Intergroup Relations.* London: Academic Press.

Charmley, John. 1993. *Churchill: The End of Glory.* London: Hodder and Stoughton.

Connor, Walker. 1990. "When Is a Nation?" *Ethnic and Racial Studies* 13(1): 92–100.

Fishman, Joshua A. 1963. "Nationality/Nationalism and Nation/Nationism." In *Language Problems in Developing Countries,* ed. Joshua A. Fishman. New York: John Wiley.

Gellner, Ernest. 1983. *Nations and Nationalism.* Oxford: Blackwell.

Hobsbawm, Eric J. 1983. "Mass-Producing Traditions: Europe 1870–1914." In *The Invention of Tradition,* ed. Eric J. Hobsbawm and Terence Ranger. Cambridge: Cambridge University Press.

Hobsbawm, Eric J. 1990. *Nations and Nationalism since 1870: Programme, Myth and Reality.* Cambridge: Cambridge University Press.

Hogg, Michael A., and Dominic Abrams, 1988. *Social Identifications: A Social Psychology of Intergroup Relations and Group Processes.* London: Routledge.

Hutchinson, John. 1994. *Modern Nationalism.* London: Fontana.

Kedourie, Elie. 1993. *Nationalism.* Oxford: Blackwell.

Moscovici, Serge. 1976. *Social Influence and Social Change.* London: Academic Press.

Moscovici, Serge. 1981. "On Social Representations." In *Social Cognition: Perspectives on Everyday Understanding* ed. John Forgas. London: Academic Press.

Moscovici, Serge. 1984. "The Phenomenon of Social Representations." In *Social Representations,* ed. Robert M. Farr and Serge Moscovici. Cambridge: Cambridge University Press.

Moscovici, Serge. 1985. "Innovation and Minority Influence." In *Perspectives on Minority Influence,* ed. Serge Moscovici and Gabriel Mugny. London: Academic Press.

Mugny, Gabriel. 1982. *The Power of Minorities.* London: Academic Press.

O'Brien, Conor Cruise. 1988. *Godland: Reflections on Nationalism and Religion.* Cambridge, Mass.: Harvard University Press.

O'Brien, Conor Cruise. 1989. "Nationalism and the French Revolution." In *The Permanent Revolution: The French Revolution and Its Legacy, 1789–1989,* ed. Geoffrey Best. London: Fontana.

Orwell, George. [1945] 1970. "The Sporting Spirit." In *In Front of Your Nose* Vol. 4 of *The Collected Essays, Journalism and Letters of George Orwell,* ed Sonia Orwell and Ian Angus. Harmondsworth: Penguin.

Ponting, Clive. 1994. *Churchill.* London: Sinclair-Stevenson.

Sherif, Muzafer. 1956. "Experiments in Group Conflict." *Scientific American* 195: 54–58.

Smith, Anthony D. 1991. *National Identity.* Harmondsworth: Penguin.

Smith, Anthony D. 1994. *Nations and Nationalism in a Global Era.* Cambridge: Polity Press.

Szporluk, Roman. 1988. *Communism and Nationalism: Karl Marx versus Friedrich List.* Oxford: Oxford University Press.

Tajfel, Henri. 1981. *Human Groups and Social Categories.* London: Academic Press.

Weber, Eugen. 1979. *Peasants into Frenchmen: The Modernisation of Rural France, 1870–1914* . London: Chatto and Windus.

Wells, George A. 1991. *Belief and Make-Believe: Critical Reflections on the Sources of Credulity.* La Salle, Ill.: Open Court.

 Article Review Form at end of book.

Color Lines

Africa and Asia in the twenty-first century

Michael Chege

Times indeed change. In the last week of March 1996, the Kenyan opposition leader Kenneth Matiba made a speech threatening to deport the country's ethnic Asians—now mainly third- or fourth-generation descendants of immigrants from India and Pakistan—should his Ford-Asili party come to power in the next election, currently scheduled for 1997. Using by-now-familiar invective, he inveighed against their "exploitation" of the people, in collusion with President Daniel Arap Moi and the corrupt and despotic cabal that rules the roost in that unhappy land. In comments clearly aimed at the African peanut gallery, Matiba upbraided "these people [Kenyan Asians] for not mixing with us."

The public reaction was instantaneous—and uniformly hostile. Former Kenyan vice president Mwai Kibaki, now in opposition to the government, asked Matiba to ponder the fate of Uganda after Idi Amin summarily expelled that nation's Asian business class in 1972. Njenga Mungai, a parliamentarian in Matiba's own party, pointed to his leader's business links with Kenyan whites and Asians and asked him to stop embarrassing himself. Press reports were overwhelmingly disapproving, calling Matiba brash and irresponsible.

The controversy over Matiba's speech stands in marked contrast to the uproar that resulted in 1967 from the publication of Paul Theroux's essay "Hating the Asians." Theroux, then a young writer teaching English at Makerere University's Extra-Mural Department, suggested in the pages of this magazine (*Transition* 33, October 1967) that Asian-baiting had been made into an art by Kenya's African political establishment and the press. Citing numerous comments on the radio, in newspapers, and in parliament, Theroux's article appeared at a time when residents of Indian and Pakistani origin were being forced to leave East Africa under the threat of "Africanization" of business and the civil service by the newly independent governments. Theroux was vilified by press and pol alike for his depiction of African prejudices.

The very week that Matiba delivered his speech, Nelson Mandela's government in South Africa held a widely advertised conference entitled "The Asian Tigers and the African Lion," attended by economic policymakers from the newly industrializing Asian countries—Thailand, Singapore, South Korea, Taiwan, and Hong Kong. Here the relevance of the "Japanese miracle" and the "Asian development model" was celebrated by all sides. In 1967, the Japanese authorities—honorary whites according to the racial dictionary of apartheid—would have been ill at ease, to say the least, with the African National Congress (ANC), then fighting an armed struggle against white supremacy from outside the country's borders. In those days, Taiwan was Pretoria's only real friend in East Asia, a strategic counter-balance to Beijing's support for the (then-socialist) ANC. It goes to show just how radically political affiliations have changed that even as the conference convened, the Mandela government was weighing the merits of opening a diplomatic mission in Beijing—it still didn't have one—and thereby risking a rupture with Taiwan, its more prosperous trading and development aid partner.

Of course, not all black Kenyans have learned to love their Asian fellow citizens—or each other, for that matter—any more than most South Africans have embraced the idea of Asian tutelage. Black bigotry is still alive and well in Africa, though it is seldom written about, and though it is frequently directed against other Africans in a perverse kind of equal-opportunity prejudice. But on the whole, African attitudes toward local Asian communities (which themselves tend to be deeply segmented on lines of caste and faith), and toward the newly rich East Asian states, reflect a new and more realistic awareness of a mutuality of interests. Predominantly black neighborhoods have elected ethnic Asians to parliament in Kenya, Zambia, and Zimbabwe. Since 1990, the Museveni government in Uganda has invited Asian exiles back and offered them compensation; there have already been a few hundred takers, including the prominent Madhvani family, owners (again) of the expansive sugar plantations at Kakira, east of the capital Kampala.

Economic realism and the course of African history since independence have much to do with the changing attitudes. As with cross-cultural and interethnic encounters throughout the world, Africa's interaction with Asians of various stripes at home and abroad is complicated by several sets of warring demands: of short-term self-interest and long-term social good, identity and difference, despair and promise. But unlike the much-contested—and well-reported—relations that characterize social and politi-

cal life between Africans and Europeans in Africa, and between the African and European diasporas in America, the evolution of African-Asian ties seldom makes headlines or feature articles, even in the African press, unless there is trouble.

This is not altogether surprising. After years of colonial domination and subjection to white racism, the African obsession with Europe and European intentions—real and imaginary—is still an overriding fact of political and intellectual life. For what they are worth—and they are insignificant, by any standard—Africa's strongest external economic ties are still with her former colonizers in Western Europe. (African exports to the European Union amounted to a mere 1 percent of total European imports in 1993.) But given Asia's projected economic importance in the coming century, and Africa's increasing poverty, it is time for Africa to look East yet again, with her feet firmly on her own multiracial ground. And she should do so in a manner that reflects the changes that have occurred since the heyday of Afro-Asian solidarity after the Bandung conference in 1955.

We are standing on the threshold of an age of globally integrated market competition between culturally diverse societies. And while there is, at least for the present, a resigned acceptance of market-based economics, ethnic differences are generating increasing friction worldwide. In order to acquire the conceptual working tools for the future, it would pay to cultivate ideas based on cool-headed national economic interests rather than blanket passions inspired by a Third World "solidarity" better suited to yesteryear. Markets reward initiative un-

equally between countries and communities, and since Bandung they have undermined whatever resemblance may have obtained between Singapore, Somalia, and El Salvador. Ways must be found to accommodate diversity, within as well as between countries. For if there is one lesson to be drawn from the first few years of the post-cold war order, it is the close statistical association between national economic wretchedness and communal warfare based on ethnic or racial prejudice, be it in Bosnia, Berbera, or Bujumbura.

Since most African states have always been ethnically or racially plural, the negotiation of difference has been part of their cultural landscape at least since the dawn of independence. Frantz Fanon in *Black Skin, White Masks* painted a riveting but one-dimensional portrait of the dilemmas of black identity on the verge of decolonization. Fanon stingingly mocked all efforts by the emerging colonial-educated black middle class to denigrate its cultural heritage in the desire to acquire the airs and mannerisms of white Europe—which in turn reacted to their every move with spite or patronizing bemusement. For Fanon, the elemental fact of white racism and European political domination was the defining social event of the age. A black Martiniquan, Fanon generously extended the term "black" to include North African Arabs and Asians of the French empire.

Fanon was right, of course, to observe that the internalization of the colonizer's culture would debilitate the self-esteem of many African blacks. But to truly understand the picture, other dimensions must be added. Since independence, there have been examples of black communities that have successfully mastered their own fate—in spite of colonialism and sometimes because of it—and who still refused to remain hapless victims or minions of Europe. (Consider the unusually high postindependence economic growth rate in Botswana.)

We have also witnessed the devastating effect of African prejudices—not just against other African peoples (pejoratively called "tribes"), as occurred during the Rwandan genocide of 1994 (and the massacres of the Kasai-Luba peoples in Shaba, Zaire, in 1993 and Kikuyus in Kenya's Rift Valley in the same year) but also against Asians in Uganda in 1972, and Arabs in Zanzibar in 1964. In each of these cases those responsible for driving out or exterminating a group inevitably resorted to a discourse of perversion, of "alien exploiters"—the familiar rhetoric of Western fascism. A successful minority, usually specializing in trade, was singled out for an alleged conspiracy to fleece the common folk. Not surprisingly, this rhetoric gets results among the dispossessed, especially in times of economic distress. In seeking to promote the interethnic tolerance currently reigning in Kenya, Uganda, South Africa, and elsewhere, therefore, it is necessary to remember that this humanistic and liberalizing trend will be fought every inch of the way by those who trade in prejudice and conspiracy theories, the extreme left as well as the hard right. The way forward to the greater, and more open, involvement which Africa must seek in Asia in the next century—and which, with time, will itself act as a solvent for bigotry and intolerance—will not be easy.

The prophecy that the twenty-first century will be the "Pacific Century" is gaining currency the closer we draw to the year 2000. The meeting between the Asian "tigers" and the South African "lion" was intended to give the latter a piece of the action. Because South Africa's GDP alone is just slightly less than that of all the other African states south of the Sahara combined, the organizers of the conference billed it as a trial run for future collaborations between the East Asian investors and a Pretoria-led group of African economies.

The idea of the "Pacific Century" reflects the emerging economic might of the Pacific Rim. A quick look at the labels on apparel and consumer goods reveals the variety and sweep of East Asian economies, in the open-air markets of tropical Africa as well as western department stores. Japan is already the second-largest economy in the world, after the United States. In the past twenty-five years the developing countries of the Pacific Basin *tripled* their share of world trade; by the year 2000, their combined share of world production will exceed that of Japan in the 1960s, when it joined the Paris-based OECD (Organization of Economic Cooperation and Development)—the official "club" of wealthy industrial economies. If it maintains its current growth rate into the next century, Southeast Asia and the Pacific may well supersede Europe as North America's most important trading and investment partner.

With the cold war receding into the background, foreign policy and international trade in many developed and developing countries are turning Japanese—or at least, Asian. During his now-expired tenure as Australia's prime minister, Paul Keating repeatedly called himself Asian as part of an attempt to forge diplomatic and commercial links with East Asian states once shunned by Australia's "white Australia" policy. Chile will soon be joining the Pacific leadership summit. About two-thirds of the private investment directed to the Third World ends up in Southeast Asia. Everyone, it seems, is scrambling for a piece of the Pacific Century.

Everybody, that is, except the Africans. And with the slowest and most problem-ridden regional economy in the world, sub-Saharan Africa has better reason to reconfigure its trade and investment patterns than most. For most of the twentieth century, Africa has been a producer of raw material destined primarily for Europe, and it appears likely to remain so into the next. As a market for East Asian goods, Africa takes an insignificant 2–3 percent of that region's exports, despite all the promise and potential.

Speakers at the Johannesburg meeting made much of a glorious, if interrupted, tradition. There is evidence of early Chinese trade in Eastern and Southern Africa. Thirteenth-century Chinese porcelain has been excavated in the Great Zimbabwe ruins, while African ivory, timber, tortoise shells, gold, and live animals made their way to India and China in the 1500s. There is also abundant evidence of Indonesian trade and settlement on the East Africa coast and Madagascar, dating to the 1400s. But all this is, literally, old news: other than as decorative anecdotes in diplomatic speeches, these museum pieces have precious little bearing on contemporary African-Asian relations.

What news there is is almost invariably bad. Twice—in 1979 and in 1989—African students in Beijing were subjected to the most outrageous racial insults and beatings, evidently for having fought off Chinese youths intent on punishing them for partying with local women. Resentment of loud African music in the dormitories, and the generous Chinese government fellowships granted foreign students, seem to have hardened antiblack feelings. By and large, the most sordid racial stereotypes of Africans and the African diaspora—imported over the years via the Western entertainment media—seem to be naively accepted as basic truths in the Far East. Most of the population knows blacks only through Tarzan-style movies, "Sambo" images from American films, goods, and services—and, of course, blacks in international sports and popular music. Since few local educators or writers have the wherewithal to suggest that these images are demeaning and wrong, they are often repeated in public, but with how much innocence or malice it is difficult to say.

At an international African-Chinese studies seminar held in Beijing in the spring of 1994, this writer listened incredulously as a young Chinese scholar, reading from a research paper, told a roomful of sympathetic African and African American intellectuals that Africans lacked any ancient civilizations or technological discoveries. As his argument came trickling through the earphones courtesy of the Mandarin-English translator, it became clear that he had lifted passages of his narrative from some old colonialist tract. When the error was pointed out to him at the end of his presentation, he appeared genuinely contrite; he had assumed that his sources had been written in good faith and he knew no others. The damage caused by the young man's gaffe was mitigated, of course, by many well-informed Chinese presentations from the old

professionals and ex-diplomats who had been to Africa. But, as these examples indicate, the whole debate on the place of Africa in world history has never been of more than passing concern to any but a very small group of experts in foreign ministries and universities; for obvious reasons, there were no sit-ins to demand African and African American studies on Asian campuses during the 1960s.

The Japanese case is similarly instructive. African Americans have been the butt of the most unflattering racial slurs, often coming from the highest places. In 1986, then-prime minister Yasuhiro Nakasone famously attributed declining American competitiveness to the low intelligence of American blacks and Hispanics. Nakasone retracted the statement after protests and a threatened boycott of Japanese goods by African American leaders, only to be followed by another gaffe by Michio Watanabe, foreign minister from 1991 to 1993, who claimed blacks have no qualms about leaving bills unpaid. In 1995 the Japanese director of the World Health Organization, Hiroshi Nakajima, appeared genuinely shocked when his remarks, delivered in halting English, to the effect that blacks could make great speeches but had difficulty writing and being efficient, provoked an uproar among African diplomats in Geneva.

In the same year, and this time without any risk of international censure, Dinesh D'Souza, a naturalized American of South Asian descent, argued in a similar vein that African Americans (and Africans) suffered from a "civilization deficit" to which other more privileged groups in the United States reacted "rationally, not racially."

Inevitably, this kind of careless talk becomes live ammunition for the bigoted fringe on the black side. The popularity of Idi Amin's expulsion order arose not least from a perception of racial arrogance among some Ugandan Asian traders. Though fully justified in his reproach of anti-Asian racism among Africans in the 1960s, Theroux seemed oblivious to the fact that Asians were capable of reciprocating, especially toward powerless employees and customers. This was aggravated by unbridgeable cultural differences—in the Indian pecking order, based on caste and fairness of skin, blacks rank lower than the darkest Indian. Call it the *Mississippi Masala* syndrome: in that film Denzel Washington plays the young black American suitor of a girl whose father, an exiled Ugandan Indian, treats him with barely disguised contempt.

This disdain on the Asian side, combined with the suspicion of outsiders that normally greets foreign traders in poor communities everywhere, produces a highly combustible political tinder that is likely to ignite at the lightest social friction. Ethnic troublemakers know all too well when and where to strike the match. In south central Los Angeles in the spring of 1992, rioters attacked Korean businesses, it was said, because of historically poor relations between the proprietors and their black customers. One incident in Los Angeles matched almost to the letter the event that touched off a riot against Taiwanese supermarket owners in Maseru, Lesotho, in early 1991. In that small southern African town, half a world away from Los Angeles, an African woman accused of shoplifting was allegedly manhandled by store management and humiliated in full view of the public. Hell broke loose as mobs of black youth proceeded to ransack supermarkets all over town, protesting the woman's innocence.

Although these events typically end in high-level reconciliations and polite apologies among political and economic elites, the rancor and mistrust they generate continue to fester. African press reaction to the incidents in Beijing in 1989 was passionately negative; although Sino-African political and economic relations have returned to normal, the Organization of African Unity felt constrained to decline a cash offer from the Chinese in compensation for the sufferings of African students following the troubles. In the United States, the Reverend Hosea Williams, former aide to Dr. Martin Luther King Jr., remarked in mid-1994 that he found "Japan to be the most racist nation in the world" days before the Japanese emperor was scheduled to pay homage at the Martin Luther King Jr. memorial in Atlanta.

There are, of course, countervailing efforts—including government-sponsored "friendship" initiatives. Since 1984, the Japanese government has sponsored an exchange program which has brought hundreds of young Japanese volunteers to African countries, and vice versa. The People's Republic of China has been an avid supporter of anticolonial movements, and her government has been a keen donor to sports and rural development programs in Africa, many of which have succeeded at a lower cost than those funded by western donors. (The Tanzania-Zambia railroad and the soccer stadium in Dar es Salaam, both built by Chinese laborers, are good examples of this.) Taiwan and South Korea have small but growing people-to-people programs with select African countries. Relations between Japanese, Korean, and Chinese technical aid specialists and their African coworkers in various African development projects have been cordial—probably less friction-prone, in fact, than those between Africans and various white western experts resident in the continent.

Furthermore, even where racist attitudes prevail, that racism takes a different form from the kind Africans have experienced in their encounters with Europeans: East is East and West is West, even in matters of prejudice. Like everyone else, Africans concerned with building diplomatic and commercial bridges to East Asia need to understand the often subtle, but substantive, differences. According to a long-term African American resident of Japan, Karen Hill Anton of the *Japanese Times*, foreigners there are despised on an equal-opportunity basis regardless of color. "Some blacks come here prepared to face and repel racism," she explained to the *New York Times* (December 10, 1995), "but if they let down their armor, they will recognize that they are first and foremost part of that larger group called *gaijin* (foreigner) . . . and that means whites too." This is corroborated in the article by long-term white residents of Japan, and also of China and Korea. Despite the profusion of stereotypes and media images, the eastern distaste for foreigners inflects their racialized prejudices. And where racial posturing in the West takes the form of domineering and contemptuous attitudes and behavior, in the East it assumes a studied, reclusive demeanor, a distant politeness, which still allows most business to be transacted in a generally amicable atmosphere. Although it would be helpful to expand the domain of the intercultural contacts already mentioned, it would be even more realistic to recognize the enduring reality of foreignness. For African business in the region must proceed, like any other, against the backdrop of that simple and inescapable fact.

This is already well understood by those small groups of African merchants who have, under very trying financial circumstances, sought to acquire merchandise for sale—not just to other African countries, but also to Europe and the Americas. Before African currencies were liberalized in the 1990s, the business which could be transacted in this manner tended to be small in scale, and surreptitious. Textiles, watches, electronics, computers, automobiles, and kitchenware have been favored product lines. While these traders have not received as much publicity as the drug pushers and smugglers (mostly Nigerian, and operative from Bangkok and Kuala Lumpur to Johannesburg, Harare, and London), they may yet provide the germ of indigenous entrepreneurship that might become the basis for expanded and institutionalized trade with the Far East. These free-lance merchants, many of them women, display greater business acumen than many African government leaders, whose entrepreneurial efforts are limited to maintaining favorable levels of aid and food relief from the West, intimidating their ethnic Asian populations, protecting domestic markets, and funneling kickbacks from all these activities into numbered Swiss bank accounts.

So far I have mostly written as if the East Asian states constitute one uniform region, which of course they do not. And I have also strayed on occasion to the Indian subcontinent, a very different scene, given the historical connection it shares with the East Africa seaboard. In attempting to sketch the broad outline of future Asian-African relations, it would be remiss to ignore the increasing diversity, even competition, between East Asian nations in their policies toward Africa, and the impact of current economic reforms in India on her diaspora in Africa—evidence of which is already visible in the rising Indian investment in Mauritius, the only African economy to have achieved full employment through export-led growth of the East Asian variety.

Although African problems are generally a low priority for East Asia, what African policies they do have are clearly drafted to serve their respective national interests. While it's well known that dealing with Beijing, for example, implies cutting ties with Taiwan, in Africa the rapidly alternating affiliations of some of the smaller states give the practice a peculiar local liveliness. (Taiwan, locked out of the international relations game since the People's Republic was seated at the UN in 1971, has been an avid suitor of repressive governments, including apartheid South Africa and the brutal government of the Gambia.) In the quest for new trade opportunities—especially for her automobile "the Proton"—Malaysia has also been eager to sell the political line of her prime minister, Dr. Mahathir Mohamed, who is dismissive of "Western" ideas of civil liberties and due process. (Sani Abacha's Nigeria has been one of the main beneficiaries.) The two Koreas, like China and Taiwan, used to court opposing sides in Africa, al-

though the North Koreans appear to have curtailed their efforts of late, amid reports of poverty, and even hunger, at home. And Japan has been eager to register African support as she bids for a bigger role in the United Nations Security Council, and global development policy generally; Africa may lack the markets, but it has over 50 votes at the UN General Assembly.

There is nothing particularly radical about these observations. They are the stuff of realpolitik, the motor of international diplomacy throughout the ages. And the challenge facing African nations is that of strengthening their own capacity to formulate national interests, and to pursue them relentlessly—just like everybody else.

Japan is particularly interesting, here: unlike the World Bank and the IMF, Japan's ideas on Third World development prescribe limited state interventions in essentially competitive markets. Japan itself may play a leading role in reconfiguring African economies—Japanese development assistance to Africa grew faster than that of any donor between 1973 and 1994, and now ranks fourth in volume after France, the United States, and Germany. A third of Japan's volunteers overseas are presently working in Africa. And while most Western donors are planning aid cuts to Africa, Japan is likely to expand its development assistance program. By targeting key states like South Africa, Kenya, Nigeria, and Egypt for trade and aid, Japan has focused her involvement on the pillars of regional integration on the continent—and the largest and most diversified markets. Nigeria and South Africa have in addition played key roles in bolstering peace and security in their

respective subregions. This is an issue that Japan has shown some interest in, as evidenced by her contribution of peace-keepers to Rwanda and Mozambique—an unprecedented development in the history of postwar Japan.

South Asia offers another set of possibilities. Even though, unlike Japan, the nations of the Indian subcontinent have per capita incomes roughly equal to those of sub-Saharan Africa, continuing reforms in that region will also affect African states as demand for African goods in that region increases. And the Asian diaspora in Africa could provide the necessary bridge between the Indian subcontinent and Africa in the same manner as overseas Chinese investors in East Asia have fueled growth in mainland China, Thailand, and Indonesia. Good working relations between minority immigrant Chinese industrialists and governments in Southeast Asia have been a key factor in facilitating that process. This is yet another reason to work to intensify the trends in racial harmony that are now emerging in East and southern Africa.

As we come to the end of the twentieth century, it is fitting to recall the prophetic words of W. E. B. Du Bois at its dawn: "The problem of the twentieth century is the problem of the color line; the relation between the darker to the lighter races of men in Asia and Africa, in America and the islands of the sea." The words were spoken at the 1900 Pan-Africanist Congress, one of several that preceded black freedom movements in Africa and the United States. Their foresight was vindicated in the wake of anticolonial nationalism and decolonization of Asia and Africa in the middle of the century. The final act in that drama was the spectacular inauguration of Nelson Mandela as president of South Africa in 1994, whose speech bore a distinct resemblance to Martin Luther King Jr.'s famous 1963 address: "The time for healing the wounds has come. Never, never, and never again shall it be that this beautiful land will again experience the oppression of one race by another. Let freedom reign. . . . Let freedom reign."

The discussions of African lions and Asian tigers in Johannesburg were about a different scene and a different century, about trade lines between the "darker" peoples of Asia and Africa and the islands of the sea, in which the "lighter" races are represented by white Africans, if at all. Still, it is only a vision, and much remains to be done. Especially in Africa.

In the 1960s estimated income per capita in Ghana, Sudan, and Zanzibar was higher than it was in South Korea. Today the citizens of South Korea, Hong Kong, and Singapore are wealthier, on average, than those of Portugal, the Russian Republic, and Greece. It is time for those now at the bottom of the list, mostly in Africa, to rethink not just economic strategy, but also the social and cultural relations that must inevitably accompany them. It no longer makes sense to dwell on a commonality of interests between peoples of non-European descent—the shared grudge against the white ex-colonial powers and the conspiracies they are still supposedly hatching against their former subjects. Color lines have in the meantime also opened within nations, and there are yet other lines to be drawn between people of the same color, lines often painted in blood. It is high time to harness the spirit of toleration to the project of increasing material opportunities. East Asia has shown how the economic part of this equation may be solved. Nelson Mandela and his government have set the pace in the resolution of the other side, the more delicate question of race. As have the courageous souls in East Africa who wish to extinguish the practice of hating the Asians—and indeed, other Africans—as a political sport.

 Article Review Form at end of book.

The Clash of Civilizations?

Samuel P. Huntington

Samuel P. Huntington is the Eaton Professor of the Science of Government and Director of the John M. Olin Institute for Strategic Studies at Harvard University. This article is the product of the Olin Institute's project on "The Changing Security Environment and American National Interests."

The Next Pattern of Conflict

World politics is entering a new phase, and intellectuals have not hesitated to proliferate visions of what it will be—the end of history, the return of traditional rivalries between nation states, and the decline of the nation state from the conflicting pulls of tribalism and globalism, among others. Each of these visions catches aspects of the emerging reality. Yet they all miss a crucial, indeed a central, aspect of what global politics is likely to be in the coming years.

Samuel Huntington, "The Clash of Civilizations?" Reprinted by permission of FOREIGN AFFAIRS, Vol. 72, No. 3, Summer 1993. Copyright 1993 by the Council on Foreign Relations, Inc.

It is my hypothesis that the fundamental source of conflict in this new world will not be primarily ideological or primarily economic. The great divisions among humankind and the dominating source of conflict will be cultural. Nation states will remain the most powerful actors in world affairs, but the principal conflicts of global politics will occur between nations and groups of different civilizations. The clash of civilizations will dominate global politics. The fault lines between civilizations will be the battle lines of the future.

Conflict between civilizations will be the latest phase in the evolution of conflict in the modern world. For a century and a half after the emergence of the modern international system with the Peace of Westphalia, the conflicts of the Western world were largely among princes—emperors, absolute monarchs and constitutional monarchs attempting to expand their bureaucracies, their armies, their mercantilist economic strength and, most important, the territory they ruled. In the process they created nation states, and beginning with the French Revolution the principal lines of conflict were between nations rather than princes. In 1793, as R. R. Palmer put it, "The wars of kings were over; the wars of peoples had begun." This nineteenth-century pattern lasted until the end of World War I. Then, as a result of the Russian Revolution and the reaction against it, the conflict of nations yielded to the conflict of ideologies, first among communism, fascism-Nazism and liberal democracy, and then between communism and liberal democracy. During the Cold War, this latter conflict became embodied in the struggle between the two superpowers, neither of which

was a nation state in the classical European sense and each of which defined its identity in terms of its ideology.

These conflicts between princes, nation states and ideologies were primarily conflicts within Western civilization, "Western civil wars," as William Lind has labeled them. This was as true of the Cold War as it was of the world wars and the earlier wars of the seventeenth, eighteenth and nineteenth centuries. With the end of the Cold War, international politics moves out of its Western phase, and its centerpiece becomes the interaction between the West and non-Western civilizations and among non-Western civilizations. In the politics of civilizations, the peoples and governments of non-Western civilizations no longer remain the objects of history as targets of Western colonialism but join the West as movers and shapers of history.

The Nature of Civilizations

During the cold war the world was divided into the First, Second and Third Worlds. Those divisions are no longer relevant. It is far more meaningful now to group countries not in terms of their political or economic systems or in terms of their level of economic development but rather in terms of their culture and civilization.

What do we mean when we talk of a civilization? A civilization is a cultural entity. Villages, regions, ethnic groups, nationalities, religious groups, all have distinct cultures at different levels of cultural heterogeneity. The culture of a village in southern Italy may be different from that of a village

in northern Italy, but both will share in a common Italian culture that distinguishes them from German villages. European communities, in turn, will share cultural features that distinguish them from Arab or Chinese communities. Arabs, Chinese and Westerners, however, are not part of any broader cultural entity. They constitute civilizations. A civilization is thus the highest cultural grouping of people and the broadest level of cultural identity people have short of that which distinguishes humans from other species. It is defined both by common objective elements, such as language, history, religion, customs, institutions, and by the subjective self-identification of people. People have levels of identity: a resident of Rome may define himself with varying degrees of intensity as a Roman, an Italian, a Catholic, a Christian, a European, a Westerner. The civilization to which he belongs is the broadest level of identification with which he intensely identifies. People can and do redefine their identities and, as a result, the composition and boundaries of civilizations change.

Civilizations may involve a large number of people, as with China ("a civilization pretending to be a state," as Lucian Pye put it), or a very small number of people, such as the Anglophone Caribbean. A civilization may include several nation states, as is the case with Western, Latin American and Arab civilizations, or only one, as is the case with Japanese civilization. Civilizations obviously blend and overlap, and may include subcivilizations. Western civilization has two major variants, European and North American, and Islam has its Arab, Turkic and Malay subdivisions. Civilizations are nonetheless meaningful entities, and while the lines between them are seldom sharp, they are real. Civilizations are dynamic; they rise and fall; they divide and merge. And, as any student of history knows, civilizations disappear and are buried in the sands of time.

Westerners tend to think of nation states as the principal actors in global affairs. They have been that, however, for only a few centuries. The broader reaches of human history have been the history of civilizations. In *A Study of History,* Arnold Toynbee identified 21 major civilizations; only six of them exist in the contemporary world.

Why Civilizations Will Clash

Civilization identity will be increasingly important in the future, and the world will be shaped in large measure by the interactions among seven or eight major civilizations. These include Western, Confucian, Japanese, Islamic, Hindu, Slavic-Orthodox, Latin American and possibly African civilization. The most important conflicts of the future will occur along the cultural fault lines separating these civilizations from one another.

Why will this be the case?

First, differences among civilizations are not only real; they are basic. Civilizations are differentiated from each other by history, language, culture, tradition and, most important, religion. The people of different civilizations have different views on the relations between God and man, the individual and the group, the citizen and the state, parents and children, husband and wife, as well

as differing views of the relative importance of rights and responsibilities, liberty and authority, equality and hierarchy. These differences are the product of centuries. They will not soon disappear. They are far more fundamental than differences among political ideologies and political regimes. Differences do not necessarily mean conflict, and conflict does not necessarily mean violence. Over the centuries, however, differences among civilizations have generated the most prolonged and the most violent conflicts.

Second, the world is becoming a smaller place. The interactions between peoples of different civilizations are increasing; these increasing interactions intensify civilization consciousness and awareness of differences between civilizations and commonalities within civilizations. North African immigration to France generates hostility among Frenchmen and at the same time increased receptivity to immigration by "good" European Catholic Poles. Americans react far more negatively to Japanese investment than to larger investments from Canada and European countries. Similarly, as Donald Horowitz has pointed out, "An Ibo may be . . . an Owerri Ibo or an Onitsha Ibo in what was the Eastern region of Nigeria. In Lagos, he is simply an Ibo. In London, he is a Nigerian. In New York, he is an African." The interactions among peoples of different civilizations enhance the civilization-consciousness of people that, in turn, invigorates differences and animosities stretching or thought to stretch back deep into history.

Third, the processes of economic modernization and social change throughout the world are

separating people from long-standing local identities. They also weaken the nation state as a source of identity. In much of the world religion has moved in to fill this gap, often in the form of movements that are labeled "fundamentalist" Such movements are found in Western Christianity, Judaism, Buddhism and Hinduism, as well as in Islam. In most countries and most religions the people active in fundamentalist movements are young, college-educated, middle-class technicians, professionals and business persons. The "unsecularization of the world," George Weigel has remarked, "is one of the dominant social facts of life in the late twentieth century." The revival of religion, "la revanche de Dieu," as Gilles Kepel labeled it, provides a basis for identity and commitment that transcends national boundaries and unites civilizations.

Fourth, the growth of civilization-consciousness is enhanced by the dual role of the West. On the one hand, the West is at a peak of power. At the same time, however, and per-haps as a result, a return to the roots phenomenon is occurring among non-Western civilizations. Increasingly one hears references to trends toward a turning inward and "Asianization" in Japan, the end of the Nehru legacy and the "Hinduization" of India, the failure of Western ideas of socialism and nationalism and hence "re-Islamization" of the Middle East, and now a debate over Westernization versus Russianization in Boris Yeltsin's country. A West at the peak of its power confronts non-Wests that increasingly have the desire, the will and the resources to shape the world in non-Western ways.

In the past, the elites of non-Western societies were usually the people who were most involved with the West, had been educated at Oxford, the Sorbonne or Sandhurst, and had absorbed Western attitudes and values. At the same time, the populace in non-Western countries often remained deeply imbued with the indigenous culture. Now, however, these relationships are being reversed. A de-Westernization and indigenization of elites is occurring in many non-Western countries at the same time that Western, usually American, cultures, styles and habits become more popular among the mass of the people.

Fifth, cultural characteristics and differences are less mutable and hence less easily compromised and resolved than political and economic ones. In the former Soviet Union, communists can become democrats, the rich can become poor and the poor rich, but Russians cannot become Estonians and Azeris cannot become Armenians. In class and ideological conflicts, the key question was "Which side are you on?" and people could and did choose sides and change sides. In conflicts between civilizations, the question is "What are you?" That is a given that cannot be changed. And as we know, from Bosnia to the Caucasus to the Sudan, the wrong answer to that question can mean a bullet in the head. Even more than ethnicity, religion discriminates sharply and exclusively among people. A person can be half-French and half-Arab and simultaneously even a citizen of two countries. It is more difficult to be half-Catholic and half-Muslim.

Finally, economic regionalism is increasing. The proportions of total trade that were intraregional rose between 1980 and 1989 from 51 percent to 59 percent in Europe, 33 percent to 37 percent in East Asia, and 32 percent to 36 percent in North America. The importance of regional economic blocs is likely to continue to increase in the future. On the one hand, successful economic regionalism will reinforce civilization-consciousness. On the other hand, economic regionalism may succeed only when it is rooted in a common civilization. The European Community rests on the shared foundation of European culture and Western Christianity. The success of the North American Free Trade Area depends on the convergence now underway of Mexican, Canadian and American cultures. Japan, in contrast, faces difficulties in creating a comparable economic entity in East Asia because Japan is a society and civilization unique to itself. However strong the trade and investment links Japan may develop with other East Asian countries, its cultural differences with those countries inhibit and perhaps preclude its promoting regional economic integration like that in Europe and North America.

Common culture, in contrast, is clearly facilitating the rapid expansion of the economic relations between the People's Republic of China and Hong Kong, Taiwan, Singapore and the overseas Chinese communities in other Asian countries. With the Cold War over, cultural commonalities increasingly overcome ideological differences, and mainland China and Taiwan move closer together. If cultural commonality is a prerequisite for economic integration, the principal East Asian economic bloc of the future is likely to be centered on China. This bloc is, in fact, already coming into existence. As Murray Weidenbaum has observed,

> Despite the current Japanese dominance of the region, the Chinese-based economy of Asia is rapidly emerging as a new epicenter for industry, commerce and finance. This strategic area contains substantial amounts of technology and manufacturing capability (Taiwan), outstanding entrepreneurial, marketing and services acumen (Hong Kong), a fine communications network (Singapore), a tremendous pool of financial capital (all three), and very large endowments of land, resources and labor (mainland China). . . . From Guangzhou to Singapore, from Kuala Lumpur to Manila, this influential network—often based on extensions of the traditional clans—has been described as the backbone of the East Asian economy.[1]

Culture and religion also form the basis of the Economic Cooperation Organization, which brings together ten non-Arab Muslim countries: Iran, Pakistan, Turkey, Azerbaijan, Kazakhstan, Kyrgyzstan, Turkmenistan, Tadjikistan, Uzbekistan and Afghanistan. One impetus to the revival and expansion of this organization, founded originally in the 1960s by Turkey, Pakistan and Iran, is the realization by the leaders of several of these countries that they had no chance of admission to the European Community. Similarly, Caricom, the Central American Common Market and Mercosur rest on common cultural foundations. Efforts to build a broader Caribbean-Central American economic entity bridging the Anglo-Latin divide, however, have to date failed.

As people define their identity in ethnic and religious terms, they are likely to see an "us" versus "them" relation existing between themselves and people of different ethnicity or religion. The end of ideologically defined states in Eastern Europe and the former Soviet Union permits traditional ethnic identities and animosities to come to the fore. Differences in culture and religion create differences over policy issues, ranging from human rights to immigration to trade and commerce to the environment. Geographical propinquity gives rise to conflicting territorial claims from Bosnia to Mindanao. Most important, the efforts of the West to promote its values of democracy and liberalism as universal values, to maintain its military predominance and to advance its economic interests engender countering responses from other civilizations. Decreasingly able to mobilize support and form coalitions on the basis of ideology, governments and groups will increasingly attempt to mobilize support by appealing to common religion and civilization identity.

The clash of civilizations thus occurs at two levels. At the microlevel, adjacent groups along the fault lines between civilizations struggle, often violently, over the control of territory and each other. At the macro-level, states from different civilizations compete for relative military and economic power, struggle over the control of international institutions and third parties, and competitively promote their particular political and religious values.

The Fault Lines between Civilizations

The fault lines between civilizations are replacing the political and ideological boundaries of the Cold War as the flash points for crisis and bloodshed. The Cold War began when the Iron Curtain divided Europe politically and ideologically. The Cold War ended with the end of the Iron Curtain. As the ideological division of Europe has disappeared, the cultural division of Europe between Western Christianity, on the one hand, and Orthodox Christianity and Islam, on the other, has reemerged. The most significant dividing line in Europe, as William Wallace has suggested, may well be the eastern boundary of Western Christianity in the year 1500. This line runs along what are now the boundaries between Finland and Russia and between the Baltic states and Russia, cuts through Belarus and Ukraine separating the more Catholic western Ukraine from Orthodox eastern Ukraine, swings westward separating Transylvania from the rest of Romania, and then goes through Yugoslavia almost exactly along the line now separating Croatia and Slovenia from the rest of Yugoslavia. In the Balkans this line, of course, coincides with the historic boundary between the Hapsburg and Ottoman empires. The peoples to the north and west of this line are Protestant or Catholic, they shared the common experiences of European history—feudalism, the Renaissance, the Reformation, the Enlightenment, the French Revolution, the Industrial Revolution; they are generally economically better off than the peoples to the east; and they may now look forward to increasing involvement in a common European economy and to the consolidation of democratic political systems. The peoples to the east and south of this line are Orthodox or Muslim; they historically belonged to the Ottoman or Tsarist empires and were only lightly touched by the shaping events in the rest of Europe; they are generally less advanced economically; they seem much less likely to develop stable democratic political systems. The Velvet Curtain of culture has replaced the Iron Curtain of ideology as the most significant dividing line in Europe. As the events in Yugoslavia show, it is not only a line of difference; it is also at times a line of bloody conflict.

Conflict along the fault line between Western and Islamic civilizations has been going on for 1,300 years. After the founding of Islam, the Arab and Moorish surge west and north only ended at Tours in 732. From the eleventh to the thirteenth century the Crusaders attempted with temporary success to bring Christianity and Christian rule to the Holy Land. From the fourteenth to the seventeenth century, the Ottoman Turks reversed the balance, extended their sway over the Middle East and the Balkans, captured Constantinople, and twice laid siege to Vienna. In the nineteenth and early twentieth centuries as Ottoman power declined Britain, France, and Italy established Western control over most of North Africa and the Middle East.

After World War II, the West, in turn, began to retreat; the colonial empires disappeared; first Arab nationalism and then Islamic fundamentalism manifested themselves; the West became heavily dependent on the Persian Gulf countries for its energy, the oil-rich Muslim countries became money-rich and, when they wished to, weapons-rich. Several wars occurred between Arabs and Israel (created by the West). France fought a bloody and ruthless war in Algeria for most of the 1950s; British and French forces invaded Egypt in 1956; American forces went into Lebanon in 1958; subsequently American forces returned to Lebanon, attacked Libya, and engaged in various military encounters with Iran; Arab and Islamic terrorists, supported by at least three Middle Eastern governments, employed the weapon of the weak and bombed Western planes and installations and seized Western hostages. This warfare between Arabs and the West culminated in 1990, when the United States sent a massive army to the Persian Gulf to defend some Arab countries against aggression by another. In its aftermath NATO planning is increasingly directed to potential threats and instability along its "southern tier."

This centuries-old military interaction between the West and Islam is unlikely to decline. It could become more virulent. The Gulf War left some Arabs feeling proud that Saddam Hussein had attacked Israel and stood up to the West. It also left many feeling humiliated and resentful of the West's military presence in the Persian Gulf, the West's overwhelming military dominance, and their apparent inability to shape their own destiny. Many Arab countries, in addition to the oil exporters, are reaching levels of economic and social development where autocratic forms of government become inappropriate and efforts to introduce democracy become stronger. Some openings in Arab political systems have already occurred. The principal beneficiaries of these openings have been Islamist movements. In the Arab world, in short, Western democracy strengthens anti-Western political forces. This may be a passing phenomenon, but it surely complicates relations between Islamic countries and the West.

Those relations are also complicated by demography. The spectacular population growth in Arab countries, particularly in North Africa, has led to increased migration to Western Europe. The movement within Western Europe toward minimizing internal boundaries has sharpened political sensitivities with respect to this development. In Italy, France and Germany, racism is increasingly open, and political reactions and violence against Arab and Turkish migrants have become more intense and more widespread since 1990.

On both sides the interaction between Islam and the West is seen as a clash of civilizations. The West's "next confrontation," observes M. J. Akbar, an Indian Muslim author, "is definitely going to come from the Muslim world. It is in the sweep of the Islamic nations from the Maghreb to Pakistan that the struggle for a new world order will begin." Bernard Lewis comes to a similar conclusion:

> We are facing a mood and a movement far transcending the level of issues and policies and the governments that pursue them. This is no less than a clash of civilizations—the perhaps irrational but surely historic reaction of an ancient rival against our Judeo-Christian heritage, our secular present, and the worldwide expansion of both.[2]

Historically, the other great antagonistic interaction of Arab Islamic civilization has been with the pagan, animist, and now increasingly Christian black peoples to the south. In the past, this antagonism was epitomized in the image of Arab slave dealers and black slaves. It has been reflected in the on-going civil war in the Sudan between Arabs and blacks, the fighting in Chad between

Libyan-supported insurgents and the government, the tensions between Orthodox Christians and Muslims in the Horn of Africa, and the political conflicts, recurring riots and communal violence between Muslims and Christians in Nigeria. The modernization of Africa and the spread of Christianity are likely to enhance the probability of violence along this fault line. Symptomatic of the intensification of this conflict was the Pope John Paul II's speech in Khartoum in February 1993 attacking the actions of the Sudan's Islamist government against the Christian minority there.

On the northern border of Islam, conflict has increasingly erupted between Orthodox and Muslim peoples, including the carnage of Bosnia and Sarajevo, the simmering violence between Serb and Albanian, the tenuous relations between Bulgarians and their Turkish minority, the violence between Ossetians and Ingush, the unremitting slaughter of each other by Armenians and Azeris, the tense relations between Russians and Muslims in Central Asia, and the deployment of Russian troops to protect Russian interests in the Caucasus and Central Asia. Religion reinforces the revival of ethnic identities and restimulates Russian fears about the security of their southern borders. This concern is well captured by Archie Roosevelt:

> Much of Russian history concerns the struggle between the Slavs and the Turkic peoples on their borders, which dates back to the foundation of the Russian state more than a thousand years ago. In the Slavs' millennium-long confrontation with their eastern neighbors lies the key to an understanding not only of Russian history, but Russian character. To understand Russian realities today one has to have a concept of the

great Turkic ethnic group that has preoccupied Russians through the centuries.[3]

The conflict of civilizations is deeply rooted elsewhere in Asia. The historic clash between Muslim and Hindu in the subcontinent manifests itself now not only in the rivalry between Pakistan and India but also in intensifying religious strife within India between increasingly militant Hindu groups and India's substantial Muslim minority. The destruction of the Ayodhya mosque in December 1992 brought to the fore the issue of whether India will remain a secular democratic state or become a Hindu one. In East Asia, China has outstanding territorial disputes with most of its neighbors. It has pursued a ruthless policy toward the Buddhist people of Tibet, and it is pursuing an increasingly ruthless policy toward its Turkic-Muslim minority. With the Cold War over, the underlying differences between China and the United States have reasserted themselves in areas such as human rights, trade and weapons proliferation. These differences are unlikely to moderate. A "new cold war," Deng Xaioping reportedly asserted in 1991, is under way between China and America.

The same phrase has been applied to the increasingly difficult relations between Japan and the United States. Here cultural difference exacerbates economic conflict. People on each side allege racism on the other, but at least on the American side the antipathies are not racial but cultural. The basic values, attitudes, behavioral patterns of the two societies could hardly be more different. The economic issues between the United States and Europe are no less serious than those between the United States and Japan, but they do not have the same political salience and emotional intensity because the differences between American culture and European culture are so much less than those between American civilization and Japanese civilization.

The interactions between civilizations vary greatly in the extent to which they are likely to be characterized by violence. Economic competition clearly predominates between the American and European subcivilizations of the West and between both of them and Japan. On the Eurasian continent, however, the proliferation of ethnic conflict, epitomized at the extreme in "ethnic cleansing," has not been totally random. It has been most frequent and most violent between groups belonging to different civilizations. In Eurasia the great historic fault lines between civilizations are once more aflame. This is particularly true along the boundaries of the crescent-shaped Islamic bloc of nations from the bulge of Africa to central Asia. Violence also occurs between Muslims, on the one hand, and Orthodox Serbs in the Balkans, Jews in Israel, Hindus in India, Buddhists in Burma and Catholics in the Philippines. Islam has bloody borders.

Civilization Rallying: The Kin-Country Syndrome

Groups or states belonging to one civilization that become involved in war with people from a different civilization naturally try to rally support from other members of their own civilization. As the post-Cold War world evolves, civilization commonality, what H. D. S. Greenway has termed the "kin-country" syndrome, is re-placing political ideology and traditional balance of power considerations as the principal basis for cooperation and coalitions. It can be seen gradually emerging in the post-Cold War conflicts in the Persian Gulf, the Caucasus and Bosnia. None of these was a full-scale war between civilizations, but each involved some elements of civilizational rallying, which seemed to become more important as the conflict continued and which may provide a foretaste of the future.

First, in the Gulf War one Arab state invaded another and then fought a coalition of Arab, Western and other states. While only a few Muslim governments overtly supported Saddam Hussein, many Arab elites privately cheered him on, and he was highly popular among large sections of the Arab publics. Islamic fundamentalist movements universally supported Iraq rather than the Western-backed governments of Kuwait and Saudi Arabia. Forswearing Arab nationalism, Saddam Hussein explicitly invoked an Islamic appeal. He and his supporters attempted to define the war as a war between civilizations. "It is not the world against Iraq," as Safar Al-Hawali, dean of Islamic Studies at the Umm Al-Qura University in Mecca, put it in a widely circulated tape. "It is the West against Islam." Ignoring the rivalry between Iran and Iraq, the chief Iranian religious leader, Ayatollah Ali Khamenei, called for a holy war against the West: "The struggle against American aggression, greed, plans and policies will be counted as a jihad, and anybody who is killed on that path is a martyr." "This is a war," King Hussein of Jordan argued, "against all Arabs and all Muslims and not against Iraq alone."

The rallying of substantial sections of Arab elites and publics behind Saddam Hussein caused those Arab governments in the anti-Iraq coalition to moderate their activities and temper their public statements. Arab governments opposed or distanced themselves from subsequent Western efforts to apply pressure on Iraq, including enforcement of a no-fly zone in the summer of 1992 and the bombing of Iraq in January 1993. The Western-Soviet-Turkish-Arab anti-Iraq coalition of 1990 had by 1993 become a coalition of almost only the West and Kuwait against Iraq.

Muslims contrasted Western actions against Iraq with the West's failure to protect Bosnians against Serbs and to impose sanctions on Israel for violating U.N. resolutions. The West, they alleged, was using a double standard. A world of clashing civilizations, however, is inevitably a world of double standards: people apply one standard to their kin-countries and a different standard to others.

Second, the kin-country syndrome also appeared in conflicts in the former Soviet Union. Armenian military successes in 1992 and 1993 stimulated Turkey to become increasingly supportive of its religious, ethnic and linguistic brethren in Azerbaijan. "We have a Turkish nation feeling the same sentiments as the Azerbaijanis," said one Turkish official in 1992. "We are under pressure. Our newspapers are full of the photos of atrocities and are asking us if we are still serious about pursuing our neutral policy. Maybe we should show Armenia that there's a big Turkey in the region." President Turgut Özal agreed, remarking that Turkey should at least "scare the Armenians a little bit." Turkey,

Özal threatened again in 1993, would "show its fangs." Turkish Air Force jets flew reconnaissance flights along the Armenian border, Turkey suspended food shipments and air flights to Armenia; and Turkey and Iran announced they would not accept dismemberment of Azerbaijan. In the last years of its existence, the Soviet government supported Azerbaijan because its government was dominated by former communists. With the end of the Soviet Union, however, political considerations gave way to religious ones. Russian troops fought on the side of the Armenians, and Azerbaijan accused the "Russian government of turning 180 degrees" toward support for Christian Armenia.

Third, with respect to the fighting in the former Yugoslavia, Western publics manifested sympathy and support for the Bosnian Muslims and the horrors they suffered at the hands of the Serbs. Relatively little concern was expressed, however, over Croatian attacks on Muslims and participation in the dismemberment of Bosnia-Herzegovina. In the early stages of the Yugoslav breakup, Germany, in an unusual display of diplomatic initiative and muscle, induced the other 11 members of the European Community to follow its lead in recognizing Slovenia and Croatia. As a result of the pope's determination to provide strong backing to the two Catholic countries, the Vatican extended recognition even before the Community did. The United States followed the European lead. Thus the leading actors in Western civilization rallied behind their coreligionists. Subsequently Croatia was reported to be receiving substantial quantities of arms from Central European and other Western countries. Boris Yeltsin's

government, on the other hand, attempted to pursue a middle course that would be sympathetic to the Orthodox Serbs but not alienate Russia from the West. Russian conservative and nationalist groups, however, including many legislators, attacked the government for not being more forthcoming in its support for the Serbs. By early 1993 several hundred Russians apparently were serving with the Serbian forces, and reports circulated of Russian arms being supplied to Serbia.

Islamic governments and groups, on the other hand, castigated the West for not coming to the defense of the Bosnians. Iranian leaders urged Muslims from all countries to provide help to Bosnia; in violation of the U.N. arms embargo, Iran supplied weapons and men for the Bosnians; Iranian-supported Lebanese groups sent guerrillas to train and organize the Bosnian forces. In 1993 up to 4,000 Muslims from over two dozen Islamic countries were reported to be fighting in Bosnia. The governments of Saudi Arabia and other countries felt under increasing pressure from fundamentalist groups in their own societies to provide more vigorous support for the Bosnians. By the end of 1992, Saudi Arabia had reportedly supplied substantial funding for weapons and supplies for the Bosnians, which significantly increased their military capabilities vis-à-vis the Serbs.

In the 1930s the Spanish Civil War provoked intervention from countries that politically were fascist, communist and democratic. In the 1990s the Yugoslav conflict is provoking intervention from countries that are Muslim, Orthodox and Western Christian. The parallel has not gone unnoticed. "The war in

Bosnia-Herzegovina has become the emotional equivalent of the fight against fascism in the Spanish Civil War," one Saudi editor observed. "Those who died there are regarded as martyrs who tried to save their fellow Muslims."

Conflicts and violence will also occur between states and groups within the same civilization. Such conflicts, however, are likely to be less intense and less likely to expand than conflicts between civilizations. Common membership in a civilization reduces the probability of violence in situations where it might otherwise occur. In 1991 and 1992 many people were alarmed by the possibility of violent conflict between Russia and Ukraine over territory, particularly Crimea, the Black Sea fleet, nuclear weapons and economic issues. If civilization is what counts, however, the likelihood of violence between Ukrainians and Russians should be low. They are two Slavic, primarily Orthodox peoples who have had close relationships with each other for centuries. As of early 1993, despite all the reasons for conflict, the leaders of the two countries were effectively negotiating and defusing the issues between the two countries. While there has been serious fighting between Muslims and Christians elsewhere in the former Soviet Union and much tension and some fighting between Western and Orthodox Christians in the Baltic states, there has been virtually no violence between Russians and Ukrainians.

Civilization rallying to date has been limited, but it has been growing, and it clearly has the potential to spread much further. As the conflicts in the Persian Gulf, the Caucasus and Bosnia contin-

ued, the positions of nations and the cleavages between them increasingly were along civilizational lines. Populist politicians, religious leaders and the media have found it a potent means of arousing mass support and of pressuring hesitant governments. In the coming years, the local conflicts most likely to escalate into major wars will be those, as in Bosnia and the Caucasus, along the fault lines between civilizations. The next world war, if there is one, will be a war between civilizations.

The West Versus The Rest

The West is now at an extraordinary peak of power in relation to other civilizations. Its superpower opponent has disappeared from the map. Military conflict among Western states is unthinkable, and Western military power is unrivaled. Apart from Japan, the West faces no economic challenge. It dominates international political and security institutions and with Japan international economic institutions. Global political and security issues are effectively settled by a directorate of the United States, Britain and France, world economic issues by a directorate of the United States, Germany and Japan, all of which maintain extraordinarily close relations with each other to the exclusion of lesser and largely non-Western countries. Decisions made at the U.N. Security Council or in the International Monetary Fund that reflect the interests of the West are presented to the world as reflecting the desires of the world community. The very phrase "the world community" has become the euphemistic collective noun

(replacing "the Free World") to give global legitimacy to actions reflecting the interests of the United States and other Western powers.[4] Through the IMF and other international economic institutions, the West promotes its economic interests and imposes on other nations the economic policies it thinks appropriate. In any poll of non-Western peoples, the IMF undoubtedly would win the support of finance ministers and a few others, but get in overwhelmingly unfavorable rating from just about everyone else, who would agree with Georgy Arbatov's characterization of IMF officials as "neo-Bolsheviks who love expropriating other people's money, imposing undemocratic and alien rules of economic and political conduct and stifling economic freedom."

Western domination of the U.N. Security Council and its decisions, tempered only by occasional abstention by China, produced U.N. legitimation of the West's use of force to drive Iraq out of Kuwait and its elimination of Iraq's sophisticated weapons and capacity to produce such weapons. It also produced the quite unprecedented action by the United States, Britain and France in getting the Security Council to demand that Libya hand over the Pan Am 103 bombing suspects and then to impose sanctions when Libya refused. After defeating the largest Arab army, the West did not hesitate to throw its weight around in the Arab world. The West in effect is using international institutions, military power and economic resources to run the world in ways that will maintain Western predominance, protect Western interests and promote Western political and economic values.

That at least is the way in which non-Westerners see the new world, and there is a significant element of truth in their view. Differences in power and struggles for military, economic and institutional power are thus one source of conflict between the West and other civilizations. Differences in culture, that is basic values and beliefs, are a second source of conflict. V. S. Naipaul has argued that Western civilization is the "universal civilization" that "fits all men." At a superficial level much of Western culture has indeed permeated the rest of the world. At a more basic level, however, Western concepts differ fundamentally from those prevalent in other civilizations. Western ideas of individualism, liberalism, constitutionalism, human rights, equality, liberty, the rule of law, democracy, free markets, the separation of church and state, often have little resonance in Islamic, Confucian, Japanese, Hindu, Buddhist or Orthodox cultures. Western efforts to propagate such ideas produce instead a reaction against "human rights imperialism" and a reaffirmation of indigenous values, as can be seen in the support for religious fundamentalism by the younger generation in non-Western cultures. The very notion that there could be a "universal civilization" is a Western idea, directly at odds with the particularism of most Asian societies and their emphasis on what distinguishes one people from another. Indeed, the author of a review of 100 comparative studies of values in different societies concluded that "the values that are most important in the West are least important worldwide."[5] In the political realm, of course, these differences are most manifest in the efforts of the United States and other Western powers to induce other peoples to adopt Western ideas concerning democracy and human rights. Modern democratic government originated in the West. When it has developed in non-Western societies it has usually been the product of Western colonialism or imposition.

The central axis of world politics in the future is likely to be, in Kishore Mahbubani's phrase, the conflict between "the West and the Rest" and the responses of non-Western civilizations to Western power and values.[6] Those responses generally take one or a combination of three forms. At one extreme, non-Western states can, like Burma and North Korea, attempt to pursue a course of isolation, to insulate their societies from penetration or "corruption" by the West, and, in effect, to opt out of participation in the Western-dominated global community. The costs of this course, however, are high, and few states have pursued it exclusively. A second alternative, the equivalent of "band-wagoning" in international relations theory, is to attempt to join the West and accept its values and institutions. The third alternative is to attempt to "balance" the West by developing economic and military power and cooperating with other non-Western societies against the West, while preserving indigenous values and institutions; in short, to modernize but not to Westernize.

The Torn Countries

In the future, as people differentiate themselves by civilization, countries with large numbers of peoples of different civilizations, such as the Soviet Union and Yugoslavia, are candidates for dismemberment. Some other countries have a fair degree of cultural homogeneity but are divided over whether their society belongs to one civilization or another. These are torn countries. Their leaders typically wish to pursue a band-wagoning strategy and to make their countries members of the West, but the history, culture and traditions of their countries are non-Western. The most obvious and prototypical torn country is Turkey. The late twentieth-century leaders of Turkey have followed in the Attatürk tradition and defined Turkey as a modern, secular, Western nation state. They allied Turkey with the West in NATO and in the Gulf War; they applied for membership in the European Community. At the same time, however, elements in Turkish society have supported an Islamic revival and have argued that Turkey is basically a Middle Eastern Muslim society. In addition, while the elite of Turkey has defined Turkey as a Western society, the elite of the West refuses to accept Turkey as such. Turkey will not become a member of the European Community, and the real reason, as President Özal said, "is that we are Muslim and they are Christian and they don't say that." Having rejected Mecca, and then being rejected by Brussels, where does Turkey look? Tashkent may be the answer. The end of the Soviet Union gives Turkey the opportunity to become the leader of a revived Turkic civilization involving seven countries from the borders of Greece to those of China. Encouraged by the West, Turkey is making strenuous efforts to carve out this new identity for itself.

During the past decade Mexico has assumed a position somewhat similar to that of Turkey. Just as Turkey abandoned its historic opposition to Europe and attempted to join Europe,

Mexico has stopped defining itself by its opposition to the United States and is instead attempting to imitate the United States and to join it in the North American Free Trade Area. Mexican leaders are engaged in the great task of redefining Mexican identity and have introduced fundamental economic reforms that eventually will lead to fundamental political change. In 1991 a top adviser to President Carlos Salinas de Gortari described at length to me all the changes the Salinas government was making. When he finished, I remarked: "That's most impressive. It seems to me that basically you want to change Mexico from a Latin American country into a North American country." He looked at me with surprise and exclaimed: "Exactly! That's precisely what we are trying to do, but of course we could never say so publicly." As his remark indicates, in Mexico as in Turkey, significant elements in society resist the redefinition of their country's identity. In Turkey, European-oriented leaders have to make gestures to Islam (Özal's pilgrimage to Mecca); so also Mexico's North American-oriented leaders have to make gestures to those who hold Mexico to be a Latin American country (Salinas' Ibero-American Guadalajara summit).

Historically Turkey has been the most profoundly torn country. For the United States, Mexico is the most immediate torn country. Globally the most important torn country is Russia. The question of whether Russia is part of the West or the leader of a distinct Slavic-Orthodox civilization has been a recurring one in Russian history. That issue was obscured by the communist victory in Russia, which imported a Western ideology, adapted it to Russian conditions and then challenged the West in the name of that ideology. The dominance of communism shut off the historic debate over Westernization versus Russification. With communism discredited Russians once again face that question.

President Yeltsin is adopting Western principles and goals and seeking to make Russia a "normal" country and a part of the West. Yet both the Russian elite and the Russian public are divided on this issue. Among the more moderate dissenters, Sergei Stankevich argues that Russia should reject the "Atlanticist" course, which would lead it "to become European, to become a part of the world economy in rapid and organized fashion, to become the eighth member of the Seven, and to put particular emphasis on Germany and the United States as the two dominant members of the Atlantic alliance." While also rejecting an exclusively Eurasian policy, Stankevich nonetheless argues that Russia should give priority to the protection of Russians in other countries, emphasize its Turkic and Muslim connections, and promote "an appreciable redistribution of our resources, our options, our ties, and our interests in favor of Asia, of the eastern direction." People of this persuasion criticize Yeltsin for subordinating Russia's interests to those of the West, for reducing Russian military strength, for failing to support traditional friends such as Serbia, and for pushing economic and political reform in ways injurious to the Russian people. Indicative of this trend is the new popularity of the ideas of Petr Savitsky, who in the 1920s argued that Russia was a unique Eurasian civilization.[7] More extreme dissidents voice much more blatantly nationalist, anti-Western and anti-Semitic views, and urge Russia to redevelop its military strength and to establish closer ties with China and Muslim countries. The people of Russia are as divided as the elite. An opinion survey in European Russia in the spring of 1992 revealed that 40 percent of the public had positive attitudes toward the West and 36 percent had negative attitudes. As it has been for much of its history, Russia in the early 1990s is truly a torn country.

To redefine its civilization identity, a torn country must meet three requirements. First, its political and economic elite has to be generally supportive of and enthusiastic about this move. Second, its public has to be willing to acquiesce in the redefinition. Third, the dominant groups in the recipient civilization have to be willing to embrace the convert. All three requirements in large part exist with respect to Mexico. The first two in large part exist with respect to Turkey. It is not clear that any of them exist with respect to Russia's joining the West. The conflict between liberal democracy and Marxism-Leninism was between ideologies which, despite their major differences, ostensibly shared ultimate goals of freedom, equality and prosperity. A traditional, authoritarian, nationalist Russia could have quite different goals. A Western democrat could carry on an intellectual debate with a Soviet Marxist. It would be virtually impossible for him to do that with a Russian traditionalist. If, as the Russians stop behaving like Marxists, they reject liberal democracy and begin behaving like Russians but not like Westerners, the relations between Russia and the West could again become distant and conflictual.[8]

The Confucian-Islamic Connection

The obstacles to non-Western countries joining the West vary considerably. They are least for Latin American and East European countries. They are greater for the Orthodox countries of the former Soviet Union. They are still greater for Muslim, Confucian, Hindu and Buddhist societies. Japan has established a unique position for itself as an associate member of the West: it is in the West in some respects but clearly not of the West in important dimensions. Those countries that for reason of culture and power do not wish to, or cannot, join the West compete with the West by developing their own economic, military and political power. They do this by promoting their internal development and by cooperating with other non-Western countries. The most prominent form of this cooperation is the Confucian-Islamic connection that has emerged to challenge Western interests, values and power.

Almost without exception, Western countries are reducing their military power; under Yeltsin's leadership so also is Russia. China, North Korea and several Middle Eastern states, however, are significantly expanding their military capabilities. They are doing this by the import of arms from Western and non-Western sources and by the development of indigenous arms industries. One result is the emergence of what Charles Krauthammer has called "Weapon States," and the Weapon States are not Western states. Another result is the redefinition of arms control, which is a Western concept and a Western goal. During the Cold War the primary purpose of arms control was to establish a stable military balance between the United States and its allies and the Soviet Union and its allies. In the post-Cold War world the primary objective of arms control is to prevent the development by non-Western societies of military capabilities that could threaten Western interests. The West attempts to do this through international agreements, economic pressure and controls on the transfer of arms and weapons technologies.

The conflict between the West and the Confucian-Islamic states focuses largely, although not exclusively, on nuclear, chemical and biological weapons, ballistic missiles and other sophisticated means for delivering them, and the guidance, intelligence and other electronic capabilities for achieving that goal. The West promotes nonproliferation as a universal norm and nonproliferation treaties and inspections as means of realizing that norm. It also threatens a variety of sanctions against those who promote the spread of sophisticated weapons and proposes some benefits for those who do not. The attention of the West focuses, naturally, on nations that are actually or potentially hostile to the West.

The non-Western nations, on the other hand, assert their right to acquire and to deploy whatever weapons they think necessary for their security. They also have absorbed, to the full, the truth of the response of the Indian defense minister when asked what lesson he learned from the Gulf War. "Don't fight the United States unless you have nuclear weapons." Nuclear weapons, chemical weapons and missiles are viewed, probably erroneously, as the potential equalizer of superior Western conventional power. China, of course, already has nuclear weapons; Pakistan and India have the capability to deploy them. North Korea, Iran, Iraq, Libya and Algeria appear to be attempting to acquire them. A top Iranian official has declared that all Muslim states should acquire nuclear weapons, and in 1988 the president of Iran reportedly issued a directive calling for development of "offensive and defensive chemical, biological and radiological weapons."

Centrally important to the development of counter-West military capabilities is the sustained expansion of China's military power and its means to create military power. Buoyed by spectacular economic development, China is rapidly increasing its military spending and vigorously moving forward with the modernization of its armed forces. It is purchasing weapons from the former Soviet states; it is developing long-range missiles; in 1992 it tested a one-megaton nuclear device. It is developing power-projection capabilities, acquiring aerial refueling technology, and trying to purchase an aircraft carrier. Its military buildup and assertion of sovereignty over the South China Sea are provoking a multilateral regional arms race in East Asia. China is also a major exporter of arms and weapons technology. It has exported materials to Libya and Iraq that could be used to manufacture nuclear weapons and nerve gas. It has helped Algeria build a reactor suitable for nuclear weapons research and production. China has sold to Iran nuclear technology that American officials believe could only be used to create weapons and apparently has shipped components of 300-mile-range missiles to Pakistan. North

Korea has had a nuclear weapons program under way for some while and has sold advanced missiles and missile technology to Syria and Iran. The flow of weapons and weapons technology is generally from East Asia to the Middle East. There is, however, some movement in the reverse direction; China has received Stinger missiles from Pakistan.

A Confucian-Islamic military connection has thus come into being, designed to promote acquisition by its members of the weapons and weapons technologies needed to counter the military power of the West. It may or may not last. At present, however, it is, as Dave McCurdy has said, "a renegades' mutual support pact, run by the proliferators and their backers." A new form of arms competition is thus occurring between Islamic-Confucian states and the West. In an old-fashioned arms race, each side developed its own arms to balance or to achieve superiority against the other side. In this new form of arms competition, one side is developing its arms and the other side is attempting not to balance but to limit and prevent that arms build-up while at the same time reducing its own military capabilities.

Implications for the West

This article does not argue that civilization identities will replace all other identities, that nation states will disappear, that each civilization will become a single coherent political entity, that groups within a civilization will not conflict with and even fight

each other. This paper does set forth the hypotheses that differences between civilizations are real and important; civilization-consciousness is increasing; conflict between civilizations will supplant ideological and other forms of conflict, as the dominant global form of conflict; international relations, historically a game played out within Western civilization, will increasingly be de-Westernized and become a game in which non-Western civilizations are actors and not simply objects; successful political, security and economic international institutions are more likely to develop within civilizations than across civilizations; conflicts between groups in different civilizations will be more frequent, more sustained and more violent than conflicts between groups in the same civilization; violent conflicts between groups in different civilizations are the most likely and most dangerous source of escalation that could lead to global wars; the paramount axis of world politics will be the relations between "the West and the Rest"; the elites in some torn non-Western countries will try to make their countries part of the West, but in most cases face major obstacles to accomplishing this; a central focus of conflict for the immediate future will be between the West and several Islamic-Confucian states.

This is not to advocate the desirability of conflicts between civilizations. It is to set forth descriptive hypotheses as to what the future may be like. If these are plausible hypotheses, however, it is necessary to consider their implications for Western policy. These implications should be

divided between short-term advantage and long-term accommodation. In the short term it is clearly in the interest of the West to promote greater cooperation and unity within its own civilization, particularly between its European and North American components; to incorporate into the West societies in Eastern Europe and Latin America whose cultures are close to those of the West; to promote and maintain cooperative relations with Russia and Japan; to prevent escalation of local inter-civilization conflicts into major inter-civilization wars; to limit the expansion of the military strength of Confucian and Islamic states; to moderate the reduction of Western military capabilities and maintain military superiority in East and Southwest Asia; to exploit differences and conflicts among Confucian and Islamic states; to support in other civilizations groups sympathetic to Western values and interests; to strengthen international institutions that reflect and legitimate Western interests and values and to promote the involvement of non-Western states in those institutions.

In the longer term other measures would be called for. Western civilization is both Western and modern. Non-Western civilizations have attempted to become modern without becoming Western. To date only Japan has fully succeeded in this quest. Non-Western civilizations will continue to attempt to acquire the wealth, technology, skills, machines and weapons that are part of being modern. They will also attempt to reconcile this modernity with their traditional culture and values. Their economic and military strength relative to the West will increase. Hence the West will increasingly have to accommodate these non-Western modern civilizations whose power approaches that of the West but whose values and interests differ significantly from those of the West. This will require the West to maintain the economic and military power necessary to protect its interests in relation to these civilizations. It will also, however, require the West to develop a more profound understanding of the basic religious and philosophical assumptions underlying other civilizations and the ways in which people in those civilizations see their interests. It will require an effort to identify elements of commonality between Western and other civilizations. For the relevant future, there will be no universal civilization, but instead a world of different civilizations, each of which will have to learn to coexist with the others.

Notes

1. Murray Weidenbaum, *Greater China: The Next Economic Superpower?*, St. Louis: Washington University Center for the Study of American Business, Contemporary Issues, Series 57, February 1993, pp. 2–3.
2. Bernard Lewis, "The Roots of Muslim Rage," *The Atlantic Monthly*, vol. 266, September 1990, p. 60; *Time*, June 15, 1992, pp. 24–28.
3. Archie Roosevelt, *For Lust of Knowing*, Boston: Little, Brown, 1988, pp. 332–333.
4. Almost invariably Western leaders claim they are acting on behalf of "the world community." One minor lapse occurred during the run-up to the Gulf War. In an interview on "Good Morning America," Dec. 21, 1990, British Prime Minister John Major referred to the actions "the West" was taking against Saddam Hussein. He quickly corrected himself and subsequently referred to "the world community." He was, however, right when he erred.
5. Harry C. Triandis, *The New York Times*, Dec. 25, 1990, p. 41, and "Cross-Cultural Studies of Individualism and Collectivism," Nebraska Symposium on Motivation, vol. 37, 1989, pp. 41-133.
6. Kishore Mahbubani, "The West and the Rest," *The National Interest*, Summer 1992, pp. 3–13.
7. Sergei Stankevich, "Russia in Search of Itself," *The National Interest*, Summer 1992, pp. 47–51; Daniel Schneider, "A Russian Movement Rejects Western Tilt," *Christian Science Monitor*, Feb. 5, 1993, pp. 5–7.
8. Owen Harries has pointed out that Australia is trying (unwisely in his view) to become a torn country in reverse. Although it has been a full member not only of the West but also of the ABCA military and intelligence core of the West, its current leaders are in effect proposing that it defect from the West, redefine itself as an Asian country and cultivate close ties with its neighbors. Australia's future, they argue, is with the dynamic economies of East Asia. But, as I have suggested, close economic cooperation normally requires a common cultural base. In addition, none of the three conditions necessary for a torn country to join another civilization is likely to exist in Austrailia's case.

 Article Review Form at end of book.

Toward the Study of Women and Politics in the Arab World

The debate and the reality

As 'ad AbuKhalil

Abstract: *This article deals with the subject of political roles of women in the Arab world. It argues that, while the conditions of women are not uniform in the region, there are some general common factors that inhibit women's participation in the political process. The article also addresses the subject of Islamic determinants—or lack thereof—of the status of women in Arab society. An analysis of the feminist debate is presented, and some trends are identified. The analysis focuses on the interaction between Islam and culture in an attempt to determine the role of each in the oppression of women. A critique of the antifeminist and "Islamic feminist" viewpoints is included. The article offers some methodological suggestions for the comparative study of women and politics in the Arab world, with special emphasis on: voting, legalistic/ constitutional method, informal vs. formal politics, and the impact of modernization. The conclusion is predicated on the belief in the limitations of a feminist struggle within the parameters of religion, any religion— in this case Islam.*

The notion that women are inferior to men permeates all cultures and most religions, including the three monotheistic religions. Even in advanced industrial societies the struggle for gender equality is far from accomplishing its aims; and women's groups in the United States were hoping in 1992 that female representation in the U.S. Senate would increase from 2 percent to 8 percent, which is, of course, far below the percentage of women in the American population.[1] (Other Western countries have higher female representation in their legislatures than the U.S. Congress, but none have female representation reflective of the female percentage in the general population).[2] While the idea of gender equality was regarded as rational by John Stuart Mill in his *The Subjection of Women*[3], Hegel warned that "when women hold the helm of government, the state is at once in jeopardy, because women regulate their actions not by the demands of universality but by arbitrary inclinations and opinions.[4] While this might not be

surprising for somebody whose political thought is associated— perhaps too simplistically—with "what is actual is rational," the idea of full gender equality is associated—even in Western countries—with radicalism and "men bashing."

This issue of women's liberation and feminist struggle is even more controversial and sensitive in the Arab world. The two most problematic aspects of the subject revolve around the interpretations of Islam and the legacy of what Leila Ahmed calls "colonial feminism."[5] Colonial feminism, according to Ahmed, refers to the tendency of colonial officials in the region to raise the banner of women's liberation in the Arab/ Muslim world while these same officials take misogynist stances in their own countries. It refers to the exploitation of the women's question by colonial administrators for purely political purposes. This exploitation left the region with a legacy that allowed misogynist thinkers and clerics to discredit feminism by associating women's liberation with colonialism, Zionism, and even Freemasonry.[6] Surprisingly, even Ahmed herself tried to discredit one of the first Arab writers on the status of women, Qasim Amin[7]—who was certainly not a feminist—, by maintaining that the idea that Amin wrote his *Tahrir Al-Mar'ah* (The Liberation of Women) in 1899 at the urging of the British consul general in Egypt "was not perhaps altogether farfetched."[8] There is no evidence, however, and Ahmed provided no evidence, to support this allegation.[9]

The Middle Eastern culture has historically been associated with the oppression of women, and the plight of Arab/Muslim women has become an issue that is often used in the West for political purposes, and sometimes to discredit and stigmatize the entire culture of the Arabs and the Islamic religion.[10] In reality, the struggle for gender equality takes place all over the region including in Israel, where Rabbi Eliezer Schach and other leading non-Hasidic Ashkenazic rabbis bitterly protested in July 1992 the appointment of a woman (Shulamit Aloni) to the Ministry of Education. According to one press account, Schach and the other rabbis stated that Aloni will "lead the children of Israel into apostasy."[11] In the Arab world, the plight of woman is more bleak and is fraught with many methodological hazards.

The historical Western (primarily Christian) attitude toward Islam has discouraged Muslims and Arabs from engaging in a frank and open discussion about the roles of women and minorities within the Islamic political—and theological—context. The Western, Christian attitude to Islam has lacked consistency; in the past

Islam was attacked for what was perceived to be its sexual permissiveness, while Islam is now associated with sexual puritanism and strictness. This inconsistency is due to the political determinants of Western perceptions, and misconceptions, of Islam which explains how Islam was approached from a purely theological Christian point of view in the past, and how Islam is now approached from a secular humanist point of view.[12] Islam, of course, has failed—in Christian, Western eyes—both tests: the Christian and the secular one.

It is not difficult to observe that women in the Arab world live under tremendous pressures and oppression; it is not accurate, however, to assume that the condition of women in the Arab world is uniform and that historically speaking the situation of women in the Middle East has been characterized by fixity. More specificity is required when one addresses the subject that involves more than half of the entire two-hundred-million Arab population. Furthermore, the historical school of Western thought that assumes Arab men and women have lived under the same conditions since the advent of Islam is erroneous. Equally fallacious is the notion that all Arab women—or in most cases all Muslim women—live under the same harsh conditions of oppression.

There is evidence, however, that a substantial section of Arab women are unhappy with their status and conditions. In a survey of women in Iraq, Jordan, Egypt, and Lebanon (and of U.S. women of the same age) conducted in the late 1950s, it was found that 53 percent of Muslim women and 48 percent of Christian women surveyed in the Arab world ex-

pressed their belief that they would have been happier as males (compared to 28 percent of U.S. women surveyed).[13] Again, it should not be assumed that levels of satisfaction of dissatisfaction are uniform throughout the Arab world.

It is also necessary to make some methodological clarifications before the subject is pursued any further. It is not useful to make assumptions about a movement if the movement involves millions of people and has many divergent trends in its body. Catherine MacKinnon, in her excellent critique of Marxism with respect to feminism,[14] treated Marxism as a monolith notwithstanding the general antifeminist trends in Marxist writings. Nevertheless, Marx, Lenin, and Trotsky treated the subject of women differently, and feminism itself is not a monolith either. One is obliged in this respect to appreciate the various trends and strands within the body of the same ideological or political movement.

For the purpose of this article, the treatment will deal with the Arab world, and not with the larger Islamic world—there is no political meaning for such a word except in the imagination of some Western writers who warn of the specter of an Islamic threat. Furthermore, the Arab world can not be taken to represent the Islamic people because the majority of Muslims are not Arabs, and the largest Muslim population is found in a non-Arab country. In the discussion of the Arab world, an emphasis will be made on the need for a comparative approach in order to underline the similarities and the stark differences in the lives and conditions of Arab women. Moreover, the role of

Islam, which is often assumed to be the underlying cause behind the oppression of Muslim women, will be investigated through a brief study of the original sources.

Islam and Culture

In her introduction to a very useful anthology of writings on and by Muslim women,[15] Fernea and Bezirgan analyze the relationship between the role (or the responsibility) of religion and culture with respect to women through the following figure:

Koran<- - - - - - - - - - - ->Tribal family and custom[16]

The figure, however, appears to misrepresent the reality of the relationship between Islam and culture (or tradition). Culture and tradition here are used to denote the set of values and patterns of behavior that characterize social relations and attitudes in the Arab world. Islam does not fully define or determine culture or tradition. Islam influences culture and has influenced tradition since its advent, but culture (the pre-Islamic culture to be specific) influenced Islam too. Consequently, the attempt at distinguishing between cultural and Islamic influences with respect to a particular issue is not always easy. The figure of Fernea and Bezirgan assumes that Islam and custom are on opposite sides of the issue of women while there is evidence that there is an area of commonality between Islam and custom regarding some aspects of women and gender.

Leila Ahmed's recent book is one of the most scholarly works dealing with the subject of women and Islam.[17] The author documents the pre-Islamic tradition of misogynist and androcentric in Mesopotamian, Persian, Hellenic, and Christian cultures.

There is enough evidence to suggest that Islamic attitudes to women (as contained in the Qur'an, the Hadith and later in the Sunnah (the presumed righteous path) were not original, but were borrowed from previous cultures and from elements of the prevailing culture in Arabia, which had some diversity of cultures and religions and which lacked uniformity in social and economic conditions. In other words, Islam accepted some misogynist views and practices, and discarded others. A diagram that would accurately represent the relationship between Islam and culture should perhaps show two intersecting circles, with a shaded area for the area of agreement between Islam and the cultural tradition.

Islam, for example rejected infanticide[18] (which victimized female children), and the Qur'an itself criticized those who considered the very birth of a female child as a social stigma.[19] It should be noted here that the task of comparing and contrasting the conditions of women before and after the advent of Islam is difficult because Arabia before Islam was a place that contained various religions and cultures and the lifestyles and social conditions of people were not uniform throughout the peninsula. Furthermore, pre-Islamic Arabia was not sufficiently studied by early Muslims and its ills and problems have always been exaggerated to glorify the role of Islam. The very word *Jahiliyyah* (Age of Ignorance) is intended to attribute negative characteristics to pre-Islamic Arabia, and our knowledge of that time was passed through the prism of Islamic apologetic. It is true that Islam laid the same obligations of belief and duties on both men and women, although the notion of

the equality-as-believers of men and women should be qualified because women are barred from performing basic religious duties during the menstrual cycle. And while Muslim apologists take pride in the fact that Islam gave women the right of inheritance[20] (half the share of the male), it is not true that females did not inherit before Islam. While information on these subjects is scant, it appears that some women in some areas did inherit and others did not. Moreover, polygamy and polyandry were both practiced in pre-Islamic Arabia. Islam, of course, legitimized only polygamy (up to four wives).

In the classical work of 'Ali ibn Abi Talib, *Nahj-ulBalaghah* (The Course of Eloquence) the plight of women was summarized as follows: Women are deficient in their minds, their lots, and their faith; the first because a woman's testimony in court equals to that of half a man, the second because women inherited half the share of men, and the third because women are not allowed to perform their religious duties during the menstrual cycle. 'Ali's assertion, from a purely logical point of view, is fallacious because the evidence for the inferiority of women is presented through a listing of restrictions that men have imposed on women. In other words, women were faulted for the very limitations that were put on them. Some Sunni apologists might consider 'Ali's views to be peculiarly Shi'ite, but the inferiority of women in general is clearly argued in the Qur'an, the Sahih of the Hadith (the authentic sections that Muslims consider to be reliable), and the basic works in Islamic jurisprudence. The Qur'an states that men are "one degree"[21] above women in rank, and that "men are *qawwamun*[22] (guardians and/or superior) to women."[23] Notwithstanding the claims of Muslim apologists and the attempts of some feminists to re-interpret Islam in ways favorable to women,[24] the ideas of female inferiority are clearly present in the Qur'anic text where the beating of women by their husbands is sanctioned.[25]

But culture can play an important role in the perpetuation of misogynist attitudes to women; in some cases cultural attitudes and patterns of behavior that favored males persisted not because of Islam but despite Islamic teachings. The birth of female children is still taken in some societies in the Middle East as a sign of bad luck; so much so that some parents name their third or fourth consecutive daughter *Kafa* (Enough) as a message to God to send a male child. Circumcision, for example, has persisted in some Islamic countries although it is not an Islamic obligation. (Some Islamic jurists, like Al-Shafi'i, praised the practice and made it an obligation.)[26] Wife beating on the other hand was sanctioned in the Qur'an and in the Hadith. Also, male jurists legitimized pre-Islamic misogynist attitudes and practices by rationalizing them and legitimizing them in Islamic language. The vast body of Hadith (which includes hundreds of thousands of deeds and utterances attributed to Muhammad) allowed male jurists and politicians to justify almost anything they wanted to justify.

But the notion of Islam (as a word that denotes the vast lands inhabited by Muslims and the millions of world Muslims) has become an ideological concept in the West. The Western usage of the word by classical orientalists like Bernard Lewis resulted in the promotion of a misconception that attributes all patterns of behavior and manifestations of political preferences to Islamic texts. The usage of—indeed the fixation with—the word has led people to assume that piety is an inherently Muslim characteristic, and that non-Islamic factors in politics and society are insignificant. And while Islam is also studied as an all-encompassing ideology, there are factions and currents of thought that use Islam for various —sometimes divergent—political interests. The scholarly obsession with Islam ignores the debate within and outside Islam about various issues of concern to the believers, including the crucial gender question. To be sure, Islam has played a legitimizing role in various contexts in Islamic countries, but it has not been the sole, dominant hegemonic ideology. In fact, Islam has served a dominant ideology that reflected the social and economic interests of ruling groups whether in the Umayyad era or in Saudi Arabia today. The ideological exploitation of Islam should lead one to investigate the role Islam plays in the legitimization of deeds of ruling elites.

Furthermore, if by Islam one means the entire span of Islamic history, one needs to consider the schematic tendencies within the body of Islam. Kharijites and Sufis have rebelled against Islamic governments by using Islamic symbols and notions. Islam does not in reality imply obedience and conformity; the history of Islamic people is full of examples of men and women who chose to avoid conformity with Islamic rules and obligations. Some of the anticonformists (including many Sufis and so-called *zanadiqah* (atheists) were, of course, killed although many others (like Abu al-Ala' al-Ma'arri and Abu Nuwwas) survived.

Islam and the Feminist Debate

The debate about the role of Islam in the gender question has led to a divergence in outlook between at least two schools of feminist thought in the Arab world. On one side of the spectrum, is the apologetic Islamic school which claims that Islam has liberated women and that Muslim women have more rights than their western counterparts. Representatives of this school exaggerate the gains that were attained by Arab women after Islam and they, predictably, misrepresent the living conditions in Arabia in pre-Islamic times. They tend to attribute a monolithic and uniform social structure to society in Arabia in *Jahiliyyah* times.[27] The Islamic apologetic school does not advocate a reinterpretation of Islamic texts; it calls for a strict application of the conservative interpretations of the *Shari'ah*.

Another branch of the Islamic apologetic school blames the harsh conditions of Arab women—and this school, unlike the previous one, acknowledges the existence of a system of gender inequality in Arab society—on male jurists who interpreted Islamic texts in a conservative and misogynist way. One interesting representative of this school is an Egyptian Sunni cleric who has a large following in the Arab/Islamic world. This man, Muhammad al-Ghazali, has been criticizing male attitudes towards women and has been attributing the harshness of women's oppression in the Arab world to a misunderstanding of Islamic texts. While Al-Ghazali dealt with the subject of women in two popular books,[28] he still accepts the inherently sexist content of Islamic texts. He also does not object to the exclusion of women from the top post of government: the Caliph position.

The third branch of the Islamic apologetic school is a feminist movement that engages in a reinterpretation of Islamic text from a female, feminist point of view. It is not inaccurate to observe that this school of thought prevails among Arab feminists (both Christians and Muslims). The power of their argument of course stems from their ability to argue their feminist point of view without being dismissed as anti-Islamic. The feminist argument from an Islamic perspective grants the feminists a position in society which they would otherwise be denied. The feminist Islamic argument is not new, it goes back to the time of the Prophet, who—according to the *tafsir* (interpreting of religious texts) of Tabari—once received a complaint from one of his wives about the absence of references to women from the Qur'an. Afterwards, the Qur'an specifically addressed both men and women although the Qur'an in general (including Surat An-Nisa' [Women]) addresses itself primarily to males.

The feminist Islamic argument focuses on the misinterpretation of the Islamic texts by male jurists. The male jurists in Islamic history did not constitute a monolith; there were—and are—conservative and liberal Islamic scholars who tend to reflect their own opinions and preferences in their reading of the Qur'anic text. The split of the liberal and the conservative is nowhere more illustrated than in the debate over women's political rights. As Mervat Hatem rightly observes: "The debate showed that Islam's position on

women's political participation was ambiguous at best."[29]

The debate about Islam and women's political rights began in the early 1950s when Egyptian feminists (mostly from the upper classes[30]) struggled to obtain political rights. Their demands caused a political and religious controversy especially when some religious authorities vehemently asserted that Islam does not recognize the political rights of women.[31] The religious authorities in Egypt tried to stifle debate about the matter when Al-Azhar issued a *fatwa*[32] (a binding religious opinion) which distinguished between private and public guardianship (*wilayah*). The *fatwa* maintained that Islam granted women rights relating to private guardianship: like the right to parenting,[33] and the right to oversee financial and *waqf* (religious charity) affairs. The opinion of Al-Azhar about political rights (what it called public guardianship) was quite categorical: it stated that public guardianship is an exclusively male realm. The opinion was based on various religious citations and it stressed the weaknesses of women: the opinion reminded believers that women are prone to emotional (non-rational) decisions and that they exhibit a preference for instinctive decisions and passions.

Al-Azhar summed up the Islamic attitude (implying, of course that there is *an* Islamic attitude) to women's political rights by invoking a *sahih* (authentic) Hadith by Muhammad in which it is claimed that he said: "A people that has a woman as their leader will never succeed." [34] This saying has been the foundation on which the clerical leadership has grounded its position regarding the exclusion of women from political leadership. The authority of

this Hadith presented the Muslim women with a difficult choice; one either accepts the authority of Islamic texts or one will be forced to argue the feminist position from a non-Islamic perspective.

Fatima Mernissi, who in earlier works argued that Islam as a religion was responsible for many of the injustices inflicted on women in their lives,[35] now argues that Islam was largely distorted by male jurists who wished to attribute to Islam misogynist tendencies that Muhammad did not possess. Mernissi's argument is based on her reading of a vast body of religious literature in order to come up with a new interpretation of some texts that feminists and their supporters find problematic. But Mernissi's position clearly fits into the Islamic apologetic school because it insists on reducing the ethical standards to religious texts and their interpretations. More importantly, the apologetic school will have far fewer texts to support its point of view than the Islamic establishment school, which has at its disposal an arsenal from the mainstream of the Islamic heritage.

It is unlikely that feminists will win by arguing according to Islamic teachings; there are far more verses and sayings in Islamic texts that can be used against feminists than the number of verses that feminists wish to reinterpret. Mernissi's book, *The Veil and the Male Elite* is the product of her frustration with what she considers male-biased interpretations that are inconsistent with Muhammad's principles. But in order for Mernissi to discredit the male jurists and the sources of the Hadith, she had to glorify and idealize the image of Muhammad. Her readings of the texts become as selective and subjective as the interpretation of Islamic texts by male jurists. In other words, Mernissi's feminism differs from the Islamic apologetic school only in its details and orientations. Both schools seem to present a picture of Muhammad which sometimes is based on a myth of his life that later Muslims constructed.[36]

As for Muhammad's admonishment of his wife 'A'ishah when he scolded her for disobeying him by saying that inside every woman there sleeps a traitor, Mernissi finds the remark "at its worst . . . tinged with tenderness."[37] Mernissi even goes farther when she justifies Muhammad's request for a female opponents head after his entry into Mecca; she calls his insistence (for her execution) "understandable." [38] Mernissi also mistakenly states that Islam opposed slavery as a matter of principle.[39] In fact, Islam regulated slavery and banned its practice only in peace time. As for the verse in the Qur'an which specifically gives the husband the right to beat his wife, Mernissi states Muhammad's disagreement with the verse and claims that Muhammad "advised against the use of violence toward women."[40] However, Muhammad himself has sanctioned this practice in his *khutbat al-wada'* (speech of farewell), according to the reliable account of his early biographers Ibn Ishaq and Ibn Hisham.[41] Like classical Muslim apologists, Mernissi exaggerates the darkness and ills of *Jahiliyyah* times although much of our knowledge of it is filtered through a Muslim apologetic perspective. And Muhammad's saying about the danger of women's political leadership can not simply be dismissed by questioning the truthfulness of its source: Abu

Hurayra.[42] Abu Hurayra's truthfulness is accepted by many Muslims and the saying does not contradict the essence of the Qur'anic attitude to women.

On the other side of the methodological spectrum is the theologocentric[43] school which focuses on Islam as the source for the explanation of all Muslim behavior and practices. This school is of course popular among some classical orientalists who find in religious and sometimes obscure texts the answers for contemporary Muslim behavior. Rather than looking at Islam as the dominant, hegemonic ideology, Islam could be seen as an element in a larger hegemonic ideology which political leaders from the seventh century until today have used. The fluctuations in the positions (on various issues) of various political leaders indicate that the impact of ideology (any ideology) on the political process is often exaggerated. The fixation with the veil is another example of the simplification of cultural attitudes and patterns of social behavior; it became a symbol of a religion that is regarded as a moral and political threat. As Mervat Hatem observes in one study of Egyptian "state feminism," in dealing with this complex phenomenon, one must analyze its socioeconomic background and "the strong sense of religiosity, which spread in the 1970s and the 1980s."[44]

The theologocentric school in Islamic studies uses the terms culture and Islam interchangeably and refuses to acknowledge the existence of non-religious factors as determinants of social behavior and political orientations. The focus on Islam and the fixation with symbols and personalities obscure the socioeconomic and cultural factors that are at play in

all societies where Muslims form a majority of the population. This tendency is also automatically inclined to make broad generalizations as it tries to explain the behavior and attitudes of millions of Muslims by quotations and citations from religious texts.[45] Another characteristic in the writings of "theologocentric feminists" is the passivity of Arab/Muslim women. The image of Arab/Muslim women as subservient and passive victims became fixed in many of the writings of theologocentrist orientalists.

The Study of Women and Politics

The study of women and politics in the Arab world could make a contribution to the general field of political science and the subfield of comparative politics of the Arab world because this topic requires an understanding of the similarities and differences in the political roles of women in the Arab world. This article does not deal with the question of Muslim women in general, and the subject cannot be approached from a generalist perspective because the status of Muslim women varies—sometimes sharply—from one Muslim country to another. This section will focus on the methodological factors that explain the male political male dominance in the region and on the ways in which females express themselves politically despite social and political pressures under which they live.

The question of Islam's compatibility with feminist ideals can not be easily resolved; Arab feminists who are already under attack by male-led organizations and religious leaders[46] find it hard to completely dissociate their positions from Islamic laws and texts. Yet the feminist battle within Islam is a losing one, not only because Islamic texts contain clear ideas of male superiority, but also because female interpreters of Islam will never have the authority of the male jurists. The question whether Islam is compatible with feminism, or democracy for that matter, should be deemed irrelevant because none of the religions of the past contained recipes for political change along democratic lines. The efforts by Islamic apologists to reconcile Islam and democracy by equating the qur'anic word *shura* (consultation) with democracy are not serious. Similarly, the efforts of Arab feminists to comb through Islamic texts for evidence of sympathy with women is a political task that will not prove to be fruitful from the feminist point of view. That these efforts of reconciliation will be futile is not an indication of the peculiarly conservative message of Islam, but is a proof that Islam—and the other two monotheistic religions—did not have modern answers to today's social and political problems. Unless Islam is treated as a religion for the believers who wish to worship in private or in public and not as a body of personal status laws to be imposed on all members of society, the chances for democratization and gender equality in the Arab world will be remote.

I. Voting

Women's suffrage has only recently been regarded as a fundamental human right and this right has not been easily attained by Western women. Swiss women, for example, were not allowed to vote in national elections until 1972.[47] In talking about voting rights in the Arab world one must emphasize that men are also unfree in most Arab countries and that Arab governments are not showing any inconsistency when they deny women (and other groups in society) their basic rights. Fatna Sabbah criticized the late Algerian president, Bumadyan, for making a speech in which he portrayed the employment of women as a problem for Algerian men, and she considered this position inconsistent with his socialism and his "ideals of democracy and equality." [48] In reality, Bumadyan came to power through a military coup d'etat and was the head of a ruthless socialist dictatorship. The anti-feminist position of Bumadyan was not inconsistent with his overall record of human rights inside Algeria.

Voting is a right enjoyed by some Arab men and women, and this right in itself does not guarantee equality of opportunity or symmetry in political roles and involvement between men and women. There are various limitations on the participatory implications of voting although voting in itself allows women (and men) to choose between various candidates. Firstly, many Arab women who vote may not be free in their exercise of that right because their fathers, brothers, or husbands may interfere in the voting choices. Of a sample survey of Libyan men and women, 43 percent of those surveyed believed that women cannot (due to various obstacles) make decisions freely.[49] Secondly, the ability of women to exercise their voting rights freely is impaired by virtue of the discrepancy in the adult literacy rates between men and women. For example, in 1980 76 percent of males in Libya were literate, but only 36 percent of females. In Morocco, the corresponding figures were 41 percent for males and 18 percent for females.[50]

Thirdly, the voting right in itself does not bring about an equality in the voting process between men and women. The Egyptian government of Nasser, for example, passed an electoral law in 1956 which stated that voter registration is compulsory for men and voluntary for women. Thus, "in 1956–57, only 1 percent of the total number of registered voters were women."[51] This number increased to 18 percent in 1986.[52] The state in those Arab countries that have recognized the women's right to vote does not consider women's political participation a priority. In fact, some of them seem to discourage women's political participation to appease the conservative segments of the population. Explaining the absence of women from the legislative election in 1984, the Moroccan minister of interior stated that the "traditions of the countryside do not allow for women's representation in parliament." [53] The significance of the latter statement should be understood in the context of the special meaning of tradition in Islamic heritage where tradition entails religious dedication and moral consistency.

In studying voting rights in the Arab world, a distinction must be made between three different types of regimes:

A. Regimes where voting rights are enjoyed by both men and women: Lebanon, Syria, Iraq, Libya[54], Jordan, Egypt, Yemen, Tunisia, Algeria, Sudan[55] and Morocco.

B. Regimes where voting rights are enjoyed by men only: Kuwait and Bahrain.[56]

C. Regimes where voting rights are nonexistent: Saudi Arabia, Qatar, UAE, Oman, Somalia, Mauritania, and Djbouti.

It is noteworthy that those countries which have voting rights for women tend to have less repressive measures toward women than the countries which do not give women voting rights. Mai Ghassoub maintains that the least repressive laws and regulations are found in a few countries where women have voting rights.[57] But the classification of regimes using the criterion of voting rights could be deceptive because the efficacy of voting as a means of political change and expression is limited in places like Syria and Iraq. In both countries, voting rights are token gestures accorded by an oppressive regime to citizens for the attainment of political legitimacy. A Syrian male or female, or an Iraqi male or female, can not change their political system, and can not even choose their political representatives by exercising their right to vote. In most cases, lists of candidates are formed by party elites in both countries, and the vote is a token measure: intended to ratify choices made by the tyrannical rulers. In the 1991 election in Syria, there was more competition between candidates and more independents were allowed to run than in previous elections under the regime of Hafidh al-Asad.

The Kuwaiti case is a special one because Kuwait has experimented with democratization—on and off—since the early 1960s. The Kuwaiti government and the political establishment in Kuwait deprived women of their political rights and theorized the virtues of this deprivation. A parliamentary committee stated in 1981 that the

proposal (by some Kuwaiti parliamentarians) for political rights for women would be rejected because "the impact of such a decision on the political life in Kuwait society can not be foreseen given its traditions and customs."[58] The Kuwaiti situation also reveals that misogynist tendencies continue to prevail among Kuwaiti women themselves. In one public opinion poll conducted in 1970, it was found that 53 percent of women polled opposed "direct political participation of women" while 47 percent agreed. And 51 percent of women polled opposed female participation in parliament, while 49 percent supported. As for the voting right for women, 58 percent of women polled opposed, and 42 percent supported.[59] Similar figures were often used by the Kuwaiti government to justify its vehement opposition to women's voting rights.

In places where women vote in the Arab world, there are still significant gaps in voter turnout between men and women. Smaller voter turnout among women was also documented in other "developing" countries in the world.[60] Many reasons explain the smaller turnout of Arab women: the small percentages of female representation in parliaments (around 5 percent in countries that have parliaments); the state's neglect of the female vote; the absence of women's issues from parties' programs; and the reluctance of some women to engage actively in politics in fear of social retribution. Even in places like Lebanon, where women faced less restriction than in other neighboring countries, some Lebanese and Palestinian men tended to discourage their wives and sisters from engaging in politics.[61]

2. Pitfalls of the Legalistic/Constitutional Method

While the study of constitutions and legal documents was popular among political scientists before the behavioral revolution, and while there can be some benefits derived from a comparative study of constitutions in Western democracies, this method is fraught with hazards in the field of Middle East politics. Arab politics has been characterized by the absence of democracy, and the dominant repressive regimes wish to attain legitimacy[62] by making certain claims about their nature that are not matched by their practices. Thus, it could be highly deceptive for one to focus on the constitutions and legal documents of Arab regimes in order to understand the decision making process in those regimes. Most Arab countries that have constitutions claim their regimes are representative democracies, and the Iraqi constitution will not help explain the brutal tyranny of Saddam Husayn.

Similarly, Arab constitutions make certain claims about the status of women that do not reflect the true situation of women. If one is to judge the status of women by reading Arab constitutions, one might draw the conclusion that gender equality prevails in the Arab world. Thus, the Algerian Mithaq talks about the "elimination of existing discrimination on the basis of . . . sex and race."[63] And the Algerian constitution authoritatively and confidently states its guarantee for "all cultural, economic, and political rights for Algerian women." In reality, the status of Algerian women began to decline steadily beginning in 1984, when the state supervised a retreat from the few gains achieved by Algerian women over the years. The Syrian constitution of 1970 makes a similar claim in article 45: "The state guarantees for woman all opportunities that allow her the full and effective participation in the economic, social, cultural, and economic life." Even the Kuwaiti constitution contains references to "equality" and "equality of opportunity."

The usefulness of studying Arab constitutions is very limited; it can, however, shed light on the discrepancy between reality and the political claims made by Arab regimes for purely political legitimacy purposes. The constitutions can help us in reading Arab public expectations based on regimes' reading of the public mood. It is clear that most Arab regimes understand the Arab popular thirst for democratization and openness, which explains the hollow words about "representative governments" and "popular sovereignty" that appear in most Arab constitutions. Saudi Arabia remains an exceptional case where the Saudi royal family has stubbornly refused to codify a constitution because it claims that the Qur'an is the only source of government. The study of women and politics in the Arab world can derive almost no benefit from the study of constitutions. Furthermore, the assertion in almost all Arab constitutions (with the exception of Lebanon) that Islam is "the source" of legislation reflects the governmental need for Islamic legitimization.

3. Informal/Local Politics vs. Formal/National Politics[64]

On the surface, women are excluded from the political process in most—if not all—Arab countries. Nevertheless, there are countries, like Egypt, Syria, Lebanon, Iraq, Jordan, Tunisia and Algeria where women have held parliamentary and/or ministerial positions. Yet, the top offices in governments have been monopolized by males since independence from Western domination. The reasons for male domination are fourfold:

Firstly, many of the top office holders in many Arab countries (like Egypt, Syria, Iraq, Libya, Algeria, Somalia, Mauritania, Djibouti, and Sudan) are military officers who came to power through coups d'etat. The power networks in those countries were woven through military connections. Secondly, some Arab governments (in Jordan, Morocco, and in Gulf countries) are led by men who follow the ancient tribal custom of leadership through a religio-political system of legitimization that excludes females. Thirdly, the ruling elites of most Arab governments are small; they tend to draw upon members of the immediate family to ensure continuity of support and loyalty. The political insecurity felt by most Arab rulers deters them from recruiting from outside the small network of supporters. Fourthly, the idea of a woman leader represents a political and religious stigma that threatens the precarious regimes of the region. Most Arab leaders have not shown a willingness to challenge the views of the clerical leadership on women's political rights. The rise of Islamist influence in politics is increasing the credibility of Islamic legitimization in the political process.

While women have not held the top positions of government in Islamic/Arab history, women have never ceased to play important political roles beginning with the influential role played by Muhammad's favorite wife, 'A'ishah. While the political roles of women (as wives, daughters, and sisters) in Islamic/Arab history should not be exaggerated, there is evidence that male clerics did not succeed in excluding women entirely from the political process. Of course, some authors blame unpopular policies of leaders on their wives, and one Egyptian writer published a book under the title: *Behind Every Dictator is a Woman.*[65] Anwar Sadat's unpopular policies in Egypt were often blamed on his wife, Jihan, who wielded significant political influence within Egypt.

The absence of women from the top echelons of government does not mean that women are completely excluded from politics in the Arab world. In fact, the self-professed revolutionary regimes of the Arab world have brought about social and, political changes that aimed at expanding the base of popular support for the new regimes. Mervat Hatem defines "state feminism" (under Nasser) as follows: "It refers to ambitious state programs that introduce important changes in the reproductive and productive roles of women."[66] While accomplishments of "state feminism" are in some countries, like Egypt (under Nasser), Syria, and Iraq, not insignificant, governments have continued to uphold religiously-based personal status laws which are all based on the inferiority of women and the dependency of the female on the "male guardian."[67]

Even regimes that extended the suffrage to women did not allow for the free and independent existence of feminist organizations. To be sure, "the revolutionary" regimes created their own version of "women's organizations" but their roles were confined to issues sanctioned by the male elite. Women's organizations became useful appendages of the state apparatus. For the Syrian and Iraqi Ba'th parties, women's organizations served as vehicles for political mobilization and party recruitment. The state would not tolerate independent feminist organizations that would set their own agendas free of state interference and manipulation. Women's organizations are not allowed to challenge the personal status laws and the legitimacy of the regimes themselves.

From works of Middle East anthropologists, one learns about the extent to which women operate politically outside the "conventional" forms of political action. In one particular case, it was observed that "as formal politics expanded . . . women's participation declined."[68] The expansion of formal politics reflected an expansion in state intrusion into social activities. The consolidation of the state in the modern Arab world introduced the governmental apparatus to branches of life that have not been accustomed to outside intrusion. The expansion of the state control over society affected women who were able to operate informally on the local level. The informal/local level accords women freedom of movement and action that would be curtailed by the formal/national version of politics. Women who played important roles locally (without holding public offices) could not transform their activities to the national/formal level due the social stigma of national exposure and publicity. Thus, Nazirah Jumblat, the mother of the late Druze leader Kamal Jumblat of Lebanon, became the leader of the Jumblati family leadership after the death

of her husband. Without holding public office, and without dealing formally with politicians, Nazirah was considered one of the most important political leaders in Lebanon in the early part of this century. Similarly, the late mother of Shi'ite *za'im* Kamil al-As'ad (also of Lebanon) participated in all major and minor decisions made by her family. She was also instrumental in the formation of electoral lists although she dealt with men from behind a curtain.

4. Modernization and Women's Rights

The fixation with modernization and westernization was a cornerstone of Middle Eastern studies until well into the 1960s. The assumption that economic developments along Western lines would bring about changes similar to the processes of change in Western societies was based on the glorification of the universality of the Western model. The replacement of communism with Western-style systems of government in Eastern Europe does not mean an end to oppressiveness and autocracy, and the area of women's rights is witnessing a retrenchment in places like Germany and Poland, where abortion rights are being increasingly curtailed. Similarly, modernization in the Arab world did not result in liberalization and democratization. It has even become clear that westernization (which has spread in the region, including Saudi Arabia) does not necessarily entail democratization. Saudi Arabia has, for example, chosen to import Western technologies and goods while refusing to copy Western-style political institutions. As far as the gender question is concerned, "economic development is largely unrelated to women's potential for political power."[69] Unless Arab

governments make official commitments to gender equality, modernization will continue to proceed while leaving women (in many aspects of social and political life) behind. The rise of Islamist political movements is increasing the pressure on governments to resist the demands of Arab feminists for gender equality.

Conclusion

Rapid political developments in the Arab world, and the antipathy to Western interests by large segments of the Arab population (for purely political reasons and not for cultural and religious reasons as some modern orientalists would have it) are making the feminist struggle more difficult. Feminism is now increasingly under attack because Islamic fundamentalists (like Christian and Jewish fundamentalists) have chosen to focus on women's issues and to discredit feminism by linking it to Western political interests. The crisis of political legitimacy among Arab governments has resulted in official accommodation of the Islamist agenda as far as the women's question is concerned. The failure by Arab governments to resolve acute political and economic problems has led to the promotion of "morality," as defined by the conservative and obscurantist clerical elite, as a main political goal. Arab feminists will not find it easy to argue their case within an Islamic framework; antifeminist thinkers and clerics have a solid base in Islamic texts to rationalize their point of view. The goals of gender equality and equal opportunity for all members of society should be regarded as desirable regardless of whether these goals conform with the essence of one religion or another.

Acknowledgment

Much of the research for this article was conducted at the Widener Library of Harvard University. The author is grateful to Prof. William Graham, director of the Center for Middle Eastern Studies at Harvard University, for his help.

Notes

1. Of the fifty U.S. governors, three are women, and women constitute 6 percent of U.S. House seats. See *Rocky Mountain News*, June 12, 1992.
2. Following are female percentages in some selected countries: Norway: 34.4 percent; Finland: 31.5 percent; Denmark: 29 percent; Sweden: 28.5 percent; Iceland: 20.6 percent; The Netherlands: 20 percent; New Zealand: 14.4 percent; Switzerland: 14 percent; Italy: 12.8 percent; Canada: 9.6 percent; Ireland: 8.4 percent; Portugal: 7.6 percent; Belgium: 7.5 percent; France and Spain: 6.4 percent; U.K.: 6.3 percent; Greece: 4.3 percent; and Japan: 1.4 percent. See *ibid*.
3. John Stuart Mill, *The Subjection of Women*, Sue Mansfield, ed. (Arlington Heights, Ill.: Harlen Davidson, 1980).
4. G. F. Hegel, *Hegel's Philosophy of Right* (Oxford: The Clarendon Press, 1942), Addition 107 (to Paragraph 166), pp. 263–264. On the general question of women in the writings of political philosophers, see Diana H. Coole, *Women in Political Theory* (Boulder, CO: Lynne Reinner, 1988).
5. Leila Ahmed, *Women and Gender in Islam* (New Haven: Yale University Press, 1992), p. 244.
6. There is a sizable body of literature in Arabic that links feminism with colonialism and Zionism. See, for example, Muhammad 'Atayyah Khamis, *Al-Harakat An-Nisa'iyyah wa Silatuha bi-l-'Isti'mar* (Feminist Movements and Their Link with Colonialism), (Cairo: Dar Al-Ansar, 1978); and Muhammad Fahmi 'Abd-ul-Wahab, *Al-Harokat An-Nisa'iyyah fi-sh-Sharq wa Silatuha bi-l-'Isti'mar wa-s-Sahyuniyyah Al-'Alamiyyah* (Feminist Movements in the East and their Link with Colonialism and International Zionism), (Cairo: Dar Al-'I'tisam, Silsilat Al-Mar'ah Al-Muslimah, No. 7, 1979). For the ostensible link between Freemasonry and feminism, see Ahmad 'Abdul-'Aziz Al-Hasin, *Al-Mar'ah Wa Makanatuha fi-l-Islam* (Woman and its Status in Islam), (Cairo: Maktabat Al-'Iman, second edition, 1981).
7. Amin is often mistakenly considered the first (male) advocate for women's rights in the Arab world. There is an earlier voice in Assad Y. Kayat, *A Voice From Lebanon* (London: Madden & Co., 1847). This book is hard to locate in U.S. libraries. I found one xerox copy of the original book in the Widener Library at Harvard University. See also the text of the speech delivered by Butrus al-Bustani in 1849 on "The Education of Women." The text was printed in the 12th volume of *Al-Jinan*, and was reprinted in this century in al-Bustani, Fu'ad Afram, *Al-Mu'allim Butrus al-Bustani: Ta'lim an-Nisa', Adab al-'Arab* (The Master Butrus al-Bustani: The Education of Women, The Literature of the Arabs), (Beirut: Manshurat al-Adab al-Sharqiyyah, 1950).
8. Leila Ahmed, *Women and Gender . . .*, *Op. cit.*, p. 159.
9. Ahmed seemed to imply in her book that most—if not all—Western female and male writers on the subject of women were either directly or indirectly serving Western political interests.
10. See Leila Ahmed, "Western Ethnocentrism and Perceptions of the Harem," *Feminist Studies*, vol. 8, no. 3 (Fall 1982). While Ahmed criticizes Western feminist misperceptions about Islam and Muslim women, her attempt at justifying defensive and apologetic treatment of the subject can not be accepted from a purely scholarly point of view.
11. *Washington Jewish Week*, July 23, 1992, p. 3. Of course, the secular politics of Aloni makes her more unacceptable to some conservative religious circles. Aloni was forced out of the Ministry of Education in 1993.
12. See the creative and original book: Hichem Djait, *L'Europe et l'Eslam* (Paris: Editions du Seuil, 1978).
13. Ibrahim 'Abdallah Muhi, *Mushkilat Al-Mar'ah fi-l-Bilad al-'Arabiyyah* (The Problems of Women in Arab Countries), (Baghdad: Matba'at al-Rabitah, 1958), p. 28.
14. Catherine A. MacKinnon, *Toward a Feminist Theory of the State* (Cambridge, MA: Harvard University Press, 1989).
15. See Elizabeth W. Fernea, and Basima Qattan Bezirgan, eds., *Muslim Women Speak* (Austin: University of Texas Press).
16. See *ibid*, p. xix. It should be noted that the figure was not replicated in full here. The main theme, however, is shown above.
17. Leila Ahmed, *Women and Gender . . .*, *Op. cit.*
18. See Surat At-Takwir, Ayats 8–9. All references to the Qur'an are from the Arabic original. Translation of Arabic is this author's.
19. See Surat An-Nahl, Ayats 58–59.
20. See, for example, Ash-Shaykh Ad-Duktur Subhi, As-Salih, *Al-Mar'ah fi al-Islam* (Woman in Islam), (Beirut: BUC, Institute for Feminist Studies in the Arab World, 1990), p. 23.
21. Surat Al-Baqarah, Ayat 228.
22. See Al-Bustani, Butrus, *Qutr al-Muhit* (Beirut: 1869).
23. Surat An-Nisa', Ayat 34.
24. See, for example, Fatima Mernissi, *The Veil and the Male Elite: A Feminist Interpretation of Women's Rights in Islam*, trans. by Mary Jo Lakeland (New York: Addison-Wesley, 1991). More on this book below.
25. Surat an-Nisa', Ayat 34.
26. See Ibrahim Muhammad Al-Jamal, *Fiqh Al-Mar'ah Al-Muslimah* (The Jurisprudence of the Muslim Woman), (Cairo: Maktabat Al-Qur'an, 1982), pp. 65–66.
27. The list of books representing this trend is too long, see, for example: Ahmad Al-Hamadani Al-Matwi, *Al-Mar'ah wa-l-Islam al-Haqq* (Women and the True Islam), (Tunisia: n.d., n.p.); Muhammad Tal'at Harb, *Fast Al-Khitab fi Al-Mar'ah Wa-l-Hijab* (The Decisive Discourse on Women and Veiling), (Cairo: Matba'at at-Taraqqi, 1901); Ahmad Ghunaym, *Al-Mar'ah Mundhu-n-Nash'ah: Bayna-t-Tajrim wa-t-Takrim* (Women since Genesis: Between Criminalization and Glorification), (Cairo: Matba'at al-Kaylani, 1980); Hasan At-Banna, *Al-Mar'ah Al-Muslimah*, (The Muslim Woman), (Cairo: Dar al-Kutub as-Salafliyah, 1983); 'Abbas Mahmud Al-'Aqqad, *Al-Mar'ah fi Al-Qur'an* (Women in the Qur'an), (Cairo: Dar Al-Hilal, 1971); Muhsin 'Atwi, *Al-Mar'ah fi-t-Tasawwur al-Islami* (Women in the Islamic Perspective), (Beirut: Ad-Dar al-Islamiyyah, 1979); and numerous other works.
28. See Al-Ghazali, Muhammad, *As-Sunnah An-Nabawiyyah: Bayna'Ahl*

al-Fiqh wa'Ahl al-Hadith (The Prophet's Sunnah: Between the Community of Fiqh and the Community of Hadith), (Cairo: Dar al-Shuruq, 1989); and *Qadaya al-Mar'ah: Bayna at-Taqalid ar-Rakidah wa al-Wafidah* (Women's Issues: Between Stagnant and Incoming Traditions), (Cairo: Dar al-Shuruq, 1990).

29. See Mervat Hatem, *The Demise of Egyptian State Feminism and the Politics of Transition (1980–1991)* (Los Angeles: The G.E. von Grunebaum Center for Near Eastern Studies, University of California, Los Angeles, Working Paper No. 3, 1991), p. 21.

30. One of their leaders at the time was Duriyyah Shafiq who declared in one statement: "It is shameful that a (male) cook can vote, while the lady who employs him in her house is deprived from that right." The statement was made in *Bint an-Nil*, March 1948, as cited in al-Siddani, Nuriyyah, *Al-Masirah at-Tarikhiyyah li-l-Huquq-i-s-Siyasiyyah li-l-Mar'a-l-Kuwaytiyyah fi-l-Fatrah ma bayna 'Amay 1971–1982* (The Historical March of Political Rights for Kuwaiti Women in the Period Between 1971–1982), (Kuwait: Dar as-Siyasah, 1983).

31. For full details of the controversy, see the account of a leading Egyptian feminist who was a prominent figure in the movement calling for women's political rights: Bint An-Nil (Duriyyah Shafiq), *Al-Kitab Al-Abyad li Huquq al-Mar'ah as-Siyasiyyah* (The White Book of Women's Political Rights), (Cairo: Al-Matba' ah al-Sharqiyyah, [1953?]).

32. The text is in *Al-Ahram*, June 11, 1952.

33. See the Azharite Kamal Ahmad 'Awn, *Al-Mar'ah fi Al-Islam* (Women in Islam), (Tanta: Al-Sha'rawi, 1955), p. 163.

34. Mernissi rendered the Arabic word *falaha* as "prospered" (F. Mernissi, *The Veil and the Male . . . , Op. cit.,* p. 1). The word actually means "to succeed."

35. See, for example, Fatima Mernissi, *Beyond the Veil* (Bloomington, IN: Indiana University Press, 1990); and Fatna Sabbah, *Woman in the Muslim Unconscious* (New York: Pergamon Press, The Athene Series, 1984). It should be noted that the identity of Mernissi as the author of *Woman In the Muslim Unconscious* was revealed in a book review.

36. The best biography of Muhammad is still Maxime Rodinson, *Mahomet* (Paris: Seuil, 1961).

37. F. Mernissi, *The Veil . . . , Op. cit.,* p. 113.

38. *Ibid*, p. 117.

39. See *ibid*, p. 129.

40. See *ibid*, p. 155.

41. See Ibn Hisham, *As-Sirah An-Nabawiyyah* (The Prophet's Biography), (Beirut: Dar Al-Jil, 1987), vol. 4, p. 186.

42. Mernissi devotes many pages to discredit Abu Hurayra.

43. I borrow this term from Maxime Rodinson, *La fascination de l'Islam* (Paris: Maspero, 1980).

44. Mervat Hatem, "Economic and Political Liberation in Egypt and the Demise of State Feminism," *International Journal of Middle East Studies*, vol. 24 (1992), p. 235.

45. For one example of this tendency, which can also apply to some leftist analysts, see Mai Ghoussoub, "Feminism—or the Eternal Masculine—in the Arab world," *New Left Review*, vol. 161, (Jan./Feb. 1987). For a penetrating critique of the article see Rema Hammami, and Martina Rieker, "Feminist Orientalism and Orientalist Marxism," *New Left Review* (July/Aug. 1988).

46. When Palestinian women organized a Women's Film Festival in Jerusalem in June 1992, Muslim fundamentalist groups sent threatening letters to the women involved. See *Al-Fajr*, July 20, 1992.

47. See Vicky Randall, *Women and Politics* (New York: St. Martin's Press, 1982), p. 36.

48. Fatna Sabbah, *Op. cit.,* p. 13.

49. See 'Abdul-Qadir 'Urabi, and 'Abdallah Al-Hamali, *Al-Mar'ah al-'Arabiyyah wa-l-Musharakah As-Siyasiyyah* (Arab Women and Political Participation), (Libya: Qar Yunis University, 1983), p. 58. Unfortunately, the usefulness of the data in this interesting book is limited because respondents are not distinguished by gender.

50. John Waterbury and Alan Richards, *A Political Economy of the Middle East: State, Class and Economic Development* (Boulder, CO: Westview Press, 1990), p. 113.

51. Mervat Hatem, *The Demise . . . , Op. cit.,* p. 9.

52. See *ibid*, p. 28.

53. As quoted in Ruqiyyah Al-Musaddaq, *Al-Mar'ah wa-s-Siyasah: At-Tamthil as-Siyasi fi al-Maghrib* (Women and Politics: Political Representation in Morocco), (Casablanca: Les Editions Toubkal, 1990), p. 48.

54. Libya is, of course, a special case given the bizarre nature of the political system constructed by Qadhdhafi. The political process is institutionalized there through the Popular Conferences in which women are encouraged to participate. Participation rights do not guarantee political effectiveness.

55. The democratic process was aborted in Sudan in 1989, when a military clique seized power.

56. The parliament was dissolved in Bahrain in 1975, and voting rights for males were also suspended.

57. See M. Ghoussoub, *Op. cit.,* p. 13.

58. The full text is in Al-Siddani, *Op. cit.,* p. 71.

59. Figures cited in *ibid*, pp. 97–98.

60. V. Randall, *Op. cit.,* p. 37.

61. For accounts of Palestinian women activists, see Julie Peteet, *Gender in Crisis* (New York: Columbia University Press, 1991).

62. On the legitimacy question, see Michael C. Hudson, *Arab Politics: The Search for Legitimacy* (New Haven: Yale University Press, 1977).

63. References to articles in constitutions are all from, Nuhad Salim, "*Huquq al-Mar'ah fi al-Watan al-'Arabi*" (Women's Rights in the Arab Homeland), *Huquq Al-Insan*, No. 23, August 1989.

64. The distinction between formal and informal politics draws on James Bill and Robert Springborg, *Politics in the Middle East*, (Boston: Little, Brown, 1989).

65. Anwar Muhammad, *Wara' Kull Diktatur 'Imra' ah* (Behind Every Dictator is a Woman), (Cairo: Dar A.M., 1990). The author chose to dedicate the book to his wife.

66. See Mervat Hatem, *IJMES, Op. cit.,* p. 231.

67. For an analysis of the Egyptian case, see *ibid*.

68. Suad Joseph, "Women and Politics in the Middle East," *Middle East Report* (January–February 1986). Joseph was citing a study published by Judith Tucker in the same issue.

69. Carol Christy, *Sex Differences in Political Participation: Process of Change in Fourteen Nations* (New York: Praeger, 1987), p. 117.

 Article Review Form at end of book.

WiseGuide Wrap-Up

Individuals who were educated to appreciate the merits of capitalism or socialism write much of comparative politics. As Tyrrell notes in Reading 62, these people largely concern themselves with issues of who controls the state and what state policies benefit which groups in society. Tyrrell argues that, to understand the political contests of the 1990s, we must give less attention to issues of state and market, and more attention to issues of nationalism and ethnic identity, especially as they help us define "us" from "them."

Africans in Asia and Asians in Africa have long complained of their treatment as minorities. Due to the successful economic development of many Asian states and many Africans' disenchantment with Western models of development, many Africans and Asians are sharing their views on development and finding new areas in which to cooperate.

In Reading 64, Huntington predicts a global clash between people who live according to the traditons of Western, Judeo-Christian values and the enlightenment, and those who live according to Confucian-Islamic traditions. Huntington believes that a Confucian-Islamic alliance will vigorously attack the traditions and security of those in the West.

In Reading 65, AbuKhalil demonstrates how important it is not to homogenize those who are different from ourselves. He analyzes, for example, the differences among Islamic states and their treatment of women.

R.E.A.L. Sites

This list provides a print preview of typical **coursewise** R.E.A.L. sites. There are over 100 such sites at the **courselinks**™ site. The danger in printing URLs is that web sites can change overnight. As we went to press, these sites were functional using the URLs provided. If you come across one that isn't, please let us know via email to: webmaster@coursewise.com. use your Passport to access the most current list of R.E.A.L. sites at the **courselinks**™ site.

Site name: Humanitarian Relief Website

URL: http://www.relief.org/

Why is it R.E.A.L.? Visit this web site and choose a civil war about which to read. Then evaluate Tyrrell's claims that issues of nationalism and ethnic identity are playing increasingly important political roles in countries around the world.

Key topic: humanitarian relief

Index

Note: References in bold type are authors of Readings. References followed by *n* are in notes.

Le Pen, Jean-Marie, 4, 8–13
Lesotho, anti-Asian rioting in, 252–53
LG, 92
Liberal Democrats (Japan)
    divisions within, 43–44
    electoral victories of, 41–42
Liberal Democrats (Russia), electoral
    support for, 35
Libya, voting rights in, 275, 280n
Lind, Amy, 126
Living standards
    in former East Germany, 26–27
    in Mexico, 58–59
Localism, in rural China, 164–65
Los Angeles, rioting in, 252

M

MacDonald, Mia, 192
Machipisa, Lewis, 101
Mairowitz, David Zane, 8
Majority, defining, 242
Majority rule, in South Africa, 177
Making Democracy Work, 105–11
Makwetu, Clarence, 82
Male domination, of Arab political
    structures, 277–78
Malnutrition
    and debt repayment, 230–31
    worldwide extent of, 224–25
Mandela, Nelson, 76, 81
    agenda for ANC, 85–86
    inauguration of, 255
Maps, and nationalism, 244
Maquiladoras, 57, 58–59
Marcos, Subcomandante, 53, 54, 55, 61
Market forces
    in Japan, 39–41
    role of supply and demand in, 120–21
    versus traditional values, 122
Marriage, in Dominican Republic, 186
Marx, Karl, 241–42
Marxism, diversity within, 270
Matiba, Kenneth, 249
Mbeki, Thabo, 86
Media
    and famine prevention, 114–15
    and nationalism, 241
    responsibilities in Southern Africa,
        103–4
Mégret, Bruno, 9, 11
Mégret, Catherine, 9
Méndez, Chico, 215n
Mernissi, Fatima, 273–74
Mexican Workers Confederation (CTM), 53
Mexico
    cultural identity of, 264–65
    democratization in, 46, 48–50
    economic crisis in, 58
    economic reform in, 50
    foreign policy of, 179–82
    resistance to globalization in, 51–62
Mexico City, 1985 earthquake, 55
Mguny, Gabriel, 242
Microenterprise, in Mexico, 60
Microfinance, and Islamic finance, 150

Middle East
    discrimination against women in,
        269–78
    effect of globalization on, 130
Migration
    to cities in China, 165–66
    from Dominican Republic, 187
Military
    post-Cold War reductions in, 266
    role in South Africa's government, 174,
        177
Military dictatorships, in Nigeria, 66–73
Military expenditures, and structural
    adjustment, 227–28
Minimal Group Paradigm, 246–47
Minimum wage, in Mexico, 60
Minorities
    defining, 242
    deprivation among, 116
    social influence of, 242
M'membe, Fred, 104
Mobility, in rural China, 161, 163, 165–66
Model C schools, 89–90
Modernization, and women's rights in Arab
    countries, 278
Monetary union, in EU. *See* European
    Monetary Union
Moral theory, 122
Mortality, among African Americans, 116
Moscovici, Serge, 242–43
Motherlands, 244
Motsepe, Godfrey, 90–91
Movement of Landless Rural Workers, 154
Moyo, Tabby, 102
Mugabe, Robert, 101
Muhammad, views of women, 273, 274
Munoz Ledo, Porfirio, 49–50
Murdoch, Rupert, 41
Myths, historical, 244

N

Namibia, status of regional governors in,
    102–3
Natal, racial makeup of, 79
Natal Indian Congress, 84
National Action Party (Mexico), 48
National Confederation of Agricultural
    Workers (CONTAG), 154
National Department for Rural Workers of
    the Unified Workers Central, 154
National Executive Committee, of ANC, 87
National Federation of Free-Trade Zone
    Workers, 185
National frontiers, 244–45
National Front Party (France)
    electoral advances of, 4, 5, 9
    politics of, 8–13
Nationalism, psychology of, 240–48
National Party (South Africa)
    Cold War politics of, 173–74
    cooperating with ANC, 76–77
    election support for, 80
    ideology and leadership of, 81
    new support from Indians, 83–85
Nations, defining, 242

Nation-state
    defined, 240
    influence of, 248
NATO, expansion of, 38
Nazi era, German views of, 28
Neofascism, in France, 4, 5, 8–13
Neoliberalism, 56
    and German unification, 132–34, 136–37
    in Mexico, 56–61, 179–82
Neves, Tancredo, 154–55
New Frontier Party (Japan), 41–42
Nicaragua
    anti-gay laws in, 127
    deforestation and agrarian reform in,
        210–12, 213, 214
Nigeria
    government repression in, 66–73
    intimidation of U.S. ambassador, 74–75
Nippon Telegraph and Telephone, 40
Noble, Kenneth B., 83
Nongovernmental organizations
    at Beijing conference, 193, 194
    cooperation with government, 108
    gay and lesbian, 126
    importance to democracy, 105–11
    for women, 190
Nonproliferation, Western support for,
    266–67
North American Development Bank, 181
North American Free Trade Agreement
    (NAFTA)
    arguments against, 181
    impact on Mexico, 56
North Atlantic Treaty Organization
    (NATO), expansion of, 38
Northern Cape province, 79
Northern Transvaal, 79
North Korea, reunification prospects with
    South, 93–95
North-West province, 79
Nuclear weapons, acquisition by non-
    Western states, 266
Nutrition, and structural adjustment
    programs, 228–29
Nyarota, Geoff, 103

O

Oasis International Equity Fund, 150
Odio, John, 73
Ojo, Godwin Uyi, 73
Olamosu, Biodun, 73
Onah, George, 72
One-child policy, 116–17
Opadokun, Ayo, 71, 72
Open society, and laissez-faire economics,
    118–25
Open Society Fund, 119
Opposition groups
    in Mexico, 51–62
    in Nigeria, 66–73
    in South Africa, 76–77, 80, 81–82, 85–88
    in South Korea, 91–93, 96–97
Oral rehydration therapy, 227
Orange Free State, 79
Organization for Tropical Studies, 209

Putting it in *Perspectives*
-Review Form-

Your name:_____   Date: _____

Reading title: _____

Summarize: Provide a one-sentence summary of this reading. _____

_____

_____

_____

Follow the Thinking: How does the author back the main premise of the reading? Are the facts/opinions appropriately supported by research or available data? Is the author's thinking logical?

_____

_____

_____

_____

_____

_____

Develop a Context (answer one or both questions): How does this reading contrast or compliment your professor's lecture treatment of the subject matter? How does this reading compare to your textbook's coverage?

_____

_____

_____

_____

_____

_____

_____

Question Authority: Explain why you agree/disagree with the author's main premise.

_____

_____

_____

_____

_____

_____

_____

_____

COPY ME! Copy this form as needed. This form is also available at http://www.coursewise.com Click on:
Perspectives.